François Cooren and Peter Stücheli-Herlach (Eds.)
Handbook of Management Communication

Handbooks of Applied Linguistics

Communication Competence
Language and Communication Problems
Practical Solutions

Editors
Karlfried Knapp
Daniel Perrin
Marjolijn Verspoor

Volume 16

Handbook of Management Communication

Edited by
François Cooren and Peter Stücheli-Herlach

ISBN 978-1-5015-2143-0
e-ISBN (PDF) 978-1-5015-0805-9
e-ISBN (EPUB) 978-1-5015-0795-3

Library of Congress Control Number: 2021934672

Bibliographic information published by the Deutsche Nationalbibliothek
The Deutsche Nationalbibliothek lists this publication in the Deutsche Nationalbibliografie;
detailed bibliographic data are available on the Internet at http://dnb.dnb.de.

© 2023 Walter de Gruyter GmbH, Boston/Berlin
This volume is text- and page-identical with the hardback published in 2021.

Typesetting: Dörlemann Satz, Lemförde
Printing and binding: CPI books GmbH, Leck

www.degruyter.com

Preface to the Handbooks of Applied Linguistics Series

The present handbook constitutes Volume 16 of the De Gruyter Mouton *Handbooks of Applied Linguistics*. This series is based on an understanding of Applied Linguistics as an inter- and transdisciplinary field of academic enquiry. The *Handbooks of Applied Linguistics* provide a state-of-the-art description of established and emerging areas of Applied Linguistics. Each volume gives an overview of the field, identifies most important traditions and their findings, identifies the gaps in current research, and gives perspectives for future directions.

In the late 1990s when the handbook series was planned by its Founding Editors Gerd Antos and Karlfried Knapp, intensive debates were going on as to whether Applied Linguistics should be restricted to applying methods and findings from linguistics only or whether it should be regarded as a field of interdisciplinary synthesis drawing on psychology, sociology, ethnology and similar disciplines that are also dealing with aspects of language and communication. Should it be limited to foreign language teaching or should it widen its scope to language-related issues in general? Thus, what *Applied Linguistics* means and what an Applied Linguist does was highly controversial at the time.

Against this backdrop, Gerd Antos and Karlfried Knapp felt that a series of handbooks of Applied Linguistics could not simply be an accidental selection of descriptions of research findings and practical activities that were or could be published in books and articles labeled as "applied linguistic". Rather, for them such a series had to be based on an epistemological concept that frames the status and scope of the concept of Applied Linguistics. Departing from contemporary Philosophy of Science, which sees academic disciplines under the pressure to successfully solve practical everyday problems encountered by the societies which aliment them, the founding editors emphasized the view that was only emerging at that time – the programmatic view that Applied Linguistics means the solving of real world problems with language and communication. This concept has become mainstream since.

In line with the conviction that Applied Linguistics is for problem solving, we developed a series of handbooks to give representative descriptions of the ability of this field of academic inquiry and to provide accounts, analyses, explanations and, where possible, solutions of everyday problems with language and communication. Each volume of the *Handbooks of Applied Linguistics* series is unique in its explicit focus on topics in language and communication as areas of everyday problems and in pointing out the relevance of Applied Linguistics in dealing with them.

This series has been well received in the academic community and among practitioners. In fact, its success has even triggered competitive handbook series by other publishers. Moreover, we recognized further challenges with language and communication and distinguished colleagues keep on approaching us with proposals to edit further volumes in this handbook series. This motivates both De Gruyter Mouton and the series editors to further develop the *Handbooks of Applied Linguistics*.

Karlfried Knapp (Erfurt), Founding Editor
Daniel Perrin (Zürich), Editor
Marjolijn Verspoor (Groningen), Editor

Contents

Preface to the Handbooks of Applied Linguistics series —— V

François Cooren and Peter Stücheli-Herlach
Introducing —— 1

Part I: Practices of management communication

Nicolas Bencherki
1 Speaking —— 27

Geert Jacobs and Daniel Perrin
2 Writing —— 47

Theresa Castor and Mariaelena Bartesaghi
3 Deciding —— 69

Philippe Lorino
4 Creating by communicating —— 87

Peter Winkler
5 Networking —— 105

Zhuo Ban and Heather M. Zoller
6 Controlling and resisting —— 123

Christine Domke and Matthias Klemm
7 Tweeting —— 143

Viviane Sergi
8 Documenting —— 161

Salla-Maaria Laaksonen
9 Posting —— 177

Part II: Forms of management communication

Florence Allard-Poesi and Laure Cabantous
10 Strategizing —— 195

J. Kevin Barge
11 Leading —— 213

Howard Nothhaft, Alicia Fjällhed, and Rickard Andersson
12 **Planning and designing** —— 231

Alex Wright and David Hollis
13 **Routinizing** —— 247

Consuelo Vásquez
14 **Branding** —— 263

Rickard Andersson and Lars Rademacher
15 **Managing communication** —— 279

Patrice M. Buzzanell
16 **Mentoring** —— 295

Peter Stücheli-Herlach and Ursina Ghilardi
17 **Counseling** —— 313

Christian Schwägerl and Susanne Knorre
18 **Developing organizations** —— 335

Bertrand Fauré
19 **Accounting** —— 355

Part III: Contexts of management communication

Susanne Tietze, Hilla Back, and Rebecca Piekkari
20 **Managing communication in multilingual workplaces** —— 373

Philipp Dreesen and Julia Krasselt
21 **Exploring and analyzing linguistic environments** —— 389

Jody L. S. Jahn
22 **Managing high reliability organizations** —— 409

Shiv Ganesh, Mohan Dutta, and Ngā Hau
23 **Building communities** —— 427

Dennis Schoeneborn and Verena Girschik
24 Managing CSR Communication —— 443

Brigitte Bernard-Rau
25 Rating social and environmental performances —— 459

Anne M. Nicotera, Melinda Villagran, and Wonsun (Sunny) Kim
26 Managing in hospitals —— 477

Amanda J. Porter, Damla Diriker, and Ilse Hellemans
27 Crowdsourcing —— 493

Sarah E. Riforgiate and Samentha Sepúlveda
28 Managing and being managed by emotions —— 511

Samir L. Vaz, Eduardo A. Figueiredo, and Gabriela X. Maia
29 Changing through communication —— 529

About the contributors —— 549

Index —— 559

François Cooren and Peter Stücheli-Herlach
Introducing

In recent scholarship, management has been understood not only as a field of formalized and instrumental action but also, in a broader sense, as a communicative practice of formal and informal conversation, text production, process stabilization, collective problem solving, identity formation, and value creation in modern organizations. The assertion that management and communication are deeply entangled results from of a shift from a scientific-technical approach to a practice perspective on management, a shift that took place during the last three decades (Holman and Thorpe 2003b; Rüegg-Stürm and Grand 2015: 48–54) and has led researchers to recognize the key role communication plays in the various spheres of action that characterize managing (Mintzberg [2009] 2011: 43–96).

1 The notion of *management communication*

To highlight this processual, discursive, and embodied aspect of management communication, each chapter of this handbook (including this one!) begins with a verb in the gerund form. We invited each contributor to focus on what people *do* when managing, an activity that, as we know since Mintzberg's (1973) landmark contribution, essentially consists of communicating. Why is communication and why are the linguistic features of this process so important in the activity of managing? To answer this question, we just have to reflect on the etymology and definition of the term itself. The verb "to manage" comes from the Latin noun *manus*, which means 'hand'. The word was originally used to speak about the handling or training of a horse, hence, the French term *manège*, which means both horsemanship and the place where these exercises occur.

We understand from this etymology why people tend not to like to be managed, as nobody likes to be treated like a horse in need of training! But what is important in this etymology is the role hands are supposed to play in this activity. Somebody who handles or, so to speak, manages a horse has to deal with a beautiful creature that could easily unseat its rider. This explains why control is always relative and finite; when thinking about control, the *autonomy* of what or who is being managed has to be taken into consideration. Handling a situation, for instance, means that we are dealing with it, that we are in charge of it, and that we might even be able to control it to some extent. However, this also implies that this situation needs to be constantly attended to and taken care of. The image of the rider who handles her horse implies that managing is a continuous *work of communication* (Kuhn, Ashcraft, and Cooren 2017).

In its multiple usages, the verb *to manage* always expresses the difficult character of this activity. For instance, *The Cambridge Dictionary* (Cambridge University Press) offers the following definitions:

https://doi.org/10.1515/9781501508059-202

To succeed in doing or dealing with something, especially something difficult (e. g., Did you manage to get any bread?)
To succeed in living on a small amount of money (e. g., After she lost her job, they had to manage on his salary.)
To be able to attend or do something at a particular time (e. g., Let's meet tomorrow – I can manage)
To be responsible for controlling or organizing someone or something, especially a business or employees (e. g., Has he had any experience of managing large projects?)

As we see, managing is not an easy task and can even sometimes take the form of a miracle. Usually, it is treated as a "controversial black box" (Rüegg-Stürm and Grand 2015: 26–27). It is little wonder managers need to communicate, because communicating is the only way they can try to minimally frame and control a situation before it gets out of hand. This handbook is thus also meant to rehabilitate the activity of "managing", which is often negatively compared with other, more noble ones such as leading, for instance. Even so-called leaders have to manage situations, as Kevin Barge aptly reminds us in one of the chapters of this volume. *Man*-aging does imply some forms of *mani*-pulation (after all, both terms share the same Latin root *manus*). However, this is the price we have to pay when we work and live together. Furthermore, handling a situation does not necessarily imply that we manage it unethically. Managing is certainly not the solution to everything. At some point, it might indeed be healthier or wiser to let things get out of hand. But management has its own merits as a communicative and thus discursive practice (Cooren 2015), and that is what this handbook is trying to demonstrate.

2 The shift to the practice and linguistic perspective

As we will see, the practice perspective we would like to put forward in this handbook is neither the result of a single scholar's work nor a consistent theoretical or methodological approach (Bourdieu 1973; Schatzki 2001; Hillebrandt 2014; Nicolini 2012; Schäfer 2013). Rather, it is characterized by a set of epistemic assumptions that underlie several conceptualizations. For example, these assumptions include the context-dependent nature of human activities and their ability to transform situations in a sense that "knowing and doing and means and ends are not held to be separate and distinct entities" (Holman and Thorpe 2003b: 5; see also Joas 1996: 218–242 as well as Philippe Lorino's contribution in this handbook). Furthermore, these assumptions take for granted the embodied, mediated, discursive, and reflective constitution of practices as well as the fact that there is never "a practice" as a singular object of research, but rather and always an "array" of practices that form a "field of practices" (Schatzki 2001: 2; see also Hillebrandt 2014: 59). Thereby, language use and communication are more generally key phenomena because discourse in interaction is seen as "a type of activity" that plays a constitutive role for practices, which are "organized around shared practical understandings" (Schatzki 2001: 3).

The shift toward the practice perspective on management was made possible by specific theoretical and methodological strands in the fields of organizational studies, management studies, and organizational communication. These include social constructivism (Weick 2001; Berger and Luckmann 1966), the ethnography of managerial work or managing (Mintzberg 1971, 2011), the interpretive approach (Burrell and Morgan [1979] 2016; Putnam and Pacanowsky 1983), the processual turn (Langley 1999, 2009; Hernes and Maitlis 2010; Rüegg-Stürm and Grand 2015), as well as the communication as constitutive of organization (CCO) approach (Putnam and Nicotera 2009; Robichaud and Cooren 2013; Brummans et al. 2014; Schoeneborn et al. 2014).

Modern management has been historically characterized by an explicit focus on the cognitive processes of decision making (Simon 1957). As Philippe Lorino (2014), points out, it is time to advocate research that investigates not only practice but also *management as practice*. Thereby, management must be understood as more than the practice of individual actors such as leaders (Bennis 1989; Mintzberg 2011), and the notion of management must not be reduced to the implementation of specific strategic instruments (Mintzberg, Ahlstrand, and Lampel 1998). In contrast to the management at the top or in the center of an organization, the notion of *management communication* leads us to think of management as something that occurs not only *at the top* or *in the center*, but mainly *throughout* an organization (Mintzberg 2011: 125).

It is a permanent, networked, and linguistically performed practice, one that deals with the uncertain development of activities, stakes, and valuations with the aim of organized *value creation* (Rüegg-Stürm and Grand 2015: 30–37) where the idea of value should not be reduced to its monetary and financial dimensions (Grand 2016: 66–148). In this sense, it is a field of socially distributed sensemaking (Weick 2001; Holman and Thorpe 2003a) and collective action (Lorino 2014; and Philippe Lorino in this handbook) to which all members of an organization potentially contribute.

3 Discursive agency and applied linguistics

Over the past thirty years, this practice perspective has revealed social and communicative aspects of management that had previously been underestimated. This, in turn, has led to an increasing interest in the communicative, linguistic, and discursive features of management practices. One might call this a communicative, linguistic, or discursive turn in the study of organizations and their management (Becker-Mrotzek and Fiehler 2002; Cooren 2015; Grant et al. 2004; Holman and Thorpe 2003b; Müller 2008; Shotter and Cunliffe 2003; Tietze, Cohen, and Mussen 2003; Westwood and Linstead 2001). However, these turns should not be interpreted as an attempt to reduce organizational life to communicative, discursive, and linguistic matters only.

Theoretical specifications and empirical evidence have so far been summarized under several key terms such as the interactional, contextual, improvisational, episodic, and multifunctional aspects of managerial performances, which contribute to the "handling" of an organization (Trujillo 1983). Others speak of controlling the situation and networking (Spranz-Fogasy 2002), of practical authorship (Shotter and Cunliffe 2003), of metaconversation (Taylor and Robichaud 2007), or even of multicommunicating (Reinsch 2008). In general, management communication also tends to be associated with the implementation of communicative roles on diverse planes of an organization (Mintzberg 2011: 48), or the enactment of the organization within its environment on distinctive levels of corporate governance and executive management, for instance (Rüegg-Stürm and Grand 2015, based especially on Weick 2001).

In all these variations of the practical performance of management communication, the use of language plays a key role. Schatzki (2001: 3) describes it as the driver of social structures and institutions. Accordingly, we understand the use of language as the "discursive agency" of management communication (Cooren 2000; Cooren et al. 2014: 4; Cooren 2015; Stücheli-Herlach 2018: 118–126). Thereby, it is neither the social status nor the hierarchical level of a "sender" that determines the *a priori* performance of managerial practices by linguistic means, but rather the interactive viability of the connections between roles, voices, artifacts, cognitive schemes, etc. that are manufactured by discursive acts and their linguistic performance.

Thus, in this sense, language use can be modeled in diverse ways (for an overview see also Tietze, Cohen, and Mussen 2003). For instance, it can be described and understood as "the performance of speech acts" (Austin 1962; Searle 1979) or "situated symbolic actions" in general (Heracleous 2006). It can be described and understood as the use of specific linguistic "form-meaning-use dynamic patterns" in the complex systems of real-life situations on various levels and in different modes of social interaction (Larsen-Freeman and Cameron 2008: 82). It can be modeled as the emergence of mediated forms (or "genres") of communication in the frame of "communication households" (Luckmann 2009). It can be seen as the emergence of collective meaning and agency in the course of "imbricating conversation" and text production in organizations (Taylor and Van Every 2011: 28–32). It can even be understood as the reproduction and transformation of discursive formations such as cognitive schemes and narratives (Boje 2008).

In this broader framework, the authors of this handbook chose their own specific approaches. This theoretical and methodological diversity is a characteristic of applied linguistics, which does not see itself as an autonomous discipline, but as a diverse, multi-perspective practice of "'doing linguistics' related to the real-life world" (Knapp and Antos 2014: xiii). Just as the objects of applied linguistics are only found in fragmentary and defective shape, the research of applied linguistics is not characterized by a compelling coherence, but by its relation of different critical and reflective approaches and methods to each other (Knapp and Antos 2014: xiv).

Therefore we understand *management* as the totality of those communicational practices that author, enact, and control an organization and its processes of value creation in specific socio-material contexts by linguistic means, this in more or less pronounced shape. And we define *management communication* as the metaconversation of all the practices, forms, and contexts of organizational communication. These activities can, of course, be planned in advance, but they can also be organized on the spot. Hence, we identify the strategic but also improvisational nature of management.

Thus the contributors to this handbook address the following questions:
- What is the specific contribution of management communication to the constitution and value creation of organizations?
- How do actors practically manage groups, projects, and organizations by "making connections" (Shotter and Cunliffe 2003: 28) and relating to each other in a professional, meaningful, decisive, and intelligible way?
- What specific events and forms of management communication can be understood as solutions for specific problems in real-world organizations (Knapp and Antos 2014)?
- How can the dynamic interplay between these practices, on the one hand, and the dynamic context of social situations, networks, and communities in organizational daily life, on the other, be described?
- What are the conditions of success and the constraints of management communication?

Answering questions such as these proves to be especially important in organizational environments where tasks are often ill defined, solutions uncertain, and flows of interaction constant. This is especially the case in the modern complex organizations of economies, state spheres, and civil societies that are highly specialized, knowledge-driven, globalized, multicultural, and multirational (Joas 1996; Baecker 2003; Danesi and Rocci 2009; Sarangi and Candlin 2011; Schedler and Rüegg-Stürm 2015).

4 The three sections of the handbook

In order to address these questions, this handbook is divided into three sections. The first section, titled *Practices of management communication* addresses specific situated activities and their discursive patterns that constitute the daily activities of management. The second section, titled *Forms of management communication* is devoted to the activities considered integral to management communication. The third section, titled *Contexts of management communication*, includes chapters that address how managing also involves dealing with specific situations and constraints that characterize the environment of an organization.

4.1 Practices of management communication

The first section, *Practices of management communication*, begins with a chapter simply titled *Speaking*, authored by Nicolas Bencherki. Although this chapter is primarily focused on orality, Bencherki deconstructs the separation that is still often established between speaking and writing today. He reminds us that any communication always involves some form of mediation. This assertion, echoing Taylor and Van Every (2000), leads him to conceive of organizations as constituted through the interplay of talk and text. Talk is marked by a certain ephemerality, while text has the capacity to endure beyond the context of a conversation, providing a certain form of stability to any collective.

In this dynamic interplay, talk is the means by which members jointly perform action and construct situations. As Bencherki demonstrates, talk builds organizational episodes not in terms of adjacency pairs, as claimed by conversation analysts, but in terms of triads where the basic organizational phenomenon can be clearly identified: request (initiation) – response (performance) – acknowledgment (closure). Talking is therefore a form of doing, and, as a form of doing, it makes up the building blocks of organization. This performativity of talk, however, needs to acknowledge that some people are prevented from speaking. So voices are not equally distributed when it comes to constituting an organization.

The second chapter offers a nice complement to the first by exploring the activity of *Writing* in a managerial context. Geert Jacobs and Daniel Perrin point out that writing constitutes a key professional practice that managers perform daily to think and decide, inform and convince, as well as integrate and motivate. Therefore, this practice needs to be mastered, because writing involves various competencies depending on the type of readership targeted or the genre the texts are supposed to belong to. Over the years, Jacobs, Perrin, and others have developed an expertise in teaching people how to increase what they call *domain-specific competences* regarding writing practices. They outline, in this handbook, some important domain-specific competences of management communication by writing texts.

To illustrate how these skills can be developed, the authors present two cases taken from their own teaching practice: a Master's-level communication course in innovation and entrepreneurship and an American-Chinese-Swiss Executive MBA. They also present a specific method called the *WAYS* (Write-As-You-Speak) writing technique, a technique that helps managers and leaders improve how they prepare and conduct their regular meetings with their employees. This method mobilizes a management instrument called *WAYSbase*, which allows managers to systematically record all agreed tasks and make them available to their employees before, during, and after each meeting. Jacobs and Perrin show that using this writing technique allows members to agree on what has to be done in a focused, transparent, and binding way.

The third chapter, *Deciding*, authored by Theresa Castor and Mariaelena Bartesaghi, explores deciding as a form of situated action where questions of agency, action, and accountability are at stake. As they remind us, reflection on decision-making processes is as old as the study of management itself. The chapter includes some key contributions from scholars such as Chester Barnard (1938) or Herbert Simon (1960). Simon highlighted what he called the *bounded character of rationality* to explain why people may select a satisfactory option instead of an optimal one when the time comes to make a decision. Deciding is messy and it is often only retrospectively that we can label what happened as having been a decision.

To study this messiness, Castor and Bartesaghi examine the process of deciding from an interactional perspective. Thus, they analyze two case studies in crisis contexts: the 2005 Hurricane Katrina and the case of Governor Andrew Cuomo's interventions during the COVID-19 crisis in New York City in 2020. Both cases show that deciding is not necessarily defined by specific speech acts and that it is not necessarily identified as a decision when it is taking place. They demonstrate that by uttering the verb "decide" in interaction, people signal an asymmetry where others are assigned positions of agency and accountability. They analyze deciding as an interactional accomplishment and as what they call a *metapragmatic* resource that helps people defer, distribute, or disclaim their own agency.

In his chapter titled *Creating by communicating*, Philippe Lorino presents a communicational view of organizations based on the pragmatist theory of *trans-actional* inquiry, initially proposed by Dewey and Bentley ([1949] 2008). According to this approach, organizations should be conceived as ongoing processes, marked by pluralist and dialogic forms of inquiry that aim not only at making situations understandable and actionable, but also at inventing possible courses of action by redefining situations through creative communication. To do so, Lorino presents two organizational episodes that illustrate this creativity. The first example involves the report of a nuclear incident to a public commission, and the second concerns the strategic transformation of a clothing manufacturer.

Through these two case studies, Lorino shows how the control paradigm, characterized by a means-ends dichotomy and a heteronomous conception of human activity, appears particularly ill-fitted when members of organizations face complex, ambiguous, and fast-evolving situations. In contrast with this paradigm, the author puts forward the principle of *trans-actional* inquiry, where people are encouraged to develop an explorative and pluralist way of collectively dealing with a problematic situation. Through this type of collective and creative inquiry, new potentials for collective action can be identified as long as people collectively remain careful, imaginative, and humble – three traits that Lorino presents as the cardinal virtues of this type of inquiry.

In his chapter, *Networking*, Peter Winkler examines this important practice, which consists of initiating and cultivating reciprocal relationships with internal and external stakeholders. While the traditional literature on networking tends to focus on the context, features, and functions of networking, the author departs from this essentialist and structural focus by exploring the communicative and linguistic dimensions of this activity. Winkler examines in detail the work of Harrison C. White (2008), a sociologist who, in his most recent work, has redefined the notions of context, features, and functions in interactional and linguistic terms.

As Winkler states, this lens allows us to identify two principal relational positions and communication styles of management that correspond to different stages of network formation in organizations. During the stage of network initiation, which White (2008) called *footing*, managers tend to preserve uncertainty, ambiguity, and indecision. During this stage, small talk is favored, and people can observe what emerges from the discussions. During the second stage, which White (2008) called *face*, the objective is to maintain the network by making formal decisions regarding questions of purpose, order, and control. These practices are supposed to lead to organizational value creation.

In their chapter on *Controlling and resisting*, Zhuo Ban and Heather Zoller address questions of power and resistance in management communication. They remind us that control is usually presented as an essential element of any organization. They draw on references from Fredrick Taylor's (1911) scientific management, which mainly focused on modes of technical control, to Elton Mayo's (2004) human relations school of management or Douglas McGregor's (1960) theory of work motivation, which were centered on persuasive methods, such as the promotion of camaraderie and self-actualization. In contrast to these traditional approaches to control and resistance, which can portray the latter as irrational, Ban and Zoller advocate for a critical/interpretive perspective that questions this functionalist agenda.

According to this critical approach, controlling should primarily be conceived as a political act by which some interests are systematically privileged over others. As the authors point out, two types of scholarship represent this approach. The structuralists, usually influenced by Karl Marx (1972) and Max Weber (1964), investigate how domination and power are cultivated and reproduced through specific communicative practices. The poststructuralists tend to be inspired by Michel Foucault (1978) and Jürgen Habermas (1984), who insist more on the fragmented and contested nature of power and control, as they both express themselves in discourse and interaction. Overall, Ban and Zoller assert that effects of power are at stake even when no conflicts or tensions appear to be present at first sight and that power can be exercised not only by people in a position of authority but also by those subjected to forms of control.

In their chapter on *Tweeting*, Christine Domke and Matthias Klemm remind us that the study of communication always appears extremely relevant when examining how managers go about their daily activities. With the rise of modern technologies of communication, such as digital texting and microblogging, managers, however, have to face new questions, which these authors explore. Twitter challenges top managers in how they present themselves through this platform. By studying the case of Siemens' CEO, Joe Kaeser, Domke and Klemm show how this executive manager deals with the necessity to represent the interests of his company within the social environment of Twitter.

With the rise of social media, CEOs often have to take the role of activists. They are supposed to raise awareness about social problems while exerting their influence on economic and political questions. This important change in management communication means that decision making seems to be repersonalized. CEOs who are using Twitter have to constantly navigate between the necessity to speak as themselves while simultaneously representing their organizations and sometimes positioning themselves as speaking on behalf of the greater good. They need to be professional, entertaining, and personal, a multiplicity of requirements that often forces them to reinvent themselves.

The chapter titled *Documenting*, authored by Viviane Sergi, deals with the common organizational practice of producing documents, whether in analog or digital format. Sergi shows that the ubiquitous character of documents renders them almost invisible, because, in organizations, we tend to take them for granted. Echoing the chapter on *Writing* (Geert Jacobs and Daniel Perrin), Sergi highlights the diversity of these documents not only in content and form (reports, budgets, procedures, policies, etc.) but also in uses (archiving, promoting, etc.) and destinations (clients, internal, etc.). She also shows how the digitalization of documents has led to their multiplication, making them more important than ever in the media ecology of an organization.

Despite its variety, Sergi also shows that the practice of documenting is characterized by the production of traces that are *a priori* considered worthy of being not only made but also kept. In other words, documenting materializes something that supposedly matters to the organization. She also points out that documents have to be relatively autonomous, given that they should be legible and usable in a near or more distant future. Their value, therefore, lies in their capacity to minimally endure. They tell us the same thing over and over, giving organizations a certain stability in terms of procedures, protocols, routines, and programs. It is this performativity of documents that Sergi also investigates throughout this chapter by showing that documents should be considered key agents in the constitution of organizations.

In her chapter, titled *Posting*, Salla-Maaria Laaksonen examines how members are inclined to use the internal social media platforms that organizations are increasingly adopting, whether they are called *enterprise social media* (ESM), *enterprise social platforms* or *enterprise social networks* (ESN). She especially focuses on the practice of writing and publishing textual updates, also known as *posts*. Posting, as she points out, not only contributes to organizational knowledge and memory but can also transcend hierarchies and boundaries by allowing employees to connect easily with each other. Even if the activity of posting demonstrates, at first sight, a certain democratic potential, Laaksonen also highlights what could be called *the dark side of posting* by revealing how these textual updates can also support surveillance and groupthink while sometimes contributing to an unhealthy work-life balance.

As she shows, these social media platforms are characterized by their technological affordance, that is, what these technologies can provide employees in terms of potential uses (Gibson 1979). These affordances also mean that these platforms are, of course, far from neutral because they definitely constrain the way people communicate. Posting, in this respect, allows employees to publish short texts that are persistent, replicable, and searchable. This also means that they increase information visibility and can potentially have positive effects on the searchability of organizational knowledge, even if concerns can sometimes be raised about security and privacy.

4.2 Forms of management communication

This section is devoted to the most basic types of management communication activities bundled to accomplish complex tasks in organizations. It begins with Florence Allard-Poesi and Laure Cabantous's chapter on *Strategizing*. The two authors examine to what extent and how communication contributes to the making of strategy. To do so, they mobilize a perspective based on John L. Austin's (1962) speech act theory, a theory that focuses on the performative dimension of language use. For Austin (1962), speaking and writing involve doing things with words, a performativity that the language philosopher analyzed by distinguishing two types of acts he called *illocutionary* and *perlocutionary* acts. While illocutionary acts refer to what people conventionally do when they say or write something (e. g., asserting, promising, asking, apologizing, etc.), perlocutionary acts correspond to the intentional or unintentional effects people produce in their interlocutors or readers when they say or write something (e. g., angering, persuading, upsetting, seducing, humiliating, etc.).

As Allard-Poesi and Cabantous note, strategy discourses rarely bring about the changes they envision, which the authors interpret as a lack of illocutionary power. The two authors attribute this lack of clout to the often ambiguous nature of this type of discourse, which frequently creates resistant employees. To circumvent this problem, this discourse can be clarified and inscribed into socio-material devices or calculative technologies. However, even this approach breaks down since the lack of ambiguity can then lead to criticism if strategic objectives are not ultimately achieved. The lack of illocutionary power does not mean, though, that these discourses do not have any perlocutionary effects. On the contrary, strategy discourses participate in positioning the persons who hold them as strategists – a prestigious status that allows this type of discourse to colonize new territories by being more frequently adopted (universities, hospitals, governmental administrations, etc.).

In the second chapter, *Leading*, Kevin Barge focuses on the interactional dimension of leadership. This approach distinguishes itself from leadership psychology, which has a tendency to center on the psychological traits that supposedly define real leaders from non-leaders. Leading, as Barge points out, is essentially about management and the coordination of human and nonhuman actants. Here, communication is conceived as constitutive of leadership, especially when it comes to building consensus – one of the key aspects of this form of management communication.

According to discursive leadership, leading is especially about the capacity to co-construct a context so that people feel that they can move forward and accomplish things together. In that respect, Barge highlights the act of framing, which he presents as an interactional accomplishment that allows people to make sense of what happens by backgrounding and foregrounding specific aspects of a situation to make some objectives and aspirations more salient. The author also shows how a plurality of agencies can also be mobilized in the activity of leading – a plurality that helps in establishing leadership presence and in building authority. Ultimately, this chapter shows how leadership practitioners have to develop a sensitivity to interaction because it is only in interaction that leading can take place.

In their chapter titled *Planning and designing*, Howard Nothhaft, Alicia Fjällhed, and Rickard Andersson also explore the performative character of communication, this time by focusing on plans and designs. While planning involves devising a program of action, designing consists of describing a main idea or vision, which usually precedes and defines the plans themselves. The authors examine the agency of plans and designs, that is, their capacity to make a difference, especially when they are concretely invoked and mobilized by managers and leaders in various situations. While things do not always work according to what is envisioned, Nothhaft, Fjällhed, and Andersson assert that this uncertainty should not discourage people from designing a future and planning accordingly.

This reflection on what one could call "bad and good governance" shows that planning and designing especially help people make sense of a situation and allow them to move forward, even if plans or designs sometimes have to be redefined in the course of action. In other words, planning and designing help people make decisions and proceed to action confidently. In a world full of uncertainties, they reassure managers and employees that they are facing a future that they can minimally anticipate and master. Although plans and designs are often criticized for acting as a smokescreen, Nothhaft, Fjällhed, and Andersson remind us that a more or less foreseeable future remains a prerequisite of good organization and management.

In their chapter on *Routinizing*, Alex Wright and David Hollis highlight the key role communication plays in routines and routinization, which are presented as the primary means by which organizing and managing take place. Routinizing is a multifunctional form of management communication that is normally tightly interlinked with other forms such as strategizing, planning, designing, and documenting. Although routines are often understood as mindless accomplishments, the authors show that their mundane and ubiquitous characters exclude a need for mindful efforts, which contributes to the creation of value. Understanding routines from a communicative viewpoint, thus, requires that we focus on their relational and performative dimensions. Routines are relational because they mobilize various elements of a situation that conjointly contribute to their achievement. And routines are performative because of their citational dimension, that is, their capacity to reiterate norms of action that legitimize what is being accomplished.

To illustrate this relational and performative dimension of routines, Wright and Hollis draw from ethnographic data collected during a nine-month period of fieldwork conducted in the UK branch of an international cosmetics company. More precisely, they focus on a makeup routine called *The Ultimate*, which comprises ten steps that must be strictly followed by the makeup artists working for this company. Despite the routine's constraints, the two authors show that each time employees follow this script, they tend to apply it for "another next first time" (Garfinkel 1967), which highlights the eventful character of this iterative performance. Through this progressive reappropriation, these employees can also affirm their organizational identity and status; these are reinforced through the invocation of this routine in face-to-face conversation and social media posts.

In her chapter, *Branding*, Consuelo Vásquez addresses what could be called the "brandization" of our societies, a tendency that can be observed today through the numerous attempts aiming at constructing coherent images for organizations, products, places, and even people. Through branding, organizations try to communicate how they want to be recognized by internal and external stakeholders, a recognition that is directly connected to the reputation they want to build for themselves. By mobilizing a communicative constitutive approach, Vásquez examines the communicative nature of branding by focusing on the meaning indeterminacy that characterizes appropriate activities and constitutes their performative force for management communication.

As this author shows, branding can be conceptualized as a semantic space of valuation where brands become the main organizing principle by which companies and other collectives structure themselves. Therefore, branding, as a collective activity, can be seen as involving conversations through which the brand is co-created and negotiated between various stakeholders. This polyphony and struggle over meaning is, according to Vásquez, what characterizes corporate branding in neoliberal capitalism. To illustrate this communicative dimension, the author examines what has happened to universities since the 1990s, through what has been called the marketization of higher education.

In their chapter, *Managing communication*, Rickard Andersson and Lars Rademacher analyze communication management as the collective practice of authoring, enacting, and controlling an organization's communication to create value. While this form of management traditionally tends to be conceived as the responsibility of a few persons (essentially, communication managers), Andersson and Rademacher approach it as a collective responsibility that can involve all organizational members. Echoing Vásquez's chapter on *Branding*, they show that managing communication has become a central concern in contemporary thought even if this practice has been labeled a "bullshit job" by some authors (Graeber 2018).

While attempts to integrate, coordinate, and orchestrate communication appear to be some key objectives of contemporary forms of organization, Andersson and Rademacher remind us that this emphasis comes at a price to the extent that it can silence contradictory and inconsistent values and identities, which contribute to the complexity and the richness of an organization's personality. The two authors argue that this polyphonic character should be considered an asset, especially when we deal with internal stakeholders, i.e., employees, who may voice dissatisfaction when they believe that communication is overmanaged by top management. Similarly, recognizing and listening to the multiple voices of external stakeholders is increasingly a central concern not only for communication management researchers but also for practitioners.

In her chapter on *Mentoring*, Patrice Buzzanell focuses on how newcomers learn from more seasoned employees. This process allows organizations to retain and diffuse critical knowledge and practices among their members. The author distinguishes between different types of mentoring, which she calls prototypical, formal, informal, and episodic. The prototypical form of mentoring enacts a standard vision of mentorship marked by high expectations and a clear hierarchical status difference between the mentor and the protégé. By contrast, other forms of mentoring generally try to deconstruct this usually male-biased heroic view by establishing more realistic objectives. Formal mentorship normally contains contractual arrangements where rights, obligations, and responsibilities are clearly defined, whereas informal mentoring is characterized by close personal relationships. Episodic forms of mentoring tend to be more fluid and spontaneous, which does not prevent them from being effective.

All in all, Buzzanell reminds us that mentoring can be defined by three main attributes, which are reciprocity, developmental benefits, and regular interaction – even if episodic mentoring may depart from this characterization. Regarding the linguistic and interactional features of mentoring, the author highlights that this type of activity mainly comprises giving and receiving advice, whether in written or oral forms. However, mentoring can also be characterized, in some contexts, by explicit or implicit directives and requests. Mentoring in general is defined as a complex and situated communicative form where questions of inclusion, linguistic choices, and satisfaction have to be considered, especially when underrepresented organizational members are involved.

The chapter titled *Counseling*, authored by Peter Stücheli-Herlach and Ursina Ghilardi, explores this specific form of management communication that is meant to help managers reflect on problems and create possible solutions. Counseling is analyzed as an interaction between at least two people where one is seeking help (the client) while the other is providing assistance (the counselor or any other person who might be playing the role of the adviser). For these two authors, counseling thus implies a form of collective reflection where the adviser acts as a sort of facilitator in charge of helping someone find a solution in his or her own way.

When this type of intervention proves to be successful, counseling can help members become more aware of their organizational practices to rationalize them. These sessions can also lead to innovations, help clarify responsibilities, and transfer knowledge. Stücheli-Herlach and Ghilardi identify four practices of counseling communication, according to topic orientation and role structures. They call these practices documentation, deliberation, analysis, and design. To illustrate how this is performed concretely, the authors analyze the details of the interactions in two case studies. The key patterns of communicative moves in these excerpts are recapitulating, conceptualizing, staging, and selecting.

In their chapter, *Developing organizations*, Christian Schwägerl and Susanne Knorre address the field of organization development (OD), which they consider to be in crisis because of its relative lack of innovation and professionalization. As they point out, this state of crisis appears even more paradoxical given the current cultural change that many organizations are experiencing with the digitalization of their communications. To show how OD can still be relevant in this new era, the authors demonstrate how the foundations of this field of knowledge can help organizations deal with this digital evolution. This field has been characterized from the beginning by a belief in the effectiveness of more decentralized organizational structures where groups play a key role in the enactment of change, development, and collective learning.

From Lewin's (1947) three-step model of *Unfreezing, Moving, and Refreezing* to the paradigmatic shift that this field has more recently experienced by addressing more volatile and unpredictable forms of development, the authors show that many successful organizations are the ones that develop ambidexterity, fluidity, and agility by both mobilizing hierarchical and heterarchical ways of enacting and dealing with change. In this context, communication plays a constitutive role through the organization of meetings, workshops, and less standard forms of interpersonal communication, such as daily stand-ups or mere conversations where people can speak up and tell others what needs to be done across hierarchical barriers.

In his chapter on *Accounting*, Bertrand Fauré shows that even if the process of financial accounting is not usually considered part of what we call management communication, this activity takes on a central role when financial accounting as a form of communication is understood as a metaconversation (Robichaud, Giroux, and Taylor 2004). Here, the question of value creation is collectively addressed and discussed. However, the author also points out that accounting has to be reconceptualized to allow organizations to create the conditions of a sustainable future. In other words, accounting needs to address the question of what is counted and how, which means that new numbers and other forms of quantification have to be processed.

Thus, Fauré explores how accounting, often called the *language of business*, can be identified as a form of communication, but also how communication itself can be reversely characterized as a form of accounting. As a form of communication, accounting involves three positions that actors can fill when they process numbers: the accountor who renders accounts, the accountee who receives them, and the accountant who makes them. This triad is often associated with capitalism and the financialization of organizations. Fauré reminds us that more social and sustainable usages of numbers have been and can be invented to make organizations more socially and environmentally responsible. Regarding communication as a form of accounting, Fauré highlights how numbers and calculations can play the role of discursive resources for several forms of management communication, making things and people visible, commensurable, and governable.

4.3 Contexts of management communication

This last section begins with a chapter titled *Managing communication in multilingual workplaces*, authored by Susanne Tietze, Hilla Back, and Rebecca Piekkari. Here, the authors explore how employees coming from various cultural and linguistic backgrounds communicate in their daily interactions. While some use English as a global lingua franca, others choose to rely on nonverbal communication or translations to interact with each other. The authors point out that even if English is often used in multilingual workplaces today, miscommunication and misunderstanding often lurk just around the corner, besides issues of inequality related to this global usage. As they also insist, the question of what language to use also depends on the situations in which people find themselves.

To analyze this complexity, Tietze, Back, and Piekkari employ the iceberg model to identify the various layers of communication that can be found in multilingual workplaces. Below the surface where English appears as the common corporate language, we find other situations, which the authors call *linguascapes*, where language use is negotiated and contested through highly interactive behaviors. Deep below the surface, the authors also find nonverbal forms of communication, which include body language, intonation, gestures, and silences, as well as visual aids. These forms of communication are sometimes the only resources employees can rely on to understand each other. All these observations lead us to acknowledge the key role multilingual and multimodal forms of communication play in the constitution of organizations.

The chapter titled *Exploring and analyzing linguistic environments*, authored by Philipp Dreesen and Julia Krasselt, shows how discourses can be investigated and monitored as the communicative environments of organizations. If organizations can indeed be considered communicatively constituted, these authors go one step further by demonstrating how organizations can manage to communicate *through* their environment, an environment that comments on what the respective organization does and is. In other words, discourses that constitute the environment of an organization can ascribe various positions and images to the latter, an attribution that can have important effects on how the organization is perceived and evaluated by its stakeholders and the general public.

Given that an important role of an executive is to serve as a mediator between the inside of the organization and its environment, Dreesen and Krasselt present an approach that is meant to help these top managers analyze the patterns of language use that can be found in these discursive environments. This method, called *Applied*

Linguistic Discourse Analysis, implies an active collaboration between the researchers and these managers to address problems that are deemed relevant, scientifically or practically speaking. As the authors point out, this approach (Dreesen and Stücheli-Herlach 2019), structured in four modules: modeling, measuring, interpreting, and simulation, aims to understand the communicative conditions of a discursive environment to improve practitioners' public communicative actions in general.

In her chapter, *Managing high reliability organizations*, Jody L. S. Jahn analyzes the role that structures and hierarchy play in the way high reliability organizations (HROs) and their members deal with weak signals. By weak signals, she means operational issues that can be easily ignored, but could sometimes lead to daring consequences if they are not quickly identified. HROs are characterized by their capacity to avoid catastrophic failures – even in situations that could be considered hard to read because of their high volatility and instability (e. g., the management of aircraft carriers, the operation of nuclear power plants, the combat of wildfires). As Jahn points out, the particularity of HROs is that, because of their constant vigilance, they can manage to prevent disasters reliably by identifying and addressing these weak signals quickly.

Noticing weak signals is, of course, the key to preventing catastrophes. However, the success of this vigilance also lies in members' capacity to voice their concerns to others, especially to their superiors. Safety communication, thus, mainly relies on the extent to which structures and managers allow subordinates to speak up when the latter feel that something is wrong. Jahn proposes a different way to understand how weak signals are talked into being through the way they are positioned, ventriloquized, and presentified. Positioning deals with the questions of rights and responsibilities, especially regarding the face-threatening or empowering dimensions of speaking up. Ventriloquizing concerns members' capacity to invoke rules, procedures, and statuses to mark the importance of the weak signals they pinpoint. Finally, presentifying refers to the way generic texts (such as rules or maps) are mobilized to alter a specific course of action.

The next chapter, titled *Building communities*, authored by Shiv Ganesh, Mohan Dutta, and Ngā Hau, addresses the need to find the means to build or rebuild communities that are currently facing the devastating impact of capitalism and its colonialist effects (Deetz 1992). By community building, they mean a form of reflexive organizing that is especially attentive to questions of marginalization. Community building strives to create the conditions of democratic communication processes that support social and economic justice. This requires, as they remind us, that these communities explicitly deal with matters of power within their own ranks, given the intractable aspects of power relations, even in this context. According to Ganesh, Dutta, and Hau, communities have to lose their innocence, so to speak, and be attentive to the issues of injustice that pervade their own activities.

The authors point out that organizers have to deal with four central communicative tensions when they are building communities: local versus global, reform versus revolution, persuasion versus coercion, and immanent versus external. The first tension – local versus global – is concerned with the scale of contention, the locations of organizing activities, as well as questions of solidarity and intersectionality. The second tension – reformation versus revolution – involves the extent of the changes envisioned by the community members in their political fights. As for the third tension, i.e., persuasion versus coercion, it deals with questions of agency and the potential use of violence, while the fourth tension – immanent versus external – concerns the locus of control in community building as well as issues of empowerment. These four tensions are illustrated through two case studies, one in Singapore and the other in New Zealand.

In their chapter titled *Managing CSR communication*, Dennis Schoeneborn and Verena Girschik recognize that organizations appear increasingly preoccupied by the social and ecological impacts they have on their environments, which leads them to approach corporate social responsibility (CSR) either reactively or proactively. Schoeneborn and Girschik show that, even if potential accusations of greenwashing and window-dressing are always near at hand, the distinction between CSR talk and CSR walk can be problematized to the extent that talking can also be constitutively construed as performing something. Talking has consequences because it tends to commit organizations to change by becoming more responsible. Talk is thus an act of commitment for which they can later be held accountable by stakeholders.

However, beyond this top-down perspective on CSR communication, Schoeneborn and Girschik also highlight more bottom-up approaches where top managers do not appear as the only CSR actors of their organizations. This is, for instance, what happens when employees become themselves activists by trying to transform their organizations from within – an activity that is not without risk. Finally, the two authors show how external stakeholders can shape CSR policies and practices when organizations become minimally responsive to these voices, a responsivity that implies the emergence of a true dialogue between the organization and all its stakeholders.

In her chapter titled *Rating social and environmental performances*, Brigitte Bernard-Rau echoes Schoeneborn and Girschik's chapter on CSR communication by exploring how social rating agencies (SRAs) evaluate companies' environmental and social performances. As she points out, investors and stakeholders in general are more and more interested in accessing rankings and indices to evaluate these types of performance indicators besides the financial results of an organization. As third parties, SRAs are able to define what it means to be a responsible company by providing assessments and measurements in an objective manner.

To illustrate how these agencies establish ratings and rankings, Bernard-Rau takes the example of oekom research AG,[1] an SRA founded in 1993, that provides information about companies' performances in terms of ecology and sustainability. The

---

1 In 2018 oekom research joined ISS to become ISS-oekom.

author discusses the agency's environmental, social, and governance (ESG) metrics and rating processes, and she shows the key role that discussions of these metrics and ratings play in the constitution of organizational and social change. In particular, Bernard-Rau shows how this SRA can be seen not only as an economic actor but also as an advocate and even activist with a clear social and environmental agenda. In other words, oekom acts as a spokesperson for environmental and societal needs.

In their chapter titled *Managing in hospitals*, Anne Nicotera, Melinda Villagran, and Wonsun (Sunny) Kim propose a new theoretical framework for hospital management communication. Hospitals are unique in the organizational world, even among other HROs, which explains why a special chapter is devoted to them in this handbook. As the authors remind us, hospitals are becoming increasingly complex, with multiple missions that are often in conflict with each other. For example, they have to take care of patients, but they also have to provide community service, train future doctors and nurses, engage in health-related research, and, in some parts of the world, make profits and represent religious values. Furthermore, hospitals not only have conflicting missions, they also include several professions and have to deal with multiple stakeholders as well as ambiguous tasks that follow various standard procedures. The authors use structurational divergence theory to examine the key challenges hospitals face. They conclude that these challenges are largely related to the tensions created by contradictory structures that enjoin members to respond to what often appear to be incompatible demands.

In this complex world, communicating appears to be the way to manage various priorities successfully. In this context, communication must, according to the three authors, create and sustain structures of accountability by the formation and maintenance of quality-monitoring and environmental scanning systems. Managers also need to be aware of their hybrid identities as well as the numerous tensions they have to face because of this increasing complexity.

In their chapter on *Crowdsourcing*, Amanda J. Porter, Damla Diriker, and Ilse Hellemans explore how digital technologies have renewed the way by which several minds cooperate to produce new ideas. Although the phenomenon is not that new and can be traced back at least to the eighteenth century in England, the term *crowdsourcing* was coined in 2006 and its practice has since grown impressively, especially in the past ten years. As the authors remind us, this type of management communication may address not only organizational issues but also societal challenges, such as poverty or climate change. Crowdsourcing literature paradoxically tends to assume a linear and information-based view of management communication, while this type of collaboration would *a priori* favor a richer view of communication.

Crowdsourcing tends to concern two main types of activity: repetitive tasks and creative tasks. Both require the definition of well-structured problems that people are asked to solve, whether individually or collectively. In some cases, these activities require no specific skills, while in others, they directly rely on the expertise brought by the participants. Other ways to differentiate types of crowdsourcing concern the incentives, the rules, the various phases of the process, the selection procedure for the best ideas as well as the implementation itself. However, the authors show that in the case of societal issues, defining the problem itself is far from unproblematic. This conclusion also means that the sources of expertise required to solve it are *a priori* difficult to define. This specificity also affects the incentives, rules, phases, selection, and implementation. So, in this case, management communication is less about engineering the process than about orchestrating the plurality of perspectives that can be mobilized to both define and tackle the problems.

In their chapter titled, *Managing and being managed by emotions*, Sarah Riforgiate and Samentha Sepúlveda address the key role emotions play in management communication. Since Hochschild's (1983) landmark book on emotion work and the success that the idea of emotional intelligence has had in recent years (Goleman 2006), researchers have explored how emotions are interpreted, shared, and managed in organizational contexts. The authors point out the negative implications that emotion management can have, especially regarding questions of suppression or control. They also highlight its positive implications when it leads to constructive outcomes, especially in terms of compassion or pride.

After exploring how emotions are nonverbally and verbally communicated, Riforgiate and Sepúlveda show how emotions can spread from one person to another and be socially reinforced and managed in organizations. They also illustrate how the word *professionalism* can be used to suppress emotions. This suppression can be extremely problematic, especially when minority groups feel that they are being disenfranchised because they are not able to express their concerns. While professionalism tends to prevent the expression of emotions, the authors show that the opposite is true for care-work positions, which are traditionally occupied by women and considered emotion-related work. Finally, Riforgiate and Sepúlveda illustrate how emotions can be managed and spread through the socialization of members, emotional labor, emotional intelligence, emotional contagion, and organizational processes and structures. They also discuss how emotion management patterns can have important destructive effects.

Finally, in their chapter titled *Changing through communication*, Samir Vaz, Eduardo Figueiredo, and Gabriela Maia explore the role discourse and sensemaking play in the management of organizational change. As they remind us, discourse represents what is supposed to drive organizational change, while sensemaking is what allows actors to deal with the uncertainty and ambiguity that typically characterize these periods of organizational transformation. According to the authors, managing organizational change thus depends on top managers' discourses and middle managers' sensemaking. Top managers are supposed to guide, through their discourses, the way middle managers make sense of this kind of situation.

To illustrate this phenomenon, Vaz, Figueiredo, and Maia present the case study of a Brazilian company – for reasons of anonymity, here called *Icarus* – which undertook a massive change management program in 2017. As they show, the discourse of this company's CEO was mainly characterized by what they call *discourses for accountability*, whereby this executive presented the plan, justified the results, and valued achievements. In parallel to this first type of discourse, this CEO also produced *discourses for engagement* through which he tried to inspire individual value behaviors while encouraging participation. Further, the authors identified two ways by which middle managers made sense of the situation, what they call *subjective confidence* and *objective skepticism*. These frameworks explain why the change process was ultimately considered a failure.

We hope you will enjoy this handbook as much as we have enjoyed composing and editing it. This volume is, we believe, a testament to the high quality of the research that is currently being done on management from a communicative viewpoint by scholars from diverse continents, working in different languages. Management is certainly not a magic bullet for all our organizational or other problems, but it is necessary for us to work and live together in a valuable way. We hope that this handbook shows how this can be accomplished in the complex situations managers have to deal with in their daily work. We also believe that this handbook can support further work of researchers, teachers, and practitioners by better illuminating, elucidating, and enacting the "black box" of management communication.

5 Acknowledgments

We would like to thank all our colleagues for their confidence and patience during the preparation of this handbook and for their willingness to contribute to this volume. We also owe many thanks to all the participants in the Sub-Theme "Putting Management Communication to the Practical Test in Its Heyday", which we organized in 2020 for the 36th EGOS Colloquium (European Group for Organizational Studies). There, we discussed some contributions that can be found in this handbook. A special thanks to Christian Schwägerl (Germany) who acted as a superb third convenor of this Subtheme. Furthermore, we express our special appreciation to Daniela Lang-Baumann (Switzerland) for her support in editing and correcting the manuscript, to Jonathan Hoare (United Kingdom) for his excellent proofreading service, and to Michaela Göbels for making this editing process as smooth as possible.

And last but not least, we are grateful for the confidence placed by the editors of the HAL series in our ability to successfully manage this project through years of communication with scholars from several disciplines and from different language regions on diverse continents.

6 References

Austin, John L. 1962. *How to do things with words*. London: Oxford University Press.
Baecker, Dirk. 2003. *Organisation und Management*. Frankfurt am Main: Suhrkamp.
Barnard, Chester I. 1938. *The functions of the executive*. Cambridge, MA: Harvard University Press.
Becker-Mrotzek, Michael & Reinhard Fiehler. 2002. Unternehmenskommunikation und Gesprächsforschung. Zur Einführung. In Michael Becker-Mrotzek & Reinhard Fiehler (eds.), *Unternehmenskommunikation*, 7–12. Tübingen: Narr.
Bennis, Warren G. 1989. Managing the dream: Leadership in the 21st century. *Journal of Organizational Change Management* 2(1). 6–10.
Berger, Peter L. & Thomas Luckmann. 1966. *The social construction of reality*. New York: Doubleday.
Boje, David M. 2008. *Storytelling organizations*. London & Thousand Oaks, CA: Sage.
Bourdieu, Pierre. 1973. *Esquisse d'une théorie de la pratique*. Geneva: Droz.
Brummans, Boris H. J. M., François Cooren, Daniel Robichaud & James R. Taylor. 2014. Approaches to the communicative constitution of organizations. In Linda L. Putnam & Dennis Mumby (eds.), *The Sage handbook of organizational communication: Advances in theory, research, and methods*, 3rd edn., 173–194. Los Angeles, CA: Sage.
Burrell, Gibson & Gareth Morgan. 2016 [1979]. *Sociological paradigms and organizational analysis*, 2nd edn. Abingdon, UK & New York: Routledge.
Cambridge University Press. 2020. *The Cambridge dictionary*. Cambridge: Cambridge University Press.
Cooren, François. 2000. *The organizing property of communication*. Amsterdam: John Benjamins.
Cooren, François. 2015. *Organizational discourse*. Cambridge: Polity Press.
Cooren, François, Eero Vaara, Ann Langley & Haridimos Tsoukas. 2014. Language and communication at work: Discourse, narrativity, and organizing. In François Cooren, Eero Vaara, Ann Langley & Haridimos Tsoukas (eds.), *Language and communication at work*, 1–16. Oxford: Oxford University Press.
Danesi, Marcel & Andrea Rocci. 2009. *Global linguistics: An introduction*. Berlin & New York: Mouton de Gruyter.
Deetz, Stanley. 1992. *Democracy in an age of corporate colonization: Developments in communication and the politics of everyday life*. Albany, NY: SUNY Press.
Dewey, John & Alfred F. Bentley 2008 [1949]. *Knowing and the known*. In Jo Ann Boydston (ed.), *Dewey: The later works, 1925–1953, Volume 16: 1949–1952*, 1–294. Carbondale, IL: Southern Illinois University Press.
Dreesen, Philipp & Peter Stücheli-Herlach. 2019. Diskurslinguistik in Anwendung: Ein transdisziplinäres Forschungsdesign für korpuszentrierte Analysen zu öffentlicher Kommunikation. *Zeitschrift für Diskursforschung* 7(2). 123–262.
Foucault, Michel. 1978. *The history of sexuality, Volume 1: An introduction*. New York: Vintage.
Garfinkel, Harold. 1967. *Studies in ethnomethodology*. Englewood Cliffs, NJ: Prentice Hall.
Gibson, James. 1979. *The ecological approach to visual perception*. Boston, MA: Houghton Mifflin.
Goleman, Daniel. 2006. *Emotional intelligence*. New York: Bantam.
Graeber, David. 2018. *Bullshit jobs*. New York: Simon & Schuster.
Grand, Simon. 2016. *Routines, strategies and management: Engaging for recurrent creation 'at the edge'*. Cheltenham, UK & Northampton, MA: Edward Elgar.
Grant, David, Cynthia Hardy, Cliff Oswick & Linda Putnam (eds.). 2004. *The Sage handbook of organizational discourse*. London & Thousand Oaks, CA: Sage.
Habermas, Jürgen. 1984. *The theory of communicative action: Reason and the rationalization of society*. Boston, MA: Beacon Press.

Heracleous, Loizos. 2006. *Discourse, interpretation, organization*. Cambridge: Cambridge University Press.
Hernes, Tor & Sally Maitlis (eds.). 2010. *Process, sensemaking & organizing*. Oxford: Oxford University Press.
Hillebrandt, Frank. 2014. *Soziologische Praxistheorien: Eine Einführung*. Wiesbaden: Springer VS.
Hochschild, Arlie R. 1983. *The managed heart: Commercialization of human feeling*. Berkeley, CA: University of California Press.
Holman, David & Richard Thorpe. 2003a. *Management and language: The manager as a practical author*. London: Sage.
Holman, David & Richard Thorpe. 2003b. Introduction: Management and language: The manager as a practical author. In David Holman & Richard Thorpe (eds.), *Management and language: The manager as a practical author*, 1–12. London: Sage.
Joas, Hans. 1996. *Die Kreativität des Handelns*. Frankfurt am Main: Suhrkamp.
Knapp, Karlfried & Gerd Antos. 2014. Linguistics for problem solving (Introduction to the handbook of applied linguistics series). In Eva-Maria Jakobs & Daniel Perrin (eds.), *Handbook of writing and text production*, vii–xvii. Berlin & Boston, MA: Walter de Gruyter.
Kuhn, Timothy, Karen Lee Ashcraft & François Cooren. 2017. *The work of communication: Relational perspectives on working and organizing in contemporary capitalism*. New York & London: Routledge.
Langley, Ann. 1999. Strategies for theorizing from process data. *Academy of Management Review* 24(4). 691–710.
Langley, Ann. 2009. Studying processes in and around organizations. In David A. Buchanan & Alan Bryman (eds.), *The Sage handbook of organizational research methods*, 409–429. Los Angeles, CA & London: Sage.
Larsen-Freeman, Diane & Lynne Cameron. 2008. *Complex systems and applied linguistics*. Oxford: Oxford University Press.
Lewin, Kurt. 1947. Frontiers in group dynamics: Concept, method and reality in social science; social equilibria and social change. *Human Relations* 1(1). 5–41.
Lorino, Philippe. 2014. From speech acts to act speeches: Collective activity, a discursive process speaking the language of habits. In François Cooren, Eero Vaara, Ann Langley & Hari Tsoukas (eds.), *Language and communication at work: Discourse, narrativity, and organizing*, 95–124. Oxford: Oxford University Press.
Luckmann, Thomas. 2009. Observations on the structure and function of communicative genre. *Semiotica* 173. 267–282.
Marx, Karl. 1972. *The Marx-Engels reader*. New York: Norton.
Mayo, Elton. 2004. *The human problems of an industrial civilization*. New York: Routledge.
McGregor, Douglas. 1960. *The human side of enterprise*. New York: McGraw-Hill.
Mintzberg, Henry. 1971. Managerial work: Analysis from observation. *Management Science* 18(2). B97–B110.
Mintzberg, Henry. 1973. *The nature of managerial work*. New York: Harper & Row.
Mintzberg, Henry. 2011 [2009]. *Managing*, 2nd edn. San Francisco, CA: Berrett-Koehler.
Mintzberg, Henry, Bruce Ahlstrand & Joseph Lampel. 1998. *Strategy safari: A guide tour through the wilds of strategic management*. New York: Free Press.
Müller, Andreas P. 2008. Aufgabenfelder einer Linguistik der Organisation. In Andreas P. Müller & Florian Menz (eds.), *Organisationskommunikation*, 17–46. München: Rainer Hampp.
Nicolini, Davide. 2012. *Practice theory, work and organization: An introduction*. Oxford: Oxford University Press.
Putnam, Linda L. & Anne Maydan Nicotera (eds.). 2009. *Building theories of organization: The constitutive role of communication*. New York & London: Routledge.

Putnam, Linda L. & Michael E. Pacanowsky (eds.). 1983. *Communication and organizations: An interpretative approach*. Beverly Hills, CA: Sage.

Reinsch, Lamar N. 2008. Management communication. In Francesca Bargiela-Chiappini (ed.), *The handbook of business discourse*, 279–291. Edinburgh: Edinburgh University Press.

Robichaud, Daniel & François Cooren (eds.). 2013. *Organization and organizing: Materiality, agency, and discourse*. New York & London: Routledge.

Robichaud, Daniel, Hélène Giroux & James R. Taylor. 2004. The meta-conversation: The recursive property of language as the key to organizing. *Academy of Management Review* 29(4). 617–634.

Rüegg-Stürm, Johannes & Simon Grand. 2015. *The St. Gallen Management Model*. Bern: Haupt.

Sarangi, Srikant & Christopher N. Candlin. 2011. Professional and organizational practice: A discourse/communication perspective. In Christopher N. Candlin & Srikant Sarangi (eds.), *Handbook of communication in organisations and professions* (HAL series 3), 3–58. Berlin & Boston, MA: de Gruyter Mouton.

Schäfer, Hilmar. 2013. *Die Instabilität der Praxis: Reproduktion und Transformation des Sozialen in der Praxistheorie*. Weilerswist: Velbrück Wissenschaft.

Schatzki, Theodore R. 2001. Introduction: Practice theory. In Theodore Schatzki, Karin Knorr Cetina & Eike von Savigny (eds.), *The practice turn*, 1–14. New York: Routledge.

Schedler, Kuno & Johannes Rüegg-Stürm (eds.). 2015. *Multirational management: Mastering conflicting demands in a pluralistic environment*. Basingstoke, UK: Palgrave Macmillan.

Schoeneborn, Dennis & Steffen Blaschke (with special contributions from François Cooren, Robert D. McPhee, David Seidl, & James R. Taylor). 2014. The three schools of CCO thinking: Interactive dialogue and systematic comparison. *Management Communication Quarterly* 28(2). 285–316.

Searle, John R. 1979. *Expression and meaning: Studies in the theory of speech act*. Cambridge: Cambridge University Press.

Shotter, John & Ann L. Cunliffe. 2003. Managers as practical authors: Everyday conversations for action. In David Holman & Richard Thorpe (eds.), *Management and language: The manager as a practical author*, 15–37. London: Sage.

Simon, Herbert A. 1957. *Models of man*. New York: John Wiley.

Simon, Herbert A. 1960. *The new science of management decision*. New York: Harper & Row.

Spranz-Fogasy, Thomas. 2002. Was macht der Chef? Der kommunikative Alltag von Führungskräften in der Wirtschaft. In Michael Becker-Mrotzek & Reinhard Fiehler (eds.), *Unternehmenskommunikation*, 209–230. Tübingen: Narr.

Stücheli-Herlach, Peter. 2018. Wertschöpfung als Wortschöpfung: Zur Modellierung des Sprachgebrauchs in der strategischen Organisationskommunikation. In Annika Schach & Cathrin Christoph (eds.), *Handbuch Sprache in den Public Relations: Theoretische Ansätze – Handlungsfelder – Textsorten*, 117–134. Wiesbaden: Springer VS.

Taylor, Frederick W. 1911. *The principles of scientific management*. New York: Harper & Row.

Taylor, James R. & Elizabeth Van Every. 2000. *The emergent organization: Communication as site and surface*. Mahwah, NJ: Lawrence Erlbaum.

Taylor, James R. & Elizabeth Van Every. 2011. *The situated organization: Case studies in the pragmatics of communication research*. New York: Routledge.

Taylor, James R. & Daniel Robichaud. 2007. Management as metaconversation: The search for closure. In François Cooren (ed.), *Interacting and organizing: Analysis of a management meeting*, 5–30. Mahwah, NJ & London: Lawrence Erlbaum.

Tietze, Susanne, Laurie Cohen & Gill Musson. 2003. *Understanding organizations through language*. London & Thousand Oaks, CA: Sage.

Trujillo, Nick. 1983. "Performing" Mintzberg's roles: The nature of managerial communication. In Linda L. Putnam & Michael E. Pacanowsky (eds.), *Communication and organizations: An interpretative approach*, 73–97. Beverly Hills, CA: Sage.

Weber, Max. 1964. *The theory of social and economic organization*. New York: Free Press.
Weick, Karl E. 2001. *Making sense of the organization*. Malden, MA & Oxford: Blackwell.
Westwood, Robert & Stephen Linstead (eds.). 2001. *The language of organization*. London & Thousand Oaks, CA: Sage.
White, Harrison C. 2008. *Identity and control: How social formations emerge*, 2nd edn. Princeton, NJ: Princeton University Press.

Part I: **Practices of management communication**

Nicolas Bencherki

1 Speaking

Abstract: While speaking is often contrasted with writing, this chapter considers that ambiguity between the two modalities confers to speaking its ability to affect organizing. The chapter conceptually discusses how these modalities have been distinguished, including by considering speaking as a human prerogative and writing as a derivative, and suggests that such distinctions are hard to justify. The chapter calls for greater attention to the performative power of speaking and to the emancipatory facet of talk, and suggests that closer attention to how people speak would reveal how they constitute a shared world. After questioning whether distinguishing talk and text is useful, the chapter shows that the two are in fact blended, especially when viewing speaking as situated action, when paying attention to conversational dynamics or when exploring its performative dimension, which leads to recognizing its critical implications in terms of giving a voice to all in constituting a collectivity.

Keywords: speaking; orality; talk and text dynamics; social interaction; performativity

Speaking is often compared to writing and deemed to have effects of its own. This chapter begins by summarizing the key distinctions that have been established between these two modalities before suggesting that, on the contrary, it is precisely the ambiguity over this distinction that grants speaking its organizing power. Several analytical perspectives are then reviewed – ethnomethodology, conversation analysis, conversational lamination, conversation/text dynamics, and speech act theory – that, each in their own way, take advantage of this ambiguity to reveal talk's contribution to organizing. Then, speaking in management is analyzed in how it offers a closer look at the distribution of voices within and around the organization. Finally, the implications of speaking for management research are considered in a concluding section, in particular by calling for greater attention to the concrete interactional practices that underly management communication.

Text and writing are often either celebrated or decried as the *sine qua non* condition of bureaucracy and rational organizing (Derrida 1996; Hull 2003; Vismann 2008) and as tools to manage complexity and stabilize change (Anderson 2004; Callon 2002; Fayard and Metiu 2013). While it is an important topic of study in literature and linguistics, orality seems to be left on the curbside of organization and management theory, including within organizational and management communication studies. This is all the more surprising given that the opposition between talk and text, or orality and literacy, is at the core of philosophical debates surrounding communication (Ong 2012).

Communication has not always defaulted to writing, as it seems to do now (Peters 1999). In Plato's *Phaedrus* (2002: 69), writing is described as "the appearance of intelligence, not real intelligence", whereas good rhetors would learn to deliver their speech orally. This tradition continues today in the United States with public speaking curricula (Boromisza-Habashi, Hughes, and Malkowski 2016). More recently, Walter J. Ong (2012: 73) similarly advocated for the priority of orality over writing:

> Because in its physical constitution as sound, the spoken word proceeds from the human interior and manifests human beings to one another as conscious interiors, as persons, the spoken word forms human beings into close-knit groups. [... When] each reader enters into his or her own private reading world, the unity of the audience is shattered, to be re-established only when oral speech begins again. Writing and print isolate.

Ong thus intimately associates talking with humanity and in particular with belonging to a community. He considers writing to be at once less connected with one's "interior" and as a solitary activity. While talking would engage with the body, writing, for its part, would reduce all sensations to visual analogues, thus impoverishing the communication experience.

In the study of organizational and management communication, literature on talk as such remains scarce. Most of it uses the notions of "talking" or "speaking" in a metaphorical sense, in particular to describe how people engage with a topic (for instance, "talking about diversity" in Auger-Dominguez 2019). Over the next few pages, we will see that this scarcity may not simply be an oversight. In fact, a clear distinction between talking and writing, or between orality and literacy, is difficult to draw. We will see that it is precisely the inability to untangle the two that makes communication so relevant to the study of organizations and management practices.

That being said, we will also propose a few avenues for a better study of talk in organizational settings. A well-established tradition in this sense is conversation analysis (Goodwin and Heritage 1990; Sacks 1992), although researchers are also pointing out that just studying talk is insufficient to fully account for interactional situations, which are inherently multimodal (Mondada 2007). We will also suggest shedding a new light on Austin's (1962) notion of "locution" as part of his speech act theory, and explore ideas of speaking up and voicing. Through a review of these research avenues, we will see that much of what goes on in organizations is done through talk, an insight that Mintzberg (1973) already suggested decades ago. More precisely, we want to argue that organizations are constituted as voices are distributed among beings (Cooren 2010). We conclude by inviting researchers to be more precise regarding the concrete practices that underlie communication, in order to discover the richness of what happens when people speak.

1 Blending talk and text

Jean-Dominique Bauby (1997) was a successful journalist until he suffered a massive stroke that left him entirely paralyzed except for his left eyelid. As he could not speak, he dictated his memoir, *The Diving Bell and the Butterfly*, by blinking his eyelid to select one letter at a time on a board that his speech therapist would show him, until he completed the book's 139 pages.

In Jordan, Doctors Without Borders renovated a hospital where a French nurse oversaw the construction of an operating theater by local workers who only spoke Arabic. She relied on informal translation by other colleagues. Over time, the workers and she developed a repertoire of gestures that allowed them to relay simple ideas even though they did not share a common tongue (Bencherki, Matte, and Pelletier 2016).

The two cases above crack open the seemingly airtight distinction between orality and writing. Neither did Bauby (1997) utter a word nor did he scribble a letter, and yet he wrote a book. As for the nurse, she did not technically "speak" or write with the construction workers. Communication is richer than implied by the either/or alternative often established between talking and writing. In both cases, Ong would surely consider that Bauby and the nurse resorted to visual analogues, and yet it would seem unfair to think of them as less in touch with their interiority or humanity than if they had actually spoken. Similar questions on what counts as talk or text could be raised with signed languages (e. g., Hodge, Ferrara, and Anible 2019) and non-verbal features of communication (e. g., Acheson 2008).

It is also not quite correct to assume that writing (in the broadest sense) requires a "medium", be it a sheet of paper or a computer, while writing oral communication would be immediate and would not need the intercession of a medium (as suggests Ong 2012: 172). The fact is that any communication situation, even in an oral form, involves some sort of mediation, at the very least because the speaker must express herself using a language that may more or less faithfully convey her intention (Derrida 1998). Her words may even betray her: she may say things she didn't mean or that could be used against her. These breakdowns are evidence of the mediated nature of oral communication (Cooren 2018a).

Furthermore, actual studies of the way people speak tend to suggest that people rarely do so in isolation. People are not just talking heads; when they talk, they do so in an embodied way (Goodwin and LeBaron 2011). To name just a few examples, they gesture to get their argument across (Brassac et al. 2008), or they refer to documents and look at blackboards together (Cooren and Bencherki 2010; Vásquez et al. 2018). Research methods now attempt to account for the "multimodal" character of interaction, for instance by developing new transcription strategies, recognizing that talk is but a portion of what occurs (Mondada 2018).

Even Ong, in what may seem like a self-contradiction, acknowledged that orality and literacy are not entirely separate domains. For instance, he recognized that

"Writing serve[s] largely to recycle knowledge back into the oral world" (Ong 2012: 117), which does give primacy to orality, but also stresses the interplay between the two. Similarly, while Ong initially appeared to argue that orality better expresses interiority and humanity, he also conceded that writing produces characters with introspection and "elaborately worked out analyses of inner states of soul and their inwardly structured sequential relationships" (Ong 2012: 149). It thus appears that the prerogatives of orality and those of literacy are not as opposed as one might think. This is made all the more true in the context of secondary and digital oralities, where people write for others to recite on television or radio, and where young people use oral-like language when chatting online and texting on their phones (Soffer 2016).

This intermingling of talk and text is crucial in communication's ability to contribute to sociality and to the constitution of collectives of all kinds, including organizations. Indeed, it has been proposed that organizations are constituted through the interplay of talk and text, the former allowing the formulation and negotiation of ways of doing, decisions and rules, and the latter allowing them to endure beyond the context of a single conversation, only to be interpreted again in talk (Taylor et al. 1996; Taylor and Van Every 2000). It is precisely the ability of language to escape the control of its author and to venture beyond her intention that offers it organizing properties (Cooren 2000). It is when language does not merely convey each individual "interior" but gains autonomy, that it may move past its expressive function and become an object of collective inquiry and possibly guide and constrain human action (Bencherki et al. 2019).

Despite the fundamental difficulty in untangling talk and text and if we caricature the opposition between the two, we must acknowledge that the "conversation" pole has been mostly ignored in organization and management scholarship. Only a few studies take the time to consider what takes place when people speak as part of their work life, for instance during strategic conversations (Samra-Fredericks 2003) and in board meetings (Cooren 2004b), in exercising leadership (Fairhurst 2007), or when people orient themselves towards a common object of work (Luff and Heath 2019). These studies have in common that they adopt ethnomethodology and conversation analysis in one way or another. The following section presents how these analytical traditions may help to value speaking in organization and management communication studies.

2 Speaking as situated action: ethnomethodology and conversation analysis

While they remain rare overall, there is an increasing number of studies looking at the detail of how people accomplish their work, especially in organizational and management studies. Typically, these studies adopt ethnomethodology or conversation analysis as a theoretical and methodological attitude, which are jointly known as EM/CA (see Llewellyn and Hindmarsh 2010). These studies reveal how apparently complex and broad organizational phenomena are in fact substantiated by seemingly "minor" conduct (Clark and Pinch 2010). One of these conducts consists of the way we talk, from everyday conversations to executive decisions (Boden 1994).

Attention to the detail of talk is justified on the premise that social order must be reconstructed in interaction "for a next time" (Garfinkel 2002: 98). Authority, for instance, is not a stable asset; rather, it must be performed by bringing into each situation absent people, principles, and things that lend their authority to the speaker (Bencherki, Matte, and Cooren 2019; Benoit-Barné and Cooren 2009; Bourgoin, Bencherki, and Faraj 2019). The same goes for other seemingly abstract organizational notions, such as property, which is accomplished in a diversity of practical ways; resorting to an ownership deed is a rare exception and is itself a communicative action as people must negotiate its meaning (Bencherki and Bourgoin 2019). As another example, it is also through situated interaction that workers address the ethical concerns that confront them by discursively challenging the demands of various standards and imperatives (Cooren 2016; Matte and Bencherki 2019). Looking at the way people talk, in each case, allows a discovery of how they, together, concretely handle issues of consequence to them in an empirical and inductive manner, rather than deducting what their behavior should be from abstract definitions.

Talk, then, is not only a means to convey a message. Thinking in terms of message exchange would be reductive of all that takes place when people interact. Instead, better analytical insight is gained when conceiving talk as social action (Pomerantz and Fehr 1997). More precisely, this means that people speaking to each other in a certain way are jointly accomplishing actions and constructing situations where expectations are imposed and accountability is demanded for violations. The building blocks for these constructions are the same ones that people use to manage their talk. For instance, the way turn-taking is accomplished can demonstrate outrage at the previous speaker's utterance by interrupting them, by hesitation, or by delaying one's turn. On the other hand, the inability to take a turn may indicate a lower social status (Sacks, Schegloff, and Jefferson 1974). In this sense, the sequence of talk, the expectation of adjacency pairs and the (dis)preference for some responses – as when a "how are you?" calls for a "good and you?" – form the basic infrastructure of social order (Schegloff and Sacks 1973).

The term *adjacency pairs* is somewhat of a misnomer given that they may be nested. For instance, "how are you?" could be followed by a second question, "are you talking to me?" and its response, "yes, you!" before resuming the main activity, "oh, I'm good, thanks!" (Heritage 1984). Furthermore, it may be more useful to think in terms of a triad than a pair, given that the confirmation that the interaction met expectations will be witnessable in the third turn of talk (Weick 1979 refers to this as a "double-interact"). For instance, if someone asks, "Can you hand me this file?" and another person responds, "Here it is!" we must wait until the first speaker answers either, "Thank you!" or, "Oh, no, I meant the other file!" to know whether the interaction succeeded and feel a sense of closure. It is only because this third turn may often be omitted (we do not always thank each other) that triads can be mistaken for pairs (Cooren and Fairhurst 2004).

Attention to the detail of interaction teaches us that collectives and organizations are built from the ground up using such triadic blocks, rather than being transcendent structures looming over our interactions. The only context of an utterance is the utterances that came before and it forms, itself, the context for the ones that come after (Pomerantz, Sanders, and Bencherki 2018). The meaning of what someone says, then, is pragmatic and comes from the saying's contribution to an ongoing flow of action (Sanders 1999). It is at least in part dependent on "its location within a sequence" (Philipsen 1990: 228). Or, to say it otherwise, hearers and speakers coordinate their actions while they infer "emerging meaning by analyzing the unfolding structure of the talk in progress" (Goodwin and Heritage 1990: 290). For instance, determining what is strategic or not to organizational members is achieved through the way matters of concern are presented and taken up in conversation (Bencherki et al. 2019). Even telling who's a member or not depends on how others perceive their contribution as participating to the ongoing activity (Bencherki and Snack 2016).

Considering speaking as a situated action, which takes place in specific interactions, thus highlights that it is an orderly, sequenced process that serves as an infrastructure for the accomplishment of seemingly "broader" activities. It also puts the emphasis on the pragmatic nature of talk, whose meaning is worked out as people participate in their joint conversational action. Talking, then, is doing.

3 Conversational lamination and text/conversation dynamics

Paying such close attention to how people talk and interact may give the impression that we are missing the bigger picture of organizational reality. However, as Boden (1994) suggests, organizational actors themselves weave together individual communicative events – conversations, decisions, declarations, etc. – into more or less coherent organizational wholes, a process she described as "conversational lamination". For instance, people, during their current interaction, may remind each other of agreements they made earlier and somewhere else, thus binding the space and time of their organization (Cooren 2004b; Vásquez and Cooren 2013). As such references take place iteratively, conversations are layered on top of each other, forming the so-called organizational structure. In this sense, there is no need for the analyst to supplement the analysis of interactions with their respective contexts since actors themselves make connections to relevant contextual features within their interactions, which in turn will make up the context for further interactions.

Context, however, may at times appear to be external and objective. This is because it is often available to us in the form of texts that inscribe and provide longevity to prior decisions and agreements. These may be texts in the conventional sense, for instance in the form of an organization's rules and regulations, or its strategic plan, which are the result of prior conversations and may again constrain future conversations. In this sense, speaking and writing flow into one another, as writing has been shown to allow elements from each conversation to be mobilized again in another context, thus allowing agreements and decisions to last beyond the situation where they were formulated in the first place (Taylor and Van Every 2000). This is the case, for instance, when people refer to notes and documents produced at previous meetings to remember what work they have already accomplished and what they still need to discuss (Cooren et al. 2015). However, writing must be made to matter in each conversation in order to make a difference in the ongoing activity, where documents, notes, and other elements are being used. Sometimes, we fail to bring up the right sheet of paper, or to recognize its meaning, or to attribute the same importance to it as we used to (Vásquez et al. 2018). While texts may participate in different ways in interactions, their mobilization in talk remains the most prominent (Brummans 2007; Cooren 2004a).

Texts can take a multiplicity of forms aside from simply written words on a sheet of paper. For instance, a piece of software is the result of numerous conversations over interests and collective action during its development and implementation phase. However, once it is deployed, it also appears as a material and immutable text that reminds its users, including those who were absent at the time it was put in place, of those previous conversations, with the inherent risk of them not being recognized if the software doesn't get the organizational text right, making it seem not to "work" (Taylor and Virgili 2008). Among management consultants, texts often take the form of Microsoft PowerPoint slide decks that encapsulate models and methods, resulting from negotiations with clients, and that consultants share with each other, thus reproducing ways of doing things (Bourgoin and Muniesa 2016; Schoeneborn 2013). The same text may be distributed among several materializations (a rule may be written in a bylaw, coded into a piece of software, and revisited during new employee training) and may become "authoritative", in the sense that it guides and, so to speak, co-authors further organizational conversations and texts (Kuhn 2008).

Through the notion of text, we are therefore able to capture the endurance of speech between conversations and its circulation from one interaction to another. We do not continuously start over and renegotiate hierarchies, roles, task distribution, and other facets of organizing because we inscribe what we say and do face-to-face (or through technological mediation) into texts of all sorts, including mnemonic traces, i.e., what we remember from one conversation to the next. We can then mobilize these texts again in the future, thus ensuring the continuity of our collectives through time and space.

4 The performativity of speaking: speech act theory and the locution

Considering talk as social action – as something that people do and through which they do things – can be captured in the notion that talk is *performative*. This term has taken a variety of meanings in organization and management studies (see Gond et al. 2016), but its origin can be traced back to John L. Austin's (1962) speech act theory. The idea of performativity was further developed by John Searle (1969) as well as Judith Butler (1990, 1993). For Austin and his followers, language does not only describe a pre-existing reality, it also actively *does* things and transforms reality, i. e., performs it. Arguably, speech act theory is not restricted to speech *per se* and it has been convincingly used to analyze the ability of texts to act on reality (e. g., Derrida 1988). However, as its name indicates, it is rooted in the way we speak.

Austin's (1962) starting point was that, while language had mostly been understood in terms of reference (i. e., the meaning of a word corresponds to the thing that it describes or expresses), reducing language to reference fails to account for many ways in which it is actually used (a view shared by Wittgenstein 1953). When considering what people tangibly do with words, we can see that many utterances cannot be explained in terms of reference, for example when someone gives an order, asks a question, commits herself, expresses condolences, and so forth. Even instances where words describe reality are, in fact, performative to the extent that describing or informing someone of something is also an action (Searle 1979, calls these "assertives"). Other instances include when someone promises to do something ("commissives"), when they give instructions ("directives"), express what they feel about a situation ("expressives"), or change the state of relations between people and things ("declarations") (Searle 1979).

One of Austin's most famous examples of this last case is when a priest says, "I now pronounce you husband and wife". In doing so, he not only describes the couple's pre-existing relationship – as if the priest was merely noticing that the couple had somehow gotten married – but produces it. Had the ceremony failed to proceed to the moment the priest said those words, depending on the country's laws, the couple may very well not be married. In organizational settings, a manager who says, "You're fired!" effectively fires you, and the one who says, "Nice work!" describes the quality of your work but also compliments you and recognizes you as a valuable member of the organization.

In addition to classifying speech acts according to the type of action they perform, Austin also offers a threefold division of the levels on which analysis can be conducted: the locutionary level looks at the fact that people speak at all (for instance, a junior employee may build up the courage to speak up during a meeting); the illocutionary level looks at what they do in speaking (she may ask a question, provide information, give instructions on how to do something, commit herself to doing something, etc.); and the perlocutionary level looks at the consequences of speaking (she impresses her manager, she contributes to the project, she prompts others to react to her suggestion, etc.).

The fact that talk is not only descriptive but also brings about a new reality has been used to understand, for example, how conversations enable organizational change (Ford and Ford 1995). The relationship between talk and action is also at the heart of corporate social responsibility communication as it allows an understanding of how promises, as illocutionary acts (namely commissives), turn into tangible actions through their perlocutionary consequences (Christensen, Morsing, and Thyssen 2019). What people do with words, therefore, is not reducible to the semantic content of their utterances. To understand the entire situation in which speaking occurs, the actions that take place when speaking must be taken into account. Such an analysis is exemplified in Judith Butler's study of hate speech, where she shows that the meaning of a speech act cannot be dissociated from "the act that the body performs in the speaking [of] the act" (Butler 1997: 11). For instance, silence can also be hurtful and complicit of hate speech when it is used to refrain from denouncing abuse (Covarrubias 2008).

Speech, then, is always performed by someone, somewhere, in a specific manner and using a corporeal body. Public speaking research emphasizes the bodily dimension of speech delivery, looking at how facial expressiveness, gestures and height, but also anxiety, play a part in talk's ability to affect audience members (Baker and Redding 1962; Beatty and Behnke 1991; Burgoon, Birk, and Pfau 1990). Consider, e. g., how being a young-looking consultant struggling to be taken seriously, or a fair-skinned woman with a British accent running a hospital ward in Kenya would influence how one speaks and interacts with others (Bourgoin and Harvey 2018; Matte and Bencherki 2019). Discounting this embodied character is a "naturalization" of the (power) relations that speech engenders (Deetz 1992).

Acknowledging that the performative power of speech acts comes from their embodied nature clarifies the relationship between speech and body/materiality. This relationship, in turn, reveals how speech also constitutes bodies and identities in an iterative manner (Butler 1990, 1993). For example, insults have been described as instrumental in forging gay identities (Eribon 2004). The connection between (hostile) speech and identity is particularly true in the workplace, where women's bodies are performatively constituted in speech (Trethewey 1999), and where being pregnant and a mother is discursively woven into professional norms and organizational narratives (Gatrell 2013).

Studies that adopt a speech act perspective, including its Butlerian variant, put the analytical emphasis on the illocutionary level – what people do when they talk – and the perlocutionary level– the consequences (anticipated or not) of their speech. This is consistent with Austin (1962: 99), for whom the guiding question was, "When we perform a locutionary act, we use speech: but in what way precisely are we using it on this occasion?" However, few studies have considered the locution itself – the fact that we use speech in the first place – as an empirically interesting fact. Turning the researchers' attention to the fact that people speak is not simply a matter of looking at how people choose talk as the appropriate "medium" or "channel" (for instance during performance appraisal; see Sorsa, Pälli, and Mikkola 2014). What is also interesting is what difference is made by the fact whether someone speaks or not in a given situation.

Without addressing this question specifically, some studies have hinted at the problematic nature of someone speaking in a particular way at a particular time. For instance, someone might speak in Swahili to avoid being understood by French expatriates during a meeting (Cooren et al. 2007). Or, the fact that a non-member speaks during a meeting may trigger a collective conversation over membership and whether or not it should be extended to that person (Bencherki and Snack 2016). Finally, some institutional contexts have specific procedures for turn-taking, meaning that the very fact of speaking out of turn may constitute a breach (Ilie 2010).

Recognizing the performative nature of talk, especially when fully taking into account the locutionary level, allows for a richer picture of what happens when people speak. However, beyond describing how talk occurs, some authors also argue that attention to *who speaks how and when* should be a normative duty for researchers.

5 Speaking up and voicing: the emancipatory facet of talk

As soon as we begin to consider speaking from a performative angle, the question of agency can be addressed: being able to speak is also being able to act within our human collectives, and being limited in the ability to speak is also a constraint on one's agency (see Ahearn 2001; Bencherki 2016; Brummans 2018). It has been suggested that, in organizational contexts, the ability to speak up and express one's voice depends on the person's power position, a relation that enforces the status quo (Islam and Zyphur 2005). Overcoming such limitations, including by defying them, thus becomes a political action through which a person reclaims her speech, her agency, and her ability to participate in her community.

Reclaiming one's speech can be understood in the broader sense of the word, as for instance marginalized populations organize media interventions to have their perspective heard (Dreher 2010). In organizations, beliefs held by managers about their employees may deter workers from expressing ideas and voicing concerns, thus requiring them to overcome their fear of negative repercussion or act covertly to contribute to their organization (Morrison and Milliken 2000). Studies of people trying to make their collectivities better, despite being prevented from speaking up, show that an important challenge is to be heard by the audience, or to have one's voice make a significant difference.

Yet, authors have pointed out the benefits of paying attention to people's voices. For instance, letting a diverse range of health professionals speak up improves patient safety (Weiss et al. 2014). As another example, "open strategizing", by allowing a wide range of stakeholders to express their interests, offers the "requisite diversity" needed for strategic planning (Seidl and Werle 2018). A *Journal of Management Studies* special issue surveyed the range of situations where being inclusive of multiple voices would benefit an organization – for instance to raise ethical issues – but where those voices may not be heard (Morrison and Milliken 2003).

However, several authors also view attention to what people have to say as a normative duty, especially when listening to populations that are historically under-privileged or actively prevented from speaking (Spivak 1988). The responsibility of listening to these subaltern voices, in the absence of other avenues for expression, is incumbent on researchers. Research strategies must therefore be devised in ways that allow for listening to these people. For instance, ethnographers spend time with dispossessed communities, talk with them, and feel it is their duty to report on their perspectives (Pal 2014). Researchers may also help people overcome linguistic limitations in multilingual settings (Barner-Rasmussen and Bor 2005). Interview strategies must be adapted to pay attention to what vulnerable populations have to say, including their refusal to speak, rather than expecting competent answers (Nagar-Ron and Motzafi-Haller 2011).

While some voices may be suppressed due to political or economic imbalance, some people are physically unable to talk in the way Western researchers expect them to. They may use a computer interface to "talk" and be perceived as lacking intelligence due to their disability, making the researcher an ally in translating and amplifying their voice (Ashby 2011). Similarly, intellectually disabled people may be unable to express their concerns, and researchers must specifically offer them an opportunity and means to speak up (McDonald, Kidney, and Patka 2013). Researchers must also take the time to listen to dying patients (Shalev 2010). Besides physical limitation, the inability to speak may have to do with *what* people are trying to express: indeed, some things, as in the case of trauma, may be unspeakable (Day 2005).

Giving a voice to others has been described as requiring a different form of theorizing. First, it must acknowledge the polyphonic nature of any situation that it attempts to describe and recognize that numerous voices may matter (Cooren and Sandler 2014). However, it must not presume that all of them are equally capable of expressing themselves, and therefore realize that it is also the researcher's duty to ensure strategies are available to listen on people's own terms (Letiche 2010). Second, scholars have warned that theorizing must not hide these voices behind the researcher's own speech, concepts, and jargon (Krippendorff 2000). Listening attentively to multiple voices also means being ready to take the risk of not liking what they have to say (Grewal 2012).

Such an agenda for theoretical work has, in part, been embraced by ethnomethodology and conversation analysis, as we saw above (Krippendorff 2000). In a more explicit way, the kind of interactional analysis EM/CA affords has been used to analyze organizational reality in terms of voices, using a perspective metaphorically termed "ventriloquism" (Cooren 2010, 2012). Ventriloquial analysis, however, extends previous research on how voice is given to others by being agnostic as to the nature of the voiceless beings who attempt to express themselves. Building on actor-network theory's notion that non-humans also participate in sociability (Latour 2005), ventriloquial analysis pays attention to how people speak on behalf of others (including absent people, things, or principles – referred to as "figures") and position themselves as both made to say or do things because of them, and as making them say and do things in the interaction. For instance, a management consultant may legitimate a suggestion by presenting it as approved by the client organization's CEO, as following a well-established auditing model, or as reflecting concerns that employees expressed during focus groups. The consultant's ability to guide collective action thus depends on her ability to channel other voices through her own (Bourgoin, Bencherki, and Faraj 2019).

Through the notion of voice and by looking at how people practically distribute it by lending voice to some beings or not, it is thus possible to realize that it is not only researchers who feel responsible for helping others talk: it is a process that a variety of people engage in regularly, e. g., when they tell a story about someone else, describe a document, or invoke a rule to lend authority to their actions (Benoit-Barné and Cooren 2009). Also, understanding how people give a voice to others helps better account for the distribution of agency and shows how people and things jointly constitute their collectives (Cooren 2010).

6 Conclusion: speaking to create a shared world

By being attentive to the fact that people *speak* (or don't), how they do so, and what they achieve by speaking – including lending their voice to other people and things – it is possible to devise a more balanced view of communication. First, it is more balanced by acknowledging that there is no reason to contrast speaking with writing, and that in fact the distinction between the two may not hold. In questioning this classical dichotomy, researchers may recognize more forms of "speaking" than just verbal speech and may be more mindful of the voices that are trying to express themselves. They may also be more aware that talk rarely comes alone, as any conversation also includes gestures, documents, and other modalities as part of talk itself.

Second, this view of communication is balanced because it does not assume an imbalance between a sender trying to cast a message over a channel to a passive receiver. These distinctions also do not hold. Instead, communication is about people trying to do something together. The meaning of what they say depends on how they contribute to the ongoing interaction and to their joint activity. In other words, speaking is *performative*: it is an achievement, and it does things in its own right. This is all the more important when considering that the act of speaking, in itself, may make a difference at the *locutionary* level. Indeed, for people who are prevented from speaking by political or physical limitations, the ability to speak may not be a given, and they must overcome these constraints in a way that allows them to participate in collective life.

This leads to the third point: a balanced view of communication means being attentive to all voices equally, specifically to how they are distributed among people and things. This may entail that it is the researcher's duty to make sure all voices are heard. However, the researcher should not assume that they will take an expected form. They may be weaker voices or express themselves in surprising ways, and they may say things that make the researcher uncomfortable. Yet, being attentive to them means being careful not to hide them behind academic jargon and accepting them for what they are.

Adopting a better understanding of speaking is of particular relevance to management and organization scholars, as it is in the way voices are distributed that collectives of all sorts, including organizations, are brought into being (Taylor and Van Every 2000). Writing and other non-verbal elements can also make a difference in this distribution, but to be of importance they must be materialized in (multimodal) talk (Cooren 2010, 2018b). In better understanding how speaking operates, including by lending a voice to absent or speechless others, it is therefore possible to observe how ways of doing things (Vásquez et al. 2018), ethical norms (Matte and Bencherki 2019), and other organizational elements are materialized and can play a part in guiding collective action.

To suggest this balanced view of communication, we had to explore several theoretical perspectives, starting with Ong's (2012) history of orality and literacy, moving to ethnomethodology and conversation analysis (Garfinkel 2002; Sacks 1992), to conversational lamination (Boden 1994), to text/conversation dynamics (Taylor and Van Every 2000), to speech act theory (Austin 1962; Butler 1997), then to perspectives on voicing (e. g., Morrison and Milliken 2003), and finishing with ventriloquial analysis (Cooren 2010). This range of perspectives, while it has a common thread, is indicative of the absence of a coherent research program on speaking, especially in the context of management and organization studies.

Future applied research on managerial communication will therefore need to be more precise about what "language", "talk", "speech", and "communication" mean. Too often, management studies employ these words in abstract ways, without being specific about the concrete practices that lie beneath them. As long as we remain evasive, we can paint categories in broad strokes and imagine oppositions between them, such as between orality and writing, or between theoretical perspectives. However, when we pay closer attention to the empirical phenomena we are supposed to be describing, we have a solid anchor to guide our theorizing in the right direction and realize that reality is both messier and more orderly than we thought.

Next, and relatedly, future research will need to describe precisely how actors themselves move across the alleged micro, mezzo, and macro levels, and create their collectivity, without presuming that communication takes place "within" an organization that forms its so-called context. In the analysis, those levels correspond to levels of vagueness more than to any actual reality. Rules, hierarchies, coordination, and the myriad of other phenomena that are of interest to management researchers are not abstract entities outside of talk and writing: they are accomplished concretely in the way people interact together and mobilize texts of all sorts, for instance through conversational lamination or through text/conversation dynamics (Boden 1994; Taylor and Van Every 2000). We must therefore analyze actual talk and interactions in search of organizing practices, rather than reduce speaking to people describing a pre-existing organizational reality. Such reduction would prevent us from understanding the profound impact speaking may have on organizational reality and would leave us bewildered at why things did not go as expected – or, what is even more amazing, why they did.

Finally, management researchers must pay greater attention to the many voices that populate organizations. Too often, management research continues to presume that the most important voice is that of top managers and only concerns itself with interviewing people in higher ranks. However, the fact is that all speech is performative in its own way and, if some voices are more powerful than others, this extra power must be explained. Indeed, as Butler (1999) pointed out, there is no "magic" in language's performativity and a lot of work is involved in making, say, a CEO's voice more powerful than that of a humble employee. Ignoring all that work not only limits our ability to understand the entire reality of an organization by focusing solely on a few necessarily partial voices, but also contributes to reproducing power relationships by assuming that it is natural for some people to sit at the top and for their contribution to be the only one that matters.

7 References

Acheson, Kris. 2008. Silence as gesture: Rethinking the nature of communicative silences. *Communication Theory* 18(4). 535–555.
Ahearn, Laura M. 2001. Language and agency. *Annual Review of Anthropology* 30(1). 109–137.
Anderson, Donald L. 2004. The textualizing functions of writing for organizational change. *Journal of Business and Technical Communication* 18(2). 141–164.
Ashby, Christine E. 2011. Whose "voice" is it anyway?: Giving voice and qualitative research involving individuals that type to communicate. *Disability Studies Quarterly* 31(4). https://doi.org/10.18061/dsq.v31i4.1723 (accessed 27 December 2019).
Auger-Dominguez, Daisy. 2019. Getting over your fear of talking about diversity. *Harvard Business Review Digital Articles*. https://hbr.org/2019/11/getting-over-your-fear-of-talking-about-diversity (accessed 12 November 2020).
Austin, John L. 1962. *How to do things with words*. Cambridge, MA: Harvard University Press.

Baker, Eldon E. & W. Charles Redding. 1962. The effects of perceived tallness in persuasive speaking: An experiment. *Journal of Communication* 12(1). 51–53.

Barner-Rasmussen, Wilhelm & Sanne Bor. 2005. Language in multilingual organizations: A review of the management and organization literature. Paper presented at the proceedings of the 18th Scandinavian Academy of Management, Aarhus, Denmark, 18–20 August.

Bauby, Jean-Dominique. 1997. *The diving-bell and the butterfly*. London: 4th Estate.

Beatty, Michael J. & Ralph R. Behnke. 1991. Effects of public speaking trait anxiety and intensity of speaking task on heart rate during performance. *Human Communication Research* 18(2). 147–176.

Bencherki, Nicolas. 2016. Action and agency. In Klaus Bruhn Jensen & Robert T Craig (eds.), *The international encyclopedia of communication theory and philosophy*, 1–13. Malden, MA: John Wiley & Sons.

Bencherki, Nicolas & Alaric Bourgoin. 2019. Property and organization studies. *Organization Studies* 40(4). 497–513.

Bencherki, Nicolas, Frédérik Matte & François Cooren (eds.). 2019. *Authority and power in social interaction* (Routledge Studies in Communication, Organization, and Organizing). New York: Routledge.

Bencherki, Nicolas, Frédérik Matte & Émilie Pelletier. 2016. Rebuilding Babel: A constitutive approach to tongues-in-use. *Journal of Communication* 66(5). 766–788.

Bencherki, Nicolas, Viviane Sergi, François Cooren & Consuelo Vásquez. 2019. How strategy comes to matter: Strategizing as the communicative materialization of matters of concern. *Strategic Organization*. https://doi.org/10.1177/1476127019890380 (accessed 12 November 2020).

Bencherki, Nicolas & James P. Snack. 2016. Contributorship and partial inclusion: A communicative perspective. *Management Communication Quarterly* 30(3). 279–304.

Benoit-Barné, Chantal & François Cooren. 2009. The accomplishment of authority through presentification: How authority is distributed among and negotiated by organizational members. *Management Communication Quarterly* 23(1). 5–31.

Boden, Deirdre. 1994. *The business of talk: Organizations in action*. Cambridge: Polity Press.

Boromisza-Habashi, David, Jessica M. F. Hughes & Jennifer A. Malkowski. 2016. Public speaking as cultural ideal: Internationalizing the public speaking curriculum. *Journal of International and Intercultural Communication* 9(1). 20–34.

Bourgoin, Alaric, Nicolas Bencherki & Samer Faraj. 2019. "And who are you?": A performative perspective on authority in organizations. *Academy of Management Journal* 63(4). https://doi.org/10.5465/amj.2017.1335 (accessed 12 November 2020).

Bourgoin, Alaric & Jean-François Harvey. 2018. Professional image under threat: Dealing with learning-credibility tension. *Human Relations* 71(12). 1611–1639.

Bourgoin, Alaric & Fabian Muniesa. 2016. Building a rock-solid slide: Management consulting, PowerPoint, and the craft of signification. *Management Communication Quarterly* 30(3). 390–410.

Brassac, Christian, Pierre Fixmer, Lorenza Mondada & Dominique Vinck. 2008. Interweaving objects, gestures, and talk in context. *Mind, Culture, and Activity* 15(3). 208–233.

Brummans, Boris H. J. M. 2007. Death by document: Tracing the agency of a text. *Qualitative Inquiry* 13(5). 711–727.

Brummans, Boris H. J. M. (ed.). 2018. *The agency of organizing: Perspectives and case studies*. New York: Routledge.

Burgoon, Judee K., Thomas Birk & Michael Pfau. 1990. Nonverbal behaviors, persuasion, and credibility. *Human Communication Research* 17(1). 140–169.

Butler, Judith. 1990. *Gender trouble: Feminism and the subversion of identity*. New York: Routledge.

Butler, Judith. 1993. *Bodies that matter: On the discursive limits of sex.* Abingdon, UK & New York: Routledge.
Butler, Judith. 1997. *Excitable speech: A politics of the performative.* New York: Routledge.
Butler, Judith. 1999. Performativity's social magic. In Richard Shusterman (ed.), *Bourdieu: A Critical Reader*, 113–128. Oxford: Blackwell.
Callon, Michel. 2002. Writing and (re)writing devices as tools for managing complexity. In John Law & Annemarie Mol (eds.), *Complexities: Social Studies of Knowledge Practices*, 191–217. Durham, NC: Duke University Press.
Christensen, Lars Thøger, Mette Morsing & Ole Thyssen. 2019. Talk-action dynamics: Modalities of aspirational talk. *Organization Studies.* http://journals.sagepub.com/doi/10.1177/0170840619896267 (accessed 21 December 2019).
Clark, Colin & Trevor Pinch. 2010. Some major organisational consequences of some 'minor', organised conduct: Evidence from a video analysis of pre-verbal service encounters in a showroom retail store. In Nick Llewellyn & Jon Hindmarsh (eds.), *Organisation, interaction and practice: Studies of ethnomethodology and conversation analysis*, 140–171. Cambridge: Cambridge University Press.
Cooren, François. 2000. *The organizing property of communication.* Amsterdam & Philadelphia, PA: John Benjamins.
Cooren, François. 2004a. Textual agency: How texts do things in organizational settings. *Organization* 11(3). 373–393.
Cooren, François. 2004b. The communicative achievement of collective minding: Analysis of board meeting excerpts. *Management Communication Quarterly* 17(4). 517–551.
Cooren, François. 2010. *Action and agency in dialogue: Passion, ventriloquism and incarnation.* Amsterdam & Philadelphia, PA: John Benjamins.
Cooren, François. 2012. Communication theory at the center: Ventriloquism and the communicative constitution of reality. *Journal of Communication* 62(1). 1–20.
Cooren, François. 2016. Ethics for dummies: Ventriloquism and responsibility. *Atlantic Journal of Communication* 24(1). 17–30.
Cooren, François. 2018a. Acting for, with, and through: A relational perspective on agency in MSF's organizing. In Boris H. J. M. Brummans (ed.), *The agency of organizing: Perspectives and case studies*, 142–169. New York: Routledge.
Cooren, François. 2018b. Materializing communication: Making the case for a relational ontology. *Journal of Communication* 68(2). 278–288.
Cooren, François & Nicolas Bencherki. 2010. How things do things with words: Ventriloquism, passion and technology. *Encyclopaideia, Journal of Phenomenology and Education* 14(28). 35–61.
Cooren, François, Nicolas Bencherki, Mathieu Chaput & Consuelo Vásquez. 2015. The communicative constitution of strategy-making: Exploring fleeting moments of strategy. In Damon Golsorkhi, Linda Rouleau, David Seidl & Eeero Vaara (eds.), *The Cambridge handbook of strategy as practice*, 370–393. Cambridge: Cambridge University Press.
Cooren, François & Gail T. Fairhurst. 2004. Speech timing and spacing: The phenomenon of organizational closure. *Organization* 11(6). 793–824.
Cooren, François, Frédérik Matte, James R. Taylor & Consuelo Vásquez. 2007. A humanitarian organization in action: Organizational discourse as an immutable mobile. *Discourse & Communication* 1(2). 153–190.
Cooren, François & Sergeiy Sandler. 2014. Polyphony, ventriloquism, and constitution: In dialogue with Bakhtin. *Communication Theory* 24(3). 225–244.
Covarrubias, Patricia Olivia. 2008. Masked silence sequences: Hearing discrimination in the college classroom. *Communication, Culture & Critique* 1(3). 227–252.

Day, Toni. 2005. Giving a voice to childhood trauma through therapeutic songwriting. In Felicity Baker & Tony Wigram (eds.), *Songwriting: Methods, techniques and clinical applications for music therapy clinicians, educators and students*, 82–96. London: Jessica Kingsley.

Deetz, Stanley A. 1992. *Democracy in an age of corporate colonization: Developments in communication and the politics of everyday life*. Albany, NY: State University of New York Press.

Derrida, Jacques. 1988. Signature, event, context. In Jacques Derrida, *Limited Inc.*, 1–23. Evanston, IL: Northwestern University Press.

Derrida, Jacques. 1996. *Archive fever: A Freudian impression*. Chicago, IL: University of Chicago Press.

Derrida, Jacques. 1998. *Monolingualism of the other, or, The prosthesis of origin*. Stanford, CA: Stanford University Press.

Dreher, Tanja. 2010. Speaking up or being heard? Community media interventions and the politics of listening. *Media, Culture & Society* 32(1). 85–103.

Eribon, Didier. 2004. *Insult and the making of the gay self*. Durham, NC: Duke University Press.

Fairhurst, Gail T. 2007. *Discursive leadership: In conversation with leadership psychology*. Los Angeles, CA: Sage.

Fayard, Anne-Laure & Anca Metiu. 2013. *The power of writing in organizations: From letters to online interactions*. New York: Routledge.

Ford, Jeffrey D. & Laurie W. Ford. 1995. The role of conversations in producing intentional change in organizations. *Academy of Management Review* 20(3). 541–570.

Garfinkel, Harold. 2002. *Ethnomethodology's program: Working out Durkheim's aphorism*. Lanham, MD: Rowman & Littlefield.

Gatrell, Caroline J. 2013. Maternal body work: How women managers and professionals negotiate pregnancy and new motherhood at work. *Human Relations* 66(5). 621–644.

Gond, Jean-Pascal, Laure Cabantous, Nancy Harding & Mark Learmonth. 2016. What do we mean by performativity in organizational and management theory? The uses and abuses of performativity. *International Journal of Management Reviews* 18(4). 440–463. https://doi.org/10.1111/ijmr.12074.

Goodwin, Charles & John Heritage. 1990. Conversation Analysis. *Annual Review of Anthropology* 19(1). 283–307.

Goodwin, Charles & Curtis LeBaron. 2011. *Embodied interaction: Language and body in the material world*. Cambridge: Cambridge University Press.

Grewal, Kiran. 2012. Reclaiming the voice of the 'Third World Woman': But what do we do when we don't like what she has to say? The tricky case of Ayaan Hirsi Ali. *Interventions* 14(4). 569–590. https://doi.org/10.1080/1369801X.2012.730861.

Heritage, John. 1984. *Garfinkel and ethnomethodology*. Cambridge: Polity Press.

Hodge, Gabrielle, Lindsay N. Ferrara & Benjamin D. Anible. 2019. The semiotic diversity of doing reference in a deaf signed language. *Journal of Pragmatics* 143. 33–53.

Hull, Matthew S. 2003. The file: Agency, authority, and autography in an Islamabad bureaucracy. *Language & Communication* 23(3–4). 287–314.

Ilie, Cornelia. 2010. Speech acts and rhetorical practices in parliamentary Question Time. *Revue roumaine de linguistique* 55(4). 333–342.

Islam, Gazi & Michael J. Zyphur. 2005. Power, voice, and hierarchy: Exploring the antecedents of speaking up in groups. *Group Dynamics: Theory, Research, and Practice* 9(2). 93–103.

Krippendorff, Klaus. 2000. Ecological narratives: Reclaiming the voice of theorized others. In Jose V. Ciprut (ed.), *The art of the feud: Reconceptualizing international relations*, 1–26. Westport, CT: Praeger.

Kuhn, Timothy. 2008. A communicative theory of the firm: Developing an alternative perspective on intra-organizational power and stakeholder relationships. *Organization Studies* 29(8–9). 1227–1254.

Latour, Bruno. 2005. *Reassembling the social: An introduction to actor-network-theory*. Oxford: Oxford University Press.

Letiche, Hugo. 2010. Polyphony and its other. *Organization Studies* 31(3). 261–277.

Llewellyn, Nick & Jon Hindmarsh. 2010. *Organisation, interaction and practice: Studies in ethnomethodology and conversation analysis*. Cambridge: Cambridge University Press.

Luff, Paul & Christian Heath. 2019. Visible objects of concern: Issues and challenges for workplace ethnographies in complex environments. *Organization* 26(4). 578–597.

Matte, Frédérik & Nicolas Bencherki. 2019. Materializing ethical matters of concern: Practicing ethics in a refugee camp. *International Journal of Communication* 13. 5870–5889.

McDonald, Katherine E., Colleen A. Kidney & Mazna Patka. 2013. 'You need to let your voice be heard': Research participants' views on research. *Journal of Intellectual Disability Research* 57(3). 216–225.

Mintzberg, Henry. 1973. *The nature of managerial work*. New York: Harper & Row.

Mondada, Lorenza. 2007. Multimodal resources for turn-taking: Pointing and the emergence of possible next speakers. *Discourse Studies* 9(2). 194–225.

Mondada, Lorenza. 2018. Multiple temporalities of language and body in interaction: Challenges for transcribing multimodality. *Research on Language and Social Interaction* 51(1). 85–106.

Morrison, Elizabeth Wolfe & Frances J. Milliken. 2000. Organizational silence: A barrier to change and development in a pluralistic world. *The Academy of Management Review* 25(4). 706–725.

Morrison, Elizabeth Wolfe & Frances J. Milliken. 2003. Speaking up, remaining silent: The dynamics of voice and silence in organizations. *Journal of Management Studies* 40(6). 1353–1358.

Nagar-Ron, Sigal & Pnina Motzafi-Haller. 2011. "My life? There is not much to tell": On voice, silence and agency in interviews with first-generation Mizrahi Jewish women immigrants to Israel. *Qualitative Inquiry* 17(7). 653–663.

Ong, Walter J. 2012. *Orality and literacy: The technologizing of the word* (New Accents), 30th anniversary edn.; 3rd edn. New York: Routledge.

Pal, Mahuya. 2014. Solidarity with subaltern organizing: The Singur movement in India. *The Electronic Journal of Communication* 24(2–3). http://www.cios.org/EJCPUBLIC/024/3/024343.html (accessed 12 November 2020).

Peters, John Durham. 1999. *Speaking into the air: A history of the idea of communication*. Chicago, IL: University of Chicago Press.

Philipsen, Gerry. 1990. Situated meaning, ethnography, and conversation analysis. *Research on Language and Social Interaction* 24(1–4). 225–239. https://doi.org/10.1080/08351819009389340.

Plato. 2002. Phaedrus (Oxford World's Classics). Edited by Robin Waterfield. Oxford: Oxford University Press.

Pomerantz, Anita & B.J. Fehr. 1997. Conversation analysis: An approach to the study of social action as sense making practices. In Teun A. van Dijk (ed.), *Discourse as social interaction*, 64–91. Thousand Oaks, CA: Sage.

Pomerantz, Anita, Robert E. Sanders & Nicolas Bencherki. 2018. Communication as the study of social action: On the study of language and social interaction. An interview with Anita Pomerantz and Robert E. Sanders, by Nicolas Bencherki. *Communiquer. Revue de communication sociale et publique* 22. 103–118.

Sacks, Harvey. 1992. *Lectures on conversation*. Cambridge, MA: Blackwell.

Sacks, Harvey, Emanuel A. Schegloff & Gail Jefferson. 1974. A simplest systematics for the organization of turn-taking for conversation. *Language* 50(4). 696–735.

Samra-Fredericks, Dalvir. 2003. Strategizing as lived experience and strategists' everyday efforts to shape strategic direction. *Journal of Management Studies* 40(1). 141–174.

Sanders, Robert E. 1999. The impossibility of a culturally contexted conversation analysis: On simultaneous, distinct types of pragmatic meaning. *Research on Language and Social Interaction* 32(1–2). 129–140.

Schegloff, Emanuel A. & Harvey Sacks. 1973. Opening up closings. *Semiotica* 8(4). 298–327.

Schoeneborn, Dennis. 2013. The pervasive power of PowerPoint: How a genre of professional communication permeates organizational communication. *Organization Studies* 34(12). 1777–1801.

Searle, John R. 1969. *Speech acts: An essay in the philosophy of language*. London: Cambridge University Press.

Searle, John R. 1979. *Expression and meaning: Studies in the theory of speech acts*. Cambridge: Cambridge University Press.

Seidl, David & Felix Werle. 2018. Inter-organizational sensemaking in the face of strategic meta-problems: Requisite variety and dynamics of participation. *Strategic Management Journal* 39(3). 630–858.

Shalev, Carmel. 2010. Reclaiming the patient's voice and spirit in dying: An insight from Israel. *Bioethics* 24(3). 134–144.

Soffer, Oren. 2016. Orality. In Klaus Bruhn Jensen & Robert T Craig (eds.), *The international encyclopedia of communication theory and philosophy*, 1–6. Malden, MA: John Wiley & Sons.

Sorsa, Virpi, Pekka Pälli & Piia Mikkola. 2014. Appropriating the words of strategy in performance appraisal interviews. *Management Communication Quarterly* 28(1). 56–83.

Spivak, Gayatri Chakravorty. 1988. Can the subaltern speak? In Cary Nelson & Lawrence Grossberg (eds.), *Marxism and the interpretation of culture*, 271–313. Chicago, IL: University of Illinois Press.

Taylor, James R., François Cooren, Nicole Giroux & Daniel Robichaud. 1996. The communicational basis of organization: Between the conversation and the text. *Communication Theory* 6(1). 1–39.

Taylor, James R. & Elizabeth J. Van Every. 2000. *The emergent organization: Communication as its site and surface*. Mahwah, NJ: Lawrence Erlbaum Associates.

Taylor, James R. & Sandrine Virgili. 2008. Why ERPs disappoint: The importance of getting the organisational text right. In Bernard Grabot, Anne Mayère & Isabelle Bazet (eds.), *ERP Systems and Organisational Change* (Springer Series in Advanced Manufacturing), 59–84. London: Springer.

Trethewey, Angela. 1999. Disciplined bodies: Women's embodied identities at work. *Organization Studies* 20(3). 423–450.

Vásquez, Consuelo, Nicolas Bencherki, Francois Cooren & Viviane Sergi. 2018. From 'matters of concern' to 'matters of authority': Reflecting on the performativity of strategy in writing a strategic plan. *Long-Range Planning* 51(3). 417–435.

Vásquez, Consuelo & François Cooren. 2013. Spacing practices: The communicative configuration of organizing through space-times. *Communication Theory* 23(1). 25–47.

Vismann, Cornelia. 2008. *Files: Law and media technology*. Translated by Geoffrey Winthrop-Young. Stanford, CA: Stanford University Press.

Weick, Karl E. 1979. *The social psychology of organizing*, 2nd edn. Reading, MA: Addison-Wesley.

Weiss, Mona, Michaela Kolbe, Gudela Grote, Micha Dambach, Adrian Marty, Donat R. Spahn & Bastian Grande. 2014. Agency and communion predict speaking up in acute care teams. *Small Group Research* 45(3). 290–313.

Wittgenstein, Ludwig. 1953. *Philosophical investigations*. Translated by Gertrude E. M. Anscombe. New York: Macmillan.

Geert Jacobs and Daniel Perrin
2 Writing

Abstract: This chapter explains why practices of writing are key for managers and leaders. It draws on two action research case studies that illustrate the needs for and benefits of empirically based knowledge on writing in management and leadership roles. An overview of the state of research shows that, besides multitudes of analyses of managerial genres as final products, only little research has been done to understand and improve the dynamic processes of writing in the field. The chapter concludes that future directions of research must include investigating how the rapidly increasing amount of written management and leadership communication comes into being and how its quality can be improved through management education. The structure of the chapter takes the readers from the topic's relevance (Section 1) to the fragmentary state of research (2), the two case studies (3, 4), and suggestions to close the research gap through a dynamic approach (5).

Keywords: writing; practice; management; leadership; professional education

Writing is an important professional practice for managers, yet little research into the processes of managerial writing has been done, and further education programs still need to be developed. This chapter explores options for the knowledge-based development of writing in management and leadership roles. Managers carry out much of their profession through communication. Writing in management processes is closely linked to thinking and deciding, informing and convincing, and integrating and motivating, as explained in Section 1. Management competence, therefore, includes domain-specific writing competence – the competence to perform management tasks in an appropriate and effective way by writing. Section 2 outlines this knowledge space and its state of research.

Section 3 uses two cases to illustrate knowledge transformation in the field: first, it presents the case of a master-level communication course in the realm of innovation and entrepreneurship that focuses on multilingual collaborative writing processes. The second case sets out to demonstrate how writing competence can be built up successfully in professional education, as shown by the case of an American-Chinese-Swiss Executive MBA. Approaching knowledge transformation from a practitioners' perspective, Section 4 discusses techniques and tools that have been developed to facilitate a key task of managers and leaders: guiding organizations through the continuous and cooperative production of meaning and commitment.

Based on the review of the knowledge base (Section 2), the two cases of knowledge transformation (Section 3), and the example of tool development (Section 4), Section 5 outlines a framework for future research.

1 Practically central

Francesco di Marco Datini, a successful Tuscan merchant who lived from 1335 to 1410, wrote everything himself. There are 140,000 letters from his hand that have been preserved.

> While the directors of other companies often had a large part of their business correspondence handled by fattori, he made a point of writing each letter himself until his old age [...]. Day after day he wrote endless letters to his wife, his factors, to tenants, bricklayers, shopkeepers, artists, and week after week business letters to the managers of all his branches. (Origo 1993: 91–92)

The company boss Datini stands for the transition from speaking to writing in European cultural history. Until the late Middle Ages, people who had something to say used to talk and dictate their thoughts; scribes did the rest. In the thirteenth century, however, more and more intellectually, economically, or politically powerful people began to write themselves. By writing at the branch office, they ran trading houses, administered cities, and unlocked knowledge. Latin gave way to the national languages, parchment to paper, the stiff book type to the fast italics (Ludwig 2005: 133).

Today, the management of a global investment bank can count on its top boss to answer very important e-mails around the clock, practically immediately, wherever she is in the world. And the director of a renowned media company reaches for his smartphone, reads and writes electronic mail as soon as he is no longer fascinated by the presentation he is attending. Written communication – ongoing, always, and everywhere or bundled into specific time windows (Hicks and Perrin 2014: 231) – has become a natural part of the daily management routine of many managers and leaders.

By *manager*, we understand an organizational role that guides teams to achieve planned goals. Success is achieved by those who know the rules, use them to the limit, and, if necessary, violate them in a targeted manner. *Leaders*, in contrast or in addition, know that the rules of the game are changing (e. g., Mayfield and Mayfield 2017). They can sense in which direction this is happening and inspire their team to move in that direction – even, under certain circumstances, without guidance from empirical data. As Peter Drucker put it: "Management is doing things right, leadership is doing the right things" (Drucker 2007; see Kodden 2019).

Both managers and leaders act symbolically and produce symbolic goods (e. g., Mintzberg's 2009 study on the nature of managerial work; see also Mintzberg 1973, 2013). In terms of practices, this means:
- Managers analyze and decide; they need to be informed and inform others; and they need to get their employees to commit to certain performance levels and to be able to monitor the success of this performance as a basis for new decisions.
- In leadership roles, designing, convincing, and connecting are added to the practices that need to be performed. Leaders must anticipate the future, perceive change, and develop their visions; they must listen to what their stakeholders say and what they are silent about; they have to empathize with others and winningly

communicate their convictions; they need to inspire groups to develop and reach shared visions and to do this as a team that is by far more than the sum of its parts (e. g., Mayfield and Mayfield 2017; Smythe and Norton 2007).
All this happens interactively, in discourses, by using signs, words, and silence (e. g., Bolden and Gosling 2006; Chang, Chou, and Han 2018; Spranz-Fogasy 2002). If the discourse contributions are to be valid beyond the moment, they must be set down in writing in texts such as memos, project proposals, minutes, annual letters, and strategy papers (see Table 1).

Table 1: Writing tasks in manager and leader roles and the corresponding text types

Management function			Text type (example)
Focus	Role	Activity	
Topic	Manager	Analyzing and deciding	Minutes
	Leader	Ideating and designing	Outline
Addressee	Manager	Informing oneself and others	White paper
	Leader	Understanding and convincing	Mission statement
Organization	Manager	Committing and controlling	Contract
	Leader	Connecting and integrating	Annual letter

Seen in this light, leadership means: managing an organization by means of spoken and written discourse contributions that raise shared involvement as much as possible. Only written contributions to the discourse will detach themselves from spontaneous expression and take on binding status. Anyone who wants to contribute to discourse with precise and effective interventions must either have them written and laboriously checked – or write them herself. This might be the reason why, in the fourteenth century, the successful Datini wrote 140,000 letters by hand, and perhaps it also explains today's ubiquitous management by smartphone.

2 Hardly explored

But why "perhaps"? Because the aspects of when and why managers and leaders write, what they want to achieve by doing so, what they actually do achieve, and how they do it, has hardly been researched so far. Writing research only sheds light on isolated aspects of writing activities in organizations, mostly activities that are also, but not only, performed by managers. The following overview follows the systematic insight that certain text production environments and domains (Section a, below), such as management, develop their typical functions (b) and the corresponding structures (c).
a) Text production is embedded in overarching linguistic and non-linguistic environments. These include, for example, the typical working environments of man-

agers or, more generally, workstations in organizations based on the division of labor. Increasingly, they entail "communication technology objects in a virtual context" (Arvedsen and Hassert 2020). Foundational research examples are the following:

Spilka (1993), Van der Geest (1996), and Jakobs (2006) worked on writing in the workplace in general; Schneider (2002) on writing in the workplace as an activity that is shaped by organizations on the one hand, but also has a formative effect on organizations on the other; Selzer (1993) on the intertextuality of writing processes in the workplace; Pogner (2003) on cooperative writing by engineers; Tapper (2000) on preparing university graduates for communication as employees; Ongstad (2005) on writing socialization in institutions; Du-Babcock and Babcock (2006) on developing language skills and intercultural competence in international business communication. Bremner (2018) provides a concise and recent overview in this area.

b) Text production fulfills certain functions in overarching contexts of action. Leaders, for example, write to achieve leadership goals such as "positioning" (Meschitti 2019). Foundational research examples are the following:

Garzone (2005) looked at cross-genre intentions of action in written and oral business communication; Spranz-Fogasy (2002, 2014) at the self-portrayal of executives in communication and at the high proportion of communicative activities in leadership behavior; Bondi (2005) at self-portrayal in business e-mails; Wolfe (2002), Melenhorst, Van der Geest and Steehouder (2005), Palaigeorgiou et al. (2006), and Rodriguez and Severinson-Eklundh (2006) at taking notes when reading texts on the computer; Severinson-Eklundh (1992) and Price (1999) at sketching out text ideas on the computer; Ortner (1995, 2000) at the connection between writing and thinking; Ortner (2002) at conditions that promote ideas when writing. The special issue on "Leadership in Interaction", by Clifton, Larsson, and Schnurr (2020) is a good place to start for some more recent work here.

c) Text production follows certain structures and leads to text products with certain structures. Typical texts from managers are, for example, memos and e-mails containing orders for employees, but also instant messages (Darics 2020). Such texts are usually created under time pressure. Especially when it comes to investigating the process-oriented aspects of such text production, studies so far have not specifically focused on managers or leaders. Foundational research examples are the following:

Levy and Ransdell (1996) examined "writing signatures", which are basic procedural patterns that are repeated in a person's writing processes; Van Waes and Schellens (2003), such basic patterns, "writing profiles" of experienced writers; Galbraith (1996), practices of inexperienced writers oriented toward drafting texts; Flyvholm Jørgensen (2005), Solbjørg Skulstad (2006), and Yli-Jokipii (2005), text types and their variation in business communication; Zhu (2005, 2006), systematic differences in writing English and Chinese business letters ("sales letters", "sales invitations") and faxes; Nickerson and De Groot (2005), editorials in annual reports. More recently, Janssen and Jansen (2018) looked at how the numeral marking of arguments influence persuasion in the writing of bad-news letters while Brühl and Kury (2019) examined rhetorical tactics in bank presidents' letters during the financial market crisis.

All in all, there is a burgeoning interest in the connection between language and language use, on the one hand, and organizational communication, on the other hand. Yet, there is still little reliable knowledge about the connection between the two: the writing processes in leadership roles. This white spot in the research landscape sharply contrasts with the fact that standardized knowledge and quality management in organizations increasingly call for transparency, specification, documentation, and traceability. Thus, they both require and foster writing and literacy. From an applied linguistics perspective, doing research in this field promises a double benefit. On a theoretical layer, it could deliver relevant insights into professional language use in the particular domain of management and leadership. On a practical layer, it could foster theoretically sound, practice-oriented measures such as training and coaching and organizational development at the interface of management, leadership, and writing.

3 Two cases: White Paper and MBA

As for the second of these two benefits, we set out on a bottom-up exploration of the link between writing, management, and the professions by analyzing the case of a Master-level communication course in the realm of innovation and entrepreneurship. We will call it the *White Paper case* because the students' writing efforts are concentrated on producing a white paper that details their ambitions with a start-up project.

3.1 The White Paper case

The white papers under investigation detail the marketing, financial, and human resources (HR) features of a start-up concept that the students have developed as part of a twelve-week course combining English and French writing and speaking skills. In this course, students are encouraged to think strategically about communication in a variety of business settings because it provides them with practice and feedback on the written and oral skills required to implement these strategies. The course is built around student-centered start-ups. In addition to writing up a white paper, the students are introduced to the fields of crisis communication (with a focus on writing press releases), recruiting (including job applications), and social media.

As for the white papers, the students started out with the following five recommendations:

(1) *Length doesn't matter.*
Tell, don't sell.
Good design is critical.
Make it easy for people to discover and get your white paper.
Leverage analytics.

Example 1: Five Recommendations

In terms of audiences, students were told that the white papers served two main "external" purposes, namely, helping position the start-up as a thought leader by informing and educating the reader and, in doing so, indirectly aiding the "selling" process. At the same time, there were also two "internal" purposes: guiding the multifaceted start-up process and serving as a roadmap and flexible working tool.

The dataset for this analysis includes a series of preliminary versions as well as the final white papers for six start-up teams. A simple close reading of the white papers provides ample evidence of how the students' multilingual (team-based) writing processes are intertwined with managerial decision-making in domains like finance, marketing, and HR. By zooming in on two distinct pairs of parameters (one focused on the idea versus the people, the other on the verbal versus the visual), we will argue that the complex activity of collaborative writing essentially guides the team's thinking process – and vice versa: the team's thinking affects the writing. In other words, the management of the text, as it unfolds across the development of the white paper, reflects and informs the management of the start-up.

Let's begin with the idea versus the people pair. The start-up idea is essentially encapsulated in the branding of the team, including the start-up's name, the tag line that comes with it, and the basic problem-solution structure that typically dominates the executive summary at the start of the white paper. All three can be seen to constitute sites of contestation, the results of a long and winding negotiation process in which team members worked toward a feasible, attractive, and financially sound business model, where writing meets marketing. The bilingual tagline for the Ghent-based Dorm-Trotter start-up, where incoming and outgoing Erasmus students can swap student rooms, is a good example:

(2) *Pour que Gand devienne plus qu'un lieu de séjour!*
 'To make Ghent not only a place to stay, but a place to live!'

Example 2: The white paper as a site of contestation (Dorm-Trotter)

The problem-solution structure is clear from the following extract from the white paper for the 2Sport app, which promises to team up students who are looking for a sports buddy:

(3) *Problem*
College days are supposed to be the best times of our lives, but as first-year students arrive in Ghent, there are many hurdles they have to overcome. They must build a whole new network of friends, they often give up their leisure activities and hobbies in their hometowns, and they have to take care of their own meals for the first time. Clearly, it should not come as a surprise that student loneliness and an unhealthy lifestyle are a growing problem.

Solution
That is why four students, passionate about playing sports, have launched the 2Sport app. Allowing students to create a profile and state their sports preferences, 2Sport matches them with their perfect sports buddy. Hence, having been confronted with unhealthy food and student loneliness themselves, the 2Sport team wants to tackle these issues by uniting Ghentian students and simultaneously motivating them to become more active between classes.

Example 3: The problem-solution structure (2Sport)

Similarly, traces of an underlying decision-making process are to be found in the complex, sometimes even conflicting ways in which the paper refers to the start-up stakeholders – the many people involved in the start-up idea. For one thing, "you" (and, for the French-language sections, *vous*) variously designates the teachers who will eventually be grading the assignment, friends and relatives who may well come to read certain sections of the white paper, and a wide range of potential customers, investors, suppliers, and competitors. This variation hints at the students' emerging awareness of the rich diversity of people who can affect the success of a start-up.

As the students increasingly realize that they need to meet wide-ranging audience expectations, the deictics of the white paper become more complicated. And conversely, as the students come to grips with whom they should address exactly, it is dawning on them that the readership is multifaceted and diverse. The direct reference to potential student customers in the Dorm-Trotter white paper is a fine example: although it draws in potential users, it excludes a wide range of other stakeholders:

(4) *Are you an international student who wants to study in Ghent, but are you having difficulty finding your bearings?*
Or are you a Ghentian student with a dorm available for only one semester, finding it hard to find a renter?

Example 4: Multiple readerships (Dorm-Trotter)

Even the single customer category can and should be broken down into several distinct so-called *personae*, i.e., fictional, idealized representations that, based on market research, can steer the would-be student entrepreneurs into tailoring their content to specific customer needs, behaviors, and concerns. The StudEx start-up aimed at finding initial work experience opportunities for students, for example, Nathalie, an architect who is looking for a trainee to help her four days a week, and Grégoire, an accounting student who would like to engage in a traineeship experience.

Finally, even the use of *I* or *we* in the white papers is dynamic. Some instances of first-person pronouns are inclusive, involving the start-up team members as well as customers or investors; others strictly identify the authors. The personal profiles, where the various team members introduce themselves, claim personal space, take up specific responsibilities, and highlight selected key skills that are considered relevant to the start-up's niche, make up a very important part of each of the white papers in our dataset.

Let us now move on to the "verbal" versus "visual" pair. At various points in the white paper, the writers were forced to make verbal, i.e., language-related, choices that impact as well as reflect managerial decisions. In the SWOT (strengths, weaknesses, opportunities, and threats) analysis, for example, the students had to look for balanced and parallel formulations to spell out the dangers and benefits underlying the start-up idea. Elsewhere, they faced similar challenges drawing up various bullet lists and a table of contents. As for the latter, this is the model that was presented to the students:

(5) *Executive Summary*
 What is this about? (Opportunity)
 – *Objectives/Mission*
 – *Keys to Success*
 – *Company Summary*
 – *Product/Services*
 Who are you? (People)
 – *Personnel Plan*
 Where and when are your activities situated? (Context)
 – *Market Analysis*
 – *Milestones*
 How much is this going to cost? (Risk and reward)
 – *Financial Plan*

Example 5: The white paper model

And this is how the input was used by the team running the Chef-Kot start-up that provides basic ingredients for students looking to cook their own dinner:

(6) *Executive Summary*
   The Story of Chef-Kot
   The People of Chef-Kot
   The Customers of Chef-Kot
   The Competition of Chef-Kot
   The Financial Plan of Chef-Kot
   The Future of Chef-Kot
   Contact Information

Example 6: Application of the white paper model (Chef-Kot)

As far as SWOT analyses are concerned, the following opportunities are identified in the StudEx white paper. Note that the formulation is not at all parallel, combining nominalizations with ing-forms and infinitives:

(7) *OPPORTUNITIES*
   Expansion from Ghent to other student cities in Belgium
   Including more academic fields in our service
   Increase partnerships with educational institutions

Example 7: SWOT (StudEx)

The students face a series of similar choices in the visual, non-verbal domain. A straightforward multimodal analysis of the white papers and of how they develop over the twelve-week writing process points to a wide range of layout and document design issues. These include the creation of a logo to match the start-up name and tag line, the choice of the document's color patterns and how they fit the target audience(s), and – perhaps most prominently – the design of a number of graphs, including Venn-diagrams with the start-up's core values, flow charts spelling out "how it works", and graphs to visualize different scenarios, budgeting options, and marketing timelines.

Again, the data reveal how deciding on both the verbal and the visual is instrumental in managerial processes and how, in turn, managerial decision-making affects the writing in terms of both the verbal and the visual.

3.2 The MBA case

Managers and leaders write for a wide range of reasons, such as being expected to make binding decisions and communicate these decisions in writing – as quickly and clearly as possible. In management training courses, therefore, training modules at the intersection of writing and leadership have proven their worth. For example, the modules can be based on classical rhetoric or linked to specific training models; at the core it is always about efficient and effective written communication.

Based on the didactic concept as explained above, we have developed and implemented such modules for various management training courses. As an example, we would like to use the communication module for the "Rochester-Bern Executive MBA", a "premium offering from a university". "Top international experts from science and business" are contracted as professors, while students from all over the world are addressed as learners before the leap to the top.

In the first communication module of this program, "The Art of Communication I", students practice four working techniques in one day, which help them get to the heart of communication when writing. The key question in the module description is: "Project reports, budget forecasts, executive summaries, comments, press releases, [...] – As a manager and program participant you often have to write texts. Yet how can you write a convincing text? And how can you do so in an efficient way?" (Perrin 2006). Texts in the above-mentioned genres are submitted by the participants before the course.

With these texts, the trainers familiarize themselves with the subject areas and the level of performance of the students. In the first half of the course, the trainers will use selected examples to present variants of core messages, argumentation, dramaturgies, and formulations for discussion. The goal is to write better texts: "The course will enable you to write professional, convincing texts in a short time and with less effort. After the course, you will 1) communicate your messages with a higher impact, 2) know how professional writing, presenting, and talking fit together, 3) enjoy communication more – and have more respect for it" (Perrin 2006, also for all the following quotations from course materials not otherwise assigned). Such a goal can only be achieved through process-oriented interventions. In the course, the participants therefore train four simple working techniques: the "Mugging Test" (Example 8), the "Finger Technique", the "Stages Technique", and the "Typo Test" (Perrin 2013). As an example, the first technique is outlined below.

(8) *The Mugging Test*
Imagine telling your story to a colleague as she is running to catch a bus that is about to leave.

In a couple of sentences, just by talking for a few seconds, outline the interesting new thing that you have to say and why it is important for your audience right now. Choose someone to mug who doesn't really want to listen to you, hardly has any time for you, and is thinking about something completely different. If your mugging victim stops, listens, and responds to your topic – then you are ready to start writing.

Don't think that your topic is much too complicated to deal with in passing [...] Sure – any subject can fill up pages and pages, and hours and hours. But you have to make it palatable and sell it to your audience as they rush by, flip pages, or zap through stations and before they stop paying attention. They'll pause, become involved with your text for a few seconds, and only continue with it if it promises something of significance.

Why should you check the main theme of your text on a live subject? Even the thought of having to verbally grab someone with your topic puts you under pressure. You mentally test the impression you make, notice that you have not yet found the right angle, change perspective, start a different way, finally risk it […] and get to the point of the text more effectively by talking than would ever have been possible by brooding over it alone. The stress of an oral situation opens the floodgates for language flow, similar to a burst of adrenaline just before a deadline. You'll become strong in self-defense, and in retrospect, you'll clearly see the best way into the text.

Example 8: The writing technique called *Mugging Test* in the Rochester-Bern Executive MBA

With four such working techniques, students can align, plan, control, and evaluate writing processes under time pressure. The "Mugging Test", for example, motivates writers to commit themselves to the meaning, addressees, topic, format, leading questions, and main statements. In other words, they must define their attempt at communication in a specific situation before they spend their limited resources on wrestling with individual formulations – the appropriateness of which they can only functionally decide on when the thrust of the communication attempt is clear to them.

As managers, students can use techniques such as the "Mugging Test" and the "Finger Technique" to check whether they can justify their decisions in a way that is appropriate for the target group and in line with their own intentions and get to the heart of the matter before they attempt to communicate. In short, they can test whether they know what they want. That someone knows what she wants before communicating and trying to inform, convince, commit, and connect others may sound self-evident. Yet, our experience in everyday life, leadership, and training shows that this effort to fully understand one's own communicational intentions and actions is worthwhile for at least two reasons:
- Many professional writers fail under time pressure because they write without a clear concept in mind. Instead, they want to develop their idea through writing (as we have seen in the White Paper case) and end up running into time problems after rebuilding their text parts over and over again. Writing in order to find out what one actually means – epistemic writing – requires time to step out of the writing process for an hour or a couple of days; to meet the written word in a new way; to read it; to discard what seems to be finished and to rebuild it until it reads as a coherent text about what one really means.

– Many professional leaders engage in presentations, conversations, and public appearances without having thought about basic questions such as: who exactly they are addressing; who else is listening; what the addressees expect; how the addressees influence the course of communication; what precedes and follows the occasion for communication and thus frames and helps shape their own communication offering; what they want to achieve and communicate themselves; how they can formulate their core concerns and statements correctly, briefly, and boldly. Only those who define the goals of their communication at an early stage will be able to fully use their resources later to cope with the current situation: to endure time and pressure, to respond to interlocutors, to remedy situational communication problems.

With techniques such as the "Mugging Test", students learn to access their resources for communication processes in general and for written communication in particular in a reflective manner. As the course progresses, they apply the new techniques in an individual writing task: "Write a short overview (maximum 1 page) of possible conflicts of interest in your company. The overview is meant to be used as an introduction to a strategy workshop of you and other executives of the company. Write the text by using the Mugging Test, the Finger Technique, and the Stages Technique".

The "Art of Communication I" module concludes with the evaluation of the students' text products and the writing experience. Later in the study program, two modules connect to this first writing module. In one of them, "The Art of Communication II", students take up the "Mugging Test" and the "Finger Technique" and use these techniques consciously to prepare presentations and conversations. In a further follow-up module, the optional module "The Art of Project Management Communication", they deepen what they have learned with writing techniques for line and committee management, such as the *Write-As-You-Speak* (WAYS) technique.

4 The WAYS writing technique and the WAYSbase®

In structured organizations, managers meet their directly subordinate employees regularly, in groups and individually, to manage day-to-day business. In complex organizations with matrix structures and many project groups, as well as in expert and agile organizations, such meetings are important. Meetings that are perceived as well-prepared, cooperative, and engaging stimulate the pulse and strengthen the identity of an organization; productive meetings can be focal points of decision-making, commitment, and involvement, stages of exemplary interaction. Unproductive meetings, on the other hand, slow down workflows and lower staff motivation.

Therefore, it is best practice for managers and leaders to prepare their regular meetings appropriately, to use the time together and to make joint decisions, and to clearly identify the new obligations that have arisen. However, all this should require as little effort as possible and, at best, be completed on-site. After a day full of meetings, little time remains to rework mountains of notes. Optimized management- and leadership-oriented writing can contribute to the effective, lean steering of committees and working groups. Such writing can be considered a direct practice of management and leadership (see above, Section 1, Table 1):

– Managers need to be able to use writing practices when analyzing and deciding; to be informed and to inform others; to commit their employees to certain performances; and to monitor success, as a basis for new decisions.
– Leaders need to be able to use writing practices when they sense the future, perceive change, and develop visions; listen to themselves, empathize with others, and win and communicate convictions; inspire groups for the common cause and thus connect them.

As linguists with a focus on professional writing, who have been entrusted for the past ten years with a growing number of management tasks in higher education and science, we have both investigated and further developed such management and leadership writing practices (see, as an illustration, the White Paper and MBA cases detailed above). In this section, we will discuss key aspects of such practices using the example of a writing technique we term Write-As-You-Speak (WAYS) and a tool we call WAYSbase. In a transdisciplinary case study of designing domain-specific writing tools, the development has made our own leadership work happier, easier, more pleasant, and more successful. There is less frictional loss in management, more leadership, and more research. In addition, many people who see us or our employees working with it are interested. So, we have brought both to a communicable level.

We teach the writing technique in the above-mentioned course "The Art of Project Management Communication" and, increasingly, in company training and coaching. The technology requires a suitable instrument, for example, the WAYSbase FileMaker database. Our main interest lies in the research potential of this package (see Section 5). But first, we outline the leadership work with WAYS and the WAYSbase, and we illustrate how strongly leadership and writing are intertwined.

WAYSbase is a management instrument for the alignment, planning, steering, and control of processes of individual and joint decision-making (4.1). Technically, WAYSbase is a content management system, a FileMaker database for management tasks, accessible via a user interface on the Internet and at all meetings (4.2). In WAYSbase applications, information, discussion points, requests, and decisions are continuously recorded (4.3). Skilled writers (4.4) – such as Diana Livingstone in the following constructed, but realistic example – can use their writing skills to benefit their leadership practice (4.5).

4.1 Management instrument WAYSbase

Diana Livingstone, the director of a large university institute, is also president of the regional section of her scientific society. Her goal is to raise the profile of both organizations and strongly expand international cooperation. She, therefore, travels a lot and wants to manage the internal business with as much focus as possible. For this purpose, she uses WAYSbase, a database in which she systematically records all agreed tasks. WAYSbase also helps her manage everything related to communication: i.e., meetings, projects, topics, actors, and working groups (Figure 1). Furthermore, she uses the database to integrate the teams.

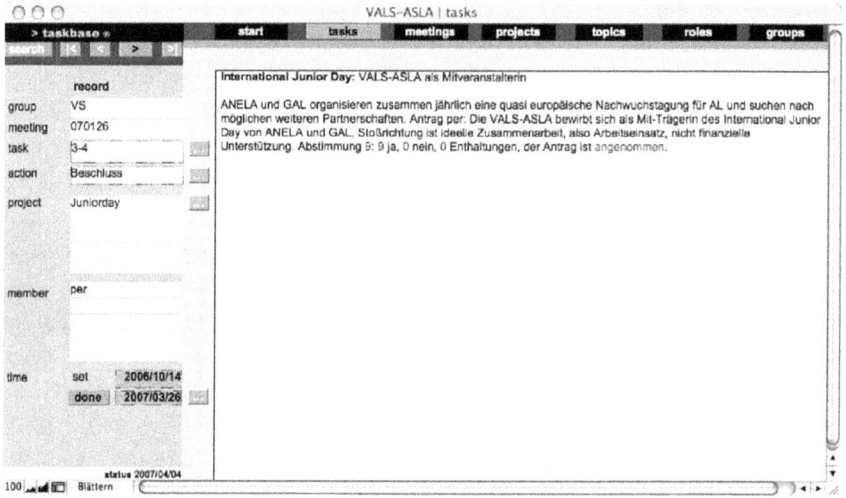

Figure 1: WAYSbase® with tasks, meetings, projects, topics, roles, groups

Whenever Diana has a thought, a proposal, or a discussion point for a later meeting, she records it as a task in the database. She formulates the text in such a way that the employees can understand it, and keywords the entry: she links it to a future meeting, to current businesses and projects, and to potential actors. Finally, she determines the speech act of the task: request, information, discussion, inquiry. Before each meeting, she puts all entries for that meeting in a certain order by numbering them. By doing so, she sets the agenda for the meeting.

4.2 On the Internet and in the meeting room

Other participants in the meeting may have also thought of topics in advance and informed Diana about them. Diana uses these contributions to formulate further entries for WAYSbase. Before the meeting, all topics are available on the Internet. The database is accessible on the network via password so that all members of the organization can see the tasks they are involved in. Preparing for the meetings is the responsibility of all participants. As a result, everybody already knows the tasks when they meet. They are ready to take a stand and negotiate solutions.

For the meetings, there are two ways of using the WAYSbase: bilateral discussions take place at a meeting table – the boss, as the representative of management and leadership roles, and the employees sit opposite each other. In small groups, Diana would sit opposite her employees, who each see the content Diana created on their own respective laptops, whereas in larger groups, the content would be projected onto the wall behind her. Thus, just like the Internet, WAYSbase can be simultaneously used by the participants involved in a project which allows them to simultaneously process the tasks step by step during the conversation.

4.3 Together from discussion to decision

As a starting point for the joint discussion, the first topic entry that has been prepared appears. During the discussion, the participants raise new issues, add aspects, and negotiate arguments. Once the positions have been defined and discussed, Diana proposes moving on to the summary. If the participants agree, she summarizes the results of the discussion in WAYSbase as a written proposal for a resolution. What is to apply from now on and who has to do what becomes visible for everyone. Misunderstandings show up immediately and can be discussed and corrected. At the end of the meeting, a joint decision closes the deal. Diana will load the next database entry only when the issue discussed in her meeting has developed into a joint decision.

In this way, the participants transfer each entry, one by one, from a basis for discussion to a binding decision. Everybody involved is present during this process; everyone can use this opportunity to add to this process during the meeting. The participants are strongly involved and experience the meetings as – literally – decisive and binding. But Diana steers the process by leading the discussion, constantly clarifying the ideas that have been put forward and specifying the wording of the resolutions.

4.4 No work after work

After the meeting, the tasks are distributed, and everyone knows what to do. The records of all the decisions made throughout the meeting are accessible on the Internet, systematically linked, through their keywords, with agents, topics, and projects. Most importantly, all the decisions and their wordings have been agreed upon by all the group members. For the participants, there is no need to wait for the minutes and there are no unpleasant surprises in the wording of resolutions. Diana does not have to revise her notes into minutes. Instead, all work has been done before and during the meeting, in a focused, transparent, and binding way. Every meeting helps the organization grow in a concrete and documented manner.

The prerequisite for this lean management of committees and working groups is the ability and skill to conceive, moderate, and discuss issues by rapidly swapping between the linguistic modes of listening and speaking as well as reading and writing. The practices include recognizing key ideas in the discussion, clarifying concepts, finding the right words – and writing them down and revising them in front of the participants. This requires leadership-specific writing competence: deciding and designing, informing and convincing, committing and involving others with writing. This competence is trained with the writing techniques from the basic module (see above, Section 3.2, Example 8). It is then used in the environment of the leadership meeting and the WAYSbase tool.

4.5 Efficient management, yes! – But leadership?

But doesn't this structured generation of decisions embody the very opposite of leadership as an attitude of "waiting" and "listening" (Smythe and Norton 2007: 87; see also Reed, Goolsby, and Johnston 2016)? Is this not an over-management of meaning-making? The relentless explicitness of the decision-making process speaks for such concerns: the vague, informal, cloudy, and fragile can be repressed in the struggle for the explicit, fixed, clear, and coherent. But vagueness and implicitness are also important for the cohesion and further development of organizations (e. g., Hargie and Dickson 2007; Lai 2019).

What speaks against such criticism, however, is that the institutionalized meetings in structured organizations are always about organizational definition. Members of the organization negotiate demanding issues, based on their role, knowledge, and "leadership-in-interaction" (Clifton, Larsson, and Schnurr 2020), and determine what applies from now on. Working with tools such as WAYSbase also makes obvious where the time has not yet come for joint determination, i.e., where waiting and listening, slowness and calmness, cooperative thinking, epistemic writing (e. g., Ortner 2002), and negotiating roles (Kim and Angouri 2019) are still appropriate to create clarity and meaning.

The writing practice presented here thus combines a certain attitude (guided common determination) with a certain method (WAYS) and a digital writing tool (WAYSbase). It enables superiors to lead an organization through systematic, continuous, and cooperative creation of meaning and commitment. This can be on-site, but also in remote meetings, "by mobilizing available information and communication technology objects in a virtual context" (Arvedsen and Hassert 2020: 548). Broken down to the core activities in management and leadership roles (see above, Section 1, Table 1), this means:

- Analyzing and deciding: all parties involved prepare decisions in such a way that they can present their position at the meeting, exchange arguments, and participate in the decision-making process. The decision-making process is visible to all parties involved. This applies not only to the key idea of a decision, but also to its – often decisive – wording.
- Informing oneself and others: decisions are uniformly indexed in the database and linked to related decisions, such as decisions from the same meeting, decisions from the same role holders, decisions on the same project, and decisions on the same topic. In this way, the organization systematically stores its decision-making knowledge on an ongoing basis and can easily access it for analyses before making any further decisions.
- Committing and controlling: decisions lead to obligations; the obligations are formulated in the database and scheduled and assigned to specific role holders. All decision makers are directly involved in this process of building commitment. The result is systematically filed, accessible to all participants at any time via password, as a basis for transparent (self-)checking.
- Ideating and designing: decisions are based, for example, on analyses and emotions, but also on ideas. Such ideas can be recorded in the database at any time, linked to projects and topics, and noted to be discussed in future meetings. After the meeting, anything that has not yet been decided remains explicitly open, as a starting point for new ideas or for new drafts in the management and leadership discourse.
- Understanding and convincing: those who have participated in making a joint decision are in a good position to understand the process of decision-making and its result and to share it convincingly with others. This is exactly what is fostered by institutionalized meetings in which decisions are made jointly, comprehensibly, and bindingly.
- Connecting and integrating: in jointly identifying, negotiating, and determining the relevant items, issues, and solutions, not only are the symbolic structures of an organization clarified and strengthened, but the continuous discourse also connects the people involved. They meet to listen to each other, to get involved, and to respond to each other in a dialogue of the community that is literally binding.

By doing so, they practice systematically what Smythe and Norton (2007: 87) describe in their profile of leadership as "listen and respond". They listen and grasp the essentials – and position themselves (Meschitti 2019). The institutionalized meetings become the focal point of "symbolic and narrative processes of collective sense making in organizations" (Bolden and Gosling 2006: 160). In remote meetings, they generate "E-leadership" (Darics 2020). It is through such on-site or online writing that manager-leaders create "choices and meanings for themselves and others" with and in front of the others (Bolden and Gosling 2006: 159).

5 Conclusion: research *and* teaching required

Resolutions, agreements, and decisions in organizations are usually fixed by writing, for example, in a genre called *minutes*. In other words, what Diana Livingstone writes using a tool such as WAYSbase, she would want to write anyway, as the minutes of her meeting. Alternatively, she could have her staff write the minutes, but then she would have to double-check them carefully. Practices such as WAYS help her reduce processes of management and leadership to the max. But there is more: the focused written nature of leadership processes in both the White Paper and the MBA case makes it easier to research how the processes work, i. e., how organizational decisions are made and resources such as knowledge and rules are developed in organizations.

Sure, the practices of leaders and organizations following the rationale of the White Paper case or choosing tools such as WAYS may not yet represent average leadership practices. As a consequence, not all conceivable questions about writing in management and leadership roles can be meaningfully researched in contexts such as outlined in this paper's two illustrative case studies. In these contexts, it makes the most sense to analyze management and leadership practices that are closely related to using digital tools of communicative decision-making. But given the increasing digitalization of the managerial workplace, systematically analyzing these practices helps us better understand and explain what it means and takes to be a manager and leader.

Research topics include the use of subtly guiding language in writing at the top: how do managers and leaders in committees, project groups meetings, and bilateral talks use language and, in particular, writing to co-create leadership (Bradford and Leberman 2019), to share values, negotiate opinions, and set and reach goals (Angouri 2012; Kim and Angouri 2019)? How do they "orchestrate" leadership (Alvehus 2019) and use language to frame what is going on when they are "powerless to control the turbulence of their environments" but find themselves able to "control the context under which turbulence [can be] seen" (Fairhurst 2005: 166)?

Using the multimethod approach of progression analysis (Perrin 2003), large corpora of domain-specific text production data could be made available for in-depth and longitudinal research (Perrin 2019). In progression analysis, a logging program records all inputs into digital devices and tools over a longer period. All formulations, with all insertions and deletions, are logged and video recorded and can be played back like a film. At a certain point in time, managers can be methodically presented with the recordings in a controlled manner, for example, to comment on their actions and thus document their repertoire of possible considerations in leadership processes.

Applying this method in entire organizations, as has been done with newsrooms (Perrin 2013), enables researchers to trace the path of decision-making from the initial idea to the shaping and communication of the decision and, finally, its uptake and implementation. The systematic evaluation of case studies of managers with different professional experience and varying degrees of success will make it possible to determine which repertoires of writing techniques and tools are used for comparable management tasks. It will also show how, for example, repertoires of experienced and inexperienced managers differ. Finally, empirically saturated best-practice trainings for effective communication in management and leadership roles, such as outlined in the White Paper case, can be derived from this analysis.

Beyond this practically oriented research interest, a systematic analysis of the writing processes of executives can provide interesting theoretical insights into a hitherto hardly recorded, but socially highly relevant variant of domain-specific writing and communication in general and its contribution to organizational value creation (Jakobs and Spinuzzi 2014). Managers and leaders can be considered as writing experts who direct their writing skills, albeit more unconscious and uncontrolled than conscious and controlled, toward practices that shape their professional field and their professional success. This situation has not changed since Francesco di Marco Datini wrote his 140,000 letters. However, the writing tools – and possible windows for research – have.

6 References

Alvehus, Johan. 2019. Emergent, distributed, and orchestrated: Understanding leadership through frame analysis. *Leadership* 15(5). 535–554.

Angouri, Jo. 2012. Managing disagreement in problem solving meeting talk. *Journal of Pragmatics* 44(12). 1565–1579.

Arvedsen, Lise D. & Liv O. Hassert. 2020. Accomplishing leadership-in-interaction by mobilizing available information and communication technology objects in a virtual context. *Leadership* 16(5). 546–567.

Bolden, Richard & Jonathan Gosling. 2006. Leadership competencies: Time to change the tune? *Leadership* 2(2). 147–163.

Bondi, Marina. 2005. People in business: The representation of self and multiple identities in business e-mails. In Paul Gillaerts & Maurizio Gotti (eds.), *Genre variation in business letters*, 303–300. Bern: Lang.

Bradford, Mark & Sarah Leberman. 2019. BeWeDō®: A dynamic approach to leadership development for co-creation. *Leadership* 15(1). 58–80.

Bremner, Stephen. 2018. Workplace writing. In John L. Liontas & Margo DelliCarpini (eds.), *The TESOL encyclopedia of English language teaching*. Oxford: Wiley. doi:10.1002/9781118784235. eelt0519 (accessed 12 November 2020).

Brühl, Rolf & Max Kury. 2019. Rhetorical tactics to influence responsibility judgments: Account giving in banks presidents' letters during the financial market crisis. *International Journal of Business Communication* 56(3). 299–325.

Chang, Tree, Shih Yung Chou & Bo Han. 2018. Silent leaders in the workplace: Forms of leadership silence, attributions of leadership silence, and accuracy of attributions. *International Journal of Business Communication*. https://journals.sagepub.com/doi/full/10.1177/2329488418777041 #articleCitationDownloadContainer (accessed 12 November 2020).

Clifton, Jonathan, Magnus Larsson & Stephanie Schnurr. 2020. Leadership in interaction. An introduction to the Special Issue. *Leadership* 16(5). 511–521.

Darics, Erika. 2020. E-leadership or "How to be boss in instant messaging?" The role of nonverbal communication. *International Journal of Business Communication* 57(1). 3–29.

Drucker, Peter. 2007. *The effective executive*. London: Routledge.

Du-Babcock, Bertha & Richard D. Babcock. 2006. Developing linguistic and cultural competency in international business communication. In Juan Carlos Palmer-Silveira, Miguel F. Ruiz-Garrido & Inmaculada Fortanet-Gómez (eds.), *Intercultural and international business communication: Theory, research, and teaching*, 55–82. Bern: Lang.

Fairhurst, Gail T. 2005. Reframing the art of framing: Problems and prospects for leadership. *Leadership* 1(2). 165–185.

Flyvholm Jørgensen, Paul Erik. 2005. The dynamics of business letters: Defining creative variation in established genres. In Paul Gillaerts & Maurizio Gotti (eds.), *Genre variation in business letters*, 147–178. Bern: Lang.

Galbraith, David. 1996. Self-monitoring, discovery through writing and individual differences in drafting strategy. In Gert Rijlaarsdam, Huub Van den Bergh & Michael Couzijn (eds.), *Theories, models and methodology in writing research*, 121–144. Amsterdam: Amsterdam University Press.

Garzone, Giuliana. 2005. Letters to shareholders and chairman's statements: Textual variability and generic integrity. In Paul Gillaerts & Maurizio Gotti (eds.), *Genre variation in business letters*, 179–204). Bern: Peter Lang.

Hargie, Owen & David Dickson. 2007. Are important corporate policies understood by employees? A tracking study of organizational information flow. *Journal of Communication Management* 11(1). 9–28.

Hicks, Troy & Daniel Perrin. 2014. Beyond single modes and media. In Eva-Maria Jakobs & Daniel Perrin (eds.), *Handbook of writing and text production*, vol. 10, 231–253. Boston, MA: De Gruyter.

Jakobs, Eva-Maria. 2006. Texte im Beruf. Schreiben, um verstanden zu werden? In Hardarik Blühdorn, Eva Breindl & Ulrich Hermann Waßner (eds.), *Text – Verstehen. Grammatik und darüber hinaus*, 310–326. Berlin: De Gruyter.

Jakobs, Eva-Maria & Clay Spinuzzi. 2014. Professional domains: Writing as creation of economic value. In Eva-Maria Jakobs & Daniel Perrin (eds.), *Handbook of writing and text production*, vol. 10, 359–384. Boston, MA: De Gruyter.

Janssen, Daniel & Frank Jansen. 2018. Persuasion by numbers: How does numeral marking of arguments in bad news letters influence persuasion? *Journal of Writing Research* 10(1). 61–84.

Kim, Kyoungmi & Jo Angouri. 2019. 'We don't need to abide by that!': Negotiating professional roles in problem-solving talk at work. *Discourse & Communication* 13(2). 172–191.

Kodden, Bas. 2019. Why Peter Drucker was wrong: The meaning of true leadership. *Management Impact*. https://www.managementimpact.nl/artikel/why-peter-drucker-was-wrong-the-meaning-of-true-leadership/ (accessed 12 November 2020).

Lai, Lisa. 2019. Managing when the future is unclear. *Harvard Business Review*. https://hbr.org/2019/01/managing-when-the-future-is-unclear (accessed 15 January 2021).

Levy, C. Michael & Sarah Ransdell. 1996. Writing signatures. In C. Michael Levy & Sarah Ransdell (eds.), *The science of writing: Theories, methods, individual differences and applications*, 127–148. Mahwah, NJ: Erlbaum.

Ludwig, Otto. 2005. *Geschichte des Schreibens: Von der Antike bis zum Buchdruck*, Volume 1. Berlin: De Gruyter.

Mayfield, Jacqueline & Milton Mayfield. 2017. Leadership communication. Reflecting, engaging, and innovating. *International Journal of Business Communication* 54(1). 3–11.

Melenhorst, Mark, Thea Van der Geest & Michaël Steehouder. 2005. Noteworthy observations about note-taking by professionals. *Journal of Technical Writing and Communication* 35(3). 317–329.

Meschitti, Viviana. 2019. The power of positioning: How leadership work unfolds in team interactions. *Leadership* 15(5). 621–643.

Mintzberg, Henry. 1973. *The nature of managerial work*. New York: Harper & Row.

Mintzberg, Henry. 2013. *Simply managing: What managers do – and can do better*. San Francisco, CA: Berrett-Koehler.

Nickerson, Catherine & Elizabeth De Groot. 2005. Dear shareholder, dear stockholder, dear stakeholder: The business letter genre in the annual general report. In Paul Gillaerts & Maurizio Gotti (eds.), *Genre variation in business letters*, 325–346. Bern: Lang.

Ongstad, Sigmund. 2005. Enculturation to institutional writing. In Triantafillia Kostouli (ed.), *Writing in context(s): Textual practices and learning processes in sociocultural settings*, 49–68. Amsterdam: Elsevier.

Origo, Iris. 1993. *"Im Namen Gottes und der Geschäfte": Lebensbild eines toskanischen Kaufmanns der Frührenaissance. Francesco di Marco Datini 1335–1410*, 3rd edn. München: Beck.

Ortner, Hanspeter. 1995. Die Sprache als Produktivkraft. Das (epistemisch-heuristische) Schreiben aus der Sicht der Piagetschen Kognitionspsychologie. In Jürgen Baurmann & Rüdiger Weingarten (eds.), *Schreiben. Prozesse, Prozeduren und Produkte*, 320–342. Opladen: Westdeutscher Verlag.

Ortner, Hanspeter. 2000. *Schreiben und Denken*. Tübingen: Niemeyer.

Ortner, Hanspeter. 2002. Schreiben und Wissen. Einfälle fördern und Aufmerksamkeit staffeln. In Daniel Perrin, Ingrid Boettcher, Otto Kruse & Arne Wrobel (eds.), *Schreiben: Von intuitiven zu professionellen Schreibstrategien*, 63–82. Wiesbaden: Westdeutscher Verlag.

Palaigeorgiou, George E., Theofanis D. Despotakis, Stavros N. Demetriadis & Ioannis A. Tsoukalas. 2006. Synergies and barriers with electronic verbatim notes (eVerNotes): Note taking and report writing with eVerNotes. *Journal of Computer Assisted Learning* 22(1). 74–85.

Perrin, Daniel. 2003. Progression analysis (PA): Investigating writing strategies at the workplace. *Journal of Pragmatics* 35(6). 907–921.

Perrin, Daniel. 2006. *Courseware: The art of communication*. Unpublished manuscript, Bern.

Perrin, Daniel. 2013. *The linguistics of newswriting*. Amsterdam: John Benjamins.

Perrin, Daniel. 2019. Working with large data corpora in real-life writing research. In Kirk Sullivan & Eva Lindgren (eds.), *Observing writing: Insights from keystroke logging*, 143–162. Leiden: Brill.

Pogner, Karl-Heinz. 2003. Writing and interacting in the discourse community of engineering. In Daniel Perrin (ed.), *The pragmatics of writing*. [Journal of Pragmatics. Special issue 35/6]. 855–867.

Price, Jonathan. 1999. *Outlining goes electronic*. Stamford, CT: Ablex/Greenwood.

Reed, Kendra, Jerry R. Goolsby & Michelle K. Johnston. 2016. Extracting meaning and relevance from work: The potential connection between the listening environment and employee's organizational identification and commitment. *International Journal of Business Communication* 53(3). 326–342.

Rodriguez, Henry & Kerstin Severinson-Eklundh. 2006. Visualizing patterns of annotation in document-centered collaboration on the web. In Luuk Van Waes, Mariëlle Leijten & Chris Neuwirth (eds.), *Writing and digital media*, 131–144. Amsterdam: Elsevier.

Schneider, Barbara. 2002. Theorizing structure and agency in workplace writing: An ethnomethodological approach. *Journal of Business and Technical Communication* 16(2). 170–195.

Selzer, Jack. 1993. Intertextuality and the writing process. In Rachel Spilka (ed.), *Writing in the workplace: New research perspectives*, 171–180. Carbondale, IL: Southern Illinois University Press.

Severinson-Eklundh, Kerstin. 1992. The use of "idea processors" for studying structural aspects of text production. In Ann-Charlotte Lindeberg, Nils Erik Enkvist & Kay Wikberg (eds.), *Nordic research on text and discourse: Nordtext Symposium 1990*, 271–287. Åbo: Åbo Academy Press.

Smythe, Elizabeth & Andrew Norton. 2007. Thinking as leadership/leadership as thinking. *Leadership* 3(1). 65–90.

Solbjørg Skulstad, Aud. 2006. Genre analysis of corporate communication. In Juan Carlos Palmer-Silveira, Miguel F. Ruiz-Garrido & Inmaculada Fortanet-Gómez (eds.), *Intercultural and international business communication: Theory, research, and teaching*, 85–108. Bern: Lang.

Spilka, Rachel (ed.). 1993. *Writing in the workplace: New research perspectives*. Carbondale, IL: Southern Illinois University Press.

Spranz-Fogasy, Thomas. 2002. Was macht der Chef? Der kommunikative Alltag von Führungskräften in der Wirtschaft. In Michael Becker-Mrotzek & Reinhard Fiehler (eds.), *Unternehmenskommunikation*, 209–230. Tübingen: Narr.

Spranz-Fogasy, Thomas. 2014. Wer redet, führt. Wie Führungskräfte kommunizieren. *Kommunikation & Management* (2). https://ids-pub.bsz-bw.de/frontdoor/deliver/index/docId/2930/file/Spranz-Fogasy_Wie+Führungskräfte+kommunizieren.pdf (accessed 31 January 2021).

Tapper, Joanna. 2000. Preparing university students for the communicative attributes and skills required by employers. *Australian Journal of Communication* 27(2). 111–130.

Van der Geest, Thea. 1996. Professional writing studied: Authors' accounts of planning in document production processes. In Mike Sharples & Thea Van der Geest (eds.), *The new writing environment: Writers at work in a world of technology*, 7–24. London: Springer.

Van Waes, Luuk & Peter Jan Schellens. 2003. Writing profiles: The effect of the writing mode on pausing and revision patterns of experienced writers. In Daniel Perrin (ed.), *The pragmatics of writing*. [*Journal of Pragmatics*. Special issue 35/6]. 829–853.

Wolfe, Joanna. 2002. Annotation technologies: A software and research review. *Computers and Composition* 19(4). 471–497.

Yli-Jokipii, Hilkka. 2005. An integrated analysis of interactive business writing. In Paul Gillaerts & Maurizio Gotti (eds.), *Genre variation in business letters*, 85–98. Bern: Lang.

Zhu, Yunxia. 2005. *Written communication across cultures: A sociocognitive perspective on business genres*. Amsterdam: John Benjamins.

Zhu, Yunxia. 2006. Cross-cultural genre study: A dual perspective. In Juan Carlos Palmer-Silveira, Miguel F. Ruiz-Garrido & Inmaculada Fortanet-Gómez (eds.), *Intercultural and international business communication: Theory, research, and teaching*, 181–196. Bern: Lang.

Theresa Castor and Mariaelena Bartesaghi

3 Deciding

Abstract: This chapter advances the conceptualization of deciding as social practice by proposing a metamodel of deciding as the discursive interplay of action, agency, and accountability. To illustrate this dynamic, data from two crisis related organizational interactions are analyzed: Hurricane Katrina Emergency management teleconference calls; and New York state Governor Cuomo COVID-19 pandemic press briefings. As a discursive practice, deciding is described as being constituted through three performative and overlapping contexts: the immediate context of utterances; a metapragmatic vocabulary; and, metaconversations. This re-conceptualization and case studies highlight the relational nature of deciding as social activity that cuts across time and place(s) and is inclusive of human and nonhuman participants. The chapter begins with a historical overview of theoretical conceptualizations of decision-making as rational and individual, proceeds to focus on discursive approaches to deciding, explains the action-agency-accountability deciding framework, and concludes with an illustrative analysis of two crisis cases.

Keywords: deciding; accountability; agency; authority; crisis

In our previous work on crisis management (e. g. Bartesaghi and Castor 2010; Bartesaghi 2014; Castor and Bartesaghi 2016), we examined deciding as situated action within a frame of agency and accountability. This chapter extends that analysis by developing an understanding of deciding as a relational arrangement of agency, action, and accountability. When we began composing this text, a Google search of the term *deciding* in the category "news" yielded ten stories on the first page on topics such as sports trades, retirement, local government, the US Supreme Court, and corporate downsizing. At the beginning of April 2020, the same search yielded nine stories on COVID-19 and one on sports (in relation to COVID-19).

These two moments – December 2019 and April 2020 – are creations and enactments of deciding. The stories about deciding perform deciding; they materialize it, calling us to act within, and account for the universe of deciding they ask us to occupy. As COVID-19 unfolded, calling us to attend to "sheltering in place", "social distancing", and "community spread", we oriented to novel understandings of bandanas, physical space, and Italy (to name a few examples), resulting in a series of prescribed actions. These unfoldings of action, agency, and accounts became attached to speakers and organizational entities in terms of "decisions", making the crisis of COVID-19 and its management a matter of deciding.

Deciding is fundamental to management science and research (Chia 1994). Niklas Luhmann (2018) defines organizations as decision systems. As a construct, decision-making originated in the early twentieth century in the writings of management theorist Chester Barnard (Buchanan and O'Connell 2006). Early notions treated decision-making as a sequence of choices, and evolved to more sophisticated treatments of deciding as an activity of bounded rationality and ambiguity that is socially constructed and discursively constituted (Buchanan and O'Connell 2006; Castor 2005; Huisman 2001). Initial decision-making models indexed a rational, prescriptive model that has been debunked (Heracleous 1994). Yet, popular cultural prescriptions provide guidance to student career-seekers on how to be rational decision-makers (e. g., Doyle 2020; Valchev n.d.).

These, along with the stories generated by our search, index a metamodel of deciding with recurring characteristics: an agent capable of rational action, accountability, causally linked choices, and an outcome based on these choices. Because deciding so conceived requires (a) rational agent(s) and a set of actions, the popular cultural metamodel of deciding appears linear. It is, however, circular: deciding leads to "a decision", where process and outcome are defined by each other. It is this appearance of linearity, kept in place by a vocabulary of rationality and the discursive illusion of distinct, ordered events that obfuscates the slippery, eventful character of *doing* deciding.

We proceed otherwise: agency, action, and accountability are key to our understanding of deciding. As Halvorsen (2010: 275–276) notes, "decisions as outcomes are frequently confused with decision-making as a process, with the presumption that the latter is related to the former in some unproblematic way". Halvorsen and Sarangi (2015: 84) claim that decisions are far from identifiable moments in a sequence of bounded actions: "Studies of meeting interaction show that it is often difficult to identify when a decision has been made and even whether a decision has been made". Deciding is fluid in terms of time and space in that where, when, and how deciding occurs can be dispersed and is socially constituted (see Weick 1995). The concept of *deciding* calls attention to how decision-making *may be realized* in the moment of its occurring *or* realized *retrospectively*. We describe how deciding is constituted through three performative and overlapping contexts:

1. the immediate context of utterances;
2. a metapragmatic vocabulary; and,
3. the metaconversations about deciding.

In the following, we briefly trace how the study of deciding moved away from a rational model. We then describe an alternative perspective that features agency, accountability, and action as well as the laminated nature of deciding as a multi-contextual practice, by analyzing spoken data in two moments of organizational deciding. Given how management studies have often connected deciding with leadership as well as crisis management, our two case analyses examine deciding in times of crisis: Hurricane Katrina and the COVID-19 pandemic.

1 Historical overview

The evolution of theorizing about deciding parallels the evolution of organizational theorizing from early scientific management, as influenced by Frederick Taylor, to perspectives that challenged the assumption of rationality (e. g., Simon 1947), to complex system orientations (e. g., Weick 1995) and perspectives that recognize the cultural and political aspects of organizational decision-making. This evolution is presented as basic knowledge found in introductory organizational communication textbooks (e. g., Eisenberg et al. 2017; Mumby and Kuhn 2018).

Buchanan and O'Connell (2006) trace the initial use of the term "decision-making" to the early twentieth century when Chester Barnard imported it from public administration into management studies (see Barnard 1938). Quoting from William Starbuck, Buchanan and O'Connell (2006: 33) elaborate on this significance: "Policy making could go on and on endlessly, and there are always resources to be allocated. Decision implies the end of deliberation and the beginning of action". Other terms associated with decision-making are: deliberation, negotiation, compromise, and problem solving (Halvorsen 2010). While these reference communicative activities that may intersect with deciding, the vocabulary of deciding implicates a set of specific actions consisting of whom, what, and how: someone(s) is (are) making a choice by means of a process.

In their analysis of problems, Rittel and Webber (1973) provide an alternative way to view deciding: problems may be ambiguous and fluid in that a purportedly clear problem may evolve into an ambiguous problem with an unclear solution (also see Grint 2005; Weick 1995). Grint (2005) argues that problems as well as solutions are socially constructed (see also Castor 2005). Herbert Simon (1960) makes a key contribution to the critique of rational decision-making through his articulation of "bounded rationality", which recognizes the limitations of human rationality (also see Cristofaro 2017). Simon (1960) delineates three phases of decision-making: "finding occasions" for decision-making; identifying choices; and then selecting a choice (also see Chia 1994). Simon (1960) points out that people tend to "satisfice" by selecting a satisfactory (in contrast to optimal) choice. While there may be *a* rationality to a given choice, it is not necessarily an ideally rational one.

Deciding and choice-selection are in dialectical relation in that the presumed result of deciding entails making a choice. Early perspectives assumed intentionality, an assumption critiqued by strategic management scholars Henry Mintzberg and James Waters (Chia 1994). As an alternative to intentionality, choice, and rationality, Cohen, March, and Olsen (1972) proposed the "garbage can model" that highlighted the ambiguous nature of deciding: deciding is not necessarily deliberate or even recognized as such until examined retrospectively (also see Weick 1995). Cohen and colleagues note that in anarchical organizations (e. g., universities, emergency operations, state governor offices), deciding can occur by flight, fight, or oversight. These methods of deciding highlight how deciding is not necessarily an intentional act: what is labeled as deciding may occur *post hoc*.

Current theorizing is disbursed, including contributions across several disciplines (e. g., psychology, management science, communication, etc.) and several different theoretical perspectives (e. g., decision theory, game theory, etc.). We describe a discursive approach to deciding that focuses on language in social interaction, noting the "messiness" of deciding in actual contexts.

2 Deciding as discourse/the discourse of deciding

Advancing Simon's (1947) work, Huisman (2001: 71) argues that "the process of decision-making is not only bounded rationally or cognitively but is also contingent upon the context of the talk, and that the 'rationale' of a decision made in interaction is a socially situated construct of the interaction". Huisman (2001: 72) describes deciding as constituted through talk in which during a decision-making episode, "participants recursively (1) formulate states of affairs, which can consist of events, situations, and actions (Dik 1981), and (2) assess those states of affairs (Pomerantz 1984)". Huisman (2001: 72) connects deciding to organizational action in that "participants form what is tantamount to a 'virtual' future reality and shape the future of the organization". Deciding is discursively enacted during organizational meetings (see Cooren 2015).

Deciding as enacted through language-in-use in social interaction is not a new conceptualization. In the development of ethnomethodology, Harold Garfinkel (1967) observed how juror deciding is an interactionally situated activity. Mehan (1983) examined the interconnection between language and institutional deciding. Boden (1994: 22) notes, "[a]s real time phenomena, decisions are, in fact, largely invisible and thus empirically unavailable, whereas decision-making can be located in the fine laminations of actions and reactions that build, from one moment to another, into the organization".

While the interconnection between discourse, interaction, management, and deciding has been recognized, application of a discursive lens to analyzing deciding has been slower in development. In Halvorsen's (2010) literature review of team decision-making, she identified sixteen studies. Kwon, Clarke, and Wodak (2009: 274) claim that little research has been done on senior management decision-making practices, and that:

> [T]his can be explained due to the tendency to play down the relations and interactions involved (Chia, 1994), resulting in a portrayal of the discursive aspect of decision-making as either: a) locally autonomous and transient (see Alvesson and Karreman, 2000), such that they are 'talked and texted into existence' (Reed, 2000, p. 525); or b) the outcome of deterministic influences of macro-institutional structures (DiMaggio and Powell, 1991) that are 'relatively immune to resistance and transformation'. (Mumby 2004: 241)

Discursive approaches must balance between the extremes of being too locally focused versus too contextually oriented. For discursive approaches to deciding to be taken seriously, context cannot be ignored. However, the claims that little work has been done in studying deciding discursively exclude research that says otherwise. These oversights speak to the challenge of identifying organizational deciding and point to the need for a multi-faceted metamodel of deciding. In the following, we examine how deciding has been examined from discursive and cultural perspectives as a precursor to presenting our metamodel.

2.1 Social and discursive forms of deciding

Building upon prior work that examines the interconnections between discourse and naturalistic deciding, we analyze the diversity of ways that deciding has been directly and indirectly studied. As a meta-analytic framework, we draw on Dell Hymes' (1962) SPEAKING mnemonic that was initially developed as a descriptive tool for conducting ethnography of speaking (also known as ethnography of communication). In applying SPEAKING as a meta-analytic tool, our purpose is to use it for comparative purposes. SPEAKING identifies: Setting or scene; Participants; Ends or goals; Act sequence; Key or tone; Instrumentalities or channels; Norms of interpretation and interaction; and Genres.

Where does deciding occur (i.e., settings and scenes)? "Decision-making" implies concrete and discrete phenomena and events. Deciding may occur in meetings (e.g., Cooren 2015; Halvorsen 2010), the office of a manager (e.g., Trujillo 1983), or other locations. Halvorsen (2010: 276) notes that "decisions are dispersed in terms of both time and space". Deciding may be dispersed rather than taking place during a specific event such as a meeting. For example, Miller (1994) showed how American and Japanese co-workers had different assumptions regarding the relationship between deciding and meetings: the former group assumed that deciding was to take place *during* a business meeting whereas the latter group assumed that deciding was to take place *before* the meeting. This example highlights two features regarding settings for deciding: (1) a group may designate that deciding is to occur within a particular setting (e.g., a meeting, the conference room, an office); and/but, (2) the interactions that contribute to deciding may take place in multiple physical locations over time.

Who gets to participate in deciding? Various textbooks in organizational communication highlight the inter-relationship between deciding and power (also see Mintzberg 1983). Political approaches to deciding in organizational contexts (e.g., Pettigrew 2014) note the relationship between power and decision-making. Shifting the notion of power as associated with persons, Kwon, Clarke, and Wodak (2009: 278) identified three ways that power and discourse are related: "i) the power in discourse; ii) power over discourse; and iii) the power of discourses". These modes highlight issues such as how rules and guidelines (stated and unstated) are developed and applied regarding who may participate in deciding.

What is the process of deciding? We are not implying that all deciding activities follow a certain process; rather, deciding is a process, and the task of analysts (as well as participants) is to identify this process. On the surface, the deciding process may be normatively prescribed (e. g., rational choice model; Robert's Rules of Order for parliamentary process). Alternatively, Cohen, March, and Olsen's (1972) garbage can model of decision-making highlights the messiness of deciding where the outcome may result in a resolution for a problem, oversight (in which a decision is made prior to or in absence of an actual problem), or flight (in which a decision is made for a problem that is no longer relevant). As Castor and Bartesaghi (2016) illustrate, a process (act sequence) may be followed without resulting in a decision.

While early notions associated decision-making with rationality, deciding cannot be separated from emotions, an issue that Hymes' (1962) SPEAKING calls attention to through key or tone. While there may be emotions associated with deciding outcomes (e. g., outrage regarding a program cut), deciding can also be construed as an emotional performance (Bailey 1983) as the Cuomo case analysis will demonstrate. One example provides an illustration of the role of instrumentality, and norms of interaction and interpretation in deciding. In Hymes' (1962) heuristic, instrumentality underscores the form and function of channels of communication. Deciding is guided through norms of interaction and interpretation: there may be expected processes to be followed. While this has some overlap with the earlier discussion of act sequence, norms emphasize the prescriptive and evaluative nature of deciding as groups have expectations on how deciding should occur.

Baxter's (1993) study of deciding at a university illustrates how norms of deciding can become a site of controversy as well as how these norms can become entangled with instrumentality. Baxter identified how university members held two divergent "codes of communication" with respect to governance. One group held a "professional management" perspective or "code of communication" that focused on written rules and policies to ensure fairness in the treatment of faculty, whereas the other group held a "collegial" perspective that emphasized "talking things through" as a way of demonstrating respect for organizational members as individuals. "Writing things down" versus "talking things through" illustrates how deciding and instrumentality are interconnected: the channels through which deciding occurs is intertwined with the social meaning of the deciding process. In addition to social meanings, there are the technological practicalities of a given communication channel. For example, Castor and Bartesaghi (2016) describe how the teleconference technology of Hurricane Katrina crisis management calls impacted the deciding process as participants were asked to mute their microphones or failed to get moderator attention through the audio-only group call.

Hymes' (1962) mnemonic ends with genre, or categorical type of speech act, or speech event. Rude (1995) directly addresses the interconnection between genre and deciding in her analysis of the genre of the written business decision report and its similarities and differences with proposals, scientific reports, and persuasive essays. As a genre, deciding intersects with other management activities as Pälli, Vaara, and Sorsa's (2009) study of strategic decision-making, Bergeron and Cooren's (2012) study of crisis management meetings, and Castor and Bartesaghi's (2016) study of crisis management teleconference calls illustrate.

Thus far, we have argued that deciding is not a sequence of choices that occurs in the head of an individual, nor is it a particular communicative "behavior" or "thing" that organizational members have at the ready and can access when it is time to make a decision. It is an organizing term that may be utilized by interlocutors *or* researchers to label activities.

2.2 Action, agency, and accountability as a deciding framework

The preceding review illustrates the challenges of studying deciding: it does not occur in a consistent way and is not associated with a specific site. What constitutes deciding is situationally and contextually variable and dispersed. Whether or not deciding has occurred may not be realized by the participants until after the fact. Multiple interactions over time and space may contribute to deciding. We argue that deciding is constituted through a metapragmatic vocabulary of action, agency, and accountability, or what we will refer to as the AAA framework.

Verschueren (2000: 439) notes regarding metapragmatics that there are "[t]wo ways in which indicators of metapragmatic awareness function in language use [...] Their functioning as anchoring devices locating linguistic form in relation to context, and their functioning as signals of the language users' reflexive interpretations of the activities they are engaged in". When interlocutors invoke a metapragmatic vocabulary, their speech highlights expectations regarding actions that should be taken or should have been taken (also see Huisman 2001). Such socially constituted actions have implications for agency in that it is presumed someone(s) or something(s) may, could, or should take action (also see Cooren 2010). Social accountability is entangled with action and agency (see Buttny 1993; Shotter 1984) in that said actions must be able to be accounted for. In utilizing a metapragmatic vocabulary, speakers may use terms that describe their own or other's activities in terms of actions that were or should be taken by someone(s).

Deciding is an activity performed at multiple contextual levels: that of utterances; by means of a metapragmatic vocabulary; and within metaconversations. The terms *decide*, *decision*, or *decision-making* may be invoked, but explicit use of these is not a necessary condition for describing those utterances as contributing to deciding. The metapragmatic vocabulary of action, agency, and accountability functions to index the performance of deciding.

Deciding is also enacted by mobilizing the epistemic norms of organizational metaconversations (Kwon, Clarke, and Wodak 2009; also see Robichaud, Giroux, and

Taylor 2004). These metaconversations, or conversations about conversations, may be enacted through institutional texts (e. g., meeting minutes, policies, reports, etc.) as well as through oral conversations. Metaconversations function to connect organizational deciding across different periods of time as well as across sites of interaction. A key function of crisis hearings and crisis investigative reports is to unpack the soundness of deciding processes according to institutional understandings of appropriate action. Rarely do such investigations point to a single situation that caused the crisis; rather, they excavate multiple failures in organizational deciding (e. g., Gephart, Steier, and Lawrence 1990; Tompkins 2005).

Crises such as the Hurricane Katrina disaster and the COVID-19 pandemic illustrate how what constitutes deciding is neither necessarily defined by specific (speech) actions nor necessarily recognized as deciding as it is occurring. Rather, deciding may be assessed as such retrospectively. As a concept that embodies agency, accountability, and action, deciding is constituted by interlocutors in ways that presume someone(s) can take an action, in a morally and socially accountable way (Shotter 1984). To illustrate these ideas, we discuss two case studies drawn from crisis management situations. We take a synthetic approach to discourse analysis understood as an umbrella term for studies in language and social interaction, such as pragmatics, conversation analysis, and critical discourse analysis (Bartesaghi and Pantelides 2018; Kwon, Clarke, and Wodak 2009; Stubbe et al. 2003).

3 Case study examples: deciding in crisis

3.1 Hurricane Katrina: on deciding and not deciding

Our first case is drawn from a series of teleconferences that took place in August 2005, in the days prior to Hurricane Katrina's landfall. The speakers, Louisiana emergency managers and other local and state officials from Louisiana and Mississippi, as well as the federal government, met for twelve teleconferences moderated by Colonel Jeff Smith, deputy director of Louisiana's Office of Emergency Preparedness over a two-day period. Actions taken in the course of these conversations later became the subject of Congressional Hearings (December 14, 2005) (see Bartesaghi 2014), as Hurricane Katrina was charged with being as much – if not more so – a social disaster as a natural disaster (Smith, N. 2006). This meant that, among the human failings and social as well as structural injustices that characterized New Orleans' vulnerability and lack of preparedness, the decisions taken by particular speakers in the calls were at fault in that they resulted in delayed evacuations and the Superdome acting as a shelter of last resort.

The calls were recorded and later made publicly available by one of the participating parish emergency operation managers. The call recordings were obtained through an open records request by the second author and transcribed verbatim using a simplified notation system (see Sacks, Schegloff, and Jefferson 1978) to indicate basic vocal features such as word emphasis, changes in volume, and overlapping speech. This analysis focuses on the second conference call that took place on August 27, 2005, at 7:30 am. With the hurricane less than twelve hours away, a number of possibilities were still in play regarding evacuation procedures and when to speak to the public.

The purpose of the meetings was to create *coordination* among multiple parties. Coordination, a key term of crisis metadiscourse that sets the stage for the metapragmatics of deciding (see Bartesaghi 2014), was a term that Jeff Smith (Hearing on Hurricane Katrina Preparedness and Response 2006) defined as a situation of communicative symmetry in which participants would be in possession of the same amount and quality of information as to be able to "speak with one voice" and "be on the same sheet". By the same token, acting outside of coordination, as Smith (Hearing on Hurricane Katrina Preparedness and Response 2006) made the case to those speakers who expressed doubts about his logic, meant acting differently than what the State's Plan dictated,[1] and therefore acting alone (and unaccounted for), with all the consequences that would bring. The production of coordination was the production of deciding: it implicated speakers' allegiance with the moderator's enforcement of the plan, committed them to the actions prescribed, and positioned those so coordinated on the right side of history, for they had not decided alone, but according to a ratified structure of accountability.

Smith (Hearing on Hurricane Katrina Preparedness and Response 2006) ensured coordination by moderating the calls. Each exchange, initiated and concluded by him, followed a predicted order of speakers, was ordered by a series of named speech activities (e.g., roll call, reports, questions) and performed by way of recipient-designed speech acts. Smith (Hearing on Hurricane Katrina Preparedness and Response 2006) verbalized categories of speech acts as they occurred, setting up a metapragmatic context for speakers' performances, and calling out breaches as "break-ins". What was unfolding by the performance of this protocol was deciding, and, crucially, the deciding of a timeline for evacuating parishes according to the dictates of "coordination".

The term *decision* was not used at all during the meeting, but *decide* was uttered eight times (two within a single speaking turn, yielding seven extracts). This tells us that deciding is an activity which does not require members' identification as such. When the term decide does appear, it refers to activities that would take place outside of the meeting, in a different setting and time and/or involving people not present at the meeting:

---

[1] The State's Plan, or "the Plan", as it was referred to in shorthand during the calls, was put in place following the 2004 disaster simulation Hurricane Pam.

1. "we'll be meeting after this conference call to do decide if we're going to activate the EOC" (parish EM).
2. "We'll move fast to decide the termination point" (DoT, official).
3. "We hadn't decided that as far as contraflow yet, we'll let ya know before we execute contraflow" (DoT official).
4. "Whenever you guys decide that we will be ready" (State Police official).
5. "Yeah, and that hadn't been decided by you guys yet [...] it has not been decided" (State Police official).
6. "Ah, we've got State Police, DOTD here and we feel like that we have to stick to time, decide that over the, ah, over the course of the next three or four hours, but that does not have to worked out specifically at this call" (moderator).
7. "And it could be that all the parties that ah are there, may decide to – to push that noon conference by a little bit" (moderator).

What can we learn from these seven extracts about the explicit use of *decide*? First, "decide" is uttered a handful of times by only four speakers. Excerpts 1, 2, and 3 refer to deciding that is to occur in the future among a different group of people than those in the teleconference call; excerpts 4 and 5 implicate deciding on the part of the meeting participants and exclude the involvement of the speaker (e. g., "whenever *you guys* decide" [emphasis ours]); and excerpts 6 and 7 appear to include features of both.

At the semantic level, decide does not actually decide anything in that closure of the action is not within the purview of the speaker at the time of speaking. Rather, it signifies action contingent on other agents or actions that are in process. Though the speaker can account for what relational and temporal arrangement *decide* requires, he cannot be held accountable for making it happen. Because "decide" grammatically favors the future tense, the location of an actual "decision" is not within any specified or known time and space. Even the delays requested by speakers in *deciding* formulations are ambiguous in terms of actual time (e. g., 6 and 7).

In each of the above examples, "decide", which operates within a crisis metadiscourse of acting together, timeliness and appropriate choice (i. e., accountable action) is dependent on agents who may and may not be accountable for deciding. This is especially clear in 1–6, where the term is associated with the first person plural pronoun "we". For instance: "whenever you guys decide that we will be ready" (State Police official).

Though the subject of the sentence is "we", "we" is moved to the object position in the utterance, calling attention to the onus placed on "you guys". The "we", for whom the speaker speaks, is waiting upon the "you", as the "whenever" signals, and it is this time element that is holding the deciding relationship together. "We" also know that the deciding relationship is distributed among the unknown membership designated by "you guys" and a group represented by the speaker's "we", for if the first party does not decide, the second will also not be able to take action. The speaker's readiness is not itself referred to as deciding: the speaker does not say "we will decide to be ready".

The speaker's readiness is presented as a response that requires no decision, because it fully depends on the interlocutor's agency as a decider.

The State Police speaker is employing "decide", "we", and "you" to accomplish three things: the first is to weigh the distribution of agency on the ambiguous "you" by placing the burden on the latter party. The second is to account for "that" which the hearer must engage in (i. e., a decision), and to note that it has yet to happen in the "whenever" of an anticipated future. Finally, the speaker from the State Police may align with the actions required of him at this point, but disaffiliates (also see Stivers 2011) himself and the "we", for whom he speaks, as parties to be held accountable in the same way as the implied decision-makers. In a sense, the speaker is deciding *not* to decide now.

Excerpt 7 presents another interesting case: "And it could be that all the parties that ah are there, may decide to – to push that noon conference by a little bit". Unlike in 1–6 above, we do not see a clear juxtaposition between the speaker's "we" and the interlocutors' "you". In this case, Jeff Smith is speaking as a moderator to an unknown interlocutor and speaking on behalf of "all the parties". Smith is neither part of the hearer's membership, nor directly included as part of those for whom he speaks. His contribution excludes his own agency in the deciding relationship, and rather, offers a suggestion about how others may conduct their deciding.

The modals – "could be" and "may" – that precede and refer to "decide", and the ambiguous time frame of "by a little bit" construct a relationship where Smith (Hearing on Hurricane Katrina Preparedness and Response 2006) is overseeing a dynamic carried out by others and assigns agency to those others ("all the parties"). The modal verbs function as negative politeness strategies that offer Smith's listener(s) the ability to disagree. The uncertainty surrounding noon as an appropriate time for a subsequent call indicates that "decide" is not about declaring a choice that might be accounted for as a "decision".

The uttering of the verb "decide" in interaction is a metapragmatic action in that it positions interlocutors in relations of action, agency, and accountability that accomplish deciding. Uttering the verb "decide" signals an asymmetry: the speaker who makes use of "decide" has interactional rights to create positions of agency and accountability for others to occupy. In the above cases, "deciding", as a metacommunicative term, amounts to deferral: the speakers' strategies are to decide not to decide. This slippage, or *différance* of deciding, means that what it "is" is never fully there, but rather invoked as a speech act that renders the deciding arrangement between the speaker and the hearer relevant and accountable.

3.2 Deciding COVID-19: the case of Andrew Cuomo

> I accept full responsibility. If someone is unhappy, if somebody wants to blame someone, or complain about someone, blame me. There is no one else who is responsible for this decision. (Andrew Cuomo, March 20, 2020)

At the time of this statement, Andrew Cuomo, governor of the hardest hit city in the hardest hit US state by COVID-19, had garnered a reputation as America's favorite governor in the midst of the ravages of the pandemic. Even in the face of controversy, Cuomo remained one of the "most charismatic leaders" of the pandemic (e. g., McBain 2020). Media outlets reported on the wisdom of his steady leadership, marveled at his 77 percent approval rating (at the time of this writing), and called him a "hot commodity". On Twitter, the governor's followers go by #cuomoforpresident, #cuomocrush, and #cuomosexual, among others (see Vásquez 2020).

His avowal of full and sole responsibility (above) supports the image of the charismatic leader popularized by psychological theories of leadership, where he embodies all agentive action, for right or wrong (Fairhurst 2008). As we argued thus far, "decision" is part of a metapragmatic vocabulary that works relationally by arranging the speaker with respect to action, agency, and accountability. The statement itself (quoted at the start of this section) claims Cuomo as a single agent for the action, and thus, solely accountable.

A closer look shows that Cuomo appears as the first person subject in the first sentence alone. The full statement is bounded at its opening and closing by two extreme case formulations (ECF) (Pomerantz 1986): "full responsibility", and "no one else to blame but me". ECFs are featured as a strategy for a speaker to account for action that may come under scrutiny, and, as in this case, to justify it as the moral action. ECFs like "everybody" and "always" normalize action, placing the speaker as part of a collective. In this case ECFs are multifunctional, defending Cuomo's action and establishing his moral authority.

We base our argument on two counts. First, Cuomo's pronominal work sets him apart from the ambiguous collective or collectives he refers to as "someone" and "somebody". Cuomo decides alone. Once "I" and "me" have been set aside from the others, Cuomo tells us what members of these other categories are doing/not doing: not taking responsibility, complaining, not being happy, blaming. As far as "no one", they are, unlike him, not making the decision. A closer look at the statement's rhetorical workings shows use of anaphora (is someone – if somebody, blame someone – complain about someone) and repetition (blame). Cuomo is not the sole agent, but the leader of a collective of agents.

Second, Cuomo's "decide" negates his version of a single-handed decision. If the decision rests only with him, then responsibility for failure is anticipated by his statement for he is also saying: there will be complaints; there will be unhappiness; there will be blame. He is not alone but part of a deciding relationship in which this account is necessary and others will be in the future. Unhappiness and complaints are discursively built into the deciding dynamic that his statement recognizes and organizes. Although Cuomo's statement locates the decision in the present moment, he has set up a web of accountable agents and necessary actions that open up the possibility of its recasting.

In an article in *Forbes* that prominently mentions Cuomo's leadership, the following observation seems to support our analysis as well as tells us something about deciding metadiscourse. "Faced with unprecedented uncertainty, leaders will need to avoid the temptation to 'stick with a decision' in an attempt to appear decisive and instead be willing to regularly review new data, information and feedback and change course if necessary" (Brownlee 2020). This is what sets Cuomo aside from Jeff Smith, on the one hand, who lost his job for following the plan he was tasked to uphold and from President Trump's bids at charisma by way of his much criticized statement that his role as president affords him absolute power. Though Smith attempted to reformulate his role in the deciding of evacuations by distributing agency to the collective "we" and calling the delay a success when questioned by the Task Force on Katrina (see Bartesaghi 2014), he failed. However, the same strategy of calling his actions a success worked for Cuomo.

We turn to a set of seven briefings during the month of April 2020. The briefings are, by definition, accounts of deciding to the public and the media. Unlike the Katrina data, the briefings are produced prospectively, marking actions as necessitating an account. In the seven Cuomo briefings, which add up to 25,322 words, a search for "decide", "deciding", "decision", and "decisions" turned up nine instances. In four of these, Cuomo used anaphora, and repeated the terms twice or more, changing our count to five. We provide all of the extracts from Cuomo, followed with a brief analysis.

1. If people wonder, "Well, where do you get these numbers, governor? How do you decide what you're going to do?" (April 1)
2. What we're doing with McKinsey is studying all of them and coming up with a moderate model that is a basis for us to make planning decisions. Because I have to make decisions. I want to make the decisions off the numbers, so that's what we're doing. (April 1)
3. It's not a government decision. It's not a political decision. The medical doctor decides. If a medical doctor decides it works, fine. (April 1)
4. We make smart decisions, you will see smart outcomes in two weeks. We make bad decisions, you will see bad outcomes in two weeks. (April 5)
5. What we do today will determine tomorrow, and we're not going to need to wait to read the history books. How do you decide? (April 25)

In each of these statements, something as yet to happen is at stake. Cuomo's accounts of deciding do important work: they presentify (i.e., make present) a collective of agents that account for his actions, supporting and authorizing them. This collective, for whom he speaks directly and indirectly, can be the medical and data experts that give warrant to his "smart decisions". They allow Cuomo to align with those who have elected him as well as those who work with him through his ambiguous "we".

The statements above are representative of Cuomo's discourse patterns in the briefings, patterns in which his most prominent strategies are pronominal work, speaking for and with facts and statistics (which "say" and "are saying"), and his unique use of PowerPoint slides as co-agents, which either echo his speech (recontextualizing its authority) or are in conversation (supporting what he is saying) (also see Cooren 2010; Kaplan 2011; Schoeneborn 2008). Much as in the Katrina data, the Cuomo briefings suggest that the term decide is not necessary to accomplish deciding.

4 Conclusion

In this chapter, we presented the notion of deciding as discursive doing. This conceptualization stands in contrast to management science's early history of locating decision-making in individual rationality. As a discursive activity, deciding is relational: it is located in shifting relational alignments and boundaries between participants. It is an interactional accomplishment *and* a metapragmatic resource for relational arrangements of agency, accountability, and action.

The hurricane teleconferences allowed us to analyze the shifting allegiances of deciding in action, and the metapragmatic work done by the seven reflexive utterances in which speakers used "decide" as a resource to defer, distribute, or disclaim their own agency in making decisions they would later be held accountable for. The data from Governor Cuomo's press briefings illustrate how accounting for deciding involves a laminated context of agency, action, and accountability. Cuomo's metapragmatic invocation of deciding terms serves to accrue his charisma as a leader by ventriloquizing the words of his supporters and detractors, as well as non-human agents such as data, PowerPoint slides, and speaking for the moral order.

The study of deciding in crisis contexts illustrates how attending to metaconversations allows for recontextualizing deciding as an iteration in time and space, across what appear as single episodes. It invites us to shift our gaze on how everything – every utterance, every exchange, for every other first time – happens in relation (Kuhn, Ashcraft, and Cooren 2017) and could, therefore, not happen at all.

5 References

Bailey, Frederick G. 1983. *The tactical uses of passion: An essay on power, reason, and reality*. Ithaca, NY: Cornell University Press.
Barnard, Chester I. 1938. *The functions of the executive*. Cambridge, MA: Harvard University Press.

Bartesaghi, Mariaelena. 2014. Coordination: Examining weather as a "matter of concern". *Communication Studies* 65(5). 535–557.
Bartesaghi, Mariaelena & Theresa R. Castor. 2010. Disasters as social interaction. *Communication Currents* 5. https://www.natcom.org/communication-currents/disasters-social-interaction (accessed 12 November 2020).
Bartesaghi, Mariaelena & Kate Pantelides. 2018. Why critique should not run out of steam: A proposal for the critical study of discourse. *Review of Communication* 18(3). 158–177.
Baxter, Leslie A. 1993. "Talking things through" and "putting it in writing": Two codes of communication in an academic institution. *Journal of Applied Communication Research* 21(4). 313–326.
Bergeron, Caroline D. & François Cooren. 2012. The collective framing of crisis management: A ventriloqual analysis of emergency operations centres. *Journal of Contingencies and Crisis Management* 20(3). 120–137.
Boden, Deirdre. 1994. *The business of talk: Organizations in action*. Cambridge: Polity Press.
Brownlee, Dana. 2020. 7 leadership traits for the post COVID-19 workplace. *Forbes*. https://www.forbes.com/sites/danabrownlee/2020/05/07/7-leadership-traits-for-the-post-covid-19-workplace/#46108a722d4d (accessed 12 November 2020).
Buchanan, Leigh & Andrew O'Connell. 2006. A brief history of decision making. *Harvard Business Review* 84(1). 34–41.
Buttny, Richard. 1993. *Social accountability in communication*. London: Sage.
Castor, Theresa R. 2005. Constructing social reality in organizational decision making: Account vocabularies in a diversity discussion. *Management Communication Quarterly* 18(4). 479–508.
Castor, Theresa & Marialena Bartesaghi. 2016. Metacommunication during disaster response: "Reporting" and the constitution of problems in Hurricane Katrina teleconferences. *Management Communication Quarterly* 30(4). 472–502.
Chia, Robert. 1994. The concept of decision: A deconstructive analysis. *Journal of Management Studies* 31(6). 781–806.
Cohen, Michael D., James G. March & Johan P. Olsen. 1972. A garbage can model of organizational choice. *Administrative Science Quarterly* 17(1). 1–25.
Cooren, François. 2010. *Action and agency in dialogue: Passion, incarnation and ventriloquism*. Amsterdam: John Benjamins.
Cooren, François. 2015. *Organizational discourse: Communication and constitution*. Cambridge: Polity Press.
Cristofaro, Matteo. 2017. Herbert Simon's bounded rationality: Its historical evolution in management and cross-fertilizing contribution. *Journal of Management History* 23(2). 170–190.
Doyle, Alison. 2020. Important decision-making skills that employers value. *The Balance Careers*. https://www.thebalancecareers.com/decision-making-skills-with-examples-2063748 (accessed 12 November 2020).
Eisenberg, Eric M., Angela Trethewey, Marianne LeGreco & Harold L. Goodall, Jr. 2017. *Organizational communication: Balancing creativity and constraint*, 8th edn. Boston, MA: Bedford St. Martin's.
Fairhurst, Gail T. 2008. Discursive leadership: A communication alternative to leadership psychology. *Management Communication Quarterly* 21(4). 510–521.
Garfinkel, Harold. 1967. Some rules of correct decisions that jurors respect. In *Studies in Ethnomethodology*, 104–115. Englewood Cliffs, NJ: Prentice-Hall.
Gephart, Robert P., Lloyd Steier & Thomas Lawrence. 1990. Cultural rationalities in crisis sensemaking: A study of a public inquiry into a major industrial accident. *Industrial Crisis Quarterly* 4(1). 27–48.
Grint, Keith. 2005. Problems, problems, problems: The social construction of "leadership". *Human Relations* 58(11). 1467–1494.

Halvorsen, Kristin. 2010. Team decision making in the workplace: A systematic review of discourse analytic studies. *Journal of Applied Linguistics and Professional Practice* 7(3). 273–296.

Halvorsen, Kristin & Srikant Sarangi. 2015. Team decision-making in workplace meetings: The interplay of activity roles and discourse roles. *Journal of Pragmatics* 76. 1–14.

Hearing on Hurricane Katrina Preparedness and Response by the State of LA before Select Comm., 109th Congress at 18 (statement of Col. Jeff Smith).

Heracleous, Loizos T. 1994. Rational decision making: Myth or reality? *Management Development Review* 7(4). 16–23.

Huisman, Marjan. 2001. Decision-making in meetings as talk-in-interaction. *International Studies of Management and Organization* 31(3). 69–90.

Hymes, Dell. 1962. The ethnography of speaking. In Thomas Gladwin & William C. Sturtevant (eds.), *Anthropology and human behavior*, 13–53. Washington, DC: Anthropology Society of Washington.

Kaplan, Sarah. 2011. Strategy and PowerPoint: An inquiry into the epistemic culture and machinery of strategy making. *Organization Science* 22(2). 320–346.

Kuhn, Timothy, Karen Ashcraft & François Cooren. 2017. *The work of communication: Relational perspectives on working and organizing in contemporary capitalism*. New York: Routledge.

Kwon, Winston, Ian Clarke & Ruth Wodak. 2009. Organizational decision-making, discourse, and power: Integrating across contexts and scales. *Discourse and Communication* 3(3). 273–302.

Luhmann, Niklas. 2018. *Organization and decision*. Cambridge: Cambridge University Press.

McBain, Sophie. 2020 Andrew Cuomo, the charismatic, controlling, combative anti-Trump. *New Statesman*. https://www.newstatesman.com/world/north-america/2020/04/andrew-cuomo-charismatic-controlling-combative-anti-trump (accessed 12 November 2020).

Mehan, Hugh. 1983. The role of language and the language of role in institutional decision making. *Language in Society* 12(2). 187–211.

Miller, Laura. 1994. Japanese and American meetings and what goes on before them: A case study of co-worker misunderstanding. *Pragmatics* 4(2). 221–238.

Mintzberg, Henry. 1983. *Power in and around organizations*. Englewood Cliffs, NJ: Prentice Hall.

Mumby, Dennis & Timothy Kuhn. 2018. *Organizational communication: A critical introduction*, 2nd edn. Thousand Oaks, CA: Sage.

Pälli, Pekka, Eero Vaara & Virpi Sorsa. 2009. Strategy as text and discursive practice: A genre-based approach to strategizing in city administration. *Discourse and Communication* 3(3). 303–318.

Pettigrew, Andrew M. 2014. *The politics of organizational decision-making*. New York: Routledge.

Pomerantz, Anita. 1986. Extreme case formulations: A way of legitimizing claims. *Human Studies* 9. 219–229.

Rittel, Horst W. J. & Melvin M. Webber. 1973. Dilemmas in a general theory of planning. *Policy Sciences* 4(2). 155–169.

Robichaud, Daniel, Hélène Giroux & James R Taylor. 2004. The metaconversation: The recursive as a key property of language to organizing. *Academy of Management Review* 29(4). 617–634.

Rude, Carolyn D. 1995. The report for decision making: Genre and inquiry. *Journal of Business and Technical Communication* 9(2). 170–205.

Sacks, Harvey, Emanuel A. Schegloff & Gail Jefferson. 1978. A simplest systematics for the organization of turn taking for conversation. In Jim Schenkein (ed.), *Studies in the organization of conversational interaction*, 7–55. New York: Academic Press.

Schoeneborn, Dennis. 2008. *Alternatives considered but not disclosed: The ambiguous role of PowerPoint in cross-project learning*. Deutscher Universitäts-Verlag & VS Verlag für Sozialwissenschaften dissertation.

Shotter, John. 1984. *Social accountability and selfhood*. Oxford: Blackwell.

Simon, Herbert A. 1947. *Administrative behavior*, 1st edn. New York: Free Press.

Simon, Herbert A. 1960. *The new science of management decision*. New York: Harper & Row.

Smith, Neil. 2006. There's no such thing as a natural disaster. *Items: Insights from the Social Sciences*. https://items.ssrc.org/understanding-katrina/theres-no-such-thing-as-a-natural-disaster/ (accessed 12 November 2020).

Stivers, Tanya. 2011. Morality and question design "of course" as contesting presupposition of askability. In Tanya Stivers, Lorenza Mondada & Jakob Steensig (eds.), *The morality of knowledge in conversation*, 27–57. Cambridge: Cambridge University Press.

Stubbe, Maria, Chris Lane, Jo Hilder, Elaine Vine, Bernadette Vine, Meredith Marra, Janet Holmes & Ann Weatherall. 2003. Multiple discourse analyses of a workplace interaction. *Discourse Studies* 5(3). 351–388.

Tompkins, Phillip K. 2005. *Apollo, Challenger, Columbia: The decline of the space program*. New York: Oxford University Press.

Trujillo, Nick. 1983. "Performing" Mintzberg's roles: The nature of managerial communication. In Linda L. Putnam & Michael E. Pacanowsky (eds.), *Communication and organizations: An interpretive approach*, 73–97. Beverly Hills, CA: Sage.

Valchev, Marin. n.d. Decision-making process: Guide with steps. *Businessphrases.net*. https://www.businessphrases.net/decision-making-process/ (accessed 12 November 2020).

Vasquez, Camilla. 2020. Leadership discourse in response to the COVID crisis: Cuomo's press briefings. *Association for Business Communication E-Lecture Series*. https://www.youtube.com/watch?v=M8zrgsTbcMA (accessed 12 November 2020).

Verschueren, Jef. 2000. Notes on the role of metapragmatic awareness in language use. *Pragmatics* 10(4). 439–456.

Weick, Karl E. 1995. *Sensemaking in organizations*. Thousand Oaks, CA: Sage.

Philippe Lorino
4 Creating by communicating

Abstract: Due to the limits of the control paradigm, static and monological, this chapter suggests that the pragmatist paradigm of "trans-actional inquiry" provides a processual and communicational alternative to study organizations in complex and uncertain situations, characterized by an unintelligible aggregate of unrelated elements; the trans-actional inquiry aims at rebuilding intelligibility and actionability, or even completely re-define the situation, through creative dialogues that involve not only verbal exchanges, but also socially meaningful acts. This framework can be applied to the "organizing" of field operations as well as organizational governance. It could be used in the future to connect organization research with political research about participative democracy. The chapter narrates two complex situations and shows the limits of the control paradigm to understand them; it presents the pragmatist concept of "trans-actional inquiry", applies it to the two narrated situations and shows how it may lead to a complete redefinition of situations; it concludes with methodological, theoretical and managerial implications.

Keywords: inquiry; pragmatism; process; situation; trans-action

1 The communicational process of organizing and the limits of the control paradigm

In light of two organizational episodes experienced by the author, this section will expose the limits of the mainstream concept of control.

1.1 Two episodes of communicational organizing

1.1.1 First example: the reporting of a nuclear incident to a commission representing the public

This incident occurred in a plant reprocessing nuclear fuel, in the west of France, in a workshop where shearing and dissolution operations are conducted (Kerveillant 2017). A logistic system evacuates nuclear waste from zones that are difficult to access to conditioning workshops using a forklift truck and a bridge crane. The bridge crane has a maximum lifting capacity of 3.2t. On May 24, 2011, it was observed that it had been used on two occasions (March 30 and May 16) to lift containers weighing up to 5.2t, above the authorized maximum weight. The company had to report the incident to a local commission representing the public of the area (Commission Locale d'Information = CLI).

During the CLI's meeting, the company presented the incident from a technical angle, going into considerable detail on the testing threshold of lifting facilities. After this presentation, one of the CLI's members, who was familiar with the equipment concerned, asked a series of precise technical questions. The responses of the company representatives plunged CLI members into a state of perplexity: the operators were skilled, the equipment, including the alarm systems, was well maintained, and the alarm had not been altered by operators. There seemed to be no identifiable cause. After a silence, the representative of the French Authority for Nuclear Safety (ASN), the controlling agency, provided some new information that had not yet been mentioned by anybody in the discussion: there had just been a change in the organization of waste transportation in the factory. The ASN representative explained that "the problem comes from the use of this type of container itself, as it has a net weight of 4.2t when empty, while the bridge crane has a maximum lifting capacity of 3.2t". It was thus impossible to complete the task in compliance with safety rules, even with an empty container! Therefore, beyond the operational conditions of bridge crane utilization, the problem involved the design of the task. The operators had faced a double bind: they had to comply with safety rules and, at the same time, they had to perform a task that could not be done without breaking those rules. The CLI inquiry experienced a significant turning point. While the problematic situation had first been viewed as a mistake in the technical operation of a bridge crane, the incident was actually a result of the faulty design of logistic operations in the engineering department, a mistake that had been made days or weeks before. Moreover, as the practices were significantly modified, a preliminary risk analysis to ensure that all important risks have been considered should have taken place, but the risk analysis had not been performed, which infringed safety regulations.

We would then have expected CLI members to go on with their inquiry, moving on to new topics: organizational change management, operators' implication in the design of new logistic operations, and compliance with safety regulations. The CLI have extensive powers to conduct such inquiries. By a law introduced in 2006, they are assigned "a monitoring, information and consultation mission". They may audition nuclear companies' employees, for example the operators directly involved in the incident, the designers of the new operations, and experts, they can get funds to order specific studies, and they can schedule specific meetings to proceed to the in-depth analysis of a specific incident. However, the inquiry came to a standstill and remained uncompleted.

1.1.2 Second example: VESTRA

VESTRA (Lorino 2018) is a clothing manufacturer, established in the 1990s, specializing in menswear (trousers and jackets). To improve VESTRA's performance, different actions take place separately and simultaneously: to increase productivity and shorten production lead time, the production department is developing robots capable of handling and laser-cutting flexible materials like fabric for clothes; to make the transmission of order data (pattern, fabric, color, size) from final points of sale (shops) to the factory quicker and more reliable, the information systems manager is testing the use of EDI (electronic data interchange); he is also experimenting with a laser-measuring device to capture customers' measurements electronically in the store when alterations are required. While the sales manager is always on the lookout for ways to extend the range of options offered to the customer, for example by increasing inventory in the shops, the logistics manager is permanently looking for methods to reduce inventories.

Through internal memos, the production manager and the information systems manager keep their colleagues informed about the progress of the robot and EDI projects, until the production manager announces that the robot is operational and can reduce production lead times for a wide range of products from one week to two days. Thanks to the flexibility of the robot (quick adaptation to different product models), production batches of just one unit should become economically viable. Then, in the monthly business review following the introduction of the robot, the logistics manager asks whether a certain proportion of customers might be prepared to wait three days for the delivery of their purchase. For such customers, it would be possible to eliminate inventory completely at the points of sale and manufacture everything to order, since the production lead time (two days) would be shorter than the customer's acceptable waiting time (three days). The sales manager answers that a large proportion of customers are already willing to wait a few days for alterations to their jackets or trousers and should therefore be prepared to wait three days for the delivery.

In the same period the laser system is successfully tested. Within a few minutes it can transmit the order data directly through EDI to the factory. The CEO then develops the idea further: the product ordered by the customer could be tailored to the customer's specific measurements through laser measurement; the measurements and personal choices (color, pattern, etc.) would then be transmitted via EDI to the factory's computer-aided design system. The sales manager comments that the range of options on offer would not then be limited by any physical inventory; any combination of patterns, fabrics, and colors could be proposed to the customer. However, this would mean a substantial change in customers' habits: they would have to choose the clothes from a catalog, not from the shelf, and they would not be able to try them on.

What looked like a series of scattered functional performance improvements (increase in manufacturing productivity, improved data transfer, better inventory management) and local changes in working habits, once combined, crystallized into a strategic transformation of the whole value chain: from production-to-inventory to production-to-order; from off-the-shelf sale to catalog sale; from standardized design to customized design. Multiple ingredients could coalesce, creating a new strategic perspective.

1.2 The conceptual and practical limits of the control paradigm

In both cases, when facing a disruptive situation, actors explore the past (incident causes; performance projects) and the future (how to make nuclear practices safer; the industrial and commercial opportunities and risks of a strategic change). However, the future does not appear as the prolongation of the past. The actors' search cannot be guided by stable norms. They are "condemned" to imagine novel options. This type of situation underlines the limits of the mainstream *control* paradigm of organizing. Control is an omnipresent theme in managerial practices and organization research (Delbridge and Ezzamel 2005: 603–604): "a central feature of organization is control and without (some form of) control organizing is not possible"; "organization theory has developed and advanced in terms of control".

The Taylorian and variance-based version of control has been widely criticized in management literature. Many "softened" versions have been developed (Eisenhardt 1985; Ouchi 1977): output control, input control, cultural control, concertive control (Barker 1993), so much so that the concept of control has become diluted and consequently assimilated with any form of organizing and coordinating collective activity. Even critical scholars tend to consider control as the only way to organize activity and try to "help organizations construct better (in ethical terms) practices of control" (Barker 2005: 795) rather than alternatives to control. To maintain a distinction between organizing and controlling and look for possible non-controlling organizing alternatives, it is necessary to identify the ultimate distinctive features of the control paradigm.

Control points to two basic characteristics: the dichotomy between means and ends, and a heteronomous conception of human activity.

- *Means/ends dichotomy*: in the control perspective, first, the ends – or goals – of collective action are defined, for example through planning procedures, and are then left outside the subsequent control loop. Control is supposed to evaluate and modify not the ends but the methods and operations activated to meet the objectives and conformance of results to goals previously assigned to collective activity. Control checks that actual behavior conforms to rational models of actions or standards. If activity appears too complex to be modeled *ex ante*, control is focused on the qualitative definition and quantitative measurement of the outcomes of activity (Ouchi 1977).
- *Heteronomous conception of human activity*: operations are supposed to be specified, organized, and regulated by norms, rules, and methods whose elaboration is external, not necessarily to acting subjects, but at least to their situated activity (Dewey [1916] 2005). Control reflects a division between designing and operating activities, either social (controllers versus controlled subjects) or psychological (mental processes of designing versus executing).

The control paradigm raises a lot of problems, more so when activity faces uncertain, complex, and fast-evolving situations, which is more and more systematically the case in organizational life. Pragmatist scholars have emphasized that the means/ends dichotomy is contradicted by the empirical observation that the determination and evaluation of means and ends are always inseparably entangled (Dewey [1939] 1988b). They have criticized heteronomous conceptions of human activity as illusory and dangerous. The pragmatists rather stress the intrinsic creative, exploratory, and experimental nature of ordinary activity (Joas 1996), because human activity is situated, and situations involve elements of novelty calling for novel responses. Dewey (2005) criticized Taylorism and promoted the idea of "industrial democracy", referring to an autonomous conception of activity and rejecting "the tendency to reduce such things as efficiency of activity and scientific management to purely technical externals" (Dewey 2005: 52).

In the CLI and VESTRA cases, actors' exploration of a doubtful situation (nuclear incident; new strategic possibilities) cannot refer to clearly established and stabilized norms. The actors try to construct relevant narratives that design means and ends in a coherent way. Complex, uncertain, and fast-changing situations are mostly beyond control, but they are not beyond inquiry and debate:

- Not beyond inquiry: the coherence and relevance of collective activity in progress must be ensured through ongoing inquiries, to answer such questions as: What happened? What to do next?
- Not beyond debate: to maintain their collective capacity to act, participants are not asked to *share* their ways of understanding and transforming the situation (Verheggen and Baerveldt 2007), since they have specific competences and missions. But they must ensure a minimum level of practical compatibility and mutual intelligibility, involving communicational practices and shared systems of signs.

2 The pragmatist concept of trans-actional inquiry

Dewey and Bentley's ([1949] 2008) concept of trans-actional inquiry can provide us with a radical alternative to the control paradigm to understand situated collective activity as a continuous, exploratory, and pluralist process.

2.1 The pragmatist concepts of habit, inquiry, and situation

Peirce (1992), the founder of pragmatism, rejected Descartes' ([1641] 1996) primacy of the individual thinker, isolated from the material and social world, subjecting everything to the doubt of the individual thinker's consciousness. Instead, he anchored his understanding of doubt in the local situated actions of ordinary living, through which we discover practical ways of coping with life's vicissitudes. For Peirce, a belief is linked with social ways of acting, habits: "[t]he essence of belief is the establishment of a habit; and different beliefs are distinguished by the different modes of action to which they give rise" (Peirce [1931] 1958: 5.398). The pragmatist inquiry is the social process through which doubt is transformed into new belief, and, through belief, into new habit. Belief and habit, not ontological truth, are thus the destination of the inquiry, while doubt is its driving force: "The irritation of doubt causes a struggle to attain a state of belief. I shall term this struggle inquiry" (Peirce 1992: 114). Any learning is an inquiry grounded in living experience.

The pragmatist inquiry is not a subjective but a full social experience: it involves a community of inquiry (Shields 2003; Lorino 2018) within which the meaning and redesign of collective activity are pursued through the confrontation between different perspectives on the situation. It is neither the context nor the inquiring body that is intrinsically doubtful, but the relationship between beliefs, habits, and circumstances. Inquiry does not unilaterally adapt habits to a situation or a situation to habits, but it acts simultaneously on the situation and on habits to rebuild their relationship.

Dewey follows Peirce in understanding inquiry as an operation activated in response to doubt, but he puts more emphasis on the concept of situation. For Peirce and Dewey, the whole is different from the sum of its parts, and perception of the whole precedes perception of the parts. Dewey applies this view to the idea of "a situation" (Dewey [1938] 1986):

> what is designated by the word 'situation' is not a single object or event or set of objects and events. For we never experience nor form judgment about objects and events in isolation, but only in connection with a contextual whole. This latter is what is called a 'situation' [...] an environing experienced world [...] in which observation of this or that object or event occurs [...] with reference to some active adaptive response to be made. (Dewey 1986: 73)

A situation is neither the passive environment of cognitive processes, nor a structure that can be objectively observed from the "outside". It is the entirety of all conditions under which, and within which, an organism functions at a given time (Dewey 1986: 72), actively connecting objects, temporal and spatial circumstances, and individuals to form a "contextual whole".

The inquiry is triggered when actors move from a habitual and therefore invisible *determinate* type of situation to a suddenly *indeterminate*, puzzling, and therefore visible situation. The indeterminate situation, a disordered and unintelligible aggregate of unrelated elements, generates doubt. The inquiry is the process that transforms the indeterminate situation into a determinate one, in which beliefs can be restored and a coherent course of action can be imagined. The situation is thus simultaneously the trigger, the site, and an emergent product of the inquiry. The relationship between the inquiry and the situation is recursive. The inquiry is triggered and, from beginning to end, influenced by the situation, but it also constantly redefines it.

The aim of inquiry is not the discovery of an antecedent fact, but rather the construction of new potentials for collective action and, thus, new practices. The situation is singular, "unique; each situation [is] an individual situation, indivisible and unduplicable" (Dewey 1986: 74). There is no strict repetition, and the inquiry is a creative accomplishment that continuously injects the possibilities of novelty into the recurring patterns of social experience (Joas 1996). At the same time, the inquiry always starts from experience, and attempts to link this situation, here and now, to past or distant situations, in hopes of revealing insights about possible futures.

2.2 The communicational dimension of the pragmatist inquiry and the concept of trans-action

Peirce (1992, 1998) and Dewey (1986) focused their attention on the communicational dimension of inquiry, so that pragmatism appears "as a tradition of communication theory" (Russill 2008: 478). For them, agency is based on dialogical verbal and non-verbal exchanges (Emirbayer and Mische 1998), "means for making a shared perspective available against the backdrop provided by the problem of incommensurability in experience" (Bergman 2008: 139).

In 1949, Dewey and Bentley published a book of epistemology in which, under the term trans-action, they developed an immanent and dynamic view of social systems that contrasts with the mainstream view of systems as objects to be modeled and controlled from an overlooking, external position. Trans-action could be metaphorically represented as the emergence of a field (in the sense of physical sciences, e. g., electromagnetic field) that results from the combined influences of acting organisms such as human beings, institutions, technological systems, concepts, tools, rules, habits, etc. The emerging field, in turn, frames the action of participants, establishes or breaks relationships, accelerates or decelerates moves, so that meaning does not emerge from one specific element, but from the overall system, "conceived as determined by the configuration and motion of that system" (Maxwell [1876] 1991, cited in Dewey and Bentley 2008: 99).

Dewey and Bentley (2008) distinguish three views of inquiry: "Self-Action, Inter-action and Transaction [...]. Self-action: where things are viewed as acting under their own powers" (Dewey and Bentley 2008: 100); for example, many pre-scientific explanations of phenomena are Self-actional ("fluids fill vacuum, because they abhor vacuum"). Inter-action intervenes when agents entering the inquiry have been adequately defined before and outside of the inquiry process, and then establish some relationship. Newtonian physics is inter-actional: objects have an invariable mass; if they get close to each other, they attract each other with a calculable force that does not modify their structural characteristics, e. g., their mass. In organizational research, the paradigm of coordination is inter-actional: actors have clearly distinct roles; they must interact from time to time and their interaction must be regulated. Trans-action intervenes when any definition of inquiry participants (of any type) is "accepted only as tentative and preliminary", so that new definitions "may freely be made at any and all stages of the inquiry" (Dewey and Bentley 2008: 113). For example, in the VESTRA case, potential strategic transformations emerge from the relationships between actors (e. g., the relationship between delivery time tolerated by customers and production lead time) and, in return, transform the identity of participating entities (the selling function moves from sales-on-the-shelf to sales-in-a-catalog, the inventories of finished products altogether disappear).

The trans-actional inquiry is a social process, but not in a holistic sense as the amalgamated expression of a collective subject, which would correspond to the Self-action view. Nor does it relate to previously defined individual participants through coordination links, which would correspond to the inter-action view. Trans-action is the overall, immanent and emergent transformation of a social situation. No single participant can have an external, overlooking, and all-embracing view or produce a transcendental model from outside: representations are just instrumental artifacts, heuristic supports, not the expression of "truth", and they participate in the trans-actional dynamics. The control paradigm expresses an inter-actional view, focused on the given existence and clear identification of distinct acting entities, with clear-cut roles.

The trans-actional inquiry expresses an immanent view in which pluralism and emergence give impulse to creative moves and redefine relationships, patterns of action, and the identity of participants. Inspired by Darwinian adaptive views, Dewey and Bentley emphasize that trans-actional inquiries are moved by an imperative of adaptive survival and existential growth. They respond to social motives, such as drawing practical conclusions from the analysis of a nuclear incident to improve safety, redesigning the value chain of a company, treating a patient, in a world that permanently moves. Motives themselves are constituents of the trans-action and can evolve at any moment.

The trans-actional view rejects both subjectivist approaches that view the inquiry as a mental process produced by one individual mind, and the objectivist approaches that view the inquiry as a logical process, producible by rational models (Lorino 2018). Trans-actional inquiries appear as combinations of situated *dialogues* through which collective activity and each participant can be transformed (Dewey [1927] 1988a: 371). Each act is a response and a call to other acts. Action meaning is thus strictly relational: "In ordinary everyday behavior, in what sense can we examine a talking unless we bring a hearing along with it into account? Or a writing without a reading?" (Dewey and Bentley 2008: 126). The very identity of participants is inseparable from their relationships within the trans-actional process: a seller is a seller because she is related to a buyer in a sales relationship. The meaning of collective activity is not the assembly of local meanings but a general shape *emerging* from the overall process: "Transaction is Fact such that no one of the constituents can be adequately specified as apart from the specification of all the other constituents of the full subject matter" (Dewey and Bentley 2008: 113), while, in the control paradigm, the identity of the controlled entity (e. g., the sales department) does not depend on the controlling relationship.

Thus, trans-action is continuously moving, acting on, and changing its own topics and tools. Concepts, names, and boundaries are transient categories and can be questioned at any moment if so required by the existential imperatives of the inquiry. In trans-action, "any knowing or known establishes itself or fails to establish itself through continued search solely" (Dewey and Bentley 2008: 48); "transaction assumes no pre-knowledge of either organism or environment alone as adequate, [...] full freedom [is] reserved for their developing examination" (Dewey and Bentley 2008: 113).

2.3 A dynamic equilibrium between difference and commonality

Trans-action involves a subtle balance between commonality and pluralism. The participants in a collective activity face disruptive situations with different, "sundry, seemingly incompatible" (Bergman 2008: 138) perspectives, for example due to professional incommensurability. The confrontation between multiple perspectives does not necessarily lead to "a shared perspective" (Bergman 2008), but rather to a redefinition of the situation, in which there are still multiple perspectives, but not the same perspectives as those prevailing at the beginning of the inquiry. The boundary between what is common and what differs can move. Pluralism is the engine of the communicational and exploratory dynamics of trans-action. The coexistence of, and controversies between, different views of the situation, e. g., different professional practices, brings about dynamic contradictions between belief systems and elicits doubt, the driving force of trans-action. Participants need each other, not despite, but because of their differences, because they do different things and think differently (Tsoukas 2009).

The actors do not necessarily produce a common representation of the situation, but no dialogue can take place without actors sharing a system of signs to express their views in ways intelligible for all participants, in "a common language" (Emirbayer and Maynard 2011: 231). The trans-actional inquiry involves a community (Woodward 2001: 71) in which commonality and pluralism are permanently converting into each other, new convergences and new divergences continue popping up, and communication is the connecting fluid of the human and non-human participants.

2.4 Non-verbal dialogue: the language of habits

The common language required by "trans-actional" dialogue does not necessarily involve verbal exchanges. In the first instance, trans-actional dialogues interrelate multiple types of utterances: texts, speeches, acts, gestures, tool uses, and facial expressions. These semiotic mediations segment the continuum of reality and stabilize segments of meaning through systems of signs, names, and designations, which provide inquiry participants with shared means of communication: "Technical names [...] serve to mark off certain portions of the scientific subject matter as provisionally acceptable" (Dewey and Bentley 2008: 113). Semiotic mediations (Lorino 2018) have a temporal function (Bakhtin 1986; Lorino and Mourey 2013). In the singular situation, here and now, signs instantiate past experiences, past meanings, anticipated meanings in the coming situations, to allow memory and projection into the future. Signs also have a social function: they instantiate in the situation distant actors, their meanings in different social environments, to allow communication and cooperation: "there are no neutral words and forms [...] All words have the taste of a profession, a genre, a tendency, a party, [...] a generation, an age group" (Bakhtin 1981: 293).

More in depth, all those semiotic mediations make sense by evoking habits, the "ultimate" semiotic mediation of action (Peirce 1998: 430). The trans-actional perspective on communication is thus discursive but not linguistic: the discursive power of acts *per se* plays a key role through a non-verbal common language, the language of habits (Lorino 2014). Acts are recognizable, nameable, socially meaningful and debatable by instantiating habits that are not subjective, but convey the history and culture of social groups, for example the usual ways of reading management indicators, of handling technical tools, of holding a meeting, or of understanding a word. The trans-action is then a permanent open-and-close communicational movement, in which each act (Lorino 2014) rebuilds the future by destroying habits, i.e., shutting off some action potentials and, at the same time, opening up new possibilities.

3 Revisiting the cases: the organizing trans-actional inquiry in operation

In the light of the cases, we can identify some characteristics of the organizing trans-actional inquiry: it is triggered by disruptive and uncertain situations; it is pluralist: new perspectives can emerge from the relationship between multiple views; it is mediated by sociocultural habits.

3.1 Facing disruption and uncertainty

The cases illustrate the permanent exposition of collective activity to de-stabilizing, threatening, or promising new situations, challenging social habits of thought and action: with pragmatism, "we are faced with the difficult challenge of pragmatically coordinating our activities in an often hostile environment", and we are "natural beings engaged in social and purposive activity" rather than "subjects striving to know (and handle) an object" (Bergman 2008: 138).

In the CLI case, the situation is first tacitly defined as an inquiry about an operational failure, the misuse of a bridge crane by operators, raising potential questions about operators' competence, task preparation, and maintenance and operation of a piece of equipment. But a long discussion leading to an apparent deadlock urged an ASN representative to bring clarification, transforming the definition of the situation. The inquiry no longer concerns an operational problem but organizational issues: defective process engineering and an infringement of safety regulations.

In the VESTRA case, the transformative processes are functional, compartmentalized, and target operational improvements. It is a situation of continuous improvement, evaluated through performance measurements such as productivity, production lead time, inventory turnover, and customer satisfaction. Now the interaction between the distinct performance projects makes a new strategic perspective emerge. The situation is redefined as an inquiry about the strategic identity and market position of the company.

3.2 Pluralism

In both cases, there is a collective process involving the communication and interaction between different perspectives. The dynamics of the situation and the emergence of new meanings result from the plurality of perspectives, what is not shared rather than what is shared.

In the CLI case, the ASN regulatory view differs from the technical view of some members of the Commission, and their collision calls for third organizational views that nobody seems to convey. The first explanations of the incident, technical (failure of the alarm system) or behavioral (operator's mistake), must make way for organizational questions. There are still multiple perspectives, but not the same as those prevailing at the start of the inquiry: some may view the problem as the result of engineers' lack of competence, others will suspect that, for the sake of profitability, logistics was reorganized in a hasty way, etc.

In the VESTRA case, each manager makes sense of the situation through distinct functional visions and professional habits. For the production manager, the situation means automation; automation means higher productivity and reduced production lead time. Reduced lead time means zero inventory for logistics. For the sales manager, it means sale on order and custom-made, made-to-measure clothes. The temporal relationship epitomized by the mathematical formulation: "production lead time < commercial delivery time" generates a qualitative transformation, with new and uncertain perspectives for the future. While actors' views may temporarily converge on the strategic interest of experimenting a new value chain, the managers still have different professional perspectives on the future.

3.3 Relational creativity

Both cases illustrate the creative power of dialogue between different perspectives. The actors' perspectives are challenged when they are exposed to other actors' perspectives. Each group is obliged to put words and figures to its beliefs and habits. The confrontation leads to the creation of new generally, temporally, and spatially more extensive perspectives, generating new definitions and reframing the situation. In the CLI discussion, the participants face two new questions: Why was the design of the new logistic organization faulty? Why was the obligation of risk assessment circumvented? In VESTRA, the logistics manager discovers that the new production lead time could allow the total elimination of the finished product inventory. The sales manager realizes that the potential elimination of store inventories could free commercial teams from the constraint of shelf availability and allow them to offer customers a huge range of options. Functional actions for performance improvement take on a different strategic meaning when addressing each other in a cross-functional arena.

3.4 Non-linguistic mediation through habits

A key question about the cases then is: why does the CLI inquiry come to a standstill and fail to explore organizational issues, while the VESTRA inquiry succeeds in defining and experimenting with new habits? To understand the course and the results of the trans-actional inquiry, beyond what is perceivable and verbally expressed, we must study the habits involved in the situation.

In the first case, there is a first set of habits, a culturally dominant way of thinking about incidents in nuclear plants: they are caused either by technical malfunctions, or by human (meaning: individual) mistakes. The first phase of the inquiry looks for such causes, but it turns out to be an impasse. Then the ASN delegate's statement, suggesting that the incident may have organizational causes, could trigger a new phase in the inquiry, focused on managerial and organizational causes. But then a second set of habits, strongly anchored in the minds of many members of the CLI, tends to inhibit this new orientation: there should be no external meddling in the internal management of nuclear operating firms, because it would compromise their accountability.

This belief is reinforced by the attitude of the nuclear company delegate, who has shown ostensible signs of irritation in answering insistent questions. However, a third set of habits might have convinced the members of the CLI to move their inquiry further into the managerial domain: the company had not complied with a regulation, which would politically justify some interference with the company management. A fourth set of habits may have neutralized this view: it is ASN's responsibility to look after regulatory compliance, and the CLI had better not interfere with ASN inspectors' controlling and regulatory missions. The ASN delegate's statement had not been made in an inviting tone. His firm tenor sounded like a way to close the discussion, conveying the tacit message: "we, ASN, are already investigating this breach of rules" and instantiated the habitual view of the ASN mission (monopoly of inspection and regulation). The 2006 "nuclear transparency and information" law promoted the new ASN mission to provide expertise to CLI inquiries, but this new mission proves to sometimes be difficult to translate into new habits of thinking and acting (Kerveillant 2017). Thus, the situation involves tacit boundaries between what is debatable and what is not in the CLI.

In the second case, explicit utterances – memos written by the managers, phone conversations, and verbal interventions in the monthly business review – per se do not make the strategic turn emerge. The whole process does not simply appear as a face-to-face discussion between actors, but rather as a remote, non-verbal interaction between separate functional improvement actions (robot development in Production, implementation of EDI in Information Systems, management of inventories in Logistics, etc.), whose practical impacts, once combined, open up a completely different perspective on organizational transformation. Behind discourses, professional habits converse with other professional habits. Thus far, VESTRA managers had followed their taken for-granted-habits: "new production technologies allow productivity increases"; "the range of options offered to the customer depends on inventories in retail shops"; "the value chain is a linear sequence design-production-transport-storage-sale". However, the managers had in mind potential new habits, fed by readings about Japanese industry, "mass customization", production-to-order, product customization, just-in-time. These were not actual practices, but virtual, imaginative resources that made new practices imaginable and debatable.

The inquiry could proceed to test radically different habits: production-to-order; selling a concept in a catalog; etc. Invisible elements participate in the trans-action: robot development project; anticipated behavior of future customers; old and new habits. Previous industrial habits remain in the background; it is their turn to become virtual resources. If the development of the robot runs into technological difficulties, or if the customers do not appear willing to forego physical contact with the product, the managers will reconsider the new practices and reintroduce their previous habits, not to reproduce them mechanically, but as resources to redesign another strategic framework.

4 The very definition of situation is at stake

The trans-actional perspective imposes a mobile and dynamic view of situations and problems and highlights the creative dimension of communication.

4.1 The definition of the situation

The situation plays a key role in trans-actional inquiries. Participants, in their "conversations-in-acts", do not only address each other, but also the overall situation. They understand their own and others' acts through the observed or anticipated changes in the situation. Therefore, they do not only make sense of the situation through dialogues, they hold dialogues through the situation. Now, the definition of the situation is not considered as given. It is contingent upon the "active adaptive response to make" (Dewey 1986: 73) and, consequently, on the definition of the problem to solve. If the inquiry leads to redefining the terms of the problem, the situation will be redefined, too.

In both cases, the definition of the situation is deeply modified. In the first case (Kerveillant 2017), the discussion reveals that the inquiry is not about the execution of a task but about its design and compliance with safety rules. The issue of task design involves different actors (those who designed the task) and different issues (non-technical but organizational). The situation now includes ASN inspection and an evaluation mission – should CLI members interfere with it? It also includes the logistic management of the company. Neither the logistic managers, nor the task designers are physically present in the room. To pursue their trans-actional inquiry, the members of the CLI should audition them.

In the VESTRA case, the very definition of the situation and its participants is at stake. The parallel development of projects to improve performances causes a strategic rupture to emerge. These moves involve a huge background of competing habits, beliefs, and values far beyond the verbal exchanges and the observable situation. For example, the perspective of moving to customization and production-to-order highlights the essential figure of the customer, physically absent from the situation: how will the customer react to the lack of physical contact with the purchased cloth? The situation, so far tacitly defined as a situation of performance improvement within the boundaries of the company, now extends to the potential transformation of cultural customs in buying clothes.

A golden rule then is revealed: to reach practical conclusions, a trans-actional inquiry must involve a community whose composition reflects the definition of the situation, i.e., the definition of the problem and its significant stakeholders. The CLI inquiry does not conform to this rule. The operators, the designers of the logistic process, the managers in charge of change management, are not invited to participate. In the second case, if the sales manager is considered as an acceptable spokesperson for future customers, all important stakeholders participate in the inquiry.

4.2 The creativity of communication

Concerned activities can occur over long time-spans and extend far beyond the perceivable space. Trans-action must often redefine its temporal, social, and spatial boundaries, the identification of its human and non-human constituents, and the relationships between them: "Transaction is inquiry which [...] proceeds with freedom toward the re-determination and renaming of the objects comprised in the system" (Dewey and Bentley 2008: 113) (in Dewey and Bentley's terminology, "objects" points to human, material, or symbolic constituents). The widening of situations to make them understandable and actionable is the basis of communication creativity. They include, not only habits that operate under normal circumstances, but also non-effected but imaginable habits (Bergman 2008), the main resource and the product of creative communication.

Communication within trans-actional inquiry does not only "coordinate" views and acts, in an inter-actional perspective, but it transforms perspectives through the dialogical construction of new "third" options: "On the basis of consequences of habitual and prospective actions, [trans-action] creates a standpoint of action that is neither ego's nor alter's but a third perspective" (Russill 2004: 105). Follett ([1933] 1995) develops the same view of *relational emergence* with her concept of *integration*: through the confrontation between A's and B's perspectives, a completely novel C perspective may emerge. The addressee/responder's unpredictable otherness provides an ongoing source of innovation through self-distance (Tsoukas 2009). New problems and new options emerge from the relationships between participants, be they human or non-human, and the habits they convey.

Creativity is not only reactive (creative responses to new problems), but it can also be proactive, through provoked de-stabilization, deliberately challenging habits through apparently insolvable problems (Lorino 2018), "[allowing] Deweyan social inquiry to perform as an active critique, *producing* problematic situations rather than merely responding to them" (Bergman 2008: 140). Arie de Geus (1988), former planning manager of Shell, used computer models of the oil market with extreme scenarios of plummeting or rocketing oil prices that should "have little relation to the real world" (de Geus 1988: 73), to oblige Shell managers to distance themselves from their own habits, imagine innovative responses, and reengineer their habits. In this abductive move, *imagination* plays a key role to grasp conceivable (and not only actual) effects (Bergman 2008).

Boundaries, then, have only an instrumental, not ontological status. In particular, the boundary between the social group and its environment is strictly instrumental and can be redefined at any moment. Humans are inseparably integrated into their environment: "[our] observation sees man-in-action, not as something radically set over against an environing world, nor yet as something merely acting 'in' a world, but as action of and in the world in which the man belongs as an integral constituent" (Dewey and Bentley 2008: 50); "we are willing to treat all of (man's) behavings as activities not of himself alone, but as processes of the full situation of organism-environment" (Dewey and Bentley 2008: 97). Thus, trans-action privileges an ecological view of agency (Woodward 2001), the agency of a milieu that includes inquirers themselves and is permanently evolving. This differs profoundly from the dualist view "in which the organism is taken as proceeding under its own powers in detachment from a comparably detachable environment" (Dewey and Bentley 2008: 81). Trans-actional inquiry teaches us a humble, non-controlling, radically immanent view of the ecological transition: there is no overlooking and omniscient inquirer or observer to sound the alarm. The communities of inquiry must therefore be highly vigilant to weak signals that can point to social and ecological turning points.

5 Conclusion: some methodological, theoretical, and managerial implications

The epistemology of trans-action leads to a methodological re-appraisal of the notion of observation (Lorino, Tricard, and Clot 2011). The observer participates in the trans-actional inquiry. Dewey and Bentley ([1949] 2008) agree with Follett's critique of the "onlooker fallacy": "We wish to do far more than *observe* our experience, we wish to make it yield up for us its riches [...] We want to find out what may be, the possibilities now open to us. This we can discover only by experiment" (Follett [1924] 1951: 2). This view of organization research rejects the dualist separation between actors or practitioners and researchers or experts. All the participants in a research field at the same time transform the situation, produce new knowledge, inquire, and are involved in inquirer-to-inquirer communication, though with different roles (Lorino, Tricard, and Clot 2011).

From a managerial and theoretical point-of-view, the concept of trans-actional inquiry can renew the stakeholder theory of governance (Freeman 1984), which sometimes tends to take for granted that stakeholders exist objectively, with clearly defined interests, and govern a given set of resources and options in an inter-actional perspective. Conversely, holding stakes in an organization is a complex and ongoing activity: "In a constantly evolving and complex world, stakeholders should be considered, not as a given, but as in an ongoing construction process" (Kerveillant 2017: 32), the process of "holding stakes", i.e., continually redefining and maintaining the proper interests and exploring and widening the space of possibilities through creative dialogues, including conflicts, in the trans-actional governance arena.

Last, "organizational governance may try to control action through algorithmic tools, but the situations are never completely controllable" (Lorino 2018: 325). As scholars and as citizens, we should be suspicious of self-complacent control discourses, rekindled by artificial intelligence and big data. We should rather be humble about our predictive competence and vigilant about novelty, often surprising, even if we use the most powerful algorithmic instruments: "More than ever, we need to consider situated action as a central object of study, taking seriously the disruptive power of situations" (Lorino 2018: 323–324).

Being careful, imaginative, and humble: the cardinal virtues of trans-actional inquiry!

6 References

Bakhtin, Mikhail M. 1981. *The dialogic imagination: Four essays*. Edited by M. Holquist. Austin, TX: University of Texas Press.

Bakhtin, Mikhail M. 1986. *Speech genres and other late essays*. Edited by Caryl Emerson & Michael Holquist. Translated by V. W. McGee. Austin, TX: University of Texas Press.

Barker, James R. 1993. Tightening the iron cage: Concertive control in self-managing teams. *Administrative Science Quarterly* 38(3). 408–437.

Barker, James R. 2005. Toward a philosophical orientation on control. *Organization* 12(5). 787–797.

Bergman, Mats. 2008. The new wave of pragmatism in communication studies. *Nordicom Review* 29(2). 135–153.

Delbridge, Rick & Mahmoud Ezzamel. 2005. The strength of difference: Contemporary conceptions of control. Introduction to the special issue. *Organization* 12. 603–618.

Descartes, René. 1996 [1641]. *Meditations on first philosophy with selections from the objections and replies*. Cambridge: Cambridge University Press.

Dewey, John. 1986 [1938]. *Logic: The theory of inquiry*. In Jo Ann Boydston (ed.), *John Dewey: The later works, 1925–1953, Volume 12: 1938*. Carbondale, IL: Southern Illinois University Press.

Dewey, John. 1988a [1927]. *The public and its problems*. In Jo Ann Boydston (ed.), *John Dewey: The later works, 1925–1953, Volume 2: 1925–1927*, 239–274. Carbondale, IL: Southern Illinois University Press.

Dewey, John. 1988b [1939]. *Theory of valuation*. In Jo Ann Boydston (ed.), *John Dewey: The later works, 1925–1953, Volume 13: 1938–1939*, 191–251. Carbondale, IL: Southern Illinois University Press.

Dewey, John. 2005 [1916]. *Democracy and education*. Stilwell, KS: Digireads.

Dewey, John & Alfred F. Bentley. 2008 [1949]. *Knowing and the known*. In Jo Ann Boydston (ed.), *Dewey: The later works, 1925–1953, Volume 16: 1949–1952*, 1–294. Carbondale, IL: Southern Illinois University Press.

Eisenhardt, Kathleen M. 1985. Control: Organizational and economic approaches. *Management Science* 31(2). 134–149.

Emirbayer, Mustafa & Douglas W. Maynard. 2011. Pragmatism and ethnomethodology. *Qualitative Sociology* 34(1). 221–261.

Emirbayer, Mustafa & Ann Mische. 1998. What is agency? *American Journal of Sociology* 103(4). 962–1023.

Follett, Mary Parker. 1951 [1924]. *Creative experience*. New York: Peter Smith.

Follett, Mary Parker. 1995 [1933]. Coordination. In P. Graham (ed.), *Mary Parker Follett: Prophet of Management*, 183–199. Washington, DC: Beard Books.

Freeman, R. Edward. 1984. *Strategic management: A stakeholder approach*. Cambridge: Cambridge University Press.

Geus, Arie P. de. 1988. Planning as learning. *Harvard Business Review* March–April. 70–74.

Joas, Hans. 1996. *The creativity of action*. Cambridge: Polity Press.

Kerveillant, Marie. 2017. *The role of the public in the French nuclear sector: The case of 'Local Information Commissions' (CLI) for nuclear activities in the west of France*. Paris: ESSEC Business School dissertation.

Lorino, Philippe. 2014. From speech acts to act speeches: Collective activity, a discursive process speaking the language of habits. In François Cooren, Eero Vaara, Ann Langley & Haridimos Tsoukas (eds.), Language and communication at work: Discourse, narrativity, and organizing, 95–124. Oxford: Oxford University Press.

Lorino, Philippe. 2018. *Pragmatism and organization studies*. Oxford: Oxford University Press.

Lorino, Philippe & Damien Mourey 2013. The experience of time in the inter-organizing inquiry: A present thickened by dialog and situations. *Scandinavian Journal of Management* 29(1). 48–62.

Lorino, Philippe, Benoît Tricard & Yves Clot. 2011. Research methods for non-representational approaches to organizational complexity: The dialogical mediated inquiry. *Organization Studies* 32(6). 769–801.

Maxwell, James C. 1991 [1876]. *Matter and motion*. Mineola, NY: Dover.

Ouchi, William G. 1977. The relationship between organizational structure and organizational control. *Administrative Science Quarterly* 22(1). 95–113.

Peirce, Charles S. 1958 [1931]. *The collected papers of Charles Sanders Peirce*. Cambridge, MA: Harvard University Press.

Peirce, Charles S. 1992. *The essential Peirce*, vol. 1. Bloomington, IN: Indiana University Press.

Peirce, Charles S. 1998. *The essential Peirce*, vol. 2. Bloomington, IN: Indiana University Press.

Russill, Chris. 2004. *Toward a pragmatist theory of communication*. University Park, PA: Pennsylvania State University dissertation.

Russill, Chris. 2008. Through a public darkly: Reconstructing pragmatist perspectives in communication theory. *Communication Theory* 18(4). 478–504.

Shields, Patricia M. 2003. The community of inquiry: Classical pragmatism and public administration. *Administration & Society* 35(5). 510–538.

Tsoukas, Haridimos. 2009. A dialogical approach to the creation of new knowledge in organizations. *Organization Science* 20(6). 941–957.

Verheggen, Theo & Cor Baerveldt. 2007. We don't share! The social representation approach, enactivism and the ground for an intrinsically social psychology. *Culture & Psychology* 13(1). 5–27.

Woodward, Wayne. 2001. Transactional philosophy and communication studies. In David K. Perry (ed.), *American pragmatism and communication research*, 65–86. Mahwah, NJ: Lawrence Erlbaum Associates.

Peter Winkler

5 Networking

Abstract: This chapter discusses the dual role of management communication in networking, understood as initiating and maintaining informal reciprocity relations in and around organizations. Drawing on cases from the literature, the chapter argues that in a stage of network initiation, managers facilitate informal network approximation by preserving uncertainty and indecision, while in a stage of network maintenance, they start to exploit emergent valuation orders in networks by making them explicit, scalable, and controllable. Previous management literature studied conditions, features, and functions of networking from an essentialist and structuralist perspective. This chapter points at promising paths for future research when studying networking from an explicitly communication-centered lens. The chapter starts with a critical overview of extant networking scholarship, it then introduces the sociology of Harrison White as key reference, and finally it elaborates on the role of management communication in the stages of network initiation and maintenance.

Keywords: informality; competition; management communication; networking; network sociology

Networking – in terms of initiating and maintaining informal reciprocity expectations and relations with internal and external stakeholders – represents a core skill in contemporary management practice. This insight finds reflection in empirical studies (Klerk 2010; Forret and Dougherty 2004), management consulting literature (Baker 2000; Baron and Markman 2000), as well as management education literature (Gibson, Hardy, and Buckley 2014; Janasz and Forret 2008). This scholarship argues that in increasingly flexible working environments, in which value creation and career responsibilities shift from the organization to the individual, employees' networking skills, and managerial networking skills in particular, are indispensable to enhance individual and organizational social capital, such as shared visions, knowledge, and support, which rest on cultivating reciprocity expectations and relations in informal networks.

Doing so, extant literature discusses the organizational *context*, *features* and *functions* of networking preliminarily from a structural and essentialist perspective (Lee 2009; Lin 1999). Regarding the *context* of networking, extant scholarship predominantly focuses on the analysis of *structural* qualities of organizational networks and their impact on individual and organization value (Rank, Robins, and Pattison 2010). Regarding the *features*, literature emphasizes an essentialist perspective, either on individual features, in terms of psychological attitudes and skills of organizational members and their impact on networking behavior and outcomes (Wolff and Kim

2012). Alternatively, this literature investigates how the organization in total benefits from aggregated networking effects (Birkinshaw and Hagström 2002).

In line with this essentialist focus on either the individual or the organization, the creation of social capital as a main *function* of networking is either reflected in a focus on how individual actors can benefit from bridging to other actors. Or social capital is analyzed from an analytic angle on the aggregated effects of network connectivity and cohesion on the organizational level. In both perspectives, the concept of social capital from networking and its relation to organizational value remain ambiguous, and scholars tend to define it *ex negativo*. Scholars distinguish social capital from established forms of market or hierarchical value, as expectations, resources, and temporality of exchange remain undecided in advance, but rest on implicit assumptions of reciprocal exchange and value creation in networks (Adler and Kwon 2002).

According to the agenda of this handbook, this chapter aims to inform and complement this essentialist and structural focus in extant management scholarship with an explicit perspective on communicative and linguistic practices. To do so, this chapter will draw on the late network sociology of Harrison C. White (2008), which itself has early roots in structural social network analysis, yet in late writings goes through an explicit communicative turn building on socio-linguistics. This approach allows for specifying the context, features, and functions of management communication and its contribution to organizational value creation from networking.

Regarding the *context*, this chapter explains in detail the distinct communicative conditions at play in different stages of network initiation and maintenance and therewith seeks to complement the current overemphasis on structural features of networks. Second, this chapter also points at the particular *features* of management communication, which holds a mediating rather than directly participating position in informal networking. Doing so, this chapter seeks to overcome the current essentialist emphasis on either the individual or the organization in total. Third, this chapter presents the *functions* of management communication, which rests in the capacity to facilitate, formalize, and exploit valuation orders emerging in informal networks on behalf of organization value creation. This explanation ultimately contributes to our better understanding of how social capital from informal networks and organizational value relate to each other. Therewith, this chapter aims to contribute to the overall agenda of this handbook to provide a more nuanced understanding of how management communication contributes to value creation in organizations.

The chapter is structured as follows: first, it lays out the conceptual foundations, introducing the network sociology of White and how to contextualize it in organizational communication and management communication in particular. Second, the chapter discusses two crucial stages of networking more in detail – network initiation and network maintenance – and how management communication facilitates and exploits them on behalf of organizational value creation. For both stages, network initiation and network maintenance, the chapter first clarifies the general communicative features and subsequently specifies concrete conditions, features, and functions of management communication drawing on examples from recent organization and management literature. The chapter ends with a brief summary of the main arguments and its overall contribution to this handbook.

1 Conceptual foundations

White's relational sociology as outlined in his late opus magnum, *Identity and Control* (White 1992, 2008) is today broadly acknowledged as a ground-breaking contribution to general sociological theory (Fuhse 2014). Different to social network analysis, in which it has its roots, this sociology seeks to overcome essentialist and structuralist explanations of social order and change from individual attributes and attitudes and their aggregated effects. Alternatively, it seeks to explain them as effects of relational communication.

1.1 Central concepts

White's relational sociology builds on the premise that communication emerges from uncertainty in meaning (White, Godart, and Thiemann 2013). White's concept of *control* is then understood as any communicative effort to come to terms with uncertainty irreducible to "domination or coercion" (White, Godart, and Thiemann 2013: 136). The concept of *identity*, in turn, is understood as "any entity to which observers can attribute meaning not explicable from biophysical regularities" (White 2008: 2). This broad understanding of identity is hence not restricted to individuals but applies to various networked social forms as long as they represent meaningful points of reference for communicative control efforts. The basic concepts of identity and control are inextricably interlinked. Identities emerge from relational control efforts, and control efforts emerge from given or assumed identity claims.

To get an analytical grip of the complex interplay of identity and control under conditions of *uncertainty*, White, Godart, and Thieman (2013) distinguish three forms of uncertainty: *ambiguity* stands for uncertainty of normative meaning; *ambage* stands for uncertainty regarding relational positioning; *contingency* stands for uncertainty on how to come to terms with particular contextual, especially material conditions at a given moment in time. Ambiguity, hence, relates to the normative question as to whether visions and values remain vague or find explicit articulation. Ambage relates to the structural question as to whether relational role expectations remain indirect and undefined or find expression. Contingency, ultimately, relates to the instrumental question as to whether given material conditions are considered incalculable or alterable and exploitable.

The emergence of identities from networking hence represents the result of relational communicative control efforts that either increase or decrease uncertainty on the above-mentioned analytic levels, which manifest in different stages of identity formation. For this chapter, the first two stages – called footing and face – are of particular interest, as they concern the conditions of initiation and maintenance of networked identity.

1.2 Application to management communication

Yet before we unfold these two stages, we first contextualize how White's (2008) approach is applicable to organizational communication and management communication in particular. To clarify the application to organizational communication, the concept of partial organization is helpful (Ahrne and Brunsson 2011). It starts from the observation that contemporary forms of organizing increasingly transcend a classic understanding of organization as formal organization. To get an analytic grip on these forms, the approach suggests a distinction between formal organizations and other forms of social organizing. This is considered a fruitful empirical starting point to reflect on hybrid organizational phenomena that borrow certain features from formal organization and other features from more general forms of social organizing, particularly institutions and networks.

Ahrne and Brunsson (2011: 89) define institutions as "stable, routine-reproduced pattern[s] of behaviour, combined with norms and conceptions that are taken for granted by larger or smaller groups of people". Networks, in turn, are defined as flexible "informal structures of relationships linking social actors [...] maintained through reciprocity, trust and social capital" (Ahrne and Brunsson 2011: 88). Organizations, ultimately, are conceptualized in terms of formal organization, and thus the ability to reproduce from decision communication (Luhmann 2018). Only by the means of decision communication, organizations, first, are able to create and maintain the idea of a joint purpose. Second, decision communication allows for explication and authorization of a chosen order, which typically finds expression in formal hierarchy and prioritization. Third, decision communication supports the organizational ability to not only create, but also control its chosen purpose and order, becoming obvious in formal forms of monitoring and sanctioning. In short, what makes an organization an organization is its ability to explicate, negotiate and formalize its purpose, ordering and controlling properties by the means of decision communication (Ahrne and Brunsson 2011). Everything that falls out of this scope, however, is then to be explained by other, more general forms of social organizing, namely institutions and networks.

While neo-institutional organizational scholarship, and its communication-centered line in particular (Cornelissen et al. 2015), reflects on the interdependencies between institutional and formal forms of organizing – that is, the interplay between unquestioned "rationalized myths" (Meyer and Rowan 1977) and organizational decisions – White's (2008) approach presents a useful explanatory basis to reflect on the interplay between informal networks and formal organization. Concretely, this concerns the question as to how informal networking relates to and can be translated into a source of organizational decision communication.

This is where management communication comes in. This chapter suggests one core function of management communication in its mediating function between informal networking attempts and formal decision communication for the sake of organizational value creation. Concretely, management communication does so by flexibly oscillating between a relational position and communicative style that preserves uncertainty and indecision and therewith facilitates network initiation, and a relational position and communicative style that exploits emergent valuation orders from networks by making them an object of formal decision communication on organizational purpose, order, and control. This oscillation plays out in two stages, to be discussed in the following based on White's first two stages of network identity – footing and face.

2 Network initiation

2.1 General features

According to White (2008), the initial stage of any identity formation from networking emerges from communicative efforts to find normative, relational, and instrumental orientation in yet unexplored or unexpected contexts. He labels this stage *footing*. Under these conditions, chances of normative misunderstanding, false relational expectations, and contextual misjudgment are high, and hence networking attempts are particularly precarious and easily decouple. This is why White (2008) argues that in a stage of footing, direct communicative control attempts are scarce, and communicative efforts rather aim to preserve uncertainty on all three analytic levels. Concretely, this is reflected in efforts to preserve high ambiguity regarding underlying normative beliefs and values, high ambage with regard to role expectations, and high contingency with regard to the overall instrumental purpose of communication. Consequently, communication remains cursory and non-binding, and information in terms of new insights rather emerge *en passant* and through indirect "social maneuvers" (Azarian 2005: 69) such as getting introduced by shared acquaintances or finding things out by hearsay. Small talk in the context of public and leisure encounters, or so-called "informal networking" in the professional context represent prime examples of communication in an early stage of footing.

Although networking attempts in a stage of footing are volatile, they present a crucial basis for social capital formation, i.e., informal value creation from reciprocity expectations and relations. Footing represents a non-binding social state, in which actors are able to communicatively detect *en passant*, tentatively approximate, and further explore if there are social compatibilities regarding normative views, relational expectations, or instrumental conduct. These perceived compatibilities, then, can turn into points of reference in future encounters and ultimately lead to social value creation from relational reciprocity, such as shared visions and beliefs, exchange of insider and background knowledge, or various forms of social support and nepotism.

2.2 Application to management communication

Obviously, the communicative features of this initial stage of footing are nothing specific or constitutive for organizations. Still, footing also emerges between organizational members all the time, particularly in case of informal talk in phases of organizational change – be it in terms of new organizational visions, new membership constellations, or new tasks and processes (Alvesson and Sveningsson 2008; Czarniawska and Sevón 1996). Further, footing does not simply emerge in organizations. Under particular conditions, management communication also systematically facilitates it. Such deliberate communicative attempts to foster a stage of footing is well known as the concept of "strategic ambiguity" in management literature (Eisenberg 1984). Yet, White's (2008) approach allows for a more systematic and explicitly network-oriented look at this concept with regard to the particular context, features, and functions of management communication.

2.2.1 Context

Extant literature proposes the following *context* as predicament for a managerial use of strategic ambiguity: "when goals are not clear, when stakeholders are not compliant, have power bases from which to resist the goal, or when achievement of the goal requires a creative engagement between the organization and its stakeholders" (Davenport and Leitch 2005: 1607). This quote directly corresponds with White's (2008) three forms of uncertainty and when management communication makes strategic use of them: under conditions of ambiguity – that is, high normative uncertainty on whether there is identification and commitment regarding an aspired goal; under conditions of ambage – that is, high relational uncertainty about who feels competent and responsible to attain this goal; and under conditions of contingency – that is, high instrumental uncertainty on the attainability and success of an envisioned goal. Under these conditions, it makes sense for managerial communication to select a language that preserves a state of formal indecision (Denis et al. 2011) and alternatively facilitates the emergence of compatible normative worldviews, relational expectations and instrumental solutions on the informal level and *en passant* instead. In the next section, we specify features of such language.

2.2.2 Features

Network scholarship describes the above discussed managerial position as an indirect observer and facilitator in terms of brokerage or "third actorhood" – because this position is not directly involved in network building, yet indirectly benefits from it, either through fostering reciprocity between compatible (*tertius ridens*) or segregating rivaling positions (*tertius gaudens*) (Burt 2007; Simmel 1964). White's (2008) distinction of three forms of uncertainty allows for concretizing the communicative features of how management communication achieves relational approximation from such a position as a third actor. His concept of ambiguity allows for closer examination of how managers preserve normative vagueness and indecision in order to avoid conflicts of interest and value.

This is typically reflected in a presentation of organizational goals in a "broad and abstract non-judgmental, non-specific way, which constructs a context in which all actions and interests are for the common good, whilst avoiding any specific points for common action" (Jarzabkowski, Sillince, and Shaw 2010: 238). Common good, best-of-all-worlds, or win-win rhetoric represent such forms of normatively ambiguous management language regarding organizational goals. White's (2008) concept of ambage, in turn, allows for further exploring how responsibility expectations remain undecided by management communication, for example by choosing a general invitational rhetoric, which addresses all members, yet leaves open who is concretely expected to do what (Sillince, Jarzabkowski, and Shaw 2012).

White's (2008) concept of contingency ultimately allows for analyzing how managerial talk remains undecided with regard to the concrete instrumental tasks and procedures in order to attain a certain goal. This is typically the case when management communication stresses lofty visions or abstract technical language. Such inaccessible language does not only create a preservative, elitist nimbus around the manager, it also leaves open to employees which concrete resources and operations they are expected to activate in order to achieve an aspired goal (Mantere and Vaara 2008).

2.2.3 Function

Besides context and features, White's (2008) approach ultimately allows for a more nuanced perspective on the particular function of strategic ambiguity with regard to organization value creation. Eisenberg (1984), the founder of the concept, considers a state of "unified diversity" as the main organizational value created by strategic ambiguity, as it allows for abstract relational co-orientation, yet remains open for multiple underlying interpretations and expectations. This affirmative focus on strategic ambiguity emphasizes how unified diversity provides a source of joint exploration and organizational learning, because visions, responsibilities, and procedures can emerge from exchange and mutually observed compatibilities in informal networks, and hence may generate more committed practices than would be the case for top-down instructions.

More critical literature (Denis et al. 2011; Paul and Strbiak 1997), however, challenges this overtly affirmative reading and rather stresses that under conditions of preserved strategic ambiguity, employee identification tends to remain weak, responsibilities remain non-binding, and action remains noncommittal. Again, White's (2008) three analytic levels of uncertainty allow for a more nuanced classification of these critical findings. On the level of ambiguity, this literature argues that in case of ongoing managerial preservation of normative vagueness, employee identification is unlikely and rather leads to the defense of vested interests (Sillince, Jarzabkowski, and Shaw 2012). Situated identification and commitment, in turn, depend on explication, concretization, and conflict of divergent interests and values at some point in time, in order to find a purpose, with which stakeholders at least temporarily can identify (Spee and Jarzabkowski 2017).

Equally, on the level of ambage, critical literature stresses the detrimental effects of management communication leaving responsibility expectations undecided. First, this literature challenges indecision on responsibilities as a source of managerial self-protection. This is particularly the case if aspired managerial goals appear to fail, in which case indecision helps to shield managers from scrutiny, for example, by denying initiative or claiming misinterpretation (Paul and Strbiak 1997). Yet, this protective function counts for employees as well, who may not only object to participation in order to avoid a managerial delegation of responsibility (Davenport and Leitch 2005). Scholars have also observed that employees, in a context of managerial indecision, start to flexibly "talk down" and "talk up" their own competencies and responsibilities, depending on whether they consider a goal to be achievable, or not (Sillince and Mueller 2007). In the long run, managerial communicative maintenance of ambiguity and ambage rather subverts than fosters aspired employee identification and responsibilization.

Ultimately, on the level of contingency, critical literature suggests that managerial insistence on abstract procedures runs the risk of provoking employees' critique of managerial aloofness and spurring situated informal practices, which only support local agendas, but decouple from overall organizational value creation (Denis et al. 2011). Achieving committed practices requires a shift in managerial language that reframes goal attainment as a collective endeavor and allows for joint evaluation of tasks and processes with regard to reaching a set goal (Mantere and Vaara 2008).

Based on these reflections, management communication fostering a stage of footing by intentionally preserving indecision on underlying interests and values, responsibility expectations, and instrumental conduct, presents itself as a fragile and temporary endeavor. Indeed, in an initial stage it can be productive, as it allows normative, relational, and instrumental compatibilities to emerge from informal experimentation and networking in a non-binding context of "unified diversity" (Eisenberg 1984). Yet, managerial communicative insistence on such context conditions has detrimental effects with regard to organizational value creation – as it not only endangers goal attainment, but it also risks erosion of employee identification and trust in managerial communication more generally.

3 Network maintenance

Given the considerations above, a closer reflection on the role of management communication in a subsequent stage of social networking is crucial. This subsequent stage focuses on the question as to how management communication can create organizational value that emerges in informal networks. The next section addresses this question, building on White's (2008) second stage of network identity, called *face*.

3.1 General features

The stage of face addresses a form of network identity in which joint control efforts decrease normative, relational, or instrumental uncertainty. In his early writings, White (2008) discusses this form of network identity in close resemblance to extant networking and social capital literature (Burt 2007; Adler and Kwon 2002). He understands network as a temporarily stable social form that is communicatively tied to and gains value from recurrent reciprocity-oriented utterances (White, Boorman, and Breiger 1976). Yet, in this early conception, White remains mostly vague regarding which concrete reciprocity expectations constitute which network value.

White (2008) becomes more specific with regard to this question in his late concept of network *disciplines*. He introduces disciplines as social "molecules" (White 1992: 22), which he defines as communicative building blocks of social order as they emerge in everyday practice. Disciplines follow very basic, often implicit communication logics, and emerge continually in virtually all areas of social life. He further proposes that we can distinguish different types of network disciplines depending on the form of uncertainty – ambiguity, ambage, or contingency – they preliminarily aim to control. These specific control efforts then lead to the emergence of binding *valuation orders* in disciplines. They provide networks with internal cohesion due to joint reciprocity expectations and assure external observability and addressability as a collective identity. Yet, these valuation orders also lead to relational asymmetries, which emerge from comparison and competition between actors, who try to adhere to a respective valuation order (White, Godart, and Thiemann 2013).

White's (2008) concept of network disciplines, hence, allows for a specification of the concept of social capital from networking in current organizational and management literature. It specifies the concrete *context* in which networks consolidate depending on the form of uncertainty they preliminarily aim to control, their constitutive communicative *features* regarding their distinct valuation orders and competitive relational asymmetries, and their specific *function* with regard to the concrete value they create. In the following, this section will first introduce the contexts, features, and functions of the three network disciplines on a general level, before it unfolds the role of management communication in formalizing their valuation orders on behalf of organizational value creation.

White (2008; White, Godart, and Thiemann 2013) distinguishes three types of disciplines: arenas, councils, and interfaces. An *arena* discipline emerges whenever relational control efforts seek to come to terms with and control ambiguity, and hence the question as to which interests, ideas, and values shall drive communication in a network and constitute network identity. Arena disciplines typically develop a valuation order of *purity*, which stands for adherence to particular affiliation criteria. These affiliation criteria often emerge randomly, remain implicit, and may even vary over time. Yet, communicative adherence to and representation of these criteria lead to relational competition and asymmetry in arena disciplines, which consolidate in internal self-affirmation and radicalization on the one hand and the seclusion and devaluation of non-conforming external values on the other. General empirical manifestations of arenas can be found, for example, in communities of faith and fandom, or resistance and protest groups.

A *council* discipline, in turn, emerges from joint efforts to reduce social uncertainty in terms of ambage, hence the question as to who is authorized to define a situation in case of competitive claims. Under these conditions, *prestige* turns into the joint valuation order. Prestige means that particular constituents achieve the status to articulate and represent valid interpretations and directives on behalf of others in a network. This valuation order, again, leads to competitive processes, the asymmetry of which results from communicative capabilities to mediate between different positions, build alliances, and mobilize support for a specific claim. All processes of authorization adhere to the logic of a council discipline. Further, council disciplines represent the basis of more institutionalized political identities, such as federations or parliaments.

An *interface*, ultimately, emerges from joint efforts to cope with social uncertainty in terms of contingency, hence the question as to how to come to terms and make instrumental use of shared material context conditions. An interface discipline typically results in a shared valuation order of *quality* and shared commitment in a network to contribute to this quality. Competitive asymmetries emerge from instrumental evaluation and up- and downgrading of individual input in accordance with what is considered useful. According to White (2002), this valuation order is empirically observable in various social settings of joint production and exchange and also presents the basis of larger institutionalized network identities such as production markets.

3.2 Application to management communication

As mentioned above, network disciplines represent very basic and emergent social phenomena, which can be empirically observed in all areas of social life. Yet, among others, network disciplines also emerge from informal networking attempts between stakeholders. Arena disciplines, for example, provide a useful approach to explain how identification with, but also rivalry in and between stakeholder groups, organizational cliques, teams, or divisions emerge from adherence to or deviance from a self-selected valuation order of affiliation purity, which often has little to do with formal stakeholder or membership status (Tichy 1973). Council disciplines, in turn, provide a useful approach to study the emergence of valuation orders of prestige regarding informal expertise and authority, which again often deviate from formal competencies and responsibilities (Baker, Gibbons, and Murphy 1999). Lastly, an interface discipline helps to better understand how instrumental valuation orders of quality emerge in informal contexts, such as in the case of informal information exchange and cooperation, which often transgress and circumvent formal tasks and procedures (Li 2007).

Research on organizational micro-politics has a long tradition in studying the emergence of such informal valuation orders in organizations, and their unintended and uncontrollable impact on culture, power, and performance in formal organizations (Crozier and Friedberg 1993; Burns 1961). Surprisingly however, it is only very recently that organizational and management scholarship began to reflect on how management, and management communication in particular, *deliberately* fosters and exploits emergent valuation orders. Concretely, this literature explores the communicative origins of value creation and competition in organizational contexts (Arora-Jonsson, Brunsson, and Hasse 2020; Kornberger 2017).

Arora-Jonsson, Brunsson, and Hasse (2020), for example, argue that managerial initiation of organizational competition depends on the communicative construction of a setting, which directs attention to a particular desire, fosters the perception of others to share this desire, and ultimately suggests that what is desired represents a scarce good. In a related vein, Kornberger (2017) points out how communicative practices of commensuration, categorization, and visualization of valuation orders are crucial to establish organizational competition. Both approaches, thereby, emphasize the crucial role of management, which in the communicative construction of organizational competition no longer represents the position of a mediating and indirectly benefiting "third actor". Rather, management switches to the position of a "fourth actor" that takes an active role in framing and formalizing competition for the sake of organizational value creation.

Yet, while this literature preliminarily focuses on the institutional context, features, and functions of inter-organizational competition, what follows is a complementary view on how management communication also serves as a "fourth actor" in the formalization of competitive valuation orders that emerge from informal networks in and around single organizations.

3.2.1 Context

While an initial stage of network footing is determined by high normative, relational, and instrumental uncertainty, a second stage of face is determined by the consolidation of particular valuation orders in emergent network disciplines. Accordingly, the relational positioning and communicative style of management changes. While in a stage of footing, managerial preservation of indecision and strategic ambiguity is key to foster open relational approximation, under conditions of emerging, more concrete, and binding valuation orders in networks, managers have to become more intervening and specific too. In order to prevent these emergent informal valuation orders to detach from or even run contrary to formal organizational purpose, order, and control, managers have to come up with new communication formats that translate and realign informal, that is, network-specific, and formal, that is, decision-based, value. Typically, this happens in the context of participatory formats, which are particularly frequent in times of organizational change and reform (Brunsson 2009). Yet, even if participatory formats share the managerial aim to translate informal into formal value, they largely differ regarding the question as to which value they aim to translate and align.

Again, the distinction between three analytic forms of uncertainty – ambiguity, ambage, and uncertainty (White, Godart, and Thieman 2013) – and arenas, councils, and interfaces as network disciplines that preliminarily engage with one of these three forms, support a systematic distinction between different participatory formats according to the value they focus on. Participatory formats focused on organizational culture, for example, preliminarily engage with the question how to align informal valuation orders of purity in emergent arena disciplines to the overall formal purpose of an organization, in terms of explicating and defining shared visions and values (Alvesson and Sveningsson 2008). Participatory formats engaging with questions of collaborative innovation and knowledge, in turn, preliminarily aim at alignment of informal prestige orders of emergent council disciplines with formal competencies and responsibilities in the organization (Heckscher and Adler 2006). Ultimately, participatory formats focused on open exchange and evaluation try to align informal quality orders of emergent interface disciplines with formal modes of organizational control (Yang and Maxwell 2011).

The communicative implementation of such participatory formats comes with a significant shift regarding relational positioning and communicative style of management. Regarding relational position, management shifts from the position of an observing and indirectly benefiting "third actor" to a more intervening position of a "fourth actor" that frames and formalizes informal valuation orders in networks in accordance with organizational value, that is formal goals, orders, and control. This shift in position goes along with a new communication style, which no longer focuses on preserving ambiguity, ambage, and contingency in terms of a vague state of "unified diversity". Quite the contrary, the communicative emphasis is now on making emergent valuation orders explicit, scalable, and controllable, and therewith transforming them into an object of formal decision communication. The subsequent section discusses core features of this shift in relational position and communicative style of management in more detail.

3.2.2 Features

Based on recent competition literature (Arora-Jonsson, Brunsson, and Hasse 2020), the genuine role of a "fourth actor" is to present particular values as commonly desirable and scarce. In the context of informal network disciplines, competition still emerges as an unintended, yet inevitable side effect of relational, often tacit expectations. Arena disciplines striving for normative coherence inevitably develop competitive valuation orders of purity, which depends on the individual adherence to or deviation from network affiliation criteria. Council disciplines striving for role clarity inevitably develop a competitive valuation order of hierarchized prestige. Interface disciplines, ultimately, striving for instrumental reliability inevitably develop a competitive valuation order of quality based on mutual grading.

Managers as a "fourth actor" communicatively seek to formalize these informal valuation orders. In a first step, they do so by communicatively directing informal valuation orders towards an overarching organizational agenda. Stressing euphemistic labels such as open culture, open collaboration, or open sharing, respectively, participatory formats orient diverse, partly conflicting informal affiliation, prestige, and quality orders that exist in and around an organization towards one shared organizational understanding of purpose, authority, and usefulness (Alvesson and Sveningson 2008; Tsoukas 2009; Stark 2009). Doing so, management communication does not only assure an explication of values that previously remained tacit. It also creates scarcity, as multiple situated and informal understandings of affiliation, prestige, and quality are now oriented towards one overarching organizational agenda.

Although these managerial efforts in creating joint orientation are conditional, they are not sufficient to assure stakeholder engagement in competition. Hence, management has to make engagement collectively desirable. Following Kornberger (2017), this is achieved by three interrelated communicative practices: commensuration, categorization, and visualization. Commensuration represents forms of communication that make hitherto incomparable contributions comparable and measurable.

Categorization represents communicative efforts to sort and re-organize commensurate contributions in accordance with evaluative schemata. Visualization ultimately represents communicative attempts to make commensuration and categorization observable to all actors involved by symbolic representation such as awards, lists, ratings, or rankings.

Again, White's (2008) three forms of uncertainty and related network disciplines help to concretize these efforts of commensuration, categorization, and visualization for different participatory formats. In the context of culture-oriented participatory settings, which are based on an arena logic where normative affiliation is central, commensuration is typically reached by facilitating the formation of so-called "joint accounts" (Spee and Jarzabkowski 2017) by means of communicative expansion, re-combination and reframing (Tsoukas 2009) of situated normative interests towards a shared vision, which most constituents can temporarily identify with. Categorization of affiliation to these joint accounts, then, typically finds expression in typologies grading stakeholder identification, ranging from labels such as ambassadors, over influencers, to advocates, and followers. These categorizations, ultimately, also find visualization in terms of guaranteeing attention to those at the top of the list by media coverage or by rewarding them (Edlund, Pallas, and Wedlin 2019).

In the context of innovation-oriented participatory settings, which are based on a council logic oriented towards prestige, commensuration is reached by the managerial implementation of various forms of expert or peer review. Such reviews do not only allow for coherent evaluation of contributions to a common project. They also contribute to a subsequent categorization and graduation of contributor rights, responsibilities, and restrictions, and hence the hierarchization of authority guaranteed to particular roles (Du Chatenier et al. 2009). Again, this categorization finds visualization, such as in the case of labels and badges indicating the prestige of particular roles, which, ironically, are particularly frequent in self-labeled "hierarchy-free" agile and holacratic collaborative participation formats (Bernstein et al. 2016).

Lastly, in the context of sharing- and evaluation-focused participatory settings, which are rooted in an interface logic, commensuration is reached most straightforwardly by implementing solution-oriented voting and polling opportunities for stakeholders involved. Categories, here, are assigned to specific contributions and their aggregated outcome. They typically find visualization in symbolic classification systems and rankings (Shore and Wright 2015; Espeland and Sauder 2007).

In sum, by means of communicative commensuration, categorization, and visualization, managerial communication formalizes emergent valuation orders in informal network disciplines, which allows exploiting, ordering, and monitoring their competitive dynamics in accordance with an overarching organizational agenda. This ultimately represents the basis for organizational value creation, as discussed in the next section.

3.2.3 Function

While in a stage of footing, the function of management communication is to foster "unified diversity" to allow for exploration and approximation of informal networking attempts, in a stage of face, the exploitation of value emerging in informal networks represents the central function of management communication. As argued above, participatory formats present the preferred context for this exploitative endeavor, and communicative commensuration, categorization, and visualization represent the particular managerial style at play. Formal organizational value ultimately stems from the systematic translation of competitive informal valuation orders into an object of formal decision communication.

Concretely, managerial attempts of commensuration facilitate decisions on purpose, because they allow for the identification of the most accepted normative "joint accounts" (Spee and Jarzabkowski 2017), the most prestigious sources of informal authority, and the most popular solutions. Categorization, in turn, facilitates decisions on formal order in terms of the prioritization of goals, the hierarchization of responsibilities, and the consideration of means, respectively. Visualization ultimately facilitates formal control, as it makes valuation orders and their competitive dynamics not only observable, but also manageable by means of positive incentives for those who adhere to the order and negative sanctions for those who underperform or ignore them.

Hence, it can be argued that management communication has a crucial role in creating organizational value from informal networks by flexibly oscillating between a facilitating position in a stage of network initiation and an exploitative position when it comes to the translation of informal network value into an object of formal decision communication on purpose, order, and control. Table 1 summarizes the main propositions on context, features, and functions of management communication in this process.

Table 1: Context, features, and functions of management communication in networking

Stage	Context	Features	Function
Network initiation	High normative, relational, and instrumental uncertainty	Maintaining indecision by strategic ambiguity, ambage, and contingency	Providing "unified diversity" as explorative context for network approximation
Network maintenance	Emergence of distinct valuation orders in informal networks	Formalizing valuation orders by means of commensuration, categorization, and visualization in participatory formats	Exploiting valuation orders for decision communication on organizational purpose, order, and control

4 Conclusion

This chapter contributes to the extant literature on networking and social capital creation in organizations by applying an explicitly communication-centered lens on the role of management practices in this process and their contribution to organizational value creation. The chapter distinguishes between two distinct relational positions and communication styles of management in different stages of informal network formation in organizations. In a stage of network initiation, management, in the position of an observing and indirectly benefiting "third actor" facilitates informal network approximation by maintaining a communicative style of indecision and high normative, relational, and instrumental uncertainty.

As soon as distinct valuation orders emerge in informal networks, however, management shifts into a more intervening position of a "fourth actor". Using participatory formats, management in this position translates informal valuations orders into organizational value by making them an object of formal decisions on purpose, order, and control. Having said that, this chapter does not only complement a predominant structural and essentialist perspective on networking in the extant management literature with an explicitly communication-centered perspective. It also clarifies the role of management communication, which goes beyond participation in informal networking in organizations but its facilitation and exploitation on behalf of overall organizational value creation.

5 References

Adler, Paul S. & Seok-Woo Kwon. 2002. Social capital: Prospects for a new concept. *Academy of Management Review* 27(1). 17–40.

Ahrne, Göran & Nils Brunsson. 2011. Organization outside organizations: The significance of partial organization. *Organization* 18(1). 83–104.

Alvesson, Mats & Stefan Sveningsson. 2008. *Changing organizational culture: Cultural change work in progress*. London: Routledge.

Arora-Jonsson, Stefan, Nils Brunsson & Raimund Hasse. 2020. Where does competition come from? The role of organization. *Organization Theory* 1. 1–24.

Azarian, Reza. 2005. *The general sociology of Harrison C. White: Chaos and order in networks*. New York: Palgrave Macmillan.

Baker, George, Robert Gibbons & Kevin J. Murphy. 1999. Informal authority in organizations. *Journal of Law, Economics, and Organization* 15(1). 56–73.

Baker, Wayne E. 2000. *Achieving success through social capital: Tapping the hidden resources in your personal and business networks*. San Francisco, CA: Jossey-Bass.

Baron, Robert A. & Gideon D. Markman. 2000. Beyond social capital: How social skills can enhance entrepreneurs' success. *Academy of Management Executive* 14(1). 106–116.

Bernstein, Ethan, John Buch, Niko Canner & Michael Lee. 2016. Beyond the holocracy hype. *Harvard Business Review* (July–August). 1–13. https://hbr.org/2016/07/beyond-the-holacracy-hype (accessed 13 November 2020).

Birkinshaw, Julian & Peter Hagström (eds.). 2002. *The flexible firm: Capability management in network organizations*. Oxford: Oxford University Press.

Brunsson, Nils. 2009. *Reform as routine: Organizational change and stability in the modern world*. Oxford: Oxford University Press.

Burns, Tom. 1961. Micropolitics: Mechanisms of institutional change. *Administrative Science Quarterly* 6(3). 257.

Burt, Ronald S. 2007. *Brokerage and closure: An introduction to social capital*. Oxford: Oxford University Press.

Cornelissen, Joep, Rodolphe Durand, Peer C. Fiss, John C. Lammers & Eero Vaara. 2015. Putting communication front and center in institutional theory and analysis. *Academy of Management Review* 40(1). 10–27.

Crozier, Michel & Erhard Friedberg. 1993. *Die Zwänge kollektiven Handelns: Über Macht und Organisation*. Frankfurt am Main: Hain.

Czarniawska, Barbara & Guje Sevón. 1996. *Translating organizational change*. Berlin: De Gruyter.

Davenport, Sally & Shirley Leitch. 2005. Circuits of power in practice: Strategic ambiguity as delegation of authority. *Organization Studies* 26(11). 1603–1623.

Denis, Jean-Louis, Geneviève Dompierre, Ann Langley & Linda Rouleau. 2011. Escalating indecision: Between reification and strategic ambiguity. *Organization Science* 22(1). 225–244.

Du Chatenier, Elise, Jos A. A. M. Verstegen, Harm J. A. Biemans, Martin Mulder & Onno Omta. 2009. The challenges of collaborative knowledge creation in open innovation teams. *Human Resource Development Review* 8(3). 350–381.

Edlund, Peter, Josef Pallas & Linda Wedlin. 2019. Prizes and the organization of status. In Göran Ahrne & Nils Brunsson (eds.), *Organization outside organizations: The abundance of partial organization in social life*, 62–83. Cambridge: Cambridge University Press.

Eisenberg, Eric M. 1984. Ambiguity as strategy in organizational communication. *Communication Monographs* 51(3). 227–242.

Espeland, Wendy N. & Michael Sauder. 2007. Rankings and reactivity: How public measures recreate social worlds. *American Journal of Sociology* 113(1). 1–40.

Forret, Monica L. & Thomas W. Dougherty. 2004. Networking behaviors and career outcomes: differences for men and women? *Journal of Organizational Behavior* 25(3). 419–437.

Fuhse, Jan A. 2014. Theorizing social networks: The relational sociology of and around Harrison White. *International Review of Sociology* 25(1). 15–44.

Gibson, Carter, Jay H. Hardy III & Ronald Buckley. 2014. Understanding the role of networking in organizations. *Career Development International* 19(2). 146–161.

Heckscher, Charles & Paul Adler (eds.). 2006. *The firm as a collaborative community: Reconstructing trust in the knowledge economy*. Oxford: Oxford University Press.

Janasz, Suzanne C. de & Monica L. Forret. 2008. Learning the art of networking: A critical skill for enhancing social capital and career success. *Journal of Management Education* 32(5). 629–650.

Jarzabkowski, Paula, John A. A. Sillince & Duncan Shaw. 2010. Strategic ambiguity as a rhetorical resource for enabling multiple interests. *Human Relations* 63(2). 219–248.

Klerk, Saskia de. 2010. The importance of networking as a management skill. *South African Journal of Business Management* 41(1). 37–49.

Kornberger, Martin. 2017. The values of strategy: Valuation practices, rivalry and strategic agency. *Organization Studies* 38(12). 1753–1773.

Lee, Robert. 2009. Social capital and business and management: Setting a research agenda. *International Journal of Management Reviews* 11(3). 247–273.

Li, Peter P. 2007. Social tie, social capital, and social behavior: Toward an integrative model of informal exchange. *Asia Pacific Journal of Management* 24(2). 227–246.

Lin, Nan. 1999. Building a social network theory of social capital. *Connections* 22(1). 28–51.

Luhmann, Niklas. 2018. *Organization and decision*. Cambridge: Cambridge University Press.

Mantere, Saku & Eero Vaara. 2008. On the problem of participation in strategy: A critical discursive perspective. *Organization Science* 19(2). 341–358.

Meyer, John W. & Brian Rowan. 1977. Institutionalized organizations: Formal structure as myth and ceremony. *American Journal of Sociology* 83(2). 340–363.

Paul, Jim & Christy A. Strbiak. 1997. The ethics of strategic ambiguity. *Journal of Business Communication* 34(2). 149–159.

Rank, Olaf N., Garry L. Robins & Philippa E. Pattison. 2010. Structural logic of intraorganizational networks. *Organization Science* 21(3). 745–764.

Shore, Cris & Susan Wright. 2015. Audit culture revisited: Rankings, ratings, and the reassembling of society. *Current Anthropology* 56(3). 421–444.

Sillince, John, Paula Jarzabkowski & Duncan Shaw. 2012. Shaping strategic action through the rhetorical construction and exploitation of ambiguity. *Organization Science* 23(3). 630–650.

Sillince, John & Frank Mueller. 2007. Switching strategic perspective: The reframing of accounts of responsibility. *Organization Studies* 28(2). 155–176.

Simmel, Georg. 1964. *The sociology of Georg Simmel*. New York: Free Press.

Spee, Paul & Paula Jarzabkowski. 2017. Agreeing on what? Creating joint accounts of strategic change. *Organization Science* 28(1). 152–176.

Stark, David. 2009. *The sense of dissonance: Accounts of worth in economic life*. Princeton, NJ: Princeton University Press.

Tichy, Noel. 1973. An analysis of clique formation and structure in organizations. *Administrative Science Quarterly* 18(2). 194–208.

Tsoukas, Haridimos. 2009. A dialogical approach to the creation of new knowledge in organizations. *Organization Science* 20(6). 941–957.

White, Harrison C. 1992. *Identity and control: A structural theory of social action*. Princeton, NJ: Princeton University Press.

White, Harrison C. 2002. *Markets from networks: Socioeconomic models of production*. Princeton, NJ: Princeton University Press.

White, Harrison C. 2008. *Identity and control: How social formations emerge*, 2nd edn. Princeton, NJ: Princeton University Press.

White, Harrison C., Scott A. Boorman & Ronald L. Breiger. 1976. Social structure from multiple networks: I. Blockmodels of roles and positions. *American Journal of Sociology* 81(4). 730–780.

White, Harrison C., Frédéric C. Godart & Matthias Thiemann. 2013. Turning points and the space of possibles: A relational perspective on the different forms of uncertainty. In Francois Dépelteau & Christopher Powell (eds.), *Applying relational sociology*, 137–154. New York: Palgrave Macmillan.

Wolff, Hans-Georg & Sowon Kim. 2012. The relationship between networking behaviors and the Big Five personality dimensions. *Career Development International* 17(1). 43–66.

Yang, Tung-Mou & Terrence A. Maxwell. 2011. Information-sharing in public organizations: A literature review of interpersonal, intra-organizational and inter-organizational success factors. *Government Information Quarterly* 28(2). 164–175.

Zhuo Ban and Heather M. Zoller

6 Controlling and resisting

Abstract: In this chapter, we discuss how power manifests in the context of management communication through the dynamic of control and resistance. The chapter covers research developments related to ideological control, disciplinary power, standpoint theory, precarity, and social change. We describe additional areas of needed development including de-centering western viewpoints and addressing macro-level social change. The chapter begins by describing different meta-theoretical influences on the study of power, followed by a discussion of major concepts related to a communicative understanding of power and resistance.

Keywords: ideological control; disciplinary power; standpoint; precarity; social change

In this chapter, we discuss power and resistance in the context of management communication. Readers will be introduced to a number of approaches to power. These approaches have emerged from distinct intellectual traditions and offer different ways to understand and address power in organizations. At the end of the chapter, readers should be able to: (1) identify and differentiate the various approaches to understanding power; (2) interpret management communication in the context of power, control, and resistance; and (3) understand how a communication perspective sheds light on the political process of management.

1 Conceptualizing power in management contexts

Researchers and practitioners alike have long observed the prevalence of power and power-related issues in organizations and management processes. Power is central to the analysis of management communication from a variety of fields, including management studies, organizational communication, psychology, sociology, and others. From the authority of the official hierarchy to the discipline of the punch card, from the silent CCTV camera to the whispers in the meeting room, from practices of employee self-management to acts of whistleblowing, power manifests as distinct patterns of control and resistance, dominance and subversion, shaping the experience of organizational members. The pervasive and promiscuous presence of power in management contexts is theorized from multiple perspectives.

1.1 Theoretical perspectives

In this section, we describe differences between scientific approaches and critical interpretive perspectives. We also elucidate two strands within the latter perspective, including structural and poststructural theorizing. These approaches, rooted in broader theoretical movements, explain communication processes from different vantage points.

The *scientific approach*, rooted in a modernist, rationalist tradition, historically offered a strategic managerial understanding of power nestled in the meta-narrative of organizational efficiency and progress. Researchers traditionally focused on the role of communication in promoting the modernist ideals of rationality, creating "purposeful, rational, and autonomous" modern subjects (Jervis 2018) within equally purposeful, rational, and autonomous organizations. Communication was largely theorized as a mechanism for managerial control, promoting the ability to "harness the forces of nature to human purposes" (Jervis 2018: 2).

The modernist epistemology seeks to establish enduring relationships between actions and outcomes across organizational situations, with a primary focus on what can be measured, tested, falsified, replicated, and generalized (Parker 1992). These methods have been employed to aid in managerial control. For example, Taylor's (1911) Scientific Management promoted ways for management to prevent systematic soldiering (workers establishing lower rates of production than their maximum potential) by using a piece-rate system incentivizing higher performance and technical control over the work process.

Scientific Management continues to influence modern organizations, most evidently in factories and fast-food restaurants, but also increasingly in places like higher education (Ritzer 2000). Social scientific approaches developed more persuasive methods to achieve managerial control. For example, Mayo's (2004) Human Relations School of management, based on his interpretations of the Hawthorne Studies, focused on manager and worker camaraderie as a route to promote productivity. Human Resource theorists such as McGregor (1960) suggested that managers promote top performance by encouraging workers to view work as a source of self-actualization. Researchers document how these relational practices have evolved over time (Carlone and Larson 2006; Johansson, Tienari, and Valtonen 2017; Kirby 2006).

Although scientific researchers traditionally viewed resistance as an irrational element to be controlled, scholars may use quantitative scholarship to address organizational power from a more employee-centered perspective. For example, Kassing, Fanelli, and Chakravarthy (2018) summarized three factors that influence employee willingness to engage in dissent, including the degree of risk, decision-making engagement, and organizational assimilation. Their research found that part-time and full-time workers differ in their dissent strategies (see also Thompson, McDonald, and O'Connor 2020).

The *critical/interpretive approach* emerged largely as a reflection on and critique of the scientific approach. Researchers questioned the idea of objectivity, given the value-laden nature of language and interpretation (Putnam and Pacanowsky 1983). Emphasizing the role of communication in constructing social reality, interpretive perspectives advocated for treating organizations as fundamentally communicative (Putnam and Pacanowsky 1983). Critical scholars expanded on this insight by situating meaning-making as a political act that favors some groups over others (Clair 1993; Conrad and Abbott 2007; Grant, Iedema, and Oswick 2009; Mumby and Clair 1997). We describe two branches of critical/interpretive research.

Structuralist scholars explore the irrational, hegemonic, and alienating aspects of power in situations of (sometimes totalizing) control and subjugation. Critical scholars who are more structuralist investigate the ways that organizations and their communicative practices are fundamentally shaped by broader social and cultural processes (Lounsbury and Ventresca 2003). Structuralist management communication theorists are interested in how domination is maintained and reproduced through communicative practices. Many of them trace their roots to Max Weber or Karl Marx (Burawoy 1982, 2012; Cloud 2005).

The foundational work of Max Weber on structuralism in the early part of the twentieth century used the concept of bureaucracy to capture the rationalized form of power and dominance in institutional settings. Weber (1964) situated organizational processes within broader social structural frameworks of political economy, power, authority, and legitimacy.

German theorist Karl Marx (1972) developed the theory of historical materialism as a framework to examine the relationship between the economic conditions and ideology in social processes. In comparison to other critical theorists like Antonio Gramsci (2000), as well as Horkheimer and Adorno (2006), and Habermas (1975) from the Frankfurt School, Marx's approach is materially deterministic, viewing ideology and consciousness as largely predetermined by class relationships.

Influenced by these scholars, structuralist studies are sensitive to how broader social structures shape communicative organizational processes. Management scholars investigate the degree to which communication works to hide or render invisible structural contradictions (McCarthy, Touboulic, and Matthews 2018; Quinlan et al. 2019; Varman and Al-Amoudi 2016; Veen, Barratt, and Goods 2020). For example, early research by Burawoy (1982) examined how management achieves worker consent through the labor process itself. More recently, Rodino-Colocino (2012) investigated how narratives of job loss by white male IT workers shift blame for precarity to offshored and H-1B workers rather than structural economic policies, highlighting the need for more inclusive forms of class consciousness.

Another branch of critical-interpretive research is the *poststructuralist* view that treats organizational power as more fragmented and contested. Heavily influenced by the linguistic turn in the Western philosophical tradition, as well as by post-Marxist critical scholars such as Gramsci (1971, 2000), Foucault (1978, 2012), and Frankfurt School scholars, including Adorno, Horkheimer (Horkheimer and Adorno 2006), and Habermas (1975, 1984), post-structuralists emphasize the role of communication in forming and negotiating relations of power, authority, and legitimacy that constitute organizations (Alvesson and Kärreman 2000).

The linguistic turn (Wittgenstein 2009, 2013) captures a philosophical movement that views language as central to understanding social phenomena. A major stream of organizational research conceptualizes organizations as discursive constructions (Fairhurst and Putnam 2004), and emphasizes how the communicative enactment of power constitutes the organizing process (Mumby 2005). Seemingly mundane interactions are sites where power structures are not merely reflected, but actually come into being. For example, Buzzanell and Liu (1994) investigated how everyday organizing processes constitute and are constituted by gender relations, contrasting the taken-for-granted dominance of values including competition, linearity, and autonomy over themes of community and connectedness.

The deconstructive tendencies and skepticism of metanarratives in poststructural research can also be traced back to influence from postcolonial research. Postcolonial research decenters Western theories and assumptions in order to theorize domination and social change from the perspective of colonized people (Broadfoot and Munshi 2007; Cruz and Sodeke 2020; Jack et al. 2011; Nkomo 2011).

1.2 Communication, power, and organizational culture

Before turning to major concepts related to communication and power, we offer an extended example describing how these theoretical perspectives influence the study of organizational culture. Functionalist, modernist researchers view normative and cultural control as tools for achieving management goals of productivity and employee commitment (Alvesson and Willmott 2012; Deetz 1996; Hodgson 2002). The interest in shared values and beliefs as a source of management control can be found in the "scientific rationalist" (Bate 1994) approach to organizational culture. Popular management authors like Peters and Waterman (1982) and White (1984) argued that organizational culture is a measurable organizational feature that can be manipulated to achieve managerial objectives.

Critical interpretive scholars challenge this view of culture as "devised by management and transmitted, marketed, sold or imposed on the rest of the organization" (Willcoxson and Millett 2000: 94). More structural scholars such as Arlie Hochschild (2005) emphasized how organizational norms about emotion management can lead to the performance of a "fake self" and estrangement from workers' "real" emotions.

Poststructural scholars, on the other hand, view these normative discourses as a constitutive element of workers' emotions, rejecting the real-fake dichotomy (Tracy and Trethewey 2005), and examine various ways these discourses influence workers. For example, Tracy (2000) described how cruise ship workers internalized cultural norms about the performance of emotions in ways that left them vulnerable to harassment by passengers. More recently, Sørensen and Villadsen (2018) described how dramatized performances by a CEO in a creative industry attempted to normalize violations of employee privacy and sexual provocations. Critical scholars also observed the development of more extreme forms of culture management, including burgeoning discourses of spirituality and even corporate "cults" (Nadesan 1999; Tourish and Vatcha 2005) that expand managerial influence over workers. Corporate participation in "fitness cults" like CrossFit promote managerial perspectives on the body, health, and fitness, although workers may interpret such efforts in myriad ways, with various degrees of acceptance and rejection (James and Zoller 2018).

We have explained a number of approaches to understanding power and communication in management communication theorizing. In the following sections, we discuss major concepts related to power, control, and resistance in managerial communication contexts.

2 Management communication and control

Management communication researchers conceptualize power and control in various ways, drawing on theories from a number of disciplines. The psychologists French and Raven (1959) represented social power as the ability to influence, including a five-fold typology of social influence: reward, coercion, legitimacy, expertise, and reference. Although communication can be theorized as an essential process through which these influences are exercised, theorists often viewed communication in a structural-deterministic manner, as an expression of existing power relations, rather than a constitutive force of social influence (Mumby 1993; Scarduzio 2011). Dahl's (1957) pluralist model, emanating from political science, conceptualized power as the ability of an individual or a group to exert influence on the behavior of another. Bachrach and Baratz (1962) added suppression as another dimension of influence, meaning that power may entail preventing others from doing something that they would otherwise do. Moreover, Lukes (1974) observed that power not only shapes decisions in open conflict and competition (decision-making power) but sets the agenda for policy debate (non-decision-making power), ultimately shaping the dominating ideology in society (ideological power). Thus, social influence may shape the desires and aspirations of others, often in the absence of apparent conflicts.

Another foundational theory that has been expanded in more communicative terms is Edwards' (1984) conception of three strategies of control. Edwards identified *simple control* as a direct, open, and interpersonal form of control that typically falls along the formal line of order, often when an owner or manager knows each employer in person. When simple control becomes ineffective in large organizations, *technical control* takes over, as managers use conveyer belts to control the speed of work, and surveillance cameras to monitor productivity. Finally, *bureaucratic control* is embedded in the social organization of the workplace characterized by established rules and standardized work flow. Tompkins and Cheney (1985) and Barker (1993) expanded Edwards' (1984) taxonomy to address *concertive control*.

Tompkins and Cheney (1985) conceptualized concertive control as an unobtrusive form of power in which workers internalize managerial values and objectives. Concertive control is "non personal, pervasive and predictable" and is achieved through "positive incentives of security, identification, and common mission" (Tompkins and Cheney 1985: 185). Barker's (1993, 1999) study of work team founds that self-management techniques led to workers surveilling and controlling themselves more stringently than supervisors would have. Unlike the bureaucratic hierarchy, authority and motivation in a concertive control system originate from the peer pressure of the team. Barker argued that these value-based systems increase the overall force of control.

2.1 Ideological control

Critical scholars often treat consensus as the manifestation of ideological domination in organizations. From this perspective, ideologies, or shared belief systems, reflect the naturalization of dominant group interests. Anthony Giddens (1979) drew from Marxism to delineate three main functions of ideology: (1) representing dominant groups' interests as universal; (2) denying social contradictions, and (3) reifying specific social relations by presenting them as natural and legitimate. Organizational consensus reflects the dominance of management interests, while other systems of significance are suppressed as unimportant or irrelevant. Mumby (1987) later proposed a fourth function of ideology as a means of control.

The Italian Marxist theorist Antonio Gramsci (1971, 2000) theorized *hegemony* as a process of moral and political subjugation of a social class by another, based in part on the consent and participation of the subjugated class. Management scholars investigate how communication establishes taken-for-granted assumptions that reaffirm the power of dominant groups (Mumby 1997). For example, workers may view management ideologies as the way things normally and naturally work, leading to the acceptance of subordination and even hazards such as occupational health risks (Zoller 2003). Women sometimes adopt management discourses that devalue women's experiences through binary distinctions such as emotionality and rationality (Ashcraft 2009; Buzzanell and Liu 2005). As we will discuss later, Gramsci was interested in hegemony as a relational negotiation, and promoted the development of a "war of position" that would establish a hegemony of subordinated classes (Mumby 1997).

2.2 Disciplinary power

Michel Foucault (2012) offered a discourse perspective on power, focusing on the role of meaning construction in defining knowledge and deploying techniques for managing the self. Foucault delineated three types of power: (1) sovereign power, which refers to the coercive, judicial type of power that has the privilege to "decide life and death" (Foucault 1978: 135); (2) biopower, which is a technology of power that functions at the population level to "incite, reinforce, control, monitor, optimize and organize" (Foucault 1978: 136), and (3) disciplinary power, which occurs through internalization of discourses regulating and organizing space, time, and everyday activities. Disciplinary power also operates through the demarcation of what counts as legitimate knowledge and areas of expertise (Foucault 2012), for example, by defining "management studies" as an area of inquiry (Carter, McKinlay, and Rowlinson 2002).

Surveillance is an integral part of the governmentality of self, and modern management engages numerous methods to inculcate internalized self-monitoring, encouraging employees to adopt, enact, and enforce organizational values. However, Foucault's conceptualizations of power are not only repressive (preventing things from happening, blocking people from acting to their desire), but also productive (making things happen, creating desire and motivations, defining competence). For example, workplace health promotion discourses not only promote policing of the body through internalized surveillance, but also contribute to employee viewpoints about what health is and how it should be achieved (Kelly, Allender, and Colquhoun 2007). Moreover, historically situated and dispersed "truths" may be internalized by individuals in ways that justify surveilling others (Dempsey and Gibson 2017).

2.3 Standpoint: theories of power and difference

Management studies scholars also investigate how organizational power relations are constituted in part based on multiple hierarchies related to identity. Researchers have demonstrated how material and symbolic relations of power are inscribed in and through relationships of difference, including gender, sexuality, race, nationality, age, and ability status (Mumby and Ashcraft 2004). Many of them have drawn in part from feminist standpoint theory (Collins 2002; Harding 2004; Hartsock 1983) to demonstrate how gendered assumptions influence taken-for-granted organizational beliefs.

Feminist research critiqued patriarchal forms of power as a system that privileges male leadership (Trethewey 2001) and questioned binary distinctions that are embedded in organizational life such as subject/object, masculinity/femininity, public/private, emotionality/rationality (Ashcraft 2009). Patriarchal values may be embedded in organizational systems. For example, Dougherty and Hode (2016) observed that management often treats sexual harassment claims as dangerous to men rather than systematically address the effects on women.

Further, constructions of sexuality reinforce heteronormativity, based on the communicative privileging of heterosexuality (Fleming 2007; Lewis 2009; Rumens and Kerfoot 2009). Lewis (2009) noted that LGBTQ individuals are not covered under civil rights laws, and that discrimination can lead to quitting, depression, and even suicide. Rumens and Kerfoot (2009) found that (white) gay men, even in "gay friendly" organizations, may struggle with the communicative negotiation of what it means to be a professional, given dominant discourse that treat sexuality and professionalism as oppositional.

Theorizing power also entails investigating racial privilege and the encoding of whiteness as an organizational norm (Ashcraft and Allen 2003; Parker and Mease 2008). Brenda Allen (1996) observed that theories of socialization that assume members transition from outsider to insider fail to consider the experiences of racial minorities, who may never be treated as insiders. Addressing connections among race, knowledge, and power, Allen (2009) also pointed out ways that white people generally determine what count as "real" incidents of racial harassment when they are reported, which is already limited.

De-centering Western assumptions that dominate managerial research, postcolonial theories interrogate the neocolonial assumptions of European management styles exported to the global South (Broadfoot and Munshi 2007). For example, Ban and Dutta (2012) explored how neo-colonialist discourses are prevalent in trade publications and mainstream news sources about doing business in China (Ban, Sastry, and Dutta 2013). Postcolonial organizational studies offer critiques "against the grain" (Prasad 2012: 21) of standard management theorizing, so that management communication is theorized from the experiences of non-Western, Indigenous, and often grassroots organizations (Cruz and Sodeke 2020; Jack et al. 2011; Pal and Dutta 2008). For example, Cruz and Sodeke (2020) re-theorized the concept of liquidity through the perspective of marginalized actors in Nigeria and Liberia. Banerjee and Tedmonson (2010) described Indigenous enterprise development in Australia and their negotiation of barriers resulting from discursive practices of whiteness (see also Spiller et al. 2020; Varman and Al-Amoudi 2016).

Intersectional research draws these issues together (Crenshaw 1989), viewing identity as a crystallization of multiple discourses of race, nationality, class, age, gender, and other forms of difference (Dougherty, Baiocchi-Wagner, and McGuire 2011; Hayden and O'Brien Hallstein 2012; Lockwood Harris 2017; Parker, Oceguera, and Sánchez 2011; Tyler 2019). Multiple assumptions about gender, race, class, and sexuality are embedded as organizational knowledge, leading workers to experience multiple forms of marginalization (Cruz 2017; Gist-Mackey 2018; Lewis 2009; Lockwood Harris 2017; Parker and Mease 2008). For example, Gist-Mackey (2018) investigated how racial and class constructions are intertwined to produce biased forms of communication training in two job search firms, placing further burdens on minoritized job seekers whose labor has devalued in the labor market. Joëlle Cruz (2017) drew from African feminisms to understand how a grassroots organization in Monrovia, Liberia, managed tensions between visibility and invisibility, delineating the communicative resources emanating from cultural logics related to temporal, relational, and structural dimensions.

3 Management communication and resistance

Organization researchers conceptualize power both in the context of exerting and resisting control. Resistance, therefore, has long been a central topic in management communication studies of organizational politics. Resistance is increasingly recognized as a routine part of the organizational processes. In this vein, the dialectical view addresses the simultaneous, interconnected nature of power and resistance (Mumby 2005). Whereas the functionalist view of organizations inferred the irrationality of any "deviance" from the authoritative view (Downes, Rock, and McLaughlin 2016), many organizational theorists also recognize the rational, productive aspect of opposition in organizational processes. Studies on organizational tensions, contradictions and paradoxes, including feminist research may view resistance as not only disruptive to the formal system of the organization, but potentially productive (Stohl and Cheney 2001, Ashcraft 2001; Putnam, Fairhurst, and Banghart 2016). For example, Ford, Ford, and McNamara (2002) argued that powerful organizational groups may be more likely to engage in conversations that open up space for alternative rationalities when they acknowledge the possibilities of resistance. Gagnon and Collinson (2017) found that whereas most teams in a global leadership program reinforced differences and exclusions, one team's resistance to parts of the program promoted both group solidarity and inclusion.

More structuralist critical researchers view resistance as a reaction to oppressive control and structural violence and often emphasize macro, overt forms of revolt against the ruling power as the route towards emancipation (Cloud 2005; Rao, Morrill, and Zald 2000; Zald and Berger 1978). Research addresses the potential of and barriers to unionization (Cloud 2005), and other forms of worker advocacy such as social movements and protests (Jiang and Korczynski 2016; Zald and Berger 1978), although such efforts are often found to be limited. For example, Varman and Al-Amoudi (2016) examined attempts by Indian workers to protest against forms of violence, finding that paternalistic management discourses undercut these efforts.

Poststructural scholars, on the other hand, recognize management as one of many political actors in an organization, and pay more attention to the everyday forms of resistance that brings out the dynamic nature of power in the organization (Alcadipani and Islam 2017). Whereas early structural researchers dismissed the potential of small acts of resistance to disrupt capitalist systems, poststructural researchers in particular have developed a rich body of evidence regarding relatively covert ways that employees resist management encroachment of their behaviors or sense of self. The focus on covert and individual forms of resistance also results from the acknowledgment that open conflict with management can be rare (Zoller and Fairhurst 2007).

Ford, Ford, and McNamara (2002) observed that authoritative management stories are foregrounded in organizations, but identified subtle resistive voices as (1) "background conversations", which can be complacent (e.g., avoidance), (2) resigned (e.g., low levels of participation), or (3) cynical (e.g., irony). Researchers have investigated the "politicking" form of defiance and struggle as well as mild, "unsupportive", "uncollaborative" forms of expression of difference (Putnam et al. 2005). Similarly, scholars have applied Scott's (1990) "hidden transcripts" to examine employee non-conformist discourse such as bitching and humor that occur outside the purview of management (Murphy 1998; Tracy 2000). This "below the radar" resistance may assert some measure of agency and define limits to dominance (Fleming 2005; Trethewey 1997).

While covert forms of resistance can be effective to some degree, they are nonetheless limited if only used as a channel to vent. Lynch (2009) distinguished between humor's role as a safety valve that allowed kitchen staff to express dissatisfaction while maintaining the status quo, and its role in creating space for workers to defy managerial controls and expectations. Similarly, hidden transcripts of bitching gave cruise ship workers the impression of control, but did not challenge managerial expectations, including those that led to harassment and burnout (Tracy 2000).

As a result, scholars called for renewed attention to ways that relatively hidden forms of resistance link to more self-consciously confrontational efforts at challenging power relationships in a variety of settings (Contu 2008; Ganesh, Zoller, and Cheney 2005). Zoller and Fairhurst (2007) theorized how discursive leadership can connect hidden transcripts of resistance with the development of social movements and other collective forms of resistance. In this vein, Zanin and Bisel (2019) investigated an athletic team that developed internal concertive control that openly flouted coach authority by refusing to identify a rule-breaker. Gossett and Kilker (2006) analyzed how hidden transcripts of employees and former employees on the website "radioshacksucks" fomented forms of overt and collective resistance by making complaints visible to management and encouraging members to participate in a lawsuit against Radio Shack. Conrad and Abbott (2007) drew from Mann (1986) to explicate the conditions under which non-elite publics assert their voice in the political process and examined the role of corporate issue management in outflanking that voice. Ganesh and Stohl (2013) investigated the communicative networks involved in fomenting large scale protests against corporate dominance in the global Occupy movement.

In the next section, we describe two areas of theoretical and practical debate related to resistance and social change. The first relates to precarity, organizational discourse and late capitalism, and the second focuses on debates about the role of the researcher in social change.

3.1 Resistance: precarious work, late capitalism, and social change

Researching resistance takes on new complexities when considering the effects of late capitalism and the dominance of neoliberal governance regimes that are driving high levels of inequality within and among countries. These inequalities undercut workers' ability to improve working conditions. Researchers have demonstrated how risk is increasingly transferred to workers through managerial practices that promote precarious forms of labor (e. g., temporary and contracted work) and more frequent unemployment. Technological changes have further facilitated downsizing, flexibilization, and offshoring (Kalleberg 2009; Pal and Buzzanell 2013; Sullivan and Delaney 2017). These changes translate to insecurity, poverty wages, and high rates of occupational illness, injury, and death for many groups, particularly marginalized supply chain workers (Chowdhury 2017).

These trends have spurred increasing attention to the dialectic of order and disorder (Ashcraft 2006). Critical scholars challenge dominant assumptions about order in organizational life (Knox et al. 2015) and call for more attention to *disorder* given that disruption and disorder are key features of neoliberal governmentality (Jiang and Korczynski 2016). Resistance to precarity ranges from contesting the mainstream rhetoric of work to organized counter-movements (Brophy 2006; Bulut 2017; De Peuter 2011; Moore 2019; Wuggenig, Raunig, and Ray 2011). For example, Wuggenig, Raunig and Ray (2011) observed cultural workers' rejection of the language of "studios", which is associated with images of glamour and leisure, preferring terms like "office" or "laboratory" that demystify the production relationship.

Research investigates new forms of worker mobilization at the intersection of social movement organizations (e. g., labor unions, grassroots activism), and CSR efforts (e. g., third-party certification). Brophy (2006) observed collective resistance among temporary "knowledge workers" at Microsoft through the formation of the Washington Alliance of Technology Workers (WashTech) union. Similarly, Jiang and Kroczynski (2016) examined the social movement organizing of domestic workers in London. The organized resistance to work precarity is often part of the general anti-capital counter-movement, although the fragmentation of political positions in workers' collective action can trigger "disavowal and exclusionary solidarity" that are detrimental to the health of the counter-movement (Neilson 2015).

3.2 Theories of power and social change

Debates have arisen regarding social change across subfields engaged in management communication research. Some Critical Management Studies scholars have called for a "performative turn" (Fournier and Grey 2000), characterized as a form of positive engagement with management, adopting an "ethic of care" orientation to research (Spicer, Alvesson, and Kärreman 2009). Critics, however, posit that such engagement ignores the potential for co-optation and lacks adequate critical reflexivity, weakening critical commitments and leading to the acceptance of the managerial status quo (Fleming and Banerjee 2016; King and Land 2018).

Similar debates about the theorist and social change take place in organizational communication studies, where scholars have called for "positive" research such as "positive deviance case selection" (Bisel, Kavya, and Tracy 2018), which involves identifying exemplary models of organizational thriving. "Positive" researchers contrast this approach with critical scholarship, which they view as focused on identifying problems to be overcome (Bisel, Kavya, and Tracy 2018). Critical scholars, on the other hand, question the commitments that guide "positive" researchers and appreciative inquiry in assessing what counts as exemplary, and for whom (Grant and Humphries 2006), promoting the selection of deviant cases through articulation of the specific relations of power that are resisted and potentially transformed (Zoller 2013).

Although Zanoni et al. (2017) saw the continued need for "anti-performative" critique, they also sidestepped a dichotomous approach by calling for more critically engaged research that investigates alternative forms of organizing (King and Land 2018). Scholars such as Parker et al. (2014) call for the investigation of organizational and economic practices that entail more affirmative articulations of what critical scholars are "for".

As management communication scholars investigate and promote alternative efforts, they highlight multiple approaches to achieving different models of organizing, and the concomitant managerial systems and values (Esper et al. 2017; Mitra and Buzzanell 2017; Parker and Parker 2017). For example, worker-owned cooperatives embrace a dual mission of generating profit and developing worker ownership and democratic participation and must learn to balance dual roles for employees as owner workers and managers (Webb and Cheney 2014). Mitra and Buzzenell (2017) investigated how "green" management consultancies balance tensions between perceived profitability and environmental protection. More broadly, efforts as time banking, LETS (Kelly 2012), and the transition movement (Ganesh and Zoller 2014) highlight the variety of democratic and networked challenges to extractive forms of corporate, capitalist management systems.

Parker and Parker (2017) observed that critical scholars must embrace the contingency inherent in assessing what are beneficial and problematic organizational practices. Bryson and Dempsey (2017) demonstrated a contingent and dialectical approach to understanding alternative change efforts within neoliberal orders. They describe their approach to studying consignment clothing workers: "Rather than resting at an easy conclusion that seasonal consignment sales practices are determined by neoliberalism, thus precluding alternatives to capitalism, we highlight their ambivalences" (Bryson and Dempsey 2017: 589). The authors acknowledged that consignment industry leaders promote neoliberal forms of entrepreneurship and gendered division of labor, but they also argued that "seasonal consignment sales provide glimpses of alternative structures of value creation outside of the wage relationship" (Bryson and Dempsey 2017: 589).

4 Conclusion

In this chapter, we have offered an overview of a number of key approaches to understanding power and its relationship to control and resistance in the management setting. We have elucidated the ways that different theorists and researchers interpret and critique management communication in the context of power, control, and resistance, and have introduced communication perspectives on the political process of management.

Researchers apply multiple frameworks regarding the communication-power relationship to illuminate both longstanding managerial practices and new developments in the face of rapidly changing organizational practices. Our review of the literature demonstrates a wide variety of approaches to understanding power. However, most researchers today agree on a number of key ideas: (1) Power operates regardless of whether there are visible conflicts or tensions. (2) Power is manifest in processes of organizing and dis-organizing, management and dis-management. (3) Power is exercised by both those who are in position of influence and dominance, and by those who are subject to control and subjugation. Increasingly, scholars also agree on a fourth stipulation: that power and resistance are fundamentally communicative phenomena.

5 References

Alcadipani, Rafael & Gazi Islam. 2017. Modalities of opposition: Control and resistance via visual materiality. *Organization* 24(6). 866–891.

Allen, Brenda J. 1996. Feminist standpoint theory: A black woman's (re)view of organizational socialization. *Communication Studies* 47(4). 257–271. doi:10.1080/10510979609368482.

Allen, Brenda J. 2009. Racial harassment in the workplace. In Pamela Lutgen-Sandvik & Beverly D. Sypher (eds.), *Destructive organizational communication*, 164–183. New York: Routledge.

Alvesson, Mats & Dan Kärreman. 2000. Varieties of discourse: On the study of organizations through discourse analysis. *Human Relations* 53(9). 1125–1149.

Alvesson, Mats & Hugh Willmott. 2012. *Making sense of management: A critical introduction*. Thousand Oaks, CA: Sage.

Ashcraft, Karen L. 2001. Organized dissonance: Feminist bureaucracy as hybrid form. *Academy of Management Journal* 44(6). 1301–1322.

Ashcraft, Karen L. 2006. Feminist-bureaucratic control and other adversarial allies: Extending organized dissonance to the practice of "new" forms. *Communication Monographs* 73(1). 55–86.

Ashcraft, Karen L. 2009. Gender and diversity: Other ways to make a difference. In Mats Alvesson, Todd Bridgman & Hugh Willmott (eds.), *The Oxford handbook of critical management studies*, 305–327. New York: Oxford University Press.

Ashcraft, Karen L. & Brenda J. Allen. 2003. The racial foundation of organizational communication. *Communication Theory* 13(1). 5–38.

Bachrach, Peter & Morton Baratz. 1962. Two faces of power. *American Political Science Review* 56(4). 947–952.

Ban, Zhuo & Mohan J. Dutta. 2012. Minding their business: Discourses of colonialism and neoliberalism in the commercial guide for US companies in China. *Public Relations Inquiry* 1(2). 197–220.

Ban, Zhuo, Shaunak Sastry & Mohan J. Dutta. 2013. "Shoppers' Republic of China": Orientalism in neoliberal U.S. news discourse. *Journal of International and Intercultural Communication* 6(4). 280–297.

Banerjee, Subhabrata B. & Deirdre Tedmanson. 2010. Grass burning under our feet: Indigenous enterprise development in a political economy of whiteness. *Management Learning* 41(2). 147–165.

Barker, James R. 1993. Tightening the iron cage: Concertive control in self-managing teams. *Administrative Science Quarterly* 38(3). 408–437.

Barker, James R. 1999. *The discipline of teamwork: Participation and concertive control.* Thousand Oaks, CA: Sage.

Bate, Paul. 1994. *Strategies for cultural change.* New York: Butterworth-Heinemann.

Bisel, Ryan S., Pavitra Kavya & Sarah J. Tracy. 2018. Making room for positive deviance in organizational communication. Paper presented at the National Communication Association Annual Convention, Salt Lake, UT, 8–11 November.

Broadfoot, Kirsten J. & Debashish Munshi. 2007. Diverse voices and alternative rationalities: Imagining forms of postcolonial organizational communication. *Management Communication Quarterly* 21(2). 249–267.

Brophy, Enda. 2006. System error: Labour precarity and collective organizing at Microsoft. *Canadian Journal of Communication* 31(3). 619–638.

Bryson, Alexis & Sarah E. Dempsey. 2017. Entrepreneurial reproductive labor as alternative economic practice: The ambivalent discourse of seasonal consignment sales. *Organization* 24(5). 589–608.

Bulut, Ergin. 2017. Can the intern resist? Precarity of blue-collar labor and the fragmented resistance of the white-collar intern in Laurent Cantet's Human Resources. *Journal of Communication Inquiry* 41(1). 42–59.

Burawoy, Michael. 1982. *Manufacturing consent: Changes in the labor process under monopoly capitalism.* Chicago, IL: University of Chicago Press.

Burawoy, Michael. 2012. The roots of domination: Beyond Bourdieu and Gramsci. *Sociology* 46(2). 187–206.

Buzzanell, Patrice M. & Meina Liu. 1994. Gaining a voice: Feminist perspectives in organizational communication. *Management Communication Quarterly* 7. 339–383.

Buzzanell, Patrice M. & Meina Liu. 2005. Struggling with maternity leave policies and practices: A poststructuralist feminist analysis of gendered organizing. *Journal of Applied Communication Research* 33(1). 1–25.

Carlone, David & Gregory S. Larson. 2006. Locating possibilities for control and resistance in a self-help program. *Western Journal of Communication* 70(4). 270–291.

Carter, Chris, Alan McKinlay & Michael Rowlinson. 2002. Introduction: Foucault, management and history. *Organization* 9(4). 515–526. doi:10.1177/135050840294001.

Chowdhury, Rashedur. 2017. The Rana Plaza disaster and the complicit behavior of elite NGOs. *Organization* 24(6). 938–949.

Clair, Robin P. 1993. The use of framing devices to sequester organizational narratives: Hegemony and harassment. *Communication Monographs* 60(2). 113–136.

Cloud, Dana L. 2005. Fighting words labor and the limits of communication at Staley, 1993 to 1996. *Management Communication Quarterly* 18(4). 509–542.

Collins, Patricia H. 2002. *Black feminist thought: Knowledge, consciousness, and the politics of empowerment.* New York: Routledge.

Conrad, Charles & Jeanna Abbott. 2007. Corporate social responsibility and public policy making. In Steve May, George Cheney & Juliet Roper (eds.), *The debate over corporate social responsibility,* 417–437. New York: Oxford University Press.

Contu, Alessia. 2008. Decaf resistance: On misbehavior, cynicism, and desire in liberal workplaces. *Management Communication Quarterly* 21(3). 364–379.

Crenshaw, Kimberlé. 1989. Demarginalizing the intersection of race and sex: A black feminist critique of antidiscrimination doctrine, feminist theory and antiracist politics. In Katherine Bartlett (ed.), *University of Chicago Legal Forum*, 139–167. New York: Routledge.

Cruz, Joëlle M. 2017. Invisibility and visibility in alternative organizing: A communicative and cultural model. *Management Communication Quarterly* 31(4). 614–639.

Cruz, Joëlle M. & Chigozirim U. Sodeke. 2020. Debunking eurocentrism in organizational communication theory: Marginality and liquidities in postcolonial contexts. *Communication Theory*. https://academic.oup.com/ct/advance-article-abstract/doi/10.1093/ct/qtz038/5820642 (accessed 13 November 2020).

Dahl, Robert. 1957. The concept of power. *Behavioral Science* 2(3). 201–215.

De Peuter, Greig. 2011. Creative economy and labor precarity: A contested convergence. *Journal of Communication Inquiry* 35(4). 417–425.

Deetz, Stanley. 1996. Crossroads—Describing differences in approaches to organization science: Rethinking Burrell and Morgan and their legacy. *Organization Science* 7(2). 191–207.

Dempsey, Sarah E. & Kristina E. Gibson. 2017. Food, biopower, and the child's body as a scale of intervention. In Pascale Joassart-Marcell & Fernando Bosco (eds.), *Food and place: A critical introduction*, 253–269. Lanham, MD: Rowman & Littlefield.

Dougherty, Debbie S., Elizabeth A. Baiocchi-Wagner & Tammy McGuire. 2011. Managing sexual harassment through enacted stereotypes: An intergroup perspective. *Western Journal of Communication* 75(3). 259–281.

Dougherty, Debbie S. & Marlo G. Hode. 2016. Binary logics and the discursive interpretation of organizational policy: Making meaning of sexual harassment policy. *Human Relations* 69(8). 1729–1755.

Downes, David, Paul E. Rock & Eugene McLaughlin. 2016. *Understanding deviance: A guide to the sociology of crime and rule-breaking*. Oxford: Oxford University Press.

Edwards, Richard C. 1984. Forms of control in the labor process: An historical analysis. *Critical Studies in Organization and Bureaucracy* 31(7). 109–142. doi:10.14452/mr-031-07-1979-11_4.

Esper, Susana C., Laure Cabantous, Luciano Barin-Cruz & Jean-Pascal Gond. 2017. Supporting alternative organizations? Exploring scholars' involvement in the performativity of worker-recuperated enterprises. *Organization* 24(5). 671–699.

Fairhurst, Gail T. & Linda Putnam. 2004. Organizations as discursive constructions. *Communication Theory* 14(1). 5–26.

Fleming, Peter. 2005. Metaphors of resistance. *Management Communication Quarterly* 19(1). 45–66.

Fleming, Peter. 2007. Sexuality, power and resistance in the workplace. *Organization Studies* 28(2). 239–256.

Fleming, Peter & Subhabrata B. Banerjee. 2016. When performativity fails: Implications for Critical Management Studies. *Human Relations* 69(2). 257–276.

Ford, Jeffrey D., Laurie W. Ford & Randall T. McNamara. 2002. Resistance and the background conversations of change. *Journal of Organizational Change Management* 15(2). 105–121.

Foucault, Michel. 1978. *The history of sexuality, Volume 1: An introduction*. New York: Vintage.

Foucault, Michel. 2012. *Discipline and punish: The birth of the prison*. New York: Vintage.

Fournier, Valerie & Chris Grey. 2000. At the critical moment: Conditions and prospects for critical management studies. *Human Relations* 53(1). 7–32.

French, John R. P. & Bertram Raven. 1959. The bases of power. In D. Cartwright (ed.), *Studies in social power*, 150–167. Ann Arbor, MI: University of Michigan.

Gagnon, Suzanne & David Collinson. 2017. Resistance through difference: The co-constitution of dissent and inclusion. *Organization Studies* 38(9). 1253–1276.

Ganesh, Shiv & Cynthia Stohl. 2013. From Wall Street to Wellington: Protests in an era of digital ubiquity. *Communication Monographs* 80(4). 425–451.

Ganesh, Shiv & Heather M. Zoller. 2014. Organising transition: Principles and tensions in eco-localism. In Martin Parker, George Cheney, Valérie Fournier & Chris Land (eds.), *The Routledge companion to alternative organization*, 236–250. Oxford: Routledge.

Ganesh, Shiv, Heather M. Zoller & George Cheney. 2005. Transforming resistance, broadening our boundaries: Critical organizational communication meets globalization from below. *Communication Monographs* 72(2). 169–191.

Giddens, Anthony. 1979. *Central problems in social theory: Action, structure, and contradiction in social analysis*. Burkeley, CA: University of California Press.

Gist-Mackey, Angela N. 2018. (Dis)embodied job search communication training: Comparative critical ethnographic analysis of materiality and discourse during the unequal search for work. *Organization Studies* 39(9). 1251–1275.

Gossett, Loril M. & Julian Kilker. 2006. My job sucks: Examining counterinstitutional web sites as locations for organizational member voice, dissent, and resistance. *Management Communication Quarterly* 20(1). 63–90.

Gramsci, Antonio. 1971. *Selections from the prison notebooks*. New York: International Publishers.

Gramsci, Antonio. 2000. *The Gramsci reader: Selected writings, 1916–1935*. NewYork: New York University Press.

Grant, David, Rick Iedema & Cliff Oswick. 2009. Discourse and critical management studies. In Mats Alvesson, Todd Bridgman & Hugh Willmott (eds.), *The Oxford handbook of critical management studies*, 213–231. Oxford: Oxford University Press.

Grant, Suzanne L. P. & Maria Humphries. 2006. Critical evaluation of appreciative inquiry: Bridging an apparent paradox. *Action Research* 4(4). 401–418.

Habermas, Jürgen. 1975. Towards a reconstruction of historical materialism. *Theory and Society* 2(1). 287–300.

Habermas, Jürgen. 1984. *The theory of communicative action: Reason and the rationalization of society*. Boston, MA: Beacon Press.

Harding, Sandra G. 2004. *The feminist standpoint theory reader: Intellectual and political controversies*. New York: Routledge.

Hartsock, Nancy C. M. 1983. The feminist standpoint: Developing the ground for a specifically feminist historical materialism. In Sandra Harding & Merrill B. Hintikka (eds.), *Discovering reality: Feminist perspectives on epistemology, metaphysics, methodology, and philosophy of science*, 283–310. Dordrecht: Springer.

Hayden, Sara & D. Lynn O'Brien Hallstein. 2012. Placing sex/gender at the forefront: Feminisms, intersectionality, and communication studies. In Karma R. Chávez & Cindy L. Griffin (eds.), *Standing in the intersection: Feminist voices, feminist practices in communication studies*, 97–124. New York: SUNY Press.

Hochschild, Arlie R. 2005. "Rent a mom" and other services: Markets, meanings and emotions. *International Journal of Work Organisation and Emotion* 1(1). 74–86.

Hodgson, Damian. 2002. Disciplining the professional: The case of project management. *Journal of Management Studies* 39(6). 803–821.

Horkheimer, Max & Theodor W. Adorno. 2006. The culture industry: Enlightenment as mass deception. In Meenakshi G. Durham & Douglas M. Kellner (eds.), *Media and cultural studies: Keyworks*, 41–72. Malden, MA: Blackwell Publishing.

Jack, Gavin, Robert Westwood, Nidhi Srinivas & Ziauddin Sardar. 2011. Deepening, broadening and re-asserting a postcolonial interrogative space in organization studies. *Organization* 18(3). 275–302.

James, Eric P. & Heather M. Zoller. 2018. Resistance training: (Re)shaping extreme forms of workplace health promotion. *Management Communication Quarterly* 32(1). 60–89.

Jervis, John. 2018. *Modernity theory: Modern experience, modernist consciousness, reflexive thinking*. New York: Springer.

Jiang, Zhe & Marek Korczynski. 2016. When the 'unorganizable'organize: The collective mobilization of migrant domestic workers in London. *Human Relations* 69(3). 813–838.

Johansson, Janet, Janne Tienari & Anu Valtonen. 2017. The body, identity and gender in managerial athleticism. *Human Relations* 70(9). 1141–1167.

Kalleberg, Arne L. 2009. Precarious work, insecure workers: Employment relations in transition. *American Sociological Review* 74(1). 1–22.

Kassing, Jeffrey W., Shea A. Fanelli & Laasya Chakravarthy. 2018. Full-and part-time dissent: Examining the effect of employment status on dissent expression. *International Journal of Business Communication* 55(4). 455–465.

Kelly, Marjorie. 2012. *Owning our future: The emerging ownership revolution*. Oakland, CA: Berrett-Koehler Publishers.

Kelly, Peter, Steven Allender & Derek Colquhoun. 2007. New work ethics?: The corporate athlete's back end index and organizational performance. *Organization* 14(2). 267–285.

King, Daniel & Christopher Land. 2018. The democratic rejection of democracy: Performative failure and the limits of critical performativity in an organizational change project. *Human Relations* 71(11). 1535–1557.

Kirby, Erika L. 2006. "Helping you make room in your life for your needs": When organizations appropriate family roles. *Communication Monographs* 73(4). 474–480.

Knox, Hannah, Damian P. O'Doherty, Theo Vurdubakis & Christopher Westrup. 2015. Something happened: Spectres of organization/disorganization at the airport. *Human Relations* 68(6). 1001–1020.

Lewis, Andrea P. 2009. Destructive organizational communication and LGBT workers' experiences. In Pamela Lutgen-Sandvik & Beverly Davenport Sypher (eds.), *Destructive organizational communication*, 203–226. New York: Routledge.

Lockwood Harris, Kate. 2017. Re-situating organizational knowledge: Violence, intersectionality and the privilege of partial perspective. *Human Relations* 70(3). 263–285.

Lounsbury, Michael & Marc Ventresca. 2003. The new structuralism in organizational theory. *Organization* 10(3). 457–480.

Lukes, Steven. 1974. *Power: A radical view*. London: Macmillan.

Lynch, Owen H. 2009. Kitchen antics: The importance of humor and maintaining professionalism at work. *Journal of Applied Communication Research* 37(4). 444–464.

Mann, Michael. 1986. *The sources of social power*. New York: Cambridge University Press.

Marx, Karl. 1972. *The Marx-Engels reader*. New York: Norton.

Mayo, Elton. 2004. *The human problems of an industrial civilization*. New York: Routledge.

McCarthy, Lucy, Anne Touboulic & Lee Matthews. 2018. Voiceless but empowered farmers in corporate supply chains: Contradictory imagery and instrumental approach to empowerment. *Organization* 25(5). 609–635.

McGregor, D. 1960. *The human side of enterprise*. New York: McGraw-Hill.

Mitra, Rahul & Patrice M. Buzzanell. 2017. Communicative tensions of meaningful work: The case of sustainability practitioners. *Human Relations* 70(5). 594–616.

Moore, Phoebe V. 2019. E(a)ffective precarity, control and resistance in the digitalised workplace. In Adam Fishwick & Heather Connolly (eds.), *Austerity and working class resistance: Survival, disruption and creation in hard times*, 125–144. London: Rowman & Littlefield.

Mumby, Dennis K. 1987. The political function of narrative in organizations. *Communications Monographs* 54(2). 113–127. doi:10.1080/03637758709390221.

Mumby, Dennis K. 1993. Critical organizational communication studies: The next 10 years. *Communications Monographs* 60(1). 18–25.
Mumby, Dennis K. 1997. The problem of hegemony: Rereading Gramsci for organizational communication studies. *Western Journal of Communication* 61(4). 343–375.
Mumby, Dennis K. 2005. Theorizing resistance in organizational studies: A dialectical approach. *Management Communication Quarterly* 19(1). 19–44.
Mumby, Dennis K. & Karen L. Ashcraft. 2004. *Reworking gender: A feminist communicology of organization*. Thousand Oaks, CA: Sage.
Mumby, Dennis K. & Robin P. Clair. 1997. Organizational discourse. In Teun A. van Dijk (ed.), *Discourse as social interaction: Discourse studies: A multidisciplinary introduction*, vol. 2, 181–205. London: Sage.
Murphy, Alexandra G. 1998. Hidden transcripts of flight attendant resistance. *Management Communication Quarterly* 11(4). 499–535.
Nadesan, Majia. 1999. The discourses of corporate spiritualism and evangelical capitalism. *Management Communication Quarterly* 13(3). 3–42.
Neilson, David. 2015. Class, precarity, and anxiety under neoliberal global capitalism: From denial to resistance. *Theory & Psychology* 25(2). 184–201.
Nkomo, Srella M. 2011. A postcolonial and anti-colonial reading of 'African' leadership and management in organization studies: Tensions, contradictions and possibilities. *Organization* 18(3). 365–386.
Pal, Mahuya & Patrice M. Buzzanell. 2013. Breaking the myth of Indian call centers: A postcolonial analysis of resistance. *Communication Monographs* 80(2). 199–219.
Pal, Mahuya & Mohan J. Dutta. 2008. Theorizing resistance in a global context: Processes, strategies, and tactics in communication scholarship. In Christina S. Beck (ed.), *Communication yearbook* 32, 41–88. New York: Routledge.
Parker, Martin. 1992. Post-modern organizations or postmodern organization theory. *Organization Studies* 13(1). 1–17.
Parker, Martin, George Cheney, Valérie Fournier & Chris Land. 2014. *The Routledge companion to alternative organization*. New York: Routledge.
Parker, Patricia S. & Jennifer Mease. 2008. Beyond the knap-sack: Disrupting the production of White racial privilege in organizational practices. *Intercultural Communication: A reader*. Belmont, CA: Thompson.
Parker, Patricia S., Elisa Oceguera & Joaquin Sánchez, Jr. 2011. Intersecting differences: Organizing [ourselves] for social justice research with people in vulnerable communities. In Dennis K. Mumby (ed.), *Reframing difference in organizational communication studies*, 219–244. Thousand Oaks, CA: Sage.
Parker, Simon & Martin Parker. 2017. Antagonism, accommodation and agonism in Critical Management Studies: Alternative organizations as allies. *Human Relations* 70(11). 1366–1387.
Peters, Thomas J. & Robert M. Waterman. 1982. *In search of excellence*. New York: Harper & Row.
Prasad, Anshuman. 2012. *Against the grain: Advances in postcolonial organization studies*. Frederiksberg, Denmark: Copenhagen Business School Press.
Putnam, Linda L., Gail T. Fairhurst & Scott Banghart. 2016. Contradictions, dialectics, and paradoxes in organizations: A constitutive approach. *The Academy of Management Annals* 10(1). 65–171.
Putnam, Linda L., David Grant, Grant Michelson & Leanne Cutcher. 2005. Discourse and resistance: Targets, practices, and consequences. *Management Communication Quarterly* 19(1). 5–18.
Putnam, Linda L. & Michael E. Pacanowsky. 1983. *Communication and organizations: An interpretive approach*. Thousand Oaks, CA: Sage.

Quinlan, Elizabeth, Susan Robertson, Ann-Marie Urban, Isobel M. Findlay & Beth Bilson. 2019. Ameliorating workplace harassment among direct caregivers in Canada's healthcare system: A theatre-based intervention. *Work, Employment and Society* 34(4). 626–643.

Rao, Hayagreeva, Calvin Morrill & Mayer N. Zald. 2000. Power plays: How social movements and collective action create new organizational forms. *Research in Organizational Behavior* 22. 237–281.

Ritzer, G. 2000. *The McDonaldization of society*. Thousand Oaks, CA: Pine Forge Press.

Rodino-Colocino, Michelle. 2012. Geek jeremiads: Speaking the crisis of job loss by opposing offshored and H-1B labor. *Communication and Critical/Cultural Studies* 9(1). 22–46.

Rumens, Nick & Deborah Kerfoot. 2009. Gay men at work: (Re)constructing the self as professional. *Human Relations* 62(5). 763–786.

Scarduzio, Jennifer A. 2011. Maintaining order through deviance? The emotional deviance, power, and professional work of municipal court judges. *Management Communication Quarterly* 25(2). 283–310.

Scott, James C. 1990. *Domination and the arts of resistance: Hidden transcripts*. London: Yale University Press.

Sørensen, Bent M. & Kaspar Villadsen. 2018. Penis-whirling and pie-throwing: Norm-defying and norm-setting drama in the creative industries. *Human Relations* 71(8). 1049–1071.

Spicer, André, Mats Alvesson & Dan Kärreman. 2009. Critical performativity: The unfinished business of critical management studies. *Human Relations* 62(4). 537–560.

Spiller, Chellie, Rachel M. Wolfgramm, Ella Henry & Robert Pouwhare. 2020. Paradigm warriors: Advancing a radical ecosystems view of collective leadership from an Indigenous Māori perspective. *Human Relations* 73(4). 516–543.

Stohl, Cynthia & George Cheney. 2001. Participatory processes/paradoxical practices: Communication and the dilemmas of organizational democracy. *Management Communication Quarterly* 14(3). 349–407.

Sullivan, Katie R. & Helen Delaney. 2017. A femininity that 'giveth and taketh away': The prosperity gospel and postfeminism in the neoliberal economy. *Human Relations* 70(7). 836–859.

Taylor, Frederick W. 1911. *The principles of scientific management*. New York: Harper & Row.

Thompson, Paul, Paula McDonald & Peter O'Connor. 2020. Employee dissent on social media and organizational discipline. *Human Relations* 73(5). 631–652.

Tompkins, Philip K. & George Cheney. 1985. Communication and unobtrusive control in contemporary organizations. In Robert D. McPhee & Philip K. Tompkins (eds.), *Organizational communication: Traditional themes and new directions*, 179–210. London: Sage.

Tourish, Dennis & Nadeed Vatcha. 2005. Charismatic leadership and corporate cultism at Enron: The elimination of dissent, the promotion of conformity and organizational collapse. *Leadership* 1(1). 455–480.

Tracy, Sarah J. 2000. Becoming a character for commerce: Emotion labor, self-subordination, and discursive construction of identity in a total institution. *Management Communication Quarterly* 14(1). 90–128.

Tracy, Sarah J. & Angela Trethewey. 2005. Fracturing the real-self ↔ fake-self dichotomy: Moving toward "crystallized" organizational discourses and identities. *Communication Theory* 15(2). 168–195.

Trethewey, Angela. 1997. Resistance, identity, and empowerment: A postmodern feminist analysis of clients in a human service organization. *Communications Monographs* 64(4). 281–301.

Trethewey, Angela. 2001. Reproducing and resisting the master narrative of decline: Midlife professional women's experiences of aging. *Management Communication Quarterly* 15(2). 183–226.

Tyler, Melissa. 2019. Reassembling difference? Rethinking inclusion through/as embodied ethics. *Human Relations* 72(1). 48–68.

Varman, Rohit & Ismael Al-Amoudi. 2016. Accumulation through derealization: How corporate violence remains unchecked. *Human Relations* 69(10). 1909–1935.

Veen, Alex, Tom Barratt & Caleb Goods. 2020. Platform-capital's 'app-etite' for control: A labour process analysis of food-delivery work in Australia. *Work, Employment and Society* 34(3). 388–406.

Webb, Tom & George Cheney. 2014. Worker-owned-and-governed co-operatives and the wider co-operative movement: Challenges and opportunities within and beyond the global economic crisis. In Martin Parker, George Cheney, Valérie Fournier & Chris Land (eds.), *The Routledge companion to alternative organization*, 64–88. Oxford: Routledge.

Weber, Max. 1964. *The theory of social and economic organization*. New York: Free Press.

White, Jerry. 1984. Corporate culture and corporate success. *Management Decision* 22(4). 14–19.

Willcoxson, Lesley & Bruce Millett. 2000. The management of organisational culture. *Australian Journal of Management and Organisational Behaviour* 3(2). 91–99.

Wittgenstein, Ludwig. 2009. *Philosophical investigations*. Hoboken, NJ: John Wiley & Sons.

Wittgenstein, Ludwig. 2013. *Tractatus logico-philosophicus*. New York: Routledge.

Wuggenig, Ulf, Gerald Raunig & Gene Ray. 2011. *Critique of creativity: Precarity, subjectivity and resistance in the 'creative industries'*. London: MayFly.

Zald, Mayer N. & Michael A. Berger. 1978. Social movements in organizations: Coup d'etat, insurgency, and mass movements. *American Journal of Sociology* 83(4). 823–861.

Zanin, Alaina C. & Ryan S. Bisel. 2019. Concertive resistance: How overlapping team identifications enable collective organizational resistance. *Culture and Organization* 26(3). 231–249.

Zanoni, Patrizia, Alessia Contu, Stephen Healy & Raza Mir. 2017. Postcapitalistic politics in the making: The imaginary and praxis of alternative economies. *Organization* 24(5). 575–588.

Zoller, Heather M. 2003. Working out: Managerialism in workplace health promotion. *Management Communication Quarterly* 17(2). 171–205.

Zoller, Heather M. 2013. Power and resistance in organizational communication. In Linda L. Putnam & Dennis K. Mumby (eds.), *The Sage handbook of organizational communication*, 3rd edn., 595–618. Thousand Oaks, CA: Sage.

Zoller, Heather M. & Gail T. Fairhurst. 2007. Resistance leadership: The overlooked potential in critical organization and leadership studies. *Human Relations* 60(9). 1331–1360.

Christine Domke and Matthias Klemm

7 Tweeting

Abstract: In this chapter top-managers' "tweeting" practice is investigated as a current challenge for organizational and management communication. The empirical analysis of selected tweets conducted by Siemens' CEO Joe Kaeser shows the emergence of the role set of the "microblogging manager" within the triangle of a critical audience, the managers' self-presentation and their occupational position as decision-makers in companies. Research conducted so far has mainly focused on the (organizational or personal) intentions or styles of Twittering, but has left out the constitutive role of the audience and its assessment of CEOs' tweets. Future research will have to take the interactional aspect of Tweeting into account. The chapter starts with theoretical reflections on digital management communication from a combined sociological and pragma-linguistic perspective, elaborates the basic structure of Twitter, discusses current findings, presents results of the analysis of CEOs' tweets and discusses their implications for further research activities.

Keywords: digital communication; top manager; self-presentation; decision-making; microblogging

It seems evident and by now a commonplace that a proper understanding and analysis of organizations has to be based on a process-orientated perspective rather than on an approach assuming rigid structures. As we know from Karl Weick's (1979) conclusive and original work, the image of an organization as based on rationality and precise objectives is misleading. Echoing March and Simon's ([1958] 1993; Simon 1945) notion of "bounded rationality" as well as their conceptions of decision-making processes as random instead of calculated ones, Weick (1979) and Luhmann (2018) have shaped the concept of organizations as social entities produced and reproduced by empirical rather than logical forms and practices of communication.

This research orientation, which focuses on ongoing processes instead of firmly established structures has had a lasting impact on organizational research as communication has been put at the center of attention in the research on organizations. Different approaches and theoretical orientations, ranging from conversation analysis (Samra-Fredericks 2004) to Luhmann's (1995) systems theory, from Critical Discourse Analysis (Fairclough 2005) to Giddens' (1984) theory of structuration, share this common interest in communication (e. g., Boden 1994; Wodak and Weiss 2001; Habscheid 2003; Domke 2006). It is also programmatically discussed under the term Communicative Constitution of Organization (CCO), as in this volume (see also Schoeneborn et al. 2014).

Since the late 1980s, CCO approaches have proposed to understand communication both as the key process bringing organizations into being and the empirical "substance" of their very existence (see Cooren et al. 2011), even if some of the theories subsumed under CCO go back further. This applies above all to the concept of decision-making, which has been an object of analysis and reflection since the 1930s (e. g., in Barnard's [1938] work) and was investigated by Luhmann (1995, 1997, 2018) and Weick (1979). Empirical studies have especially highlighted decision-making as a crucial practice in the "making" of organizations (Boden 1994; Domke 2006; Menz 2000).

This orientation towards decision-making, i. e., organizing as an ongoing practice, has also led to a large number of studies in which different practices such as advising, negotiating, selling, and different genres of communication such as meetings, emails, and telephone calls in the organization were examined as constitutive of organization (see Domke 2011). Today, the analysis of communication thus appears extremely relevant for the development of management theory. For management itself has to be seen as a (more or less reflexive) bundle of techniques and practices of communication, too. This is even more the case in the light of newly emerging forms of communication triggered by the larger process of the digitalization of society and its communicative infrastructure.

With new forms of communication, such as digital texting and multimodal storytelling (Remus and Rademacher 2018), the choice of appropriate communication has to be considered as a permanent challenge for any organization and especially its management (see below). Surprisingly, there are still few empirical studies on the challenges that management and today's managers are facing due to the establishment of these new digital practices. In this chapter, we would therefore like to highlight one of these current communicative tasks, that is, CEOs' use of Twitter. We assume a growing relevance of managerial self-presentation in social media, a self-presentation that also reshapes the contemporary interpretation of what management consists of. We thus propose to combine a sociological approach to management with a pragma-linguistic perspective on organizational communication in order to understand how CEOs present themselves through Twitter texting.

Our empirical study of Twitter posts conducted by Siemens' CEO Joe Kaeser focuses on two aspects: the use of Twitter by CEOs in its basic structure, on the one hand, and the link of this new communicative challenge to the changing profile of management, on the other. While Section 1 discusses managers' current profile, Section 2 explains the basic logic of Twitter as a social media platform. In Section 3, we then present tweeting as a new practice – and challenge – for CEOs, a presentation that is followed, in Section 4, by our empirical analysis *per se*. The results are summed up in Section 5.

1 Theory of management, theory of communicating management

An approach towards organizations that focuses on communication as mentioned above must, on the one hand, distinguish communication procedures and practices from other forms of action, e.g., bodily performance. For instance, a company producing and selling cars needs people to move things around, use skills and technology to build, transport, and hand over sold products and so on. We refer to these kinds of "doings" when we speak of bodily performance. Very roughly speaking, communication can then be understood as the formative and reflexive part of organizational action whereas bodily (and technical) aspects can be seen as translating the meaning circulating in communication into practical and material levels of performance. In other words, communication has its own "place" in time-space-activity, it has its own material and medial dignity and logic (Alexander 2019; Brandom 2001; Luhmann 1995; Schatzki [2010] 2013), which has been focused on and elaborated by approaches such as ethnomethodology, workplace studies, and conversation analysis (Domke and Holly 2011) as well as the CCO approach in organizational studies (Cooren et al. 2011). This first line of inquiry leads to the conclusion that management is always and necessarily a communicative form of doing.

On the other hand, we have to distinguish different contexts of communication. Everyday life communication within organizations is not always identical with decision-making communication, let alone with management. For example, private communication at the desk with colleagues is *as such* not considered to be part of formal organizational communication. And regardless of whether management is understood more narrowly as decision-making or in broader terms as the hierarchical structuring of power relations in general, many utterances, knowledge-based reports, technical innovations, and the like cannot and should not be understood as managerial processes.

But how should we theoretically distinguish between communication as a managerial process and other forms of organizational communication? Unfortunately, management theory often reflects on action taken by management as being opposed to organizational action as if the control of a social system could be set apart from the system in question (see Gottwald et al. 2007). In contrast to this externalistic view, management can be better described with the CCO framework. For instance, McPhee and Zaug (2000) suggested to differentiate "communicative flows" with respect to interorganizational functions, i.e., "membership negotiation", "self-structuring", "activity coordination", and "institutional positioning".

Although this typological approach carries a certain functional bias, it highlights the autogenetic dynamic of organizational structuring: it is within "communicative flows" that management has to be made visible and explicit as specific binding and directional speech acts carried out by people appointed to legitimately do so (see

Bourdieu 1992). As Mintzberg (1989) discussed and Luhmann (2018) elaborated, management has to be formally defined as an occupational position providing power and status. Management theory, which we will refer to as management concepts in the following sections, further elaborates managerial appearance in organizational communication.

Early management concepts stressed individual exceptionality as managers' defining characteristics who, back then, still mostly were company owners. The idea of the manager as a business leader or entrepreneur with highflying skills and outstanding decision competences can still be found in theories of leadership, especially in the global context (Bartlett and Ghoshal 2003). These approaches to leadership carry on Schumpeter's (1942) way of conceiving of entrepreneurship as well as his concept of "creative destruction".[1] However, at the same time, business theorists started to conceptualize management as a (scientific) profession set apart from the question of ownership (Pross and Boetticher 1971). In this line of argumentation, management is not made visible by outstanding performers of management roles but by rationalized and formalized decision programs of business administration. In recent debates, the idea of a post heroic management came up emphasizing a horizontal relationship between management and the organization (Baecker 1994).

However, Mintzberg (1989: 354) strongly rejects the aforementioned vision of a rational and therefore more or less technical form of management, which he calls "thin management", and presents as "aggregated, analytical, detached". He also claims that Fayol's classical theory of leadership (planning, organizing, coordinating, and controlling) is more "folklore" than reality. In contrast to this model, he shows that management activities are highly fractioned and have much to do with fulfilling external expectations in a constant flux of talking to different stakeholders within and outside the firms. Mintzberg (1989) works on a descriptive rather than a prescriptive model of management and identifies three clusters of empirical management roles: interpersonal, informational, and decisional roles. He then develops no less than ten roles of managerial action, which are in part contradictory but add up to a "gestalt" of the modern management to be performed by people holding managerial positions in companies (the "figurehead", "leader", "liaison", "monitor", "disseminator", "spokesman", "entrepreneur", "disturbance handler", "resource allocator", and "negotiator") (Mintzberg 1989: 15–24).

This short discussion of how management is generally conceived thus defines this activity as the ongoing result of communicative practices carried out by people occupying a social position called manager. The position is part of an occupational system provided by organizations and at the same time embedded into the organizational environment. We can identify at least three dimensions of these practices: first,

---

[1] Critics argue that this kind of personalizing management task serves the need for legitimizing high incomes for the management class (e. g., Hansen 1992).

we find functional prerequisites within the organizational division of labor, i.e., classical management tasks; second, management deals with the accountability of decision-making, allowing to remember, alter, and develop the past, present, and future decisions; third, visibility and accessibility of organizations via management allows the establishment of an organizational identity in different medial environments.

These dimensions can only be developed if communication procedures are made explicit, media channels make them accessible, and positions within the occupational system of a company such as executive ranks are legitimately connected to their fulfillment. The question then arises as to how management is altered if the communicative media environment undergoes a far reaching social and technical change. Social media and – in our case – Twitter as a microblogging service represent and enhance such a changing medial environment of organizations. We assume that microblogging poses additional expectations towards professional managerial appearance and adds new tasks to the list of management competencies. At the same time, we assume that conceiving of CEO's texting as a managerial practice and microblogging as a new form of management communication sheds some light on how social media use alters the extension of what it means to be a manager, especially regarding the relation between organization, top management, and personal responsibility.

In the next sections, we will discuss the most recent changes in a manager's appearance in relation to microblogging in general and to Twitter in particular and present the basic logic of this recent trend of management communication in relation to media history. Afterwards, we will elaborate on this communication form as new and formative for the role of today's managers using the example of Kaeser's Twitter account.

2 Twitter, tweets, and tweeting: basic structure and logic of a new communication form

Founded in 2006, Twitter is a microblogging service that currently has approximately 330 million active users per month. Around 145 million people use this digital service worldwide every day (see, e.g., Poleshova 2020). In the USA, for example, usage is more widespread than in Germany: while about 68 million or rather a good 20 percent of Americans tweet monthly, in Germany it is an estimated 2 million or almost 3 percent a day (see, e.g., ARD/ZDF-Forschungskommission 2020). In contrast to other members of the social media family, Twitter therefore has relatively few users. However, since a comparatively large number of so-called multipliers such as journalists and politicians actively use Twitter, the spread of tweets and thus the communicative potential is much higher (see Mergel 2012; Pleil and Zerfass 2014). This is one of the reasons why Twitter has received a lot of attention as a relevant practice of communication, which has been widely discussed in the field of politics (e.g., Thimm, Dang-Anh, and

Einspänner 2014, 2011; Emmer 2017), but less so in the field of management (e. g., Kubowicz Malhotra and Malhotra 2016).

Twitter initially enabled short messages with only 140 unicode characters, but since 2017 this has been expanded to 280 characters. Twitter can be reached via a website of the same name and is viewed as a social network that Thimm, Dang-Anh, and Einspänner (2011) refer to as a "discourse system". Twitter enables the creation of an account (there are currently around 1.4 billion worldwide) and the posting of short messages as well as the subscription and reading of messages from others, which is also possible without having accounts but only through self-search and with some restrictions. The discrepancy between the number of Twitter accounts and that of active twitterers illustrates different forms of benefit: relatively few active twitterers generate a lot of attention and obviously a lot of reading material and information for a large number of only "passive" readers (see below).

In terms of media-linguistic terminology, Twitter can initially be seen as a communication practice that can be used for different pragmatic purposes (see below). It is primarily visually perceptible, it can be produced via non-place-bound media such as notebooks or smartphones, and it makes it possible to directly address a selected group of followers. This selective form of addressing of a locatable and numerable group at the meso level (see Domke 2014: 159–180) is a decisive advantage of using Twitter as interested subscribers can be addressed quickly, economically, and systematically (Mergel 2012; Pleil and Zerfass 2014).

Tweets' semiotic resources are words, images, and gifs, even if words are given a central function, given the shortness of the messages (Dang-Anh, Einspänner, and Thimm 2013: 150–151). The brevity often corresponds to a speech act performed on a specific topic (e. g., through comments, evaluations, arguments) and shapes the linguistic creativity which can be disseminated and linked by four Twitter operators (Dang-Anh 2019; Klemm and Michel 2014; Thimm, Dang-Anh, and Einspänner 2011): (1) the operator @ makes it possible to address and mention someone and therefore to communicate directly with this person; (2) a hyperlink or URL facilitates linking to a website and thus referring to complex texts and other semiotic resources; (3) the retweet function allows the retweeting of a posting in order to comment, multiplicate, and cite it; and (4) the hashtag (#) enables keywording, indexing, and (re-)contextualization.

It is the fourth operator, the hashtag, which is the central characteristic of Twitter texts. Mergel (2012: 38) describes this function: "A hashtag, denoted by the # sign in front of a keyword, is used as a categorization technique: the hashtag highlights specific keywords in a tweet that can then be used as search terms throughout the Twitter universe". As we will see, its pragmatic potential seems particularly important for CEO's postings. With one or more hashtags, a topic can be stated concisely and at the same time a context can be established through the resulting inter- and intramedial connection to other – even future – texts, in which the respective text is to be understood (Dang-Anh 2019: 146–148, see below).

The more a hashtag is used, the more attention is paid to the subject tagged with it, which means that this subject may become a "trending topic" (Mergel 2012: 38). By using a hashtag, a tweet (re-)produces – in the ethnomethodological sense of "ongoing accomplishment" (see Domke and Holly 2011: 266) – the context in which the contribution has to be interpreted (see Domke 2006: 62–64): "In this sense hashtags as contextualization hints are practical to the core: They refer to trans-situational practical contexts, create them, modify them" (Dang-Anh 2019: 151, our translation). For the CEOs' use of Twitter, there is an advantage to this practice, which enables topic setting and contextualization at this meso level instead of using established (and often tedious) mass media channels (Pleil and Bastian 2016). It is not uncommon for topics to be established at the (digital) meso level via Twitter or Facebook, the success and relevance of which can then be seen in the successive dissemination through mass media reports (see below).

It is, so to speak, constitutive for hashtags to refer to other texts and to generate text (types) networks and thereby to ensure continuous communication. This means that there is a considerable communication potential for users interested in reaching the general public and customers as well as influencing opinions. By using Twitter and using hashtags functionally, CEOs have the opportunity to initiate topics "and influence online conversations. Rather than waiting for impressions to be driven by the media or individuals with ulterior motives, CEOs can use tweeting to help shape their public image and that of their companies" (Kubowicz Malhotra and Malhotra 2016: 74). This includes both opportunities and challenges for managers, which will be discussed in the next section.

3 CEO-tweeting: a new managerial role set?

According to what we highlighted above, the communicative construction of management in general and of the role of executive management in particular have evolved in the course of time. The different ways of conceiving of management reflect its changing meaning and the evolution of the different tasks managers are expected to exert. Specific tasks, as we saw, are connected with the CEOs' role. Individuals who are CEOs both represent "their" companies to the outer world and are also expected to set the basic strategy and the moral compass of "their" companies with respect to the workforce. They are therefore supposed to bridge the gap between the organization and its various social environments. In the past, this role was shaped by the ideas of industrial leadership to be later associated with the function of professional bureaucrats (executives) often defined as highly distinguished members of the social elite of the host countries of their companies (see Boltanski and Chiapello 2005; Pohlmann and Bär 2009).

With the rise of social media, a new type of CEO is said to have emerged: the CEO as an "activist" (Chatterji and Toffel 2019). Chatterji and Toffel (2019) discuss a change in the CEOs' action from a "traditional" orientation, which was rather "nonconfrontational" (Chatterji and Toffel 2019: 48), to an orientation that consists of "raising awareness" for societal problems (e. g., with reference to discrimination or climate change) and "exerting economic influence" (Chatterji and Toffel 2019: 48). Kubowicz Malhotra and Malhotra (2016) identify four types of CEOs who use Twitter: "generalists", "expressionists", "information mavens", and "business mavens". With reference to the CEO as an "activist" as discussed above, here it is the "expressionist" who uses Twitter "extensively for non-business content sharing" (Kubowicz Malhotra and Malhotra 2016: 75). While the authors doubt that the influence of this group is important, they generally attribute a lot of potential to Twitter in addressing stakeholders and customers (Kubowicz Malhotra and Malhotra 2016: 72).

This is also noted by Mergel (2012) and Pleil and Zerfass (2014), the latter emphasizing that there still seems to be no agreement on the appropriate and optimal use of Twitter (Pleil and Zerfass 2014: 3). A more recent case study of a Swedish bank CEO comes to a similar conclusion: an intensification of Twitter use is observed, albeit in a rather impersonal style. The authors conclude that a discrepancy can be observed between far reaching but hypothetical expectations connected to the use of microblogging on the one hand and missing empirical knowledge on CEOs' Twitter use and their effects on business and reputation on the other hand (Grafström and Falkman 2017). Obviously, social media and especially Twitter do play a role in the genesis of new types of CEO role sets, e. g., the "activist". However, this new option must be treated with caution: it is currently not clear what consequences this new level of media performance will have for the expectations of CEOs and their profile. The relation between person and role is another area of uncertainty.

To sum up the Twittersphere holds specific challenges for CEOs. These challenges are often mentioned and can also be explained by the basic communication structure of Twitter (see above). These challenges include the following dynamics and aspects of social media, especially Twitter:

- communication on Twitter is asymmetrical (one to some) between active producers and far more passive consumers or specifically addressable followers (see Domke 2019: 178–179). This asymmetry only partially enables interaction in the sense of mutual exchange (see Geser 2011);
- most members of the Twittersphere are consumers, while a relatively small group of distinct users such as journalists, activists, and scientists drives the action, using Twitter to multiply content, get information, and generate relevance on the meso level of selected addressing and dissemination;
- Twitter is a mobile device of communication that enables inexpensive communication anywhere at any time and carries the potential to generate attention in a short period of time (Kubowicz Malhotra and Malhotra 2016);
- the impact of Twitter reaches beyond the digital sphere: for many professional users, Twitter represents the place of the "crystallization of public judgement" (see Geser 2011: 16), which is then carried to other media channels.

Many company leaders are not yet represented on Twitter. And up to now, tweeting cannot be regarded as an institutionalized aspect of the CEO's role (see also Porter, Anderson, and Nhotsavang 2015). Furthermore, CEOs' postings are postings of individuals who also happen to be executives of large companies. In other words, they are not part of the official Twitter accounts of their respective companies. But if CEOs tweet, the following questions seem central in the light of the considerations so far:

1) How do CEOs deal with Twitter's own challenge of brevity and creativity?
2) For what pragmatic purposes do CEOs use Twitter?
3) Which requirements for the "new" profile of the manager become clear? Does using Twitter impose distinctive requirements on managers?
4) To what extent does the use of Twitter and other forms of microblogging become a balancing act between personal and functional communication?

Taking up these questions, the CEO-Twitter relation is empirically examined in the next section. We will develop three interrelated theses: first, the CEO's microblogging under examination revolves around the distinction between the individual character who also occupies the role of a CEO and the professional CEO role. Second, intensification and reciprocal interaction occur in cases when other Twitter users put the CEO's self-presentation in question. Third, the CEO's role in the making is not a question of voluntary action but is shaped by the digital co-users and consumers as well as media-driven expectations.

4 CEOs and the Twittersphere

As mentioned above, the CEOs' Twitter use is associated with numerous questions and challenges. So far, there has been comparatively little empirical research that explores the pragmatics and consequences of authentic CEO postings. We are interested in the influence of Twitter on the profiling of CEOs as high-rank managers in the occupational structure of companies. In the context of this chapter, we would like to concentrate only on one account: Jo Kaeser's, CEO of Siemens, a so-called global operating company with its headquarters located in Germany.

The empirical dataset consists of about 120 tweets that Kaeser posted from January 2019 until March 2020, including the follow-up comments by the audience. We will also refer to public debates in other media, but only if they are directly connected to the Twitter practices. All data used in our analysis is publicly available. We analyzed them from a sociological and media-linguistic perspective, as mentioned above. To expand the empirical basis of our research and differentiate the relation between form and function, we selectively compared Kaeser's microblogging activity with postings from other prominent CEOs: Elon Musk and Mary Barra (numbers of followers in 07/2020: Musk 37.8 million; Joe Kaeser: 34.8 thousand; Mary Barra: 51.6 thousand). We applied a typological approach clustering posts with respect to their pragmatic custom. We were then able to identify four dominant modes and functions of postings. Some of the functions are also being investigated in other studies (see above) and all of them can also be found in the Musk and Barra accounts. However, our main focus will be restricted to Kaeser's activity.

4.1 CEOs and Twitter: posts in the personality-profession-audience triangle

First, Kaeser, as any other CEO account we found, is presented as an individual with a picture and personal description. The profile picture shows him facing the viewer with a friendly smile. The cover photo, which is the larger photo behind the profile photo on Twitter, shows him together with Siemens employees, as part of a physically working team. In the picture, we see him interacting with men, apparently at a construction site of the group. Kaeser's special status comes into its own here because everyone is facing him. He is, so to speak, the focus of their attention. In the description of his profile ("One of 386,000 dedicated Siemens employees worldwide. Passionate about innovation, inclusive capitalism & transformation of business & society. Enjoys 70s music"), he makes himself linguistically an equal part of a team "one of …" and specifies personal preferences by referring to 1970s music. There is no identification of him as a CEO of Siemens, only the Siemens logo, which is visible in the picture, and the link in the description to Siemens make the connection clear. It is therefore the absence of a functional description that clarifies his special status: you just know or should know.

The post we have chosen to analyze for this section is from January 24, 2019. The post's written text reads: "We can't change history, but will make sure that the Holocaust is never forgotten! We'll fight #antisemitism and any kind of #racism and #intolerance. #WeRemember #Auschwitz75 #HolocaustMemorialDay". The post also includes a photo with Kaeser standing in front of a fence, immediately indicating the context of a concentration camp. He is holding a note with "#WeRemember" on it. At the time of our screenshot, the post had 53 likes, 873 comments, and 128 retweets. The two syntactically closed sentences of the post contain statements about the culture of remembrance in relation to Nazi crimes and thus topics that obviously include non-business content (see below).

The hashtags #antisemitsm, #racism, and #intolerance are syntactically embedded in the second sentence and thus appear not only as contextualization hints (see Section 3), but also as keywording for the discourses they call up. The personal attitude towards the memory discourse, racism, and anti-semitism is visually marked by the placement of Joe in front of the fence with the sign in his hand. His facial expression is serious, the use of the hashtag on the sign seems noticeable: the call for reminder in the form of a hashtag uses the functions of hashtags (keywording, topic setting, etc., see Section 3), but also the option of media processing (distribution, follow-up communication, etc.). At the same time, it transforms the memory discourse through the sign into the Twittersphere: collective memory on the Internet can or should take place in this way (see, e. g., Burkhardt 2017; Titze 2020). Regarding the function of hashtags (see Dang-Anh 2019: 148–150) we could identify this post as "stance making".

The author put himself in the position of traditional moral authorities such as church representatives. Reactions to these forms of self-presentation in the comments were mostly negative (e. g., as "cheap marketing", as Hajo Müller wrote in an answer on February 4, 2019) fueled by moral conflicts in which the company is entangled. People appeared not to buy it and to reject the CEO's moral authority because he is identified with a negative image of a rent-seeking company, exploiting, destroying, or wasting ecological resources. The CEO's call for moral action was therefore interpreted as a distraction from the alleged immoral behavior of the company (related, in this case, to environmental issues). In other words, the audience, which he addressed via the choice of historical and moral hashtags (see Dang-Anh 2019: 153), forced the role as CEO of Siemens onto Kaeser, whether he was actually tweeting as Siemens' CEO or not. The audience held him responsible as Siemens' CEO even if he has not established his account as CEO and chose a non-professional topic.

As Kaeser actually performed his "new" role as a moral authority in this posting, the audience reacted to it by addressing him as CEO with a special responsibility for company decisions. This type of role conflict and ambivalence can also be found in other of his posts.

4.2 CEOs and Twitter: (re-)presenting images of the company – and of its leaders

Other posts seem directly connected to company activities. To be more precise, they deal with changes in the company's policy with regard to public expectations. In the post from November 8, 2019, Kaeser took up the topic "diversity" while congratulating Siemens' new Chief Diversity Officer, Maria Ferraro.

Figure 1: Post by Joe Kaeser on November 8, 2019

The posting includes a retweet from a post in the press department with Kaeser's own comment: he congratulates the employee as the new diversity officer and thanks her. By listing outstanding features such as work-family balance and a "metropolitan mindset", this post delivers both a content-based explanation and legitimation for choosing Maria. At the same time, it becomes clear what he, as CEO, understands by core competencies for a diversity officer. By formulating it and congratulating her, one could also affirm that he also refers to his own competence in assessing the field of diversity and its challenges.

The direct naming of "Maria" as well as the listing of her competencies suggests familiarity with and knowledge of each other. The company thus appears progressive, family-friendly, women-promoting, a company that carefully chooses the best-fitting individuals for top management tasks. Two exclamation marks emphasize his statement, which implies that the "diversity" topic seems to arouse enthusiasm. In short, the post carries a specific modern image of the company and its management crew (in a way that one would expect it also from a company newsletter). Furthermore, it demonstrates a form of social proximity of the group of top managers, both personal and skill-related, to which the CEO and now also Maria belong. But note that the CEO himself is projected as not having taken a direct part in Maria's nomination. Rather, he congratulates, in the sense of Goffman (1981), as a "bystander" who is part of the top management.

4.3 CEOs and Twitter: choosing topics and drawing attention

Less prominent but nevertheless important are posts that obviously react to public arousal regarding the behavior of Siemens as a capitalist company. The following posts deal with Kaeser reacting to moral accusations directed towards his company. In this case, he directly addresses a specific audience and acknowledges their moral authority and concerns:

Figure 2: Post by Joe Kaeser on December 15, 2019

This type of outwards-directed post reacting to claims regarding responsibility or moral concerns is often taken up and further disseminated and discussed through different media channels such as television or newspapers – just as the initial topic had started outside of Twitter. An economic engagement of Siemens regarding the delivering of parts for an Australian coal mine had indeed led to a major public outcry. In various media, activists from the "Fridays for Future" movement accused the German company of environmental destruction and having a bad business model.

We can identify five relevant elements in the post: first, from the outset, we see Kaeser accepting the moral authority of "everyone" while protest is turned into "reaching out", that is, into a legitimate call for an explanation. In addition, criticism is gratefully accepted, which means that the "accused" – at least linguistically – becomes a "friendly actor" thanking others. Second, he presents himself as "I", which amounts to positioning him as the legitimate addressee of the call but not necessarily as one who has actual oversight of the case in question. For a CEO, this seems to be a rather surprising reaction ("I was not aware [...]") as it displays a form of detachment from certain company decisions. Third, he then displays his functional authority within the company as he promises to investigate the matter. Fourth, he sends direct assurance to both his readers and the Siemens company, addressed via @Siemens, claiming that his action might or might not change prior decisions of the company. Fifth, in the last sentence, the audience is again addressed, but now in a different manner: as concerned citizens who "deserve" something and to whom he, Kaeser, personally promises an answer.

The promised answer was in fact given via Twitter on January 12, 2020, roughly three weeks after the first post. Kaeser texted: "Just finished our extraordinary Management Board Meeting. We evaluated all options and concluded: We need to fulfil our contractual obligations [...]". In contrast to the original post, this text now refers not to an individual "I" but to a collective "we" (the management board). Kaeser refers to organizational accountability and the basic economic rule "*pacta sunt servanda*" ('agreements must be kept'). As a member of the management board, his hands seem to be tied by different types of obligation, i.e., the ethos of the businessman running a trustworthy organization.

The discrepancy between the person and the function surfaces yet again and thus, in a certain way, the risks of personal tweeting. This serious negotiation of the position as a person and as CEO of a company is also made clear by the fact that the posts have few hashtags: the contextualization is not the public discourse as analyzed in Section 4.1 but takes place through personal and organizational statements. With the exception of #Adani, the addressing of an audience takes place specifically through personal pronouns, not through the usual Twitter operators (such as @ and #, see Section 3). This is "only" about him and Siemens.

4.4 CEOs and Twitter: self-referentiality or discussing the CEO microblogging role

We picked one last post that stands out from the others because it is written not in English but in German. On November 8, 2019, Kaeser found himself charged with criticism regarding his style of microblogging, as his blogs were described as too "pathetic" and "philosophical". In this tweet, he compared his style to that of a US CEO who was not named but described as a hash-smoking individual. Kaeser complained about his colleague getting positive attention as a visionary for speaking about "*Peterchens Mondfahrt*" ('Little Peter's journey to the Moon') while he, Kaeser, is criticized for his "proactive" steering of Siemens towards a better future.

Kaeser's post was immediately heavily attacked both on Twitter and in the business press. The audience immediately delivered the information that Kaeser did not directly mention in his post. They named the attacked CEO, his projects and style as well as internal leadership decisions at Siemens: Kaeser spoke of Elon Musk, his company SpaceX (which is as Tesla an important customer of Siemens), and an appraisal of Musk's "dreams" and visions by another senior Siemens manager (again posted on Twitter). It was also mentioned that Musk has far more followers on Twitter than Kaeser (see above). Musk's postings do in fact contain more entertaining content and information which are far more personalized and private than any of Kaeser's tweets.

In our analysis of this high-impact and cross-medial conversation about the role of CEO's posts, we can identify two types of pressure that appear to reshape digital management communication: the media logic of self-presentation beyond the functional role and the role set of management itself. Musk, like some others such as Steve Jobs or Mark Zuckerberg, is perceived not only in his role of CEO but also as a represent of the revival of the business leader who acts as a charismatic societal entrepreneur. In fact, Musk acts and presents himself accordingly (visionary, individually, disregarding ordinary rules of behavior). His digital "habitus" (e. g., posting a dog meme on March 3, 2019) seems to fit best to the overall logic of Twitter: the topics chosen in his posts such as business, entertainment, and events create a lot of followers and everything he does seems to be of public interest. In contrast, CEOs like Kaeser are seen as high-ranking officers, i. e., as employees. Their "me-forming" activities (Riemer et al. 2011: 2) and moral statements are therefore made with respect to their occupational role in the company (even if they do not explicitly mention it).

5 Conclusion

As we tried to show, management and management communication are changing under the influence of social media. Prescriptive models of managerial self-presentation are put to the test in these highly volatile arenas of communication. The "gestalt" (Mintzberg 1989) of managerial appearance is altered when CEOs and other administrative members enter the microblogging sphere in their double role as individuals and company representatives. The digital transformation of managerial communication is still on its way.

So far, organizational research has often stressed the general challenges and opportunities provided by Twitter and other social media platforms (Kubowicz Malhotra and Malhotra 2016; Mergel 2012; Pleil and Zerfass 2014). However, from a CCO perspective, management can also be seen as constituted via communication practices, forms, and contexts (see, e. g., Cooren et al. 2011). Following this approach, we focused on a CEO's pragmatic use of microblogging by discussing a small sample of his posts. Our findings suggest that the new role of the microblogging manager emerges in the triangle of occupational expectations, a new need for medial individual self-presentation, and an ever-watching audience critically assessing what these microblogging managers post. This holds especially true for the relation between the manager's moral integrity as a publicly accessible individual and the decisions made by "her" company. Microblogging as a collaborative interaction of managers and the audience seems in our view to re-personalize decision-making at the top of large-scale companies.

Digital media are currently changing the visibility of the role of the CEO, which means that they need to adapt to these changing environments. One central result of our analysis is that the categorical attribution of twittering CEOs either as, for instance, generalists or expressionists (Kubowicz Malhotra and Malhotra 2016) is not tenable. All of the accounts examined include professional, entertaining, and personal posts – albeit with different frequencies. The role of the CEO as a microblogger obviously cannot be determined by focusing on the topic managers' posts or by the self-presentation they adopt. The reshaping of the "gestalt" takes place in public communication within the personality-profession-audience triangle.

6 References

Alexander, Jeffrey C. 2019. *What makes a social crisis? The societalization of social problems*. Cambridge: Polity Press.
ARD/ZDF-Forschungskommission. 2020. Nutzung von Social Media/WhatsApp 2020. ARD/ZDF Onlinestudie. http://www.ard-zdf-onlinestudie.de/whatsapponlinecommunities/ (accessed 17 August 2020).
Baecker, Dirk. 1994. *Postheroisches Management. Ein Vademecum*. Leipzig: Merve Verlag.
Barnard, Chester I. 1938. *The functions of the executive*. Cambridge, MA: Harvard University Press.
Bartlett, Christopher A. & Sumantra Ghoshal. 2003. What is a global manager? *Harvard Business Review* August. 101–108.
Boden, Deirdre. 1994. *The business of talk: Organizations in action*. Cambridge: Polity Press.
Boltanski, Luc & Ève Chiappelo. 2005. *The new spirit of capitalism*. London: Verso.

Bourdieu, Pierre. 1992. *Language and symbolic power*. Cambridge: Polity Press.
Brandom, Robert B. 2001. *Begründen und Begreifen. Eine Einführung in den Inferentialismus*. Frankfurt am Main: Suhrkamp.
Burkhardt, Hannes. 2017. Erinnerungskulturen im Social Web. Auschwitz und der Europäische Holocaustgedenktag auf Twitter. In Uwe Danker (ed.), *Geschichtsunterricht – Geschichtsschulbücher – Geschichtskultur. Aktuelle geschichtsdidaktische Forschungen des wissenschaftlichen Nachwuchses. Mit einem Vorwort von Thomas Sandkühler*, 213–236. Göttingen: Vandenhoeck & Ruprecht.
Chatterji, Aaron K. & Michael W. Toffel. 2019. The new CEO activists. In *HBR's must reads. The definitive management ideas of the year from Harvard Business Review*, 47–65. Boston, MA: Harvard Business Review Press.
Cooren, Francois, Timothy Kuhn, Joep P. Cornelissen & Timothy Clark. 2011. Communication, organizing and organization: An overview and introduction to the special issue. *Organization Studies* 32(9). 1–22.
Dang-Anh, Mark. 2019. *Protest twittern. Eine medienlinguistische Untersuchung von Strassenprotesten*. Bielefeld: Trancript. https://doi.org/10.14361/9783839448366 (accessed 17 August 2020).
Dangh-Anh, Mark, Jessica Einspänner & Caja Thimm. 2013. Kontextualisierung durch Hashtags. die Mediatisierung des politischen Sprachgebrauchs im Internet. In H. Diekmannshenke & T. Niehr (eds.), *Öffentliche Wörter. Analysen zum öffentlich-medialen Sprachgebrauch*, 137–159. Stuttgart: Ibidem.
Domke, Christine. 2006. *Besprechungen als organisationale Entscheidungskommunikation*. Berlin: De Gruyter.
Domke, Christine. 2011. Organisationale Kommunikationstypen. In Stephan Habscheid (ed.), *Textsorten, Handlungsmuster, Oberflächen*, 206–230. Berlin & Boston, MA: De Gruyter.
Domke, Christine. 2014. *Die Betextung des öffentlichen Raumes. Eine Studie zur Spezifik von Meso-Kommunikation am Beispiel von Bahnhöfen, Innenstädten und Flughäfen* (Reihe Wissenschaft und Kunst, Band 26). Heidelberg: Verlag Winter.
Domke, Christine. 2019. Meso-Kommunikation zwischen Stadt/Netz. Zur Struktur alternativer Kommunikationswege. In Stefan Hauser, Roman Opilowski & Eva L. Wyss (eds.), *Alternative Öffentlichkeiten. Soziale Medien zwischen Partizipation, Sharing und Vergemeinschaftung* (Edition Medienwissenschaften, Band 35), 167–190. Bielefeld: Transcript.
Domke, Christine & Werner Holly. 2011 Foundations: Ethnomethodology and Erving Goffman. In Wolfram Bublitz & Neal R. Norrick (eds.), *Foundations of pragmatics* (Handbooks of Pragmatics 1), 261–287. Berlin: Mouton de Gruyter.
Emmer, Martin. 2017. Soziale Medien in der politischen Kommunikation. In Jan-Hinrik Schmidt & Monika Taddicken (eds.), *Handbuch Soziale Medien*, 81–99. Wiesbaden: Springer VS.
Fairclough, Norman. 2005. Peripheral vision: Discourse analysis in organization studies: The case for critical realism. *Organization Studies* 26(6). 915–939.
Geser, Hans. 2011. Has Tweeting become inevitable? Twitter's strategic role in the World of Digital Communication. *Sociology in Switzerland* July. https://socio.ch/intcom/t_hgeser26.pdf (accessed 17 August 2020).
Giddens, Anthony. 1984. *The constitution of society: Outline of the theory of society*. Berkeley and Los Angeles, CA: University of California Press
Goffman, Erving. 1981. *Forms of talk*. Philadelphia, PA: University of Pennsylvania Press.
Gottwald, Markus, Matthias Klemm, Gerd Sebald & Jan Weyand. 2007. Die Heterogenität von Wissen als Herausforderung für organisationales Wissens- und Innovationsmanagement. In Herbert Gronau (ed.), *4. Konferenz Professionelles Wissensmanagement. Erfahrungen und Visionen*, 202–210. Berlin: GITO-Verlag.

Grafström, Maria & Lena Lid Falkman. 2017. Everyday narratives: CEO rhetoric on Twitter. *Journal of Organizational Change Management* 30(3). 312–322.

Habscheid, Stephan. 2003. *Sprache in der Organisation. Sprachreflexive Verfahren im systemischen Beratungsgespräch*. Berlin & New York: De Gruyter.

Hansen, Klaus P. 1992. *Die Mentalität des Erwerbs. Erfolgsphilosophien amerikanischer Unternehmer*. Frankfurt am Main & New York: Campus.

Klemm, Michael & Sascha Michel. 2014. Social TV und Politikaneignung. Wie Zuschauer die Inhalte politischer Diskussionssendungen via Twitter kommentieren. *De Gruyter Mouton Zeitschrift* 60(1). 3–35.

Kubowicz Malhotra, Claudia & Arvind Malhotra. 2016. How CEOs can leverage Twitter: Rather than waiting for impressions about a company to be driven by others in social media, CEOs can help shape the conversation. *MIT Sloan Management Review* 57(2). 72–80.

Luhmann, Niklas. 1995. *Social systems*. Stanford, CA: Stanford University Press.

Luhmann, Niklas. 1997. *Die Gesellschaft der Gesellschaft* (Erster und zweiter Teilband). Frankfurt am Main: Suhrkamp.

Luhmann, Niklas. 2018. *Organization and decision*. Cambridge: Cambridge University Press.

March, James G. & Herbert A. Simon. 1993 [1958]. *Organizations*. Cambridge, MA: Wiley.

McPhee, Robert D. & Pamela Zaug. 2000. The communicative constitution of organizations: A framework for explanation. *Electronic Journal of Communication* 10(1–2). http://www.cios.org/EJCPUBLIC/010/1/01017.html (accessed 17 August 2020).

Menz, Florian. 2000. *Selbst- und Fremdorganisation im Diskurs. Interne Kommunikation in Wirtschaftsunternehmen*. Wiesbaden: Deutscher Universitäts-Verlag.

Mergel, Ines. 2012. *Working the network: A manager's guide for using Twitter in government*. Syracuse, NY: Syracuse University Press.

Mintzberg, Henry. 1989. *Mintzberg on management: Inside our strange world of organizations*. New York & London: Free Press & Collier Macmillan.

Pleil, Thomas & Matthias Bastian. 2016. *Soziale Medien in der externen Organisationskommunikation*. Wiesbaden: Springer Fachmedien.

Pleil, Thomas & Ansgar Zerfass. 2014. Internet und Social Software in der Unternehmenskommunikation. In Manfred Piwinger & Ansgar Zerfass (eds.), *Handbuch Unternehmenskommunikation*, 2nd edn., 731–753. Wiesbaden: Gabler.

Pohlmann, Markus & Stefan Bär. 2009. Grenzenlose Karrieren? – Hochqualifiziertes Personal und Top-Führungskräfte in Ökonomie und Medizin. *Österreichische Zeitschrift für Soziologie* 34(4). 13–40.

Poleshova, A. 2020. Statistiken zu Twitter. Statistika ZHAW. https://de.statista.com/themen/99/twitter/ (accessed 17 August 2020).

Porter, Michael C., Betsy Anderson & Mary Nhotsavang. 2015. Anti-social media: Executive Twitter "engagement" and attitudes about media credibility. *Journal of Communication Management* 19(3). 270–287.

Pross, Helge & Karl W. Boetticher. 1971. *Manager des Kapitalismus*. Frankfurt am Main: Suhrkamp.

Remus, Nadine & Lars Rademacher (eds.). 2018. *Handbuch NGO-Kommunikation*. Wiesbaden: Springer VS.

Riemer, Kai, Stephan Diederich, Alexander Richter & Paul Scifleet. 2011. Short message discussions: On the conversational nature of microblogging in a large consultancy organisation. Paper presented at the 15th Asia Conference on Information Systems (PACIS), Queensland University of Technology, 7–11 July.

Samra-Fredericks, D. (2004). Talk-in-interaction/conversation analysis. In Catherine Cassell & Gillian Symon (eds.), *Essential guide to qualitative methods in organizational research*, 214–227. London: Sage.

Schatzki, Theodore R. 2013 [2010]. *The timespace of human activity: On performance, society and history as indeterminate teleological events*. Lanham, MD: Lexington Books.

Schoeneborn, Dennis, Steffen Blaschke, François Cooren, Robert D. McPhee, David Seidl & James R. Taylor. 2014. The three schools of CCO thinking: Interactive dialogue and systematic comparison. *Management Communication Quarterly* 28(2). 285–316.

Schumpeter, Joseph A. 1942. *Capitalism, socialism & democracy*. New York: Harper & Brothers.

Simon, Herbert A. 1945. *Administrative behavior: A study of decision-making processes in administrative organizations*. New York: The Free Press.

Thimm, Caja, Mark Dang-Anh & Jessica Einspänner. 2011. Diskurssystem Twitter: Semiotische und handlungstheoretische Perspektiven. In Mario Anastasiadis & Caja Thimm (eds.), *Social Media: Theorie und Praxis digitaler Sozialität*, 265–286. Frankfurt am Main & New York: Peter Lang Verlag.

Thimm, Caja, Mark Dang-Anh & Jessica Einspänner. 2014. Mediatized politics: Structures and strategies of discursive participation and online deliberation on Twitter. In Friedrich Krotz & Andreas Hepp (eds.), *Mediatized worlds: Culture and society in a media age*, 253–269. Basingstoke, UK: Palgrave Macmillan.

Titze, Antonia. 2020. Hashtag KZ? KZ-Gedenkstätten und Social Media. *ComSoc Communicatio Socialis* 53(1). 97–108.

Weick, K. E. (1979). *The social psychology of organizing*. New York: Random House.

Wodak, Ruth & Gilbert Weiss. 2001. "We are different than the Americans and the Japanese!" A critical discourse analysis of decision-making in European Union meetings. In Marcelo Dascal & Edda Weigand (eds.), *Negotiation and power in dialogic interaction*, 39–62. Amsterdam: John Benjamins.

Viviane Sergi
8 Documenting

Abstract: This chapter addresses the contribution of documents to management communication. It describes the centrality of documents and documenting practices in organizations and develops an overview of how documents have been conceptualized in a variety of studies. Taking an active and performative view on documenting, it reflects on how documents are fundamentally about value and temporality. Building on insights from the CCO perspective, the chapter finally calls for a renewed interest in the study of documents and documenting, which is deemed especially timely in the context of the current digitalization of organizational activities.

Keywords: documents; documenting; texts; CCO; materialization

Is there anything more banal and ubiquitous in organizations than documents? Documents – in their material or digital form – are so pervasive in organizational settings that we tend to neglect them, take them for granted, or even dismiss them. But when one starts to think about their presence, production, circulation, diffusion, or dissimulation, invocation, manipulation, and archiving – to only name a few of the activities devoted to them – suddenly, the size of the iceberg begins to reveal itself. So many occupations, activities, and processes develop documents and rely heavily on them; so many actions take place before, with, around, and after documents. And so, the scope of writing about documents and documenting looms over whoever attempts to undertake this task. Documenting might seem easy and quick to cover, at first sight, exactly because everybody knows what documents are and how they are produced, especially in the context of managerial practice and organizations. The word evokes a pack of sheets, or a file with words, numbers, and/or figures, all serving to carry information. But as one continues to ponder documents in organizations, the image complexifies, for the simple reason that documents multiply: the more you consider them, the more you note their presence (or imagine their absence and its implications).

Let's do a little exercise: think about a document. What is this mysterious document? Is it a report, a plan, a series of figures? Is it a one-pager, is it in a nice binder, or is it so voluminous that it requires a document holder? Is it fresh out of the printer, is it a PDF file, or has it been retrieved from an obscure (and probably dusty) archive? Is that document to be given to someone, or is it only useful for its author? When was it written? Where is that document going: to someone's desk, to a meeting, to a client outside the organization? Is it meant to stay as an important trace, or was it made in the spur of the moment, only to be put in the recycling bin at the end of the day? And why has this document appeared in this organization (are you too imagining a large organization, vaguely bureaucratic and neutral in color?), why did someone spend time and energy producing it, what role(s) does it fulfill?

The more we project ourselves into this organizational *rêverie*, trying to peel away the layers of what documents are *in* and *to* organizations, the more we feel that a neat and well-circumscribed understanding of them – and of the act of making them – slips away. If documents' physical features can be described without too much trouble, their variety is difficult to grasp and their presence in organizations appears massive. The conclusion quickly becomes obvious: given that documents are everywhere in organizations, documenting must be essential in and to management. Procedures and policies are documents. Standards are documents. Mission statements and strategies are documents. Meeting minutes, forms, budgets, analyses, charts, reports of all kinds, plans, charters, contracts, and bills are all documents.

More importantly for this chapter, each of these documents – and all the others I have not listed here, for the sake of brevity – derive from the act of documenting, in the many forms that it can take. These documents are key in various organizational processes, and they all have to be developed, circulated, and archived, at some point. It does not take long to come to the conclusion highlighted many years ago by Smith (1974, 1984, 2001): documents and documentary practices constitute organizations at an ontological level. Documents and documenting are so integral to what organizations are and to managerial practices that an entire set of encyclopedias could be devoted to exploring all their facets.[1]

This chapter is much more modest in scope. A variety of fields, while touching upon managerial practices, have considered the contribution of documenting to management communication: management and organization studies (MOS) of course, but also science and technology studies (STS), sociology, anthropology, communication, nursing, and social work among many others. This wide variety of studies makes it near to impossible to cover everything that pertains to documenting. I will hence start by offering some elements of description of the centrality of documents and documenting in organizations and will then consider ways in which documents have been studied, developing a short overview of how they and their making have been conceptualized. Highlighting the different ways we can conceive of documents will allow me to get closer to the act of documenting. Building on insights from an array of studies, I will then reflect on two central features of documenting, features that are brought up in a vivid way by a communicative perspective.

This chapter hence has no pretension to be exhaustive; rather, my aim is to provide an overview of documenting, in order to underline the potential of devoting more attention to documents and acts of documenting. This chapter should also be viewed more as a meditation on documenting and documents than a thorough review

---

[1] The same could be said about the use of documents in research and, in fact, such an encyclopedia exists: Prior's four volumes of texts on documents in social research, published in 2011.

of everything that pertains to documents. Prior (2003: 48) summarizes eloquently both the extent of the task of opening up documents, and its relevance:

> Dismantling documents is not an easy task, but it is a worthwhile one, not least because every document is packed tight with assumptions and concepts and ideas that reflect on the agent who produced the document, and its intended recipients, as much as upon the people and events reported upon. For what is counted and how it's counted are expressive of specific and distinctive ways of thinking, acting and organizing.

Convinced of the significance not only of documents, but of their study, both for the fields of organizational communication and organization studies, this chapter will emphasize the potential of taking an active and performative view on documenting. In an age where digitalization is set to transform – albeit partially and in a still unknown fashion – organizations and management, I contend that understanding documenting is more important than ever. Digitalization does not spell the end of documents: in fact, it heightens them, multiplies them, and opens the door to processes of unprecedented scale that may involve documents produced by human and nonhuman actors. It may be more important than ever to give more thought and more consideration to documenting.

1 A first foray into documenting

Before beginning the proposed overview, it can be useful to turn to etymology to shed a first light on documents and documenting. The word *document* is both a noun and a verb in English. As a noun, document comes from the Latin *documentum*, meaning "example, proof, lesson" (Online Etymology Dictionary); in Medieval Latin, document meant an "authoritative paper"; and at the turn of the eighteenth century, document came to mean "written or printed paper that provides proof or evidence". The verb form of the word seems to have appeared in the English language around the same time, meaning "to support by documentary evidence". Modern English tells us that document, as a noun, refers both to something that conveys information (written or created through the use of a computer) and to a form of evidence. As for the verb, to document now commonly designates "to furnish documentary evidence of" something, and simply "to furnish with documents" (Merriam-Webster Dictionary). These etymological and definitional elements highlight a few key aspects of documents: that they derive from writing or inscribing, that they represent proof or evidence of something, and that they offer support.

While these elements are basic, we can already see why documents and documenting are so crucial to organizations: as traces that can carry information through space and time, documents sustain activities. These etymological elements will reappear, from time to time, in the course of this chapter. Documents and texts can be used interchangeably, but in this chapter, documenting refers to a communicative act aiming at keeping a trace of something that is happening and/or attesting to something. Documenting should also be viewed in both its physical (i.e., paper) and its digital form. Documenting can be performed with solely individual aims, or to contribute to collective action. On a more individual basis, keeping a diary can be seen as a form of documenting one's life.

If acts of making documents only for individual use do belong to the broad practice of documenting (and this surely happens in organizational settings for valuable reasons that could be explored), this chapter focuses primarily on documenting intended for others, being part of managerial activities, such as planning, leading, coordinating, regulating, etc. Hence, it mainly considers documenting and documents in the context of interactions, and as pertaining to collective processes. Broadly speaking, I also define documenting as a practice, understood in the sense of Nicolini and Monteiro (2017: 114): "practices are meaning-making, order-producing, and reality-shaping activities. That is, orderly sets of materially mediated doings and sayings aimed at identifiable ends". Applied to documenting, the concept of practice highlights the situated production of an activity and considers how such doing is productive; it also allows inquiring into the structuring of action and into the stabilization and/or destabilization of organization.

Beyond these elements, offering a panorama of documenting is a colossal task because the study of documents is scattered among objects of inquiry, empirical contexts, and even branches of social sciences. Given the highly specialized organization of research, to be exhaustive would imply looking for all forms of documenting, such as memos (e.g., Yates 1989), PowerPoint slides (e.g., Schoeneborn 2013), annual reports (e.g., David 2001), etc., as studies on what belongs to the vast category of documents are not necessarily united by an overarching keyword or perspective. This study is also dispersed in empirical settings: for example, Rot, Borzeix, and Demazière (2014) offer a list of no less than twenty-seven very different contexts in which studies of documenting have been conducted (including shorthand typists, bailiffs, sea workers, inspectors, and farmers, among others), pointing to the wide range of situations in which this practice happens, has been considered, and has been shown as crucial to collective and coordinated action. Furthermore, documenting has been studied by several disciplines, each mobilizing its own set of concerns as prisms to address this practice: beyond organizational communication and organization studies, documenting can be investigated from an information technology (IT) angle, looking at more technical dimensions of documents (the software used to make them, issues pertaining to compatibility of formats, storage and access to documents), or with a library science approach, dealing with the organization and preservation of documents. Finally, to complicate things even more, key aspects of documenting could be discussed in studies that do not have this practice as a main focal point: indeed, since documenting and documents are closely embedded in a wide range of activities, how they pertain to these activities and how they contribute to action may be featured in these studies.

Hence, while documenting appears here and there in social sciences, it is not a unified object of inquiry.[2] This fragmentation, both in theoretical and empirical terms, may explain why research published on documents regularly underlines that not enough attention is given to all forms of documents and paperwork in organizational settings. The issue may not be that of a limited attention, but of a lack of convergence in the studies that attend to documents. At the same time, this lack of convergence may also reveal something quite fundamental and even slightly paradoxical about documenting: while this act belongs to the banal or the mundane (documents are produced all the time in all contexts), its effects can be quite significant (by shaping, structuring, sustaining, etc. – in a word, by contributing to organizing what is done). This makes documenting simultaneously endemic to organizational life, hardly visible and barely noticeable.

Following this observation, where does one start, if one is still interested by documents and not defeated by the above challenges? I propose that a fruitful way to attend to both dimensions of documenting – its mundane character and its organizing effects – is to anchor the inquiry in a resolutely active and performative view. Documenting, understood as a management communication phenomenon and as a practice, focuses on what document making does *in* and *for* managerial practices. The active and performative view, I suggest, is influenced by ideas stemming from different streams of research, the most notable being actor-network theory (Latour 1986, 1987, 2005), workplace studies (Heath, Knoblauch, and Luff 2000), Dorothy E. Smith's institutional ethnography (2005), the French line of studies that consider the mundane practices of writing in working situations (e. g., Grosjean and Lacoste 1998; Fraenkel 2001; Denis 2011) and the CCO (communication as constitutive of organization) perspective (e. g., Cooren 2004; Kuhn 2008). Notably, the performative take I propose builds on a relational epistemology, which among others rests on the ideas of treating humans and nonhumans in a symmetrical way (Latour 2005).

Although this list of theoretical influences may seem disparate, and ontological and epistemological differences exist between them, all can be united based on their connection, in one form or another, with ethnomethodology, on their unwavering commitment to what is happening in situations and in interactions as well as on their keen sensitivity, even their core concern, for the materiality of social phenomena. All the insights coming from these perspectives move away from seeing documents as passive and/or as secondary actors in organizational action, and view documenting as accomplishing and performing managerial activities – and consequently, organi-

---

[2] At least, it does not appear as unified in management and organization studies, in sociological investigations of work or even in organizational communication. The situation might be different in library science and in archival science, disciplines where the notion of document and the act of documenting are obviously of prime importance. However, given that this chapter is anchored in the fields of management communication and organization studies, and that the core objects of inquiry differ between fields, this literature has not been included.

zations themselves. Without leading to the development of a new or specific theory of documenting, the combination of these insights allows us to better recognize the roles of documenting as a form of management communication, and to reflect on what this act, repeated as a practice, produces for organizations and managerial activities.

2 Looking at documents to delve deeper into documenting

A first step to enter the proposed reflection on documenting is to consider what results from it, in basic terms: documents themselves. In organizational settings, the act of making a document can happen virtually anywhere, can be done by any actor (human and even nonhuman; think of all technologies that can record and produce texts), and is connected in one way or another to most, if not all processes that are part of management and organizations.[3] Following this, it can be complicated to know where to start, when it comes to documenting understood as a general term (i.e., in opposition to the already circumscribed act of documenting, like the work of making meeting minutes). Investigating more carefully what documents do in organizations will reveal their important role for action.

One of the key features of documents is that they possess the capacity to remain the same. Unless deliberate attempts are made to change them, or a process corrupts them, documents have a certain fixity (Levy 2016) that makes them endure over time. This fixity pertains to their content, not their location: again, unless efforts are consciously made to lock them up, by definition, documents can circulate with a relative ease. This is exactly why Latour (1986) identified documents as belonging to what he called *immutable mobiles*: artifacts that can change place while their content remains the same. Documents also exhibit another feature that makes them useful for carrying out action: they can make visible things that otherwise would be difficult to see, as Latour (1987) documented when he highlighted the importance of inscriptions in scientific practices – traces produced by various machines that hence materialize phenomena.

Moreover, studies that place documents at their focal point reveal a variety of effects, deriving from their production and circulation. Documents play an important role in coordinating work, managerial activities, and relationships (Callon 2002; Fraenkel 2001). As Geisler (2001) aptly underlined, texts at the same time inscribe activities in them and prescribe other activities, thus playing a role in coordination.

---

[3] If you find this claim a tad too generalizing, look at the table of contents of this book. I personally find it very easy to see document making and the use of documents to be part of most, if not all, of the aspects of management communication that this book covers. But I may tend to see documents everywhere ...

For her part, Henderson (1991), referring to drawings in sketches in engineering documents, coined the term *conscription device* to highlight their notable contributions to collective work, including structuring work and sustaining the collective. Part of their organizing effects comes from their capacity to provide order, although the fact that they rest on language does not ensure that these ordering effects will be reproduced elsewhere, when the document moves in time and/or space, what Vásquez, Schoeneborn, and Sergi (2016) have deemed the (dis)ordering effects of texts. Given the features that they exhibit, and in spite of the potential disorder that may arise around them over time, documents can model collective action by forcing a specific comprehension of reality (Winsor 2006).

Most of these actions rely on the content of documents: it is in the textual reality (Bloomfield and Vurdubakis 1994; Anderson 2004) that they create that one of their most powerful sources of influence lies. The importance of texts has been heightened by the CCO perspective (especially by the Montréal school) by building on Taylor and Van Every's (2000) idea of text-conversation as a central communicative dynamic that sustains and/or transforms organizations. If, according to this perspective, texts should not be restricted to actual, physical artifacts, or documents – and the act of documenting, as happening in situation – actively contributes to the formalization and routinization of organizations – to establish organizational features that can, partially, endure.

The communicative take on reality that can be found in the Montréal school version of CCO (Cooren 2015, 2018) rests on a performative view of communication, hence the emphasis on the verb *constituting*. Building on Austinian performativity, a few studies located in this perspective have explicitly conferred to documents a form of agency, a textual agency, linked to what documents can do (Cooren 2004; Sergi 2013; without using this expression, Rot, Borzeix, and Demazière [2014] also allude to a performative take on documents). If recent developments in this perspective (e. g., Cooren 2018, 2020) might find the notion of textual agency as still carrying too much of a separation between what is commonly labeled "the social" and "the material",[4] these studies remain relevant to build a finer understanding of what documents actually do when they are placed in managerial and organizational situations.

Documents result from the course of documenting and can subsequently act. Yet, I contend that because documents are traces, evidence, testaments, looking into them represents an appropriate point of entry in documenting, especially in empiri-

---

[4] Indeed, arguing for a relational ontology in communication and showing the artificiality and the fruitlessness of such a separation can be seen as one of the key objectives of Cooren's recent work (see, most notably, Cooren [2018], an article dedicated to dismantling the idea that there is such a thing as a separation between the social and the material by reflecting on the nature of communication). Following this relational ontology, agency is not to be found "inside" actors – humans or nonhumans – but is always a conjoint accomplishment in situation. The label "textual agency" may not capture in full the idea of hybrid agency as it identifies too much of a location for agency.

cal terms. Considering the various studies that discuss documents, three avenues of research can be distinguished. These three avenues should not be viewed as mutually exclusive, as they coexist in all documents. They should be conceived more as vantage points from which documents can be approached and investigated, a choice that the researcher can make depending on the specific nature of her inquiry. Up to now, theorizing on documents has not developed a specific and overarching framework that would allow the investigation of the various forms of implication in organizational action that documents can adopt.

I have thus combined different literatures that have for the most part remained separated to conceptualize documents in these three different ways. The identification and the combination of these three ways are at the same time a possibility to theorize what documents are and a first attempt at building a framework that could be used to carry out fieldwork. In the following paragraphs, I briefly present these three ways of conceiving documents. This presentation is not meant to be exhaustive but aims at showcasing the variety of theoretical perspectives and methodological choices that exist for researchers who want to explore documents.

First, documents can be viewed as *products*. Documents can be studied as the result of several practices, most notably documenting. Studies that consider documents as products tend to consider the social processes – such as negotiating and building alignment – that surround the production and circulation of documents and investigate documenting itself, which may or may not be defined as a practice of textualization (some researchers do, for example Anderson [2004], while others do not make this argument). In this line, questions guiding the inquiry are: What documents are produced through social interactions happening in situation? How is this production done – and by whom, with which means? However, it could be said that a majority of studies, in any theoretical perspective, that looks at documents as part of a setting belongs to this first approach, as it rests on the neat and traditional separation between the social and the material. Consequently, it is difficult to clearly identify theoretical perspectives that belong to this stream. In general, this way of conceiving documents recognizes their importance but may tend to see them as objects to be used in a more passive light and not as elements actively doing things.

A second way to approach documents is to conceive of them as *sites*. With this approach, the focus moves toward documents themselves, not by dislocating them from their situation but by zooming in on what is inside them, that is, their content. With this approach, more attention is devoted to linguistic aspects, to figures, tables, styles, genres, aesthetic choices, rhetorical strategies, among many possibilities. Generally, this approach aims at considering what has been inscribed in writing (following document making) and at investigating what these documents present and offer. Studies of documents that belong to this category often belong to discourse analysis, in one form or another. Questions in this form of investigation of documents could be: What does this document mean, express, represent? Or, what is inscribed, articulated, and delineated in this document?, often paying attention to rhetorical features (Nørreklit 2003; Young 2003). For example, Espeland (1993) describes government documents as sites where power is expressed, revealing the rhetorical tactics that objectify and include/exclude issues. With this way of viewing documents, we are getting closer to their inner workings and to the managerial and organizational implications of what they are made of (words, structuring, ideas or values inscribed in them, etc.).

Finally, a third way to conceptualize documents is to opt for the performative view described above, and to define documents as *actors*. Viewed not simply as appearing in action, or being produced by human actors, documents can also be considered as themselves intervening in action, as doing things. In this approach, it is their participation and contribution to activities, events, and more largely encompassing processes that are at the center of studies. Generally, contributions belonging to this approach discuss how documents can make people act, hence being imbued with a form of authority. This approach is more likely to argue for an altogether different relational ontology of organizations than the first two. The questions asked in this line underscore this relational ontology, for example: When seen as actors, how do documents contribute to the unfolding of organizational action? Or, how do documents materialize and sustain organizations?

This approach aims to reveal the responsibilities or tasks actively delegated to documents and to identify the actions that documents do, like formalizing work (e. g., Berg 1997), contributing to leading (e. g., Sergi 2016), and materializing concerns that will shape how a strategy will be developed (Vásquez et al. 2018). Beyond specific actions, contributions according to this approach could be seen as illustrating what Smith described as the objectifying capacity of texts and documents, an objectification that she defines as central to the making of organizations. This final stream is most notably influenced by research pertaining to science and technology studies and the CCO perspective (e. g., Callon 2002; Cooren 2004; Kuhn 2008).

As mentioned, this separation into products, sites, and actors is neither impervious nor complete. As is the case with any typology, other categories could be added to the three just described; moreover, these categories could be debated. Also, beyond theoretical perspectives and their ontological and epistemological commitments, it might be more productive to combine these approaches. For example, a rhetorical analysis of a standard (where the document is first viewed as site) could be interestingly complemented with a study of what this standard does in various situations (how it is invoked and hence justifies decisions, what is done in the name of the standard, how the standard brings people together in order to actualize what it prescribes).

Other combinations could be imagined on the basis of these three categories. This echoes Barry, Carrol, and Hansen's (2006) suggestion to consider both texts (a focus that they label *endotextual*) and contexts (named *exotextual*). This combination of approaches has also been promoted by other researchers, such as Michaud (2017), who has argued for inquiring into documents and what happens around them as a way to enrich the study of paradoxes. To this general methodological approach, I suggest that a line of questioning documents specific to them might further elevate such empirical investigations. Maybe several of such lines exist. In the following, I turn back to documenting, the act of making documents, to make one proposal.

3 Back to the nature of documenting: a proposal

Documenting refers to creating a text that pertains to an activity, a process, an aspect, or a function of an organization. It is not bound to a context: it can be done in the present of a situation to serve the task at hand, just as it can be done for the sake of posterity, for a long future; it can be done in the most informal or idiosyncratic way, or practiced in formalized settings or with a highly codified language. Documenting happens in the course of an action people perform, ranging from the sole individual to states, and including groups of all sizes in-between. Documenting can serve no other purpose than being a transient repository of notes with little value outside the moment when it is done, to serve as official proof or evidence of lasting influence.

Documenting is also practiced very differently depending on the organizational setting where it happens; and even when it sustains a managerial activity that can be found in most organizations (for example, accumulating materials to feed a process of strategy making), many aspects of it will vary: the manner in which it is done, who is responsible for it, the tools used, etc. It is mainly done through language, but is not restricted to it: documenting may imply numbers, measurements, rates, etc.; words can be accompanied or even replaced with visual elements, such as drawings, sketches, and photos. It can adhere to a strict linearity (like in meeting minutes, in which topics are re-presented in the order in which they happened, or in observation notes where the time of events is recorded; such linearity is also visible in documenting that is done with a formal document, like a form or a chart with already defined categories to be filled), but it can also proceed in free form, on a blank page, without any constraints.

But in spite of all of the diversity that surrounds the act of documenting, there is an important commonality: whatever the scope, the parameters, the objectives, documenting creates traces that are deemed to be worthy of being made and, possibly, of being kept. To borrow Cooren's (2015) vocabulary, in two words that are in an intimate, even unbreakable relationship, documenting *materializes* something because this something is supposed to *matter* (see Cooren, Fairhurst, and Huët 2012; Cooren 2015, 2018). Everything else about documenting can vary, from act to act; but I suggest that this materializing effect stemming from documenting is a stable feature of this action, in the sense of a feature that will, in one way or another, always manifest itself.

If something is documented, it is because it matters enough in the present to be understood (or felt) to keep mattering for a while (in the short term, or in a longer term). The perceived value of keeping a trace, of keeping in mind, of remembering can lead to different actions like memorizing and recording. While these actions may be interpreted as acts of documentation, documenting may be more useful, conceptually, when restricted to the notion of document making, as it helps in circumscribing this action and facilitating its study. In the case of documenting, this perceived value of keeping a trace calls for materialization in what will become a document, the fruit of documenting. Documenting is materializing in a specific way: in relation to action that is in the process of happening, to preserve some aspects of it, in something that will be self-contained but not necessarily closed (some documents can be annotated, augmented, becoming a collective elaboration over time; others cannot be altered, once completed, signed, and stamped).

It also involves effort, and it is this effort that signals that what is being captured (never completely accurately, never fully) is conceived as having a form of value for action somewhere in the future. This future action should be understood in the plural, just as plural are the contexts in which documenting takes place and the documents that result from it. Beyond its communicative nature, documenting is linked with temporality, an effort unfolding in the present, trying to grasp what is becoming the past, in order to keep it for the future. Past, present, and future are visibly connected both in the act of documenting and in the document hence produced. Combining these elements, I suggest that documenting is an act that rests on the recognition (not necessarily in full) of the worthiness of what is happening (its value), a worthiness perceived as, at least potentially, lasting (what is happening here and now may still matter later and elsewhere), hence triggering or calling forth the effort of capturing what is happening. In this sense, documenting is linked to making something endure: thus, it is fundamentally about value and/in time.

Recognizing this copresence of value and temporality in documenting opens a different research program to those we commonly find in the literature that discusses documents and documenting, as described by the three approaches briefly covered earlier. As overviewed in the previous section,[5] the study of documents is not an integrated field of study. Based on how I just described documenting, I see another path into the study of this act and of its effects: building on insights from CCO, I suggest that it would be quite generative to explore this intertwinement of *value* and *temporality* around documenting for organization. I believe that a dedicated focus on these two aspects – each resting on vast and rich literatures – could help researchers conceptualize documenting and documents in a complementary manner to what has up to

---

[5] The incompleteness of the presentation I developed in that section is further made visible when one realizes that I, deliberately, did not include in it any reference to methodological reflections on documenting. Indeed, documenting is a central methodological concern in a wide variety of fields. For example, the kind of study I do – qualitative, inspired by the ethnographic tradition, concerned with action as it is happening in situation and over time – rests on extensive and heavy documentation of the matter at hand. Even when narrowing the focus to these kinds of studies, there is an abundance of articles and books devoted to methodological issues linked to documenting. Again, documenting overflows! While it was important to signal this aspect, it cannot be covered with the appropriate depth in the course of this chapter.

now been pursued. This also echoes, albeit in differ terms, what Taylor and Van Every (2000) and Smith (2001) made central in their work: without texts, there would be no organization. The production, maintenance, and invocation of documenting of these texts (many of them actual documents) play a key role in developing, maintaining, and transforming organizations.

I would add that once something has been made more durable through a document, the features of documents can not only make the document endure, but they can contribute to amplifying it: a document can be copied, and since the invention of the printing machine, we have means to reproduce documents in an infinite manner (something that is only made even easier with the digital format). In this sense, the circulation of documents (something that happens after documenting) can contribute to materializing *even more* – that is, materializing beyond the creation of the document itself. This is one of the implications of the idea of materialization as *degrees* (Cooren 2020), an idea that directly points to processes of either amplification or deflation. Documenting, as a communicative phenomenon, may therefore represent a central practice of investigating this idea, and its multiple implications in terms of organization.

4 Concluding remarks

In 1999, Linstead argued that the textual nature of organizations had been largely understudied in management and organization studies. Two decades later, and in spite of a multiplication of studies about how texts are fundamental to organizations, the potential of considering more closely all forms of texts in managerial practices and processes has not been exhausted. Especially with the rise of the CCO perspective, texts in general and documents more specifically have been receiving much-needed attention. In this chapter, I have defined documenting as a practice and have suggested that a performative take on documents would deepen our understanding of what they do in and for organizations. Building on insights from a CCO perspective, I have also proposed to decorticate how value and temporality become inscribed and intertwined through documenting, hence contributing to the understanding of what makes documents so significant for organizations.

Such an understanding can never be fully abstracted from empirical investigations. If documents are integral to organizing and organizations, not all of them are created equally. Some instances of documenting can be mundane, both in scope of what is collected and used of the resulting document, while others will yield more influence. The effects of documenting always have to be appreciated in situation, as what appears as mundane might turn out to have long-lasting influences on organizations. In this sense – and despite the many studies already conducted on documenting and documents – much remains to be explored with regard to documenting. This applies to the study of specific acts of documenting, but also to the chaining of documenting that happens in organizations. If documenting can be seen as taking place in specific circumstances, in association to identifiable actions in organizations, it is also a pervasive act, genuinely constitutive of organizational life. Documenting most likely has an accumulative effect that should also be considered.

That studies are still needed on documenting might be especially true in the face of the current digitalization of organizations and organizational activities. This digitalization rests on a complex architecture that may not always make itself visible, and one which foregrounds texts – in the form of code and algorithms, for example. Not all the textual aspects of digitalization belong to documenting, as I have defined it in this chapter, but some do. Lambotte (2019) alludes to this in his study of how social media analytics perform analysis of the digital traces we produce, viewing these tools as an editorial infrastructure. Opening the black box of social media analytics reveals that these tools produce documents, including visualizations. What especially raises questions is the invisibility of such tools and their implications. Critical investigations of the effects of algorithms have been expanding in recent years, and documenting, understood as I have proposed, might be a relevant angle to extend such inquiries. Given how salient these engines of digitalization are becoming, documenting and documents may also rise in criticality, calling forth a renewed interest in their study.

Finally, from a theoretical standpoint, investigating the proposal I have made in this chapter may represent a way to answer Kuhn's (2020) call to practice-based studies to fully embrace a constitutive perspective. Instead of seeing communication as one practice among others inside organizations, Kuhn argues that adopting a CCO perspective implies viewing all practices as communication; it also signifies that practices are not simply about producing the activity they designate (e. g., strategizing or collaborating), but that in doing so, they (re)create the organization. Kuhn suggests that doing so allows a better pursuit of critical inquiries of organizing. Hence, in the light of what I have argued, with regard to documenting, opting for such a perspective on communication may not only lead to novel theorizing, but may open the door to renewed critical inquiries into managerial and organizational phenomena.

5 References

Anderson, Donald L. 2004. The textualizing functions of writing for organizational change. *Journal of Business and Technical Communication* 18(2). 141–164.

Barry, David, Brigid Carroll & Hans Hansen. 2006. To text or context? Endotextual, exotextual, and multi-textual approaches to narrative and discursive organizational studies. *Organization Studies* 27(8). 1091–1110.

Berg, Marc. 1997. Of forms, containers, and the electronic medical record: Some tools for a sociology of the formal. *Science, Technology, Human Values* 22(4). 403–433.

Bloomfield, Brian P. & Theo Vurdubakis. 1994. Re-presenting technology: IT consultancy reports as textual reality constructions. *Sociology* 28(2). 455–477.

Callon, Michel. 2002. Writing and (re) writing devices as tools for managing complexity. In John Law & Annemarie Mol (eds.), *Complexities: Social Studies of Knowledge Practices*, 191–217. Durham, NC: Duke University Press.

Cooren, François. 2004. Textual agency: How texts do things in organizational settings. *Organization* 11(3). 373–393.

Cooren, François. 2015. In medias res: communication, existence, and materiality. *Communication Research and Practice* 1(4). 307–321.

Cooren, François. 2018. Materializing communication: Making the case for a relational ontology. *Journal of Communication* 68(2). 278–288.

Cooren, François. 2020. Beyond entanglement: (Socio-)materiality and organization studies. *Organization Theory*. https://journals.sagepub.com/doi/10.1177/2631787720954444 (accessed 13 November 2020).

Cooren, François, Gail Fairhurst & Romain Huët. 2012. Why matter always matters in (organizational) communication. In Paul M. Leonardi, Bonnie A. Nardi & Jannis Kallinikos (eds.), *Materiality and organizing: Social interaction in a technological world*, 296–314. London: Oxford University Press.

David, Carol. 2001. Mythmaking in annual reports. *Journal of Business and Technical Communication* 15(2). 195–222.

Denis, Jérôme. 2011. Le travail de l'écrit en coulisses de la relation de service. *Activités* 8(2). 1–21.

Espeland, Wendy. 1993. Power, policy and paperwork: The bureaucratic representation of interests. *Qualitative Sociology* 16(3). 297–317.

Fraenkel, Béatrice. 2001. La résistible ascension de l'écrit au travail. In Anni Borzeix, Béatrice Fraenkel & Josiane Boutet (eds.), *Langage et travail. Communication, cognition, action*, 113–142. Paris: CNRS éditions.

Geisler, Cheryl. 2001. Textual objects: Accounting for the role of texts in the everyday life of complex organizations. *Written Communication* 18(3). 296–325.

Grosjean, Michèle & Michèle Lacoste. 1998. L'oral et l'écrit dans les communications de travail ou les illusions du "tout écrit". *Sociologie du travail* 4(98). 439–461.

Heath, Christian, Hubert Knoblauch & Paul Luff. 2000. Technology and social interaction: The emergence of 'workplace studies'. *The British Journal of Sociology* 51(2). 299–320.

Henderson, Kathryn. 1991. Flexible sketches and inflexible data bases: Visual communication, conscription devices, and boundary objects in design engineering. *Science Technology Human Values* 16(4). 448–473.

Kuhn, Timothy. 2008. A communicative theory of the firm: Developing an alternative perspective on intra-organizational power and stakeholder relationships. *Organization Studies* 29(8–9). 1227–1254.

Kuhn, Timothy. 2020. (Re)moving blinders: Communication-as-constitutive theorizing as provocation to practice-based organization scholarship. *Management Learning*. https://doi.org/10.1177%2F1350507620931508 (accessed 13 November 2020).

Lambotte, François. 2019. A communication perspective on the fabric of thinking infrastructure: The case of social media analytics. In Martin Kornberger, Geoffrey C. Bowker, Julia Elyacher, Andrea Mennicken, Peter Miller, Joanne Rando Nucho & Neil Pollock (eds.), *Thinking infrastructures* (Research in the Sociology of Organizations, 62), 307–319. Bingley, UK: Emerald Publishing.

Latour, Bruno. 1986. Visualisation and cognition: Thinking with eyes and hands. In Henrika Kuklick (ed.), *Knowledge and society studies in the sociology of culture past and present*, vol. 6, 1–40. Greenwich, CT: Jai Press.

Latour, Bruno. 1987. *Science in action*. Cambridge, MA: Harvard University Press.

Latour, Bruno. 2005. *Reassembling the social: An introduction to actor-network theory*. Oxford: Oxford University Press.

Levy, David M. 2016. *Scrolling forward: Making sense of documents in the digital age*. New York: Arcade.

Linstead, Stephen. 1999. An introduction to the textuality of organizations. *Studies in Culture, Organizations and Societies* 5(1). 1–10.

Michaud, Valérie. 2017. Words fly away, writings remain: Paradoxes in and around documents. *Qualitative Research in Organizations and Management* 12(1). 35–52.

Nicolini, Davide & Pedro Monteiro. 2017. The practice approach: For a praxeology of organizational and management studies. In Ann Langley & Harisimos Tsoukas (eds.), *The Sage handbook of process organization studies*, 110–126. Thousand Oaks, CA: Sage.

Nørreklit, Hanne. 2003. The balanced scorecard: What is the score? A rhetorical analysis of the Balanced Scorecard. *Accounting, Organizations and Society* 96(5–6). 379–389.

Prior, Lindsay. 2003. *Using documents and records in social research*. Thousand Oaks, CA: Sage.

Rot, Gwenaële, Anni Borzeix & Didier Demazière. 2014. Introduction. Ce que les écrits font au travail. *Sociologie du Travail* 56(1). 4–15.

Schoeneborn, Dennis. 2013. The pervasive power of PowerPoint: How a genre of professional communication permeates organizational communication. *Organization Studies* 34(12). 1777–1801.

Sergi, Viviane. 2013. Constituting the temporary organization: Documents in the context of projects. In Daniel Robichaud & François Cooren (eds), *Organization and organizing: Materiality, agency, discourse*, 190–206. New York: Routledge.

Sergi, Viviane. 2016. Who's leading the way? Investigating the contributions of materiality to the study of leadership-as-practice. In Joe Raelin (ed), *Leadership-as-practice: Theory and applications*, 110–131. New York: Routledge.

Smith, Dorothy E. 1974. The social construction of documentary reality. *Sociological Inquiry* 44(4). 257–268.

Smith, Dorothy E. 1984. Textually-mediated social organization. *International Social Science Journal* 36(1). 59–75.

Smith, Dorothy E. 2001. Texts and the ontology of organizations and institutions. *Studies in Cultures, Organizations and Societies* 7(2). 159–198.

Smith, Dorothy E. 2005. *Institutional ethnography: A sociology for people*. Lanham, MD: Altamira.

Taylor, James R. & Elizabeth J. Van Every. 2000. *The emergent organization: Communication as its site and surface*. New York: Routledge.

Vásquez, Consuelo, Nicolas Bencherki, François Cooren & Viviane Sergi. 2018. From 'matters of concern' to 'matters of authority': Studying the performativity of strategy from a communicative constitution of organization (CCO) approach. *Long Range Planning* 51(3). 417–435.

Vásquez, Consuelo, Dennis Schoeneborn & Viviane Sergi. 2016. Summoning the spirits: Organizational texts and the (dis)ordering properties of communication. *Human Relations* 69(3). 629–659.

Winsor, Dorothy. 2006. Using writing to structure agency: An examination of engineers' practice. *Technical Communication Quarterly* 15(4). 411–430.

Yates, JoAnne. 1989. The emergence of the memo as a managerial genre. *Management Communication Quarterly* 2(4). 485–510.

Young, Joni J. 2003. Constructing, persuading and silencing: The rhetoric of accounting standards. *Accounting, Organizations and Society* 28(6). 621–638.

Salla-Maaria Laaksonen

9 Posting

Abstract: This chapter discusses posting status updates in internal social media as a practice of management communication, a way of voicing decisions, issues, ideas, and concerns in organizations. Posting is conceptualized as a technology-mediated textual form and an intra-organizational communication practice, which functions by transmitting and mediating organizational voices and by constituting the organization and its culture. Current research typically explores the possibilities and constraints imposed by technological affordances of the digital platforms or mobilizes digital discourse approaches to explore the linguistic features of posts. This chapter maintains that posting is not only shaped by the technology, but also by the organizational context, and their socio-technical reconfigurations should be considered when studying posting. The chapter first shows how posting, as both text and practice, is shaped by the affordances of digital platforms, then discusses different functions of posting in organizations, and concludes with a discussion of power relations connected to posting.

Keywords: social media; enterprise social media; digital communication; technology; affordance

During the past decades communication in organizations has seen the proliferation of various technological platforms on which messages are published and disseminated. While surveys show that e-mail still remains the most popular communication tool for organizations (Purcell and Rainie 2014; Cardon and Marshall 2015), organizations are increasingly adopting internal social media platforms to facilitate organizational and team-based communication; tools such as Yammer, Jive, Slack, or internal Google and Facebook tools (Sinclaire and Vogus 2011). There is a vast variety of terms for such platforms: enterprise social media (ESM), enterprise social platforms, enterprise social networks (ESN), or online collaboration software. They commonly give all members of the organization access to features that enable communication, collaboration, and file sharing.

In one of the earliest conceptual accounts, Leonardi, Huysman, and Steinfield (2013: 2) define ESM as:

> Web-based platforms that allow workers to (1) communicate messages with specific coworkers or broadcast messages to everyone in the organization; (2) explicitly indicate or implicitly reveal particular coworkers as communication partners; (3) post, edit, and sort text and files linked to themselves or others; and (4) view the messages, connections, text, and files communicated, posted, edited and sorted by anyone else in the organization at any time of their choosing.

As evident in the definition above, as platforms of communication, these tools have given rise to a new modality of communication in organizations: writing and publishing short textual updates known as posts or status updates.

The variety of communication types under the umbrella of posting is vast: it ranges from one-to-many, organization-wide, or even public posts in external social media by top management to one-to-few type of posts in restricted team environments. Posting as a word, however, has longer historical roots than any modern platforms. According to Merriam-Webster, the verb *post* originally referred to the practice of affixing something as a public notice to a place publicly available, such as a wall or a billboard. A more recent meaning stands "to publish (something, such as a message) in an online forum (such as an electronic message board)". Thus, the materiality of the board has perhaps changed, but the meaning of the word and the related practice is closely tied to making something *public*.

Public communication arenas have existed in organizations before ESM. Previous platforms for posting were indeed noticeboards, physical surfaces where public messages were posted. After becoming popular online, blogs were adopted to organizational use around the turn of the millennium, perhaps first introducing the noun *a post* to intra-organizational use. To some extent, ESM platforms replicate functionalities of bulletin boards or blogs, but with a new twist: by offering a virtual, always available platform for social interaction and collaboration, they host the modern placard; the social media post. Posts are short, usually textual updates published on a social media platform. As placards, posts are usually visible to several others and can also be commented on, shared, and endorsed.

Research focused on enterprise social media platforms has highlighted their distinct nature as a communication environment. In their review, Paul Leonardi and Emmanuelle Vaast (2017) conclude that ESM provide various implications for organizational processes of communication, collaboration, and knowledge sharing. They potentially facilitate and increase communication and networking among individuals in an organization (DiMicco et al. 2009; Leonardi, Huysman, and Steinfield 2013; Kim and Pilny 2019), create organizational knowledge and memory by acting as an archive (Ellison, Gibbs, and Weber 2015), and connect individuals over hierarchies and geographical boundaries (Gibbs et al. 2015). Posting, thus, is only one specific but perhaps the most central and visible use of ESM. This chapter builds on ESM literature, affordance theory, and computer-mediated communication research to explore posting as a practice of management communication; as intra-organizational communication, a way of voicing decisions, issues, ideas, and concerns in organizations.

1 The affordance approach

A concept widely used to describe the influence and possibilities of technological tools and platforms is *technological affordance*, which refers to the potentials of action offered to the user by the technology (Gibson 1979; Norman 1988; Stanfill 2015; Bucher and Helmond 2017; Hutchby 2001). The original conceptualization by Gibson (1979) related to animal perception and to the action potentials provided to them by the environment. Later, the concept was adopted in technology design studies and human-computer interaction research, which highlighted how affordances are designed to objects (Norman 1988), as well as in ESM studies (Leonardi, Huysman, and Steinfield 2013).

By seeking to explain the potentials offered by technology, the concept of affordance emphasizes the productive power of the technological interface to reinforce certain social logics (Stanfill 2015). The influence of the technology, however, is considered relational (Hutchby 2001): some technologies are better afforded to certain actions than others. The affordance approach accentuates framing instead of determining: affordances are not features of technology but relationships between people and the objects they use (Hutchby 2001; Treem and Leonardi 2013). Technological affordances are, thus, simultaneously material and perceptual, objective and subjective (Nagy and Neff 2015; Gibson 1979). They are shaped in the interaction between the observer and the environment. From this approach, technologies are materialities in organizations, and they both constrain and enable social action (Faraj and Azad 2012; Laitinen and Sivunen 2020). Through their design, they make things possible but also limit what can be done with technology. Thus, a technological platform encourages certain actions – for example, posting certain types of posts – but these suggestions can be rendered differently by different people in different contexts.

The affordances emblematic to social media underline social action and interactivity: the platforms afford posting content and commenting, endorsing, or sharing content posted by others, and storing posts and related actions in an archive (see Manovich 2001). Danah Boyd (2010) posits that the four central affordances of networked technologies are persistence, replicability, scalability, and searchability. Together, these affordances affect the ways digitally mediated texts and contents differ from other forms of communication. Exploring the realization of these characteristics, studies have investigated how online platforms intervene in flows of communication (e. g., Gillespie 2015; Alaimo and Kallinikos 2017). This research highlights that technologies are not neutral platforms that mediate and enable communication, but they shape the communication on them. For example, platforms affect the social relationships they mediate (e. g., Baym 2015) or the political conversations taking place on them (e. g., Nelimarkka et al. 2020).

In the context of organizational communication, several authors have explored the influence of ESM from an affordance approach, showing that they have implications for organizational processes of communication, collaboration, and knowledge sharing (for a review, see Leonardi and Vaast 2017). The affordances of ESM relate not only to communication such as posting, but also to the collaboration and connections between individuals as well as knowledge sharing in an organization, by, for example, making the associations between individuals and topics visible (Treem and Leonardi 2013). These studies highlight that affordances not only make actions possible, but also constrain them (e. g., Laitinen and Sivunen 2020). Next, building on this work, this chapter discusses how posting, as a practice of management communication, is shaped by the affordances of digital platforms.

1.1 Posting is persistent and editable

Digital content is stored in databases (Manovich 2001; Miller 2011), and thus, can be retrieved from storage. Therefore, a pertinent affordance of digital platforms for posting is that posts become *persistent*, *replicable*, and *searchable* (Treem and Leonardi 2013; Boyd 2010). This leads to a public space where speech acts and expressions are automatically archived and can be accessed later – perhaps even by new organization members. Therefore posting, unlike conversations that are located and situated, endures time. Posts can be replicated (as copied text or as a screenshot) or transferred even outside the organization (Leonardi 2017; Wilner, Christopoulos, and Alves 2017) and they can have consequences later (Treem and Leonardi 2013). Posts as acts of communication thus are unique because they can be browsed, searched, and analyzed to produce new knowledge (Erickson and Kellogg 2000). By forming a growing database of contents, they sustain situated knowledge over time and create robust modes of communication that help to build organizational memory and common ground for communication (Treem and Leonardi 2013).

Despite their relative persistency, posts are often *editable* and *variable*: not only can the digital expression be crafted while writing, but several ESM platforms also allow the author to edit the content later. This makes posts unfinished products, potentially reassembled objects that change over time, or disappear if deleted. Literature largely presents editability as a positive affordance that improves information quality. Treem and Leonardi (2013), for example, suggest that editing allows users to improve information and communication quality, as they can better tailor messages to the audience based on their responses. However, it can also have destabilizing consequences for management communication: to what extent, for example, is it appropriate to modify an organization-wide post by the CEO? Many platforms make editing transparent and show the editing history of a post, but this feature is not always available. Posting, thus, is persistent, but the exact form and content of the message can be altered, and the change history is not necessarily visible to all.

1.2 Posting as interactive visibility

Another prominent element of digital communication technology is *interactivity* (e. g., Miller 2011). Interacting with a published post is an emblematic affordance of nearly all social media platforms that encourage users to comment, like, or share content. As Lev Manovich (2001) argues, interactivity is embedded in digital media in multitudinous ways, which could be considered an expansion of editability: users can modify the digital environment they use. This ability has been considered one of the main features and value adding properties of digital technologies. As an affordance related to posting, interactivity makes posting simultaneously a call for conversation and commenting, thus, effectively supports two-way communication.

A central affordance identified in ESM research has been *visibility* (Treem and Leonardi 2013; Leonardi 2014; Van Osch and Steinfield 2018; Treem, Leonardi, and van den Hooff 2020): social media platforms make knowledge, networks, and behavior in the organization visible. Posting in organizational social media thus could be argued to be communication that increases information visibility, enables social connections between organization's members as their knowledge becomes visible, and potentially also strengthens latent connections (Treem and Leonardi 2013; Kim and Pilny 2019). Leonardi (2014) argues that communication visibility increases metaknowledge in organizations: knowledge of who knows what and communicates with whom. These benefits are recognized for ESM in general, and indeed, posting can potentially work as a mode of communication that makes knowledge and management visible. Therefore, it could be argued that posting increases the possibility of multiple voices being heard in organizations (Ruch, Welch, and Menara 2017).

However, as posting practices and platform features vary, the visibility facilitated by posting cannot be taken for granted. Many platforms offer options to limit the post visibility to specific audiences only, or the user can opt to post only in a specific group, such as her team. Further, recent studies highlight that not all want to post: visibility of posts and actions might discourage individuals from sharing information due to security concerns (Gibbs, Rozaidi, and Eisenberg 2013; Leonardi 2017; Laitinen and Sivunen 2020). Studies also identify strategic uses of visibility on enterprise social media. For example, Van Osch and Steinfield (2018) show how visibility affords the enactment of different types of boundary-spanning depending on the strategic choices and resources needed by a team: teams can strategically communicate visibly in order to mobilize certain network structures and organizational outcomes. Posting can thus be a strategic act of visibility management (Flyverbom et al. 2016), a communicative process of deciding what to disclose, when and to whom. In this vein, studies have shown that communication on internal social media platforms is not only unselfish information sharing, but also a form of self-presentation, a performance of presence-building in the workplace (Danis and Singer 2008; Ellison, Gibbs, and Weber 2015).

Finally, if not the content generation, at least its presentation is increasingly automated on digital platforms (Miller 2011; Manovich 2001; Nagy and Neff 2015). Similar to public social media, posts are shown in newsfeeds and are often selected and ordered by algorithms that seek to promote the most important posts. This means the platform is potentially intervening in defining the importance of issues posted about. Journalism has covered cases in which algorithms are affecting the visibility of posts also on organizational social media. Most ironic, perhaps, was the story of Facebook content moderation subcontractor Cognizant, where the employees missed important changes in their internal guidelines because of algorithmic ordering (Newton 2019). The information was posted on Cognizant's Facebook Workspace, the enterprise version of Facebook, whose algorithmically organized newsfeed pushed the new guidelines away from the top and instead highlighted an older post with higher engagement numbers. The logics of social media platforms thus affect the sharing and presentation of information also inside organizations.

1.3 Posting as computer-mediated text

The above-mentioned affordances emphasize contextual and practice-related perspectives on posting. But posting is also a textual form and distinguished from other practices of management communication by technological mediation, which renders posting a textual form of computer-mediated communication (CMC). Understanding the specificities of such text is supported by computer-mediated communication and digital discourse studies, where scholars have worked for decades exploring and explaining how communication is changed when it is mediated by technologies (e. g., Herring 2003; Thurlow 2018; Yao and Ling 2020).

While the variety of digital communication is constantly growing, some characteristics are quintessential to it. First, in computer-mediated communication the author and reader typically are physically located in separate locations, and the communication is asynchronized (Baym 2015; Baron 2008). As most ESM platforms allow commenting, communication can be two-way, but rarely synchronous. Then again, posting is always *on* (Baron 2008); unlike meetings or internal briefings, platforms for posting are open around the clock, making us infinitely available (Gumbrecht 2011). Research suggests that in the context of work, this feature has increased working off-hours and thus contributes to exhaustion (van Zoonen, Verhoeven, and Vliegenthart 2016; Boswell and Olson-Buchanan 2007). At the same time, however, *timelessness* means that users have the possibility to control when and with whom they interact (Baron 2008), unlike with phone calls and meetings, for example. As all posts are available regardless of the time, they can be accessed anytime – or left unnoticed.

Second, early accounts of digital communication have highlighted missing social cues and non-verbal communication, suggesting that CMC is an impoverished type of communication and that messages can be more easily misinterpreted (Herring 2003; Baym 2015). However, studies have shown that people invent compensating mechanisms to express missing gestures and audio, thus enabling them to express and interpret feelings as well as build social relationships and structures online (e. g., Baym 2015; Herring 2003). The lack of cues can also be an advantage: Treem and Leonardi (2013) suggest that the lack of non-verbal cues is not an issue when posting, as editability allows the author to focus on forming the content and meaning of the message more carefully. Further, not all posting is text-based: public social media platforms are turning increasingly multimodal, focused on images, video, and the creative use of gifs and emojis (Highfield and Leaver 2016; Thurlow 2018). While such visual practices are not yet common inside organizations, they are in external corporate and strategic communication. Platform-specific visual features are prominent in marketing campaigns, and many political leaders frequently use visual platforms such as Instagram to communicate with voters.

Third, computer-mediated communication, particularly on social media, makes an explicit connection between the author and the text. In principle, a post is typically shown together with the user account who published it, often accompanied with a profile picture. In this sense, posts are tightly coupled with their creators – a connection sensed both when posting or when reading content by others. Individuals use posting for presence-building and profile work (Danis and Singer 2008; Uski and Lampinen 2016) as well as indicators to learn about their peers (DiMicco et al. 2009). However, the variability of potential interfaces to access the digital content bestow the user with autonomy to browse the content and reconstruct their own paths in the system of communication – for example by using search tools or text analytics. Such alternative interfaces might give differently structured views to the content. Indeed, researchers of digital discourse note that the digital form also allows a potential disconnection of the text and the author, as posts on digital media can be distributed, searched, and retrieved through various interfaces (e. g., Manovich 2001).

Finally, the lexicon and genres of digital discourse are evolving to include textual and linguistic features of their own. Even as a pure text, computer-mediated, digital language has been considered a mixed register (Ferrara, Brunner, and Whittemore 2009; Baron 2008) that combines features and styles of written and spoken language – however, such mixing and recontextualizing is, to some extent, a feature of all language use (Thurlow 2018). Further, social media posts are often a combination of formal and informal styles (Baym 2015; Baron 2008). For example, emojis are slowly entering the workplace lexicon despite the warnings presented in netiquettes (Skovholt, Grønning, and Kankaanranta 2014). But digital language is not standardized, as Baym (2015) reminds: it is always shaped by the circumstances and contexts in which it is used. Similarly, Yates and Orlikowski (1992) remind how organizational genres of communication evolve over time as they are used and modified by individuals coupled with institutional practices and media types. Thus, when posting in an organization, where hierarchies and performance expectations might be present, communicators presumably limit the use of the informal register they would use in private conversations.

2 Functions of posting

As described above, posting as a practice and as textual form is influenced by the technological affordances of the hosting platform. However, as the relational nature of affordances reminds us, affordances are a relationship, not a feature of technology. Social processes and technological artifacts are interrelated in complex ways and their relationship is socially constructed. That is why posting takes different forms in different organizations by different people. Users commonly shape the technological tools and their affordances so that they suit their purposes (Nagy and Neff 2015) and use them in ways different of those which the tools were originally designed for (Bijker and Law 1992). The styles of using e-mail are as wide as its user base is (Baron 2008) and posting seems to follow suit. Posting, thus, is a practice formed in a sociotechnical relationship, which widens the variety of its functions. It is reasonable to expect that communication climate (Gibb 1961) and organizational culture (e. g., Geertz 1973) also influence posting. The following sections highlight two clear functional uses for posting and discuss their characteristics and limitations: (1) transmitting and mediating organizational voices and (2) constituting organization and its culture.

2.1 Posting for information transmission and voicing

From a simple transmission perspective, posting could be considered as a digital, technologically mediated practice of communication where the management communicates and transfers information to the members of the organization. In such use, posting serves to transmit and disseminate management voices in the organization as a part of leadership communication. For example, Huang, Baptista, and Galliers (2013) explored the importance of ESM communication by senior management for strategic organizational rhetoric, however, emphasizing the increasing multivocality and fluidity introduced by ESM. The connection between leadership communication and organizational performance has also been investigated, for example, by exploring how leaders effectively communicate through ESM. Research suggests that active digital leadership communication cultivates organizational culture and emotional capital, which in turn increases the organization's performance and employee engagement (Huy and Shipilov 2012; Men 2014; Cardon, Huang, and Power 2019).

Posting, however, is rarely limited to management, but a practice available to all members of the organization (Leonardi and Vaast 2017). This makes ESMs spaces where downward, upward, and lateral voices are present at the same time, possibly in shared spaces (Ashford, Sutcliffe, and Christianson 2009; Huang, Baptista, and Galliers 2013). Therefore, posting can work horizontally to transfer information among organizational members, bringing visible – and potentially searchable and analyzable – employees' voices across the hierarchies of the organization. Posting, thus, can make voices heard, things known, and issues articulated in an organization, in a searchable and potentially visible way, by generating a technologically mediated space and practice for voice opportunity (Ashford, Sutcliffe, and Christianson 2009). This is why posting indirectly supports digital listening practices (Cardon, Huang, and Power 2019; Ruck, Welch, and Menara 2017): by reading and analyzing the posts, management can listen and pay attention to employees' ideas and concerns, thus supporting employee engagement and participation. Huang, Baptista, and Newell (2015) refer to coping with such voice opportunities as *communicational ambidexterity*: the learned ability of an organization to manage both management-led and employee-led communication. They identify the simultaneous existence of these modes of communication as a potential tension but also a possibility and suggest that ESM has potential to support both as complementary modes (also Huang, Baptista, and Galliers 2013).

However, as any communication, posting is open to multiple interpretations, and takes place in the social context of the particular organization. It is difficult to circumvent conditions such as existing hierarchies (Kim 2018): for example, despite the increased opportunities, managers post to subordinates more often than the other way around (Gibbs et al. 2015). Also, the ways in which management encourages and supports ESM use, as well as how the organizational culture generally shows support for openness, asking questions and voicing concerns, all affect how the practice of posting unfolds in an organization (Ellison, Gibbs, and Weber 2015; Ashford, Sutcliffe, and Christianson 2009; Laitinen and Sivunen 2020). Further, the transmission can be hindered with potential ambiguities in the meaning of the message, unclear communication by the sender, or receivers misinterpreting the message. ESM affordances such as persistence, interactivity, and editability help with potential unclarities with regard to the meaning: it is possible to revisit the message (*persistence*), ask the original poster for clarification (*interactivity*), or modify the message (*editability*). In order for these affordances to be realized, however, the communicating individuals need to act.

2.2 Posting for organizational culture and constitution

Posting also functions as a constituting process for the organization and its culture. Posting, if actively practiced and followed, can result in an increasing awareness of the organization, its activities, and networks. Studies on ESM use show that communicating and consuming the information on internal social media helps employees to orient towards the organization (Treem and Leonardi 2013; Treem, Leonardi, and van den Hooff 2020). Posting, thus, could be considered as a flow of communication that contributes to the constitution of the organization as a sub-stream of the dynamic process of communication as organizing (e. g., Ashcraft, Kuhn, and Cooren 2009). Such a perspective suggests that posting, or other forms of communication, are not reflections or products of the organization and its members, but essential processes of organizing that bring the organization into existence as an entity and an actor (Cooren et al. 2011). In this sense, the often-emphasized democratic idea of posting as a form of communication available to everybody in an organization (Leonardi and Vaast 2017) becomes intriguing: posting is a visible stream of organizational constitution to which all its members contribute. Empirical studies imply that posting can be a form of organizational identity building for its members (Madsen 2016), also when organization-related content is posted on a public social media site (Sias and Duncan 2018).

From this communication-centric perspective, management-led communication also emerges as a process of social construction which establishes organizational structures, realities, and hierarchies (Ashcraft, Kuhn, and Cooren 2009). Management becomes a symbolic action for that constitution, and leaders act as managers of meaning, whose leadership is meaning making and framing, a process of defining the reality for others (Pfeffer 1981; Smircich and Morgan 1982). To succeed, leaders need to orient individuals in the organization towards the desirable direction for the organization by supporting their sensemaking. A central way to achieve this is to communicate and engage in interaction – which is well afforded by posting. In this vein, posting can be conceptualized as an ongoing, socially constructed performance of leadership and authority, where positions and hierarchies are constituted and reinforced (Koch 2017; Kim 2018).

It needs to be acknowledged that not all ESM content is work- or organization-related, but nevertheless bears a meaning for the organization. Studies show that if ESM communication reveals the coworkers' personalities and personal lives, it works as a motivating factor (DiMicco et al. 2009; Ellison, Gibbs, and Weber 2015). Thus, freedom of expression in intra-organizational posting seems beneficial. It could be argued that allowing and encouraging phatic communication (Jakobson 1960), communication that essentially serves a social purpose only, can be important for organizational culture: it helps members to keep in touch, generate a sense of intimacy for collaboration, reinforce relationships, and potentially find new connections. Yet, many organizations explicitly deny posting non-work-related content and aim to control what is being posted on their internal platforms (Vaast and Kaganer 2013). Perhaps it is another imagined affordance of control produced by technology: the ability to follow and analyze the communication it sustains.

3 Posting and power – critical remarks

The use of ESM, particularly in business contexts, but somewhat also in academic literature, is glazed with technology hype. These platforms are seen as efficient facilitators of communication and collaboration, which directly contribute to the organization's performance and workplace culture. Another big narrative that relates to ESM platforms is that they allegedly make communication more transparent and democratic. However, in most organizations, employees still seldom use the digital platforms, which hinders their potential effectiveness for organizational communication processes (Cardon, Huang, and Power 2019; Li 2015). Studies imply that organization members consider traditional, more rich forms of communication more satisfactory and effective than digital communication channels, for both team communications (Cardon and Marshall 2015) and leadership (Men 2014). Further, as employees are often aware of the public nature and surveillance possibilities offered by the platforms, they carefully consider what information to share and how to participate (Denyer, Parry, and Flowers 2011; Ellison, Gibbs, and Weber 2015; Laitinen and Sivunen 2020).

Posting, thus, does not necessarily represent all the voices of an organization but just the loud, active, and technologically savvy minority, who have nothing to hide. The potential asymmetries are further complicated by the technological infrastructure that uses power by algorithmically organizing content and by allowing more rights to users such as administrators and community managers. The key question is whether the micro-level everyday acts of communication such as posts on an ESM can actually contribute to the macro-level discourses of ideology and power in the organization (Alvesson and Deetz 1999). This distinction could be conceptualized through the well-known distinction between macro-level, constituting and shaping big-D Discourse and local interaction-level small-d discourse (Alvesson and Kärreman 2000). Posting indeed produces more small-d discourse and makes the multiplicity of voices in an organization more visible through everyday textual interactions, but with what organization-level consequences? Are posts considered just a form of everyday talk or are they denoted with power to shape organizational reality? Such questions are important both for management and for the researcher who studies posting. In order to generate value in an organization, the practice of posting needs to be planned and managed so that the visibility, flexibility, and editability it affords are harnessed so that they benefit both the organization and its members.

Finally, as pointed out by Treem and Leonardi (2013), social media platforms and their features enter organizations after they have been adopted in public. Therefore, the practices of posting are heavily affected by what happens on the public consumer side of social media. The technological affordances built into the systems are commonly similar in both consumer and corporate versions of the platforms, and they are institutionalized across the platforms. Through the adaptation of the existing designed affordances, the practices afforded by them also enter organizations. Therefore, technology feeds features from public communication to the internal communication practices in organizations (Treem et al. 2015). This is a value-related question: are we asked to like and share our coworkers' posts because it is beneficial for the organization, or just because an engineer invented such a feature back in 2007?

Further, posting connects to rankings and metrics that are a common affordance of social media: datafication and commensuration of social action are deeply intertwined in the infrastructure of social media platforms (e. g., Scott and Orlikowski 2012; Alaimo and Kallinikos 2017). This means that organizational interactions taking place on ESM can be explored as quantified data, which can be leveraged for management purposes. For instance, Yammer, a platform owned by Microsoft (2019), offers reports that track user activity and engagement as well as provides tips on how to "measure success" across your groups. Thus, it is a matter of conscious decision-making and, again, of the particular organizational context whether ESMs support digital participation and listening or digital surveillance (see Hafermalz 2020).

4 Conclusion

This chapter set out to explore posting as an intra-organizational practice of management communication and conceptualized it as a communication practice as well as a textual form, both of which are enabled and constrained by affordances of the technological platforms on which posting takes place. Highlighting the socio-technological nature of posting, this chapter argued that, similar to other processes of using voice in an organization (Ashford, Sutcliffe, and Christianson 2009), posting as a practice of communication is intertwined with the organizational context and culture, but also with the technology that makes it possible. However, neither of these relationships is deterministic: technological affordances are a relationship, not a coercive feature of technology (Hutchby 2001), and organizations and organizational realities are constantly reconfigured (Ashcraft, Kuhn, and Cooren 2009).

Therefore, as proposed by Flanagin (2020), research of posting should not focus on the particular, contemporary technologies, but on the interlinked processes of communication and the ways in which they are technologically mediated. The forms and nuances of posting as a practice of management communication cannot be derived directly from their organizational or technological context, as they take different forms in different organizations by different people. While ESM platforms are often sold, adopted, and even studied with great enthusiasm, given their productive and democratic potential, this chapter highlights the sociotechnical nature of the communication process of posting. As Cardon (2016: 141) reminds us, "the transformative potential of these platforms depends on a communication perspective". The platforms support visibility, democracy, spatial and temporal flexibility, and collaboration across boundaries, but also surveillance, clique formation, unhealthy work-life balance, and impetuous interactions. The beneficial outcomes of ESM use are not necessarily the same for the organization and the individuals. This means there is no all-encompassing blueprint for posting to leverage value in the organization, but the sociotechnical practice needs to be carefully adjusted with the related processes, practices, and organizational culture.

5 References

Alaimo, Cristina & Jannis Kallinikos. 2017. Computing the everyday: Social media as data platforms. *The Information Society* 33(4). 175–191.

Alvesson, Mats & Stanley Deetz. 1999. Critical theory and postmodernism: Approaches to organizational studies. In Stewart R. Clegg & Cynthia Hardy (eds.), *Studying organization: Theory & method*, 185–211. London: Sage.

Alvesson, Mats & Dan Kärreman. 2000. Varieties of discourse: On the study of organizations through discourse analysis. *Human Relations* 53(9). 1125–1149.

Ashcraft, Karen Lee, Timothy R. Kuhn & François Cooren. 2009. Constitutional amendments: "Materializing" organizational communication. *The Academy of Management Annals* 3(1). 1–64.

Ashford, Susan, Kathleen M. Sutcliffe & Marlys K. Christianson. 2009. Speaking up and speaking out: The leadership dynamics of voice in organizations. In Jerald Greenberg & Marissa Edwards (eds.), *Voice and silence in organizations*, 175–202. Bingley, UK: Emerald.

Baron, Naomi. 2008. *Always on: Language in an online and mobile world*. Oxford: Oxford University Press.

Baym, Nancy. 2015. *Personal connections in the digital age*. Malden, MA: Polity Press.

Bijker, Wiebe & John Law. 1992. *Shaping technology/building society: Studies in sociotechnical change*. Cambridge, MA: MIT Press.

Boswell, Wendy & Julie Olson-Buchanan. 2007. The use of communication technologies after hours: The role of work attitudes and work-life conflict. *Journal of Management* 33(4). 592–610. https://doi.org/10.1177/0149206307302552.

Boyd, Danah. 2010. Social network sites as networked publics: Affordances, dynamics and implications. In Zizi Papacharissi (ed.), *A networked self: Identity, community, and culture on social network sites*, 39–58. New York: Routledge.

Bucher, Taina & Anne Helmond. 2017. The affordances of social media platforms. In Jean Burgess, Thomas Poell & Alice Marwick (eds.), *Handbook of Social Media*, 233–253. London: Sage.

Cardon, Peter. 2016. Community, culture, and affordances in social collaboration and communication. *International Journal of Business Communication* 53(2). 141–147.

Cardon, Peter, Yumi Huang & Gerard Power. 2019. Leadership communication on internal digital platforms, emotional capital, and corporate performance: The case for leader-centric listening. *International Journal of Business Communication*. https://doi.org/10.1177/2329488419828808 (accessed 13 November 2020).

Cardon, Peter & Bryan Marshall. 2015. The hype and reality of social media use for work collaboration and team communication. *International Journal of Business Communication* 52(3). 273–293. https://doi.org/10.1177/2329488414525446.

Cooren, François, Timothy Kuhn, Joep Cornelissen & Timothy Clark. 2011. Communication, organizing and organization: An overview and introduction to the special issue. *Organization Studies* 32(9). 1149–1170.

Danis, Catalina & David Singer. 2008. A wiki instance in the enterprise: Opportunities, concerns and reality. In *Proceedings of the 2008 ACM conference on Computer Supported Cooperative Work (CSCW '08)*, 495–504. New York: Association for Computing Machinery. https://doi.org/10.1145/1460563.1460642 (accessed 4 November 2020).

Denyer, David, Emma Parry & Paul Flowers. 2011. "Social", "open" and "participative"? Exploring personal experiences and organizational effects of enterprise 2.0 use. *Long Range Planning* 44(5–6). 375–396. https://doi.org/10.1016/j.lrp.2011.09.007.

DiMicco, Joan, Werner Geyer, David Millen, Casey Dugan & Beth Brownholtz. 2009. People sensemaking and relationship building on an enterprise social network site. Paper presented at the Proceedings of the 42nd Annual Hawaii International Conference on System Sciences, Big Island, HI, USA, 5–8 January.

Ellison, Nicole, Jennifer Gibbs & Matthew Weber. 2015. The use of enterprise social network sites for knowledge sharing in distributed organizations: The role of organizational affordances. *American Behavioral Scientist* 59(1). 103–123.

Erickson, Thomas & Wendy Kellogg. 2000. Social translucence: An approach to designing systems that support social processes. *ACM Transactions on Computer-Human Interaction* 7(1). 59–83.

Faraj, Samer & Bijan Azad. 2012. The materiality of technology: An affordance perspective. In Paul M. Leonardi, Bonnie A. Nardi & Jannis Kallinikos (eds.), *Materiality and organizing*, 237–258. Oxford: Oxford University Press.

Ferrara, Kathleen, Hans Brunner & Greg Whittemore. 2009. Interactive written discourse as an emergent register. *Written Communication* 8(1). 8–34.

Flanagin, Andrew J. 2020. The conduct and consequence of research on digital communication. *Journal of Computer-Mediated Communication* 25(1). 23–31.

Flyverbom, Mikkel, Paul M. Leonardi, Cynthia Stohl & Michael Stohl. 2016. The management of visibilities in the digital age. *International Journal of Communication* 10(1). 98–109.

Geertz, Clifford. 1973. *Local knowledge: Further essays in interpretive anthropology*. New York: Basic Books.

Gibb, Jack. 1961. Defensive communication. *Journal of Communication* 11(3). 141–148.

Gibbs, Jennifer, Julia Eisenberg, Nik Rozaidi & Anna Gryaznova. 2015. The "megapozitiv" role of enterprise social media in enabling cross-boundary communication in a distributed Russian organization. *American Behavioral Scientist* 59(1). 75–102.

Gibbs, Jennifer, Nik Rozaidi & Julia Eisenberg. 2013. Overcoming the "ideology of openness": Probing the affordances of social media for organizational knowledge sharing. *Journal of Computer-Mediated Communication* 19(1), 102–120.

Gibson, James. 1979. *The ecological approach to visual perception*. Boston, MA: Houghton Mifflin.

Gillespie, Tarleton. 2015. Platforms intervene. *Social Media + Society* 1(1). https://doi.org/10.1177/2056305115580479 (accessed 4 November 2020).

Gumbrecht, Hans. 2011. Infinite availability: About hypercommunication [and old age]. In Timothy Kuhn (ed.), *Matters of Communication*, 13–22. New York: Hampton Press.

Hafermalz, Ella. 2020. Out of the panopticon and into exile: Visibility and control in distributed new culture organizations. *Organization Studies*. https://doi.org/10.1177/0170840620909962 (accessed 13 November 2020).

Herring, Susan C. 2003. Computer-mediated discourse. In Deborah Schiffrin, Deborah Tannen & Heidi Hamilton (eds.), *Handbook of discourse analysis*, 612–634. Malden, MA: John Wiley & Sons.

Highfield, Tim & Tama Leaver. 2016. Instagrammatics and digital methods: Studying visual social media, from selfies and GIFs to memes and emoji. *Communication Research and Practice* 2(1). 47–62.

Huang, Jimmy, João Baptista & Robert Galliers. 2013. Reconceptualizing rhetorical practices in organizations: The impact of social media on internal communications. *Information and Management* 50(2–3). 112–124. https://doi.org/10.1016/j.im.2012.11.003.

Huang, Jimmy, João Baptista & Sue Newell. 2015. Communicational ambidexterity as a new capability to manage social media communication within organizations. *Journal of Strategic Information Systems* 24(2). 49–64.

Hutchby, Ian. 2001. Technologies, texts and affordances. *Sociology* 35(2). 441–456. https://doi.org/10.1177/S0038038501000219.

Huy, Quy & Andrew Shipilov. 2012. The key to social media success within organizations. *MIT Sloan Management Review* 54(1). 73–81.

Jakobson, Roman. 1960. Linguistics and poetics. In Thomas Sebeok (ed.), *Style in language*, 350–377. Cambridge, MA: MIT Press.

Kim, Heewon. 2018. The mutual constitution of social media use and status hierarchies in global organizing. *Management Communication Quarterly* 32(4). 471–503.

Kim, Heewon & Andrew Pilny. 2019. The use of enterprise social media and its disparate effects on the social connectivity of globally dispersed workers. *International Journal of Business Communication*. https://doi.org/10.1177/2329488419877233 (accessed 13 November 2020).

Koch, Jochen. 2017. Organization as communication and the emergence of leadership: A Luhmannian perspective. In Steffen Blaschke & Dennis Schoeneborn (eds.), *Organization as Communication: Perspectives in Dialogue*, 143–162. New York: Routledge.

Laitinen, Kaisa & Anu Sivunen. 2020. Enablers of and constraints on employees' information sharing on enterprise social media. *Information Technology and People*. https://doi.org/10.1108/ITP-04-2019-0186 (accessed 21 January 2021).

Leonardi, Paul M. 2014. Social media, knowledge sharing, and innovation: Toward a theory of communication visibility. *Information Systems Research* 25(4). 796–816.

Leonardi, Paul M. 2017. The social media revolution: Sharing and learning in the age of leaky knowledge. *Information and Organization* 27(1). 47–59.

Leonardi, Paul M., Marleen Huysman & Charles Steinfield. 2013. Enterprise social media: Definition, history, and prospects for the study of social technologies in organizations. *Journal of Computer-Mediated Communication* 19(1). 1–19.

Leonardi, Paul M. & Emmanuelle Vaast. 2017. Social media and their affordances for organizing: A review and agenda for research. *Academy of Management Annals* 11(1). 150–188.

Li, Charlene. 2015. Why no one uses the corporate social network. *Harvard Business Review*. https://hbr.org/2015/04/why-no-one-uses-the-corporate-social-network (23 December 2019).

Madsen, Vibeke. 2016. Constructing organizational identity on internal social media: A case study of coworker communication in Jyske bank. *International Journal of Business Communication* 53(2). 200–223.

Manovich, Lev. 2001. *The language of new media*. Cambridge, MA: MIT Press.

Men, Linjuan. 2014. Strategic internal communication: Transformational leadership, communication channels, and employee satisfaction. *Management Communication Quarterly* 28(2). 264–284.

Microsoft. 2019. Measure success in Yammer. https://support.office.com/en-ie/article/measure-success-in-yammer-f6047dff-8dc3-4d1e-a939-617e02211f3e (accessed 23 December 2019).

Miller, Vincent. 2011. *Understanding digital culture*. London: Sage.

Nagy, Peter & Gina Neff. 2015. Imagined affordance: Reconstructing a keyword for communication theory. *Social Media + Society* 1(2). https://doi.org/10.1177/2056305115603385 (accessed 13 November 2020).

Nelimarkka, Matti, Salla-Maaria Laaksonen, Mari Tuokko & Tarja Valkonen. 2020. Platformed interactions: How social media platforms relate to candidate-constituent interaction. *Social Media + Society* 6(2). https://doi.org/10.1177/2056305120903856 (accessed 13 November 2020).

Newton, Casey. 2019. The trauma floor: The secret lives of Facebook moderators in America. *The Verge*. https://www.theverge.com/2019/2/25/18229714/cognizant-facebook-content-moderator-interviews-trauma-working-conditions-arizona (29 December 2019).

Norman, Don. 1988. *The design of everyday things*. New York: Basic Books.

Pfeffer, Jeffrey. 1981. Management as symbolic action: The creation and maintenance of organizational paradigms. *Research in Organizational Behavior* 3. 521–552.

Purcell, Kristen & Lee Rainie. 2014. Technology's impact on workers. *Pew Research*. https://www.pewresearch.org/internet/2014/12/30/technologys-impact-on-workers/ (28 December 2019).

Ruck, Kevin, Mary Welch & Barbara Menara. 2017. Employee voice: An antecedent to organizational engagement? *Public Relations Review* 43(5). 904–914.

Scott, Susan V. & Wanda J. Orlikowski. 2012. Great expectations: The materiality of commensurability in social media. In Paul M. Leonardi, Bonnie A. Nardi & Jannis Kallinikos (eds.), *Materiality and organizing*, 113–133. Oxford: Oxford University Press.

Sias, Patricia & Kaylin Duncan. 2018. Not just for customers anymore: Organization Facebook, employee social capital, and organizational identification. *International Journal of Business Communication* 57(4). 431–451.

Sinclaire, Jollean & Clinton Vogus. 2011. Adoption of social networking sites: An exploratory adaptive structuration perspective for global organizations. *Information Technology and Management* 12(4). 293–314.

Skovholt, Karianne, Anette Grønning & Anne Kankaanranta. 2014. The communicative functions of emoticons in workplace e-mails: :-). *Journal of Computer-Mediated Communication* 19(4). 780–797.

Smircich, Linda & Gareth Morgan. 1982. Leadership: The management of meaning. *The Journal of Applied Behavioral Science* 18(3). 257–273.

Stanfill, Mel. 2015. The interface as discourse: The production of norms through web design. *New Media & Society* 17(7). 1059–1074.

Thurlow, Crispin. 2018. Digital discourse: Locating language in new/social media. In Jean Burgess, Thomas Poell & Alice Marwick (eds.), *Handbook of social media*, 135–145. New York: Sage.

Treem, Jeffrey, Stephanie Dailey, Casey Pierce & Paul M. Leonardi. 2015. Bringing technological frames to work: How previous experience with social media shapes the technology's meaning in an organization. *Journal of Communication* 65(2). 396–422.

Treem, Jeffrey & Paul M. Leonardi. 2013. Social media use in organizations: Exploring the affordances of visibility, editability, persistence, and association. *Communication Yearbook* 36(1). 143–189.

Treem, Jeffrey, Paul M. Leonardi & Bart van den Hooff. 2020. Computer-mediated communication in the age of communication visibility. *Journal of Computer-Mediated Communication* 25(1). 44–59.

Uski, Suvi & Airi Lampinen. 2016. Social norms and self-presentation on social network sites: Profile work in action. *New Media and Society* 18(3). 447–464.

Vaast, Emmanuelle & Evgeny Kaganer. 2013. Social media affordances and governance in the workplace: An examination of organizational policies. *Journal of Computer-Mediated Communication* 19(1). 78–101.

Van Osch, Wietske & Charles Steinfield. 2018. Strategic visibility in enterprise social media: Implications for network formation and boundary spanning. *Journal of Management Information Systems* 35(2). 647–682.

Wilner, Adriana, Tania Pereira Christopoulos & Mario Aquino Alves. 2017. The online unmanaged organization: Control and resistance in a space with blurred boundaries. *Journal of Business Ethics* 141(4). 677–691.

Yao, Mike & Rich Ling. 2020. "What is computer-mediated communication?" An introduction to the special issue. *Journal of Computer-Mediated Communication* 25(1). 4–8.

Yates, Joanne & Wanda J. Orlikowski. 1992. Genres of organizational communication: A structurational approach to studying communication and media. *Academy of Management Review* 17(2). 299–326.

Zoonen, Ward van, Joost Verhoeven & Rens Vliegenthart. 2016. Social media's dark side: Inducing boundary conflicts. *Journal of Managerial Psychology* 31(8). 1297–1311.

II. Forms of management communication

Florence Allard-Poesi and Laure Cabantous
10 Strategizing

Abstract: In this chapter, we use Austin's view of performativity as a framework to comprehend the effects of strategic discourse on strategic outcomes. Our review of the literature reveals a paradox: On the one hand, and contrary to what many managers believe, strategic discourses have limited illocutionary power – they seldom engender the reality they describe. On the other hand, strategic discourses have important perlocutionary effects – for instance, they have a significant impact on organizational members' identity. In the conclusion of our chapter, we outline some avenues for future research on the performativity of strategic discourses.

Keywords: Austin; strategic discourse; performativity; illocutionary effects; perlocutionary effects

In the autumn of 2019, the director of the subsidiary of an international building company asked us to help them "make sustainability performative". When we questioned him about what he meant by that, he explained that they wanted sustainability and social responsibility to become a reality in every department and action of the organization as well as the number one priority of its suppliers. In other words, he wanted the strategic discourse of sustainability to engender sustainability, a little bit like saying "I baptize you" leads to the baptism of the designated person.

This anecdote echoes an increasing interest among researchers in the effects of strategy discourses and communication on strategy: To what extent and how does communication, and in particular strategic discourses, contribute to the making of strategy? Does talking of strategy help the performance of strategy? Following the discursive turn in organizational analysis, strategy scholars have increasingly been interested in organizations' strategy discourses, including strategic plans, CEO's public communications regarding the overall strategy, or strategic managers' conversations. As several review papers have shown (e.g., Balogun et al. 2014), research on strategy discourses is lively and mobilizes a diversity of theoretical lenses (sensemaking, sociomateriality, etc.) and research methods (critical discourse analysis, conversational analysis, etc.). An important idea guiding this body of work is that strategy discourses – be they approached as a body of knowledge (Knights and Morgan 1991, 1995), narratives (Fenton and Langley 2011), or conversations (Samra-Fredericks 2003) – can help make sense of strategic action and thus fully take part in strategic practices and strategizing (Schatzki 2001; Balogun et al. 2014), with some scholars being more critical (Alvesson and Kärreman 2011).

While past research on strategy discourses has often explored the effects of strategy discourses – e.g., do these discourses change organizational actors' identity and behavior? And if so, how? – few scholars have explicitly adopted a performative lens in their inquiries. The notion of performativity has been extensively mobilized in philosophy and the social sciences – e. g., analytical philosophy (Austin 1962), gender studies (Butler 1997), continental philosophy (Derrida 1979), sociology (Callon 2007) – to shed light on the ways in which our writing and saying do not just reflect or describe an external world, but help to create it. In other words, the languages we speak are *performative*.

In this chapter, we rely on Austin's (1962) view of performativity and use it as a framework to analyze the effects of strategic discourses on strategic outcomes. We choose this view because it puts to the fore two effects of discourses – namely their illocutionary and perlocutionary effects – which are highly pertinent in the context of strategic discourses. We suggest that this view reveals an intriguing paradox: on the one hand, while many managers believe that adopting the *rules of statements* of strategy discourse will engender the reality they describe, research shows that this is rarely the case – strategic discourses have limited illocutionary power. On the other hand, strategic discourses have important perlocutionary effects – for instance, they have significant impact on organizational members' identity.

The chapter is organized as follows. We first define strategic discourses before outlining Austin's (1962) view on performativity. Using this framework, we critically review past works to appreciate to what extent and how strategic discourses can be said to be performative. We finally discuss these results and describe some avenues of research that we think can be fruitful to pursue.

1 Strategic discourses: three complementary perspectives

Strategic discourse is a broad notion that traditionally refers both to the sets of discursive (or communicative) practices through which people communicate about strategy (e. g., texts, talks) and to the assemblages of ideas about strategy that are conveyed through these practices (Balogun et al. 2014). This notion thus inherently points to the duality between the action of talking about strategy and strategy ideas. Such a duality is similar to the distinction between conversation, which refers to the practices of communication, and text, which refers to the ideas, concepts, and notions developed through these practices, a distinction introduced by CCO (Communication as Constitutive of Organization) scholars (Taylor and Robichaud 2004).

While strategy researchers adopt micro, meso, or macro perspectives on strategy discourses (see Vaara 2010) – in between the *small d* or *textual* and *big D* or *paradigmatic* perspectives respectively (Alvesson and Kärreman 2000, 2011) – they all consider both the practices and ideas conveyed by such practices in their studies. They nonetheless adopt different perspectives on strategic discourse, defining it as a body of knowledge (i.e., the *big D* perspective), a (set of) narrative(s), or (set of) conversation(s) (i.e., the *small d* perspective) (Vaara 2010). In order to clarify and exemplify what *discourses* mean in strategy research, we briefly review each of these three streams below.

1.1 Strategy discourse as a discursive formation or body of knowledge

First, following Foucault's (1977) concept of discursive formation or *body of knowledge* (*savoir* in French),[1] some strategy scholars have defined strategy discourse as "a set of ideas and practices which condition our ways of relating to, and acting upon, particular phenomena" (Knights and Morgan 1991: 253). Strategic discourse as a *discursive formation* is marked by a wide variety of statements, concepts, and theories. This variety, however, is limited by a number of rules (Foucault 1969, 1991) that make certain statements read as "strategic", while excluding others. The task of the researcher then is to define these "rules of statements" that render specific statements possible (and others not) and create a specific discursive formation or "reading system" (Lilley 2001: 69). Adopting this perspective, researchers underscore that the strategic discourse has powerful effects thanks to its conventional dimensions: it helps those who use it to get a favorable position during interactions (e.g., Kornberger and Clegg 2011) and contributes to creating, along with other practices, particular realities and subjectivities (Knights and Morgan 1991; Oakes, Townley, and Cooper 1998).

Strategy scholars inspired by Foucault's (1977) work have primarily investigated the characteristics of strategy discourse envisaged as a body of knowledge. Their research has shown that this kind of discourse emphasizes the links between the organization and its environment, and typically describes the environment as hostile and changing, thereby endangering the organization's future (e.g., Lilley 2001; Vaara, Kleymann, and Seristö 2004; Crilly 2017). Another central characteristic of strategy discourse is that it focuses on the idea of *strategic change*, where change is considered both as rational and necessary, given the threats of the environment. For instance, Kornberger and Clegg (2011: 144) have demonstrated how the strategists of the City of Sydney 2030 argued "for the need to respond to a completely new set of issues" and how, in particular, "global warming […] was presented as 'a burning platform' that necessitate[d] a 'dramatic and rapid shift in thinking and action'".

---

[1] Foucault (1991) defined the concept of discursive formation as a "limited practical domain which [has] [its] boundaries, [its] rules of formation, [its] conditions of existence" (61), and that defines "what is actually said" (63).

The necessity of change that is ingrained in strategy discourse suggests, implicitly at least, that the people in charge of the organization and its strategy are able to conduct such a change. Hence, the very idea of strategy discourse goes hand in hand with the figure of the strategist: an individual who masters, at least in part, the organization's environment and destiny (Lilley 2001), who has projects and goals, and is able to transform the organization to its benefit (Knights and Morgan 1991, 1995). This portrait of the strategist, which is arguably highly attractive, greatly contributed to the rapid diffusion of strategy discourse in the private sector after World War Two, and later, in the public and nonprofit sectors (e. g., Oakes, Townley, and Cooper 1998; Kornberger and Clegg 2011).

1.2 Strategy discourses as narratives

A second stream of research, inspired by Boje (1991, 1995) and Barry and Elmes (1997), considers strategic discourses as *narratives*. In this perspective, strategic discourses – be they official (e. g., activities, financial reports, or strategic plans) or informal (e. g., minutes of strategic meetings or workshops) – are seen as imposing a temporal order on the flow of experiences and events of the organization and its environment. They define the organization's frontiers, its allies and enemies, the past realizations, as well as the future actions to undertake. While strategy researchers initially underlined the coherence and argumentative force of strategic discourses – what Fenton and Langley (2011) called the narrative infrastructure – they have progressively recognized the ambiguity, fragmented and conflictual aspects of strategic narratives (Abdallah and Langley 2014).

Vaara, Kleymann, and Seristö (2004) provide a neat illustration of this narrative perspective on strategy discourses. These authors analyzed strategic discourses held by the CEOs, managers, and frontline members of airline companies regarding strategic alliances. Their analysis demonstrated that if alliances are unanimously considered as inevitable and beneficial to one's airline company, they also generated ambiguous responses. Middle managers and some CEOs emphasize both synergy and cooperation as potential benefits of alliances, while considering sovereignty and independence as unnegotiable dimensions of their company's strategy.

1.3 Strategic conversations

Finally, following Weick (1995) and Ford and Ford (1995), a third stream of research has investigated strategic conversations between organizational members – or between them and the organization's clients or diverse stakeholders – with the aim of developing a deeper understanding of how people strategize through their talk. Conversations refer to the sets of interactions whereby people construct meaning through their talk, eye contact, gestures, or attitudes (Goffman 1967, in Mengis and Eppler 2008: 1287). In keeping with conversational analytic principles (see Samra-Fredericks 2003, 2005), particular attention is given to the sequences of participants' verbal and non-verbal behaviors considered as the medium through which they construct – or not – mutual understanding, and enact power and resistance relationships in the making of strategy (see Allard-Poesi 2015b; Alvehus 2019).

For instance, Alvehus (2019) investigated how a manager in a high-tech company framed the discussion and decision made during a core-values session with his team. Described as having a light leadership style, he seemed to follow the team members' opinions regarding what changes were acceptable or not in the organization's policy (e. g., the suppression of "skunkworks", projects developed during working hours that are not approved by management, but that can lead to new projects and successful products and programs). However, he strongly influenced the team's reactions to top management proposals by simply announcing that a new core value would be the suppression of "skunkworks", and mentioning ironically that he did not do any "skunkwork" in the past – although he successfully did.

2 Performativity as a heuristic framework to account for strategy discourses' effects

In line with Austin (1962), we consider that some strategic utterances have *illocutionary effects*, others have *perlocutionary effects*, while some have no effects at all. An illocutionary act constitutes what a specific utterance *conventionally* does in being pronounced. For instance, in saying, "We should be careful about our small competitors", manager X might be warning her interlocutor Y. Austin would analyze this situation by saying that *in* mentioning small competitors, X warned Y against their potential danger. In other words, this utterance consists of producing a speech act that can be conventionally identified as a warning.

In comparison, perlocutionary acts consist of conveying what the manager is doing in terms of the consequences of her utterances, expected or not, by the simple fact that they have been produced. For instance, *by* mentioning small competitors, manager X could anger manager Y. The notion of perlocutionary acts underscores that some utterances create realities (e. g., anger) that go beyond what is actually said. In line with this distinction, Austin (1962) defined performative acts as utterances that *do* something, either *in saying* it (the utterance is an illocution) or *by the fact of saying it* (perlocution), or both.

In the following developments, we apply the notions of illocutionary and perlocutionary acts and their related power and effects beyond face-to-face speech acts to encompass the different levels and definitions of discourses previously exposed. While the distinction between illocutionary and perlocutionary acts as defined by

Austin is not, in practice, always easy (see Austin 1962: lecture IX),[2] we contend that it is heuristically very helpful to capture some important issues related to strategic discourses and their effects. The adoption of an Austinian performative lens reveals the paradoxical effects of strategy discourses. On the one hand, many managers and strategists believe that "talking strategy", that is, adopting the *rules of statements* or conventions of strategy discourse, can engender the reality they describe, although it is rarely the case, as we will see. Said differently, strategic discourses have limited illocutionary power. On the other hand, strategic discourses sometimes have significant consequences on organizational members' power balance and identities. These discourses also keep diffusing among various types of organizations around the world, which means that they can have important perlocutionary effects.

In the next two sections, we critically review prior works investigating the effects of strategic discourses and seek to explain this paradox.

3 The limited illocutionary effects of strategic discourses

Our review of prior research suggests that strategy discourses rarely perform the strategic changes they describe or prescribe. We interpret this finding as evidence of a lack of illocutionary power. We also point to some studies that help in identifying some of the conditions (or dynamics) that seem important for the occurrence of illocutionary effects.

3.1 Ambiguity and contradictions of strategic discourses

Strategic discourses are often ambiguous because they have to be oriented towards an uncertain future while being designed to mobilize organizational members and channel their efforts towards sometimes unclear or multiple organizational ends. They typically point to unspecific criteria to take actions (e. g., "being relevant" [Abdallah and Langley 2014]); mention indeterminate objectives (e. g., become a "Top 10 university" when university rankings did not yet exist [Gioia and Chittipeddi 1991]); aim at achieving contradictory goals (e. g., "cutting costs", "increasing performance", and "being a team" [McCabe 2010]; "being creative and achieving commercial success" [Abdallah and Langley 2014]); and sometimes also call for multiple, unprioritized ori-

---

[2] This distinction has also been contested by Searle (1969) for whom illocutionary effects are limited to the audience's understanding of the illocutionary acts, all other effects being perlocutionary (see also Cooren 2000).

entations (Abdallah and Langley 2014). Such ambiguity, however, is a double-edged sword. Whereas it has been said to encourage multiple initiatives and creativity while favoring consensus among organizational members at the beginning of the change process (Eisenberg 1984; Davenport and Leitch 2005), it might also limit, if not nullify, strategic discourses' performative power.

Equivocal or contradictory orientations and goals are liable to encourage the inflation of initiatives that can interfere with one another, resulting in loss of energy and resources as managers seek to rein back these initiatives and as conflicts emerge between people having different orientations (Abdallah and Langley 2014). If a particular orientation is chosen at the expense of the other, organizational members may feel frustration and resentment, arousing cynicism and withdrawal attitudes (McCabe 2010; Davenport and Leitch 2005). Finally, unclear goals and orientations in organizational change imply that managers must make sense of these, which may result in conflict and power struggles as efforts to change the organization can also lead to a redefinition of the business units and participants' roles as well as power balance (Balogun and Johnson 2004, 2005; Allard-Poesi 2015b).

Longitudinal studies of strategic change initiatives also underscore that ambiguous strategic discourses can generate more or less passive forms of resistance from organizational members who consume, albeit differently, these strategic discourses (Suominen and Mantere 2010). While some may adhere to these discourses because they interpret them as serving their particular interests, others may adopt a rather playful, ironic, and distanced reading of those same discourses. If, however, the discourse is understood as undermining the participants' roles in the organization or as endangering their social identity as organizational members, they may develop counterarguments and discourses, and engage in active resistance (Laine and Vaara 2007; McCabe 2010).

In sum, strategic discourses, when they are ambiguous, fail to have illocutionary power: they do not enact the actions they talk about or reach the goals (e. g., strategic change) they set. Yet, these very same ambiguous strategy discourses result in multiple and unintended perlocutionary consequences, from multiple initiatives to active resistance. By contrast, strategic discourses that are clear, consistently defended by managers over time and across orientations – e. g., promoting "excellence of research" and its positive, synergetic consequences for both education and the development of professional courses (Jarzabkowski and Silince 2007) – are liable to enact what they say.

3.2 The mixed effects of management discourse and devices coupling with strategy discourses' performativity

Other scholars have highlighted that for strategy discourses to have tangible effects, they need to be coupled with socio-material devices (e. g., calculative technologies), which underlines the role technology plays in the performativity of strategy discourse. This body of work, which approaches strategy discourses as a body of knowledge, builds on two research traditions: Foucauldian analysis and the sociological research on the performativity of scientific theories (Callon 2007; MacKenzie, Muniesa, and Siu 2007).

Management scholars inspired by a Foucauldian perspective (e. g., Ezzamel and Willmott 2008; Ezzamel, Willmott, and Worthington 2008) adopt Foucault's (1991) concept of discourse as implying an assemblage between discursive and non-discursive practices. Their research shows that strategic discourses acquire a transformative power *when* they are linked to accounting metrics. Ezzamel, Willmott, and Worthington's (2008) study of strategic change at a chemical company shows how the CEO's strategic discourse – focused on the creation of value for shareholders – was performed thanks to the development and use of accounting metrics and technologies. The use of these metrics enabled staff to translate the CEO's strategic discourse into measurable objectives as well as to link operational actions to strategic objectives and promote those actions that transform the organization in a manner consistent with shareholder value. By linking operational actions (e. g., cutting costs) and performance objectives (in terms of share price, for instance), accounting technologies thus allowed the strategy discourse to become performative, that is, to focus organizational members' efforts on the creation of value.

More recently, some researchers interested in the effect of strategy discourses on practice, have adopted another perspective, rooted in Actor-Network Theory, and developed in sociology by Callon and his colleagues (Callon 2007; MacKenzie, Muniesa, and Siu 2007). This perspective studies the processes whereby economic theories (e. g., finance and marketing theory) become self-fulfilling – i. e., how theoretical discourses eventually bring about the reality they describe and contribute to the creation of the social world they assume. Research on the performative power of theories underscores the role of socio-material devices in performativity (Callon 2007; Gond et al. 2016).

In strategic management, this perspective has been adopted by Ligonie (2018) to study the processes by which a strategy discourse aiming at creating "shared value" (Porter and Kramer 2011) transformed a European gambling company. Her analysis shows, among other things, that the translation of the strategy discourse into a set of calculative devices and measurable objectives enabled organizational actors to draw explicit (causal) links between their actions and the strategic objectives of the company. In a similar vein, Vargha (2018) shows how the strategic change envisioned by the top management team of a Hungarian bank was brought about, partly thanks to the use of a specific technology – a Customer Relationship Management (CRM) software. Vargha's (2018) analysis also shows how the use of the CRM software was crucial in transforming the bank clerks' subject positions and identities.

While there are important differences between the Foucauldian research tradition and Callon and colleagues' work (e. g., Aggeri 2017), we contend that these two bodies of work converge on the same broad message, when they are used to study strategic discourses: for strategy discourses to have illocutionary effects, they need to be inscribed into socio-material devices (e. g., software) or some forms of calculative technology (e. g., accounting metrics). These assemblages between strategic discourses and socio-material devices are, however, not without side-effects: While the deployment of metrics focuses organizational members' efforts and resources on the chosen objectives and orientations, it also renders the organization's results highly visible and so vulnerable to critics if objectives and orientations are not reached. For instance, Ezzamel and Willmott's (2008) study showed how the adoption of performance metrics helped critics to better see and assess the negative impact of some of the CEO's strategic choices, thereby justifying both the CEO's ousting and a (new) strategic change.

On the whole, our review of this body of work suggests that strategy discourse has a rather uncertain illocutionary power when it is not accompanied by socio-material devices.

4 The perlocutionary effects of strategic discourses

Meanwhile, the work of other researchers interested in the power effects of strategy discourses suggests that such discourses can have tremendous effects at the individual, interindividual, organizational, or societal levels. In other words, and using Austin's (1962) conception of performativity, strategy discourses can have important perlocutionary effects as they can affect people and reality beyond what these discourses are saying or prescribing.

4.1 Constructing the *strategist*

Following Knights and Morgan (1991), researchers have investigated how strategic discourse enacts both subjectivation – i. e., the transformation of one's identity into that of a strategist – and subjection – i. e., disempowering effects related to what being a strategist implies (e. g., making one's desires and plans visible, accounting for the organization's performance) (see Allard-Poesi [2015a] for a review). Holding a strategic discourse constructs the person who holds that discourse as a strategist, that is, someone with high analytical and innovation skills who has particular goals for the organization (Lilley 2001), is oriented towards the future, and is able to exercise leadership (Dick and Collins 2014; Knights and Morgan 1991; Laine et al. 2016). This attractive identity, by the same token, also implies entering a "visibility field" (Brighenti 2007), that is, a metaphoric arena wherein one's attitude and discourse will be scrutinized by the organizational members and the stakeholders. Being a strategist also means being accountable and responsible for the organization's performance and results. In becoming a strategist, one is endowed with a highly desirable, powerful identity, but one is also, at the same time, disempowered by the duties and achievements this identity implies (Dick and Collins 2014; Laine et al. 2016).

Based on an in-depth analysis of interviews with nineteen senior executives of five family-owned industrial companies in Finland, Laine et al. (2016) outline how these top managers submitted to a rather conventional strategic discourse of rationality, control, and leadership. These top managers displayed their mastery of strategy discourse by repeatedly referring to their ability to conduct rational analyses, to develop and to communicate better than others a deep understanding of the business as well as their capacity to implement a significant change compared to their predecessors. They only marginally subverted this rational discourse by mentioning their intuition or their openness to dialogue with clients or employees in the making of strategy. This reluctance can be interpreted as a fear of endangering their social identity as strategists in the eyes of the interviewers.

In a similar perspective, Dick and Collins (2014) underscore how resisting strategic discourse in order to underline one's personal contribution as a manager to the success of a subsidiary is difficult, if not impossible. The vice president of an Irish subsidiary of a US company could not argue that the company's success was due to its business model – hence downplaying his room for maneuver and own contribution to the company's success – while claiming that this success depended on his personal strategic management skills. If holding a strategic discourse has rather ambivalent effects on the strategist herself, as it implies both empowering and disempowering effects, holding that same discourse can be an effective practice to convince others or silence opponents during interactions.

4.2 Gaining a favorable position in a strategic conversation

Individuals who master strategic discourses' rules, vocabularies, and tools might also get a favorable subject position during conversations in the organization. Samra-Fredericks (2003, 2005), for instance, showed how a manager turned a conversation to his advantage –at the expense of one of his colleagues – during a strategy meeting. This manager was able to acquire a favorable position thanks to the use of specific rhetorical skills and through categorizing the view defended by his colleague as managerial as opposed to strategic. These discursive practices progressively eroded his colleague's position and, in the eyes of the other participants, constructed himself as a strategist, that is, someone who is able to embrace the organization's interests, issues, and future. Generally, scholars who have studied discursive practices show that people who behave and talk strategy are often able to undermine others' positions – which are then categorized as "non-strategic" (e. g., as "political" [Whittle et al. 2014]) – and to acquire a leadership position within the group (Samra-Fredericks

2003, 2005; Whittle et al. 2014). These studies also show that those who master the rhetoric of strategy during strategic conversations can not only change the immediate course of action but also significantly modify the power balance within the organization as well as its strategic orientations.

However, when several participants master strategic discourse, conversations may lead to destructive power struggles (Patriotta and Spedale 2009; Allard-Poesi 2015b). Allard-Poesi's (2015b) analysis of strategic conversations between the director and the managers of a social organization reveals that participants' will to power leads them to depict others' position as lacking strategic commitment, innovation, or realism – thereby underlining the incongruence of the strategy with environmental constraints. This power struggle was all the more violent as the conversation also aimed at clarifying the participants' roles in the definition of strategy. When several participants master strategic discourse and use it to gain a favorable position during the conversations, talking strategy can only result in destructive sensemaking and collective paralysis (see also Patriotta and Spedale 2009).

Although strategic discourse has little illocutionary power, mastering its rule permits the disciplining of the strategist, and, to a certain extent, his/her potential opponents who, if they do not master strategic discursive rules, are liable to lose any advantage in the conversation and even be silenced. This may explain why, in spite of its limited illocutionary power, strategic discourse keeps proliferating and colonizing new organizations and spheres of the society that were initially foreign to strategy.

4.3 Colonizing new territories

Universities, hospitals, research agencies (Davenport and Leitch 2005), cultural and social organizations (Oakes, Townley, and Cooper 1998), and even cities (Vaara, Sorsa, and Pälli 2010; Kornberger and Clegg 2011) have progressively adopted strategic discourses, tools, and practices as a way to legitimate their orientations and actions. One may interpret this colonization as powerful – and even necessary – means for organizations to meet external stakeholders' expectancies and pressures by acquiring or reinforcing their legitimacy (DiMaggio and Powell 1983) and, by the same token, attracting the resources and skills necessary for their survival (Pfeffer and Salancik 1978). With neo-institutionalism, mimesis and search for legitimacy can be seen as powerful mechanisms that have contributed to the diffusion and adoption of strategic discourses and practices. However, this does not explain why a particular discourse – here, strategic discourse – gained the advantage over alternative discourses at a particular point in time.

Following Knights and Morgan (1991), one may suggest two complementary explanations. First, strategic discourse since World War Two has benefited from the development of collaborative practices among business schools, enterprises, and consulting firms. Second, strategic discourses, along with accounting and reporting techniques, appeared as adequate solutions to the problem of control and surveillance that firms were facing as they progressively internationalized their activities and developed new business units and subsidiaries. These issues became all the more thorny as top managers have been increasingly expected to report on their organization's activities and results to stockholders. Together with accounting and reporting techniques, strategic discourses have participated in a control-at-a-distance assemblage that clearly responded to the transformation of the firm (Hoskin, Macve, and Stone 2006) after World War Two, and then of the European states in the 1970s.

Even if it participates in surveillance dispositive, strategic discourse is usually not understood as such. On the contrary, it is said to value responsibility and intentionality (Lilley 2001), which contributes to its adoption and diffusion among various types of organizations. Strategy, as demonstrated by Knights and Morgan (1991), is equivalent to having objectives and intentions that justify action plans and orientations. This idea of intentionality and, relatedly, of being in control of one's destiny – a highly "masculine" discourse (Knights and Morgan 1991) that is specific to strategic discourse – was and still is, in our view, a determinant driving force of its adoption and proliferation. Kornberger and Clegg (2011) as well as Vaara, Sorsa, and Pälli (2010) also showed how cities' strategic discourses help to depoliticize issues and then neutralize potential opponents.

While, on the whole, strategic discourses' performative power appears rather limited, it nonetheless proliferates, colonizing new spheres of the economy. In our view, it is also this failure to perform what it says that makes strategic discourse so successful. We conclude by summarizing the main results reviewed above and then discuss this idea further.

5 Conclusion and discussion

To summarize, the strategy literature delivers a complex message about the effects of strategy discourses. In this chapter, we offered a performative reading of this body of work. Austin's (1962) conception of performativity allowed us to reveal the paradoxical effects of strategy discourses. On the one hand, we have outlined that few strategy discourses are effective in bringing the change they envision – they have little illocutionary power. On the other hand, we have shown that strategic conversations have important effects within organizations and that strategy discourse has gained legitimacy in many organizational fields. In other words, strategy discourse has important perlocutionary power.

To conclude, while these findings may seem paradoxical, we contend that they are in fact intrinsically linked. The ineffectiveness of many strategy discourses in enacting the state of affairs they envision should not be considered as evidence of strategy's failed performativity. On the contrary, we contend that the failure of a particular strategy discourse in one organization, at a given point in time, is what justifies – given the persistence of environmental threats and change – the development of a new strategy discourse for this organization. This idea was particularly well illustrated by Ezzamel and Willmott (2008). As the deployment of calculations and reporting techniques made apparent the inability of the strategy to create value for the stockholders, it seemed rational to replace the CEO and call for a new strategy. The local performative failure of any given strategy discourse accordingly is accompanied by a global performative effect, whereby entire organizational fields come to be imbued by strategy vocabulary, tools, and logic.

Hence, a performative interpretation of the literature on strategy discourse, in calling attention to the illocutionary and perlocutionary effects of strategic discourse, invites researchers to consider both the complex and multifaceted aspects of strategic discourse, thereby taking distance from the "all-powerful" view of discourse against which Alvesson and Kärreman (2011) warned us. By the same token, it also helps defining the conditions and processes that appear necessary for a strategic discourse to produce some performative effects (Varlet and Allard-Poesi 2017).

Three sets of research questions are, in our view, worthy of investigation. The first one deals with the conditions and processes that facilitate or hinder the performativity of strategic discourse. Whereas one can easily understand that calculative technologies help organizational members connect their activities to cost-reduction strategies, the contribution of these technologies to the performativity of strategy expressed in qualitative terms – e.g., improving creativity or social responsibility – might be less self-evident. In such cases, what type of translation work is needed? What assemblages of strategic discourse with calculative technologies and material devices are required? How do "acts of calculation" and "acts of writing" (Aggeri 2017) interplay and conjunctively contribute to the performativity of strategy discourse? While some scholars have started to study these questions (Gond, Cabantous, and Krikorian 2018; Ligonie 2018), further investigations are needed. For instance, one may even assume that the use of calculative technologies can deter the strategy from its initial objectives through the translation process these technologies would imply. Collaborative studies between researchers in strategic management and accounting, management control, and/or information systems would be fruitful to investigate these assemblages between strategic discourses and socio-material devices.

In a similar perspective, following research in management inspired by conversational analysis (see Samra-Fredericks 2003; Whittle et al. 2014), one may seek to investigate further the characteristics of strategic discourse that contribute to its performativity. If prior works have underlined some "rules of statements" of strategic discourses (see Kornbeger and Clegg 2011; Vaara, Sorsa, and Pälli 2010), they did not investigate the effects of their use and of related discursive devices (e.g., use of vagueness, of metaphors) on the audience.

A second avenue of research would be either to enlarge our concept of performativity and approach the quest for performativity as a cultural condition, as Muniesa

(2018) suggests in his provocative essay on the performativity of strategy (see also Cabantous, Gond, and Wright 2018), or to consider performativity as a mindset (Garud, Gehman, and Tharchen 2018; Cabantous and Sergi 2018), or both. Approaching performativity in one of these two ways shifts the emphasis from the study of outcomes (e. g., performative success, failure) as it invites studying performativity as an ongoing journey. This broader approach thus puts the emphasis on the fragility of performativity as the latter "can never be a settled state of affairs" (Garud, Gehman, and Tharchen 2018: 502). It could be used to explore how some spheres of our societies are permanently inhabited by the strategy discourse while others seem to resist this colonization, thanks to the active involvement of actors who keep proposing alternative initiatives, and strive to perform alternative projects (Leca, Gond, and Barin-Cruz 2014; Esper et al. 2017).

Finally, an intriguing but, yet, omitted question deals with the strategists' beliefs in the power of their discourses. To what extent do strategists – as the director of the subsidiary mentioned in our introduction – think that their strategy talk can produce the change they describe? If one resists their discourse, is it mainly because one does not understand it? In our view, this collective wisdom rests on an unquestioned faith in strategy understood as an institution that, if one follows its conventions, will produce the changes that strategy supposes. But strategy discourse today, as other (scientific) disciplines and institutions, is increasingly contested for both its ambiguity and vacuity, and for the significant, negative consequences that it keeps silencing. On the whole, turning a performative lens on strategic discourse helps to uncover the paradoxical and contested processes at stake in the discursive dimension of strategizing.

6 References

Abdallah, Chahrazad & Ann Langley. 2014. The double edge of ambiguity in strategic planning. *Journal of Management Studies* 51(2). 235–264.

Aggeri, Franck. 2017. Qu'est-ce que la performativité peut apporter aux recherches en management et sur les organisations. Mise en perspective théorique et cadre d'analyse. *M@n@gement* 20(1). 28–69.

Allard-Poesi, Florence. 2015a. A Foucauldian perspective on strategic practice: Strategy as the art of (un)folding. In Damon Golsorkhi, Linda Rouleau, David Seidl & Eero Vaara (eds.), *Strategy as Practice, Theory, Epistemology, Methodology*, 2nd edn., 234–248. Cambridge: Cambridge University Press.

Allard-Poesi, Florence. 2015b. Dancing in the dark: Making sense of managerial roles during strategic conversations. *Scandinavian Journal of Management* 31(3). 338–350.

Alvehus, Johan. 2019. Emergent, distributed, and orchestrated: Understanding leadership through frame analysis. *Leadership* 15(5). 535–554.

Alvesson, Mats & Dan Kärreman. 2000. Taking the linguistic turn in organizational research: Challenges, responses, consequences. *The Journal of Applied Behavioral Science* 36(2). 136–158.

Alvesson, Mats & Dan Kärreman. 2011. Decolonializing discourse: Critical reflections on organizational discourse analysis. *Human Relations* 64(9). 1121–1146.

Austin, John L. 1962. *How to do things with words: The William James Lectures delivered at Harvard University in 1955*. London: Oxford University Press.

Balogun, Julia, Claus Jacobs, Paula Jarzabkowski, Saku Mantere & Eero Vaara. 2014. Placing strategy discourse in context: Sociomateriality, sensemaking and power. *Journal of Management Studies* 51(2). 175–201.

Balogun, Julia & Gerry Johnson. 2004. Organizational restructuring and middle manager sensemaking. *Academy of Management Journal* 47(4). 523–549.

Balogun, Julia & Gerry Johnson. 2005. From intended strategies to unintended outcomes: The impact of change recipient sensemaking. *Organization Studies* 26(11). 1573–1601.

Barry, David & Michael Elmes. 1997. Strategy retold: Toward a narrative view of strategic discourse. *Academy of Management Review* 22. 429–452.

Boje, David. 1991. The storytelling organization: A study of story performance in an office-supply firm. *Administrative Science Quarterly* 36(1). 106–126.

Boje, David. 1995. Stories of storytelling organization: A postmodern analysis of Disney as "Tamara-Land". *Academy of Management Journal* 38(4). 997–1035.

Brighenti, Andrea. 2007. Visibility: A category for the social sciences. *Current Sociology* 55(3). 323–342.

Butler, Judith. 1997. *Excitable speech: A politics of the performative*. London: Routledge.

Cabantous, Laure, Jean-Pascal Gond & Alex Wright. 2018. The performativity of strategy: Taking stock and moving ahead. *Long Range Planning* 51(3). 407–416.

Cabantous, Laure & Viviane Sergi. 2018. See the potentialities at the intersection: A reflexion on performativity and processuality mindsets. *M@n@gement* 21(4). 1229–1243.

Callon, Michel. 2007. What does it mean to say that economics are performative? In Donald MacKenzie, Fabian Muniesa & Lucia Siu (eds.), *Do economists make markets? On the performativity of economics*, 311–357. Princeton, NJ: Princeton University Press.

Cooren, François. 2000. *The organizing property of communication*. Amsterdam & Philadelphia, PA: John Benjamins.

Crilly, Donal. 2017. Time and space in strategy discourse: Implications for intertemporal choice. *Strategic Management Journal* 38(12). 2370–2389.

Davenport, Sally & Shirley Leitch. 2005. Circuits of power in practice: Strategic ambiguity as delegation of authority. *Organization Studies* 26(11). 1603–1623.

Derrida, Jacques. 1979. Scribble (writing-power). *Yale French Studies* (58). 117–147.

Dick, Penny & David Collins. 2014. Discipline and punish? Strategy discourse, senior manager, subjectivity and contradictory power effects. *Human Relations* 67(2). 1513–1536.

DiMaggio, Paul & Walter Powell. 1983. The iron cage revisited: Institutional isomorphism and collective rationality in organizational fields. *American Sociological Review* 48(2). 147–160.

Eisenberg, Eric M. 1984. Ambiguity as strategy in organizational communication. *Communication Monographs* 51(3). 227–242.

Esper, Susana, Laure Cabantous, Luciano Barin Cruz & Jean-Pascal Gond. 2017. Supporting alternative organizations? Exploring scholars' involvement in the performativity of worker-recovered companies. *Organization* 24(5). 671–699.

Ezzamel Mahmoud & Hugh Willmott. 2008. Strategy as discourse in a global retailer: A supplement to rationalist and interpretive accounts. *Organization Studies* 29(2). 191–217.

Ezzamel, Mahmoud, Hugh Willmott & Franck Worthington. 2008. Manufacturing shareholder value: The role of accounting in organizational transformation. *Accounting, Organizations and Society* 33(2–3). 107–140.

Fenton, Christopher & Ann Langley. 2011. Strategy as practice and the narrative turn. *Organization Studies* 32(9). 1171–1196.
Ford, Jeffrey D. & Laurie W. Ford. 1995. The role of conversations in producing intentional change in organizations. *Academy of Management Review* 20(3). 541–570.
Foucault, Michel. 1969. *L'Archéologie du savoir*. Paris: Gallimard.
Foucault, Michel. 1977. *The archaeology of knowledge*. London: Tavistock.
Foucault, Michel. 1991. Politics and the study of discourse. In Graham Burchell, Colin Gordon & Peter Miller (eds.), *The Foucault effect: Studies in governmentality*, 53–72. Chicago, IL: University of Chicago Press.
Garud, Raghu, Joel Gehman & Thinley Tharchen. 2018. Performativity as ongoing journeys: Implications for strategy, entrepreneurship, and innovation. *Long Range Planning* 51(3). 500–509.
Gioia, Dennis A. & Kumar Chittipeddi. 1991. Sensemaking and sensegiving in strategic change initiation. *Administrative Science Quarterly* 12(6). 433–448.
Gond, Jean-Pascal, Laure Cabantous, Nancy Harding & Mark Learmonth. 2016. What do we mean by performativity in organizational and management theory? The uses and abuses of performativity. *International Journal of Management Reviews* 18(4). 440–463.
Gond, Jean-Pascal, Laure Cabantous & Frédéric Krikorian. 2018. How do things become strategic? 'Strategifying' corporate social responsibility. *Strategic Organization* 16(3). 241–272.
Hoskin, Keith, Richard Macve & John Stone. 2006. Accounting and strategy: Towards understanding the historical genesis of modern business and military strategy. In Alnor Bhimani (ed.), *Contemporary issues in management accounting*, 165–190. Oxford: Oxford University Press.
Jarzabkowski, Paula & John Silince. 2007. A rhetoric-in-context approach to building commitment to multiple strategic goals. *Organization Studies* 28(11). 1639–1665.
Knights, David & Gareth Morgan. 1991. Corporate strategy, organizations and the subject: A critique. *Organization Studies* 12(2). 251–273.
Knights, David & Gareth Morgan. 1995. Strategic management, financial services and information technology. *Journal of Management Studies* 32(2). 191–214.
Kornberger, Martin & Steward Clegg. 2011. Strategy as performative practice: The case of Sydney 2030. *Strategic Organization* 9(2). 136–162.
Laine, Pikka-Maaria, Susan Meriläinen, Janne Tienari & Eero Vaara. 2016. Mastery, submission, and subversion: On the performative construction of strategist identity. *Organization* 23(4). 505–524.
Laine, Pikka-Maaria & Eero Vaara. 2007. Struggling over subjectivity: A discursive analysis of strategic development in an engineering group. *Human Relations* 60(1). 29–58.
Leca, Bernard, Jean-Pascal Gond & Luciano Barin Cruz. 2014. Building 'critical performativity engines' for deprived communities: The construction of popular cooperative incubators in Brazil. *Organization* 21(2). 683–712.
Ligonie, Marion. 2018. The 'forced performativity' of a strategy concept: Exploring how shared value shaped a gambling company's strategy. *Long Range Planning* 51(3). 463–479.
Lilley, Simon. 2001. The language of strategy. In Robert Westwood & Stephen Linstead (eds.), *The language of organization*, 66–88. London: Sage.
MacKenzie, Donald, Fabian Muniesa & L. Siu. 2007. *Do economists make markets? On the performativity of economics*. Princeton, NJ: Princeton University Press.
McCabe, Darren. 2010. Strategy-as-power: Ambiguity, contradiction and the exercise of power in a UK building society. *Organization* 17(2). 151–175.
Mengis, Jeanne & Martin J. Eppler. 2008. Understanding and managing conversations from a knowledge perspective: An analysis of the roles and rules of face-to-face conversations in organizations. *Organization Studies* 29(10). 1287–1313.

Muniesa, Fabian. 2018. Grappling with the performative condition. *Long Range Planning* 51(3). 495–499.

Oakes, Leslie S., Barbara Townley & David J. Cooper. 1998. Business planning as pedagogy: Language and control in a changing institutional field. *Administrative Science Quarterly* 43(2). 257–292.

Patriotta, Gerardo & Simone Spedale. 2009. Making sense through face: Identity and social interaction in a consultancy task force. *Organization Studies* 30(11). 1227–1248.

Pfeffer, Jeffrey. & Gerald R. Salancik. 1978. *The external control of organizations: A resource dependence perspective*. Stanford, CA: Harper & Row.

Porter, Michael E. & Mark R. Kramer. 2011. Creating shared value. *Harvard Business Review* 89. https://hbr.org/2011/01/the-big-idea-creating-shared-value (accessed 13 November 2020).

Samra-Fredericks, Dalvir. 2003. Strategizing as lived experience and strategists' everyday efforts to shape strategic directions. *Journal of Management Studies* 40(1). 141–174.

Samra-Fredericks, Dalvir. 2005. Strategic practices, 'discourse' and the everyday interactional constitution of 'power effects'. *Organization* 12(6). 803–841.

Schatzki, Theodor. 2001. Practice mind-ed orders. In Theodore Schatzki, Karin Knorr Cetina & Eike Von Savigny (eds.), *The practice turn in contemporary theory*, 42–55. London: Routledge.

Searle, John. 1969. *Speech acts: An essay in the philosophy of language*. Cambridge: Cambridge University Press.

Suominen, Kimmo & Saku Mantere. 2010. Consuming strategy: The art and practice of managers' everyday strategy usage. *Advances in Strategic Management* 27. 211–245.

Taylor, James R. & Daniel Robichaud. 2004. Finding the organization in the communication: Discourse as action and sensemaking. *Organization* 11(3). 395–413.

Vaara, Eero. 2010. Taking the linguistic turn seriously: Strategy as a multifaceted and interdiscursive phenomenon. *Advances in Strategic Management* 27. 29–50.

Vaara, Eero, Birgitt Kleymann & Hannu Seristö. 2004. Strategies as discursive constructions: The case of airline alliances. *Journal of Management Studies* 41(1). 1–35.

Vaara, Eero, Virpi Sorsa & Pikka Pälli. 2010. On the force potential of strategy texts: A critical discourse analysis of a strategic plan and its power effects in a city organization. *Organization* 17(6). 685–702.

Vargha, Zsuzsanna. 2018. Performing a strategy's world: How redesigning customers made relationship banking possible. *Long Range Planning* 51(3). 480–494.

Varlet, Marion & Florence Allard-Poesi. 2017. A quelles conditions un discours stratégique peut-il produire un changement ? Analyses et apports d'Austin, Searle, Butler et Callon. *Revue Française de Gestion* 263(2). 71–96.

Weick, Karl E. 1995. *Sensemaking in organizations*. Thousand Oaks, CA: Sage.

Whittle, Andrea, William Housley, Alan Gilchrist, Frank Mueller & Peter Lenney. 2014. Category predication work, discursive leadership and strategic sensemaking. *Human Relations* 68(3). 1–34.

J. Kevin Barge
11 Leading

Abstract: This essay focuses on discursive approaches to leading as opposed to leadership psychology by centering on leading's linguistic and interactional accomplishment. It presents the primary task of leading as the management of meaning and the coordination of networks of human and nonhuman actants, giving attention to issues regarding framing, sense making, temporal sequencing, materiality, and hybrid forms of agency. Future research should explore how leadership studies can integrate quantitative and qualitative linguistic analysis, facilitate uptake of theory and research on leading by leadership practitioners, and take seriously the role of ethics and morality within leading practices. The chapter begins by distinguishing leading discursively from leadership psychology and unpacking key linguistic practices as well as analytical choices and tools that academic scholars and leadership practitioners may engage when analyzing leadership interaction, and concludes by examining future research directions

Keywords: leadership; discursive leadership; leadership psychology; reflexive agency; discourse analysis

This chapter focuses on discursive leading as opposed to leadership psychology by giving attention to the interactional processes of leading as opposed to the entities of leadership: individuals who occupy leadership roles, the characteristics and functions of leadership messages, and the various individual, organizational, or cultural structures that enable or constrain certain forms of leadership. Discursive leading centers on the linguistic construction of leadership with an emphasis on meaning making as opposed to a prediscursive approach to leadership that is rooted in leadership psychology with a focus on the measurement of the qualities or dimensions of entities such as individuals, message characteristics, structures, and their interrelationships. Drawing on studies of discursive leading, this contribution: (1) distinguishes between leading discursively and leadership psychology, (2) presents the primary work of leading as meaning management and coordination of networks of human and nonhuman actants, and (3) highlights key analytical choices for discursively oriented academic researchers and leadership practitioners.

1 Leading discursively and leadership psychology

Fairhurst (2007a) positions discursive leadership as a complementary alternative to leadership psychology. Leadership psychology approaches operate from an entitative viewpoint which focuses attention on specific entities-individuals who perform leadership roles as well as structures that affect their performance (Hosking and Shamir 2012). For example, many leadership theories such as "Great Man" theory, neo-trait theory, and transformational leadership presume that leaders have particular essences in the form of cognitive and personality structures that distinguish them from non-leaders. Moreover, structural entities exist within the larger environment such as formal organizational networks and hierarchies as well as national and organizational culture that impact the appropriate and effective performance of leadership. An excellent example of an entitative approach to leadership is situational leadership where certain leadership qualities such as personality traits or dispositions are assumed to generate particular outcomes such as team performance which may be moderated or mediated by environmental structures such as the quality of leader-member relations, task structure, and goal clarity (Yukl 2011). Leadership psychology treats communication as a transmissive process of conveying information where communication is simply one of many behaviors that leaders may perform such as decision making, conflict management, and planning.

Discursive leadership operates from a different set of assumptions than leadership psychology. Discursive leadership views communication as a primary social process that is involved with managing meaning. Communication is constitutive as the way we talk and act creates our social worlds that comprise personal and professional identities, relationships, organizations, institutions, and cultures. Discursive approaches to leadership open up the "blackbox" of leading, and directly explore how talk and text constructs the performance of activities such as consensus building (e.g., Choi and Schnurr 2014). Rather than view context as something that is distinct and apart from human communication, context is viewed as a discursive phenomenon where the objects that make up the context are constructed through human communication. For example, Grint's (2005) analysis of Bush's rhetoric regarding the decision to invade Iraq demonstrated how he used rhetoric to create a crisis context that legitimated his use of command leadership.

This set of assumptions is embodied in a process-oriented definition of discursive leadership that focuses on interaction. Barge and Fairhurst (2008: 232) define leadership as, "a co-created, performative, contextual, and attributional process where the ideas articulated in talk or action are recognized by others as progressing tasks that are important to them". Different forms of leading are co-created by people in everyday interaction as they draw on various arrays of practices when sequencing their talk and text. People also make attributions whether leading (in some form) has occurred based on what they have witnessed and the context that has been created at that moment.

Discursive leadership distinguishes between little-d discourse (signified by a lower-case d) and big-D Discourse (signified by an upper-case D) (Alvesson and Kärreman 2000). Drawing on Foucault, Discourse is conceptualized as a worldview that provides people a way of orienting to their social worlds while discourse refers to the talk and text that is produced through interaction among interlocutors. Studies of leading focusing on *D*iscourse tend to articulate the assumptions and practices associated with a particular worldview and are concerned with understanding the interpretive resources that *D*iscourse provides people to understand what counts as leading and what actions or action sequences they consider to be permitted, prohibited, or obligated. For example, studies such as Fine's (2009) examination of women's discursive accounts of leadership, Fairhurst et al.'s (2011) study of executive coaching, and Elliott and Stead's (2018) analysis of leadership representations of women in relation to crisis, highlight the gendered assumptions that inform the practice of leading.

Little-d discourse studies focus on the interactional accomplishment of leading and the conversational dynamics associated with leading, unpacking in granular detail the way that utterances and sequences of utterances work when leading. An illustrative example is provided by Wodak, Kwon, and Clarke's (2011) study that investigated how consensus building was accomplished through interaction. They articulated five discursive practices they termed *strategies*, that meeting chairs used to facilitate consensus building: (1) bonding, (2) encouraging, (3) directing, (4) modulating, and (5) re/committing. For example, the strategy of bonding was associated with individual utterances and sequences of utterances that used the plural pronoun "we" to collectivize responsibility, and words like "think" and "perceive" to hedge one's commitment to particular positions, and disclaimers. Such linguistic devices signaled a willingness by individual meeting chairs to listen to the views of others and forge consensus.

It is through talk and text that *d*iscourse invokes and reproduces the presence of *D*iscourse within interaction or mixes them together in different ways through practices such as bricolage (Pearce 1994). For example, Clifton (2019a) used a celebrity interview involving Jack (former CEO of GE) and Suzy Welch to explore how existing leadership Discourses are drawn on and used within discourse. During the interview, they framed effective leadership using metaphors such as "leader-as-doctor", "leader-as-savior", and "leader-as-loving parent" that drew on a prevalent existing transformational leadership Discourse, which positions the transformational leader as the only individual who can revive an ailing company. Their storytelling invoked and reproduced a transformational leadership Discourse during the interview. Individuals may unknowingly depend on and reference Discourse in their talk. If they have a certain level of reflexive agency (Fairhurst 2007a), an awareness of the existence/presence of different Discourses and their effects on reality construction, they may then use this awareness to strategically encourage preferred forms of interaction and outcomes.

2 Discursive leading and managing

The primary work of discursive leading involves the co-construction of meaning and the coordination of networks of human and nonhuman actants. The former draws heavily on framing studies of leading (Fairhurst 2011) while the latter is heavily influenced by the Montreal School (Cooren 2000, 2012), which is informed by Latour's (1999) Actor Network Theory.

2.1 Managing meaning making

Studies of discursive leading that focus on meaning making typically explore the ways that frames are created and used during interaction to shape the social construction of meaning. Fairhurst and Sarr (1996: 3) define framing as choosing "one particular meaning (or set of meanings) over another" and when we share the frames we use to make sense of the world with others, we are asserting that "our interpretations should be taken as real over other possible interpretations". It is by backgrounding and foregrounding particular frames within the flow of interaction that certain goals and aspirations become more or less salient and preferred pathways of action for leading are determined and pursued. For example, during the COVID-19 pandemic in 2020, political leaders actively debated as to whether to use a public health or economic frame when determining plans for reopening public spaces for social and economic commerce. Depending on which frame or combination of frames is adopted, the reality of COVID-19 is understood and acted on differently.

Framing research explores the types of frames that can be used when leading, how frames are introduced and sustained, and how frames are broken and supplanted through the process of reframing. For example, Fairhurst (2011; Fairhurst and Sarr 1996) offered a typology of linguistic framing tools that are central to reality construction, including metaphors, jargon and catchphrases, contrast, spin, and stories that can be used to shape and crystallize meaning around particular ideas and concepts. Framing assumes that the frames enacted during leading will influence the sensemaking process. For example, Minei, Eatough, and Cohen-Charash (2018) demonstrated how using acknowledgment or explanation to frame an illegitimate task request influenced people's sensemaking and emotional experience.

Minei (2015) also explored the framing-to-sensemaking relationship. She found that harmonious sensemaking occurred when the framing by company leaders through company mottos, guiding principles, and position descriptions were well integrated with each other and free of ambiguity. This facilitated an alignment between the leader's intent and employee expectations. However, discordant framing-to-sensemaking was characterized by multiple competing messages about the company's future direction, company values, and leadership roles, which led employees to have negative perceptions of the company as they interpreted the absence of a consistent frame as lacking transparency and made inaccurate conjectures about the company's state of affairs.

Framing is an interactional accomplishment. Dewulf et al. (2009) observe that an interactional approach to framing differs from a cognitive approach, which is closely tied to leadership psychology, as it positions individuals as lay rhetoricians where frames are invoked in participants' language use and either taken up or rejected by others. Barge's (2004a) study of systemic constructionist leadership suggests that it is important for individuals wishing to create leadership positions to use language that connects with the grammar and logics of others if they are to shape the meaning-making process. This requires individuals to have a sense of relational reflexivity regarding the effects of their talk on others as well as to have access to a variety of discursive resources such as Discourses or interpretive repertoires.

The ability to sustain a frame during interaction depends on the way the frame is managed during interaction. Clifton (2012: 162) observes that management of meaning is about epistemic primacy, what counts as reality in the moment, and that establishing epistemic primacy depends on the sequencing of interaction. Using the notion of adjacency pairs, he argues that "going first makes a claim to epistemic primacy in the management of meaning and going second can be seen as following somebody else's lead. However, the first-position assessment can be neutralized through collaborative completion which claims joint epistemic primacy [...] or it can be challenged through upgrades". The establishment of epistemic primacy depends on the conjoint interaction among persons – whether the first-person position assessment is presented in a compelling way and whether the second-person position assessment challenges, neutralizes, and affirms the first-person position assessment. As Clifton (2012) observes, the use of particular membership categorization devices that are tied to identity may create different kinds of power dynamics that influence people's ability to frame the situation in desired ways.

The notion of interactional sequences, as it relates to establishing and challenging the epistemic primacy of frames, necessitates giving consideration to how interaction facilitates frame-breaking and reframing. Whittle et al.'s (2015) study of discursive leadership explored how categorization practices were used during strategic change and their relationship to frame-breaking and reframing. They observed that sensemaking is directly tied to the "category predicates", the knowledge and associated reasoning processes that are connected with particular categories, which serve as frames that people use to make sense of situations and events. Their study suggested that master frames such as who typically undertakes strategic change work need to be "broken" and reframed in order to create new possibilities for organizational change. Frame-breaking requires degradation work and employing contrasting classes of categories that allow individuals to establish challenges and problems within existing frames that then can be addressed through reframing.

2.2 Managing networks of human and nonhuman actants

Rather than reduce agency solely to the domain of human actors, Actor Network Theory (ANT) (Latour, 1999) presumes a plurality of agencies that may be "textual, mechanical, architectural, natural, and human" that are networked with one another from within the flow of interaction thus creating a hybrid agency (Fairhurst and Connaughton 2014: 410). The use of Actor Network Theory by the Montreal School has led to numerous studies that explore the way that hybrid agency is created within interaction and how leadership structures are altered over time. It has been used to engage with a number of key leadership issues such as leadership presence, power, organizing, and shared leadership.

One area of ANT-inspired research has focused on leading as the hybrid production of presence(s). Fairhurst (2007a) argued attributions by New York citizens after 9/11 that Rudy Giuliani's leading was charismatic could be explained by the network of human actants (the desires, needs, and wants of New York citizens) and nonhuman actants such as the setting of press conferences. Fairhurst and Cooren (2009) subsequently argued that presence is an effect, something that is produced materially or through a given discourse, to a specific audience. They developed the notion of macro acting which permits leaders or followers to speak on behalf of their organizations and intervene in the name of the organization. Presence becomes an argumentative technique, whereby some specific aspects of reality are made present to a given audience that is produced materially or through a given discourse. This attention to presence during leading directs our attention to the "cyborg-like couplings" that human actants knowingly or unknowingly create with nonhuman actants to create presence (Fairhurst and Cooren 2009: 471).

Clifton (2017: 301) notes the role that talk plays in creating these networks observing that "social actors can talk into being a 'leader identity', which is not necessarily a purely physical presence, but can also be a hybrid presence of human and nonhuman actants". Drawing on Cooren's (2012) notion of ventriloquism, he examined how speakers animated networks of human and nonhuman actants (including textual actants) during their conversation. He found that human actants ventriloquized other human and nonhuman actants in three ways: (1) they can speak on their behalf – individuals may ventriloquize nonhuman actants such as budgets where the budget is also presented as making them speak; (2) they can ventriloquize other human actants that may not be present in the situation – an individual may ventriloquize someone by claiming they know what they think; and (3) they can ventriloquize other human actants by using plural pronouns such as "we" – claiming to know what they want and to speak on the other's behalf, which assumes an alignment between their needs.

Leading through ventriloquizing activates different networks of human and nonhuman actants and these networks may be more or less persuasive and likely to gain compliance depending on what elements constitute the network. Fairhurst and Cooren's (2009) study analyzing Louisiana Governor Blanco's response to Hurricane

Katrina demonstrated how human and nonhuman agents can organize their networks of meaning and how one network can take hold and influence another. For example, Hurricane Katrina activated a powerful network of nonhuman agents such as flooding and property destruction that diminished Blanco's ability to create an alternative narrative that would portray her as successfully managing the crisis, leading her to be viewed as "flustered" and "overwhelmed".

A second area of leadership research informed by the Montreal School has explored how sequences of organizing are initiated, elaborated, and closed within space and time. Using schemata theory, Cooren and Fairhurst (2004) developed a template that utilized Weick's (1979) notion of double interacts, conversational analysts' concept of adjacency pairs (Sacks, Schegloff, and Jefferson 1974), and Greimas' (1983) approach to narrative schemas to examine how human and nonhuman actants contribute to the opening and closing off of sequences of organizing. They argue that organizational worlds are spatially and temporally ordered by human and nonhuman actants (including textual actants) through communication processes. Simply, the space in which people organize is not merely the physical building they work in or a prespecified set of hours such as a work week. Rather, the space they work in is communicatively achieved, which highlights the importance of how persons-in-conversation manage overlapping spacing and timing for multiple activities, how they manage transitions from one space to another, and the strategies they use to open and close off spaces.

A final area of research informed by concepts drawn from the Montreal School is hierarchical and shared leadership. Holm and Fairhurst (2018) used Taylor and Van Every's (2014) concept of authoring and grants to conduct an interaction process study that examined the relationship between hierarchical and shared leadership as it occurred over time. Their study revealed the presence of many different types of authoring claims based on organizational position, expertise, and advancing the task. Moreover, their analysis suggested that hierarchical and shared leadership are intertwined and that attributions of their utility are a function of time and timing. At the micro-level of the meetings, leading was shared as various team members contributed authoring claims. Across several meetings or at a meso-level of analysis, the discussion of topics was organized by hierarchical forms of leading where the appointed leader bookended the discussion by initially introducing the topic as well as setting an agenda for its discussion and ending the discussion with the creation of an authoritative text. Holm and Fairhurst (2018: 715) observed that "The participation in decision-making that may be welcomed initially at the micro-level of the team meeting eventually grows tiresome at the meso-level across meetings, as team members wanted a stronger hierarchical presence – not to tell them what to do, but to help contain the excesses of too much participation". Hierarchical and shared forms of leading are both useful, but attributions of their utility depend on issues of time and timing.

3 Analyzing leading

A variety of analytical tools and methods drawn from applied linguistics, conversational analysis, and interactional coding exist to unpack the way leading is performed within the flow of interaction. Fairhurst and Uhl-Bien (2012) highlight a number of organizational discourse analytical tools and strategies that academic practitioners (read researchers) can employ to unpack the interactional accomplishment of mundane pragmatic activities such as consensus building, visioning, and collaborating. More recently, Clifton (2019b; Darics and Clifton 2019) has argued the tools of applied linguistic analyses are equally relevant to leadership practitioners as they work within their organizations and communities.

3.1 Academic practitioners

Analyzing talk-in-interaction has focused on both the category of utterances individuals perform and their associated effects, as well as how these individual utterances cohere into larger patterns of leading and the consequences they create. Fairhurst (2007a; Fairhurst and Uhl-Bien 2012) has identified a number of tools and methods that facilitate academic practitioners taking a rigorous exploration of how leading unfolds within conversation over time including: membership categorization devices; Weick's (1979) notion of acts, interacts, and double interacts; turn taking and adjacency pairs; narrative schemas and episodes; and cognitive and behavioral scripts. Academic practitioners typically make four important analytical choices when designing studies to engage the way interaction contributes to accomplish various pragmatic tasks: (1) quantitative and/or qualitative data, (2) individual messages and/or message sequences, (3) interaction and/or interview data, and (4) singular and/or multiple contingencies.

3.1.1 Quantitative and/or qualitative data

Fairhurst (2007b) observes that quantitative and qualitative data can be used depending on the particular research question that is posed. Quantitative interaction analyses can be very useful for determining whether patterned sequential regularities within interaction exist, as a first cut into a particular area (answering "what" and "why" questions) that may be pursued further by fine-grained textual analysis (answering "how" questions), and by focusing on longer temporal sequences beyond individual interaction episodes in order to explore spatio-temporal forms and phases over time. For example, Fairhurst, Rogers, and Sarr (1987) used a relational control coding interaction scheme to explore whether patterned sequential regularities could be used to differentiate among different kinds of leader-member exchange (LMX) relationships.

This study then served as a springboard for using discourse analysis to perform a more granular discourse analysis of LMX relationships that revealed important differences in the patterns of communication as high LMX relationships tended to be characterized by communicative patterns regarding values convergence, insider markers, and polite disagreement, while low LMX relationships were not (Fairhurst 1993).

3.1.2 Individual messages and/or message sequences

Some academic practitioners focus their analyses on the effects that individual messages produce. The former is represented by studies that use experimental designs and content analysis to test the effects of certain discursive moves on people's perceptions of messages. Minei, Eatough, and Cohen-Charash (2018) used an experimental vignette design where they manipulated whether a manager provided an acknowledgment or explanation when making an illegitimate task request and whether these different linguistic moves mitigated perceptions of illegitimacy or anger. Aritz et al. (2017) used content analysis to code transcripts of small group decision-making meetings and examined how the frequency of question type and response to question influenced the establishment of leadership roles in groups and the role of gender in asking questions.

Other academic practitioners are interested in how turn-by-turn sequenced interaction coheres into larger units of patterned interaction that address issues such as control and managing relationships or exemplify a particular genre of leading. Such studies employ a variety of analytical tools to explore in granular detail the patterning of interaction using quantitative methods such as interaction process analysis (Fairhurst, Rogers and Sarr 1987) as well as qualitative methods drawn from conversational analysis. Aritz and Walker (2014) used turn-taking patterns and interaction analysis to examine how the style of leading may influence the participation and feelings of satisfaction and inclusion within multicultural groups. Wodak, Kwon, and Clarke (2011) articulated interactional patterns associated with authoritative and transformational leadership. Regardless of working with quantitative or qualitative data, it is important to keep in mind that the unit of analysis is not individual leaders but rather the flow of interaction that is conjointly produced among interlocutors that perform and coordinate leading.

3.1.3 Interaction and/or interview data

Organizational discourse analyses of leading can employ interactional or interview data. Interactional data typically comprises recordings and transcriptions of interaction as well as field notes derived from ethnographic work to capture how certain activities such as control and organizing are performed (Fairhurst and Uhl-Bien

2012). Such data allows discourse analysts to go beyond simple thematic analyses that articulate the strategies and functions associated with different forms of leading to focus on how they are performed and sequenced during interaction. The use of interview data allows academic practitioners to examine the sensemaking processes that individuals use to interpret leading and how issues of pacing, sequence, and choice making enter into leading. It uses analytical tools such as reflexive narration and membership category devices to unpack the sensemaking and identity work that individuals attribute to leading.

3.1.4 Discursive and/or discursive-material hybridization

Hybridization refers to mixing elements of different origins. Some studies on leading have focused on the language of leadership, carefully documenting the linguistic moves and strategies associated with particular practices such as framing (e. g., Fairhurst and Sarr 1996; Minei, Eatough, and Cohen-Charash 2018; Aritz et al. 2017). However, such analyses may ignore how practices of leading draw on and combine various Discourses in different ways. Studies focusing on *discursive hybridization* examine how alternative Discourses that have different origins are managed through interaction. For example, Crevani et al. (2015) showed how a new academic culture within a university setting was created by professors as they drew on resources provided by Discourses of Academic Professionalism/Impartial Bureaucracy and Managerialism/Leaderism. Their analysis revealed that members of the university community worked with these discourses in ways that confirmed elements of both, re-formulated elements of one into another, rejected elements of each. Similarly, Hall (2011) explored how Discourses of Jamaicanization, Nationalism, and Westernism interacted to affect the leading practices of Jamaican managers.

Analyses of leading have also pursued the study of *discursive-material hybridization*. Such analyses examine the interplay between the linguistic and non-linguistic world and explore how linguistic performance brings the non-linguistic into play during leading. For example, Ford et al.'s (2017) study used interview data to articulate a lay theory of leadership of material presence by having participants talk about the role of appearance in leadership and the differences it created. Similarly, Fairhurst and Cooren (2009) examined how textual and nondiscursive elements combined to create leadership presence(s).

3.2 Leadership practitioners

An area that has received scant attention in discursive leading is how leadership practitioners within organizations and communities may use the tools and methods associated with organizational discourse analysis to make sense of and intervene in their own leading practices. Clifton (2019b) laments the lack of uptake by leadership practitioners in the use of organizational discourse analysis in order to become aware of how linguistic practice shapes leading and organizing. However, different linguistic tools and pedagogical or training initiatives have emerged recently that aim to build the capacity of leadership practitioners to reflect on their linguistic experience.

Darics and Clifton (2019) offer diagnostic listening as a tool that can help leadership practitioners attend to the discursive realities they engage in. Diagnostic listening is based on positioning and narrative theory and presumes that individuals need to give attention to the stories that people tell about their social worlds that have occurred in the past (storyworld), how they tell the story in the present and what this reveals about their identity (the performance), and how the story and the storytelling may be connected to other larger stories within the organization. Leadership practitioners are provided a number of prompts that promote listening to and reflecting on their stories regarding agency, change, sameness/otherness, and evaluation.

Tracy (Tracy and Donovan 2018; Tracy et al. 2015) and her colleagues have generated an ontological, phenomenological, phronetic, and transformative approach (OPPT-in) that focuses attention on the communicative constitution of leadership. An OPPT-in approach differs significantly from conventional approaches to leadership training by: (1) assuming that communication is constitutive of leadership, (2) that practicing the being of leadership is more important than learning about leadership, and (3) communication theory and practice should form an integrative whole. OPPT-in emphasizes the importance of individuals being in a first-person position where they experience the practice of leadership first-hand and use the resources of theory and research to reflect on their communicative experience. This approach differs from conventional approaches to leadership by using the first-hand experience of individuals versus third-person case studies to learn leadership.

While some leadership training programs do emphasize self-reflective learning models (e. g., Brynne, Crossan, and Seijts 2018), OPPT-in is different in that it foregrounds reflection on one's communication and the communication patterns that constitute leadership within a situation as opposed to more general issues regarding power, authority, and agency. For example, students complete exercises where they are asked to engage in different conflict and negotiation scenarios, reflect on what they experience, report back to the class how these conversations went, and practice difficult conversations that may enable them to manage conflict and negotiation differently in the future.

Finally, the systemic constructionist community of leadership practice within Europe offers another training model for moving individuals to critically inspect the co-created interactional patterns they observe and participate in (see Barge 2007, 2012). It draws on a variety of discursive theories, including Harré and van Langenhove's (1999) positioning theory, Coordinated Management of Meaning theory (Pearce 1994, 2007), Shotter's (1993, 2011) relationally responsive approach to communication, and Appreciative Inquiry (Cooperrider 2008). The practices that comprise this community of practice are designed to facilitate leading practices attuned to the linguistic accomplishment and performance of leading such systemic story making (Barge 2004a) and relational reflexivity (Barge 2004b) as well as the linguistic capacities that individuals wishing to perform leading with others need to develop such as sensemaking, positioning, and playing with meaning making (Barge 2012, 2014). This focus aligns well with other studies on language-reflective practice (Habscheid 2003).

A good example of how leadership practitioners can use particular tools for reflecting on their linguistic experience is provided by Hedman-Phillips and Barge (2017). They studied a top management team of a Finnish international manufacturing company as part of an external consultation that the first author conducted to improve "team spirit" in the midst of industrial decline and a corporate turnaround. This study identified several key interventions that were made by the consultant to help the team explicitly and implicitly reflect on their linguistic environment and how it shaped their team culture.

First, the consultant designed activities that encouraged *explicit reflection* on the team's linguistic practice such as directly reflecting on team transcripts using concepts drawn from the Coordinated Management of Meaning (CMM) and explicitly focusing reflection on the collective communication of the team versus individual communication behavior. This moved team members to focus on specific conversational episodes and to take a deep dive into the sequential construction of the conversation and its effects. The consultant also facilitated sessions where team members reflected on the themes that characterized their team culture given attention to how these themes come into existence, how they were cast as useful or not, and how these themes might be elaborated or transformed in the future. By examining concrete transcripts of their interaction and critically reflecting on how certain outcomes are produced through collective inquiry, the team members systematically analyzed their linguistic experience and its consequences. Second, the consultant fostered *implicit reflection* on the team's experience by role modeling different forms of communication such as appreciative and dialogic forms of communication. By modeling different forms and approaches to communication such as positive storytelling, team members were provided models for new ways of communicating that they could compare and contrast to their current model.

4 Moving leading forward

Drawing on literature from discourse theory, social constructionism, and linguistics, a discursive approach to leading focuses on the interactional accomplishment of leading and how meaning making is managed among individuals and within communities and organizations. Actor Network Theory has been used in a number of studies and has focused attention on issues relating to the way networks of human and nonhuman actants are coordinated and their effects on leading as well as how issues related to the sequencing and timing of utterances are coordinated during interaction. There are three areas that seem profitable for future research: (1) integrating quantitative and qualitative linguistic analysis, (2) facilitating uptake of discursive leading with leadership practitioners, and (3) examining issues of ethics and moral positioning within leading practices.

First, an opportunity exists to develop creative ways to integrate quantitative and qualitative linguistic analyses. With some exceptions (e. g., Walker and Aritz 2015), most discourse analyses of leading tend to focus on a specific case, be it an individual or team, and use textual examples to illustrate how particular strategies or activities are performed. While such granular analyses of individual or team interaction are valuable, how can we scale up such analyses to encompass organization-wide studies of leading and integrate quantitative and qualitative linguistic analyses? Following Fairhurst's (2007a) suggestion, one could envision using corpus linguistics or semantic networks as an initial strategy to map out the linguistic landscape of the organization which could be followed up with an explication of the conversational enactment of leading suggested by specific themes or patterns revealed through the initial quantitative analysis.

Drawing on techniques from progressive discourse analysis (PDA) and experimental critical discourse analysis (CDA) (Kampf & David 2019), one could then create conversational vignettes that could be placed in a survey in order to assess quantitatively the perception and uptake of particular conversational forms within the organization. Given the emergence of analytical tools that facilitate the analysis of language within large systems, finding ways to integrate the quantitative and qualitative approaches to language seems useful as the fine-grained granular analyses of leading can also be supplemented by quantitative tools that allow us to address issues regarding the dispersion and uptake of patterns of leading within organizations, how different conversational patterns are coordinated across units and teams, and how interventions for introducing new patterns of leading can be introduced into the organization.

Second, additional work needs to be done regarding training leadership practitioners in linguistic analysis. To be sure, the idea of reflective practice has been central to many models of leadership development (Byrne, Crossan, and Seijts 2018). However, it is important to develop ways to facilitate the ability of leadership practitioners to describe, critique, and transform their joint linguistic activity. For example, Collinson and Tourish (2015) argue that critical approaches to leadership training offer ways of critiquing the role of power in leading, how culture and context affects leading, and the role of followership. By engaging in critical discourse analysis we have a powerful set of tools that allow individuals to explore how linguistic practices construct power relations.

The challenge is how to translate the resources that linguistic analysis offers leadership practitioners that are user friendly. If linguistic analysis is to have uptake with leadership practitioners, then training exercises and programs need to be developed that speak to their lived experience. For example, could training exercises be developed that foster leader practitioner's awareness of how language positions individuals into certain identities and subjectivities using mundane communication artifacts within organizations such as memos and emails? Could training exercises be developed to facilitate leadership practitioners' understanding of how member categories such as the use of the pronouns (I, you, we) can shape issues such as competition, collaboration, and consensus? Developing relatively simple tools leadership practitioners can use that demonstrate how language choice and sequencing has real world consequence makes uptake by leadership practitioners more likely.

A third area for future research centers on issues of aesthetics and ethics. Current studies linking linguistic practice to issues of aesthetics and ethics provide insight into leading that can be subsequently translated into best practices. For example, Holm and Fairhurst (2018) have demonstrated empirically that managing the transitions between hierarchical and shared forms of leading require individuals to use bookending. However, if we think about linguistic analysis and practice from within the flow of interaction as leadership practitioners must do, this requires us to focus attention on how issues of moral accountability and relationality enter into leading in the moment (Cunliffe 2009; Shotter 2011).

Leadership practitioners must make choices about how to shape, coordinate, and intervene in their conjoint activity with others and must make decisions, consciously or not, as to what kinds of relationships they wish to keep with others, what tasks are significant at the moment, and what it means to progress a task. This requires leadership practitioners to develop wisdom (Grint 2007), ontological acuity (McKenna and Rooney 2008), or work with sensibility (Barge and Little 2008) in the interactional moment to determine how to shape the conversation. Leadership practitioners are often change agents, and our linguistic analyses need to take into account the aesthetic and ethics of change and intervention.

5 References

Alvesson, Mats & Dan Kärreman. 2000. Varieties of discourse: On the study of organizations through discourse analysis. *Human Relations* 53(9). 1125–1149.

Aritz, Jolanta & Robyn C. Walker. 2014. Leadership styles in multicultural groups: Americans and East Asians working together. *International Journal of Business Communication* 51(1). 72–92.

Aritz, Jolanta, Robyn Walker, Peter Cardon & Zhang Li. 2017. Discourse of leadership: The power of questions in organizational decision making. *International Journal of Business Communication* 54(2). 161–181.

Barge, J. Kevin. 2004a. Reflexivity and managerial practice. *Communication Monographs* 71(1). 70–96.

Barge, J. Kevin. 2004b. Antenarrative and managerial practice. *Communication Studies* 55(1). 106–127.

Barge, J. Kevin. 2007. The practice of systemic leadership: Lessons from the Kensington Consultation Centre Foundation. *OD Practitioner* 39. 10–14.

Barge, J. Kevin. 2012. Systemic constructionist leadership and working from within the present moment. In Sonia M. Ospina & Mary Uhl-Bien (eds.), *Advancing relational leadership theory: A conversation among perspectives*, 107–142. Charlotte, NC: Information Age Publishing.

Barge, J. Kevin. 2014. Pivotal leadership and the art of conversation. *Leadership* 10(1). 56–78.

Barge, J. Kevin & Gail T. Fairhurst. 2008. Living leadership: A systemic constructionist approach. *Leadership* 4(3). 227–251.

Barge, J. Kevin & Martin Little. 2008. A discursive approach to skillful activity. *Communication Theory* 18(4). 505–534.

Byrne, Alyson, Mary Crossan & Gerard Seijts. 2018. The development of leader character through crucible moments. *Journal of Management Education* 42(2). 265–293.

Choi, Seongsook & Stephanie Schnurr. 2014. Exploring distributed leadership: Solving disagreements and negotiating consensus in a 'leaderless' team. *Discourse Studies* 16(1). 3–24.

Clifton, Jonathan. 2012. A discursive approach to leadership: Doing assessments and managing organizational meanings. *The Journal of Business Communication* 49(2). 148–168.

Clifton, Jonathan. 2017. Leaders as ventriloquists. Leader identity and influencing the communicative construction of the organisation. *Leadership* 13(3). 301–319.

Clifton, Jonathan. 2019a. Investigating the dark side of stories of "good" leadership: A discursive approach to leadership guru's storytelling. *International Journal of Business Communication* 56(1). 82–99.

Clifton, Jonathan. 2019b. Using conversation analysis for organizational research: A case study of leadership-in-action. *Communication Research and Practice* 5(4). 342–357.

Collinson, David & Dennis Tourish. 2015. Teaching leadership critically: New directions for leadership pedagogy. *Academy of Management Learning & Education* 14(4). 576–594.

Cooperrider, David L. 2008. *The appreciative inquiry handbook: For leaders of change*. San Francisco, CA: Berrett-Koehler.

Cooren, François. 2000. *The organizing property of communication*. Amsterdam: John Benjamins.

Cooren, François. 2012. Communication theory at the center: Ventriloquism and the communicative constitution of reality. *Journal of Communication* 62(1). 1–20.

Cooren, François & Gail T. Fairhurst. 2004. Speech timing and spacing: The phenomenon of organizational closure. *Organization* 11(6). 797–828.

Crevani, Lucia, Marianne Ekman, Monica Lindgren & Johann Packendorff. 2015. Leadership cultures and discursive hybridization: On the cultural production of leadership in higher education reforms. *International Journal of Public Leadership* 11(3–4). 147–165.

Cunliffe, Ann L. 2009. The philosopher leader: On relationalism, ethics and reflexivity – A critical perspective to teaching leadership. *Management Learning* 40(1). 87–101.

Darics, Erika & Jonathan Clifton. 2019. Making applied linguistics applicable to business practice: Discourse analysis as a management tool. *Applied Linguistics* 40(6). 917–936.

DeWulf, Art, Barbara Gray, Linda Putnam, Roy Lewicki, Noelle Aarts, Rene Bouwen & Cees van Woerkum. 2009. Disentangling approaches to framing in conflict and negotiation research: A meta-paradigmatic perspective. *Human Relations* 62(2). 155–193.

Elliott, Carole & Valerie Stead. 2018. Constructing women's leadership representation in the UK press during a time of financial crisis: Gender capitals and dialectical tensions. *Organization Studies* 39(1). 19–45.

Fairhurst, Gail T. 1993. The leader-member exchange patterns of women leaders in industry: A discourse analysis. *Communication Monographs* 60(4). 321–351.

Fairhurst, Gail T. 2007a. *Discursive leadership: In conversation with leadership psychology.* Thousand Oaks, CA: Sage.
Fairhurst, Gail T. 2007b. "Standing by" numbers and statistics in organizational discourse analysis. *Communication Methods and Measures* 1(1). 47–54.
Fairhurst, Gail T. 2011. *The power of framing: Creating the language of leadership.* San Francisco, CA: Jossey-Bass.
Fairhurst, Gail T., Marthe L. Church, Danielle E. Hagen & Joseph T. Levi. 2011. Leadership discourses of difference: Executive coaching and the Alpha Male syndrome. In Dennis Mumby (ed.), *Reframing difference in organizational communication studies: Research, pedagogy, and practice*, 77–100. Thousand Oaks, CA: Sage.
Fairhurst, Gail T. & Stacey L. Connaughton. 2014. Leadership. In Linda L. Putnam & Dennis Mumby (eds.), *The Sage handbook of organizational communication*, 401–423. Thousand Oaks, CA: Sage.
Fairhurst, Gail T. & François Cooren. 2009. Leadership as the hybrid production of presence(s). *Leadership* 5(4). 469–490.
Fairhurst, Gail T., L. Edna Rogers & Robert A. Sarr. 1987. Management-subordinate control patterns and judgements about the relationship. In Margaret McLaughlin (ed.), *Communication yearbook 10*, 395–415. Beverly Hills, CA: Sage.
Fairhurst, Gail T. & Robert A. Sarr. 1996. *The art of framing: Managing the language of leadership.* San Francisco, CA: Jossey-Bass.
Fairhurst, Gail. T. & Mary Uhl-Bien. 2012. Organizational discourse analysis (ODA): Examining leadership as a relational process. *The Leadership Quarterly* 23(6). 1043–1062.
Fine, Marlene G. 2009. Women leaders' discursive constructions of leadership. *Women's Studies in Communication* 32(2). 180–202.
Ford, Jackie, Nancy Helen Harding, Sarah Gilmore & Sue Richardson. 2017. Becoming the leader: Leadership as material presence. *Organization Studies* 38(11). 1553–1571.
Greimas, Algirdas Julien. 1983. *Structural semantics: An attempt at a method.* Lincoln, NE: University of Nebraska Press.
Grint, Keith. 2005. Problems, problems, problems: The social construction of leadership. *Human Relations* 58(11). 1467–1494.
Grint, Keith. 2007. Learning to lead: Can Aristotle help us find the road to wisdom? *Leadership* 3(2). 231–246.
Habscheid, Stephan. 2003. *Sprache in der Organisation, Sprachreflexive Verfahren im systemischen Beratungsgespräch.* Berlin & New York: De Gruyter.
Hall, Maurice L. 2011. Constructions of leadership at the intersection of discourse, power, and culture: Jamaican managers' narratives of leading in a postcolonial cultural context. *Management Communication Quarterly* 25(4). 612–643.
Harré, Rom & Luc van Langenhove. 1999. *Positioning theory.* Oxford: Blackwell Publishing.
Hedman-Phillips, Erika & J. Kevin Barge. 2017. Facilitating team reflexivity about communication. *Small Group Research* 48. 255–287.
Holm, Flemming & Gail T. Fairhurst. 2018. Configuring shared and hierarchical leadership through authoring. *Human Relations* 71(5). 692–721.
Hosking, Dian Marie & Boas Shamir. 2012. A dialogue on entitative and relational discourses. In Mary Uhl-Bien & Sonia M. Ospina (eds.), *Advancing relational leadership theory: A conversation among perspectives*, 463–477. Charlotte, NC: Information Age Publishing.
Kampf, Zohar & Yossi David. 2019. Too good to be true: The effect of conciliatory message design on compromising attitudes in intractable conflicts. *Discourse & Society* 30(3). 264–286.
Latour, Bruno. 1999. *Pandora's hope: Essays on the reality of science studies.* Cambridge, MA: Harvard University Press.

McKenna, Bernard & David Rooney. 2008. Wise leadership and the capacity for ontological acuity. *Management Communication Quarterly* 21(4). 537–546.

Minei, Elizabeth M. 2015. Discursive leadership: Harmonious and discordant framing-to-sensemaking outcomes. *Journal of Creative Communications* 10(2). 141–160.

Minei, Elizabeth M., Erin M. Eatough & Yochi Cohen-Charash. 2018. Managing illegitimate task requests through explanation and acknowledgement: A discursive leadership approach. *Management Communication Quarterly* 32(3). 374–397.

Pearce, W. Barnett. 1994. *Interpersonal communication: Making social worlds*. New York: HarperCollins.

Pearce, W. Barnett. 2007. *Making social worlds: A communication perspective*. Malden, MA: Blackwell Publishing.

Sacks, Harvey, Emmanuel A. Schegloff & Gail Jefferson. 1974. A simplest systematics for the organization of turn-taking for conversation. *Language* 50(4). 696–735.

Shotter, John. 1993. *Conversational realities: Constructing life through language*. London: Sage.

Shotter, John. 2011. *Getting it: Withness-thinking and the dialogical … in practice*. Cresskill, NJ: Hampton Press.

Taylor, James R. & Elizabeth J. Van Every. 2014. *When organization fails: Why authority matters*. New York: Routledge.

Tracy, Sarah J. & Matthew C. J. Donovan. 2018. Moving from practical application to expert craft practice in communication: A review of the past and OPPT-ing into the future. In Phillip J. Salem & Erik Timmerman (eds.), *Transformative practices and research in organizational communication*, 202–220. Hershey, PA: IGI Global.

Tracy, Sarah J., Tara M. Franks, Margaret M. Brooks & Trisha K. Hoffman. 2015. An OPPT-in approach to relational and emotional organizational communication pedagogy. *Management Communication Quarterly* 29(2). 322–328.

Walker, Robyn C. & Jolanta Aritz. 2015. Women doing leadership: Leadership styles and organizational culture. *International Journal of Business Communication* 52(4). 452–478.

Weick, Karl E. 1979. *The social psychology of organizing*, 2nd edn. New York: McGraw-Hill.

Whittle, Andrea, William Housley, Alan Gilchrist, Frank Mueller & Peter Lenney. 2015. Category predication work, discursive leadership and strategic sensemaking. *Human Relations* 68(3). 377–407.

Wodak, Ruth, Winston Kwon & Ian Clarke. 2011. 'Getting people on board': Discursive leadership for consensus building in team meetings. *Discourse & Society* 22(5). 592–644.

Yukl, Gary. 2011. Contingency theories of effective leadership. In Alan Bryman, David L. Collinson, Keith Grint, Brad Jackson & Mary Uhl-Bien (eds.), *The Sage handbook of leadership*, 286–298. London: Sage.

Howard Nothhaft, Alicia Fjällhed, and Rickard Andersson

12 Planning and designing

Abstract: The chapter addresses planning and designing by asking a threefold question: 1) How does talk about plans and designs mobilize specific understandings of the organization, its environment, future and purpose? 2) How do plans and designs have *agency* in organizations? 3) How do management concepts affect planning and designing? The chapter draws on various illustrative examples – from Babylonian metaphysics to the U.S. Constitution, from Hobbes's *Leviathan* to Prussian military doctrine – to suggest that 'talk' about planning and designing has more fundamental implications than previously theorized. Prosperous civilization, the chapter argues, requires plannability of the future and purpose to human action. After a brief etymological exploration and preliminary definition, the chapter explores this idea against the CCO-framework's backdrop and key assumptions: that communication is constitutive of organizations.

Keywords: planning; designing; strategy; CCO; ventriloquism; smoke and crystal; future; purpose

After a brief etymological exploration and preliminary definition, the chapter will explore plans and designs, planning and designing, against the backdrop of the communication as constitutive of organization (CCO) framework and its key assumption. Three complexes will be addressed: (1) In what ways does talk about plans and designs invoke specific understandings of the organization and its environment, especially with regard to *future* and *purpose*? (2) In what way do plans and designs have *agency* in organizations? (3) How do management concepts affect planning and designing, plans and designs? The chapter begins and ends with a plea for a nuanced view. While critical and deconstructive academics rightfully expose ego-centric managers who utilize the discourse of plans, designs, and strategy to "bullshit" their way (Christensen, Kärreman, and Rasche 2019), a "plannable" future and constancy of purpose remain prerequisites of civilization.

1 The place for industry and the uncertainty of fruits

The ability to envision the future and one's own projected position in it has long been identified as a defining characteristic of *homo sapiens*. Thomas Hobbes (1651), in *Leviathan*, devotes considerable space to anticipation and judges it both a blessing and a curse. In times of peace and order, the ability to think ahead lies at the root of any complex, purposive endeavor (or "design"). When peace and order erode, it is the very same anticipation of the future that accelerates the breakdown of civilization, as agents foresee the futility of long-term efforts in a world where they are easily robbed: "In such condition, there is no place for industry; because the fruit thereof is uncertain" (Hobbes 1651: 2165).

The concern of political philosophers like Hobbes is the relationship between individuals and the state; the terms preferred by Hobbes' heirs are big ideas like *power*, *ideology*, and *structure*. Management communication addresses a more modest, yet equally important concern: the relationship between individuals and the organizations and institutions. The CCO perspective, here, is singularly well suited to bring together the macro- and meso-concern.

The CCO perspective's axiomatic assumption is that communication not only "goes on" in companies and authorities, but is, in fact, the constitutive principle of an organization. Communication, i. e., the communicative actions of managers, communication professionals, employees, suppliers, hangers-on, fans, etc. (Cooren et al. 2011), is what organizations are made of. The consequences are far-reaching. If management is understood not merely as running an organization, but as enacting and authoring it, everyday talk matters in more profound ways than previously theorized. Metaphorically speaking, it "creates the world".

With regard to planning and designing, the key problem mirrors the one identified by Hobbes: To what degree does this creation ensure and guarantee certainty of fruit, and consequently, a place for industry? Once you strip away the inherent metaphor in terms like *structure*, the question remains *how exactly* creation happens. Our point of departure, then, lies in the observation that managers, be they corporate CEOs, military people, heads of state, popes, or chiefs of tribes, talk a lot about plans and designs, explicitly and implicitly. When they do, we argue, they necessarily invoke two powerful notions: *future*, as it is tied up with plans; *purpose*, as it is tied up with design. The first aim of our contribution, therefore, is to explore the following question:

1) In what ways does the talk about plans and designs invoke specific understandings of the organization and its environment, especially with regard to the future and the purposefulness of endeavor?

However, plans and designs do not speak for themselves. If we take the US constitution as a plan, we have not established how and why a document authored in the late eighteenth century still "does things" today. Non-human agency, how things do things, is the particular interest of the Montréal School, which is perhaps best understood as a branch of the CCO-tradition. Inspired by the work of Bruno Latour among others, adherents to the Montréal School (see Brummans et al. 2014), e. g., James Taylor, Elizabeth Van Every, and François Cooren, have developed a theoretical apparatus that expands the notion of agency to non-human entities. In the view of the Montréal School, texts, logos, websites (see Cooren's answer in Schoeneborn et al. 2014: 298) carry agency. Our second complex of exploration is, therefore, the following question:

2) In what way do plans and designs have *agency* in organizations?

Finally, there is a third notion on a meta-level. In modern organizations, manager talk is not naïve. While necessities and requirements shape manager talk, it is also shaped by managers' reflexive attempts as professionals to reconstruct themselves communicatively. Managerial communication will be affected not only by the bare necessity to perform and achieve but also by what is *en vogue* in their specialized profession (say, logistics, human resources (HR), or retail). It is here that the study of management communication as a meta-conversation investigating the effects of management concepts comes into play. Our last question is, therefore:

3) How do management concepts affect planning and designing, as well as plans and designs?

2 Planning and designing

Etymologically, the word *plan* derives from Latin *planum* for 'level or flat surface', and later it was used as a verb for our ability to draw on a surface a scheme of action. *Design*, in turn, traces its roots back to the Latin word *designare*, roughly 'to mark'. In English, design acquired the meaning of 'scheming' or 'projecting' and carried less artistic and aesthetic connotation than today. As Shakespeare has Richard III say in the play of the same name: "And be not peevish-fond in great designs". The difference is preserved in modern French, where *dessein* continues to mean 'deliberately', 'intentionally', 'in accordance with a purpose or plan', whereas *dessin* roughly equals 'designs' as artistic concepts, as in drawings or sketching as a technique.

For our argument, we will differentiate plans and designs. We do not claim that there is only one correct meaning of each, but we maintain that agents who invoke the discourse of planning and designing must fulfill linguistic and logical requirements. As the etymology indicates, the prototypical plan is a reduced, often two-dimensional representation of a more complex, often three-dimensional, reality. Architectural plans or blueprints come to mind, but we can also imagine prehistoric humans scratching into soil a scheme of action, perhaps for approaching a gathering of beasts from multiple directions. The idea of a plan is thus to *coordinate action*. In that way, a plan is the functional equivalent of communication.

Management studies offer various typologies of plans. *Symbolic planning* is connected to a broader, long-term plan; *rational planning* features action plans that divide a formal planning process into smaller units or steps of action. *Transactive planning* emphasizes the iterative and constructive character of plans; *generative planning* encourages innovation (Brews and Purohit 2007), while *draft plans* are "explicitly designed to enhance debate inside companies and simulate strategic imagination" (Giraudeau 2008: 291).

On a general level, the imperative of the plan remains *here-is-what-we-will-do-in-time-and-space*. Expressed in the terminology of speech act theory, plans are *directive* and *commissive* (Searle 1979). Plans are not merely a directive device that tells agents what to do but constitute, *commissively* in Searle's terms, the promise of collaborative success under the condition that everyone cooperates as agreed. Christensen, Morsing, and Thyssen (2013) suggest, furthermore, that many plans in the business world are not really meant as directive devices but are somewhat aspirational.

Designs are as much devices of coordination as plans are, but their imperative is different. Designs place less emphasis on the representation of actions in time and space, more on the conceptualization of *purpose*, i.e., a desirable end-state and reason-why. Our prehistoric humans agree that the purpose of the scheme is to herd the beasts into a gorge, for example. The imperative of designs, thus, is *here-is-the-idea*. Terzidis (2007: 69) describes designs as "the spark of an idea or the formation of a mental image" that precedes and shapes the frame for the plan.

> While planning is the act of devising a scheme, program or method worked out beforehand for the accomplishment of an objective, design is a conceptual activity involving formulating an idea intended to be expressed in a visible form or carried into action. (Terzidis 2007: 69)

Explorations of the plan/design nexus are easily confused by the existence of what we term *design plans* and *symbolic purposes*. If you have designed the perfect tin can opener and want to mass produce it, you will have to give detailed production instructions in the form of plans in time and space. If you automate the production, the machine will be ignorant of the opener's purpose; it will not pursue your design but execute the plan devised by the production engineers. *Symbolic purposes* come into play when agents are secondarily interested in the functionality of an item, but primarily in what it communicates. The "real" purpose of a ridiculously expensive designer can opener is to communicate that its owner can afford costly household items: cheap imitations aside, the opener is a costly signal (see Zahavi and Zahavi [1997] for costly signals in organisms, for economic signaling theory, see Spence [1973] or "conspicuous consumption" in Veblen [1899]). The functionality of the opener remains an integral part of its symbolic value, however, and makes the can opener different from a "purpose-free" piece of art.

How do planning and designing go together with the perhaps grandest, most controversial of management terms, namely *strategy*? The strategic plan has been described as a genre of texts characterized by its typical *elements* (e.g., aims, objectives, strengths, weaknesses), characteristic *tone* (directive, authoritarian and at the same time educational, future-oriented, and optimistic) as well as its ambiguity (see review in Piette, Rouleau, and Basque 2014). In *Strategy Safari: Your Complete Guide through the Wilds of Strategic Management*, Mintzberg, Ahlstrand, and Lampel (2009) present ten strategy schools, among which are the *planning school* and the *design school*. Designing strategy, in their account, is concerned with conceiving an overarching, guiding idea – a purpose. Planning, in contrast, is a matter of drawing up plans that are implemented and their implementation reviewed. Mintzberg, Ahlstrand, and Lampel (2009) make clear from the beginning, however, that their approach of distinguishing one-dimensional schools resembles the story of the blind men trying to fathom what an elephant is. Confusingly, strategies take the shape of designs as well as plans. Strategizing happens at the intersection of planning and designing, coordinating action, and imbuing purpose (for further exploration of strategy and strategizing, see the contribution of Allard-Poesi and Cabantous, in this volume).

3 Re-creating the world

Let us turn to our first question: In what ways does management communication about plans and designs invoke specific understandings of the organization and its environment?

3.1 Making the world mysterious or comprehensible

Max Weber's ([1905] 1920) argument in *The Protestant Ethic and the Spirit of Capitalism* is perhaps the best-known account of how metaphysical assumptions can impact organizations, institutions, and even the prosperity of civilizations. We will provide a less-known example. Recently, Woods (2012) argued that modern Europe would be unthinkable without the Catholic Church. Drawing on the works of Father Stanley Jaki (1924–2009),[1] Woods (2012) argues that medieval and early modern Catholicism, rather than suppressing inquiry into nature, largely catalyzed modern science (a fact obscured by the popular fixation on Galileo's case). In his historical-philosophical work *Science and Creation*, Jaki (2017) argues that many advanced civilizations – such as the Arabic, Babylonian, Chinese, Egyptian, Greek, Hindu, Mayan – arrived at astonishing scientific discoveries, yet did not institute science as we know it today. Science as a "formal and sustained inquiry" into nature suffered "stillbirths" because of the metaphysical frameworks underpinning these civilizations and, presumably, pervading their "management talk".

---

[1] Stanley Jaki OSB, a historian of science and philosopher, is ranked among the five most scientifically influential Catholic priests together with Copernicus (1473–1543), the father of genetics Gregor Mendel (1822–1884), the volcanologist Giuseppe Mercalli (1850–1914), and the physicist and astronomer Georges Lemaître (1894–1966), who first formulated the theory of the expanding universe.

Catholicism, as a monotheist faith, maintains that a transcendent, ultimately benevolent, and supremely rational creator endowed the world with consistent physical laws. Jaki (2017) shows that Augustine (354–430), one of the church fathers, repeatedly drew attention to order and consistency in creation. Augustine often quoted Solomon 11:20, in which God is praised for arranging everything in an orderly fashion: "but thou hast ordered all things in measure and number and weight" (KJV, Solomon 11:20).

As the Catholic Church postulates a lawfully ordered world, not only does inquiry make sense, Jaki (2017) argues, but attempts to understand the cosmic design might even please the creator. However, a metaphysically ordered world is not to be taken for granted. Despite developing early astronomy and elementary algebra, the Babylonians "perceived the natural order as so fundamentally uncertain that only an annual ceremony of expiation could hope to prevent total cosmic disorder" (Woods 2012: 77–78). The pantheism of ancient Greece, with a multitude of deities engaging in soap-opera-like antics, did not do much to anchor inquiry into the natural world as a systematic endeavor, despite a flowering of philosophical and metaphysical ideas. In ancient China, Taoism suggested that the world was far too sophisticated to be governed by rules imposed by a creator. As Joseph Needham (1954: 581, quoted in Woods 2012: 78) puts it in his exploration of science and civilization in China: "The Taoists, indeed, would have scorned such an idea as being too naïve for the subtlety and complexity of the universe as they intuited it".

Jaki's (2017) argumentation affirms the constitutive effect of communication. In his view, exegesis of scripture that reconstructed nature as governed by stable, rational, and comprehensible laws, with the supreme being only intervening occasionally, encouraged scientific inquiry. Exegesis that reconstructed nature as capricious and willful undermined it. Similarly, management discourse that emphasizes a relatively stable, predictable competitive environment will catalyze a planned, scientific approach to business, whereas a discourse of chaos and disruption will catalyze hustle.

3.2 Making the world interesting or dangerous

All advanced cultures and religions construe the cosmos as beyond intuitive human comprehension. Presumably, this reflects that advanced civilization as a social environment *is* beyond human cognitive capacity. Anthropologist Robin Dunbar (1996), extrapolating from the observable group size of other primates in relation to their brain size, suggested that humans can maintain stable relationships with about 100–230 others – far less than the population of a medium-sized company. *Dunbar's number*, normally given as 150, is reflected in many social settings, such as the estimated number of academics in a sub-specialization (roughly 200), the size of a military company (roughly 80–150), or the number of meaningful relationships in social networks.

However, overload of human cognitive capacity stems not only from numbers but from assumptions about the world. Some metaphysical systems, like Stoicism, construe the cosmos as beyond human control yet *disinterested* in human fate. Here, plans are restrained by the fact that the world beyond the known is a confusing place. Randomness, not good or evil, is the challenge. The conviction that the universe is impartial stands in stark contrast to other metaphysical systems, in which the world is pervaded by forces that take a *personal interest* in individuals' fate.

Whether metaphysical concerns or business practice, the point is choice. Although business and operations determine how the environment is construed to a considerable degree, there is also an element of favoring one view over the other. Ramírez and Selsky (2016: 91) conceptualize strategic planning as "a process that supports the creation of future value through the identification, definition, production, assessment, and application of goals and resources, and by selecting or making one or more chosen market spaces". By emphasizing "identification", "definition", and "selection", Ramírez and Selsky (2016) mark that strategic planning requires choice. The automotive sector is a good example. Management discourse could emphasize as the primary challenge either the intricacies of technology, innovation, and worldwide supply chains or competitors' machinations. In the first case, the critical problem of planning would lie in complexity, the second in competition (for the performativity of strategy, see, e. g., Vargha 2018).

Augier et al. (2018) see a very similar difference in the contrast between *scenario planning* and its "intellectual cousin", *wargaming*. The authors contend that "[s]cenario planning is designed to grapple with exogenous uncertainty relating to possible contextual shifts in the organization's task environment". In other words, scenario planning predominantly explores ways to cope with randomness. "In contrast, wargaming is designed to tackle endogenous uncertainty relating to an organization's interactions with competitors and other stakeholders" (Augier et al. 2018: 512). Wargaming, places emphasis on simulating dynamic interaction with allies and antagonists.

3.3 Making the world small or large

According to the CCO perspective, the social dimension of planning and designing is captured by identifying three steps: "(1) voicing and collectively negotiating matters of concern, (2) transporting and materialising matters of concern through text, and (3) recognising matters of concern as legitimate (i. e., authorised or authored)" (Vásquez et al. 2018). Princeton historian of ideas Peter Paret (2009), one of the world's foremost authorities on Clausewitz, offers a wide-ranging case study of a fundamental change, effectively a total *volte-face*, in a highly complex organization. Exploring the reforms of the Prussian army after the defeat at the hands of Bonaparte in 1806, Paret not only investigates how a new military doctrine was re-negotiated and rematerialized in text but also traces how the new ideal of the nationally inspired, flexible fighting was culturally anchored – i.e., legitimized – in society via broadsheets, fine art, and literature.

When Frederick the Great died in 1786, the Prussian army was the most feared military machine on the European continent. Only twenty years later, still organized along the same lines, it was catastrophically beaten by Bonaparte's revolutionary army. What had happened? In modern terms, the Friderician army had been a "dumb" organization: the emphasis was on drill and obedience; any initiative was discouraged, the common soldier harshly disciplined, the officer required to be brave, not necessarily smart. The "dumbing down" of the rank and file went so far that drill discouraged any attempt at *aiming*. Soldiers were to discharge their weapons in the general direction of the enemy, then busy themselves with reloading the musket. In the terminology of the CCO perspective, the fusilier's matter of concern ended at the tip of the musket. Drawn from the lowest ranks of society or foreigners, with very little to gain in a decidedly non-meritocratic organization, the world of the Friderician foot soldier, his legitimate concern, was very small. Prussian fusiliers, in Paret's (2009: 745) words, became *automata*: "men, who had been drilled to move only on command and in unison, who had never been taught to aim their muskets, let alone to think for themselves".

The catastrophe of 1806 brought to the fore reform-minded military men like von Scharnhorst (1755–1804), von Gneisenau (1760–1831), and von Clausewitz (1780–1831), who had studied Bonaparte's approach and identified national spirit and flexibility as the key. Thus, while the Prussian military certainly did not invent flexible tactics, the Prussian military in the aftermath of its defeat was the first armed force to *deliberately* "re-empower" soldiers and officers by design, i.e., top-down (Nothhaft and Schölzel 2015). Developed further in the nineteenth and twentieth centuries, the Prussian tradition laid the groundwork for what would become the most pervasive, doctrinally anchored expression of the empowered soldier – known as *Auftragstaktik* in World War Two, "mission command"[2] today (for a variety of perspectives on mission command see Vandergriff and Webber 2017, 2018). In effect, the new doctrine re-enlarged the soldier's world. His world did not end at the tip of the musket anymore but comprised the bigger picture, all the way through national resurgence and liberal ideals.

Paret (2009) shows that enormous not only military but cultural and societal efforts were required to effect the change, i.e., to voice and re-negotiate matters, to transport and materialize, and recognize as legitimate. On the military side, hitherto

---

[2] Mission command, in its modern form, prescribes that superior commanders should not task subordinate commanders with the execution of a *plan* worked out by the superior staff, but with the achievement of an objective. Mission command is the accepted doctrine, although not always the reality, in many modern armed forces nowadays. The Prussian army was the first armed force, however, that was *designed* to react flexibly.

brutal corporal punishment was much reduced. Examination by board replaced nobility as a precondition for a commission, opening new and meritocratic career paths in the officer corps. Regarding materializing in texts, field regulations were rewritten in briefer, more concise terms: the old Prussian infantry regulations of 1788 comprised 546 pages; the new version covered the same ground in 131. On the cultural and societal level, serfdom and many privileges of the nobility were abolished. Not only for the soldier but also the citizen, the world grew larger.

4 The agency of plans and designs

Our second question is in what way do plans and designs have *agency* in organizations. How are "matters of concern" transformed into "matters of authority" when talk solidifies in text and artifacts (Vásquez et al. 2018).

4.1 From talk to artifacts

The US Constitution provides a fascinating example of talk solidifying into artifact. Where it sketches the institutions of republican government (e. g., president, congress, etc.) and its system of checks and balances, the US constitution is a *plan*; where it codifies the purpose of the state, it is a *design*. Defining *text* (or communication) as manifested through material documents or "mediums of communication" and immaterial talk or "collections of interactions" (Putnam and Cooren 2004), organizations exist in-between a state of *crystal* and *smoke* (Taylor and Van Every 2000) where "portions of smoke-like conversation are preserved in crystal-like texts that are then articulated by agents speaking on behalf of an emerging collectively" (Weick 2006: 1725). The text solidified in documents is thus the talk that gained enough legitimacy to be preserved in an artifact.

The US Constitution has not only been subject to a series of amendments but has continuously been interpreted and re-interpreted to reflect changes in society. Thus, Weick (1993) proposes that the emphasis should be placed on plan*ning* and design*ing*, i. e., the dynamic verbs rather than the static nouns. Organizations are construed in a constant state of redesign: "Repetitive cycles of texts, conversation, and agents define and modify one another and jointly organize everyday life" (2006: 1725). Furthermore, the plan will not only have agency over members' behavior but will also be echoed in other plans (Giraudeau 2008; Pälli, Vaara, and Sorsa 2009). The US constitution echoes the *English Bill of Rights* and the *Magna Carta Libertatum*, for example.

4.2 Enactors

There is also a social, strongly identity-related element in planning and designing. Organizational members and the organization itself are engaged in *consubstantialization*, i.e., the co-creation of sameness, as organizational identity is shaped. The construction of a document, be it a plan or something else, is far from a neutral process, as "organizational members attempt to negotiate, debate, fix, and/or change the process of consubstantialization" (Chaput, Brummans, and Cooren 2011: 263). The negotiations that took place during the drafting of the Constitution and resulted in the *Great Compromise of 1787* offer a fascinating case study.

Who are the agents that ascribe agency to the plan? Traditional management literature, beginning with authors like, e.g., Henri Fayol (1841–1925) or Frederick W. Taylor (1851–1915), tended to conceptualize senior management as unmoved movers, the true authors of the organization. The senior managers' task was to "initiate new rules, procedures, and processes; inscribe them into the text; and announce and 'sell' them by various means" while the employees' task was to implement the change, that is, "translate these texts into social practices" (Jian 2007: 13). Thus, in the traditional view, only top management, and ultimately only the owner/entrepreneur, bestowed legitimacy. Employee engagement at odds with top management's ideas tended to be viewed as troublesome.

While Taylor, in particular, sought to design organizations like machines (Morgan 2006), the military, generally regarded as the most machine-like organization, experimented with doctrines that emphasized flexibility and initiative, as we have seen. Purpose and direction were given from above, but the plan was to be made by the agents tasked with executing it; strategic ambiguity was built into directions. Weick's (1993: 347) late twentieth-century description fits the early nineteenth century: "responsibility for the initiation of redesign is dispersed, interpretation is the essence of design".

The CCO perspective is interested in what the plan does to the planner. Cooren (2012) conceptualizes actors who *ventriloquize* the text in a way that ultimately raises the question as to "who is the ventriloquist and who is the dummy". In Cooren's way of thinking, the plan affects the enactor simultaneously as it is being affected. In other words, actors take advantage of linguistic devices, strategic ambiguity, and multiple interpretations (see Eisenberg 1984) to engage in an "intersubjective and intertextual process in the actual production and consumption of strategy texts" (Pälli, Vaara, and Sorsa 2009: 310–311).[3]

---

[3] Studies of art organizations have consequentially found that their plan includes "a number of linguistic devices, including juxtapositions, a rhetoric of certainty and ambiguity" (Daigle and Rouleau 2010) that function as a set of "micro-compromises" between the management's need for order and the artist's need for creative flexibility.

4.3 A cycle of agency

If an *agent* is considered as what or who appears to make a difference and the *agency* the capacity to make a difference, the *agents* of plans and designs can be described as the document (crystal) through which the talk (smoke) materializes, and the agency of plans and designs could be envisaged as resting on other agents' enactment of the document. This leads to "the general problematic of agency" pinpointed by Cooren (2006: 82):

> [T]he socioconstructivists are right to start from interaction, but they need to widen the extension (and intention) of this concept to recognise that non-humans also do things. As for the materialists, they are right to notice that humans are acted on as much as they act, but they need to recognise that using analytical shortcuts like "structures", "power", or "ideology" to account for what influences human action and discourse does not do justice to the complexity of the phenomena they study.

In this sense, the world is "filled with agencies" (Cooren 2006: 82). Agency comprises both the non-human articulations of communication through smoke and crystal as well as the human beings that affect and are being affected by communicative artifacts. Just as the organization resides between smoke and crystal, between non-human and human agents, so does agency reside in all levels of communicative interactions.

5 The management discourse: meta-communication about plans and designs

Our third question, finally, addresses how management concepts affect planning and designing as well as plans and designs. Management concepts, be they generic and lasting or merely fads, tell agents what to do and how to speak, not only to be successful but to appear as managerial. Management communication, as a scholarly discipline, explores what to think about management ideas on a meta-level. There is a limit, however. When meta-communication about one's discursive practices engenders sensitivity to the preconceptions embedded in talk about plans, designs, functions, purposes, etc., that is commendable. To call out "bullshit" in strategizing – like Christensen, Kärreman, and Rasche (2019) do – hopefully leads to better plans and more successful designs. Nevertheless, there comes the point where agents substitute "real" planning and design skills for mastery of the meta-discourse.

By and large, the scholarly meta-discourse in management communication began as a critical counterweight to overly optimistic and functional approaches. Classical and neo-classical management theory seemed to suggest that proper planning and designing could, in principle, be perfected to the point of securing a permanent competitive advantage: a promise of eternal life for companies. The scholarly discourse in organization and management studies deconstructed these heroic, pseudo-scientific models. Plans and designs, it was shown, were often not more than mere coping mechanisms at best: a balm for the frayed nerves of managers. Moreover, what was mostly missing in these accounts, some of which go back to the early 1950s, was a sensitivity towards the recursive effects designs and plans have on the human agent. These were matters brought to the fore by the linguistic or narrative turn.

However, a critical and deconstructive perspective only makes sense against the backdrop of real planning and design competence. It serves as a *counterweight* against managerial egocentrism, but it does not carry weight on its own. Many academics who delight in the vocabulary of "anything goes" would be outraged if the airline supposed to fly them to the next conference took them by their word. That neither side was ever entirely right or wholly wrong is easily illustrated. In *Sensemaking in Organisations*, Weick (1995: 345–346) tells the delightfully deconstructive anecdote of a detachment of Hungarian soldiers that gets lost in a snowstorm in the Alps. Panicked, the soldiers make the mistake of walking around aimlessly in whiteout conditions. Then one of the soldiers discovers a map in his backpack. That calms the men. They pitch their tent, huddle together, and wait out the storm. Once the weather clears, they sit down with their map, figure out where they are, and make it back to camp. Their commanding officer, worried about having sent his men to their death, is much relieved. He asks how they made it back, and they tell him how they got lucky with their map. Puzzled, the officer asks to see the thing and discovers that it was not a map of the Alps but of the Pyrénées.[4]

Weick's point is that "when you are lost any old map will do" (Weick 2005: 1040). His argument, which ascribes a good deal of agency to the map, is by no means naïve or trivial. Not only did the map restore the men's confidence. Mountain ranges, like organizations, Weick (2005: 1055) argues, share *generic qualities*: "a map of the Pyrenees can still be a plausible map of the Alps because in a very general sense, if you have seen one mountain range, you have seen them all".

But is it true that any old map will do? The anecdote obscures that the soldiers were lucky. Although mountain ranges share generic qualities, that does not matter if you exhaust your strength in a dead pass. The soldiers' rescue was not *due* to the map. Surely, it would have been better to issue an appropriate map. Scholars enamored with anecdotes where organizations stumble to success tend to disregard the detachments perished, and organizations foundered because their maps, i.e., their representations

---

4 Weick (2005) has been criticized by Thomas Basbøll and Henrik Graham (2006) for plagiarizing the story word-for-word from a poem by Miroslav Holub published in a 1977 *Times Literary Supplement* (see Andrew 2012). There is a similar story about a Gurkha serving in Burma. When the Chindits were dispersed by the Japanese, the soldier was separated from his unit and for several days hacked his way through the jungle. He made it to the British lines clutching a map he swore saved his life. When he was persuaded to give up this precious possession, it turned out to be a diagram of the London Underground (see Latimer 2017: 183).

of their environment, were wrong. Scholars enamored with attention to detail and meticulous planning disregard the failures of the ostensible masterminds. Numerous are the examples of meticulous planners and grand leaders who led their detachments, organizations, corporations, nations into disaster.

With the adoption of the CCO perspective, a more nuanced view is taking hold. Christensen and Christensen (2018), for example, make a strong case for a "dialogic" of deliberate and emergent perspectives. A nuanced perspective acknowledges that preparing plans is essential – "proper planning prevents piss-poor performance", as the six Ps go. At the same time, it acknowledges that its importance does not always derive from what the plan ostensibly does. A plan does not always have to precisely predict the future to catalyze action, just as Weick's (2005) map did not have to represent the territory to calm the soldiers. Moreover, going through the motions of a scientific planning process might obscure, i.e., bury under "bullshit", what every common-sensical outsider quickly sees: that the emperor is naked, the whole endeavor nonsensical. That does not mean, however, that there can *never* be a good map, or that everyone claiming to know the way must be inherently mistrusted.

Similarly, while purpose is important, it is not single-handedly provided by great leaders, handed down by infallible founding fathers, or inspired by supreme beings. Purpose, or sense, grows over time, is negotiated and re-negotiated. Not only the crystal – the table of ten commandments or the exact wording of the US Constitution – counts. The smoke, i.e., meaning reproduced over the years, decades, centuries, and millennia, counts as well. Augustine could have emphasized, i.e., ventriloquized, other passages in the Bible. That would have resulted in an entirely different conception of the world, yet equally consistent with scripture.

6 Conclusion: plannability and constancy of purpose

Our investigation began with Hobbes' (1651) observation that human anticipation of the future constitutes a blessing as well as a curse. The tragedy of failed states worldwide suggests that Hobbes' (1651) observation about the uncertainty of fruit remains valid. Collier (2007) estimates that presently around a billion humans live in failed or collapsed states. Ghani and Lockhart (2009: 3) put the number higher, suggesting two billion trapped in states which are "either sliding backward and teetering on the brinks of implosion or have already collapsed".

Many reasons have been suggested for the failure and collapse of states. Among the varied explanations – malaria, colonial heritage, civil war, etc. – one frequently re-occurs: *bad governance*. Collier (2007) ranks bad governance as one of four traps that keep countries in poverty. Ghani and Lockhart (2009: 3) diagnose that failed states trap their citizens in state-like structures but fail to provide them with "any certainty about or control over their own futures". Acemoglu and Robinson (2012: 372) diagnose that "[n]ations fail today because their extractive economic institutions do not create the incentives needed for people to save, invest and innovate".

Notwithstanding big ideas like *power*, *ideology*, *structure*, state failure, then, is perhaps more properly diagnosed as the failure of the organizations that constitute the state, its institutions. If saving, investing, and innovating are keys to prosperity, a prosperous civilization depends on establishing organizations and institutions that guarantee plannability, i. e., a future stable enough for long-time, planned efforts on one side, a sense of purpose in human affairs on the other.

The CCO perspective is especially valuable here because it emphasizes that perception of the future and subjective experience of purpose is not merely a function of objective, material conditions. The predictability of the future and the purposefulness of the cosmos are also communicatively constituted, are a function of the way groups see the world, and how they are *made* to see the world. It is here that political philosophy and the study of management communication intersect, the concerns for viable states and effective organizations merge. Some communities, be they countries, cultures, or organizations, prove highly resilient vis-à-vis the uncertainty of fruits. Perhaps for religious, perhaps for cultural reasons, they continue to pursue long-term plans and maintain a coordinated, cooperative society despite "environmental jolts" (Meyer 1982). In other societies, coordination and cooperation quickly collapse: beyond family and kin, the reality quickly becomes the war of all against all, the "natural state" so dreaded by Hobbes (1651). The CCO perspective, with its emphasis on communication and a more nuanced view of planning and designing, is singularly well suited to explore why and how.

7 References

Acemoglu, Daron & James A. Robinson. 2012. *Why nations fail: The origins of power, prosperity and poverty*. New York: Crown.

Andrew. 2012. "Any old map will do" meets "God is in every leaf of every tree". *Statistical Modeling, Causal Inference, and Social Science*. https://statmodeling.stat.columbia.edu/2012/04/23/any-old-map-will-do-meets-god-is-in-every-leaf-of-every-tree/ (accessed 13 November 2020).

Augier, Mie, Nicholas Dew, Thorbjørn Knudsen & Nils Stieglitz. 2018. Organizational persistence in the use of war gaming and scenario planning. *Long Range Planning* 51(4). 511–525.

Basbøll, Thomas & Henrik Graham. 2006. Substitutes for strategy research: Notes on the source of Karl Weick's anecdote of the young lieutenant and the map of the Pyrenees. *Ephemera* 6(2). 195–204.

Brews, Peter & Devavrat Purohit. 2007. Strategic planning in unstable environments. *Long Range Planning* 40(1). 64–83.

Brummans, Boris H. J. M., François Cooren, Robichaud Daniel & James R. Taylor. 2014. Approaches in research on the communicative constitution of organizations. In Linda L. Putnam & Dennis K. Mumby (eds.), *The Sage handbook of organizational communication*, 173–194. Thousand Oaks, CA: Sage.

Chaput, Mathieu, Boris H. J. M. Brummans & François Cooren. 2011. The role of organizational identification in the communicative constitution of an organization: A study of consubstantialization in a young political party. *Management Communication Quarterly* 25(2). 252–282.

Christensen, Emma & Lars Thøger Christensen. 2018. Dialogics of strategic communication. *Corporate Communications: An International Journal* 23(3). 438–455.

Christensen, Lars Thøger, Dan Kärreman & Andreas Rasche. 2019. Bullshit and organization studies. *Organization Studies* 40(10). 1587–1600.

Christensen, Lars Thøger, Mette Morsing & Ole Thyssen. 2013. CSR as aspirational talk. *Organization* 20(3). 372–393.

Collier, Paul. 2007. *The bottom billion: Why the poorest countries are failing and what can be done about it*. Oxford: Oxford University Press. [Kindle Edition].

Cooren, François. 2006. The organizational world as a plenum of agencies. In François Cooren, James R. Taylor & Elisabeth J. Van Every (eds.), *Communication as organising: Empirical and theoretical explorations in the dynamic of text and conversation*, 81–100. New York: Routledge.

Cooren, François. 2012. Communication theory at the center: Ventriloquism and the communicative constitution of reality. *Journal of Communication* 62(1). 1–20.

Cooren, François, Timothy Kuhn, Joep P. Cornelissen & Timothy Clark. 2011. Communication, organising and organization: An overview and introduction to the special issue. *Organization Studies* 32(9). 1149–1170.

Daigle, Pascale & Linda Rouleau. 2010. Strategic plans in arts organizations: A tool of compromise between artistic and managerial values. *International Journal of Arts Management* 12(3). 13–30.

Dunbar, Robin. 1996. *Grooming, gossip and the evolution of language*. London: Faber & Faber.

Eisenberg, Eric M. 1984. Ambiguity as strategy in organizational communication. *Communication Monographs* 51(3). 227–242.

Ghani, Ashraf & Clare Lockhart. 2009. *Fixing failed states: A framework for rebuilding a fractured world*. Oxford: Oxford University Press. [Kindle Edition].

Giraudeau, Martin. 2008. The drafts of strategy: Opening up plans and their uses. *Long Range Planning* 41(3). 291–308.

Hobbes, Thomas. 1651. *Leviathan*. Printed for Andrew Crooke, at the Green Dragon in St. Paul's Churchyard. http://www.gutenberg.org/files/3207/3207-h/3207-h.htm (accessed 13 November 2020).

Jaki, Stanley L. 2017. *Science and creation: From eternal cycles to an oscillating universe*. Fort Collins, CO & New Hope, KY: Gondolin & Real View Books. [Kindle Edition].

Jian, Guowei. 2007. Unpacking unintended consequences in planned organizational change: A process model. *Management Communication Quarterly* 21(1). 5–28.

Latimer, Jon. 2017. *Burma: The forgotten war*. London: Thistle.

Meyer, Alan D. 1982. Adapting to environmental jolts. *Administrative Science Quarterly* 27(4). 515–537.

Mintzberg, Henry, Bruce Ahlstrand & Joseph Lampel. 2009. *Strategy safari: Your complete guide through the wilds of strategic management*, 2nd edn. Harlow, UK: Pearson Education.

Morgan, Gareth. 2006. *Images of organization*. Thousand Oaks, CA: Sage.

Needham, Joseph. 1954. *Science and civilisation in China*, vol. 1. Cambridge: Cambridge University Press.

Nothhaft, Howard & Hagen Schölzel. 2015. (Re-)reading Clausewitz: The strategy discourse and its implications for strategic communication. In Derina Holtzhausen & Ansgar Zerfass (eds.), *The Routledge handbook of strategic communication*, 18–33. New York & Abingdon, UK: Routledge.

Pälli, Pekka, Eero Vaara & Virpi Sorsa. 2009. Strategy as text and discursive practice: A genre-based approach to strategising in city administration. *Discourse & Communication* 3(3). 303–318.

Paret, Peter. 2009. *The cognitive challenge of war: Prussia 1806*. Princeton, NJ: Princeton University Press. [Kindle Edition].

Piette, Isabelle, Linda Rouleau & Joelle Basque. 2014. Credibility and defamiliarization in strategic plans: A narrative analysis. *Academy of Management Proceedings* 2014(1). 1021–1026.

Putnam, Linda L. & François Cooren. 2004. Alternative perspectives on the role of text and agency in constituting organizations. *Organization* 11(3). 323–333.

Ramírez, Rafael & John W Selsky. 2016. Strategic planning in turbulent environments: A social ecology approach to scenarios. *Long Range Planning* 49(1). 90–102.

Schoeneborn, Dennis, Steffen Blaschke, François Cooren, Robert D. McPhee, David Seidl & James R. Taylor. 2014. The three schools of CCO thinking: Interactive dialogue and systematic comparison. *Management Communication Quarterly* 28(2). 285–316.

Searle, John R. 1979. *Expression and meaning: Studies in the theory of speech acts*. Cambridge: Cambridge University Press.

Spence, Michael. 1973. Job market signaling. *The Quarterly Journal of Economics* 87(3). 355–374.

Taylor, James R. & Elizabeth J. Van Every. 2000. *The emergent organization: Communication as its site and surface*. Mahwah, NJ: Erlbaum.

Terzidis, Kostas. 2007. The etymology of design: Pre-Socratic perspective. *Design Issues* 23(4). 69–78.

Vandergriff, Donald & Stephen Webber. 2017. *Mission command: The who, what, where, when and why: An anthology*. CreateSpace Independent Publishing Platform. [Kindle Edition].

Vandergriff, Donald & Stephen Webber. 2018. *Mission command: The who, what, where, when and why: An anthology*, volume 2. CreateSpace Independent Publishing Platform. [Kindle Edition].

Vargha, Zsuzsanna. 2018. Performing a strategy's world: How redesigning customers made relationship banking possible. *Long Range Planning* 51(3). 480–494.

Vásquez, Consuelo, Nicolas Bencherki, François Cooren & Viviane Sergi. 2018. From 'matters of concern' to 'matters of authority': Studying the performativity of strategy from a communicative constitution of organization (CCO) approach. *Long Range Planning* 51(3). 417–435.

Veblen, Thorstein. 1899. *The theory of the leisure class*. Gutenberg. https://www.gutenberg.org/ebooks/833 (accessed 14 November 2020).

Weber, Max. 1920 [1905]. *The Protestant ethic and the spirit of capitalism*. New York: Scribner.

Weick, Karl E. 1993. Organizational redesign as improvisation. In George P. Huber & William H. Glick (eds.), *Organizational change and redesign: Ideas and insights for improving performance*, 346–382. Oxford: Oxford University Press.

Weick, Karl E. 1995. *Sensemaking in organizations*. Thousand Oaks, CA: Sage.

Weick, Karl E. 2005. Plans in case you are stuck. In Bruce Ahlstrand, Henry Mintzberg & Joseph Lampel (eds.), *Strategy bites back*, 72–75. Upper Saddle River, NJ: Pearson Prentice Hall.

Weick, Karl E. 2006. Faith, evidence, and action: Better guesses in an unknowable world. *Organization Studies* 27(11). 1723–1736.

Woods, Thomas E. Jr. 2012. *How the Catholic Church built Western civilization*. Washington, DC: Regnery Publishing.

Zahavi, Amotz & Avishag Zahavi. 1997. *The handicap principle: A missing piece of Darwin's puzzle*. Oxford: Oxford University Press.

Alex Wright and David Hollis

13 Routinizing

Abstract: An understanding of organizing routines as phenomena that are constituted by communication is advanced. Data drawn from an ethnography of a cosmetics firm illustrates the performative power of a communicationally formed makeup routine. We argue that framing organizational routines as relational accomplishments, unfolding on the *terra firma* of interaction, extends existing debates that fail to account for how work actually gets done. The chapter points towards the need for future research to center how the communicational moves of actors (in human and nonhuman entanglements) produce routinized practice. Following a short introduction, how routines are regarded in organization and management theory is briefly reviewed; this is followed by an outlining of a communication-inspired understanding of routinization that centers relationality and performativity; next, data from our empirical setting is analyzed and discussed; a conclusion ends the chapter.

Keywords: routines; CCO; performativity; relationality; routinizing

This chapter discusses and explicates the pivotal role of routines and routinization in management communication. It begins by giving an overview of the study of routines in organization and management theory (OMT). This is then followed by a brief consideration of how a more communication-centered understanding of routinization has emerged in contrast to the dominant OMT view. This perspective is developed in this chapter, with particular emphasis laid on its relational ontology and on the role of performativity. To illustrate this argument, ethnographic data crafted from fieldwork in the United Kingdom sales and education department of a major international cosmetics company, Ella May, are drawn from. A discussion of the implications of a developed, communicational framing of organizational routines for managers and researchers follows.

Several key points are developed throughout the chapter. First, we explain that while routines have become recognized as the primary means by which managing and organizing are accomplished, their traditional framing has limited the usefulness of this realization for crafting insights into how work actually unfolds in organizations. Second, we advance a communicative understanding of organizing routines based on a communication constitutes organization (CCO) perspective (Schoeneborn, Kuhn, and Kärreman 2019); we contrast this with how routines have traditionally been comprehended. Next, we show how a relational understanding of routine practices privileges both an interweaving of conversation and text (Taylor et al. 1996) for their emergence, and highlights how individual routines always interrelate with other emerging routines during organizing. Then, we call attention to the performative quality of some routines; here, we argue that it is the repetitive, citational feature of routine communication that distinguishes it from mere performance and helps to explain the transformational property performative routines exercise. We draw from an empirical study of a management routine to illustrate and substantiate our key arguments and discuss these with reference to our understanding of relationality and performativity. We close with a short concluding section.

1 Routines in organizational and management theory

Researchers such as Martha Feldman and Brian Pentland have been very successful in advancing the study of organizational routines into the mainstream of academic research, particularly within the top North American journals (e. g., *Academy of Management Journal, Administrative Science Quarterly*, and *Organization Science*). Their venture has been to move thinking about routines on from a limiting evolutionary perspective (Nelson and Winter 1982) that considers them from a purely output perspective and disregards any processual dimension. The evolutionary theory of routines and its neglect of process is characteristically criticized as conceiving routines as mindless accomplishments enacted by highly automated human actors working unconsciously (Zbaracki and Bergen 2010). Workplace routines in this framing are mundane phenomena and are felt to contribute little to organizing's unfolding.

Feldman, Pentland and their colleagues' great contribution has been to question the assumptions of an evolutionary understanding and to successfully argue that organizational routines are much more than previously thought. They declare that far from being mindless accomplishments, routines require mindful effort for them to unravel in ways that contribute to the creation of value (Bertels, Howard-Grenville, and Pek 2016). Workplace routines, in this view, require actors to consciously act so that each routine can fulfill its function. Some if not most organizational routines are still acknowledged as being *mundane*, but mundanity is not viewed as a reason not to study them. Mundane routine action is regarded as the default position in most organizations, so if we wish to understand better how value is created we should focus upon what has previously been dismissed: the routine and the mundane. Now, organizational routines are being promoted as the primary means through which work gets done (Feldman et al. 2016). It is for this reason that communication scholars need to pay more attention to the organizing routines that swirl around in our organizations.

Feldman et al. (2016) posit that in their unfolding, routines contribute to both stability and change in organizations, and to investigate these vital phenomena, emphasis is placed on what is seen as the internal dynamics of routines. They achieve this in quite a novel way, but one that is not without its problems. From Bruno Latour (1986), they adopt the terms *performative* and *ostensive*, but they do not use these terms in the ways Latour advanced (Wright 2013, 2016). Rather, they appropriate them to present a structuration-inspired framing of routines. Performative and ostensive are linked to Anthony Giddens' (1984) idea of a structure/agency duality in society, with performative equated to agency and structure seen as commensurate with ostensive. In this view, the performative aspect of the routine relates to its specific performances that are held to appear in specific places and at specific times (Feldman et al. 2016). And, the ostensive aspects are considered to be the abstracted patterns or scripts of the routine that guide and shape how it is performed (Bertels, Howard-Grenville, and Pek 2016). The dynamism within a single routine is said to occur with the ostensive framing how the performative is accomplished. Change in a routine is assumed to happen through the performative enactments feeding back into how ostensives account for the routine.

Existing routines research that adopts these constructs in the way they have been described has been criticized for how both the performative and the ostensive have been understood and applied. Gond et al. (2016) criticize the notion of performative adopted by routines' researchers, describing it as a unique construct created within OMT and having little connection to existing descriptions of the notion. Wright (2016) points out that the idea of performative Feldman et al. (2016) promulgate fails to get us close enough to the actual doings of work-based routines. While *people* are acknowledged in the OMT literature as being human contributors to how routines progress, they tend to be regarded as disembodied actors whose corporeality is not seen as significantly influencing how routines emerge (Wright 2019). The level of analysis such a conceptualization invites is always too far removed to develop insight into how routines are actually constituted. Gond et al. (2016) further criticize that existing routines research of ostensive patterns neglects to connect how they are influenced by theories or ideas in their performance of specific collections of knowledge.

Unfortunately, such criticisms have tended to be ignored and not seriously engaged with by routines researchers. This is regrettable because the research by Feldman, Pentland and colleagues has undoubtedly made significant strides in moving work-based routines into the consciousness of a broader, general management readership. In the remainder of this chapter we articulate a CCO understanding of organizational routines, designed to address the problems we discern in the existing literature and to stimulate communication scholars to take up the challenge of researching this pervasive but still little understood organizational phenomenon. Our CCO-inspired conceptualization of organizational routines stresses their relational citationality, conversation and text dialectic, embodied quality, and assumes that some, but not all, will have performative effects.

2 A CCO understanding of routinization

So, how can a CCO-framing of routine organizational practices address the limitations of the dominant OMT understanding, and how can it help illuminate management communication in modern organizations? We address this by first considering the ubiquity of routine interaction in our organizations. Much of what we engage in and experience can be considered routine, in the sense that it is a recognizable repetition of what has gone before. This does not mean that a routine experienced today will be exactly the same as it was experienced yesterday or the day before. Rather our experiencing of a routine is better understood as another next first time (Garfinkel 1967). Each time a routine unfolds it will be a uniquely experienced temporal and spatial entwinement of conversation and text that resembles previous experiences but does not mirror them. Workplace routines are not merely mindless accomplishments enacted by unthinking automatons as the evolutionary perspective suggests. Routines that make a difference to how value is created are indeed effortful accomplishments. Some examples illustrate our point.

If one thinks of the industry that, as either students or educators, we are familiar with, i.e., higher education, it can be recognized that our organizational lives are enmeshed in the routine. Educators prepare their lecture material following established processes that have been used previously and therefore offer some assurance that through their re-enactment a competent lecture will be delivered. These processes involve the materializing of texts, be they concrete or figurative, such as academic articles and textbooks, theories and concepts; additional texts such as PowerPoint help to frame the lecture and conversations with others about the appropriateness of what is being assembled: "at what level are the students, undergraduate or postgraduate?", "what are the aims of the module?", "what are the learning outcomes attached to the module?", "what is the assessment?", "how does this lecture fit with others in the module?". The preparation of a lecture involves acts that will not be exactly the same as those that were accomplished the last time a lecture was prepared, but there exists a routineness about them that means they are recognizable as acts necessarily undertaken for a lecture to be prepared.

The authoring of assignment essays, articles, book chapters, and books is both a routine process and a creative activity. Over time, most authors, when they write, develop a routine or rhythm that suits their preferred way of working. Temporality is important, when writing is done is both a pragmatic choice – when we can make or find the time to write – and indicative of the preference of authors. Some may feel they write better first thing in the morning, therefore they will aim to set out their day to allow themselves this time. Others could feel that writing late at night is when they are most productive and factor this into their daily schedules. The tools used for writing: laptop, desktop, paper journal; what font to use: Garamond, Arial, Times New Roman; whether the preference is for silence, music, or background noise; and, where one locates oneself when writing: university office, home office, coffee shop are all texts that interplay in the writing routine. Such texts enable the author's creativity; they facilitate the creativity required to produce one's written work. As CCO scholars are well aware, ideas do not only reside in the minds of authors, be they student or faculty, to be reproduced unaltered on the screen or page; routinized writing also produces an author's ideas in text form.

Managers are largely routine workers and management is a function characterized by its routinization (Mintzberg 1973). Managers spend most of their time in formal and informal communicative acts: talking, listening, writing, etc. For example, the recruitment process can be understood as involving an array of routine practices. The placing of a job advert involves repetitive acts that when undertaken in a certain sequence will result in the posting of a vacancy. Shortlisting is often a conversation and textual encounter whereby the relative merits of each application are discussed with reference to texts, documents, that outline the requirements of the job and the essential and desirable skills and experience deemed necessary for the role to be effectively accomplished. The interview itself, often a site of impression management by both the interviewee and the interviewer, is a formal conversation where multiple texts, both concrete (PowerPoint) and figurative (ideas and experiences), are materialized and help to direct the trajectory of the conversation. The selection process is similarly arranged so that talk is based upon texts in order that a decision can be made. Finally, a telephone call to offer the post to the preferred candidate completes this stage of the recruitment process; references are still to be obtained and a contract needs to be signed, of course.

If we wish to understand more deeply how recruitment processes in organizations are managed and accomplished, we argue, we need to follow the flows of communication of the recruitment routine. We need to understand that every enactment of the recruitment process is another next first time, each interview of candidates, even where scripted questions are followed, will be a unique but recognizable rendering of the interview routine. Acknowledging the routineness of processes like recruitment through a CCO lens offers the promise of developing new insights into how routinized management communication is realized. We develop this argument further by discussing two qualities of a communicative understanding of routinization: its privileging of a relational ontology and discerning when language is performative. We begin with relationality.

2.1 Relationality

Understanding routines as constituted by communication rejects the dominant structuration-inspired duality ontology assumed to exist within the OMT community and replaces it with a relational take on organizational phenomena. This is important, we argue, because when managers are recruiting new staff for example, they are, fundamentally, communicating and it is through inter-related communicative acts that managerial actions like recruitment are achieved. A structure/agency ontology assumes a hierarchy whereby agency at the micro level is determined by macro structuring forces. The assumed recursive relationship between the two levels is always shrouded in mystery and characterized as a *black box* that largely defies explanation (Pentland and Feldman 2005). Alternatively, the relational approach we advocate embraces the assumption that understanding more about how work actually unfolds in organizations is best realized by never leaving the *terra firma* of interaction (Kuhn, Ashcraft, and Cooren 2017; Schoeneborn, Kuhn, and Kärreman 2019).

This approach does not deny that more *macro* influences can make a difference to what happens in the *micro* of everyday interactions, rather, it assumes that such texts exert their authority on action through how they motivate and shape the conversations that drive managing and organizing interactions. There is no black box at the ground level, however. At a practice's site of unraveling there is only communicational unfolding that is relationally accomplished as agency unfurls in a conversational talk and textual (both modest and authoritative) interplay (Sandberg and Tsoukas 2011).

Relationality advances that creating value in organizations through routine practices emerges from, and is performed in, communication (Kuhn, Ashcraft, and Cooren 2017: 27). Traditional separations of human and nonhuman actors situate them as separate phenomena that connect when they are brought together in action. Moving toward a relational understanding questions whether such an approach can adequately account for how, for example, preparing and delivering an academic lecture unfolds. Are texts brought together for the authoring that produces a lecture; or, do the texts and human conversations *conjointly* (Kuhn, Ashcraft, and Cooren 2017) materialize in the acts necessary for lecturing to take place?

Kuhn, Ashcraft, and Cooren (2017: 31) explain that the texts that are required for lecture delivery "are not pre-bounded entities that exist before they come into contact with humans". Such an assumption would suggest that texts are somehow and somewhere waiting to be activated in human practice and are called upon and called down when they are needed. Also implied is that such a *calling down* calls into being texts unaltered from how they reside in the ether awaiting their human call. Rather, in their materializing on the *terra firma* of interaction, texts are formed another next first time each time they co-mingle with conversations. Texts then, do not exist to be called down, but only exist in their material relating with other texts and conversations (Kuhn, Ashcraft, and Cooren 2017).

Routinizing, therefore, becomes a form of managerial practice that involves material relating that resembles similar forms of material relating. A routine's resemblance to previous occurrences facilitates and takes advantage of familiarities, foibles, and whimsical language patterns that, though meaningful in the context of the routine, would lose their meaning if demonstrated away from it. Such felicity conditions (Austin 1975) contribute to the routineness of a routine. Acts of posting an advert, shortlisting, interviewing, selecting, and offering a job to a desired candidate are only meaningful when they occur as part of the recruitment routine. Were shortlisting and interviewing, for example, to occur as part of, say, the routine of strategy implementation, they would be deemed infelicitous and lack meaning.

During the recruitment routine, styles and traits of communication not necessarily customary elsewhere are accepted and deemed appropriate and necessary for the routine to maintain its trajectory. For example, during an interview the bodily communications of interviewees are scrutinized by interviewers, and interviewers' corporeality is carefully observed by interviewees much more closely than would be the case during other interactions. Styles and types of dress are also taken account of and noted that, once the successful applicant begins in her new post, go unrecognized. After all, this is why we *dress* for an interview. And silences, when an interviewee may be thinking of a response to an interviewer question, are interpreted for the meanings that may lie behind them; was the interviewee caught off-guard (for we assume that interviewees are on-guard during the interview interaction), for example?

Conceiving of organizational routines through a relational ontology as opposed to a duality of structure ontological stance encourages investigators to remain firmly at the level of practice, while recognizing that what happens there is influenced by what is not present. The accomplishment of a routine materializes the interplay of text and talk in a unique unfolding that is recognizable as a routine practice because of the communicational familiarity of interaction. Although much of what we do and encounter can be considered routine, each iteration is a complex, creative, and precarious accomplishment (Kuhn, Ashcraft, and Cooren 2017). Academic lectures could emerge differently if the interplay of conversations and texts materializes differently. The outcome of a recruitment process could have been different had the communicative cues been conjointly assembled differently to how they formed on that particular day at that particular time. Organizational routines, we argue, are much more than is commonly assumed. In the next section we discuss how routines can performatively constitute those they implicate.

2.2 Performativity

The origin of our communicational take on performativity can be found in the work of philosopher J. L. Austin. Austin (1975) distinguished between words and utterances that do things and those that merely express, transmit, or represent things. Most research on communication in management tends to neglect the *performative* power of language and instead concentrates solely on *constative* utterances (Austin 1975). McKinlay (2010a: 123) argues that constatives, while not performatives themselves, could become the basis, what he describes as the "sub-set" upon which performatives are formed. And yet, we understand little about how such performatives emerge. We know far more about constative expressions, transmissions, and representations in management; those that attempt to convey pre-existing meaning in a neutral way, than we do about performative utterances that, in their saying, *do* something; they create that to which they refer, and in their creating they constitute new organizational realities.

Austin's (1975) focus on felicity conditions demonstrates the importance of where communication takes place, who is communicating, the authority invested in the communicator, and what other communicative processes are invoked. What Austin did not explicitly consider is the vital role of repetition and how recurring communication authorizes communication-induced transformation and change. For insights into this and how this accounts for some routines' performative quality we turn to the work of philosopher and gender theorist Judith Butler. As our interest in this chapter is on routinization and routinizing, we focus here on Butler's (1993) discussion of citationality, which is how she terms the reiterative practice "by which discourse produces the effects that it names" (Butler 1993: 2). It is the citationality of gender discourses, Butler argues, that produce societal understandings of gender, sex, and bodies.

We distinguish between the terms *performance* and *performativity*. Performance tends to denote the following of a script (McKinlay 2010b), which has little or no long-term lingering effect (Fox and Alldred 2015) on those who are involved with it; either on their corporeality or intellectual outlook. Performativity, by contrast, implies greater significance and suggests that the effects of performative practice transform bodies and intellectual perspectives, changing how sense is made of social worlds. Performative action can, like performances, follow managerially imposed scripts (e. g., standards, protocols, work instructions, etc.); however, in the following of a script a routine becomes performative when the effects of it transform those implicated in the script in terms of what they do, who they are, how they make sense, and how they regard themselves and become perceived by others. The writings on routines by Feldman, Pentland and colleagues contains the tautological implication that *all* routines are performative because they all possess a performative aspect. Our reading of this literature is that when reference is made to a routine's performative aspect, scholars are largely referring to a routine's performance, as the level of analysis is frequently too far removed from the *terra firma* of practice for a judgment about a routine's performative consequences to be made.

For Butler (1993: 2), performativity must "be understood not as a singular or deliberate 'act,' but rather as [a] reiterative and citational practice". Performativity is not achieved through one-off communicational acts but can be accomplished through relatively rare utterances that have a social as well as linguistic content (Austin's felicity conditions) that impact on our worlds (McKinlay 2010a). Through recognizable and repetitive conjoinings of conversation and text, materialized communication becomes stabilized over time to produce practice that becomes accepted and regarded as routine. Identifying workplace routines is of analytical interest and promise because it opens up new possibilities for insight to be crafted into how management unfolds. Routines that have a performative impact are those citational practices that transform employees, workplaces, and society.

The importance of routine communicating to performativity is acknowledged by Butler (1993: 14) when she describes her project as being about "the reworking of performativity as citationality". While we noted above that our relational ontological framing of routines assumes that conversations and texts materialize in their coming together in the moment of practice, their materializing is also a kind of citationality (Butler 1993). Citational materialization needs to contain the reiteration of plausible associative norms that legitimize any performative intent. Most types of performatives in management are verbal or written statements that, in their uttering, accomplish a certain action that exercises an authoritative and disciplining power. Performativity can be discerned in management when speech and text aim to "confer a binding power" (Butler 1993: 225) on those addressed. Such an exercise of power transforms both those managed and those that are managing into norm-affirming materializations.

In our next section we provide an empirical illustration of management routines as communicative constitutions. We explain how the founder of a company imposed a relational routine on staff and how their repetitive enactment of the routine performatively produced transformational consequences.

2.3 Ella May and *the Ultimate* routine

The ethnographic data we draw from for our empirical illustration of routinizing management communication centers on fieldwork conducted in the UK sales and education department of a major international cosmetics company (Hollis 2018). The firm is eponymously named after its US founder. So, our reference to "Ella May" denotes both the founder and the company name. Fieldwork comprised nine months of on-site data collection where approximately 640 hours were spent working, observing, and conversing with largely female makeup artistry teams and observing how managerial visits were conducted. The remaining time was taken up attending meetings (85 hours) and training courses (65 hours). Our attention was on how a specific makeup routine, referred to by participants as the Ultimate, was managerially imposed on makeup artists who were required to apply it on their own faces, and then to perform it on and sell its application, associated products (e. g., blush), and accoutrements (e. g., brushes) to clients. As our focus is on the managerial aspects of communicative routinizing, we emphasize how an organizational routine, the Ultimate, performatively acts in disciplining and transforming artists' bodies.

Pages 20 through to 76 of the eighty-seven-page Basic School Training Workbook (Ella May 2016) are dedicated to how to apply the Ultimate. New artists receive this workbook and are instructed to follow the ten steps in the order below. A "face chart" text acts as a prescription for how makeup should be applied on clients' faces, an explanation for what makeup has been applied, and a prompt for the customer to purchase further cosmetic products. The "face chart" is typically presented to clients at the completion of their treatment as a record of what makeup has been applied and, of course, as a cue for them to purchase Ella May cosmetic products (Ella May 2016: 3):

1. Skincare
2. Corrector & Concealer
3. Foundation
4. Powder/Bronzer
5. Blush
6. Lips
7. Brows
8. Eye Shadow
9. Eye Liner
10. Mascara

The sequential order of steps is important as Ella May believes that, with regard to its customers, it allows its artists to "create a beauty regime that's right for you" (Ella May 2015: 2). From a managerial perspective, however, makeup artists are also required to have applied and wear the makeup in the same prescribed manner. Such an imposition is managerially controlled and surveyed.

The Ultimate is a managerially designed routine that is the main source of both reputational (internal and external) and economic (external) value for Ella May. It is viewed internally as its unique selling point with its customers. This approach to cosmetically making up the face distinguishes it from its main competitors and gives Ella May its commercial edge. An artist who had worked for one of Ella May's main competitors described the difference in approach of the two firms: "xxx products can be used in various ways but at Ella, products have to be used in the 'Ella way' [...] there's a different ethos with Ella. You follow the face chart and it's less creative than xxx" (field note).

Ella May requires that all its makeup artists apply makeup upon themselves in the same ten-step order as they do on their clients. This is a non-negotiable condition of employment. During recruitment, candidates are visually assessed and judgments are made on whether, through applying the Ultimate upon themselves, they can be transformed into embodying what Ella May designates as her/its preferred beauty aesthetic. Phrases such as "can we Ella her?" and "is she Ella?" were overheard when managers were discussing the potential suitability of candidates. One new starter reported how she had been interviewed for a position at Ella May six months previously but had not been successful. She said she had gone away and changed how she had applied her own makeup to more closely align with the Ella May "look" (interview).

During an interview with an Ella May counter manager, she related how adopting the mandatory ten steps as her own makeup regime caused her to change the order that she cosmetically made up her face:

Before working for Ella, because a lot of people do this, I always [did] my eye makeup before doing lip and cheek, and when I came to work for her I was like, "This is weird, we're doing lip and cheek beforehand". So when I asked it was explained to me that we do it in that certain order because every stage is enhancing [...] It was initially explained to me if the fire alarm went off and I had to go outside, if I've got my eye makeup on but I've got no lips and cheeks on I look half done. But they were like, "If your lip and cheek is done and you've got no eye makeup on still, that still works" [...] So it's just saying at every stage just add an additional stage [...] Yes, so we're enhancing at each stage, that's why we go through it in that specific order that Ella's put together. (Counter Manager interview)

It is not just a change in the order of application that the Ultimate requires. It also changes the way individuals look and feel about themselves. The routine's repeated enactment has a performative effect in that through a conjoining of the texts necessary for the Ultimate to be accomplished with the conversations that inform its trajectory, actors who were previously not deemed "Ella" are transformed into the socially desirable status of self-styled *Ella-ettes* (field note).

Ella-ettes, those staff that fully embody the Ella look, present a homogeneous beauty aesthetic characterized as a dewy complexion, with light hued skin foundation that makes the darker-painted eye area "pop" (i.e., stand out), and blusher on the "balls" of the cheeks to resemble the color of skin after it is "pinched" (field note).

The Ella May look is racially ambivalent and does not account for the different shapes faces can be. Makeup artists with different ethnic heritages were required to apply the makeup with the same results as white artists. One artist was observed to be self-conscious about what she perceived to be her round-shaped face and she resisted adopting the mandated makeup routine. This was addressed by managers during their routine surveilling of on-counter makeup artists. Following discussion, a manager sat down with the artist and touched-up her makeup using the Ultimate's constituent steps so that it appeared more aligned with the preferred ideal (field note). Managers were observed to ask artists who they suspected of not following the ten-step routines correctly to "talk me through your ten steps" (field note) to explain how they had applied makeup to their faces.

Peer pressure to conform was often less overt. Ella May made extensive use of social media where artists were encouraged to post photographs of their made-up faces, displaying the Ella look. Transformational photographs, before Ella and after Ella, were also encouraged and these often elicited effusive comments from peers as well as managers about the positive effects of applying the Ultimate. Comments such as "you look lovely", "looking very Ella", and "amazing" were common. Claims for the performative transformations the ten steps had achieved were extravagant. Ella-ette artists were described as being much more "confident" and through making up their faces as having become "another pretty [and] powerful woman" (field notes).

Figure 1, taken from Ella May's UK staff-only Facebook group, illustrates the Ultimate's performative effects after its managerially mandated application by artists. The post appeared underneath an ebullient title; "Amazing, fun and inspiring breakfast meeting":

Figure 1: A Facebook post showing the Ultimate routine being performed

The manager's post shows artists' enactment of the Ultimate and details its claimed transformational and therefore performative effects. Labeled as a "(F)ace chart competition", artists must copy the manager's application of the ten steps (one of which, corrector, is shown being administered in the top-left image) and accomplish Ella May's aesthetic ideal (top-right image) on their colleagues' faces by applying "Red" or "Pink" shaded products in the prescribed "face chart" order (as emphasized by another manager pictured holding the face chart in the bottom-right image). Fulsome remarks such as "Dream team", "Saviour", and "We are ready to smash February" mark a transformational achievement as artists' bodies, identities, and attitudes are felt to be optimized before the store opens and clients are served.

In the next section we draw on our data to discuss how this communicative managerial routine can stimulate insights into our relational ontological understanding of organizational routines and their performative quality.

3 Discussion

The Ultimate routine is depicted in textual form as a ten-step process that new starters to Ella May are introduced to during their basic training (Ella May 2016). Conventional approaches to investigating organizational routines would characterize this script as a macro phenomenon bearing down upon, or as being drawn from in the micro interaction of artists applying makeup to both their own faces and the faces of their clients. Our relational ontology framing of organizational routines enables us to present a more nuanced and finely grained interpretation that allows us to understand management communication more deeply.

The ten steps do not reside in a fixed state that is external to the site of interaction to be called upon to act in combination with human conversation. Rather, their invoking creates each step anew as it conjoins with actors in their sites of unraveling (Kuhn, Ashcraft, and Cooren 2017; Sandberg and Tsoukas 2011). These sites of unraveling differ; they can be in an artist's own home as she hurriedly applies her makeup prior to heading off to work, or, in a large department store as she conducts a makeup lesson with a customer prior to the client enjoying a social evening out. Each individual step and the ten steps as a whole only exist in their material relating with other texts and conversations that revolve around organizing actors. These other conversations and texts influence how the routine is accomplished. A new starter eager to please is likely to take great care over how the routine is applied and display awkward movements as she concentrates on getting her brush strokes, etc. just right. Whereas, a more experienced colleague, a manager for example, may apply her makeup with little conscious thought as to the hand movements and facial contortions necessary for the cosmetic products to be transferred from their containers to her face. In both cases the ten steps materialize in different, but recognizably similar, acts of embodied practice.

A relational privileging of organizational routines recognizes that each embodied unfurling of a routine occurs in contexts of overlapping, inter-relating routines of different varieties and types. The routines that an ambitious new starter is embedded within as she applies the Ultimate routine are different to those that a young female customer is emplaced within when it is applied upon her. When organizations implicitly recognize this, the temptation is to construct routine standards and procedures that are tighter and tighter, and to establish more and more elaborate means of control. And yet, however tight the script and intricate the monitoring, routines will always be accomplished in ways that depart from the prescribed instruction, for another next first time (Garfinkel 1967).

This is inevitable when we consider the complexity of modern organizations that are entangled in an ever-evolving communicational milieu. Instead of assuming that authoritative routines can be followed in the way organizations dictate, managers would be better advised to appreciate the fluidity of their prescriptions and be open to recognizable, but necessarily imperfect, repetitions from which they can learn. For example, the ten-step order of the Ultimate is sometimes subverted when at industry fashion shows, time restrictions do not allow for the ten steps to be applied sequentially as more than one makeup artist is working on the model at any one time. And further, a particular makeup artist recalled being more comfortable reversing the order of two steps within the Ultimate's prescribed ten steps, while still accomplishing its mandated aesthetic effect: "[the ten step] just doesn't work for me. Me personally, if I'm going anywhere I do my eyes first and my foundation and it works for me" (makeup artist). The same organizational routine then, can be accomplished differently and still achieve the same desired outcome. Their significance lies not just in their individual achievement, but in how they associate with the other routines they inevitably implicate and effect.

While not all routines are performative, as is frequently claimed in the OMT literature, all routines hold the potential to become performative (Butler 1993), if, through their unfolding, they transform those to whom they are aimed into new realities. Routines are phenomena whose repeatability has effects. Through citationality, routines can produce effects on the body. This is something that the existing literature is yet to fully address. Communication can change bodies (Ashcraft, Kuhn, and Cooren 2009). As was witnessed, makeup artists were largely willing participants in altering their physical appearance to one that more closely resembled that prescribed by Ella May. The longitudinal nature of our fieldwork allowed us to observe that the effects of repeated daily (and hourly) applications of the ten-step process ran deeper than mere superficial, surface-level restylings of appearance. The artists who self-disciplined to embrace this routine transformed themselves into "gorgeous Ella-ettes" (field note), whose desirable status was consistently reinforced through face-to-face conversation and social media posts. When actors resist the Ultimate's performative intent, managerial surveillance and corrective action is taken. However, resistance has consequences and reduces a routine's performative power.

Performativity in organizations then, is a particular form of communicative language that produces the effects it names. History both precedes and conditions such instances of language use so that when they are materialized their transformational power is mobilized (Butler 1993). As Butler (1993) notes when considering the performative construction of gender, performativity tends to work, in part, by covering over the means by which communication *claims* its performativity, thus masking both performativity's power and its authoring. The Ultimate is not presented by Ella May and its managers as an attempt to performatively transform those to whom it is aimed into homogenized replicants of beauty. It is offered in more benign terms as a means of helping women become both "pretty" and "pretty powerful" (field note). Understanding performativity as citational communicating is important if we are to develop our knowledge of how managers constitute, maintain, and direct organizing in ways they can disguise or simply be unaware of.

4 Conclusion

In this chapter we have outlined a communicational understanding of organizational and management routines. Our focus has been on demonstrating how a communicative understanding, one embedded in a communication constitutes organization (CCO) (Schoeneborn, Kuhn, and Kärreman 2019) approach, attends to the deficiencies and problems existing organization and management theory perspectives exhibit. In particular, we show the benefits of a relational ontological framing of routines and how a more developed and historically based conceptualization of performativity can help researchers determine when language changes and transforms organizational reality, not just performs it. As our illustration centering on UK makeup artists within a multinational cosmetics company highlights, citationality (Butler 1993) is the construct that extends performances into performativity. For communication scholars interested in management communication and how value is constituted, privileging workplace routines as the dominant means by which work unfolds and gets done opens up new possibilities to refine our understanding of how organizational practices are communicationally produced and reproduced.

5 References

Ashcraft, Karen L., Tim R. Kuhn & François Cooren. 2009. Constitutional amendments: "Materializing" organizational communication. *The Academy of Management Annals* 3(1). 1–64.

Austin, John L. 1975. *How to do things with words*, 2nd edn. Edited by J. O. Urmson & Marina Sbisà. Cambridge, MA: Harvard University Press.

Bertels, Stephanie, Jennifer Howard-Grenville & Simon Pek. 2016. Cultural molding, shielding, and shoring at Oilco: The role of culture in the integration of routines. *Organization Science* 27(3). 573–593.

Butler, Judith. 1993. *Bodies that matter: On the discursive limits of "sex"*. New York: Routledge.

Ella May. 2015. *Menu of lessons*. Unpublished.

Ella May. 2016. *Basic training workbook*. Unpublished.

Feldman, Martha S., Brian T. Pentland, Luciana D'Adderio & Nathalie Lazaric. 2016. Beyond routines as things: Introduction to the special issue on routine dynamics. *Organization Science* 27(3). 505–513.

Fox, Nick J. & Pam Alldred. 2015. New materialist social inquiry: Designs, methods and the research assemblage. *International Journal of Social Research Methodology* 18(4). 399–414.

Garfinkel, Harold. 1967. *Studies in ethnomethodology*. Englewood Cliffs, NJ: Prentice Hall.

Giddens, Anthony. 1984. *The constitution of society: Outline of the theory of structuration*. Oxford: Polity Press.

Gond, Jean-Pascal, Laure Cabantous, Nancy Harding & Mark Learmonth. 2016. What do we mean by performativity in organizational and management theory? The uses and abuses of performativity. *International Journal of Management Reviews* 18(4). 440–463.

Hollis, David J. D. 2018. *"It's the secret to the universe": The communicative constitution and routinization of a dominant authoritative text within a UK cosmetics company*. Milton Keynes, UK: The Open University PhD thesis.

Kuhn, Tim, Karen L. Ashcraft & François Cooren. 2017. *The work of communication: Relational perspectives on working and organizing in contemporary capitalism*. New York: Routledge.

Latour, Bruno. 1986. The powers of association. In John Law (ed.), *Power, action and belief: A new sociology of knowledge?*, 264–280. London: Routledge & Kegan Paul.

McKinlay, Alan. 2010a. Performativity: From J. L. Austin to Judith Butler. In Peter Armstrong & Geoff Lightfoot (eds.), *'The leading journal in the field': Destabilizing authority in the social sciences of management*, 119–142. London: MayFlyBooks.

McKinlay, Alan. 2010b. Performativity and the politics of identity: Putting Butler to work. *Critical Perspectives on Accounting* 21(3). 232–242.

Mintzberg, Henry. 1973. *The nature of managerial work*. New York: Harper & Row.

Nelson, Richard R. & Sidney G. Winter. 1982. *An evolutionary theory of economic change*. Cambridge, MA: Harvard University Press.

Pentland, Brian T. & Martha S. Feldman. 2005. Organizational routines as a unit. *Industrial and Corporate Change* 14(5). 793–815.

Sandberg, Jörgen & Haridimos Tsoukas. 2011. Grasping the logic of practice: Theorizing through practical rationality. *Academy of Management Review* 36(2). 338–360.

Schoeneborn, Dennis, Tim R. Kuhn & Dan Kärreman. 2019. The communicative constitution of organization, organizing, and organizationality. *Organization Studies* 40(4). 475–496.

Taylor, James R., François Cooren, Nicole Giroux & Daniel Robichaud. 1996. The communicational basis of organization: Between the conversation and the text. *Communication Theory* 6(1). 1–39.

Wright, Alex. 2013. Organizational routines: Toward a communicational perspective. *Sciences de la Société* 88. 21–57.

Wright, Alex. 2016. Organizational routines as embodied performatives: A communication as constitutive of organization perspective. *Organization* 23(2). 147–163.

Wright, Alex. 2019. Embodied organizational routines: Explicating a practice understanding. *Journal of Management Inquiry* 28(2). 153–165.

Zbaracki, Mark J. & Mark Bergen. 2010. When truces collapse: A longitudinal study of price-adjustment routines. *Organization Science* 21(5). 955–972.

Consuelo Vásquez
14 Branding

Abstract[1]: This chapter explores the contribution of the communicative constitution of organization (CCO) approach to corporate branding by focusing on the organizing properties of branding as a discursive practice. The current state of research in corporate branding has been rather dominated by linear models of communication. The CCO approach challenges such view by considering branding as an emergent and polyphonic communicative process characterized by the indeterminacy of meaning, by acknowledging the productive capacities of the "receivers" of the brand, and the agency of non-human actors. Future research can develop a more responsible approach to branding that considers other stakeholders, such as citizens and nature. The chapter presents the key premises of the CCO approach and the theoretical developments in the corporate branding literature that propose communicational explanations to branding. Then, it offers an illustration in the context of university branding. It concludes with theoretical lessons and practical orientations for management communication.

Keywords: CCO approach; corporate branding; meaning indeterminacy; university branding; brand management

Brands have, in the past decades, pervaded social reality. Everything from products, services, people, places, and organizations are branded: branding is thus seen as a key element in the constitution of overall "relationships between consumer actions, the marketplace, and cultural meanings" (Arnould and Thompson 2005: 868). Accordingly, brand literature has evolved from focusing on output (the product) to branding as a social process in which multiple stakeholders are involved in the co-creation of brand value (Merz, He, and Vargo 2009). One example of this shift of orientation is corporate branding literature (e. g., Balmer and Gray 2003; Hatch and Schultz 2002), which includes a whole range of activities around strategy and vision, communication, marketing, reputation, and organizational culture (Balmer 2012).

Generally speaking, the traditional view of corporate branding follows Aaker's (1997: 347) definition of a brand: "the set of human characteristics associated with an organization". These characteristics relate to the physical, aesthetic, rational, and emotional dimensions of an organization. In this traditional view, the brand is not the organization itself, but the image that the organization wants the public or audi-

---

[1] I would like to thank Sophie Del Fa for her critical and constructive comments on this chapter as well as Viviane Sergi and Benoit Cordelier for our rich discussions around university branding.

ence to have of it. Branding is seen as a process through which organizations define who they are and communicate that definition to others (Argenti 2000). In this sense, branding is often associated with corporate identity and corporate image, the former related to internal processes of identification, the latter to external stakeholders.

It follows that the main goal of branding is to create a strong brand that articulates organizational identity and image to build and/or increase the corporation's reputation. As Wæraas and Solbakk (2008) noted, a common understanding of branding in this traditional perspective is the idea of capturing the "essence" of an organization in order to develop a clearly defined branding proposition that will increase the identification of the target audience. The brand acts here as "the set of meanings by which it allows people to describe, remember and relate to it" (Celly and Knepper 2010: 140). In this sense, corporate branding strategies aim to reinforce the involvement of the stakeholders in the construction of the brand.

Cornelissen, Christensen, and Kinuthia (2012) have argued that corporate branding scholarship has been rather consensus-driven and somewhat guarded and restricted, insulating itself from important theoretical development around discourse and processes of communication. More importantly, they stress the dominance of linear or conduit models of communication, which "often assume one-way communication processes from the organization to its stakeholders (e. g., Abratt 1989; Olins 1989) with images being projected and installed into the stakeholders' minds" (Cornelissen et al. 2012: 1097). Also, this linear model of communication tends to separate identity from image formation, the former shaping the latter (but not the other way around). The authors sketch out several important limitations of these models of communication (Cornelissen et al. 2012: 1098; see also, Axley 1984): (a) an underlying presupposition that meaning construction is an uncomplicated process of sending/receiving messages, the outcome of this process being predetermined or given; (b) a discredited view of communication as a mere means of revealing and transferring cognitive representations, which set aside any formative effect of language; (c) a reduced conception of individual agency and interpretative capabilities, in which receivers of corporate messages are seen as passive targets that align with the representations provided to them. Hence, they call for developing constitutive models of communication that emphasize the processual, context-dependent, and negotiated character of corporate branding, in which meaning construction is not only "in" the product but at the core of the process of value creation and identity formation. For Cornelissen et al. (2012), the contribution of communication and discourse-oriented perspectives to scholarship on branding will "certainly enrich its theoretical vocabulary and research and arguably strengthen its explanations and predictions" (Cornelissen et al. 2012: 1094; see also, Aggerholm, Andersen, and Thomsen [2011], for a similar argument regarding employer branding).

Following this invitation, the purpose of this chapter is to probe the contribution of a communication as constitutive of organization approach (hereafter CCO), to explore branding as a discursive practice in terms of its organizing properties. The

CCO approach offers an interesting way to do so, namely by questioning the communicative nature of the brand, one that is characterized by meaning indeterminacy. Hence, this approach addresses questions such as: How is value communicatively negotiated in the context of branding initiatives? How does this negotiation unfold in practice? How do organizational actors create a sense of who they are collectively and individually? This chapter is structured as follows: First, we present the key premises of the CCO approach and, accordingly, the theoretical developments in the (corporate) branding literature that propose communicational explanations to branding. Second, based on our work regarding branding in higher education, we offer some illustrations of adopting a CCO approach. We conclude with some future theoretical directions and practical orientations for management communication.

1 What are (corporate) brand and branding? Some elements of answers from a CCO approach

In the field of organization studies, the fundamental and formative role of communication in organizational phenomena of all kinds is particularly emphasized in the stream of literature known as the CCO approach (Brummans, Cooren, Robichaud and Taloy 2014). The proponents of this approach claim that communication does not solely express social realities, but "is the means by which organizations are established, composed, designed, and sustained" (Cooren, Kuhn, Cornelissen and Clark 2011: 1150). The constitutive role of communication is in fact the overarching principle (Ashcraft, Kuhn, and Cooren 2009; see also Craig 1999) of the CCO approach. This idea stems from the recognition that the existence of organizations is the result of dynamic and collective processes of meaning negotiation, which arises from the possibility of multiple interpretations and ways of contextualization that derives from the inherently open-ended nature of communication (Vásquez, Schoeneborn, and Sergi 2015; see also Kuhn 2012). Indeed, as soon as people communicate, meanings multiply. This, in turn, leads to the possibility of struggles over meaning and resistance to dominant readings.

Insights from a CCO approach have been mobilized to account for a variety of organizational phenomena, including diversity management (Trittin and Schoeneborn 2015), leadership (Blaschke, Frost, and Hattke 2014), and strategy making (Cooren, Bencherki, Chaput and Vásquez 2015). Few scholars, however, have expressly mobilized this approach to branding (some exceptions: Ashcraft, Muhr, Rennstam and Sullivan 2012; Cordelier, Vásquez, and Sergi 2020; Hansen 2018; Kärreman and Rylander 2008; Mumby 2016, 2019; Vásquez, Sergi, and Cordelier 2013; Vásquez, Del Fa, Sergi and Cordelier 2017). Yet, the CCO approach can be especially fruitful to engage with ontological questions regarding branding mainly because it challenges transmission models of communication and highlights the formative role of communicative practices in creating, reinforcing, and transforming the brand. This has direct practical implications for management communication, as I develop in the concluding section of this chapter.

With this in mind, I present next the few works that have, to some extent, engaged with these orientations in order to sketch out the communicative dimensions that explain how (corporate) branding operates. From the outset, I specify that not all the authors mobilized in this section will proclaim themselves as CCO scholars; yet I see in their work some similarities with the main CCO premises. I have thus taken the liberty to read their work through a CCO lens in order to highlight the constitutive force of communication for branding.

1.1 Branding as a semantic space of valuation

Inspired by critical consumer culture studies, Kornberger (2010, 2015) defined the brand as an organizing device that structures the fields of consumption and production through the creation of value. Similar to the critical consumer perspective (see Ardvisson 2006), he placed branding at the intersection of marketing strategies and consumer practices, the brand being here defined as an interface. He qualified this mediating function of the brand as an "organizing device" that structures the fields of consumption and production, mostly through two practices: visualization and valuation. To illustrate his argument, Kornberger (2015: 106) took the example of books and questioned the "practices, technologies, and methodologies" through which "they are made valuable in the first place". He concluded that the value of a product is made by "evaluation devices", which constitute a space he calls "the brand". In his words: "The sum of visualizations and valuation practices generates the values associated with and attached to an object. A brand is fundamentally about these values, and not about price" (Kornberger 2015: 108).

Following these arguments, Kornberger (2015: 108) proposed to define the brand as "a semantic space of valuation" that creates an interface between consumer and producer, a new sociability and new forms of imagined communities. He used the metaphor of the shop window to explain this idea:

> [The brand] is a translucent surface upon which the inside meets the outside. Metaphorically speaking, the brand represents the evolution of the shopping window. Being neither inside nor outside, it belongs to both the consumer and the producer. It is the translucent canvas that reflects economic realities and social relations. The shopping window and the brand are both border operations, exchange mechanisms, interfaces. (Kornberger 2015: 108)

This metaphor has three important implications for unpacking the organizing properties of the brand from a communication-centered view. First, the brand erases the consumption and production categories: "the brand is the space where consumer activities become productive" (Kornberger 2015: 109). This is nicely illustrated by Facebook and other social media such as Instagram that are based on consumer production. Second, the brand dissolves the differentiation between global and local environments. Evaluation devices function at the level of day-to-day practice, yet once aggregated, they reveal global orders and dynamics. For example, searching in Google is a routine activity, yet it generates big data regarding users' preferences that feeds the system (Kornberger 2015: 109). Third, the social and the technological merge and produce new forms of organizations. Brands create new forms of imagined communities that function as a resource for individual identity and collective identification. These communities are materialized in evaluation devices. For instance, the brand "Harvard University" is associated with its elite status in global rankings (Kornberger 2015: 109).

This "organizing" perspective can be seen as "setting the table" for developing a constitutive communication approach to branding by recognizing that "brands are increasingly becoming the internal organizing principle of business" (Kornberger 2010: 22).

1.2 Branding as a conversational space of stakeholder interaction

In the stakeholder perspective, brands are seen as dynamic and social processes in which many parties are portrayed as a network of co-creators of the brand, thus actively participating in the branding process. For example, Merz, He, and Vargo's (2009) framework recognizes that the creation of value largely depends on interactions between the firm and customers, the various employees and other stakeholders, as well as brand communities. Extending this framework, Iglesias, Ind, and Alfaro (2013: 670) have developed an organic view of branding, which rests on the idea that "brand value is *conversationally* co-created by many different stakeholders in a fluid space subject to constant negotiation and often develops beyond the strategic aims set by brand managers [emphasis mine]". From this perspective, they argue that "building a brand is an *interactive* process in a *conversational* environment" (Iglesias et al. 2013: 673 [emphasis mine]. The conversational space is a place where consumer and organizations, as well as other stakeholders interact. In this space, interaction is made possible through brand interfaces and frontline employees. Iglesias et al. (2013) highlight the role of new information technologies in the process of brand value creation, and more particularly the part they take in the ways in which brands interact with consumers. They note the importance of the conversations between consumers in a brand community, and how these conversations can alter subsequent interactions with brand interfaces and employees.

In her dissertation, Hansen (2018: 168) applies the concept of conversational space to the physical site of "doing branding", a site where the discourse of branding can be "talked into existence". She shows how some of these spaces are strategically set up (e. g., steering group meetings), while others emerge spontaneously and are created by external stakeholders. Her analysis also underlines the key role played by non-human actors, such as charts, codes of conduct, and legislation in these conversational spaces, which can be physically or discursively mobilized in interaction. According to Hansen (2018), conversational spaces are polyphonic: the brand is constituted by a plethora of voices.

The notion of conversational space has two implications for our understanding of (corporate) branding from a communication-centered perspective: first, it highlights the interactive nature of branding processes, in which many actors (or stakeholders) participate. Of interest is Hansen's (2018) study, which extends the stakeholder perspective to include non-human actors, thus showing that the boundaries of such conversational spaces are fluid and constantly negotiated in communication. Second, this concept emphasizes the interlocking of multiple conversations "inside and outside" the organization in brand value creation. Iglesias et al. (2013) considerations regarding the influence of brand communities, in which consumers will interact with other consumers or other stakeholders about a brand, is quite revealing of this intertextuality – a phenomenon increased by the use of social media.

1.3 Branding as a discursive practice of communicative capitalism

In a critical essay, Mumby (2016: 5) argues that branding is "a principal medium and outcome of 'communicative capitalism'". This concept, borrowed from Dean (2009), puts forth the "conjuncture of economic, political, and discursive formations that organizes work, identity, and democracy in specific ways under neoliberalism" (Mumby 2016: 2). Mumby (2016) identifies three elements – floating signifiers, communicative labor, and affect – that characterize how branding operates in the process of creating economic value, which, he notes, is realized through everyday practices of communication, social interactions, and societal discourses.

Noteworthy is Mumby's (2016) emphasis on the indeterminacy of meaning as a key characteristic of communicative capitalism expressed in branding. As he notes, "precisely because they are rooted in indeterminacies and struggles around meaning, possibilities for resisting corporate branding practices exist within the domain of branding itself" (Mumby 2016: 18). Mumby's (2016: 7) definition of branding sheds light on the contradictory nature of the brand: "brands embody a contradiction – they rely on the productivity of the social and the communicative labour of social actors, but at the same time are increasingly unable to fully capture that sociality". This contradiction, he argues, is at the heart of a "dialectic of branding": brands try to fix meaning and yet are always subject to appropriation and contestation.

Following this work, Mumby (2019) has more recently called for an alternative CCO perspective, one that interrogates the relation between Communication, Capital, and Organization. Within this framework, the question is "how communication mediates and constructs the capital-labour relationship, and hence renders the indeterminacy of labour power more determinate in the production of surplus value" (Mumby

2019: 133). Branding moves this problematization beyond the organization to life itself as living labor: the brand – as communicative capitalism – mediates the relationship between capital and everyday life, a mediation that deeply rests on indeterminacy. Mumby (2019: 135) explains this by two key features of brands: "[they] strive on a surplus of meaning that is never fully determinate. A brand whose meaning becomes fixed eventually dies" and "[they] engage in political ambivalence", in which they mediate the tension between the entrepreneurial neoliberal self and a collective and communal self, formed around political and social issues.

In a similar vein, Leitch and Richardson (2003) develop a discursive framework they call the "brand web model", which addresses interconnectivity and decentralization for constructing brand alliances in a new economy. While their model does not critically engage with neoliberal capitalism, it puts forth the idea of multiple discourses competing with one another in the creation of brand value. As Leitch and Richardson (2003: 1068) suggest,

> Brands are discursive constructs that occupy discursive space which is the space in which meaning is created (Fairclough 1992; Leitch and Richardson 2000). Discursive space is made up of multiple discourses that compete with one another for dominance. There is also competition among discourses of what things – including the brand – means.

With their web brand model, Leitch and Richardson (2003) intend to illustrate how different brand discourses – such as those of competitors, media, or suppliers – may intertwine, collide, overlap, and be in opposition to each other. Hence, meaning is not inherent to things or words but created in these discursive struggles. Hansen (2018) applies this idea to her conceptualization of corporate branding as a discursive brand space. She argues that the discursive brand space is constituted by macro discourses – what Alvesson and Kärreman (2000) named Discourses with a capital "D" – and micro discourses or talk (small "d" discourses; Alvesson and Kärreman 2000). Interestingly, Hansen (2018) notes that Discourses with a capital "D" are activated as a frame of reference in small "d" discourses: informing the interlocutors about what is deemed right or wrong, good or bad, or how things ought to be done.

These discursive renderings of branding put forth the struggle over meaning, and the inherent indeterminacy of the process of meaning construction, as a key feature of contemporary capitalism. Moreover, these perspectives highlight the power of discourses about and around branding in enacting a particular worldview. As these frameworks suggest, discourses play a key role in strengthening people's argument to give weight to a proposal. The possibility to work within these discursive struggles is an interesting avenue for unpacking the polyphonic character of corporate branding and its anchoring in neoliberal capitalism.

2 Illustrations from branding in higher education

Since the 1990s, universities have faced major challenges due to the transformation and evolution of the context of higher education (Dill and Sporn 1995). Researchers have referred to this transformation as an "industrialization", a "corporatization", a "marketing shift", a "consumerist turn", or, more commonly, as the "marketization" of higher education (Molesworth, Nixon, and Scullion 2009; Natale and Doran 2011). In a context of increasing competition, in which rankings and certifications are objects of attention, branding has emerged as a strategic tool for universities to recruit faculty members and students and attract financial donors (Chapleo 2010). This focus on branding has brought into question what defines universities and how they are viewed. Most of the scholarly work has engaged in this reflection by proposing tools and strategies for creating a coherent and powerful brand (Celly and Knepper 2010; Wæraas and Solbakk 2008). A more critical stance has emerged in the critical management literature, which aims to denounce the consequences of these branding practices on education and knowledge (Butler and Spoelstra 2012).

In the past years, I have been working on a research project on branding in higher education with Sophie Del Fa, Viviane Sergi, and Benoit Cordelier. Based on a communication-centered perspective, we conducted two case studies in a Canadian university that focus on the development of a departmental website and the conception and launching of a university advertising campaign. In this section, I share some of our findings in order to offer an empirical illustration of a CCO approach to branding.

The first study (Vásquez et al. 2013) articulated practice-based and CCO approaches to explore the organizing dimensions of the brand by focusing on what we called "representation practices": "actual day-to-day communicative practices through which people collectively engage in representing the organization, and by doing so participate in creating its brand(s)" (Vásquez et al. 2013: 135). This pragmatic lens allowed us to account for both the symbolic and the performative characters of the brand, and thus the negotiated and ongoing nature of branding. Drawing on two departmental meetings and email exchanges between the chair of the department and his colleagues, we were able to trace the interactional dynamics through which issues regarding the new webpage were discussed. In the article, we argued that branding "implies an ongoing negotiation of representations, which affects both what and who is being branded" (Vásquez et al. 2013: 136).

In this case study, the negotiation of representations mainly revolved around a struggle over the question, "Who are we as a collective?" More specifically, this struggle was manifested as a tension between presenting a unified image of the academic department and putting forth the diversity of its members, who, in this case, were all professors. As we noted, "Each pull toward an attempt at unifying their collective identity was somewhat answered by a reaction against it, as a form of resistance to this reduction of diversity" (Vásquez et al. 2013: 138). Interestingly, our analysis showed that these negotiations were both framed by branding logic and influenced the branding process itself. As such, economy, market, aesthetic, and technical dimensions were constantly brought to the table. In the end, a marketing rhetoric was privileged over the academic one.

These findings illustrate Mumby's (2016) argument on the contingencies of economic and political discourses that are at work in branding, which, while affecting the workplace, go far beyond it. They also demonstrate that for these discourses to operate, they have to be evoked, negotiated, and even resisted in actual practices of communication. Our study shows that through these representational practices, the brand is mobilized as a frame and/or a boundary that foregrounds and includes particular discourses, aiming to align the multiple interpretations. Yet, because of the indeterminacy of meaning that characterizes branding, and because of its direct association with identity issues, alignment is never to be taken for granted: questions over "who am I" and "who are we" remained opened in this case. Finally, this first study highlights the negotiations, conflicts, and contradictions around branding that stem from its ideological and political nature (see also the special issue of *International Studies of Management and Organization* [Drori, Tienari, and Waeraas (2015)] for a similar argument).

The second case study (Vásquez et al. 2017) followed the development of the advertising campaign of a Canadian university over roughly three years. Conceptually speaking, we drew on Cooren's (2010) notion of figures to analyze how the student was represented in the different stages of the campaign, as well as the ways that actual students were enrolled in this branding process. Cooren (2010) highlights that for a figure to exist, it must be re-presented; this is how the figure can be recognized as such. It is also by this process of re-presentation in and through communication that the figure operates. Moreover, figures are excellent discursive resources: they give weight to an argument by incorporating a variety of agents.

Our main argument in this study revolved around the idea of commodification of the student as a brand: "[i]t is through the combination of figures – or (re) configurations – that the student is commodified" (Vásquez et al. 2017: 151). We approached the communicative reconfiguration of students from a critical pragmatic stance (Spicer, Alvesson, and Kärreman 2009) which implied focus on the practices and lived experiences through which the advertising campaign evolved. This echoes Korberger's (2010, 2015) idea, also developed in consumer culture theories (Arvidsson 2006), that branding organizes the relations between producers and consumers and that these relations go about creating and negotiating the brand.

Our results showed that students were branded as consumers, as producers of the university brand, and as a commodity, i.e., the brand itself. Moreover, our findings showed how the marketization of higher education can be masked behind more "noble" discourses, disguising the attempts to brand the student and exploit her in a form of free labor. In the case we studied, "this masking was realized through the discourse of creativity, which configured the actual students and the alumni as co-creators of the university brand and as an inspiration for the creative process"(Vásquez et al. 2017: 148). We also found a collaborative and participative discourse of prosumption that enhanced student's free labor in "living the brand".

These findings resonate with studies based on critical discourse analysis (CDA), which focus on discursive material produced by universities to explore the shifts stemming from the marketization of higher education (e. g., Fairclough 1993; Kheovichai 2014; and Han 2014). Their conclusion is quite straightforward: the university is colonized by business discourses. Yet, for these discourses to make a difference, they must be materialized in job announcements, speeches, advertising campaigns, and, as we argue, embodied in students. Hence, to show concrete occurrences of the marketization of universities, one must focus on discursive artifacts, bodies, and day-to-day interaction.

In a different analysis of the same advertising campaign (Cordelier, Vásquez, and Sergi 2020), we drew on Lévi-Strauss's (1950) notion of floating signifiers to analyze the discursive attempts through which the actors involved in the advertising campaign negotiated the university's identity and image. The semiotic approach developed in this paper allowed us to capture the discursive struggle between the "neoliberal market" and "humanist university" discourses and show how this struggle contributed to branding the university (in one way or another). Some of our main findings suggest the collision of two opposed visions of the university, which recall a perennial debate regarding the mission of universities in society (Derrida, Porter, and Morris 1983).

Interestingly, our analysis showed that opposing ideological stances are not completely isolated from one another, and that actors involved in branding processes are able to overcome these oppositions by enacting local organizational discourses. More broadly, our findings suggest that branding in higher education is driven by a central question: what makes up the value of the university? A CCO approach revealed that this valuation process is a continuous negotiation between the different parties involved. This negotiation takes place in conversational spaces, to borrow Hansen's (2018) term, where this question is debated. As in our previous studies, this one shows that marketization deeply influences the branding process by valuing consumers and business-driven orientations.

3 Concluding remarks

In this section, we propose some theoretical and practical implications of adopting a CCO approach to (corporate) branding and outline some linguistic features of management communication. As mentioned in the introduction, a constitutive model of communication challenges existing and dominant models of branding that follow linear and conduit models of communication (Cornelissen et al. 2012).

A first challenge is ontological: CCO approaches do not consider organizations and their brands as a given, but as emerging from communication. This performative account of corporate branding suggests that brands are constantly reproduced, and thus subjected to transformation. It also implies that multiple individual and collective voices (employees, clients, stakeholders, and brand community, for instance) take part in the constitution of the brand. This polyphonic nature of branding questions the privileged perspective of brand managers and challenges the assumption that the organization exists *ex ante* (Cornelissen et al. 2012).

A second challenge to mainstream approaches to branding concerns the role of communication. A CCO approach assumes that any representation of an organization is relational, hence interactively constituted at a particular place and time, what we named representation practices (Vásquez et al. 2013). The process of branding and its outcome (the brand) lie in the act of communication itself: branding is indeed a semantic, conversational, semiotic, or discursive space where multiple beings and things (the organization and its stakeholders, the competitors, citizens) are being connected. Of importance here is the way that through these relations a collective sense about the organization and its value is constantly being negotiated. This process of meaning making is both local – it emerges from the interactions of people and their talk – and global, as discourses of consumption (and of neoliberal capitalism) frame branding conversations. Moreover, what triggers this constant negotiation over the identity and image of an organization is the indeterminacy of meaning that characterizes branding. As Mumby (2016; see also Cordelier et al. 2020) noted, the brand is both a floating signifier that allows for multiple and even divergent meaning and a deliberative intent to fix meaning. This dialectic of the brand explains the processual and political nature of branding as an ongoing discursive/communicational struggle.

A third challenge to the conduit model that dominates current approaches to branding concerns agency. On the one hand, a CCO approach allows accounting for the interpretative capacities of the "receivers": employees, consumers, and other stakeholders are not just passive actors that receive and decode a message designed by the organization and managers. They actively participate in co-constructing the brand and ultimately the organization (Cornelissen et al. 2012). Worth noticing here is the blurring of lines between the production of the brand and its consumption. Prosumers, as our case study of student branding showed (Vásquez et al. 2017), are key actors, actively involved by universities to consume, produce, and live the brand. Critical scholars denounce this form of "free" or "cheap" labor, which enrolls consumers by mobilizing an entrepreneurial and communal conception of the self as a form of individual validation and recognition (Ritzer 2015). On another hand, the CCO approach extends the notion of agency to include other actors or figures that take part in the communicational scene where issues of branding are at stake. Hansen's (2018) dissertation, for example, showed the importance of charts and organizational mission statements.

These lessons from a CCO approach can be seen as an invitation to brand managers to understand that despite the strategies and tools, there is no such thing as a unique selling proposition to brand their organization. First, formal branding initiatives are not the only communicational events where branding is at work. Any conversational space where questions regarding the organization's identity and/or representations are discussed also constitutes the organization's brand. Moreover, any time someone or something talks on behalf of the organization, she/he/it is representing the organization, thus participating in constructing its brand. To this, may we add that these spokespersons and spokesobjects will also (even if unintendedly) represent other organizations and their interests, betraying, to some extent, their "official role" (Vásquez and Cooren 2011). Hence, brand managers should pay attention to the various and unfolding narratives of the organization as manifested through conversations, texts, objects, and symbols.

Second, as noted, branding is defined by the indeterminacy of meaning. This means that even if the manager's intent is to fix meaning through offering a representation of the organization, meaning will inevitably be opened. Indeterminacy lies not only in the interpretative capacities of the organization's stakeholders, but also – and we would argue mainly – in its communicative nature (Vásquez, Schoeneborn, and Sergi 2016). As such, brands will always be negotiated, contested, and thus re-instantiated. If meaning is completely fixed, the brand ceases to exist. To some extent, struggles over meaning are what makes a brand live. Embracing the dialectics of the brand is thus a way for brand managers to envisage their role: instead of silencing conflicts to avoid a bad reputation, or finding a perfect value fit between the organization and its consumers, managers should create a space of dialogue in which stakeholders and the organization converse about collective and individual identities and representations. Conceiving the brand as a dialogical space can open interesting avenues for managing the brand without trying to control it. Taking the idea of the brand as a floating signifier (Cordelier et al. 2020), for example, brand managers can foster negotiation between seemingly opposing discourses and thus strengthen the appropriation of the brand.

A third and last practical implication of adopting a CCO lens to branding regards the pervasiveness of marketing and business-oriented discourses that frame branding practices and initiatives, reinforcing consumerist frameworks and neoliberal capitalistic logics. Here we would like to make a call for a more responsible and ethical approach to branding, one that evolves from a self-referential corporate asset centered on the organization to a socially inspired asset that considers other stakeholders such as citizens and nature (Biraghi, Gambetti, and Schultz 2017). Brands and branding have a profound impact on our societies –many of those can be potentially affected by branding decisions. Brand managers should take this into consideration. Communicatively speaking, and related to our previous discussion on agency, this implies both extending the notion of receivers of corporate messages and shifting towards a more (inter)active view of reception. Branding emerges from the ongoing conversations between the organization and society. Brand managers should thus envisage building a societal brand community that opens up the discussion on what we should value as a society.

4 References

Aaker, Jennifer. 1997. Dimensions of brand personality. *Journal of Marketing Research* 34(3). 347–356.
Abratt Russell. 1989. A new approach to the corporate image management process. *Journal of Marketing Management* 15(1). 63–76.
Aggerholm, Helle Kryger, Sophie Esmann Andersen & Christa Thomsen. 2011. Conceptualising employer branding in sustainable organisations. *Corporate Communications: An International Journal* 16(2). 105–123.
Alvesson, Matt & Dan Kärreman. 2000. Varieties of discourse: On the study of organizations through discourse analysis. *Human Relations* 53(9). 1125–1149.
Argenti, Paul. 2000. Branding b-schools: Reputation management for MBA programs. *Corporate Reputation Review* 3(2). 171–178.
Arnould, Eric J. & Craig J. Thompson. 2005. Consumer culture theory (CCT): Twenty years of research. *Journal of Consumer Research* 31(4). 868–882.
Arvidsson, Adam. 2006. *Brands: Meaning and value in media culture*. Abingdon, UK: Routledge.
Ashcraft, Karen L., Thimothy Kuhn & François Cooren. 2009. Constitutional amendments: 'Materializing' organizational communication. *Academy of Management Annals* 3(1). 1–64.
Ashcraft, Karen L., Sarah Muhr, Jens Rennstam & Katie Sullivan. 2012. Professionalization as a branding activity: Occupational identity and the dialectic of inclusivity-exclusivity. *Gender, Work & Organization* 19(5). 467–488.
Axley, Stephen R. 1984. Managerial and organizational communication in terms of the conduit metaphor. *Academy of Management Review* 9(3). 428–437.
Balmer, John M. T. 2012. Strategic corporate brand alignment: Perspectives from identity based views of corporate brands. *European Journal of Marketing* 46(7–8). 1064–1092.
Balmer, John M. T. & Edmund R. Gray. 2003. Corporate brands: What are they? What of them? *European Journal of Marketing* 37(7–8). 972–997.
Biraghi, Silvia, Rossella C. Gambetti & Don E. Schultz. 2017. Advancing a citizenship approach to corporate branding: A societal view. *International Studies of Management & Organization* 47(2). 206–215.
Blaschke, Steffen, Jetta Frost & Fabian Hattke. 2014. Towards a micro foundation of leadership, governance, and management in universities. *Higher Education* 68(5). 711–732.
Brummans, Boris H. J. M., François Cooren, Daniel Robichaud & James R. Taylor. 2014. Approaches to the communicative constitution of organizations. In Linda L. Putnam & Denis Mumby (eds.), *The Sage handbook of organizational communication: Advances in theory, research, and methods*, 173–194. London & New York: Sage.
Butler, Nick & Sverre Spoelstra. 2012. Your excellency. *Organization* 19(6). 891–903.
Celly, Kirti S. & Brenda Knepper. 2010. The California State University: A case on branding the largest public university system in the US. *International Journal of Nonprofit and Voluntary Sector Marketing* 15(2). 137–156.
Chapleo, Chris. 2010. What defines 'successful' university brands? *International Journal of Public Sector Management* 23(2). 169–183.

Cooren, François. 2010. *Action and agency in dialogue: Passion, incarnation and ventriloquism.* Amsterdam & Philadelphia, PA: John Benjamins.

Cooren, François, Nicolas Bencherki, Mathieu Chaput & Consuelo Vásquez. 2015. The communicative constitution of strategy-making: Exploring fleeting moments of strategy. In Daniel Golsorkhi, Linda Rouleau, David Seidl & Eero Vaara (eds.), *Cambridge handbook of strategy as practice*, 365–388. Cambridge: Cambridge University Press.

Cooren, François, Thimothy Kuhn, Joep P. Cornellissen & Timothy Clark. 2011. Communication, organizing and organization: An overview and introduction to the special issue. *Organization Studies* 32(9). 1149–1170.

Cordelier, Benoit, Consuelo Vásquez & Viviane Sergi. 2020. Branding the university: Building up meaning through ideological oppositions. *Journal of Marketing for Higher Education*. 1–19. https://doi.org/10.1080/08841241.2020.1761507.

Cornelissen, Joep, Lars Thøger Christensen & Kendi Kinuthia. 2012. Corporate brands and identity: Developing stronger theory and a call for shifting the debate. *European Journal of Marketing* 46 (7–8). 1093–1102.

Craig, Robert T. 1999. Communication theory as a field. *Communication Theory* 9(2). 119–161.

Dean, Jodi. 2009. *Democracy and other neoliberal fantasies: Communicative capitalism and left politics*. Durham, NC: Duke University Press.

Derrida, Jacques, Catherine Porter & Edward P. Morris. 1983. The principle of reason: The university in the eyes of its pupils. *Diacritics* 13(3). 3–20.

Dill, David D. & Barbara Sporn. 1995. The 'marketization' of higher education: Reforms and potential reforms in higher education finance. In David D. Dills & Barbara Sporn (eds.), *Emerging patterns of social demand and university reform: Through a glass darkly*, 170–193. Bingley, UK: Emerald.

Drori, S. Gili, Janne Tienari & Arild Waeraas. 2015. Strategies of building and managing higher education brands. [Special issue]. *International Studies of Management and Organization* 45(2).

Fairclough, Norman. 1993. Critical discourse analysis and the marketization of public discourse: The universities. *Discourse & Society* 4(2). 133–168.

Han, Zhengrui. 2014. The marketization of public discourse : The Chinese universities. *Discourse & Communication* 8(1). 85–103.

Hansen, Heidi. 2018. *Communication as constitutive of brands*. Odense: University of Southern Denmark PhD dissertation.

Hatch, Mary Joe & Majken Schultz. 2002. The dynamics of organizational identity. *Human Relations* 55(8). 989–1018.

Iglesias, Oriol, Nicholas Ind & Manuel Alfaro. 2017. The organic view of the brand: A brand value co-creation model. *Journal of Brand Management* 20. 670–688.

Kärreman, Dan & Anna Rylander. 2008. Managing meaning through branding: The case of a consulting firm. *Organization Studies* 29(1). 103–125.

Kheovichai, Baramee. 2014. Marketized university discourse: A synchronic and diachronic comparison of the discursive constructions of employer organizations in academic and business job advertisements. *Discourse & Communication* 8(4). 371–390.

Kornberger, Martin. 2010. *Brand society: How brands transform management and lifestyle*. Cambridge: Cambridge University Press.

Kornberger, Martin. 2015. Think different. *International Studies of Management & Organization* 45(2). 105–113.

Kuhn, Timothy R. 2012. The (dis)ordering force of communication: Thought leadership for organization theory. *Management Communication Quarterly* 26(4). 543–584.

Leitch, Shirley & Neil Richardson. 2003. Corporate branding in the new economy. *European Journal of Marketing* 37(7–8). 1065–1079.

Lévi-Strauss, Claude. 1950. *Introduction à l'œuvre de Marcel Mauss*. Paris: Presses Universitaire de France.

Merz, Michael A., Yi He & Stephen L. Vargo. 2009. The evolving brand logic: a service-dominant logic perspective. *Journal of the Academy of Marketing Science* 37(3). 328–344.

Molesworth, Mike, Elizabeth Nixon & Richard Scullion. 2009. Having, being and higher education: The marketisation of the university and the transformation of the student into consumer. *Teaching in Higher Education* 14(3). 277–287.

Mumby, Dennis K. 2016. Organizing beyond organization: Branding, discourse, and communicative capitalism. *Organization* 1(24). 884–907.

Mumby, Dennis K. 2019. Communication constitutes capital: Branding and the politics of neoliberal dis/organization. In Consuelo Vásquez & Timothy Kuhn (eds.), *Dis/organization as communication*, 125–147. New York: Routledge.

Natale, Samuel M. & Caroline Doran. 2011. Marketization of education: An ethical dilemma. *Journal of Business Ethics* 105(2). 187–196.

Olins, Wally. 1989. *Corporate identity: Making business strategy visible through design*. Boston, MA: Harvard Business School Press.

Ritzer, George. 2015. Prosumer capitalism. *Sociological Quarterly* 56(3). 413–445.

Spicer, Andre, Mats Alvesson & Dan Kärreman. 2009. Critical performativity: The unfinished business of critical management studies. *Human Relations* 62(4). 537–560.

Trittin, Hannah & Dennis Schoeneborn. 2015. Diversity as polyphony: Reconceptualizing diversity management from a communication-centered perspective. *Journal of Business Ethics* 144(2). 305–322.

Vásquez, Consuelo & François Cooren. 2011. Passion in action: An analysis of translation and treason. In Paolo Quattrone, Chris McLean, François Puyou & Nigel Thrift (eds.), *Imagining organizations: Performative imagery in business and beyond*, 191–212. London & New York: Routledge.

Vásquez, Consuelo, Sophie Del Fa, Viviane Sergi & Benoit Cordelier. 2017. From consumer to brand: Exploring the commodification of 'the student' in a university advertising campaign. In Matt Benner, Tony Huzzard & Dan Kärreman (eds.), *The corporatization of the business school: Minerva meets the market: Exploring and experiencing the corporate business school*, 146–164. London & New York: Routledge.

Vásquez, Consuelo, Dennis Schoeneborn & Viviane Sergi. 2016. Summoning the spirits: Exploring the (dis)ordering properties of organizational texts. *Human Relations* 69(3). 629–659.

Vásquez, Consuelo, Viviane Sergi & Benoit Cordelier. 2013. From being branded to doing branding: Studying representation practises from a communication-centred approach. [Special Issue: Being Branded]. *Scandinavian Journal of Management* 29(2). 125–136.

Wæraas, Arild & Marianne N. Solbakk. 2008. Defining the essence of a university: Lessons from higher education branding. *Higher Education* 57(4). 449–462.

Rickard Andersson and Lars Rademacher
15 Managing communication

Abstract: This chapter deals with communication management as a specific form of management communication responsible for authoring, enacting, and controlling an organization's communication to create value. The chapter covers central ideas in the communication management literature, the practices, forms and contexts of communication management, and how the communication management literature has approached the concept of value creation. The authors encourage researchers interested in communication management to investigate what forms and practices of communication management could stimulate stakeholder polyphony and employee voice. The first section contains a brief overview over central ideas in the communication management literature, the second section focuses on the practices, forms and contexts of communication management, the third section contains a review of communication management and value creation, the fourth section highlights the usefulness of the Communication as Constitutive (CCO) approach for analyzing contemporary developments in communication management, and the last section contains the conclusions and future directions.

Keywords: communication management; value creation; CCO; strategic communication; management communication

Managing communication strategically has become an increasingly central management concern in contemporary organizations. In this chapter, we zoom in on communication management to advance the understanding of the ways of thinking, and the collective communicative practices, that constitute communication management as a specific management practice in contemporary organizations. In line with the editors' definition of *management* as a collective practice of authoring, enacting, and controlling an organization and its value creation in specific socio-material contexts, and *management communication* as the metaconversation of all the practices, forms, and contexts of organizational communication, we define *communication management* as the collective practice of authoring, enacting, and controlling an organization's communication to create value.

Communication management is usually understood as those purposeful external and internal communication activities and campaigns communication managers and other managers author, enact, and control with the aim to support organizational operations and contribute to overall goal fulfillment (e. g., Hallahan et al. 2007). We do, however, zoom in on the contemporary streams within communication management research arguing that communication management should be understood and approached as a collective responsibility of all organizational members in their daily work (e.g., Gulbrandsen and Just 2016; Heide et al. 2018), to more comprehensibly account for how communication contributes value to organizations. Thus, in this chapter, and especially when we outline how recent developments in communication management theory and practice can be analyzed through a CCO lens, we are giving particular attention to the increasingly common understanding of communication management as a collective responsibility of all organizational members whose communication behavior contributes to value creation.

Throughout the chapter, we generally use communication management interchangeably with public relations, corporate communication, and strategic communication. However, in the section on *central ways of thinking in communication management*, the contribution of each area of interest will be highlighted given that they all, during different time periods, have contributed new ways of thinking about communication management.

The body of the chapter is divided into four sections. In the first section, we briefly review the central ideas in the body of knowledge to explicate the dominant ways of thinking that have contributed to constitute how the management of communication is communicatively constituted and practiced in contemporary organizations. In the second section, we shift our attention to the contemporary communicative practice and explicate the practices, forms, and contexts central to contemporary communication management. In the third section, we shift our attention to the concept of *value creation* which, parallel to the growing centrality of communication management in contemporary organizations, has become a central concept to consider for communication managers. In the fourth section, we highlight the usefulness of the *communication as constitutive* (CCO) approach for analyzing contemporary developments in communication management as communication managers vie for influence over the "authoritative texts" (Kuhn 2008) that influence and shape organizational members' collective practices. Lastly, in the conclusion, we summarize the arguments put forth in the chapter and stake out some future directions in relation to the function of communication management for solving practical challenges faced by managers in contemporary organizations.

1 Central ways of thinking in communication management: from strategic public relations to strategic communication

To understand the contemporary practice of communication management, it is important to briefly review the central ways of thinking that have emerged since the 1970s, and gradually have become embedded in the communicative practices of communication managers. Common to all the different *bodies of knowledge* interested in the management of communication, such as communication management, public relations, corporate communication, and strategic communication, is that they all encourage a *strategic* approach to communication management, whether in the form of strategic public relations, strategic corporate communication, or strategic communication. While this emphasis on strategic communication management in communication management research partly reflects the transformation of the practice of communication management from a *tactical* to strategic management practice, the adoption of the strategy discourse should also be understood as having enabled researchers and practitioners to claim communication management's place as a strategic management practice with a legitimate claim to intra-organizational power and status (Andersson 2020).

Already in the 1980s, Grunig and Hunt (1984) and most notably the influential *Excellence project* (e. g., Dozier, Grunig, and Grunig 1995; Grunig 1992) contributed to establishing communication management as a strategic management function given that the strategic management of publics and relationships were argued to be inseparable from the strategic management of an organization. Therefore, communication managers should take a seat at the decision-making table, and communication managers and departments should work strategically with communication, meaning that principles from strategic management theory, such as the idea of goal alignment and the central two-step process of *strategy formulation* (i. e., analyzing, planning, and setting goals) followed by *strategy implementation* (i. e., controlling and evaluating activities), should direct how communication managers and communication functions structure their work.

Together with ideas put forth by other public relations researchers, Grunig (1992) contributed to contest the, at the time, predominant view of communication management as a tactical function (Moss and Warnaby 1998). The following quote from Webster (1990: 18) aptly captures both the normative strategic ideal conceived by the expanding public relations body of knowledge, as well as the growing ambition to turn communication management into a legitimate and influential management practice:

> To be strategic, public relations must pass one basic test: At a minimum, everything done must be aligned with the corporate vision or mission – the company's reason for being – and must substantially contribute to achieving the organization's objectives. Ideally, public relations should be part of the team helping to create the corporate mission and set the objectives.

In the early to mid-1990s, following developments in academic fields related to communication management and in "real world" organizations (Argenti 1996), corporate communication began emerging as both a concept and a practice in organizations and academia. According to Argenti, this was a consequence of (1) the tendency of business schools to educate more communication managers, (2) the increasing tendency of publics to question the sole monetary purpose of many organizations forcing organizations to interact more with stakeholders, and (3) the introduction of new laws. Together, these developments gradually "forced" organizations to take a more *deliberate approach* towards communication management. Following the emergence of corporate communication as a body of knowledge and practice, several new aspects for communication managers to consider were introduced in the communication management discourse, such as the *corporate identity*, *strategic vision*, *corporate image*, *organizational culture*, *corporate reputation*, and *consistency* in internal and external communication (e. g., Hatch and Schultz 1997, 2001, 2003; van Riel 1997; van Riel and Balmer 1997). From the mid-1990s, interest in the idea of corporate communication continued to grow, constituting an understanding of communication management emphasizing *integration*, *coordination*, *orchestration*, and *alignment* (Christensen and Cornelissen 2011).

During the first two decades of the twenty-first century, communication management researchers' and practitioners' engagement with the strategy discourse has continued, and strategy became the dominant buzzword during this period. In organizations, the term *strategic communication* became increasingly popular for describing the communication management units and practices in both private and public organizations (Hallahan et al. 2007). Additionally, there were signs that communication management was on its way to become an institutionalized practice and mindset taken into account in the broader collective practices of management such as strategic planning and decision-making (e. g., Swerling and Sen 2009; Tench, Verhoeven, and Zerfass 2009; Zerfass 2009). In research, the practice of strategic communication management is defined as communication activities and resources of substantial relevance to an organization (Zerfass et al. 2018).

2 Practicing communication management

Several societal and intra-professional developments, have changed the prerequisites for the practice of communication management in contemporary organizations. Firstly, societal developments, such as expectations on organizations to be transparent and communicate coherently and the emergence of "new media" (e. g., Christensen and Langer 2009; Christensen, Morsing, and Cheney 2008; Gulbrandsen and Just 2016; Kornberger 2010), have contributed to convince organizational leaders that it is necessary to take a deliberate approach to communicative dimensions such as the brand, image, and reputation. Secondly, the deliberate effort from communication managers to "professionalize" the practice of communication management and increase the intra-organizational status of communication managers to thereby gain inclusion in the top management team (Frandsen and Johansen 2015) must also be taken into account. Central to this process of "professionalization" has been the adoption of the strategy discourse (Andersson 2020; Nothhaft and Schölzel 2015; Sievert, Rademacher and Weber 2016), in tandem with the "scientification" of communication management (see also Macnamara 2015), which has provided communication managers with new linguistic tools and discursive means to participate in the communicative practice and "lingua franca" of strategic management.

Traditionally, the practice has been characterized by its technical nature, where the communication department and the communication managers mainly have been producing content for various channels. Although this production or operational side still is one of the core constituents of the practice, the rising popularity and significance ascribed to strategy has resulted in a linguistic re-framing of the practice through which a strategic approach to various communicative practices is emphasized. Communication managers' adoption of the strategy discourse, understood as a specific body of knowledge (e. g., Knights and Morgan, 1990, 1991), especially manifests in how the role of communication management and communication managers in contemporary management is discursively re-framed as communication managers, similarly to other professions, increasingly claim the role of experts whose expertise is of vital importance to the long-term success of the organization.

This strategic re-framing of the practice entails that communication managers, instead of producing content commissioned by other managers and organizational members, take charge of the organization's communication to ensure that the output and work of communication management contributes to the organizations' long-term goal fulfillment. This entails that communication managers to a greater extent act as advisors to the top management, other managers, and employees regarding how to manage communication issues of strategic importance to the organization (Zerfass and Franke 2013) such as public relations, corporate communications, corporate social responsibility, media relations, public affairs, employee communication, and corporate branding.

While the profession has strived to gain a seat at the strategic decision-making table, much of the daily operational praxis consists of the production of *concrete* texts with varying degree of *relative permanence* (Kuhn 2008). Firstly, texts such as organizational communication strategies, corporate brand strategies, and communication policies are intended to endure over time with long-term effects on how especially the organizations' communication activities and the communication function organize and coordinate so that communication management contributes to the organizational goal fulfillment. Secondly, texts produced in relation to specific communication campaigns, for example the release of a new car model, are intended to endure throughout the duration of the campaign. Thirdly, the daily production of channel content online and offline, such as replies to customers on social media, the production of newsletters, and intranet content and news with varying degree of relative permanence depending on whether it is intended for the immediate setting only or an information text intended to endure and remain relevant beyond a specific conversation.

3 Communication management and value creation

How communication management contributes to value creation in organizations is a central concern for both communication managers and researchers. In the 2015 edition of the *European Communication Monitor* (ECM), the world's largest annual survey inquiring into the perceptions of communication managers around the globe, 4,200 practitioners in eighty-two countries responded that they see linking communication and business strategy as a key challenge for communication management (Zerfass et al. 2015). Additionally, 4,483 practitioners interviewed for *The Global Study of Public Relations and Communication Management* ranked "improving the measurement of communication effectiveness to prove value" as a top priority for communication management practitioners (Berger and Meng 2014).

Traditionally, the languages of quantitative research and mathematics have framed how researchers, not the least in communication management, have approached and talked about value creation (Macnamara 2015). In his literature review of measurement and evaluation research in communication management, Macnamara (2015) found that research has tended to focus on how communication management can generate value by studying how organizations can quantify everything – perceptions, attitudes, opinions, trust, engagement, loyalty, relationships, behaviors, etc. – to measure and evaluate the value created by communication management. Furthermore, Macnamara (2015) discussed two potential ways by which communication management creates value: by *increasing* sales, reputation, and employee loyalty and by *decreasing* costs or risks.

In contemporary communication management, both professional associations/institutes and academic institutes have placed great emphasis on developing management tools and models to help organizations to understand and communication managers to explain how communication management creates value. However, in their review of widely used evaluation models around the world, Macnamara and Gregory (2018) concluded that the models limit the potential of showing how communication management creates value. They argued that the established models are predominately organization-centric and top-down, focusing on evaluating one-way messages rather than enabling a two-way perspective on evaluation and measurement. The lack of a two-way perspective on communication measurement and evaluation was highlighted by Macnamara (2015) and Macnamara and Gregory (2018) as especially problematic as the communication management function thereby misses an opportunity to move beyond the control focus, currently predominant in communication management, in favor of a practice which:

> [...] recognizes the realities of the modern communication environment in which two-way communication is not only increasingly expected and demanded by stakeholders and publics, but is also more ethical. It takes into account the view that organizations have an obligation to stake-

holders and society. Organizations' effectiveness in listening to and responding to these broader perspectives is therefore key to operationalizing corporate social responsibility and maintaining a 'licence to operate'. (Macnamara and Gregory 2018: 483)

Inspired by Porter's (1985) ideas on value-based management and the contemporary understanding of stakeholder rather than solely shareholder value, Zerfass and Viertmann (2017) proposed a generic framework of how communication management contributes value to the organization. This framework stretches beyond the classical understanding of reaching out to stakeholders and instead aims to capture the multi-faceted value contribution of communication management. In their framework, communication management is depicted as contributing value in four ways; by: (1) *enabling operations* (publicity, customer preferences, and employee commitment), (2) *ensuring flexibility* (relationships, trust, and legitimacy), (3) *adjusting strategy* (thought leadership, innovation potential, and crisis resilience), and (4) *building intangibles* (reputation, brands, and corporate culture).

Several communication management research papers also emphasize the importance of *alignment* between communication goals and organizational goals for communication management to create value. In their review of previous research on alignment, Volk and Zerfass (2018) discussed the centrality of alignment and propose a definition of alignment that distinguishes between *primary* and *secondary* alignment, where the former highlights value creation through alignment of communication strategy with corporate strategy, and the latter highlights value creation through integrated communication.

To conclude this section, the practitioner and academic debate regarding the value creation of communication management highlights that it is considered an essential, albeit complex, issue. While researchers have argued that the value created by communication management is difficult to quantify and measure, a situation that most practitioners are aware of, quantifying output and outreach still is a common practice given the pressure on communication departments and managers to demonstrate their return on investment and contribution to the organization.

4 Communication management through a CCO lens

In this section, we aim to exemplify how communication management increasingly is discursively and linguistically framed as a collective practice that all organizational members must author, enact, and control to create value. To illustrate the usefulness of the CCO lens for analyzing how communication management is discursively and linguistically framed as a collective practice, we take inspiration from Vásquez et al.'s (2018) framework for understanding the performativity of strategy through paying attention to how *matters of concern* become *matters of authority*, and draw upon it to analyze text excerpts from the communication policy and the branding platform of a Swedish municipality with approximately 10,000 employees. Drawing upon the framework presented by Vásquez et al. (2018), we argue that these texts demonstrate how communication managers are framing communication management as a matter of concern for all organizational members. Through producing texts that linguistically frame communicative dimensions such as the brand, image, and reputation as the collective concern of all organizational members, communication managers thereby attempt to discursively frame communication management as a central concern for organizations.

We argue that this framing should be viewed both as an indication that communication managers are increasingly perceived as a legitimate management practice by the top management, but also as an indication that communication managers themselves vie for greater intra-organizational influence and authorship of the abstract "authoritative texts" that "define [...] boundaries and exert [...] 'official' influence over practice" (Kuhn 2008: 1236). Thus, communication managers attempt to turn communication management into a matter of authority that simultaneously *authorizes*, i.e., permits and enables, organizational members to act on behalf of the organization, and *author*, i.e., assign organizational members a formal responsibility to make the organization present in a specific way, when *presentifying*, i.e., making present (Benoit-Barné and Cooren 2009) the organization in conversations with stakeholders.

However, communication management still struggles to be perceived as a "strategic" management practice with a legitimate claim to the collective practice of management. Therefore, it is important to note that while communication managers increasingly frame communication management as a collective concern through texts stressing that all organizational members must understand their communication responsibility (Andersson 2019), this does not automatically turn communication management into a matter of authority acknowledged by other organizational members whose communicative practices it aspires to author. Nonetheless, we argue that these texts demonstrate communication managers' *aspirational talk* (Christensen, Morsing, and Thyssen 2013), and their ambition to advance their intra-organizational status and influence (see also Andersson 2020; Knights and Morgan 1991), and simultaneously turn communication management into a central management practice enabled to co-author those "authoritative texts" (Kuhn 2008) that influence the decisions and actions central to processes of organizing.

The illustrative examples originate from the case mentioned above and are taken from the city's communication policy and brand platform. At the start of the communication policy, the document is described as a "normative" text providing "principles and guidelines" as well as "directives" for "how we communicate in the city". The information given at the branding platform states that it is intended as an aid for organizational members to understand how they can contribute to ensure that the city reaches its long-term vision, to become "the creative, pulsating, common, global, and balanced, city for people and businesses" in 2035. Given the authors' intention that the texts should act as guidelines for all organizational members, and not only the communication management function and communication managers, we argue that they provide a telling illustration of how communication managers discursively and linguistically attempt to frame communication management as essential for the organization and as a collective responsibility of all organizational members.

Through this re-framing, the ambition is to make communication management evolve beyond its current main form as a "functional derivative of the general strategic management of the organization" (Zerfass et al. 2018: 497). More specifically, this entails moving beyond its form as a management process through which mainly communication managers, through planning, implementing, and evaluating communication activities, "manage the communication of strategic significance with regard to a focal entity" (Zerfass et al. 2018: 497). Instead, the ambition is to make communication, and the management of it, a concern and responsibility taken into consideration by all organizational members in their daily work, be it in interactions with colleagues or interactions with customers.

As argued by Vásquez et al. (2018), matters of concern must be provided endurance by inscribing them into more permanent texts, understood broadly, to enable them to travel through time and space and make a difference beyond the current situation and influence future talk and action. The following excerpts from the communication policy and branding platform illustrate how communication managers transport and materialize their matters of concern into text:

> The city's operations are to a large extent built on human interactions. The coworkers in the city have an important role as knowledge bearers and representatives of the organization. A prerequisite for achieving high quality communication with the citizens is therefore that the coworkers in the organization have access to relevant information about the organization and its goals. (Communication policy)
>
> Say the city name to a citizen and that person will have some form of perception or get an image on its retina. This applies regardless of whether we talk about the city as an organization or a physical place. This implies that our brand exists regardless of whether we work with it or not. Therefore, we want to create a strong and common expression for the city that facilitates acts and communication in spirit of the vision [...] Branding is not a one-time effort, but a long-term work where we all contribute in our meetings with our stakeholders and through how we communicate. (Branding platform)

By (1) describing "human interactions" as a core task, (2) translating the city (i.e., organization) into a communicative accomplishment, i.e., a brand, and (3) framing communication management as a long-term collective effort constituted in communication processes to which all members "contribute", as shown in the two excerpts above, the authors of the texts manage both to frame the organization as an ongoing unstable accomplishment that always needs to be made present for the very first time, and to frame communication management as a collective responsibility of all organizational members. Matters of concern drive actors to, among other things, justify objectives and account for actions (Vásquez et al. 2018).

Through their framing of communication management in the communication policy and the branding platform, communication managers voice that managing communication is central to the organization and that it is a collective responsibility of all organizational members. This framing of communication management as a concern for all organizational members is further legitimized in another text on the branding platform which attempts to explain what a brand is:

> This [the brand] includes attitudes, associations, thoughts and emotions that surface in the receiver's consciousness when they come in contact with the brand. Immediately, we understand that a brand is not owned by the organization, but its receivers. And the organization cannot control it, *only influence it*.

Here, the communication managers stress that the communicative processes in which the organization is constituted cannot be controlled by the organization, but is co-created as citizens and other stakeholders come in contact with it through the representatives of the organization. This framing of communication management as a collective responsibility that cannot be controlled by the organization can be interpreted as a way for communication managers to dissociate themselves from the operational side of communication management. As the stakeholders' perception of the brand/organization is described as largely depending on "human interaction" and coworkers' "meetings" with stakeholders, the communication managers seemingly attempt to make coworkers aware of their own responsibility for communication. Thereby, by transferring and materializing their matters of concern into texts intended to be principles and guidelines for all organizational members, the communication managers seem to at least have been given the mandate to produce texts with "authoritative" ambition that aim to define "boundaries and exert 'official' influence over practice" (Kuhn 2008: 1236).

Framing the organization as a communicative accomplishment, and communication as a responsibility of all organizational members, can be understood as a way for communication managers to vie for greater intra-organizational authority by framing communication as a central concern for all organizational members. Thus, the texts can be understood as exemplifying the tendency of communication management to voice their concern and thereby engaging in the ongoing struggle over meaning and power, which characterizes the communicative process of co-orientation as various intra-organizational actors vie for authorship of the dominant "authoritative" text (Kuhn 2008). However, as pointed out by Vásquez et al. (2018), matters of concern must become matters of authority if they are to have performative consequences on other organizational members' decisions and actions.

Thus, while the empirical illustrations we have included in this section illustrate how communication managers discursively and linguistically frame communication management as a central concern for all organizational members, the transformation of these concerns into concrete interventions demands that they be perceived as legitimate by the organizational members that the texts are intended to guide. Thus, we settle for arguing that what we have demonstrated is the voicing of matters of concerns, and the aspirational talk (Christensen, Morsing, and Thyssen 2013), of communication managers. The presence of such texts indicates that communication management is perceived as a management practice that is legitimate enough to at least voice them in organizational contexts.

There are several readings that can be made of these texts. On the one hand, they can be read as communication management being on its way to becoming a continuation of normative control and identity-regulation (Alvesson and Willmott 2002; Christensen, Morsing, and Cheney 2008), which has been described as "brand-centered control" (Müller 2017). On the other hand, it can also be read as a trend towards decentralizing the authorship of the organization, as this increasingly common discursive and linguistic framing of communication management, as a matter of concern for all organizational members besides the control dimension, also contains an element of empowerment (see also Müller 2018). In addition to disciplining employees, this discursive and linguistic framing also acknowledges the co-constituted nature of organizations where a plethora of actors, both "inside" and "outside" the organization, contribute to make it present over time.

It can thus be read as an authorship that acknowledges the polyphonic rather than monolithic nature of the communicative co-orientation process through which the organization is constituted (Christensen and Cornelissen 2011). This highlights that the mindset and collective practice of communication management, as it gains traction and begins to influence organizational conversations and texts, should be studied from several perspectives so that its contribution to value creation and the management of contemporary organizations, as well as its "darker" implications such as potential "colonization" and "exploitation" of the "life worlds" of organizational members is acknowledged as well. Given that communication management to a large extent, as highlighted in the example above, can take the form of the management of the communicative constitution of organizations when communication managers are authorized to influence collective practices, this makes it especially relevant for CCO researchers to address (see also Christensen and Cornelissen 2011).

5 Conclusions and future directions

Nowadays, communication management is considered an increasingly institutionalized "thought structure" performed by senior managers in top-level decision-making and strategic planning (Tench, Verhoeven, and Zerfass 2009) and a mindset shared and reproduced by several different actors "inside" and "outside" the organization

(Christensen and Cornelissen 2011). In this chapter, we have aimed to advance our understanding of the ways of thinking and the collective communicative practices that constitute communication management as a specific management practice in contemporary organizations by reviewing central ideas in the constantly expanding body of knowledge of communication management, its relation to value creation, and by exemplifying how communication managers, by discursively and linguistically framing communication as a central organizational concern and responsibility of all organizational members, are enabled to voice their matters of concern and thereby vie for greater intra-organizational influence over the collective practice of management.

Societal and organizational developments have resulted in that communicative dimensions and communication management increasingly are becoming a central concern in contemporary management. Simultaneously, communication management is one of the practices labeled a "bullshit" job contributing little to no value to society at large (Graeber 2018). The increasing adoption of a corporate branding "way of thinking" in public sector organizations, with its emphasis on coherency and consistency, is not unproblematic given that imposing these ideals risks downplaying the strengths and uniqueness of contradictory and inconsistent values and multiple identities usually characterizing these organizations (Wæraas 2008).

Thus, future studies using a CCO approach when studying the collective practice of communication management could focus on how polyphony is encouraged in and through communication management. As pointed out by Christensen and Cornelissen (2011), the conceptual toolbox of organizational communication opens up for greater consideration the dimensions of polyphony, politics, and employee voice in the communicative co-orientation processes in and through which the organization is constituted. This is because the toolbox of organizational communication generally is more attentive to the individual voices of organizational members than traditional communication management literature which tends to focus more on the voice of the top management. This approach would fruitfully challenge the dominant mindset of communication management emphasizing coherence, integration, and consistency.

There are studies demonstrating the risks of failing to do justice to the polyphonic nature of internal stakeholder positions on a topic when externally communicating on controversial issues (Henderson, Cheney, and Weaver 2014). Similarly, a recent study on reputation management practices highlighted that traditional forms of communication management, which emphasize and strive to create a single corporate voice, produce employee dissatisfaction (Wæraas and Dahle 2020). Moreover, there is an increasing understanding among communication management researchers of the centrality to consider and "listen" to the interests and concerns of stakeholders and society when evaluating the value created by communication management (Macnamara and Gregory 2018). Thus, future research could focus on inquiring into what forms and practices of communication management could stimulate stakeholder polyphony and employee voice.

6 References

Alvesson, Mats & Hugh Willmott. 2002. Identity regulation as organizational control: Producing the appropriate individual. *Journal of Management Studies* 39(5). 619–644.

Andersson, Rickard. 2019. Employee communication responsibility: Its antecedents and implications for strategic communication management. *International Journal of Strategic Communication* 13(1). 60–75.

Andersson, Rickard. 2020. Being a 'strategist': Communication practitioners, strategic work, and power effects of the strategy discourse. *Public Relations Inquiry* 9(3). 257–276.

Argenti, Paul A. 1996. Corporate communication as a discipline: Toward a definition. *Management Communication Quarterly* 10(1). 73–97.

Benoit-Barné, Chantal & François Cooren. 2009. The accomplishment of authority through presentification: How authority is distributed among and negotiated by organizational members. *Management Communication Quarterly* 23(1). 5–31.

Berger, Bruce K. & Juan Meng (eds.). 2014. *Public relations leaders as sensemakers: A global study of leadership in public relations and communication management*. New York: Routledge.

Christensen, Lars T. & Joep Cornelissen. 2011. Bridging corporate and organizational communication: Review, development and a look to the future. *Management Communication Quarterly* 25(3). 383–414.

Christensen, Lars T. & Roy Langer. 2009. Public relations and the strategic use of transparency: Consistency, hypocrisy, and corporate change. In Robert L. Heath, Elizabeth L. Toth & Damion Waymer (eds.), *Rhetorical and critical approaches to public relations II*, 129–153. New York: Routledge.

Christensen, Lars T., Mette Morsing & George Cheney. 2008. *Corporate communications: Convention, complexity, and critique*. Los Angeles, CA: Sage.

Christensen, Lars T., Mette Morsing & Ola Thyssen. 2013. CSR as aspirational talk. *Organization* 20(3). 372–393.

Dozier, David. M., Larissa A. Grunig & James E. Grunig. 1995. *Manager's guide to excellence in public relations and communication management*. Mahwah, NJ: Laurence Erlbaum Associates.

Frandsen, Finn & Winnie Johansen. 2015. The role of communication executives in strategy and strategizing. In Derina R. Holtzhausen & Ansgar Zerfass (eds.), *The Routledge handbook of strategic communication*, 229–243. New York: Routledge.

Graeber, David. 2018. *Bullshit jobs*. New York: Simon & Schuster.

Grunig, James E. (ed.). 1992. *Excellence in public relations and communication management*. Hillsdale, NJ: Laurence Erlbaum Associates.

Grunig, James E. & Todd Hunt. 1984. *Managing public relations*. New York: Holt, Rinehart & Winston.

Gulbrandsen, Ib T. & Sine N. Just. 2016. In the wake of new media: Connecting the who with the how of strategizing communication. *International Journal of Strategic Communication* 10(4). 1–15.

Hallahan, Kirk, Derina Holtzhausen, Betteke van Ruler, Dejan Verčič & Krishnamurthy Sriramesh. 2007. Defining strategic communication. *International Journal of Strategic Communication* 1(1). 3–35.

Hatch, Mary J. & Majken Schultz. 1997. Relations between organizational culture, identity and image. *European Journal of Marketing* 31(5–6). 356–365.

Hatch, Mary J. & Majken Schultz. 2001. Are the strategic stars aligned for your corporate brand. *Harvard Business Review* 79(2). 128–134.

Hatch, Mary J. & Majken Schultz. 2003. Bringing the corporation into corporate branding. *European Journal of Marketing* 37(7–8). 1041–1064.

Heide, Mats, Sara von Platen, Charlotte Simonsson & Jesper Falkheimer. 2018. Expanding the scope of strategic communication: Towards a holistic understanding of organizational complexity. *International Journal of Strategic Communication* 12(4). 452–468.

Henderson, Alison, George Cheney & C. Kay Weaver. 2014. The role of employee identification and organizational identity in strategic communication and organizational issues management about genetic modification. *International Journal of Business Communication* 52(1). 12–41.

Knights, David & Gareth Morgan. 1990. The concept of strategy in sociology: A note of dissent. *Sociology* 24(3). 475–483.

Knights, David & Gareth Morgan. 1991. Corporate strategy, organizations, and subjectivity: A critique. *Organization Studies* 12(2). 251–273.

Kornberger, Martin. 2010. *Brand society: How brands transform management and lifestyle*. Cambridge: Cambridge University Press.

Kuhn, Timothy. 2008. A communicative theory of the firm: Developing an alternative perspective on intra-organizational power and stakeholder relationships. *Organization Studies* 29(8–9). 1227–1254.

Macnamara, Jim. 2015. Breaking the measurement and evaluation deadlock: A new approach and model. *Journal of Communication Management* 19(4). 371–387.

Macnamara, Jim & Anne Gregory. 2018. Expanding evaluation to progress strategic communication: Beyond message tracking to open listening. *International Journal of Strategic Communication* 12(4). 469–486.

Moss, Danny & Gary Warnaby. 1998. Communications strategy? Strategy communication? Integrating different perspectives. *Journal of Marketing Communications* 4(3). 131–140.

Müller, Monika. 2017. 'Brand-centred control': A study of internal branding and normative control. *Organization Studies* 38(7). 895–915.

Müller, Monika. 2018. 'Brandspeak': Metaphors and the rhetorical construction of internal branding. *Organization* 25(1). 42–68.

Nothhaft, Howard & Hagen Schölzel. 2015. (Re-) Reading Clausewitz: The strategy discourse and its implications for strategic communication. In Derina R. Holtzhausen & Ansgar Zerfass (eds.), *The Routledge handbook of strategic communication*, 18–33. New York: Routledge.

Porter, Michael E. 1985. *Competitive advantage: Creating and sustaining superior performance*. New York: Free Press.

Riel, Cees B. M. van. 1997. Research in corporate communication: An overview of an emerging field. *Management Communication Quarterly* 11(2). 288–309.

Riel, Cees B. M. van & John M. Balmer. 1997. Corporate identity: The concept, its measurement and management. *European Journal of Marketing* 31(5–6). 340–355.

Sievert, Holger, Lars Rademacher & Anna Weber. 2016. Business Knowledge as a limited success factor for Communication Managers: Results of a Survey in the German-Speaking Context. In: Peggy Simcic Brønn, Stefania Romenti, Ansgar Zerfass (eds.), *The Management Game of Communication: Advances in Public Relations and Communication Management*, Vol. 1. Bingley: Emerald Publishing Group Limited, pp 3–21.

Swerling, Jerry & Chaiti Sen. 2009. The institutionalization of the strategic communication function in the United States. *International Journal of Strategic Communication* 3(2). 131–146.

Tench, Ralph, Piet Verhoeven & Ansgar Zerfass. 2009. Institutionalizing strategic communication in Europe – An ideal home or a mad house? Evidence from a survey in 37 countries. *International Journal of Strategic Communication* 3(2). 147–164.

Vásquez, Consuelo, Nicolas Bencherki, François Cooren & Vivane Sergi. 2018. From 'matters of concern' to 'matters of authority': Studying the performativity of strategy from a communicative constitution of organization (CCO) approach. *Long Range Planning* 51(3). 417–435.

Volk, Sophia. C. & Ansgar Zerfass. 2018. Alignment: Explicating a key concept in strategic communication. *International Journal of Strategic Communication* 12(4). 433–451.

Webster, Phillip J. 1990. Strategic corporate public relations: What's the bottom line? *Public Relations Journal* 46(2). 18–21.

Wæraas, Arild. 2008. Can public sector organizations be coherent corporate brands? *Marketing Theory* 8(2). 205–221.

Wæraas, Arild., Dag Y. Dahle. 2020. When reputation management is people management: Implications for employee voice. *European Management Journal* 38(2). 277–287.

Zerfass, Ansgar. 2009. Institutionalizing strategic communication: Theoretical analysis and empirical evidence. *International Journal of Strategic Communication* 3(2). 69–71.

Zerfass, Ansgar & Neele Franke. 2013. Enabling, advising, supporting, executing: A theoretical framework for internal communication consulting within organizations. *International Journal of Strategic Communication* 7(2). 118–135.

Zerfass, Ansgar, Dejan Verčič, Howard Nothhaft & Kelly Page Werder. 2018. Strategic communication: Defining the field and its contribution to research and practice. *International Journal of Strategic Communication* 12(4). 487–505.

Zerfass, Ansgar, Dejan Verčič, Piet Verhoeven, Angelos Moreno & Ralph Tench. 2015. *European Communication Monitor 2015. Creating communication value through listening, messaging and measurement. Results of a survey in 41 countries*. Brussels: EACD/EUPRERA, Helios Publishing.

Zerfass, Ansgar & Christine Viertmann. 2017. Creating business value through corporate communication: A theory-based framework and its practical application. *Journal of Communication Management* 21(1). 68–81.

Patrice M. Buzzanell
16 Mentoring

Abstract: Mentoring is a reciprocal developmental relationship that often is constructed, analyzed, and evaluated through examination of types, functions, and outcomes for mentors and mentees, as well as their organizations. Although formal, informal, and episodic or spontaneous mentoring are compared against the idealistic and prototypical mentor-protégé relationship, mentoring often is enacted as a blend of different types and functions. These functions are enacted through advice, directives, and requests in situated communicative interactions and with varied single- and multi-level consequences. Future research should explore how mentoring is constituted in specific contexts and with diverse groups of people to better understand the complexities of this vital managerial communication process.

Keywords: mentor-mentee relationships; mentoring types; mentoring functions; linguistic features; mentoring goals

Mentoring focuses on the development of individuals, groups, and organizations through human and AI (artificial intelligence)-assisted management communication. Although there are different types of mentoring, they all involve key linguistic and interactional features that vary based on participants' expertise, power, and goals for the mentorship. This chapter notes ways to make mentoring more productive for all parties. Mentoring is the process by which people learn from others who are perceived to have more experience or knowledge in particular areas. Mentoring occurs throughout lifespans – when children begin to navigate relationships with the help of siblings and parents, to employment situations where workers and entrepreneurs learn from others in their actual and/or aspirational organizations and industries. Unlike consultancies or coaching, where experts are hired to provide professional opinions or to develop a client more broadly, mentoring benefits organizations and individuals by assisting in the development and retention of critical knowledge and practices over the course of career- and life-spans, and of individuals for key roles.

Scholarship and practice focus on mentorship types (formal, informal, and episodic), mentoring reasons or functions (career developmental, psychosocial, or personal and professional support, as well as role modeling), and outcomes for mentees, mentors, and organizations (continuum of positive through dysfunctional consequences). Ideally, mentorship is a reciprocal relationship in which mentors and mentees – as individuals or as groups – switch roles for beneficial processes and results. Addressing power control and tensions in mentoring communication designs and implementations is a fundamental task for management. To discuss communicative characteristics and practices of mentoring, this chapter describes (1) types of mentoring, (2) linguistic and interactional features of mentoring, and (3) lessons for mentoring.

1 Types of mentoring

The types presented here are ideal insofar as their descriptions are based on their primary characteristics, outcomes, and logical assumptions. From the idealized functions and benefits codified in (a) prototypical mentoring through (b) formal and (c) informal to (d) episodic moments, individuals and groups obtain career, psychosocial support, and/or role modeling assistance in online and face-to-face encounters that often (e) blend types. Management's encouragement of participants' shifts in mentor-mentee roles and associated linguistic and interactional features can promote more satisfactory mentoring regardless of type.

1.1 Prototypical mentoring

When individuals and organizations think about mentoring, they often subscribe to the "master narrative of mentoring" that promotes prototypical dyadic relationships of single mentors who guide, assist in overcoming obstacles, advocate for, and revel in protégés' success. The prototypical arrangement is marked by clear hierarchical status differences and by the ways in which protégés' objective successes, indicated by promotion and pay, reflect mentors' worth and legacies. This archetypical imagery portrays how protégés, as epic heroes, enact masculine career scripts with male actors and upward linear trajectories toward success in public arenas (Buzzanell and Goldzwig 1991).

Ideal mentors often are leaders: decisive, aggressive, competitive, confident, and courageous (Holmes 2017). These mentorship actors willingly engage with each other, sometimes at the behest of rulers or organizational managers, to form bonds of affection and trust that can span decades and work-life boundaries. Sometimes these relationships become the stuff of lore over centuries as Homer's Odysseus left his son, Telemachus, in the care of Mentor (Irby et al. 2020: 19); sometimes these mentorships become popular media classics across generations and galaxies, like Obi-Wan Kenobi to Luke Skywalker and Luke Skywalker to Rey in the *Star Wars* films. Regardless of context, prototypical mentorship is the standard against which people compare their experiences.

In their comparisons, people make value or cost-benefit judgments. There is tacit understanding that mentors are measured and selected for what they can bring to the table, as are protégés (or mentees, to lessen power differentials linguistically). Thus, managers need to be mindful that cultural understandings, or macrodiscourses, of assessment, power and control, productivity, worth, accountability, competition, and exceptionalism drive mentoring practice. People may experience disillusionment and organizations may lose talent if mentorships are not perceived as ideal or, minimally, as functional and inclusive. To combat expectations of prototypical mentoring, managers and employees can establish realistic goals and contexts. Managers can be vigilant in terms of how mentoring is and can be constituted through talk and interaction to develop and sustain diverse mentorship structures of equity, career promise fulfillment, and retention of organizational and industry expertise (Ibarra 1995). Recognizing that mentoring is situated, that is, that people interact to construct their realities (Sillince 2007), fosters agency and responsibility in aspirational and everyday mentoring types and content.

1.2 Formal mentoring

Formal mentorship is arranged by outside parties, often contractually with rights, obligations, and responsibilities for specified times and resources (Kram and Ragins 2007). Formal mentorship may be dyadic, clustered, networked, arranged into affinity groups, or tied specifically to career developmental and/or work-life exigencies for limited time periods. Formal mentorship may use face-to-face and online formats, including use of influencers in social media, gatherings, and websites or businesses devoted to mentoring others, and mentor chatbots. For instance, in academe, faculty might use the services of Rockquemore's (2020) National Center for Faculty Development and Diversity (NCFDD), with its Monday Motivator emails and virtual mentoring groups organized by career developmental stage (e.g., postdocs or assistant professors).

Formal mentorship is motivated by external rewards and career development with the label derived from the initial impetus for the arrangement. In businesses, formal mentorship may be part of position responsibilities or set up as contracts through Human Resources (HR) functions and/or corporate initiatives. The impetus could be assistance in role transitions, such as moves from technical to managerial career ladders in engineering, but it also could be the need to create more inclusive cultures by creating opportunities for those who might not be mentored otherwise (e.g., cross-gender, -race and ethnicity, -class, -nationality and immigrant status; for overviews, see Ragins and Kram 2007). Furthermore, formal reverse mentoring, "where knowledge is transferred from younger to older individuals" (Kaše, Saksida, and Mihelič 2019: 57), operates from differential motivations for older and younger learners. Implications for managers are that reverse mentoring rewards for mentors and mentees need to be consistent with career and lifespan phases, cognizant of difference, and in keeping with organizational cultures (Kaše, Saksida, and Mihelič 2019) and reward systems.

Because formal mentorship is officially arranged, it is embedded in the hierarchical nature of organizing and has several implications not fully explored in mentorship, scholarship, and practices. First, one premise is that mentors provide advice, and mentees ask for explanations, clarifications, and elaborations but generally follow mentors' directives and requests. Discussion of linguistic, interactional, role, and contextual aspects provide insight into the complexities of formal mentoring when viewed from a communicatively constituted lens (for discussion of linguistic and interactional processes, see Section 3). Second, formal mentoring might be considered as a process designed to assist with adaptation to current or anticipated circumstances, much like communication for newcomer socialization and role transitions (i.e., Jablin 2001). In these cases, formal mentoring success could be determined by the effective and efficient means by which mentees (and mentors in reverse mentoring) fulfill their responsibilities and obligations. This adaptation assumes that the organization for which people are being mentored is healthy and that both parties understand and comply with their roles. However, Allen (2000) described the ways in which she as newcomer or mentee and her departmental colleagues or mentors faced challenges posed by changing academic systems, diversity initiatives, and higher education institutional norms in which she was positioned as an insider-outsider. Allen (2000) pulled lessons for newcomers, administrators, peers, and scholars from her deep and nuanced feminist standpoint analysis of microaggressions that she, and other faculty of color, face on a daily basis (for microaggressions, or interpersonal assaults, and macroaggressions, or race-based systemic injustices, see Sue et al. 2019).

As a final consideration, the hierarchical nature of formal mentoring assumes that those with power and expertise would willingly mentor others and know how to do so, whereas those designated as mentees are *mentorable*. Although there is very little research on being mentorable, my personal observations indicate that *mentorability* assessments are based on one's vantage points. To be mentorable, mentees would want to be open-minded, flexible, and persistent as first-generation students of color indicated in their interviews on this topic (Black et al. 2019). To these, I add that mentees need to be vulnerable, humble, and willing to ask questions and take risks in trusting the mentor and in admitting lack of knowledge and skills in particular areas.

Managers interested in being mentored or matching employees for formal mentoring might consider displays that they or others might perceive as indicating (un) mentorability. If they take pride in being able to figure out and do things on their own, they might need coaching to work effectively with mentors. They may be the one and only in a given situation and perceive that there is no one like them to which they could turn, especially if they have not had positive interactions with majority group members in mentorships or other contexts, or if mentoring communication seems to come from majority perspectives making the content difficult to translate to mentee experiences (for mentoring based on white male paradigms, see Blake-Beard, Murrell, and Thomas 2007).

Finally, being mentorable likely falls along a continuum. Mentees may not recognize themselves as tending toward being (not) mentorable. Mentors might not recognize how their dominant group membership(s) encourage them to label others in this way. Straightforward talk about and careful matching of mentor-mentee dyads, clusters, or affinity groups, and developmental networks can support people in these initiatives and offer starting points for conversation about how talk and interactions can constitute healthy mentoring (for successful matching criteria based on mentoring program objectives, see Blake-Beard, O'Neill, and McGowan 2007).

1.3 Informal mentoring

Just as the metaphor for formal mentoring is a contract, the metaphor for informal mentoring is a close personal relationship. Informal mentoring is motivated by attraction (liking), interest, admiration, and mentors' and mentees' beliefs that they could work well together as dyads or in group contexts. Organizational position or some other status marker can function as a proxy for expertise in initial mentor and mentee selection. Often, mentees in informal relationships, particularly men, receive more favorable career outcomes than formally mentored and non-mentored employees (Ragins and Cotton 1999). Informal mentoring may benefit from different expectations (compared to formal and episodic mentoring) and long-term friendships (Baugh and Fagenson-Eland 2007).

With regard to different expectations and associated linguistic choices, informal mentoring discussions can resemble the development and language of personal relationships since both are based on liking and attraction. Indeed, Chao (1997) described phases in mentoring relational development – initiation or mutual discovery, cultivation or relationship maturation, separation or independence (relational break-up), and redefinition or relationship transformation that ends the mentorship but could shift into another kind of relationship. Kalbfleisch's (2002) Theory of Enactment proposed communicative strategies for facilitating and maintaining informal mentoring relationships. Whether phases or enactments, little is known about how mentors and mentees identify with each other at the start and throughout the mentorship (Humberd and Rouse 2016).

Informal mentorships are difficult to form and sustain for different groups of people. Saffie-Robertson (2020) found that women in male-dominated and masculine fields such as STEM (science, technology, engineering, and math) faced four significant barriers – demonstrating capability, need for fit, trust in the mentor, and commitment to the mentor. Although practical implications recommended mentoring program and culture development, how one communicates explicitly to overcome these barriers is not explicated.

Saffie-Robertson (2020) positions communication as a tool to advance women's interests, but not as the constitutive process through which mentorship comes into being, meaning that attention to linguistic choices and interactions that might unintentionally undermine these relationships would be critical for managers and mentoring participants. As a second example, Kalbfleisch and Eckley (2003) found that internet-enabled mentoring offers assistance for underrepresented group members trying to initiate and maintain mentorships. Sample posts showed how the parties negotiated what they could bring to the relationships and what their hopes were for mentoring. Mentees felt able to request advice and often perceived support and affirmation.

These materials indicate that people find it difficult to initiate and sustain informal mentoring. Yet managers and/or HR functions can provide training and resources to assist in face-to-face and virtual informal mentoring by considering its ideal type. Informal mentoring ideally approaches the relationally responsive interplays and understandings about which Shotter and Cunliffe (2002) write, namely, those in which jointly structured activity is incomplete and participants engage in listening and responding to each other and to the circumstances. As mentors and mentees co-produce meaning, their moments of involvement and commitment enable them to engage in co-authoring "possibilities for action" (Shotter and Cunliffe 2002: 26). This authoring of mentoring, like leadership processes, likely unfolds as claims of expertise and mentoring roles are navigated *in situ*, such as through negotiating identity group memberships, work-life experiences, and tasks or developmental learnings associated with hierarchical passages, trajectories, and reputations (for authoring, see Holm and Fairhurst 2018).

1.4 Episodic mentoring

Episodic mentoring draws from Fletcher and Ragins' (2007) Relational Cultural Theory (RCT), in which relational mentoring challenges traditional notions of hierarchy, distinct roles, and outcomes for mentees by infusing mentoring with understandings of power, fluidity in expertise, mutual development in proficiencies, and two-directional learning. Mentoring operates as a continuum of mentoring episodes, notably, one interaction at a time with "a set of evaluative criteria that can be used to determine whether growth and learning occurred within a given interaction, thus allowing us to classify the interaction as mutually growth fostering or not" (Fletcher and Ragins 2007: 381). This definition enables RCT researchers to distinguish mentoring relationships from other learning and developmental processes. This definition also requires that both parties are asked about their mentoring experiences to determine mutuality and growth-fostering nature (Fletcher and Ragins 2007), criteria not always met in studies (e. g., Schwarts and Holloway 2014).

Long et al. (2014) adhere to these distinctions by defining episodic mentoring "as consisting of developmental interactions that occur at a specific point in time when two parties exchange knowledge, engage in relationship building, and enact social support [...] [and] are agreed on explicitly or tacitly as mentoring by mentors and mentees" (392). These characteristics are similar to relationally responsive understandings insofar as mentoring episodes operate as the communitive building blocks or units of relational mentoring (Shotter and Cunliffe 2002). RCT maintains that healthy growth-fostering relationships include and generate "Five Good Things" (Jordan 2010): energy, knowledge, movement, self-worth, and a desire for connection. Schwartz and Holloway (2014) found that some but not all of the Five Good Things, for mentoring episodes, could be considered high quality.

Buzzanell (2009) notes that spontaneous mentoring may occur within, or build to, a mentoring relationship. These spontaneous moments may be discrete and influential learnings; they may be overheard and ascertained through observations of role models. Furthermore, spontaneous mentoring might produce a ripple effect insofar as the mentees may check in with other human and non-human sources then pass along what they learned. Although there is much to learn about episodic mentoring and how it functions as a mentoring type in and of itself and in combination with other mentoring types, managers can encourage and role model spontaneous mentoring. Spontaneous mentoring can be as simple as posting a new technique or resource on WeChat for employees whom one knows would benefit from this knowledge. Managers could also set up face-to-face and virtual meetings in which sharing of new learnings directed to all or some members of the unit is accomplished. Episodic mentoring is less costly in time and other resources and can develop a culture of mentoring.

1.5 Blending mentoring types

To summarize this section, four main types of mentoring – prototypical, formal, informal, and episodic or spontaneous – can be distinguished based on how and why they begin and unfold communicatively, and the imagery associated with each – idealized mentor-protégé, contract, close personal relationship, and just-in-time moments. Regardless of these differences, mentoring has (a) key characteristics that distinguish this process from other learning and socializing models, (b) popular notions that mentoring is essential for positive outcomes, and (c) critique that mentoring is not as straightforward as it is rendered in scholarship and practice.

First, key characteristics distinguish mentoring from other processes. Akin to coaching, supervising, teaching, and parenting, Haggard et al. (2011) propose that three main attributes of mentoring in workplaces are reciprocity, developmental benefits, and regular interaction. These attributes serve to characterize mentoring relationships but might not be consistent with spontaneous or episodic mentoring moments that can be incorporated or blended into other mentorship types. Managers' repertoire of mentoring types can enable them to foster and/or change types as needed by their employees.

Second, people and organizational documents talk about this process as positive and essential for learning how to manage diverse career and personal life events and relationships over the lifespan. In their meta-analysis of career benefits for mentees, Allen et al. (2004) found that individuals who had been mentored for their careers experienced greater objective career success (total annual compensation, salary growth, and self-reported promotions) and subjective career success (career satisfaction, advancement expectations, career commitment, and job satisfaction) than those who had not been mentored. Their findings suggested that career and psychosocial mentoring were both important for career and job attitudes. However, since Allen et al.'s meta-analysis, studies have found small to moderate effects of mentoring on mentee outcomes although beliefs in benefits persist (Eby and Robertson 2020). In other words, mentoring may be helpful for traditionally researched outcomes, but managers should consider mentoring for other reasons such as inclusive cultures and reputations as growth-facilitating organizations, for recruitment, and retention.

Third, the mentoring process is not as straightforward as some might assume. First, little to no research takes a life- and/or career-span approach to what mentoring means and how it evolves for individuals and in collectivities. Little is known about what people learn from early childhood experiences or even intergenerational mentoring patterns although there are glimmers in memorable messages and occupational osmosis studies whereby people learn from stories or observations of others' work (e. g., Gibson and Papa 2000). Long et al. (2018) propose evolutionary career networks of human and non-human (e. g., website) mentoring to provide longitudinal insights. Second, most research taking an intersectional or multiple identity(ies) approach (Cho, Crenshaw, and McCall 2013; Collins and Bilge 2016) examines gender and/or race in particular contexts, such as STEM majors in college and careers, from preconceived social identity groupings and contexts without attention to how these and other, even invisible, identities emerge in situated interaction. For instance, gender and race or ethnicity might interact with nationality, age, educational institutions through which individuals matriculated, previous life and career experiences, and so on. In any given instance, these different identities may come into play in unique ways that make some identities more salient than others and that could alter expected mentoring processes and outcomes. Third, little research examines how mentoring is constituted in the moment (exception: McAllum 2019) meaning that additional studies need to examine linguistic and interactional features.

2 Linguistic and interactional features of mentoring

Much of the literature on mentoring gives a nod to advice and complex interactional enactments without delving into these communicative processes per se. In other words, mentoring materials indicate that mentors and mentees communicate advice and engage in interactions and relationship development and maintenance, yet few discuss exactly how these communicative functions are constituted *in situ*. As mentioned in the discussion of formal mentoring (Section 2.2), a premise of mentoring is that mentors give (a) advice, likely through (b) directives and requests, and mentees ask for advice but also explanations, clarifications, and elaborations. Informal and episodic mentoring assume give-and-take qualities as well as role switching. The other feature that is typically noted is that mentoring is (c) a complex and situated communicative practice.

2.1 Mentoring as advice

Central to mentoring is advice-giving and -receiving. In these discussions, advice is a communication tool for doing the work of mentoring. Mentoring might involve directives, particularly in official or formal mentoring situations where the mentor traditionally has legitimate power. Often those in leadership roles would frame their recommendations as advice to provide guidance and empower their mentees (Vine 2022: 171–172). When advice is given as part of mentoring, such advice could function as career oriented and/or supportive, but advice relies on a disparity of experience such that advice-givers would be perceived as having expertise (MacGeorge and Van Swol 2018). Mentoring messages and interactions focus on the other's actions, with future orientations and intents to guide behavior in ways that advice-givers believe would help others with issues or problems. Advice is an influence attempt, often conducted in one-to-one situations. In managerial communication contexts, advice-giving could occur in group or networked sessions.

Professional advice-giving is conducted in written or oral forms with occupation- and problem-specific considerations. Attorneys must consider if they are functioning as advisors of legal rights and obligations, or as advocates, negotiators, or evaluators (Kong 2014). In medical contexts, there are other roles and potential liabilities particularly in life threatening cases or end-of-life interactions. In academe, graduate students might not want to contradict formal mentors' advice because of advice-givers' disciplinary reputation and authority (Long, Selzer King, and Buzzanell 2018). In managerial contexts, mentoring involves advice but also directives and requests, among other linguistic features.

2.2 Mentoring as directives and requests

As Vine (2022: 55) notes, directives, or attempts to get others to do something, are "contextually complex", can be implicit and explicit, and can take many forms depending on context and power dynamics. Whereas directives tell mentees to do something, requests ask them to do it. When subordinates make requests, they often do so with justifications more so that managers do (Kong 2014). In formal mentoring, mentors have legitimate rights (or authority) to give directives, but mentees may enact agency to refuse or modify these directives. The right of refusal is contextually determined. In less formal mentoring, where role boundaries are less defined, the development and attribution of expertise happens interactionally and linguistic forms may shift from what one might presuppose from ideal mentoring types. For instance, interrogative (question) forms might be used to soften directives especially when there is no sense of urgency.

2.3 Mentoring as complex and situated communicative practice

Linguistic and interactional processes through which mentoring is constituted are complex and situated through (a) context, (b) identities, (c) agency, (d) culture, and (e) motivations. Regarding context, McAllum (2019) provides a detailed case of how mentoring emerges linguistically and interactively in emergency situations where professionals need to talk through and enact safety. She describes how mentoring intends to meet relational goals but also to socialize individuals into communities of practice with shared tools, language, jargon, and tasks. Her work indicates that directives on ways to act may be implicit and/or explicit but can attend to relational goals or collegiality by phrasing and explanations during or after crises. Similarly, Tolbert et al. (2016) use a ventriloquial approach to describe how certain linguistic patterns and accepted ways of critiquing projects are normal for particular groups. During design critiques, linguistic patterns emerged such as directives and direct criticism leveled at novice designers. These critiques might seem harsh to those who are not part of an industrial arts and engineering community but they are received as part of the design review and critique genre.

Second, regarding identities, many studies focus on a particular identity group (e. g., women in STEM) or identity clusters (e. g., women engineering managers of color). As noted earlier, most mentoring researchers often start with already established identities or roles rather than seeing how identities emerge as salient in certain situations. For instance, there is a large body of research focusing on outcomes of same- and cross-gender mentoring relationships (e. g., Ragins and McFarlin 1990). A recent study in this vein indicated that same-gender and -race of mentors and mentees affect mentees' occupational choices in military branch assignment preferences (Kofoed and McGovney 2019). However, using a poststructuralist feminist narratological and intersectional approach, complex mentoring enactments and assessments can be found (Buzzanell et al. 2015). These enactments depended on mentees' positions in institutional hierarchies, as well as their career stage, previous history with and expectations about mentoring, spirituality, type of engineering work, countries of origin and cultural expectations, race, relational status (including dependents), and age. Complicated identities embedded in power-laden stories of mentoring, career, and personal life emerged. These stories displayed ambiguities, ambivalences, and contradictions in mentorship. Thus, mentoring identities come together differently for groups.

Third, agency or ability to act comes to the forefront in mentoring scholarship when mentors and mentees switch roles, transition through different mentorship phases, and make decisions about face-to-face and online mentoring. For instance, e-mentoring – "a mutually beneficial relationship [...] through e-mail and other electronic means (e. g., instant messaging, chat rooms, social networking spaces, etc.)" (Ensher and Murphy 2007: 300) – expands the reach of mentoring through technological affordances. Its advantages are boundaryless mentoring: greater access to mentors by removing geographic and organizational barriers and by lessening biases associated with difference. Disadvantages focus on potential miscommunication through less information-rich media and technological savvy. However, formal e-mentoring programs have been successful for career and management development as long as mentor-mentee matching was carefully done and aligned with program goals and technological skills (Headlam-Wells, Gosland, and Craig 2005).

More sophisticated mentoring systems have become increasingly boundaryless. Labeled as distributed and networked mentoring, they rely on internet-enabled geographically distributed and collectively managed systems for requesting and providing feedback with role fluidity. For Campbell et al.'s (2016: 1) fan communities, distributed mentoring is "community-based learning and mentoring that is uniquely facilitated by the technological affordances of the Web" and that resembles spontaneous mentoring more so than formal, informal, or episodic relational mentoring. Mentoring incorporated varied linguistic features from many different individuals in reciprocal processes: "In some cases, respondents would provide advice to the original poster independently without referencing what other respondents stated, but in other cases respondents would debate, correct, or agree with the advice provided by other respondents, often adding to it" (Campbell et al.'s 2016: 6).

For Pruchniewska (2019), a private feminist Facebook™ group offered network mentoring opportunities befitting feminist fourth wave activists. These women collectively mentored each other but ironically reproduced cultural hierarchies of power that reaffirmed normative whiteness. Although these two examples are not set in managerial communication contexts, they do indicate the kinds of collaborative mentoring that promote different and more fluid or boundaryless mentoring types, roles, and linguistic features. These qualities are consistent with peer mentoring (Kram and Isabella 1985) and developmental network mentoring (Higgins and Kram 2001). However, these examples still involve humans as mentors and mentees, whereas mentoring systems enabled by artificial intelligence (AI) do not.

AI mentoring systems depend on algorithms that produce chatbots with different voices and responses to diverse group members' mentoring needs at specific career phases with attention. Chatbots that are more emotionally relatable through user interface and content enable mentees to share sensitive content (Mendez et al. 2019). Through phenomenological designs with focus group data, future faculty in Mendez et al.'s (2019) study felt supported when they discussed isolation and the extra service that they do as people of color. These same considerations would apply to workplaces where chatbots could engage in different types of mentoring.

According to Kravčík, Schmid, and Igel (2019), requirements for AI mentoring systems to meet diverse needs include: affect detection, metacognitive support, opportunities for lifelong mentoring, and prediction consistent with known mentoring aspects. In some contexts, mentors develop algorithms with mentees to become diversity champions (e. g., Girls Who Code; AI4ALL) and admit that "greater focus [is] needed on ethical and moral mentoring" (Smith and Green 2018; see also Daugherty, Wilson, and Chowdhury 2019). The field of Critical Algorithms Studies examines fairness, accountability, and transparency in machine learning (e. g., for sociocultural processes such as newcomer socialization, Geiger 2017; see also Chah 2019). Chatbots typically are responsive to mentee questions and requests, including advice-seeking aligned with formal mentoring. Chatbot mentoring also could be classified as episodic and/or spontaneous depending on the perceived relationships or just-in-time responses. Chatbots offer opportunities to establish mentoring as safe and satisfying foundations on which managers can personalize.

Fourth, culture influences mentoring. Since what constitutes mentoring is socially constructed, mentoring is shaped by (and shapes) everyday talk and interaction within socio-political-economic, and historical macro understandings. Mentoring itself and what is desirable or considered good mentoring in type, content, and delivery (e. g., online, distributed, face-to-face, or bot<–>human) shifts. For example, Irby et al. (2020) discussed the importance of justice in Ptah-hotep's ancient Egyptian texts, whereas Vine (2022) noted that people in collectivist cultures might wait to be asked to contribute rather than just inviting themselves to participate (see also "Maria" who waited for faculty mentoring lunch invitations in Buzzanell et al. 2015).

Zhou, Lapointe, and Zhou (2019) conducted in-depth interviews to understand Chinese mentoring. They found many similarities with Western features but also some distinctive aspects that they attributed to Confucianism. In particular, mentoring was family-like: "The family is the prototype of all social organizations. In China, the *jia-ren* (family) relationships are characterized by relatively stable, long-lasting, and expressive relationships in which the welfare of the other is part of one's duty" (Zhou, Lapointe, and Zhou 2019: 436). Mentoring phases are similar to those studied in Western contexts, but Chinese pre-mentoring contact differs from the formal beginning of mentorship. Chinese formal mentoring relationships often are ritualized with official ceremonies that mark their start. Another difference is that these relationships are embedded in mentors' and mentees' social networks rather than having stand-alone dyadic mentoring as is prominent in Western mentoring. Although mentoring becomes more like friendships and peer relationship over time in the West, the relationship remains as a mentoring arrangement throughout its lifespan in China.

Furthermore, culture might also connote social identity communities in particular contexts. Harris and Lee (2019) discussed the need to do advocate-mentoring. This form of mentoring functions as a means of taking active and assertive roles on behalf of marginalized people in academe and in other contexts. Advocate-mentors embody deep commitments to social justice. They defend and champion mentees' intellectual abilities, research interests, value, and career advancement. Above all, they provide emotional safety. Similarly, micro-, meso-, and macro-level institutional mentoring support can be found in programs that move toward transformational change with regard to gender and other forms of difference through questioning norms, workplace practices, peer support networks, and creation of new stories (Leenders, Bleijenbergh, and Van den Brink 2019).

Finally, motivations differ in mentoring relationships with most research examining mentor and mentee reasons for participation. The assumption is that mentoring produces positive outcomes. However, dysfunctional and toxic mentoring can be embedded within an institutional culture where leadership models behaviors of self-interest, sabotage, maliciousness, and exploitation (Pelletier, Kottke, and Sirotnik 2019) that then become normalized and enacted in mentors' and mentees' behaviors. When toxic mentoring is normalized by unit and organizational cultures or by one's past experiences with mentoring, the damage to individuals' careers, personal well-being, and economic health can be extensive. In addition, dysfunctional mentoring might occur inadvertently such as when mentors provide advice that is outdated or they do not recognize their own behaviors as detrimental. Similarly, mentees' communication can be negative such as when mentees fail to hold confidences or engage in unethical and manipulative behaviors (Eby and McManus 2004). Rather than either-or categorizations or typologies of mentoring, such toxicity can be arrayed along a continuum from high quality to marginal to dysfunctional (Ragins, Cotton, and Miller 2000).

In sum, this section on mentoring as complex and situated communicative practice points out managers' responsibilities to attend to departmental and organizational cultures of inclusion and functionality, role modeling of linguistic choices and professional interactions, and mentors and mentees' development through and satisfaction with their relationships.

3 Lessons for mentoring

Because mentoring is a prized resource for individuals and organizations, strategies have been designed to create greater opportunities for all organizational members, but particularly for underrepresented group members. These opportunities leverage the advantages of specific mentoring types and their combinations, but also generate more distributed and collective forms through media affordances and more individualized and safe environments through artificial intelligence. Inherent in mentoring is power, control, and resistance. Managers would do well to consider what priorities are embedded in the ways that they establish and enact mentoring. For instance, they might examine the benefit and potential consequences – for good or for ill – of mentoring program design, selection, and matching of people into dyadic and group mentoring, and training and resources for participants. This chapter draws attention to the profound complexities regarding linguistic and interactional choices for meeting relational, task, community and occupational, and/or advocacy goals in mentoring.

4 References

Allen, Brenda J. 2000. Learning the ropes: A Black feminist standpoint analysis. In Patrice M. Buzzanell (ed.), *Rethinking organizational and managerial communication from feminist perspectives*, 177–208. Thousand Oaks, CA: Sage.

Allen, Tammy D., Lillian T. Eby, Mark L. Poteet, Elizabeth Lentz & Lizzette Lima. 2004. Career benefits associated with mentoring for protégés: A meta-analysis. *Journal of Applied Psychology* 89(1). 127–136.

Baugh, S. Gayle & Ellen Fagenson-Eland. 2007. Formal mentoring programs: A "poor cousin" to informal relationships? In Belle Rose Ragins & Kathy Kram (eds.), *The handbook of mentoring at work: Theory, research, and practice*, 249–272. Thousand Oaks, CA: Sage.

Black, V. G., Z. Taylor, Richard J. Reddick & J. Smith. 2019. Being mentorable: First-generation students of color define "Mentorability". [Special Issue 1]. *UNM Mentoring Institute, The Chronicle of Mentoring & Coaching* 2.

Blake-Beard, Stacy, Audrey Murrell & David Thomas. 2007. Unfinished business: The impact of race on understanding mentoring relationships. In Belle Rose Ragins & Kathy Kram (eds.), *The handbook of mentoring at work: Theory, research, and practice*, 223–248. Thousand Oaks, CA: Sage.

Blake-Beard, Stacy, Regina O'Neill & Eileen McGowan. 2007. Blind dates? The importance of matching in successful formal mentoring relationships. In Belle Rose Ragins & Kathy Kram (eds.), *The handbook of mentoring at work: Theory, research, and practice*, 617–632. Thousand Oaks, CA: Sage.

Buzzanell, Patrice M. 2009. Spiritual mentoring: Embracing the mentor-mentee relational process. *New Directions for Teaching and Learning* 120. 17–24.

Buzzanell, Patrice M. & Steven Goldzwig. 1991. Linear and nonlinear career models: Metaphors, paradigms, and ideologies. *Management Communication Quarterly* 4(4). 466–505.

Buzzanell, Patrice M., Ziyu Long, Lindsey Anderson, Klod Kokini & Jennifer Batra. 2015. Mentoring in academe: A feminist poststructural lens on stories of women engineering faculty of color. *Management Communication Quarterly* 29(3). 440–457.

Campbell, Julie, Cecilia Aragon, Katie Davis, Sarah Evans, Abigail Evans & David Randall. 2016. Thousands of positive reviews: Distributed mentoring in online fan communities. In *Proceedings of the 19th ACM Conference on Computer-Supported Cooperative Work & Social Computing*, 691–704. New York: Association for Computing Machinery.

Chah, Niel. 2019. Down the deep rabbit hole: Untangling deep learning from machine learning and artificial intelligence. *First Monday* 24(2). https://doi.org/10.5210/fm.v24i2.8237.

Chao, Georgia. 1997. Mentoring phases and outcomes. *Journal of Vocational Behavior* 51(1). 15–28.

Cho, Sumi, Kimberlé Williams Crenshaw & Leslie McCall. 2013. Toward a field of intersectionality studies: Theory, applications, and praxis. *Signs* 38(4). 785–810.

Collins, Patricia Hill & Sirma Bilge. 2016. *Intersectionality*. Malden, MA: Polity.

Daugherty, Paul, H. James Wilson & Rumman Chowdhury. 2019. Using artificial intelligence to promote diversity. *MIT Sloan Management Review* 60(2). 1.

Eby, Lillian & Stacy McManus. 2004. The protégé's role in negative mentoring experiences. *Journal of Vocational Behavior* 65(2). 255–275.

Eby, Lillian & Melissa Robertson. 2020. The psychology of workplace mentoring relationships. *Annual Review of Organizational Psychology and Organizational Behavior* 7(1). 75–100.

Ensher, Ellen & Susan Murphy. 2007. E-mentoring: Next generation research strategies and suggestions. In Belle Rose Ragins & Kathy Kram (eds.), *The handbook of mentoring at work: Theory, research, and practice*, 299–322. Thousand Oaks, CA: Sage.

Fletcher, Joyce & Belle Rose Ragins. 2007. Stone center relational cultural theory. In Belle Rose Ragins & Kathy Kram (eds.), *The handbook of mentoring at work: Theory, research, and practice*, 373–399. Thousand Oaks, CA: Sage.

Geiger, R. Stuart. 2017. Beyond opening up the black box: Investigating the role of algorithmic systems in Wikipedian organizational culture. *Big Data & Society* 4(2). 1–14.

Gibson, Melissa & Michael Papa. 2000. The mud, the blood, and the beer guys: Organizational osmosis in blue-collar work groups. *Journal of Applied Communication Research* 28(1). 68–88.

Haggard, Dana, Thomas Dougherty, Daniel Turban & James Wilbanks. 2011. Who is a mentor? A review of evolving definitions and implications for research. *Journal of Management* 37(1). 280–304.

Harris, Tina & Celeste Lee. 2019. Advocate-mentoring: A communicative response to diversity in higher education. *Communication Education* 68(1). 103–113.

Headlam-Wells, Jenny, Julian Gosland & Jane Craig. 2005. "There's magic in the web": E-mentoring for women's career development. *Career Development International* 10(6–7). 444–459.

Higgins, Michael & Kathy Kram. 2001. Reconceptualizing mentoring at work: A developmental network perspective. *Academy of Management Review* 26(2). 264–288.

Holm, Flemming & Gail T. Fairhurst. 2018. Configuring shared and hierarchical leadership through authoring. *Human Relations* 71(5). 692–721.

Holmes, Janet. 2017. Leadership and change management: Examining gender, cultural and "hero leader" stereotypes. In Cornelia Illie & Stephanie Schnurr (eds.), *Challenging leadership stereotypes through discourse*, 15–43. Singapore: Springer.

Humberd, Beth & Elizabeth Rouse. 2016. Seeing you in me and me in you: Personal identification in the phases of mentoring relationships. *Academy of Management Review* 41(3). 435–455.

Ibarra, Herminia. 1995. Race, opportunity, and diversity of social circles in managerial networks. *Academy of Management Journal* 38(3). 673–703.

Irby, Beverly, Nahed Abdelrahman, Rafael Lara-Alecio & Tammy Allen. 2020. Epistemological beginnings of mentoring. In Beverly Irby, Jennifer Boswell, Linda Searby, Frances Kochan, Rubén Graza & Nahed Abdelrahman (eds.), *Wiley international handbook of mentoring*, 19–28. Hoboken, NJ: Wiley Blackwell.

Jablin, Fredric. 2001. Organizational entry, assimilation, and disengagement/exit. In Fredric Jablin & Linda Putnam (eds.), *The new handbook of organizational communication: Advances in theory, research, and methods*, 732–818. Thousand Oaks, CA: Sage.

Jordan, Judith. 2010. *Relational-cultural therapy*. Washington, DC: American Psychological Association.

Kalbfleisch, Pamela. 2002. Communicating in mentoring relationships: A theory for enactment. *Communication Theory* 12(1). 63–69.

Kalbfleisch, Pamela & Valina Eckley. 2003. Facilitating mentoring relationships: The case for new technology. *Informing Science* 6. 1581–1590.

Kaše, Robert, Tina Saksida & Katarina Mihelič. 2019. Skill development in reverse mentoring: Motivational processes of mentors and learners. *Human Resource Management* 58(1). 57–69.

Kofoed, Michael & Elizabeth McGovney. 2019. The effect of same-gender or same-race role models on occupation choice evidence from randomly assigned mentors at West Point. *Journal of Human Resources* 54(2). 430–467.

Kong, Kenneth. 2014. *Professional discourse*. Cambridge: Cambridge University Press.

Kram, Kathy & Lynn Isabella. 1985. Mentoring alternatives: The role of peer relationships in career development. *Academy of Management Journal* 28(1). 110–132.

Kram, Kathy & Belle Rose Ragins. 2007. The landscape of mentoring in the 21st century. In Belle Rose Ragins & Kathy Kram (eds.), *The handbook of mentoring at work: Theory, research, and practice*, 659–692. Thousand Oaks, CA: Sage.

Kravčík, Milos, Katharina Schmid & Christoph Igel. 2019. Towards requirements for intelligent mentoring systems. In *Proceedings of the 23rd International Workshop on Personalization and Recommendation on the Web and Beyond*, 19–21. New York: ACM.

Leenders, Joke, Inge Bleijenbergh & Marieke Van den Brink. 2019. Myriad potential for mentoring: Understanding the process of transformational change through a gender equality intervention. *Gender, Work & Organization* 27(3). 379–394.

Long, Ziyu, Patrice M. Buzzanell, Lindsey Anderson, Jennifer Batra, Klod Kokini & Robyn Wilson. 2014. Episodic, network and intersectional perspectives: Taking a communicative stance on mentoring in the workplace. *Annals of the International Communication Association* 38(1). 387–422.

Long, Ziyu, Patrice M. Buzzanell, Klod Kokini, Robyn Wilson, Jennifer Batra & Lindsey Anderson. 2018. Mentoring women and minority faculty in engineering: A multidimensional mentoring network approach. *Journal of Women and Minorities in Science and Engineering* 24(2). 121–145.

Long, Ziyu, Abigail Selzer King & Patrice M. Buzzanell. 2018. Ventriloqual voicings of parenthood in graduate school: An intersectionality analysis of work-life negotiations. *Journal of Applied Communication Research* 46(2). 223–242.

MacGeorge, Erina & Lyn Van Swol. 2018. Advice across disciplines and contexts. In Erina MacGeorge & Lyn Van Swol (eds.), *The Oxford handbook of advice*, 3–20. Oxford: Oxford University Press.

McAllum, Kirstie. 2019. Delegation-based and directive mentoring relationships in high reliability organizations: Negotiating the reliability-resilience tension in ambulance work. *Communication Monographs*. 200–222. https://doi.org/10.1080/03637751.2019.1677926 (accessed 14 November 2020).

Mendez, Sylvia, Valerie Conley, Katie Johanson, Kinnis Gosha, Naja Mack, Comas Haynes & Rosario Gerhardt. 2019. The use of chatbots in future faculty mentoring: A case of the engineering professoriate. *Proceedings of the 2019 ASEE Annual Conference*. Tampa, FL: American Society for Engineering Education.

Pelletier, Kathie, Janet Kottke & Barbara Sirotnik. 2019. The toxic triangle in academia: A case analysis of the emergence and manifestation of toxicity in a public university. *Leadership* 15(4). 405–432.

Pruchniewska, Urszula. 2019. "A group that's just women for women": Feminist affordances of private Facebook groups for professionals. *New Media & Society* 21(6). 1362–1379.

Ragins, Belle Rose & John Cotton. 1999. Mentor functions and outcomes: A comparison of men and women in formal and informal mentoring relationships. *Journal of Applied Psychology* 84(4). 529–550.

Ragins, Belle Rose, John Cotton & Janice Miller. 2000. Marginal mentoring: The effects of type of mentor, quality of relationship, and program design on work and career attitudes. *Academy of Management Journal* 43(6). 1177–1194.

Ragins, Belle Rose & Kathy Kram (eds.). 2007. *The handbook of mentoring at work: Theory, research, and practice*. Thousand Oaks, CA: Sage.

Ragins, Belle Rose & Dean McFarlin. 1990. Perceptions of mentor roles in cross-gender mentoring relationships. *Journal of Vocational Behavior* 37(3). 321–339.

Rockquemore, Kerry Ann. 2020. National Center for Faculty Development & Diversity™. https://www.facultydiversity.org/ (accessed 14 November 2020).

Saffie-Robertson, Ma Carolina. 2020. It's not you, it's me: An exploration of mentoring experiences for women in STEM. *Sex Roles* 83. 566–579.

Schwartz, Harriet & Elizabeth Holloway. 2014. "I become a part of the learning process": Mentoring episodes and individualized attention in graduate education. *Mentoring & Tutoring: Partnership in Learning* 22(1). 38–55.

Shotter, John & Anne Cunliffe. 2002. Managers as practical authors: Everyday conversations for action. In David Holman & Richard Thorpe (eds.), *Management and language: The manager as a practical author*, 15–38. London: Sage.

Sillince, John. 2007. Organizational context and the discursive construction of organizing. *Management Communication Quarterly* 20(4). 363–394.

Smith, Ashley & Mark Green. 2018. Artificial intelligence and the role of leadership. *Journal of Leadership Studies* 12(3). 85–87.

Sue, Derald Wing, Sarah Alsaidi, Michael N. Awad, Elizabeth Glaeser, Cassandra Z. Calle & Narolyn Mendez. 2019. Disarming racial microaggressions: Microintervention strategies for targets, White allies, and bystanders. *American Psychologist* 74(1). 128–142.

Tolbert, DeLean, Patrice M. Buzzanell, Carla Zoltowski, Antonette Cummings & Monica Cardella. 2016. Giving and responding to feedback through visualisations in design critiques. *CoDesign* 12(1–2). 26–38.

Vine, Bernadette. 2022. *Introducing language in the workplace*. Cambridge: Cambridge University Press.

Zhou, Abby, Émilie Lapointe & Steven Zhou. 2019. Understanding mentoring relationships in China: Towards a Confucian model. *Asia Pacific Journal of Management* 36(2). 415–444.

Peter Stücheli-Herlach and Ursina Ghilardi

17 Counseling

Abstract: This chapter describes counseling as a form of management communication whose function is to reflect on problems and to design possible solutions for them. The chapter unfolds a theory of counseling communication and analyzes the case of a single conversation and the case of a larger project drawn from the context of communication consulting. The focus is not on the aspects of institutionalization, but on the linguistic performances of emergent and interactive counseling processes. First, a distinction is made from other forms of management communication such as leading (Section 1). Then the chapter presents defining features of counseling communication as well as typical schemes and patterns of language use in this framework (2, 3). The focus on counseling communication raises new possibilities for research as well as for counseling practices in various professional fields (4).

Keywords: counseling communication; consulting; management communication; systemic approach; patterns of language use

Counseling communication is a form of management communication whose function is to reflect on problems and to create possible solutions. It thus supports other forms of management communication, such as leading or planning and controlling, respectively. Specific characteristics of communicative procedures are the prerequisites for the emergence of discursive consulting systems, which can provide services for processes of value creation. They serve to chain, link, and entangle various individual activities of counseling communication. Research on counseling communication can simultaneously expand knowledge about counseling and support the counseling praxis.

1 Leading and counseling

Management communication emerges in different forms of practice, each of which solves different problems in organizational value creation. Leading, for example, can be understood as a form of proactivity whose function it is to determine situational contexts, thus initiating and framing discourses (Fairhurst 2008, 2011; Fairhurst and Sarr 1996; see also Barge, as well as Jacobs and Perrin in this handbook). Meanwhile, counseling emerges in a reactive manner from situations that participants perceive as problematic and in which leading would be too risky or resources are still lacking. Thus, counseling is a variant of management communication that contributes to organizational value creation by reflecting problems *ex-post* and creating possible solutions *ex-ante*. Herein, we find also a crucial difference to executive management, which deals with the simultaneity of value creation procedures ("From our many conversations [...] with executives we know: Either you can say the essentials in a few sentences or you are out of the race" (see Grand and Bartl 2011: 15)).

As leading and "managing executively" can be institutionalized, for example by training personal competencies, establishing professional roles and routinizing practices (it is then commonly called *leadership* (see Rumsey 2012), or *executive management* (see Grand and Bartl 2011)), so can counseling. In such cases, the term *consulting* usually is applied (Kipping and Clark 2012; Deelmann 2019). However, this terminology carries the danger of confusing the practical form of communication with its sturdy institutionalization. Thus, research on "consulting" repeatedly raises the question as to whether "management consultants are really helping their clients" (Czarniawska and Mazza 2012: 427). Furthermore, a common topic in the research literature is the "ambivalent roles of consultants in driving management innovation as well as management fashions" (Cerrutti, Tavoletti, and Grieco 2018: 902).

If we want to investigate emergent forms and success criteria of a communicatively constituted management practice, we do not first have to ask about its institutionalization, but about its empirical communicative performance. Hence, the term *counseling* is used here to describe the communicative processes of reflecting on problems and creating possible solutions by using language in organizational contexts. By doing so, it is not solely to McLeod (1998, 2007) that we owe this term. It is also inspired by the theory of the communicative constitution of organizations (Brummans et al. 2014), to the extent that we try to work out the organization-building and value-adding performance of communicative procedures.

Furthermore, we follow two important German-speaking variants of this approach (Kieser and Seidl 2013). On the one hand, a systemic approach (in the sense of Niklas Luhmann, see Kieser and Seidl 2013: 292–293) and, on the other hand, Ludwig Wittgenstein's perspective on language games (see Kieser and Seidl 2013: 293). As far as we follow the systemic approach, we focus on the emergence of consulting systems (or "contact systems") through the mutual "interactive openness" of client systems and consulting systems (Kieser and Seidl 2013: 295–296). Following Wittgenstein's approach, we search for patterns of language use that can become "attractors" for such complex and dynamic discourse systems of counseling (Larsen-Freeman and Cameron 2008: 163, matching the argumentation with regard to Wittgenstein, see Kieser and Seidl 2013: 293).

In this specific sense, we understand counseling as "not something done to one person by someone else; counseling is an interaction between two people" (McLeod 2007: 12). If so, the term refers to the "consulting process in action", whereby the reciprocal action of those involved consists in seeking and giving help (Lippitt and Lippitt 2015: 3). We choose the term *counseling communication* to denote this linguistic object of study. Of course, counseling communication produces and reproduces patterns of language use and thus attractors of organizational discourses (Cooren 2015: 3–8), which can also break the interactive dyad socially, temporally, and thematically. In such cases, counseling Discourses (*big D*) emerge from counseling discourses (*small d*) (Cooren 2015: 4–8). This can occur during press conferences, for instance, when someone uses the pattern "we face some huge challenges" or "something is meanwhile clear" – by speaking or by writing – and thus refers to preceding processes of internal consultations and their results. This can occur if collectively shared cognitive concepts are used in business reports and analyst conferences, for instance, such as *change management*, *megatrends*, *dynamic markets*, or *changing customer needs* and thus refer to analyses, for instance, that have been consulted in the process of decision making. It can also occur if members of organizations use single discourse markers as "we" in order to express that they have developed, through long series of controversies and processes of strategy development, a common sense of identity (see Larsen-Freeman and Cameron 2008: 161–195; and overall see Bamberger and Wrona 2012). Therefore, counseling communication consists of diverse practices that scale up and down between micro-, meso-, and macro-levels (Deppermann, Feilke, and Linke 2016: 12–13; for text production, see Perrin 2016: 431–434) and are entangled with other practices of management communication.

According to this understanding, the term counseling communication refers not primarily to the structures of the professional institutionalization of consulting, but to a form or genre of management communication in the sense of this handbook (see chapter "Introducing" by Cooren and Stücheli-Herlach as well as Fuchs 1994). In their interaction, counselors and their clients (who are seeking advice) thus develop linguistic attractors for a common discursive system, the *counseling system*. Essentially, the development of this system is promoted by the fact that the participants mutually grant each other the right to communicate ("permissions to speak") and by the fact that they not only respect each other's differences but also recognize these differences as trustworthy (McLeod 2007: 12–13). Counseling communication can be realized in explicit or embedded variants (McLeod 2007: 17–19), in rapid or extended executions (McLeod 2007: 19–20), within the organization or together with external participants (McLeod 2007: 17–20; Wohlgemuth 2010: 81–132; Heusinkveld and Benders 2012). And in these manifold manifestations, counseling communication has a significant influence on the "site and surface" of modern organizations and their communication (Taylor and Van Every 2000).

2 Defining features of counseling

If proactive leading in management communication is too risky or not possible, by reflecting on problems and jointly creating possible solutions, reactive counseling is the best way to help each other. Besides the execution of consulting being a communicative process, it is also assumed that the causes of the problem at hand and the possible solutions are communicatively constituted. At any rate, the aspirational capacity (Christensen, Morsing, and Thyssen 2013: 373), the organizing property (Cooren 2000), and thus the performative effect of counseling arise from the processing of this dilemma. Hence, we must assume a double functionality of counseling communication (similar to the case of leading with the defining interpretation of contexts as well as their framing by the same procedures): it has to display organizational problems and reflect them coincidently. Furthermore, counseling communication must create new solutions and design them likewise in a communicatively viable manner.

Following such a systemic-linguistic understanding of the "helpfulness" of counseling communication, the emergence of this form of management communication can be explained in specific terms using a concrete example. Let us imagine that someone falls into a hole again and again when she is walking to her organization or her workplace (according to Radatz 2000: 29). Doing counseling in such a situation means neither describing this problem as naturally given – and therefore inevitable – nor helping the person again and again directly out of the hole without any longer communication-based assistance. Rather, counseling means entering into an interaction with the affected person with the aim of helping her by using communicative procedures of reflection and problem-solving to avoid the problem in the future.

Consulting communication can now be characterized as follows (Schützeichel 2004: 279–284, see also Radatz 2000: 29): it evolves problem-related reflections and possible solutions in time-limited sequences in order to avoid further systemic problems and let the client solve her problems communicatively in her own way. Thus, it differs from (didactic) instruction over longer curricula and it does not define and select the alternatives for action in advance. Moreover, it differs from care services insofar as it does not take away from the person who falls into a hole the decision about different alternatives but helps her reflect on them. In other words, neither does it present the person who constantly falls into a hole with the ready-made solution of filling up the hole with gravel nor does it instruct the person to bypass it in the future. However, counseling communication develops individual and communicatively viable solutions together with the client, lets the client try them out, and supports her in the evaluation of her attempts.

Through these characteristics, processes of counseling communication generate effects such as an awareness and rationalization of organizational practices and innovations, a clarification of responsibility (Schützeichel 2004: 280–284) as well as knowledge transfer (Enoch 2011). They do not replace but complement and support other forms and practices of management communication such as leading, planning and controlling, or strategizing. They also scale up and down through different levels of interaction (Fuchs and Mahler 2000: 359): organizations advise other organizations (as, for example, in political consulting) or they advise individuals (as, for example, in career development processes); individuals advise organizations (as, for example, in management consulting) or they advise individuals (as, for example, in personal coaching for executives).

The characteristic feature of a counseling system on a social level (the level of relationships) is thus a discourse regulated by parity between those seeking and those providing help. On a thematic level, a counseling system not only answers directly and explicitly asked questions or sum up ready-made solutions to obvious cases but also searches for causal correlations in problematic situations and develops multi-variant, sustainable approaches for communicatively viable solutions. And on the temporal level, it is not a matter of permanent processes (that would already be collaborative executive management), but rather of limited sequences of interaction such as conversations or projects, which can be divided into separate phases such as opening, reflection, and solution development as well as closing (on the temporal structuring of appropriate conversations see Nothdurft, Reitemeier, and Schröder 1994, summarized in Habscheid 2003: 127–130 as well as Lippitt and Lippitt 2015: 17–52; on the structure of systemic counseling in general, see Steiner 2009: 89–105).

Although we emphasize the perspective of the manifold emergence of counseling communication (Taylor and Van Every 2000), it can be described exactly as a phenomenon of language use. Admittedly, its research has not yet had a long tradition (Preusse and Schmitt 2009: 78–79; Scherf 2011: 101). However, the robust practical-theoretical framework and linguistic empiricism make it possible to expand professional knowledge by means of case studies. The results will deepen the knowledge on the communicative constitution of organizations and its value creation practices.

3 Specific practices of counseling communication

Counseling communication results from the combination of different recursive practices, which combine specific language actions in specific roles, on relevant topics, and with suitable media instruments and artifacts. The identification of such practices (and their comprehensive categorization) plays a crucial role in ethnomethodology (Garfinkel 1967: 1–2) as well as in all the recent research on the practice turn (Schatzki 2001; Hillebrandt 2014: 58–61). So far, research on counseling has distinguished between various "counseling architectures", "counseling designs", and "counseling tools" (Königswieser and Hillebrand 2009: 54–101; on the "tools" see also Brüggemann, Ehret-Ivankovic, and Klütman 2007 as well as Schwing and Fryszer 2007), or it defines structures and principles of counseling interaction, which it understands "as exemplary communicative problem solutions that can, of course, be adapted to the context" (Habscheid 2003: 176). To further sharpen these previous approaches for linguistic research, we consistently follow the "flat ontology" of the practice turn (Schatzki 2016) and identify dynamic patterns of linguistic practices in complex discursive systems that constitute and permeate modern organizations (Larsen-Freeman and Cameron 2008; see Figure 1). These practices are neither temporally delimited from one another nor are they always explicit to the same extent (as has to be expected in the "imperfect world" of language and communication; Knapp and Antos 2014: xiii). Rather, they can overlap, repeat, accelerate, and slow down in communicative procedures.

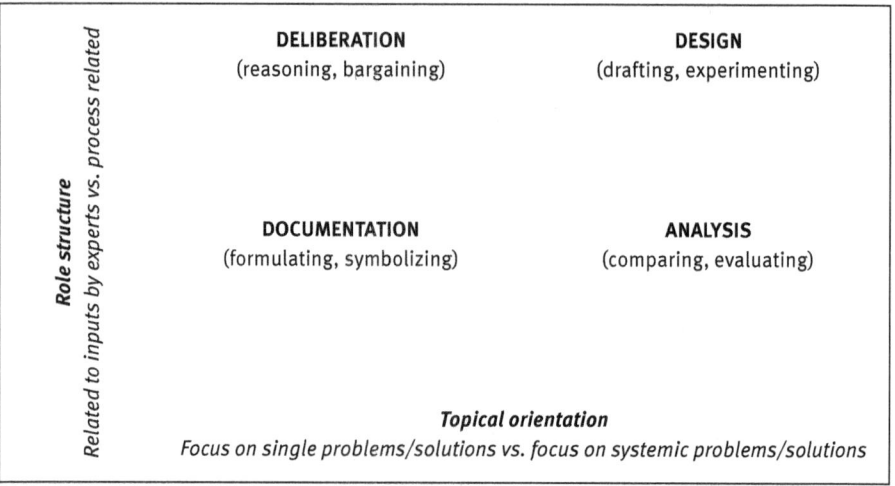

Figure 1: Practices of counseling communication according to topical orientation and role structure

Practices of documentation consist in the attempt to make communication problems and solutions available to the counseling system in singular appearance as "problematic" or "successful" "cases". This can be accomplished in conversations by formulating (also explicating, structuring, illustrating, conveying, etc.) and in projects by documenting interviews, or other forms of data collection and evaluation such as analyses of the position of actors or organizations in their linguistic environment (see Dreesen and Krasselt in this handbook; Königswieser and Hillebrand 2009: 54–101).

Practices of deliberation consist in the attempt to work on communication problems and solutions not only in the interactive dynamics of a counseling system, but also by making purposeful use of these dynamics and controversies. This can be accomplished in conversations by arguing for or against certain positions (also animating, criticizing, moderating, etc.), in projects by negotiating and bargaining roles that are suitable for the process, or by defining goals and procedures of the process. Regarding the client that constantly falls into a hole, it would in any case be reasonable for a counselor to indicate that she unconditionally accepts her obvious plight – or, alternatively, the counselor could try to lure the client out of her reserve with targeted provocation in order to be able to bring up a fully new perspective on the case ("shaking up the client") and establish a solution-oriented relationship in the system.

Practices of analysis consist in the attempt to reflect and evaluate communication problems and solutions in their systemic contexts and interactions. This can be done in conversation by using tools of comparison (also schematizing, categorizing, scaling, circular questions, etc.) and in projects by establishing sound judgment devices (also classifications, generalizations of problems and of possible solutions). In relation to the client, who constantly falls into a hole in the case study, it would in any case be reasonable for the counselor to determine in conversation what the deeper social or cultural reasons for the incidents might be (perhaps a strange ritual in the daily life of the client) and what precautions would have to be taken in the environment to resolve the problem (even this would only be a better explanation of the behavior for the client's peers).

Practices of design consist in the attempt to develop communication solutions for problems by creating perspectives that do not seem real or realizable in the given situation, but are indeed imaginable, potentially feasible, and, above all, desirable (on the concept see Schön 1983: 132; Simon 1996: 4). This can be done in conversations by using tools and techniques of design (as projecting, prototyping, fantasizing, etc.) and in projects by experimenting with possible solutions (simulating, testing, role-playing, etc.). The concept of design that is being proposed here thus goes beyond the design concept of systemic organizational consulting (in the sense of *counseling designs*, see above) and is based on the design-scientific idea of a collective development of discursive artifacts (Krippendorff 2006: 6) or, even more broadly, on "possible futures in a complex world" (Grand 2012: 165). In relation to the client, who is constantly falling into a hole, it would in any case be reasonable if the counselor could, through various measures, create the idea of a less painful or less irritating behavior in the future in order to motivate and initiate the process of finding solutions and develop concrete criteria for this purpose – even if the solutions still seem far away or almost unattainable at the moment of counseling.

Competent contributions to counseling communication must be both appropriate and effective (Rickheit, Strohner, and Vorwerg 2008: 25–26). Both the criterion of appropriateness and the criterion of effectiveness refer, on the one hand, to the situational conditions and thus to individual activities (individual turns in discussions, text contributions in projects) of counseling interaction. On the other hand, these contributions are expected to lead to a reflection on communication problems and to enable the development of sustainable, multi-variant systemic solutions. Thus, these contributions must be designed and controlled in such a way that the participants do not attempt to perform the counseling practices as separate accomplishments but in a way that links the practices to each other and even entangles them situatively. This can be done by a circular, recursive, and from time to time even partial performance of the practices.

4 Schemata and patterns of counseling communication

According to linguistic research, the concatenation and entanglement of specific practices in the course of a conversation or a counseling project follows certain schemata (Nothdurft, Reitemeier, and Schröder 1994, summarized by Habscheid 2003: 127–130). From the documentation of a case, those involved in counseling can switch to free deliberation about its interpretation and the further counseling process, its rules and goals, when they begin to analyze the case as a "problem" and when they clarify the mutual, at least provisional roles in the "contact system". In the example of the hole case, this would mean that counselors and clients agree, in the course of a short analysis, on the negative consequences of the case and establish strongly asymmetrical roles (the client may have become aware of her strong need for help only by anticipating the analysis).

From a "later" or repeatedly performed deliberation, those involved in the counseling process switch again back to the analysis of the problem if they decide to deepen their understanding, e. g., theses on possible cause-effect relationships or comparative perspectives. In the case study, this would mean that counselor and client would try to make it clearer whether the problem was merely an oversight or whether the person concerned is suffering from a disadvantageous disposition, for example, in psychological terms. They progress from analysis to design when they try to draft desirable solutions and are willing to work them out. In the case study, this would mean that alternative solutions (structural measures, alternative routes, join forces with others, etc.) would be designed and weighed against each other. And from the design to the renewed documentation they change as they resolve the situation by presenting each other their assessments of the previous process and its provisional results and by jointly evaluating them, respectively. They then agree either to end the process or to start a new counseling sequence, in case, for instance, the chosen solution did not work (see Figure 2).

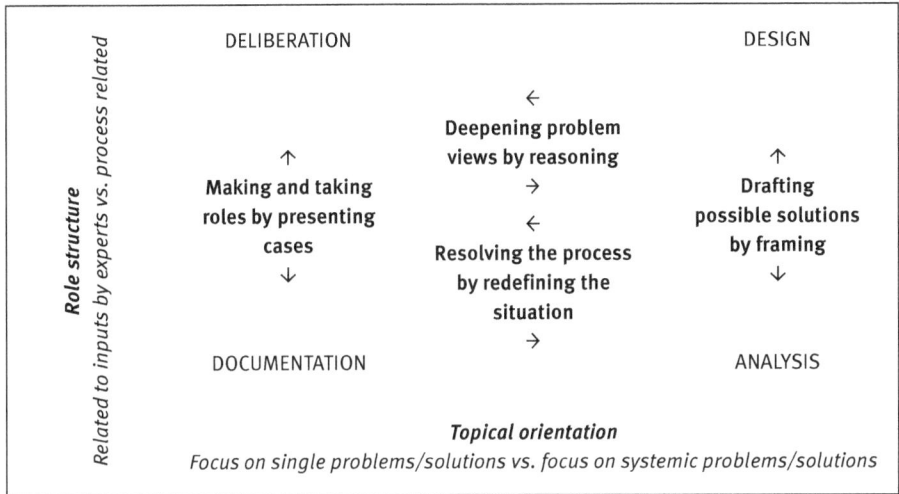

Figure 2: Interactive schemes of systemic counseling communication for linking and intertwining communicative practices over time

The deductively determined theoretical model of counseling communication can be sharpened and deepened on the basis of empirical data and findings. In doing so, it is important to address the related caveats that arise from the specifics of counseling research. In its field, it has to struggle with considerable communication, trust, and disciplinary barriers as a result of a lack of tradition, strong competitive pressure, and disparate professionalization in the respective professional fields (Scherf 2011: 103–106). Accordingly, we present here two case studies in an exemplary manner, each from different contexts. Both are of an auto-ethnographic nature (Denzin 2014). The first case study comprises several sequences of a consulting process between an expert in organizational communication and a student at the level of executive, professional training. The aim was to develop personal skills in management consulting in the corporate communications sector. The second case study is based on a collection of data from a project to develop a corporate newsroom in a large Swiss company in Switzerland (Seiffert-Brockmann and Einwiller 2020). Both case studies were conducted within the last six years under the direction of the first-mentioned author, while, the second-mentioned author contributed in a non-participating role to the analysis.

Our approach aims at developing a documentary reconstruction of linguistic patterns in which interactive schemes for linking and intertwining consulting practices are realized (Bohnsack 2008; Vogd 2009; Vogd and Amling 2017; on patters of language use, see Larsen-Freeman and Cameron 2008: 79–114). The data are analyzed using conversation and thus sequence analysis (Deppermann 2008), which is based on individual cases (even just specific sequences of a conversation) and aims to develop a comparative typology (Deppermann 2008; Kelle and Kluge 2010). The theoretical model outlined above serves as a sensitizing concept (Kelle and Kluge 2010: 28–30). Its application to the empirical data provokes deductive as well as abductive conclusions, which, in turn, have been and can be used for further qualitative sampling, further inductive coding, dimensionalization, and typologization of empirical data (Kelle and Kluge 2010: 21–40).

The investigated communication praxis is implemented by means of more or less sophisticated knowledge about counseling communication. This knowledge is accessible for professional practice in easily understandable formats (for example, Fiehler, and Sucharowski 1992; Ertelt and Schulz 2002; Migge 2005; McLeod 2007; Bachmair et al. 2011). However, in the field of communication consulting examined here, it has only been partially received and partially routinized (Stücheli-Herlach 2015: 7–8). Thus, the choice of auto-ethnographic methods entails both their opportunities and their risks, but it is typical of the current state of research and appropriate for the subject of counseling insofar as participating observations support the process of documentary and thus interpretative reconstruction of frameworks for action (Albrecht and Perrin 2013: 26–31). In both cases, we present some exemplary extracts from transcripts according to the GAT conventions (Gesprächsanalytisches Transkriptionssystem, a conversation-analytic transcription system adapted for the German language, Deppermann 2008: 119–121). The numbering of the lines follows a document with the collected excerpts; information about the time course is inserted into the transcript itself (hours:minutes:seconds). Since counseling action is interactive action, we present here selected sequence patterns (Deppermann 2008: 76–78), consisting of several successive turns.

As a first example we present here the case of a counseling interview – conducted in Swiss German – between the first author as counselor (CO, in the Swiss German transcript RG, *Ratgeber*) and a communication consultant as client (CL, in the Swiss German transcript RS, *Ratsuchende*). Since the beginning of her professional career, the client has worked for a smaller public relations agency. The topic was an assessment of personal counseling skills in the context of digitalized communication management (Röttger and Zielmann 2009; Rademacher and Andersson in this handbook).

4.1 Recapitulating

After an introduction with an exchange about the spatial setting, CO/RG (from here on called CO) opens the main conversation. By asking specific questions, he tries to lead CL/RS (from here on called CL) to confirm agreements made, thereby linking the documentation process with the deliberation process. We call this pattern *recapitulation*. By using this pattern, it is possible to implement the scheme of creating roles and presenting the topics in the context of a given situation – in a way that opens up a perspective for the further course of the discussion. In the following, we present the relevant excerpt from the conversation transcript and supplement it with a summarizing English translation:

```
29   RG: .hh und mier hend de gseid, mier machid en <<rall>> ↑'berater-
         sprächstOHD> #00:00:27-4#
30
31   RS: ↑'geNAU #00:00:28-0#
32
33   RG: und hend gseid, mier machid das mal FOIF 'mal: [(.)] #00:00:30-
         9#
34   RS:                                              [`´mhhm] ((bejahend)) #00:00:30-2#
35
36   RG: a eis bis zwei ↑⁻sTUND #00:00:31-8#


38   RS: genau! #00:00:32-7#
39
40   RG: .hh ähmmmm (3) <<p> und etz fangemer 'ah:> #00:00:36-9#
41
42   RS: <<p> guet> #00:00:39-9#
43
44   RG: <<p> und jetzt chasch du mier doch mal e chli> ↑'verZÄHLE .h
         #00:00:41-5#
45
46   RS: söll [ich dier VERzähLE?] #00:00:42-8#
47   RG:      [uf was es GAHT öberhaupt] ((lachend)) #00:00:43-9#
48
49   RS: [.hhh] ((stark hörbares Einatmen)) #00:00:43-7#
50   RG: [.hh] #00:00:56-2#
```

Summarizing translation

CO:	We said that we will talk on counseling.
CL:	Right.
CO:	And we said that we would do it five times, each time for one or two hours.
CL:	Exactly.
CO:	And now we begin!
CL:	Good.
CO:	And now you can tell me a little bit about what this is all about.

4.2 Conceptualizing

After CL's introductory description, CO leads into a discussion about the concept of counseling and counseling competences in order to realize the scheme of developing a problem view. This serves to link the practices of deliberation and analysis. After all, in order to ensure a successful systemic process, the problem analysis should not simply be done outside the counseling system but developed within it. This switching between deliberation and analysis, we call an interactive *conceptualization*. The pattern of verbal conversation is characterized by the fact that CO, based on a negotiated concept (the "counseling skills"), tries to lead CL to apply the concept to her own situation in such a way that different aspects of problems and approaches to solutions become apparent in that situation. One result of the pattern in the present case is that CL identifies two concrete aspects of "counseling skills", namely the ability to "give quick advice" (line 59) and to "take a better overall view" (line 67).

```
55   RG:  ähmmm (-) ETzt wäre total wichtig, wenn du chöntisch churz e
          chli beschribe,
56        was DU under beraterKOMpetenz [↓verstahsch.] #00:03:03-2#
57   RS:  [mhm] ((bejahend)) (.) <<all> also> BERaterkompetenz
58        hed für mich .hh ZWEI:: siite,
59        einersits ischs ähmmm <<acc> de schnälli ↑`ratschLAG> (-) zu
          `JEDere ´ziit (-) ähmmm (2)
60        dass ich us em us em stehgreif gwössi (-) <<rall> BERatigs-
          frage> so chli klassischi
61        beratigsfrage `chan ↑¯beantworte (-) ähmmm (1) ↑¯SCHNÄller als
          ich das jetzt chan (.)
62        und INTUItiver als ich das jetzt ↓chan (2) das (.) beinhaltet
          au m meh ↓´sicherHEIT (-) und meh
63        sicherheit bedüted au (.) dass es bim chund (.) kompetenter
          achond (2) <<t> mini erfahrig
64        bis jetzt> #00:03:44-7#
65
66   RG:  [mhhhm] #00:03:44-5#
67   RS:  [das ischs] ↑¯EINte (-) und s andere isch .h ähmmmm (.) en
          BEssere GSAMTblick ↑`öbercho (.)
68        gad i de strategische ↑_`beratig (-) ähmmmm (2) de WÄG:: ähhh
          MEH gseh för de ↑chund (-)
69        meh MERke was för de chund guet wär und was för taktig dass mer
          chönti ↑neh #00:04:08-6#
```

Summarizing translation

CO: Now it would be very important that you briefly describe what you understand by counseling skills.
CL: For me, counseling skills has two sides. On the one hand, it is quick advice at any time; that I can answer certain questions, classic counselor questions so to speak, right off the bat, faster and more intuitively than I can today. This also means more security, and more security also means greater competence from a client's point of view. That has been my experience so far.
CO: Mmmh [...]
CL: That is one thing. The other is a better overall view, in strategic counseling especially. It means being able to better see the path for the client, to better understand what would be good for the client, and what tactics should be chosen.

4.3 Staging

Towards the middle of the conversation, the actors analyze the concept of "counseling skills" with regard to the specific situation of CL on the basis of concrete examples of good communication counseling and concrete negative examples. In order to develop possible career prospects for CL (scheme of solution development), CO introduces a sequence in which CL is asked to develop a vision of her own future counseling activities. This sequence is introduced and executed in a pattern of *staging and dramatization* with specific features: CO's introduction is characterized by her imagination of the future, in a way that dramatizes the intended difference from the current situation by saying that CL should imagine a striking improvement. CL completes the scheme by developing the idea of a "smoother" project process (line 91), in the course of which work steps, but also content-related tasks, would be "easier to go through" (line 94). The "design" of a mental vision of the future is remarkable under aspects of sensual experience ("smoother") and systemic networking of the solution in terms of content and time (lines 93 and 94).

```
74   RG:  .h was glaubsch `DU (3) ALso agno mier schaffid jetzt ↑¯DA: und
          ähmmm ((Schnalzen))
75        .h oder oder DU schaffsch no in andere KONtext (irgendwie)
          THEMene und ↓´FRAge [mhhmm]
76        oder mier schaffid ZÄME no imne ↑`KURS oder imne (xxx) oder was
          au ↑'immER .h <<cresc> UF
77        jede FALL> 'agno (-)es passiert öbis (.) und du wirsch (.)
          plötzlich (.) Oder im lauf vo
78        dim ↑'prozÄSS .h plötzlich en <<cresc> marKANT!> BESSeri
          beraterin. (mhhmm) was passiert denn?
79        (-) i dim umfeld? (-) was seid denn de N. N.*? (.) was sägid
          dini chU:nde? #00:12:08-8#
```

80
81 RS: .h ich bin NID sicher, öb sie das Sofort wördid merke. [mhhm] du seisch jetzt zwar ↑⁻MARkant (.)
82   [mhmm (.) mal agno] <<all> jaja> #00:12:19-5#
83
84 RG: mer schaffid en MARkante [sprung] #00:12:19-8#
85
86 RS: [GEnau:] aso (-) ich bin NID sicher, öb mer das Sofort wörd ↑⁻merke
87   oder s (.) öb mers eifach <<rall>> a de projektverläuf wör ↓merke.> [⁻ja] (.) aso ich hans gfÜHL (.)
88   en (.) beratig wo ned <<rall> Optimal> 'isch (1) HEMMT de projektverlauf und erschWÄRT verschiedeni
89   projekt. [.h ja!] aso di di BESSeri beratig macht s projekt au ↓'EIfacher (.) es gid projekt wo IMM:er
90   schwirig sind. [mhmm] Egal wie guet s de berater [mhmm] isch. .h Aber es gid sicher optimierigspotential
91   (.) ZUM projekt so chli (.) gschmeidiger ↑mache ähmmm (-) also ich säge jetzt mal, wenn du es guets
92   projektmanagement ↓HEsch [mhmm] (.) denn ichs es projekt au eifach z ↓'handhabe (.) und wenn du ebe gUEt
93   berA:tisch (.) au im hinblick uf de ablauf vom projekt, au im hinblick uf die uf die inhaltliche sache vom
94   projekt .h ´`ja! ds es gAht eifach liechter ´dure (3) #00:13:15-7#
95
96 RG: was heisst LIEchter ´`dure? Wird's GÜNschtiger? wirds SCHNÄLLer? #00:13:21-1#
101 RS: es wird es wird ↑`schNÄLLER [mhmm] (.) es wird nöd weniger ↓'ufwändig. das [ja] wird's nie. [ja] (.)
102   A:ber es wird ähmmm (1) es wIRd au för de chund ↓'eifacher. (-) also [ja] es isch för MI::ch eifacher z
103   handhabe, well wells klari asage und meinige ↑gid [mhmm] und klari ↑'awisige .h und för de chund ischs
104   eifacher (.) ähmmm well er meh orientierig ↓hed. [mhmm] (2) inhaltlich wie au: (.) ↓´projektverlauf.
105   #00:13:51-5#

*Names of RS's supervisors

Summarizing translation

CO:	Let's say we create now, or you create here and in other contexts, on other topics and questions [...] or we create together in a class or whatever: either way, something happens and you suddenly – or in the course of this process – become a remarkably better consultant. What happens then in your environment? What does your boss say then? What do your customers say?
CL:	I'm not sure if they would notice it immediately. Now, you say "remarkably better" [...] suppose [...]
CO:	[...] We manage a striking leap [...]
CL:	[...] Exactly, so I'm not sure whether one would notice it immediately or whether one would simply notice it later in the course of the project. Well, I have the feeling that suboptimal counseling hampers the progress of the project and makes various projects more difficult. Better counseling makes a project easier. There are projects that are always difficult, no matter how good the counseling is. But there certainly is a potential for optimization to make projects a bit smoother. Well, let's say you have good project management, a project is easy to handle. And if you have good counseling, also with regard to the course of the project, also with regard to the content aspects, then it's simply easier to go through [...]
CO:	[...] What does "easier" mean? Does it become cheaper, does it become faster?
CL:	It gets faster. It will not become less complex, it never will. But it will be easier for me to use because there are clear announcements and opinions and clear instructions. And it's easier for the client because he has more orientation, both in terms of content and in the course of the project.

4.4 Selecting

Towards the end of the conversation, the task is to come out of the designed future projection and to a conclusion but, at the same time, to secure the results for the subsequent systemic activities of CL, which in this case will consist of a further consultation. In this sense, the scheme for resolving the situation combines the practices of design and documentation. This is realized in the present case by *selecting* certain criteria, which the documented basics should meet for the next consultation.

```
110  RG:  etzt nur zur ´`hUUsufgab [genau] <<h> isch es guet [en huusuf-
          gab?>] #00:59:06-6#
111  RS:                          [<<h> ja das isch
          guet, ja klar] #00:59:07-8#
112
113  RG:  .h ähmmm (2) ähmmm (5) <<len> ich fendis gUET> wenn du dier ufs
          nächscht mal ↑`chöntisch (2) en (3)
114       <<len> ganz en kOnkrEte FALL schildere> [mmhhm] .h (-) wo du
          scho erläbt ↑häsch (1)und de fall muess
115       zwEI bedingige ´`erfülle (-) bedingig Eis isch .h de fall muss
          so goi si, dass du seisch: DA wär
```

116	beratig (.) wECHtig ↑gsi [mhmm].h UND (.)DA hani si nÖd i dem mass chöne ebe ↓⁻leischte (.) wieni hed
117	sölle [mhmm] oder wieni hed welle. [mhhm ja!] (1) [mhmm] .hh und de FALL wenn du de fall (.) chöntisch
118	´`beschribe (1) bitte (3) unter foni folgende ↑pönkt: erschtens .h ähmmm wie wie isch dezue ↑cho?
119	[mmmhm] aso: wEr hed dich wie agfrögt oder wie bisch <<acc> demit eifach konfrontiert worde
120	mit dem fall?> [mhmm].h zweitens was sind (.) vorussetzige gsi uf dinere chUNDe-
121	oder ↑`klientesiite? (1) [mhmm].h DRITTens was sind vorussetzige gsi be DIER!? (-) uf
122	dINere ↑siite? [mhmm] (3) h. (und) VIERtens (.) wie 'isch de `verlauf gsi (.) a dem ↓fall.
123	[ja!] aso wa was ISCH pAssiert? [mhmm] füre TIMEline, e gschICHT (.) <<dim> oder so> [ja] (1) [mhmm]
124	<<all> du das> chöntsch ↓mache. [guet.] .h das chasch mache: du chaschs ders äh ´`öberlegge und denn
125	mündlich ↑`säge [mhmm] oder (.) chasch es au schribe<<f> GERN>
126	
127	RS: [(mit notize ja)]
128	RG: [natürli.] oder chasch mers sogar vORher lah zuecho lah, denn (.) [ja] chöntemer under
129	umstände de chli zIIt äh [okay.] spare (.) natürli

Summarizing translation

CO: No, as a sort of homework [...] is that good?
CL: Yes, that is good, of course.
CO: I would like it if next time you could describe a very concrete case that you have experienced. This case must fulfill two conditions: condition one is that the case has made you say: counseling would have been important, but since (and that would be condition two) I was not able to provide it to the extent that it would have been necessary or I would have wanted. And if you could please describe the case under the following points: first, how did it come about? So, who asked you or how were you simply confronted with the case? Second: What were the conditions on the client's side? Third: What were the requirements on your side? And fourth: What was the process in this case like? So, what happened, on a timeline, a story or something. If you could do that. You are welcome to think it over, then report it orally or you can write it down.
CL: With notes, yes.
CO: Or you can send it to me beforehand, so we can save a bit of time.

As a second case study, we summarize here some results of a documentary analysis of a project aimed at the implementation of a corporate newsroom by one of the larger enterprises in Switzerland. The project lasted for about seven months and struggled with a huge social and topical complexity as well as with a tight schedule. The following project map in terms of counseling communication (see Figure 3) is reconstructed based on project documents, a final qualitative interview with one of the project co-leaders, and protocols of participatory observation.

The schemata of counseling communication were carried out typically by *demanding attractive incisive slides* from the team of the client as well as from the counselors, by *interpreting and anticipating decisions* of a member of the top management (in the project called "sponsor"), by *launching and processing thought experiments*, and, finally, by *interrupting the process of organizational and competence development*. The top management decided to implement a top-down restructuration by using some of the results of the previous counseling process.

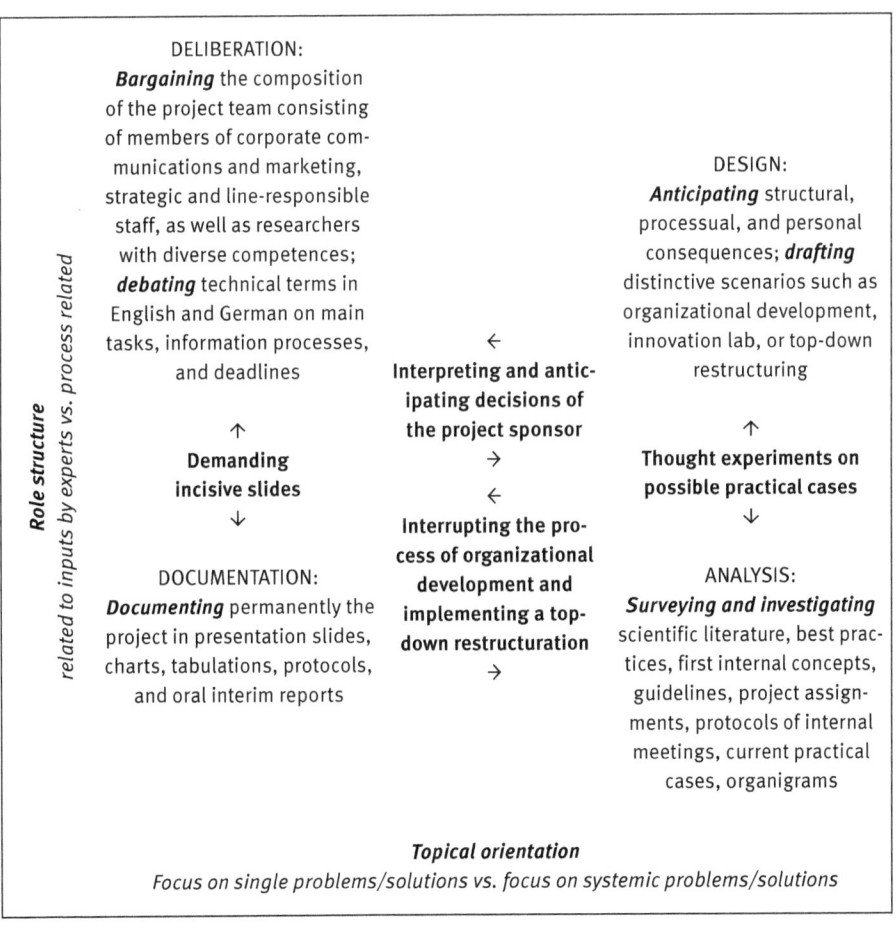

Figure 3: Project map of a counseling project to implement a corporate newsroom

It is possible to identify some patterns of language use that are typical for counseling communication not only on the level of the project as a whole but also on the microlevel of situative interactions. The following examples will demonstrate this. In the course of a more than one-hour discussion in the project team, the aim was to model future process flows in the company's corporate newsroom by "thought experiments" and role-playing (*in vivo* code from project documents, translated from Swiss German; here, this notion stands for the practice of design). The cognitive concepts repeatedly used by the participants to denote such case-based thought models were "examples" and "stories" (translated from Swiss German). The counselor motivated such design procedures recursively by using patterns of *invitations to design* ("Please tell us what could happen", "What happens then ...?", "Let's play through the different variants", "What does that mean in concrete terms?"; translated from Swiss German). The clients answered these in turn by thinking aloud using patterns of *self-questioning* (such as "Where are potential stories hidden and how do we get there?", by *adopting different perspectives, simulating process flows,* and by *imagining appropriate working tools and interfaces* for management practices. By doing so, participants could anticipate potential synergies between functional roles (such as newsroom managers and content producers), conflicts, and technical problems of the future corporate newsroom.

5 Perspectives for research and professional practice

Counseling communication is a form of management communication that complements and supports other forms such as leading or planning and controlling and is therefore one of the prerequisites for their success. Despite its importance for organizational value creation, this form is not always anchored and consolidated in institutional structures; rather, it emerges in a more or less explicit way in the manifold discourses/Discourses of an organization.

Scientific research can not only provide knowledge on counseling practices in specific domains. It can also provide valid problem-solving knowledge across the domains and disciplines. The pertinent form of this service could be called "scientific counseling on counseling communication for consultants". According to this understanding, counseling research is a variety of applied, transdisciplinary, and "engaged" communication research (Frey and Cissna 2009; Seibold et al. 2009: 346; Perrin 2012). It supports professional actors in practicing and establishing communicative procedures to reflect on systemic problems and create viable solutions, at the level of both individual discussions and entire projects. This is a contribution to narrowing the gap between the growing importance of counseling in organizational communication and the lack of scientific investigation to date (Preusse and Schmitt 2009: 77). In practice, this opens up the possibility of deriving specific competence requirements for counseling in the context of value-added processes, which can contribute, among other things, to determining the current status of career development, evaluating organizational processes, or designing business models in the field of institutionalized consulting.

6 References

Albrecht, Christine & Daniel Perrin. 2013. *Funktionales Zuhören als Gesprächskompetenz im Coaching*. Wiesbaden: Springer VS.
Bachmair, Sabine, Jan Faber, Claudius Hennig, Rüdiger Kolb & Wolfgang Willig. 2011. *Beraten will gelernt sein. Ein praktisches Lehrbuch für Anfänger und Fortgeschrittene*. Weinheim & Basel: Beltz.
Bamberger, Ingolf & Thomas Wrona. 2012. *Strategische Unternehmensberatung: Konzeptionen – Prozesse – Methoden*. Wiesbaden: Gabler.
Bohnsack, Ralf. 2008. *Rekonstruktive Sozialforschung: Einführung in qualitative Methoden*, 7th edn. Opladen: Barbara Budrich.
Brüggemann, Helga, Kristina Ehret-Ivankovic & Christopher Klütman. 2007. *Systemische Beratung in fünf Gängen: Ein Leitfaden*, 2nd edn. Göttingen: Vandenhoeck & Ruprecht.
Brummans, Boris H. J. M., François Cooren, Daniel Robichaud & James R. Taylor. 2014. Approaches to the communicative constitution of organizations. In Linda L. Putnam & Dennis Mumby (eds.), *The Sage handbook of organizational communication: Advances in theory, research, and methods*, 3rd edn., 173–194. Los Angeles, CA: Sage.
Cerrutti, Corrado, Ernesto Tavoletti & Cecilia Grieco. 2018. Management consulting: A review of fifty years of scholarly research. *Management Research Review* 42(8). 902–925.
Christensen, Lars T., Mette Morsing & Ole Thyssen. 2013. CSR as aspirational talk. *Organization* 20(3). 372–393.
Cooren, François. 2000. *The organizing property of communication*. Amsterdam & Philadelphia, PA: John Benjamins.
Cooren, François. 2015. *Organizational discourse*. Cambridge: Polity Press.
Czarniawska, Barbara & Carmelo Mazza. 2012. Consultants and clients from constructivist perspectives. In Matthias Kipping & Timothy Clark (eds.), *The Oxford handbook of management consulting*, 427–443. Oxford: Oxford University Press.
Deelmann, Thomas. 2019. Consulting: Characterization of concepts and connections. In Volker Nissen (ed.), *Advances in consulting research: Contributions to management science*, 31–52. Cham: Springer.
Denzin, Norman K. 2014. *Interpretive autoethnography*. Los Angeles, CA: Sage.
Deppermann, Arnulf. 2008. *Gespräche analysieren: Eine Einführung*, 4th edn. Wiesbaden: VS Verlag.
Deppermann, Arnulf, Helmuth Feilke & Angelika Linke. 2016. Sprachliche und kommunikative Praktiken: Eine Annäherung aus linguistischer Sicht. In Arnulf Deppermann, Helmuth Feilke & Angelika Linke (eds.), *Sprachliche und kommunikative Praktiken*, 1–23. Berlin & Boston, MA: Walter de Gruyter.
Enoch, Clinton. 2011. *Dimensionen der Wissensvermittlung in Beratungsprozessen: Gesprächsanalysen der beruflichen Beratung*. Wiesbaden: Springer.
Ertelt, Bernd-Joachim & William E. Schulz. 2002. *Handbuch Beratungskompetenz: Mit Übungen zur Entwicklung von Beratungsfertigkeiten in Bildung und Beruf*. Leonberg: Gabler Verlag.

Fairhurst, Gail T. 2008. Discursive leadership: A communication alternative to leadership psychology. *Management Communication Quarterly* 21(4). 510–521.
Fairhurst, Gail T. 2011. *The power of framing: Creating the language of leadership*. San Francisco, CA: Jossey-Bass.
Fairhurst, Gail T. & Robert A. Sarr. 1996. *The art of framing: Managing the language of leadership*. San Francisco, CA: Jossey-Bass.
Fiehler, Reinhard & Wolfgang Sucharowski (eds.). 1992. *Kommunikationsberatung und Kommunikationstraining*. Opladen: VS Verlag für Sozialwissenschaften.
Frey, Lawrence R. & Kenneth N. Cissna (eds.). 2009. *Routledge handbook of applied communication research*. New York: Routledge.
Fuchs, Peter. 1994. Die Form beratender Kommunikation. Zur Struktur einer kommunikativen Gattung. In Peter Fuchs & Eckhart Pankoke (eds.), *Beratungsgesellschaft*, 13–25. Schwerte: Katholische Akademie Schwerte.
Fuchs, Peter & Enrico Mahler. 2000. Form und Funktion von Beratung. *Soziale Systeme* 6(2). 349–368.
Garfinkel, Harold. 1967. *Studies in ethnomethodology*. Englewood Cliffs, NJ: Prentice-Hall.
Grand, Simon. 2012. Research as design: Promising strategies and possible futures. In Simon Grand & Wolfgang Jonas (eds.), *Mapping design research*, 155–175. Basel: Birkhäuser.
Grand, Simon & Daniel Bartl. 2011. *Executive Management in der Praxis: Entwicklung – Durchsetzung – Anwendung*. Frankfurt am Main: Campus.
Habscheid, Stephan. 2003. *Sprache in der Organisation: Sprachreflexive Verfahren im systemischen Beratungsgespräch*. Berlin: De Gruyter.
Heusinkveld, Stefan & Jos Benders. 2012. Consultants and organization concepts. In Matthias Kipping & Timothy Clark (eds.), *The Oxford handbook of management consulting*, 267–284. Oxford: Oxford University Press.
Hillebrandt, Frank. 2014. *Soziologische Praxistheorien: Eine Einführung*. Wiesbaden: VS Verlag für Sozialwissenschaften.
Kelle, Udo & Susann Kluge. 2010. *Vom Einzelfall zum Typus: Fallvergleich und Fallkonstrastierung in der qualitativen Sozialforschung*, 2nd edn. Wiesbaden: VS Verlag für Sozialwissenschaften.
Kieser, Alfred & David Seidl. 2013. Communication-centered approaches in German management research: The influence of sociological and philosophical traditions. *Management Communication Quarterly* 27(2). 291–302.
Kipping, Matthias & Timothy Clark (eds). 2012. *The Oxford handbook of management consulting*. Oxford: Oxford University Press.
Knapp, Karlfried & Gerd Antos. 2014. Linguistics for problem solving (Introduction to the handbook of applied linguistics series). In Eva-Maria Jakobs & Daniel Perrin (eds.), *Handbook of writing and text production*, vii–xvii. Berlin & Boston, MA: Walter de Gruyter.
Königswieser, Roswita & Martin Hillebrand. 2009 [2004]. *Einführung in die systemische Organisationsberatung*, 5th edn. Heidelberg: Carl-Auer Verlag.
Krippendorff, Klaus. 2006. *The semantic turn: A new foundation for design*. Boca Raton, FL: Taylor & Francis.
Larsen-Freeman, Diane & Lynne Cameron. 2008. *Complex systems and applied linguistics*. Oxford: Oxford University Press.
Lippitt, Gordon & Ronald Lippitt. 2015. *Beratung als Prozess*, 4th edn. Wiesbaden: Springer Gabler.
McLeod, John. 1998. *An introduction to counselling*. Buckingham, UK: Open University Press.
McLeod, John. 2007. *Counselling skill*. Maidenhead, UK: Open University Press.
Migge, Björn. 2005. *Handbuch Coaching und Beratung: Wirkungsvolle Modelle, kommentierte Falldarstellungen, zahlreiche Übungen*. Weinheim & Basel: Beltz.

Nothdurft, Werner, Ulrich Reitemeier & Peter Schröder. 1994. *Beratungsgespräche: Analyse asymmetrischer Dialoge*. Tübingen: Narr.
Perrin, Daniel. 2012. Transdisciplinary action research: Bringing together communication and media researchers and practitioners. *Journal of Applied Journalism and Media Studies* 1(1). 3–23.
Perrin, Daniel. 2016. Vom vielschichtigen Planen: Textproduktions-Praxis empirisch erforscht. In Arnulf Deppermann, Helmuth Feilke & Angelika Linke (eds.), *Sprachliche und kommunikative Praktiken*, 431–455. Berlin & Boston, MA: De Gruyter.
Preusse, Joachim & Jana Schmitt. 2009. Zum Status Quo der PR-Beratungsforschung: Stand und Perspektiven eines vernachlässigten Forschungsfeldes. In Ulrike Röttger & Sarah Zielmann (eds.), *PR-Beratung: Theoretische Konzepte und empirische Befunde*, 75–86. Wiesbaden: VS-Verlag für Sozialwissenschaften.
Radatz, Sonja. 2000. *Beratung ohne Ratschlag: Systemisches Coaching für Führungskräfte und BeraterInnen*. Wien: ISCT.
Rickheit, Gert, Hans Strohner & Constanze Vorwerg. 2008. The concept of communicative competence. In Gert Rickheit & Hans Strohner (eds.), *Handbook of communication competence*, 15–62. Berlin & New York: Mouton de Gruyter.
Röttger, Ulrike & Sarah Zielmann (eds.). 2009. *PR-Beratung: Theoretische Konzepte und empirische Befunde*. Wiesbaden: VS Verlag für Sozialwissenschaften.
Rumsey, Michael G. (ed.). 2012. *The Oxford handbook of leadership*. Oxford: Oxford University Press.
Schatzki, Theodore R. 2001. Introduction: Practice theory. In Theodore R. Schatzki, Karin Knorr Cetina & Eike von Savigny (eds.), *The practice turn*, 1–14. New York: Routledge.
Schatzki, Theodore R. 2016. Practice theory as flat ontology. In Gert Spargaaren, Don Weenink & Machiel Lamers (eds.), *Practice theory and research*, 28–42. New York: Routledge.
Scherf, Michael. 2011. Herausforderungen der empirischen Erforschung der Organisationsberatungsinteraktion: Am Beispiel einer Studie zur Professionalisierungsbedürftigkeit der Organisationsberatung. In Eva-Maria Graf, Yasmin Aksu, Ina Pick & Sabine Rettinger (eds.), *Beratung, Coaching, Supervision*, 101–114. Wiesbaden: VS Verlag für Sozialwissenschaften.
Schön, Donald A. 1983. *The reflective practitioner: How professionals think in action*. New York: Basic Books.
Schützeichel, Rainer. 2004. Skizzen zu einer Soziologie der Beratung. In Rainer Schützeichel & Thomas Brüsemeister (eds.), *Die beratene Gesellschaft: Zur gesellschaftlichen Bedeutung von Beratung*, 273–285. Wiesbaden: VS Verlag für Sozialwissenschaften.
Schwing, Rainer & Andreas Fryszer. 2007. *Systemisches Handwerk*, 2nd edn. Göttingen: Vandenhoeck & Ruprecht Verlage.
Seibold, David R., Daisy R. Lemus, Dawna I. Ballard & Karen K. Myers. 2009. Organizational communication and applied communication research: Parallels, intersections, integration, and engagement. In Lawrence R. Frey & Kenneth N. Cissna (eds.), *Routledge handbook of applied communication research*, 331–354. New York: Routledge.
Seiffert-Brockmann, Jens & Sabine Einwiller. 2020. Content-Strategien in der Unternehmenskommunikation: Themensetzung, Storytelling und Newsroom. In Ansgar Zerfass, Manuel Piwinger & Ulrike Röttger (eds.), *Handbuch Unternehmenskommunikation*, 1–17. Wiesbaden: Springer Nature.
Simon, Herbert A. 1996. *The sciences of the artificial*, 3rd edn. Cambridge, MA: The MIT Press.
Steiner, Adrian. 2009. *System Beratung: Politikberater zwischen Anspruch und Realität*. Bielefeld: transcript Verlag.
Stücheli-Herlach, Peter. 2015. *Beratungskommunikation in der Kommunikationsberatung* (Working Papers in Applied Linguistics 8). Winterthur: ZHAW.
Taylor, James R. & Elizabeth Van Every. 2000. *The emergent organization: Communication as its site and surface*. New York & London: Taylor & Francis.

Vogd, Werner. 2009. *Rekonstruktive Organisationsforschung: Qualitative Methodologie und theoretische Integration*. Opladen: Verlag Barbara Budrich.

Vogd, Werner & Steffen Amling. 2017. Ausgangspunkte und Herausforderungen einer dokumentarischen Organisationsforschung. In Steffen Amling & Werner Vogd (eds.), *Dokumentarische Organisationsforschung: Perspektiven der praxeologischen Wissenssoziologie*, 9–40. Opladen: Verlag Barbara Budrich.

Wohlgemuth, André C. 2010. *Unternehmensberatung (Management Consulting)*, 11th edn. Zürich: Hochschulverlag.

Christian Schwägerl and Susanne Knorre
18 Developing organizations

Abstract: This chapter reviews organizational development (OD) as networked managerial practices and investigates the role these practices play in contemporary strategic management and in management communication. Our analytical overview of studies finds that the literature lacks empirical evidence on the linguistic properties of OD's practices as these properties have not been researched in OD but in settings where change is solely approached as a planned process. To fill this gap, we propose a research framework to inquire into OD's verbal, paraverbal, and nonverbal practices. After a *tour d'horizon* of OD's and change management's ontological and epistemological paradigms, we outline the implications of the practice perspective of OD for strategic management, then narrow our focus to empirical studies' prominent outcomes on discursive practices in change processes, and conclude with a framework for future research.

Keywords: organizational development; change management; management communication; emergent strategy; organizational communication

In the context of the disruptive changes associated with digitization, including Big Data use that affects both industry and service sectors, we could imagine that organizational development (OD) would currently play a significant role in the applied science of management. However and paradoxically, OD is said to suffer from a deficit in innovation (Burke 2018) and professionalization (Kauffeld and von Ameln 2019). This deficit falls precisely during disruptive social and economic changes when OD is needed as an action-guiding concept. In this "Enterprise 2.0" era (McAfee 2006), digitized communication across hierarchies and departments appears constitutive of any form of collaborative work across organizations (Schwägerl 2020), which is frequently described as a massive cultural change (Capgemini Consulting 2017).

Presently, other concepts, in particular leadership, agility, or entrepreneurship, are in the foreground (as evident on leading business schools' websites[1]), despite their basis in OD's basic ideas, albeit implicitly. This suggests, in accordance with the emergence of "digital leadership", that OD's transition into the digital age can succeed with the establishment of connections between leadership and organizational change. Therefore, we investigate which OD foundations and findings can facilitate organizations' adjustments to a digitized world.

---

[1] For this study, we collected samples from two leading business schools each in the USA and Europe: HBS and MITSloan and LBS and INSEAD, respectively (accessed 18 August 2019).

We focus on organizational members' discursive practices that co-create shared understandings, concepts, and interactions aimed to move the value creation process towards an intentional goal. In keeping with this understanding of practices, we propose to conceive of organizational change as a social accomplishment made of collective action and collaboration, rather than as a plannable, linear process initiated and controlled solely by management. In the context of management communication, we inquire into how these practices' linguistic features and their purposeful enactment achieve the social accomplishment of organizational change.

To do so, we first review OD's evolution as a specific "array" (Schatzki 2001: 11) of managerial practices, which previous research has addressed through long-term observations. We then investigate, which fundamental ideas may facilitate change in current strategic management practices. Furthermore, we narrow our focus and examine how organizational discourse theory and linguistics literature inquire into these practices' linguistic features. Through this examination, we acknowledge the prominent outcomes of empirical studies devoted to the detailed study of discursive activities and linguistic features in organizational change processes. Finally, we suggest a research framework which can initiate examination into the discursive practices and structural features of management communication in face-to-face encounters, especially those in the emerging change processes of contemporary organizations.

1 OD as an explanatory context for management communication

Management communication in OD aims to change value creation processes in varying degrees. Given OD's systemic spirit, we explore the management communication spectrum without limiting it to managers' discursive activities intended to affect others' practices and states: speech acts that managers may "use to create, sustain, focus, and complete a change" (Ford and Ford 1995: 541). Rather, management communication occurs in an array of observable discursive practices, involving all members in the way change processes are communicatively constituted (Cooren et al. 2011; Cooren 2017; Stücheli-Herlach 2018). We consider that verbal, nonverbal, and paraverbal practices make OD an interactive and collective process among the actors involved, creating viable networks in their roles-relationships and identities in formal and informal communication (Stücheli-Herlach 2018). This network of practices establishes OD as a social process, rather than as an instrumental action initiated and controlled by management, which leads us to investigate the daily practices members carry out and make accountable. Despite this, it appears that research on OD's fundamental ideas is mostly characterized by a prescriptive stance that does not pay much attention to interactional processes, even when OD is viewed as a collective activity.

1.1 OD as controlled change

OD's history reflects a normative paradigm shift, which initially viewed human beings as the centers of creative leadership in organizations, while assuming that change can and should only be steered by organization members' attitudes, perspectives, and behaviors (Wimmer 2004). By replacing strict hierarchical and bureaucratic structures with more decentralized and participatory ones, the group could become a structural organizational unit; this idea was then perceived as a form of socio-political progress, Wimmer explains (2004). Empirical field research in the 1950s and 1960s observed that groups are better equipped for change, because they can reflect on each other, and as such, question structures, roles, and communication patterns more effectively. Therefore, OD involved practices and methods of initiating, accompanying, and evaluating such group processes. The survey feedback method, representing a broad range of typical OD interventions, was present for decades in the hardly questioned corporate management action spectrum (Wimmer 2004).

Lewin's (1947) basic three-step model of Unfreezing, Moving, and Refreezing also implied that an organization's transition to its desired goals can be controlled if the three phases consider force fields, action concepts, and intervention methods (Burnes 2014). Changing-as-three-steps also creates a confusing abundance of other step models for planned change and change management (Bridges 2017; Cummings, Bridgman, and Brown 2016). The conceptual shift from OD to change management from the 1980s onwards indicates a shift in focus to carefully planned and strictly controlled change processes. This corresponded with dominant management schools' views, whose basic linear action sequences involved analysis, planning, and controlling implementation, which nourished the desired idea of an organization's plan-determined success.

However, this perspective created a paradox: a top-down controlled change for the entire company that should, according to OD's principles, be based on participatory approaches at the employee team level. Therefore, incompatibility between management thinking oriented toward efficiency, and the comparatively time-consuming participation procedure in groups appears indeed quite obvious. This discussion on whether planning can control change or whether organizations' developments are primarily emergent (Burnes 2013) continues. Accordingly, it is a matter of promoting emergent processes in order to influence or build the desired environmental conditions through one's own communicative activities (Rüegg-Stürm and Grand 2017). Therefore, companies adopt this emergent change perspective to address the quick, complex, and unpredictable development of their environment, resulting in no predictable change process (Burnes, Cooper, and West 2003). Change is rather a "complex analytical, political and cultural process of challenging and changing the core beliefs, structure and strategy of the firm" (Pettigrew 1987: 650).

The idea of learning organizations (Argyris 1977; Burnes, Cooper, and West 2003; Senge 2006) positions itself in this temporal context: collecting, storing, and evaluating knowledge. Apparently, learning also implies the ability to repeatedly question organizational knowledge. Thus, learning organizations should develop forms of a management practice wherein its members consistently verify their actions, correct mistakes, and find new answers for risky conditions. This concept of a constantly learning or rather processing organization is connected to the concept of High Reliability Organizations being attentive to failures, simplifications, operations, resilience, and distributed expertise (Jahn 2016; Roberts, Stout, and Halpern 1994; Weick and Sutcliffe 2001; Weick, Sutcliffe, and Obstfeld 1999; Weick 1987).

Learning is a collective task that includes all organization members, potentially assembled through shared values, unified future visions, and collaborative cooperation. Compressed in single-loop and double-loop learning models, managers have a clear task within learning organizations: "The chief executive officer and his immediate subordinates are the key to success, because the best way to generate double loop learning is for the top to do it" (Argyris 1977: 116). A learning organization's "fifth discipline" (Senge 2006: 57), i.e., the meta-learning about organizational learning processes through continuous self-reflection, also views corresponding communicative management actions as organizational quality. Thus, the postulates of more democratic and humanistic organizations shaped the normative direction of OD development, based on the optimistic view, if not bias, of human beings as committed, fact-oriented, and progressive employees, and on extensive empirical research.

1.2 The paradigm shift: emergence and contingency as structural principles of change

Organizational environments are increasingly perceived as volatile and unpredictable; consequently, the assumptions of OD's stability and re-frozen states of equilibrium being in a process of change seem unrealistic. Since the turn of the millennium, the perception of OD as basically dealing with hierarchical systems, unwilling and incapable of changing and only to be developed in a normative manner through more participatory forms, appears as an outdated perspective and has led to a paradigm shift (Wimmer 2004). Currently, every conception of change must assume a wide range of organizational structures located in the entire continuum between hierarchy and heterarchy. In fractal organizations models (heterarchical), respective status results solely from self-steering subunits' interactions (Laloux 2015).

However, organizations predominantly adopt the principle of ambidexterity (Birkinshaw and Gibson 2004; Duwe 2016; Schreyögg and Geiger 2016), involving the ability to equally address hierarchical and heterarchical elements within an organization. Thus, OD and change management focus less on hierarchies' flexibility and permeability than on the consequences of decentralization and the existence of several operating systems (i.e., project or network organizations). Consequently, the objectives in organizational change alter. The importance of overcoming members' resistance to change (Coghlan 1993), particularly pronounced in prescriptive change management literature, as well as the normative image of a "more democratic" organization have become less urgent. Instead, more recent approaches focus on general adaptability and resilience (Buchholz and Knorre 2012). The abstract goal is to secure one's existence in an unstable environment, but individual, temporary measures, or OD projects are not sufficient to achieve this goal.

Alternatively, the concept of agility demands that an organization and its members act in a consistently agile manner (Doz and Kosonen 2010). This involves fast decision paths, short planning and implementation cycles as well as flexible structures with high decentralization, semi-autonomous teams, and close networks. Agility opposes plan-driven management and departs from slow stability-seeking OD. In this context, overcoming resistance is irrelevant, as organizational agility replaces this focus by consistently understanding members' changes in attitude and behaviors. Collective action, focusing on the critical mass' or small groups' potential for change, conforms with these new OD directions (Gladwell 2002; Granovetter 1973; Rogers 2003). Agility proves to be compatible with leadership (Kotter 1990), which is supposed to inspire change through entrepreneurial vision, personal charisma, and being one's own role model, while admitting mistakes to oneself and others to survive in a volatile environment (Baecker 2015; Au 2016). Similarly, the concept of effectuation, postulated by Sarasvathy (2008), is a leadership action that relies on an intuitive impetus to recognize and seize unexpected opportunities.

The interdisciplinary abundance of contributions emanating from this shift in goals and priorities (Buchholz and Knorre 2017) is a renewed paradigm shift, characterized by contingency and emergence, two structural principles inherent in company environments and markets that also shape corporate management (Buchholz and Knorre 2019; Rüegg-Stürm and Grand 2017). Contingency refers to multi-optionality in decision-making that is based on permanently incomplete information. Therefore, companies exist in a state of permanent instability, as they can potentially find more promising alternatives. Consequently, wrong decisions, which eventually must be corrected, are unavoidable. By contrast, emergence requires a system's individual parts to build relationships with each other, resulting in new elements emerging from interactions that cannot be reduced from the knowledge of these parts and cannot or should not be planned. The objective is a fundamental openness to emergent effects from diverse stakeholder dialogues, effects that cannot be foreseen, even if the company favored them (Rüegg-Stürm and Grand 2017).

Contingency and emergence can neither be overcome by higher steering efforts, nor by heroic leadership ambitions. Rather, they must represent the organization's collective practice, made effective through its purpose and objectives. For management communication, this involves a "metaconversation" in which a collective identity is constituted, which allows a "multivocal" organization to act as one (Robichaud, Giroux, and Taylor 2004; Taylor and Robichaud 2007). This metaconversation explains emergence and contingency effects as structural principles of change that enable an organization's members to address rapid direction changes, mistakes, and failures, while promoting the organization's agility and scaling through observations, self-reflection, and creativity (Rüegg-Stürm and Grand 2019).

Accordingly, management authors argue that an organization's purpose is to convey how its existence benefits society (Buchholz and Knorre 2019). A purpose is a strategic instrument intended to unfold a common frame of reference for a continuous "verification of identity", once initially diffused through the organization (Rüegg-Stürm and Grand 2017: 237). This idea entails that organizational members can orient to this frame of reference even when they work autonomously. However, the predominantly prescriptive literature on OD scarcely elaborates on the microlevels of interactional procedures, which involve the actors effecting change or meaning negotiation processes. The literature has also avoided detailed elaborations on the conversational practices as well as the practices of text production by which organizational members understand the perceived urgency to change and co-create knowledge, concepts, and interactions aimed to intervene in the value creation process.

1.3 The current relevance of OD: implications for strategic management and management communication

The essential elements of the new paradigm of change, as manifested today mainly in the agility concept, are based on OD's basic ideas. When OD's fundamental ideas are translated into contemporary strategic management practices, the following practical concerns emerge:

- To secure long-term existence, organizations must continuously be aware of the changes in their stakeholder environment and adapt to these changes and unforeseeable environmental conditions. They must permanently initiate and evaluate discourses between the organization and its environment, and within the organization (Meyer 2019).
- Change occurs in both planned and emergent forms. Planning refers to the extent that an organization strives for goals and meaning, most effectively achieved by promoting emergent forces within itself and in the environment. Organizational change begins with executives' changes in communicative behaviors, stemming from self-reflection (Burnes 2014; Rüegg-Stürm and Grand 2017).
- All management decisions have alternatives; mistakes are an integral part of management practice, which requires a continuous questioning of current strategies and a sensitivity to changes in stakeholders' environments. Alternatives and mistakes are stored in narrations and are subjects of future discourses, promoting the collective learning ability (Buchholz and Knorre 2019).
- Only an array of communicative practices can manage contingency and emergence throughout an organization, and discursive agency is necessary for facilitation (Stücheli-Herlach 2018). This requires awareness and reflections on the

linguistic practices with which situations, forms, and accounts can be managed to facilitate strategic decisions. Thus, management communication assumes a meta-communicative role (Robichaud, Giroux, and Taylor 2004; Taylor and Robichaud 2007). It must decipher the interplay of contextual variables in organizations' interpersonal communications, and how members' communicative routines, which might inhibit open communication across hierarchical, departmental, and cultural barriers, can be resolved systematically.

- As organizations favor more heterarchic and agile structures (Laloux 2015), communicative exchanges, with which organizational members make sense of contingency and network these practices throughout the organization to socially accomplish their purpose, should be the primary inquiry focus.
- Sensemaking practices bring about change processes in organizations (Rüegg-Stürm and Grand 2017). The conceptual and empirical analysis of verbal, paraverbal, and nonverbal practices may reveal members' attitudinal parameters, co-orientations, and sensemaking processes, thus revealing its significance.

In a communication-centered management model (Buchholz and Knorre 2019; Rüegg-Stürm and Grand 2017), OD's unchanged relevance can thus appear in value creation and securing organizational existence contexts. Wimmer (2004: 38) can indeed rightly claim that "abundant knowledge on change has been accumulated in the rich pool of many OD projects, which, combined with an adequate understanding of the current dynamics in organizations, could be valuable in the future, especially for their central survival issues" (our translation).

2 Communication and OD perspectives

We propose to review conceptual and empirical works on communicative practices and organizational change, specifically elaborating on OD's microlevel foundations. We perpetuate our idea of OD as interactively viable for all involved actors and as being majorly constituted of interpersonal communicative exchanges. Within the literature on strategic management, organizational theory, or linguistics, *organizational change* appears more frequently than OD. Thus, we acknowledge that OD is an overarching concept that includes change management and include *change* and *change management* in our research.

2.1 Theoretical views on discursive actions and organizational change

In a rationalist view, organizational change is a deliberate, controllable, episodic occurrence, and linear process (Barrett, Thomas, and Hocevar 1995; Ford and Ford

1995; Johansson and Heide 2008; Marshak and Grant 2008). Thus, communication is purposefully employed by management to announce, explain, and legitimize change for internal stakeholders (Ford and Ford 1995; Johansson and Heide 2008; Marshak and Grant 2008; McClellan 2014).

In this paradigm, communication is deliberately employed *a posteriori* to implement a preceding managerial decision for organizational change, and, regarding meaning and sensemaking, is an amorphous process that occurs alongside formal organizational hierarchies in top-down, bottom-up, and lateral directions. Rather than developing a nuanced reflection of how communication and social processes are entangled, the perspective implies that messages be transmitted between managers and employees (Johansson and Heide and 2008). Despite recommendations to involve employees in implementational questions to convey a sense of participation, the impression of having a voice, and to ensure commitment (Johansson and Heide 2008), people are objectified as senders and receivers.

By contrast, constructivist approaches view organizations as communicatively constituted social realities (Dunford and Jones 2000; Ford and Ford 1995; Ford 1999; Ford and Ford 2002; Jacobs and Heracleous 2006; Marshak and Grant 2008). Meaning is socially constructed, rather than transmitted in a message authored by management and disseminated to the internal public among which desired effects are intended to emerge (Barrett, Thomas, and Hocevar 1995; Darcis and Clifton 2018; Ford 1999; Johansson and Heide 2008). The literature on communication's constructive force in change processes originates from organizational theory and linguistics (Grant and Iedema 2005). These works conceptualize discourse as organizational change's nucleus, making language use a theoretical and empirical focus. Scholars from both fields refer to discourse studies that examine oral and written communication and investigate the relation between utterances and objectives/effects (functions) through hearer/reader interpretations (Renkema 1993).

Oral communication writings center on discourse's constitutive force to construct intersubjective realities resulting in a change in larger social structures. Discursive activities both express and constitute organizational realities as interlocutors decipher their social world through these activities (Ford 1999; Jacobs and Heracleous 2006). Change, according to Grant et al. (2005: 8), is "brought into being" by mediated and conversational practices "so that it becomes a material reality in the form of the practices that it invokes". From this perspective, social reality, social structure, and organizational structure are ongoing accomplishments (Garfinkel 1967). Regarding communicative exchanges, interlocutors act in and against a shared local context, accomplishing a subjective "here-and-now" and becoming "fully real" to each other (Berger and Luckmann 1966: 43) by viewing "the other's subjectivity [as] available to me through a maximum of symptoms". If change is seen as a phenomenon that "necessarily occurs in a context of human interactions" (Ford and Ford 1995: 542), then communication is constitutive for the change process, rather than being a mere *a posteriori* tool to effectively implement predetermined change (Ford and Ford 1995).

Heracleous and Barrett (2001) identified four approaches on change and communication within organizational discourse studies: namely, the functional, interpretive, critical, and structurational research streams. According to them, the functional stream identifies practical implications from the social constructive interpretive paradigm: "Discourse is a communicative tool at the actors' disposal" (756). Discourse is here presented as purposefully articulated to intervene in an existing reality and facilitate a new reality's construction (Grant and Iedema 2005). Thus, decision makers "author" realities by changing the organization's communicative practices (Ford and Ford 2002).

By contrast, the interpretive stream includes works that are descriptive, as they aim to understand the entanglement of discourses, peoples' guiding interpretations of written and oral discourse, meaning construction, and actions (Jacobs and Heracleous 2006). The critical stream explores the ways practices both mirror and constitute the structural power relations insinuated in discourse. Critical approaches aim to disclose subtly blurred and implicit power relations between discourse participants, and how these representations reflect and amount to larger hegemonic power structures in organizations (Mumby and Clair 1997). Finally, Heracleous and Barrett (2001) suggested a structurational stream which views discourse as a duality of observable communicative actions and deep discursive structures.

The four approaches in organizational change emphasize the entanglement of discursive practices and formations, as well as meaning and action. Some studies disclose how meaning's co-construction proceeds in interactions. Jabri, Adrian, and Boje (2008) claimed, for instance, that meaning construction is only created through interactions, supporting Bakhtin's (1986) concept of written and oral communication and meaning. As Ford (1999: 487) wrote, "change is an unfolding of conversations into already existing conversations". He suggested intervening in this conversation network to "add, weed out, supplement, reintegrate, and organize conversations in order to construct a reality" (Ford 1999: 488–489).

Conversations, according to Bakhtin (1986), recursively refer to a speaker's (or others) past utterances that will potentially reappear in future utterances (e. g. Jabri, Adrian, and Boje 2008; see also Taylor and Robichaud 2007; Robichaud, Giroux, and Taylor 2004). Hence, interlocutors construct meaning within a myriad of utterances, whose meanings are suggested and negotiated within the current situation. This perspective encourages viewing communication in change to "engage persons in ongoing conversations about what they see and what needs to be done" (Jabri, Adrian, and Boje 2008: 679) and contradicts the perception of organizational change to be accomplished by a management's crafted consensus. Instead, it invites dissenting views. This finding alludes to modern management approaches that rely on questioning knowledge and strategic decisions.

2.2 Findings from empirical and conceptual works

Empirical studies on discursive practices in organizational change are rare and only apply to planned change occurrences. We present works grounded in speech act theory (Ford and Ford 1995; Pieterse, Caniëls, and Homan 2012) and conversation analysis (Aggerholm and Asmuß 2016; Vacek 2009, 2016).

Ford and Ford (1995) addressed speech acts' capacities to deliberately induce and implement organizational change, referring to verbal practices that typically occur during changes made by decision makers to construct a local reality. They defined conversations as verbal exchanges between interlocutors (Ford and Ford 2002) and Ford (1999) extended this view to nonverbal and paraverbal practices. Using a functional approach, they described these practices' capacities to facilitate change. They referred to "intentional" change as a deliberate pursuit of a desired situation. Drawing on Searle's (1969, 1979) speech act theory, they explained that speakers change their situational realities when using assertives, directives, commissives, expressives, and declarations on local communicative exchange levels. Conversations range from longer interrelated speech act sequences to single turns, and differ within organizations.

However, regarding intentional change, Ford and Ford (1995: 546) identified four distinct, yet interrelated conversations that facilitate the desired outcome: "initiatives, understanding, performance, closure". While initiatives serve to gain attention and acceptance for a specific issue, participants in "understanding" conversations negotiate the initiative, typically using assertions and expressives. They discuss the initiatives' assumptions, obtain information on expectations, create a common ground, and decipher the presented issue.

During this process, three byproducts emerge: (1) "satisfaction" appearing in participants' agreements on measurable outcomes or "a priori specifications that define the intended end point of the change", (2) "involvement, participation, support" emerge as participants interpret and discuss the change's relevance and meaning, and present "concerns, ideas and suggestions", and (3) decision makers' "interpretations" of "what changes can or should be produced next or in the future" (Ford and Ford 1995: 548–549). Additionally, "performance" conversations specifically focus on directives and commissives (requests and promises), in which participants express and negotiate actions to measurably induce the desired results. "Closures" apply assertions, expressives, and declarations to reveal a change's finalization and convey appreciation to the participants. Moreover, they may address problems that arose within the new situation and imply connecting points for future changes.

Ford and Ford (1995) suggested that conversation types imply that intentional change is a finite process. However, prior to local social dynamics in conversation, they did not assume that the four conversation types necessarily proceed in a successive fashion, from initiative to closure conversations. Conversations, such as "understandings", can be skipped, suspended, or reverted, or may, as in "performances", produce new "initiatives" (555). Conversation breakdowns may threaten change, when inferiors' initiatives in an organization are ignored, not expressed, or gain no traction. This is possible as semantics and local-level politics between participants impact conversations. Overall, language is and can be a strategic instrument: change occurs in communication and managers have an impact on this process, given language's performative character.

By contrast, using participatory methods, other authors empirically explore the verbal practices of managers endorsing change (Aggerholm and Asmuß 2016; Vacek 2009) and actors appointed by decision makers in planned changes' legitimization and implementation phases (Pieterse, Caniëls, and Homan 2012; Vacek 2009, 2016).

Pieterse, Caniëls, and Homan (2012) examined the discrepancies in various professional group members' discursive practices within an organization. Some actors supported a change project (implementation of a technology system), while others voiced their skepticism. The authors coded the actors' conversational and negotiation styles; conversational styles refer to Ford and Ford's (1995) previous findings, while negotiation styles involve "cooperative" practices, such as asking for understanding, confirmation, information, stipulations, and general requests, and "non-cooperative" practices, such as criticizing, denying, and rejecting. In interviews, the study reports, the system's "key users", responsible for development and testing, expressed interest and enthusiasm. Through informal conversation, this group voiced their skepticism about the system's benefits. Similarly, managers questioned the project's long-term benefits in interviews while their written documents endorsed it (Pieterse, Caniëls, and Homan 2012).

Differences in discursive activities and a lack of speakers' reflections on these differences may hint at poor cooperation. Pieterse, Caniëls, and Homan (2012) concluded that while project managers mostly used assertives in workshops and informal discussions, general managers frequently used meta-communication (practices that conclude, close, engage, offer promise, propose, remind, repeat, resume, and/or specify). In the workshops, the negotiation style was cooperative among general and project managers, but not sufficient to proceed to the "understanding" phase or to "performance" and "closure". However, the authors did not elaborate on the interactional procedures adapted to the sequential talking context.

Studies grounded in conversation analysis address speech's sequential context at the local level. Aggerholm and Asmuß (2016) investigated the verbal practices of a public sector organization's CEO that served to articulate a restructuring initiative's rationale (downsizing) in all-employee and senior management meetings. The authors elaborated on three appearing discursive practices: First, the use of direct speech and pronouns when representing the initiative in a socioeconomic context. Second, representing downsizing as stemming from a lack of alternatives and as an extraordinary situation, placing the CEO's and the management team's accountability in perspective (205). Third, using an idiomatic expression in a management meeting can be read as an achievement of legitimation (205). The authors concluded that changes in discursive practices according to organizational contexts provides a metaperspective of the overall conflictual situation and insinuates that common sense guides the discussion.

Vacek's (2009, 2016) study examined a global automobile manufacturer's site manager's speech before lower-level managers, and discursive practices through a question round. The author (2009, 2016) wrote that an ambiguous audience question offered different readings. The site manager's and one other discussant's responses to the question exhibited their perceptions of the event as a form of practices normatively aimed at achieving a consensus, rather than a platform where participants display dissent. The author showed that the site manager's response implicitly assumed the audiences' allegiance and support. Before the question round closed, however, another senior manager on the podium had disqualified the audience question as dissenting from expected allegiance. The site manager's discursive practices strongly regulated the situation, restoring control over the audiences without discussing the question as a constructive request (Vacek 2009). Moreover, Vacek (2009) reported that change implementation in a meeting of superiors and subordinates was a meta-communicative event wherein participants followed their formal obligations to report to higher levels.

Conversation analysis may clarify social situation dynamics. The sequential analysis brought out the practices with which members participate in interactions, co-create meanings, and negotiate role relationships and professional identities. However, the literature lacks empirical evidence specifically acknowledging organizational change's interactive nature, which would convey a broader picture of observable linguistic practices in OD.

3 OD as arrays of management communication practices: a research framework

Our research framework addresses strategic management tasks, since OD helps to direct change and manage contingency. Previous research has not yet empirically investigated OD's concrete verbal, nonverbal, and paraverbal practices, or created a research framework addressing practitioners' problems in tackling contingency and emergence. These require critically examining and contemplating decisions. Practically facilitating a discourse that allows decisions' critical examinations requires interpersonal communication across hierarchical barriers (for the relevance of political processes in contemporary OD, see Marshak and Grant 2008). The literature on workplace and communication in organizational settings may provide empirical insights on communicative practices and hierarchical relations among interlocutors. These studies mostly explore interactional asymmetries in formal communicative encounters, e.g., team and supervisor-supervisee meetings (Holmes, Stubbe, and

Vine 1999; Müller 1997; Schmitt 2006), and communicative practices that locally establish interactional and social order (Deppermann, Schmitt, and Mondada 2010; Drew and Heritage 1992; Have 2007; Müller 2018).

Hierarchy is a quality of the talk context. As a sequential organization of speaker turns, talk is a fleeting construct constituted by coordinated activities representing the local context that sets the discursive background for the interpretations and production of utterances (Goodwin and Duranti 1992; Heritage 1997; Schegloff 1992). Participants may lean toward extrasituational contextual variables, such as background knowledge on the setting's social and cultural characteristics. In sum, context involves local coordinating activities, interactants' background knowledge on participants, social norms, and normative situational expectations of speakers' cooperation (Deppermann 2008).

One central resource for participants' background knowledge in organizational settings may be underlying institutional hierarchy, a non-interactional concept that maps inferiority/superiority, but not necessarily a contextual variable that guides interlocutors' practices (Müller 2018). Questioning current strategies and plans requires local-level politics to avoid involvement in participants' activities. Rather, managers ask questions, express doubts, and criticize, while employees can promote strategic management, discussing strategies, using a discourse commonly associated with executives' "right to know" (Have 2007: 181; Heritage 1997: 178), contrasting the *need to know* principle practiced in hierarchical systems. Managers' "controlling" attempts (Müller 1997; Spranz-Fogasy 2002) and activities with which executives "do power" (Holmes, Stubbe, and Vine 1999) have the opposite effect.

Müller (1997) developed a model illustrating local-level workplace politics' dynamics, based on conversation analyses examining interlocutors' interdependent verbal, nonverbal, and paraverbal controlling activities. Participants majorly oriented to each other's formal positions ("statuses"), as shown in the formal organization of the examined conversations: participants' observable contributions to the conversation's sequential organization appeared through turn allocation and timing (Müller 1997). However, if topical aspects, such as participants' responsibilities within their realms of expertise and roles, are addressed, formal status fades (Müller 1997).

Another variable is "situation", the formal attributes characterizing an interaction's course (Müller 1997). In conversations, this is generally created and shaped by participants' verbal, paraverbal, and nonverbal means to coordinate activities, and consistently reorient their focus within each other, while considering activities' contextual implications for subsequent turns (Müller 1997). Müller also assumed the regulation of social distance between participants. Finally, "activity type" involves practices (formal meeting, discussion, banter, etc.) and their tone (informal, formal, humorous, etc.) within an identifiable long, sequential interaction segment. Activities encompass conversation types, topics, and "participation role" – participants' expectations of the predetermined configuration of individuals in a situation (Müller 1997).

Speech that considers contingency presupposes "openness" in communication, inviting dissenting views and obscuring local-level politics to negotiate the contingent state of affairs and its related activities. Mobilizing Bakhtin's concept of written and oral communication and meaning, Jabri, Adrian, and Boje (2008) viewed meaning as continuously accomplished through a "discovery" process, part of which involves encountering dissenting interpretations that serve to inform and enlighten. Thus, communication regarding change should "engage persons in ongoing conversations about what they see and what needs to be done" (Jabri, Adrian, and Boje 2008: 679). In this sense, management communication embeds and shapes metaconversations on a paradox: organizing that allows for collective identity while dealing with contingent decisions in the locally grounded "multiverses" of fragmented communities and their respective practices (Robichaud, Giroux, and Taylor 2004).

Methodologically, it is best to first inquire into manager-employee-peer communication or to arrange observations during days where communicative events on strategy topics are on the agenda (workshops, meetings, etc.) (Spranz-Fogasy 2002), while emphasizing an open knowledge and opinion exchange. For analysis, we suggest examining sequential properties, dissent, and topic organization: How is an interest topic made relevant? Does it assume interactional relevance in further sequences? How does dissent emerge in interactions? Is it negotiated and resolved?

Table 1: A research agenda examining the practices of contemporary OD

Practices	Analysis Levels
Sequential properties	– Turn-taking. – Interactional asymmetries and symmetries.
Topic organization	– Verbal, nonverbal, and paraverbal means to make topics relevant in interaction. • Practices that introduce topics at turn-taking organization levels. • Making topics relevant (activities displaying how interlocutors want their turn to be understood). • Argument presentations. • Interactional consequences. Practices employed to order and end topics. • Activities creating, unfolding, and resolving dissent in interactions.
Guiding activities	– Activities indicating orientation to extrasituational contexts: background knowledge on expected normative cooperation rules in discussions, where contingency topics assume interactional relevance, as observable in speakers' turns. – Activities indicating orientation to participants' status. – Activities indicating intertextual relations between the local level of talk and the metaconversation (Robichaud, Giroux, and Taylor 2004; Taylor and Robichaud 2007).

These interdependent variables form a communicative genre (Müller 2018; Stücheli-Herlach 2018), a type of practices. Accordingly, management communication involves different practices: eliciting knowledge during turn-taking, managers not interrupting participants, allocating turns, or exercising topic control (progressing through an agenda), etc. Furthermore, meta-communicative actions' occurrences and formulations aimed at praising, encouraging, justifying, and expressing doubt are also worth exploring.

Finally, inspired by the organizational discourse literature outlined in this chapter, we suggest examining the use of metaphors, the performativity of language, and the structural power relations insinuated in written formal and informal communication produced in OD contexts: texts announcing and legitimizing change to internal audiences (e.g., Barrett, Thomas, and Hocevar 1995), texts developed in the context of OD methods, e.g., minutes, slide shows, or dialogical scripts (Marshak and Grant 2008), and texts in Enterprise Social Media (posts).

4 Concluding remarks

In the context of theoretical and applied sciences of strategic management and communication, OD assumes practical relevance in ambidexterity and post-bureaucratic organizing to facilitate contemporary organizations' agility. Management communication prioritizes the meta-communicative task of reflecting on practices that facilitate communicative exchanges across hierarchies and departments. Practices eliciting no constraints on socially permitted contributions require managerial sensitivity to shape such contexts in interpersonal communication. Moreover, management should regularly establish formal types of management communication speech events, such as meetings, workshops, and practices associated with agile methods, such as daily stand-ups where the behavioral environment and participation roles are regulated (prestructured). However, the prestructuring of these speech events would still occur locally.

5 References

Aggerholm, Helle & Birte Asmuß. 2016. A practice perspective on strategic communication: The discursive legitimization of managerial decisions. *Journal of Communication Management* 20(3). 195–214.

Argyris, Chris. 1977. Double loop learning in organization. *Harvard Business Review* (9). 115–125.

Au, Corinna von. 2016. Paradigmenwechsel in der Führung: Traditionelle Führungsansätze, Wandel und Leadership heute. In Corinna von Au (ed.), *Wirksame und nachhaltige Führungsansätze. System, Beziehung, Haltung und Individualität*, 1–42. Wiesbaden: Springer Fachmedien.

Baecker, Dirk. 2015. *Postheroische Führung: Vom Rechnen mit Komplexität*. Wiesbaden: Springer Gabler.
Bakhtin, Mikhail M. 1986. Speech genres and other essays. In Caryl Emerson & Michael Holquist (eds.), *Speech genres and other late essays*. Austin, TX: University of Texas Press.
Barrett, Frank J., Gail Fann Thomas & Susan P. Hocevar. 1995. The central role of discourse in large-scale change: A social construction perspective. *Journal of Applied Behavioral Science* 31(3). 352–372.
Berger, Peter L. & Thomas Luckmann. 1966. *The social construction of reality: A treatise in the sociology of knowledge*. Harmondsworth, UK: Penguin.
Birkinshaw, Julian & Christina B. Gibson. 2004. Building ambidexterity into an organization. *MIT Sloan Management Review* 46(2). 47–57.
Bridges, William. 2017. *Managing transitions: Making the most of change*. London: Brealey.
Buchholz, Ulrike & Susanne Knorre. 2012. *Interne Unternehmenskommunikation in resilienten Organisationen*. Heidelberg: Springer.
Buchholz, Ulrike & Susanne Knorre. 2017. *Interne Kommunikation in agilen Unternehmen: Eine Einführung*. Wiesbaden: Springer Gabler.
Buchholz, Ulrike & Susanne Knorre. 2019. *Interne Kommunikation und Unternehmensführung: Theorie und Praxis eines kommunikationszentrierten Managements*. Wiesbaden: Springer Gabler.
Burke, W. Warner. 2018. The rise and fall of the growth of organization development: What now? *Consulting Psychology Journal: Practice and Research* 70(3). 186–206.
Burnes, Bernard. 2013. A critical review of organizational development. In H. Skipton Leonard, Rachel Lewis, Arthur M. Freedman & Jonathan Passmore (eds.), *The Wiley Blackwell handbook of the psychology of leadership, change, and organizational development*, 379–404. Hoboken, NJ: Wiley Blackwell.
Burnes, Bernard. 2014. *Managing change*. Harlow, UK: Pearson.
Burnes, Bernard, Cary Cooper & Penny West. 2003. Organisational learning: The new management paradigm? *Management Decision* 41(5). 452–464.
Capgemini Consulting. 2017. Culture first! Learning from the pioneers of the digital revolution. *Change Management Study 2017*. https://www.capgemini.com/consulting-de/wp-content/uploads/sites/32/2018/01/pdf_changestudie2017_rz_en.pdf (accessed 4 November 2019).
Coghlan, David. 1993. A person-centred approach to dealing with resistance to change. *Leadership & Organization Development Journal* 14(4). 10–14.
Cooren, François. 2017. Organizational communication: A wishlist for the next fifteen years. In Barbara Czarniawska (ed.), *A research agenda for management and organization studies*, 79–87. Cheltenham, UK: Edward Elgar.
Cooren, François, Timothy Kuhn, Joep P. Cornelissen & Timothy Clark. 2011. Communication, organizing, and organization: An overview and introduction to the special issue. *Organization Studies* 32(9). 1149–1170.
Cummings, Stephen, Todd Bridgman & Kenneth G. Brown. 2016. Unfreezing change as three steps: Rethinking Kurt Lewin's legacy for change management. *Human Relations* 69(1). 1–29.
Darics, Erika & Jonathan Clifton. 2018. Making applied linguistics applicable to business practice: Discourse analysis as a management tool. *Applied Linguistics* 40(6). 917–936.
Deppermann, Arnulf. 2008. *Gespräche analysieren: Eine Einführung*. Wiesbaden: VS Verlag.
Deppermann, Arnulf, Reinhold Schmitt & Lorenza Mondada. 2010. Agenda and emergence: Contingent and planned activities in a meeting. *Journal of Pragmatics* 42(6). 1700–1718.
Doz, Yves L. & Mikko Kosonen. 2010. Embedding strategic agility: A leadership agenda for accelerating business model renewal. *Long Range Planning* 43(2). 370–382.

Drew, Paul & John Heritage (eds.). 1992. *Talk at work: Interaction in institutional settings*. Cambridge: Cambridge University Press.

Dunford, Richard & Deborah Jones. 2000. Narrative in strategic change. *Human Relations* 53(9). 1207–1226.

Duwe, Julia. 2016. *Ambidextrie: Führung und kommunikation. Interne kommunikation im Innovationsmanagement ambidextrer Technologieunternehmen*. Wiesbaden: Springer Gabler.

Ford, Jeffrey D. 1999. Organizational change as shifting conversations. *Journal of Organizational Change Management* 12(6). 480–500.

Ford, Jeffrey D. & Laurie W. Ford. 1995. The role of conversations in producing intentional change in organizations. *Academy of Management Review* 20(3). 541–570.

Ford, Jeffrey D. & Laurie W. Ford. 2002. Conversations and the authoring of change. In David Holman & Richard Thorpe (eds.), *Management and language: The manager as a practical author*, 141–156. London: Sage.

Garfinkel, Harold. 1967. *Studies in ethnomethodology*. Englewood Cliffs, NJ: Prentice-Hall.

Gladwell, Malcom. 2002. *The tipping point: How little things can make a big difference*. Boston, MA: Little, Brown.

Goodwin, Charles & Alessandro Duranti. 1992. Rethinking context: An introduction. In Alessandro Duranti & Charles Goodwin (eds.), *Rethinking context: Language as an interactive phenomenon*, 1–42. New York: Cambridge University Press.

Granovetter, Mark. 1978. Threshold models of collective behavior. *American Journal of Sociology* 83(6). 489–515.

Grant, David & Rick Iedema. 2005. Discourse analysis and the study of organizations. *Text* 25(1). 37–66.

Grant, David, Grant Michelson, Cliff Oswick & Nick Wailes. 2005. Guest editorial: Discourse and organizational change. *Journal of Change Management* 18(1). 6–15.

Have, Paul ten. 2007. *Doing conversation analysis*. London: Sage.

Heracleous, Loizos & Michael Barrett. 2001. Organizational change as discourse: Communicative actions and deep structures in the context of information technology implementation. *Academy of Management Journal* 44(4). 755–778.

Heritage, John. 1997. Conversation analysis and institutional talk: Analysing data. In David Silverman (ed.), *Qualitative research: Theory, method, and practice*, 161–182. London: Sage.

Holmes, Janet, Maria Stubbe & Bernadette Vine. 1999. Constructing professional identity: 'Doing power' in policy units. In Srikant Sarangi & Celia Roberts (eds.), *Talk, work and institutional order: Discourse in medical, mediation and management settings*, 351–385. Berlin & New York: De Gruyter.

Jabri, Muayyad, Allyson D. Adrian & David Boje. 2008. Reconsidering the role of conversations in change communication: A contribution based on Bakhtin. *Journal of Organizational Change Management* 21(6). 667–685.

Jacobs, Claus D. & Loizos Th. Heracleous. 2006. Constructing shared understanding: The role of embodied metaphors in organization development. *Journal of Applied Behavioral Science* 42(2). 207–226.

Jahn, Jody L. S. 2016. Adapting safety rules in a high reliability context: How wildland firefighting workgroups ventriloquize safety rules to understand hazards. *Management Communication Quarterly* 30(3). 362–389.

Johansson, Catrin & Mats Heide. 2008. Speaking of change: Three communication approaches in studies of organizational change. *Corporate Communications: An International Journal* 13(3). 288–305.

Kauffeld, Simone & Falko von Ameln. 2019. Change management. *Gruppe. Interaktion. Organisation. Zeitschrift für Angewandte Organisationspsychologie (GIO)* 50(2). 97–99.

Kotter, John P. 1990. *A force for change: How leadership differs from management*. New York: The Free Press.
Laloux, Fredric. 2015. *Reinventing organizations: A guide to creating organizations inspired by the next stage of human consciousness*. München: Vahlen.
Lewin, Kurt. 1947. Frontiers in group dynamics: Concept, method and reality in social science; social equilibria and social change. *Human Relations* 1(1). 5–41.
Marshak, Robert J. & David Grant. 2008. Organizational discourse and new organization development practices. *British Journal of Management* 19(1). 7–19.
McAfee, Andrew P. 2006. Enterprise 2.0: The dawn of emergent collaboration. *MIT Sloan Management Review* 47(3). 21–28.
McClellan, John G. 2014. Announcing change: Discourse, uncertainty, and organizational control. *Journal of Change Management* 14(2). 192–209.
Meyer, Lisa. 2019. The future of OD from a stakeholder perspective. *Organization Development Review* 51(3). 31–35.
Müller, Andreas. 1997. *'Reden ist Chefsache'. Linguistische Studien zu sprachlichen Formen sozialer 'Kontrolle' in innerbetrieblichen Arbeitsbesprechungen*. Tübingen: Narr.
Müller, Andreas. 2018. Sprache und Hierarchie. In Stephan Habscheid, Andreas P. Müller, Britta Thörle & Antje Wilton (eds.), *Handbuch Sprache in Organisationen*, 105–125. Berlin & Boston, MA: De Gruyter.
Mumby, David & Robin P. Clair. 1997. Organizational discourse. In Teun A. van Dijk (ed.), *Discourse as social interaction*, 181–205. Los Angeles, CA, London, New Delhi & Singapore: Sage.
Pettigrew, Andrew M. 1987. Context and action in the transformation of the firm. *Journal of Management Studies* 24(6). 649–670.
Pieterse, Jos, Marjolein Caniëls & Thijs Homan. 2012. Professional discourses and resistance to change. *Journal of Organizational Change Management* 25(6). 798–818.
Renkema, Jan. 1993. *Discourse studies: An introductory textbook*. Amsterdam & Philadelphia, PA: John Benjamins.
Roberts, Karlene H., Suzanne K. Stout & Jennifer J. Halpern. 1994. Decision dynamics in two high reliability military organizations. *Management Science* 40(5). 614–624.
Robichaud, Daniel, Hélène Giroux & James R. Taylor. 2004. The meta-conversation: The recursive property of language as the key to organizing. *Academy of Management Review* 29(4). 617–634.
Rogers, Everett M. 2003. *Diffusion of innovations*. New York: Free Press.
Rüegg-Stürm, Johannes & Simon Grand. 2017. *Das St. Galler Management-Modell*. Bern: Haupt.
Rüegg-Stürm, Johannes & Simon Grand. 2019. *Das St. Galler Management-Modell. Management in einer komplexen Welt*. Bern: Haupt.
Sarasvathy, Saras D. 2008. *Effectuation: Elements of entrepreneurial expertise*. Cheltenham, UK: Edward Elgar.
Schatzki, Theodore R. 2001. Introduction: Practice theory. In Theodore R. Schatzki, Karin Knorr Cetina & Eike von Savigny (eds.), *The practice turn in contemporary theory*, 10–23. London & New York: Routledge.
Schegloff, Emanuel A. 1992. On talk in its institutional occasions. In Paul Drew & John Heritage (eds.), *Talk at work: Interaction in institutional settings*, 101–134. Cambridge: Cambridge University Press.
Schmitt, Reinhold. 2006. Interaction in work meetings. *Revue Française de Linguistique Appliqué* 2(11). 69–84.
Schreyögg, Georg & Daniel Geiger. 2016. *Organisation: Grundlagen moderner Organisationsgestaltung*. Wiesbaden: Gabler.
Schwägerl, Christian. 2020. Ubiquitäre Kommunikation und Kollaboration in Digitalen Arbeitsplätzen. In Sabine Einwiller, Sonja Sackmann & Ansgar Zerfaß (eds.), *Handbuch*

Mitarbeiterkommunikation. Wiesbaden: Springer Gabler, https://doi.org/10.1007/978-3-658-23390-7_20-1 (accessed 16 September 2020).

Searle, John R. 1969. *Speech acts: An essay in the philosophy of language*. London: Cambridge University Press.

Searle, John R. 1979. *Expression and meaning: Studies in the theory of speech acts*. Cambridge: Cambridge University Press.

Senge, Peter. 2006. *The fifth discipline: The art and practice of the learning organization*. London: Random House.

Spranz-Fogasy, Thomas. 2002. Was macht der Chef? – Der kommunikative Alltag von Führungskräften in der Wirtschaft. In Michael Becker-Mrotzek & Reinhard Fiehler (eds.), *Unternehmenskommunikation*, 209–230. Tübingen: Narr.

Stücheli-Herlach, Peter. 2018. Wertschöpfung als Wortschöpfung. Zur Modellierung des Sprachgebrauchs in der strategischen Organisationskommunikation. In Annika Schach & Catrin Christoph (eds.), *Handbuch Sprache in den Public Relations. Theoretische Ansätze – Handlungsfelder – Textsorten*, 117–134. Wiesbaden: VS Verlag.

Taylor, James R. & Daniel Robichaud. 2007. Management as metaconversation: The search for closure. In François Cooren (ed.), *Interacting and organizing: Analyses of a management meeting*, 5–30. Mahwah, NJ: Lawrence Erlbaum.

Vacek, Edelgard. 2009. *Wie man über Wandel spricht. Perspektivische Darstellung und interaktive Bearbeitung von Wandel in Organisationsprozessen*. Wiesbaden: Verlag für Sozialwissenschaften.

Vacek, Edelgard. 2016. Agile Kommunikation in Veränderungsprozessen – Ein Beitrag aus diskursanalytischer Perspektive. In Inga Ellen Kastens & Albert Busch (eds.), *Handbuch Wirtschaftskommunikation: Interdisziplinäre Zugänge zur Unternehmenskommunikation*, 294–329. Tübingen: Narr Francke Attempto.

Weick, Karl E. 1987. Organizational culture as a source of high reliability. *California Management Review* 29(2). 112–127.

Weick, Karl E. & Kathleen M. Sutcliffe. 2001. *Managing the unexpected: Assuring high performance in an age of complexity*. San Francisco, CA: Jossey-Bass.

Weick, Karl E., Kathleen M. Sutcliffe & David Obstfeld. 1999. Organizing for high reliability: Processes of collective mindfulness. *Research in Organizational Behavior* 21. 81–123.

Wimmer, Rudolf. 2004. OE am Scheideweg. Hat die Organisationsentwicklung ihre Zukunft bereits hinter sich? *OrganisationsEntwicklung* 1(4). 26–39.

Bertrand Fauré
19 Accounting

Abstract: This chapter deals with a counterintuitive form of communication: accounting. It shows how accounting can be seen as organizing through communicating, a position that is illustrated through two cases of budget making in the contexts of construction industry and humanitarian intervention. Reversely, this approach allows to conceive of communication *as* a form of accounting, a perspective that appears particularly relevant in the digital age. This view also shows how accounting and communication professions might struggle in the future about the definition of what should be accounted, how and by whom. The first section explores theoretical arguments about the links between accounting and communication while the second section develops the practical implications of this view

Keywords: organizational communication; accounting; performativity; social media; social change

> *What is most difficult here is to put this indefiniteness, correctly and unfalsified, into words.*
> (Wittgenstein 1953: 227)

While accounting is not usually considered part of management communication practices and specialties such as business communication, strategic communication, or public relations, it becomes a central form of management communication when the latter is defined as the metaconversation (Robichaud, Giroux, and Taylor 2004) of all contributions to collective value creation by modern organizations. If it is true that creating value or not underlies, orients, and limits most organizational conversations, knowing how value is calculated and accounted for becomes almost synonymous with management communication: the supreme metaconversation. Indeed, the first speech act (Searle 1969) that gives birth to any modern organization is an accounting act. Just as Austin (1962) famously showed that we constantly do things with words, we have to acknowledge that we can do a lot of things with numbers.

The study of the performativity of accounting has a long tradition of research (Goody 1996; Weber 1978), a tradition that is still vivid today and explores how accounting not only describes the reality it is supposed to account for but also contributes to its construction (Morgan 1988) by rendering what (and who) is counted more visible and controllable (Burchell et al. 1980; Miller and O'Leary 1987). Capitalism would indeed not be the same if "capital accounting" had not been invented (Chiapello 2007; Sombart 1930). Management also would not be possible without the striking capacity of accounting signs to "act at a distance" (Robson 1992). This performativity is so strong that it has even been argued that numbers can become "more real than reality, i. e. hyperreal" (Macintosh et al. 2000). Building on this literature about what numbers have already proven to be able to do, research is also exploring how to do more with numbers (Vollmer 2007). If numbers are so powerful, why not use them to build a better world? (Gray 2002).

Acknowledging that the accounting metaconversation is constitutive of modern organization and thus also of management communication enables us to develop theoretical arguments about the role of accounting and communication in organizing a sustainable future. These theoretical arguments are presented in the first section. The second section discusses their implications for management communication and accounting professions. Despite their current heyday, both professions might be closer than imagined to a rough competition for supremacy in social change: will community managers become heads of the accounting and finance department, telling accountants what to count and how? Or will they become a subservice called "social media accounting" within an extended accounting and finance department?

1 Theoretical arguments about the relation between communication and accounting

This first section presents theoretical arguments about the relationship between accounting and communication: how accounting can be seen as a form of communication and reversely how communication can also be seen as a form of accounting.

1.1 Accounting as a form of communication

Accounting is so deeply embedded in every aspect of management that it is sometimes even called "the language of business" (Bloomfield 2008). This language is taught in business schools and in specialized academic programs. The profession is flourishing and communication skills are increasingly recognized as important aspects of the job (Alvesson and Willmott 2003). If accounting was just writing numbers and calculation, why would we spend so much time speaking about them, trying to make them speak, or speaking in their name? Research shows that accounting talk is not a waste of time but on the contrary a "complex processes of enacting the orders which accounting engenders" (Ahrens 1997: 617). As shown in Figure 1 (from Fauré et al. 2010: 1264), this enactment involves three roles and positions strongly embedded into management doctrine and theory (Ijiri 1975): the accountor who renders accounts, the accountee who receives them, and the accountant who makes them.

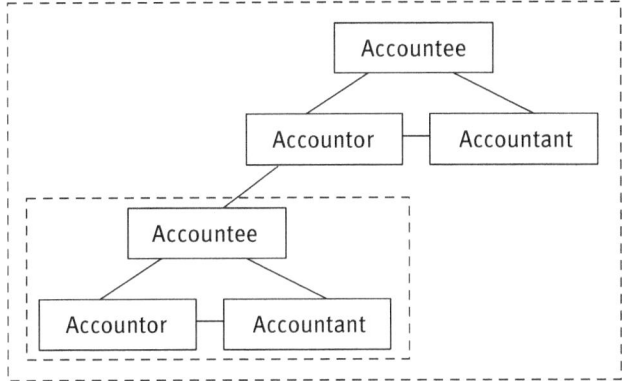

Figure 1: Embedded triad of accounting relationships (from Fauré et al. 2010: 1264)

Whether you are a local logistician (Fred) and a regional coordinator (Luc) trying to budget how to construct an incinerator and a waste pit in the Democratic Republic of Congo (Fauré, Cooren, and Matte 2019: 346) or a site engineer (SE), a management controller (MC), and an operations manager (OM) talking about a deficit during a budgetary control meeting (Fauré et al. 2010), ways of making numbers speak are the same. Questions about missing numbers or possible mistakes are addressed to the accountor by the accountant under the authority of the accountee. Depending on the answers given and their estimated usefulness, plausibility, and acceptability (Fauré and Rouleau 2011), questions can be reframed as *orders-to-respond*: silence or non-response are out of the question (see Excerpt 1). Most of the time, the accountee does not have to be physically present and the role of the accountant is precisely to ask questions in her place. The accountant herself can be rendered present during the conversations between accountors (see Excerpt 2). This presentification of the authority of numbers (Benoit-Barné and Cooren 2009) is the essence of management at distance and a key factor of the development of this form of management.

See for example how close together the two following excerpts are. In the first one, the site engineer (SE) is the accountor, the management controller (MC) is the accountant, and the operations manager (OM) is the accountee. All the members of the triad are present during a budgetary control meeting. The meeting begins with a question about "the number at the bottom of the summary sheet" and will continue line by line until an acceptable answer is found. This pattern is perfectly enacted in just a few turns of talk.

Excerpt 1: "I hadn't seen the number …" (Fauré et al. 2010: 1861)

MC: I hadn't seen the number at the bottom of the summary sheet. What is it?
SE: It's the number.
MC: What happened?
SE: Some things were forgotten.
MC: What?
MC: ((Silence))
OM: I would dare to hope that there are some mistakes.

The same pattern is at stake during a conversation between Fred and Luc, two logisticians working for Médecins sans frontières (also known as Doctors Without Borders) in the Democratic Republic of the Congo. As we see, they are both accountors of the budget of their mission, making the accountant (Mike) speak at distance.

Excerpt 2: "It must be clear for Mike" (Fauré, Cooren, and Matte 2019: 360)

FRED: But, it's the same, I have to put it back in the budget.
LUC: No no they are there.
FRED: No no but yes the labor.
LUC: Ah.
FRED: I have to note everything. I will justify everything, I'm gonna make a narrative, you see (.) so that he can follow and then that – so that Mike – It must be clear for Mike.
LUC: Um ((silence)).
FRED: I'm telling you, I did it line by line, we looked and um.

In this situation, Fred and Luc are both accountors of the budget. The accountant evoked by Fred (Mike) and the accountee (MSF) are rendered present through talk and language use during the exchanges between them. This personification of absent figures of the accounting triad is a foundational pattern of numbers' authority and organizational performativity. This triad can also be upscaled to a higher triad in which it is embedded: the one of MSF as the accountor of financial resources rendering account to public and private donors (accountees) with the help of independent auditors (accountants). This embeddedness of accounting triads contributes to empowering and weighting the authority of questions as *orders to answer*: Fred describes a situation where he will have to face Mike's questions. Luc's silence is an implicit agreement that answers will have to be given, as with the management controller's silence in Excerpt 1.

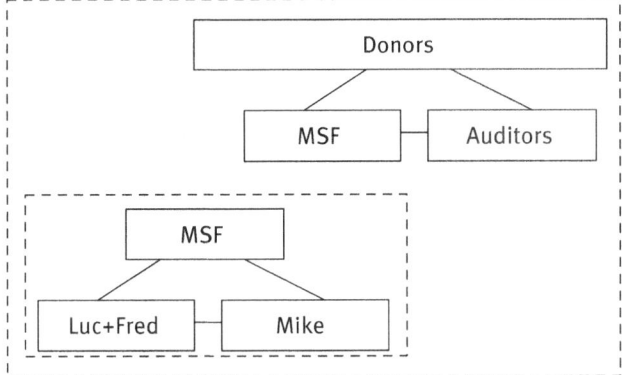

Figure 2: Luc and Fred as accountors within embedded accounting triads

As illustrated in the previous excerpts, just as we can do things with words (Austin 1962), we can do things with numbers. Their power is often undeniable, especially when they manage to impose silence. Even if the meaning of silence is not always something easy to grasp, as silence has no syntax or lexis, its performativity can be felt. In the excerpts, silence indeed consists of implicitly accepting the existing order and established patterns of communication. The silence of the management controller echoes Luc's relative silence: these silences signal the success of a previous performance, namely the performance of numbers that were *made to speak*.

The language of numbers is the same in every culture, dialect, and sector of activities. Management by numbers is often associated with fierce capitalism and short-term profit (Ezzamel, Willmott, and Worthington 2008) but nothing should prevent us from imagining more social and sustainable usages of numbers (Gray 2002) and, indeed, the last two decades have paved fruitful avenues of research for the future (Vollmer 2007). The accounting field has deeply changed over the years: several techniques, tools, and standards of the last century have been rebranded and issues that were previously neglected begin to be taken into account (sustainable development, corporate social responsibility; see the contribution of Schoeneborn and Girschik, in this volume). Viewing accounting as a form of management communication not only provides theoretical arguments for a positive approach to the performativity of numbers, but also helps to reveal why management communication can be viewed as a form of accounting.

1.2 Communication as form of accounting

Knowing how accounting organizes through communication is helpful to understand the specific function of management communication regarding value co-creation, especially in comparison with other fields of organizational communication such as strategic communication, business communication, and professional communication. Managerialism is not necessarily a "threat to communication professionalism" (Simonsson 2019) and business (re)branding is not necessarily the "dark side of communicative capitalism" (Mumby 2019). The field of corporate social and environmental responsibility that could still be compared through the lens of the "mafia metaphor" ten years ago (Gond, Palazzo, and Basu 2009) is now a much more constraining game of reputation making (Cho et al. 2015). It has become more and more difficult to claim, on one side, exemplarity in management and to accept, on the other side, sponsorship from celebrities involved in sex scandals. Numbers that were previously disclosed on different documents, through different media, with different agendas are now much more easily connected, aligned, and commented. Online firestorms cannot be reduced to a public relation or digital marketing issue (Pfeffer, Zorbach, and Carley 2014): if they can cause huge financial losses, it is because they disrupt existing boundaries and distinctions.

What is crucial in the use of accounting language is to establish a contrasted reciprocity with numbers, what Fauré, Cooren, and Matte (2019) proposed to call ventriloquial resistance. Numbers can indeed tell us a lot of things, but not everything we want, especially if knowledgeable people are listening. It is, on the contrary, precisely because they sometimes contradict or betray us that they can speak for themselves, give us authority, and give a voice to neglected aspects of reality. Value creation through accounting change is not a peaceful and quiet story. To paraphrase Wittgenstein (1953: 227), "What is most difficult here is to put this indefiniteness, correctly and unfalsified, into *numbers*".

How accounting numbers are daily used by managers to interpret and shape situations through specific discursive means is involuntarily illustrated by Shotter and Cunliffe (2002) in their study of leadership as practical authorship. Following Wittgenstein (1953), and in line with the linguistic turn in management communication, Shotter and Cunliffe (2002: 28–29) propose to distinguish what they identify as *six aspects of talk*:

> Wittgenstein's later work (1953) offers a number of resources for grasping these practical and taken-for-granted aspects of our talk. They may be summarized as follows:
> 1) Noticing in practice: 'giving prominence to distinctions which our ordinary forms of language easily make us overlook' (no. 132): 'stop' 'look', 'listen to this', 'look at that' (breaking routine ways of responding by pointing out features of the flow from within the flow) (no. 144);
> 2) New connections and relations: 'a picture held us captive' (no. 115): the use of new metaphors to reveal new possible connections and relations between events hidden by the dead metaphors in routine forms of talk;
> 3) To continue to gather examples: 'don't think, but look!' [...] 'and the result of this examination is: we see a complicated network of similarities overlapping and crisscrossing' (no. 66);
> 4) Making comparisons: to bring some order to our experiences by making comparisons using (sometimes invented) 'objects of comparison which are meant to throw light on the facts of our language by way not only of similarities but dissimilarities' (no. 130);

5) Establishing 'an order in our knowledge of the use of language: an order with a particular end in view [so that we can all participate in discussions toward that end]; one out of many possible orders, not the order' (no. 132);

6) Seeing not something behind or underlying appearances: but seeing 'something that lies open to view and that becomes surveyable by a rearrangement' (no. 92).

This Wittgensteinian framework enables us to grasp how accounting numbers and calculations play the role of discursive resources for management communication. Table 1 reports citations about numbers (interview, records) found for each of the six aspects of talk distinguished by these two authors in order to "focus on interactive moments in which opportunities occur for constructing shared significances, and draw attention to the type of dialogue in which such moments of connection and meaning may be created" (Shotter and Cunliffe 2002: 28).

Table 1: Examples of the performative use of numbers in talk (from Shotter and Cunliffe 2002)

Aspects of talk	Examples of the performative use of numbers
Noticing	"I say, 'Okay, first tell me about all the casualties, I want to **set priorities**. What are the things that might take us out of business today?'" (Shotter and Cunliffe 2002: 25)
Connecting	"If someone comes in and says, 'Gee **the numbers look really bad** this quarter, but I think I've found a way.'" (Shotter and Cunliffe 2002: 30)
Comparing	"Other program managers, who have the same job description, **have different measures** and different things they key in on." (Shotter and Cunliffe 2002: 18)
Gathering	"If you ask somebody **'How much is it going to cost?'** 'Well I don't know – you tell me.'" (Shotter and Cunliffe 2002: 29)
Ordering	"To provide leadership in saying, **'this is where we are heading**, this is what's important, this is what we need to do together.'" (Shotter and Cunliffe 2002: 20)
Arranging	"**We've set a goal that 95 per cent** of the issues I hear about shouldn't go further than me – only 5 per cent should go to the next level of managers." (Shotter and Cunliffe 2002: 15)

As shown in Table 1, management communication is about noticing, connecting, comparing, gathering, ordering, and arranging denumerable things and management communication does so through various performative uses of numbers: rendering things and people visible (Morgan 1988), commensurable (Espeland and Stevens 1998), and governable (Miller 2001). This second-hand analysis of Shotter and Cunliffe's (2002) discursive material shows how deeply numbers are embedded into management communication practices and how strongly numbers' uses shape the form taken by management communication.

2 Practical implications for communication and accounting

What are the practical implications of these theoretical arguments about the links between accounting and management communication? We saw that accounting is a performative language deeply involved in the constitution of modern capitalism and organizations and thus of modern management communication. We also saw that management communication is not only shaped by accounting norms and languages but also is itself a discursive form of accountability in the sense of rendering things and people visible, commensurable, and governable. It now remains to discuss how these theoretical arguments on the relationships between accounting and management communication provide insight into their practical roles in social changes.

2.1 Communication as a unit of value

One of the most challenging paradoxes facing management communication is that if the latter can claim to be a critical discipline in theory (Mumby and Stohl 1996), it unfortunately remains, in practice, subservient to an economic system that deserves to be criticized, i.e., capitalism (Mumby 2019). This is why management communication, as a practice, can be used, for instance, to support water-as-business storytelling despite critical evidence of the ecological consequences of this practice (Boje 2019). This is also why this discipline suffers from a lack of legitimacy and identity: Although it is involved in every aspect of organizational life, even if it is hard to quantify and evaluate its contribution in financial terms, it has never been able to develop its own system of metrics and performance indicators (Simonsson 2019). If it is true that communication constitutes the basic building blocks of organizational existence and change (Taylor 1993; Taylor et al. 1996; Taylor and Van Every 2000), speech acts should therefore be considered the units to be counted in order to determine value creation in organizations: the more organizations speak (communicate through talks and texts), the higher their value.

Of course, this axiom does not work in all cases: marketing campaigns can fail to gain new consumers and total quality policies can fail to improve anything. Not all words have positive perlocutionary effects (Austin 1962). In a certain way, communication as a science can be described as the search for the laws and rules of the performativity of language (Searle 1969). The paradox is that science is also a language and thus also has performative effects, so that performativity is both the object of communication science and its property as language use. A perfect communication science – i.e., a science that would be able to account for all communication acts and to predict all their effects – would therefore be the science of all other sciences. Talking at scientific conferences and writing research papers are acts of communication: accounting for these acts and calculating their impact is more than ever a crucial issue for the future of science as specialized knowledge (Hirsh 2005), as well as for its place and role in society as a performative language (Harzing and Van Der Wal 2009).

Citation indexes, of course, tell nothing about the content of the research that is ranked or about its intrinsic scientific value, and predict very imperfectly its scientific and social impact. Despite these limits as performance indicators, the existence and increasing calculability of citation indexes disrupt scientific practices and institutions. Science must communicate or perish (Harzing and Van Der Wal 2009) and how scientific communication is accounted for and evaluated determines how science is ultimately funded and thus oriented towards one direction instead of others. The same applies for management and business: they cannot exist and develop without a form of communication accountability, that is, without ways to measure how they communicate successfully.

An organization – but also a religion, an institution, etc. – that does not communicate (anymore) does not exist (anymore) as a participant in the social life. Most civilizations die (Valéry 1957), but some manage to last centuries and colonize continents. Jesus Christ's language (Aramaic) is not spoken anymore and the laws authorizing his public execution (crucifixion) would nowadays be seen as crimes against humanity. Yet his words have changed the world and his commandment ("Love your neighbor as yourself") still speaks to millions of believers. Everything that has been said and done since then is now situated in time before and after his date of birth: historical events, national calendars, or family agendas (birthdays, weddings, and funerals). In modern management terms, Jesus Christ's start-up is now a multinational corporation and a model of communication in several domains of community management: team-building (the apostles), story-telling (the gospels), branding (the cross), and marketing (Christmas).

The higher the citation index of Jesus Christ's theory of love, the more profitable Christian business. To the extent that *Mein Kampf* is still published, read, and talked about, the same could, unfortunately, be said of Hitler. Furthermore, the business model of modern social networks such as Facebook or Google relies on real-time micro accounting of communicative acts (texts, talks, pictures) and the sophisticated calculations of their social reception (comments, reactions) and impact (shares, reaches). The value created by these communities directly depends on the volume of members and the frequency of their interactions, whether they speak about cats' behaviors, border walls, or women's rights. Fake news, hate speech, and pornography also are very profitable businesses. This is why they are so difficult to forbid: they cannot be fought without being accounted for, and if they are accounted for, their value can also be calculated, thus rendering their whole business more manageable and accountable.

Primarily conceived as tools of communication, social networks have also introduced new numbers and forms of quantification that have disrupted management in general and communication in particular, as well as accounting. These new numbers refer to what can be called by the generic term *like*. In its simplest form, the like is a button displayed next to an online content, a button that can be pressed only once by each user and is then visible by the other users and added to the total number of previous likes with the same value as whatever the button represents: thumb up, middle finger, smiley, all count for one like or one dislike (Sumner, Ruge-Jones, and Alcorn 2018). This innovation was not desired or planned by governments or researchers but is now deeply challenging the accounting and management communication profession.

On the accounting side, the like increasingly appears as a new unit that could potentially replace traditional monetary ways of counting value and making exchanges. The shift is considerable. What was still science fiction a few years ago with the Black Mirror episode *Nosedive* (2016) is now close to becoming real with the generalization of the Chinese social scoring system: individuals' social scores determine their purchasing power. On the communication side, the like constitutes a new indicator of performance that could help the profession to gain autonomy from financial indicators. This shift is also considerable. If the like is the new money, then one of the specialties of management communication, such as community manager, almost becomes an accounting job.

Who will count the likes in the future and how they will be accounted for and reported will thus be determinant for both professions. If so, a promising direction of research, as shown in Figure 3, will consist in defining and characterizing more precisely the role and relationship between the figure of the *likor* (the one in charge of gaining likes and accountable for this performance), the *likee* (the one who receives this account of like performance), and the *likant* (the one in charge of controlling the account). Who will be the likant tomorrow: the community manager or the traditional accountant? While still purely theoretical, this question might soon become very practical.

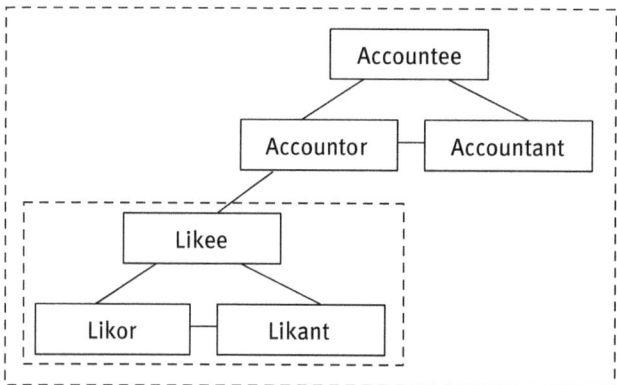

Figure 3: Triad of liking process embedded into an accounting triad (from Fauré et al. 2010: 1264)

The issue of this struggle between accounting and management communication is highly uncertain. Management communication is historically subordinated to accounting language but could take over the strategic advantage of being entitled to define what counts and what does not. However, accounting could also reinvent itself and maintain its own position of authority.

2.2 Accounting for the unaccountable

Just as for management communication performativity, the critique of management accounting performativity is an unfinished task (Spicer, Alvesson, and Kärreman 2009). Demonstrating the perverse effects of existing numbers does not help much to develop better ones (better calculation, better performativity). The development of accounting practices such as counting worktime, measuring work results, and calculating labor cost have contributed, however, to the social construction of a governable person (Miller and O'Leary 1987), not only in the private sector and for-profit organizations but also in the public sector and not-for-profit organizations (Deetz 1992). Even if not initially calculated for this aim, these numbers can later help to demonstrate social or gender inequality at work (Ashcraft and Mumby 2003), and thus be used for developing business ethics and corporate responsibility (Igalens and Gond 2005).

Accounting for absence/presence reflects not only who and what contributes to value creation (Catasús 2008) but also the underlying performative work of numbers making (Fauré et al. 2010). Accounting for information value depends on the value of what is counted and of its usefulness for decision making. A short and close list of important assets, debts, and liquidities and a large and open list of small transactions are more reliable, and thus useful, if they account for the same cumulated value: connecting them is a strategic issue for the accounting profession. Accountants have their own interest in saying who and what should be accounted for and how: extending the volume and scope of what is accounted for is profitable under the limit of accounting for something accountable, i.e., connectable and equalizable with others accounts and numbers through repeated interactions staging the three roles involved in accounting talk: accountor, accountant, and accountee (Fauré et al. 2010).

A zero carbon accounting strategy therefore works if constructed interactively and consistently with other accounting documents such as a strategic plan, a partnership contract, a conformity certificate, etc. (Aggeri and Le Breton 2018). On the contrary, sophisticated and costly statistics can be denied and defeated by one single fact. This is what happened, for instance, when managers representing private healthcare centers in the Democratic Republic of the Congo highlighted that some grass had been growing in front of their doors while statistics *gathered* by MSF were supposed to prove that its presence (and unfair competition) did not affect their profitability (Fauré, Cooren, and Matte 2019).

As Alfred Einstein might have allegedly said, "Not everything that counts can be counted and not everything that is counted counts" (apocryphal). Acknowledging the performative functions and discursive features of accounting talk in organizations could help us better know when we have "to speak or not to speak the language of numbers" (Fauré, Cooren, and Matte 2019). Numbers' performativity begins (1) when they do not say what we want them to say (by contradicting, denying, or betraying what we would like them to say), (2) when they give a voice (providing materiality, visibility, and authority) to other things or beings that could have been neglected, and (3) when we make them speak the same language (unit of counting, list of accounts, calculation of aggregates).

How can we know whether these numbers are ethical or not (Cooren 2016)? Numbers give great power to their spokespersons, which means that they also give them great responsibility, especially in terms of social change. Unaccountability does not equate with inexistence or insignificance (Messner 2009). On the contrary, being "invisible to the eyes [and thus *a fortiori* for numbers]" (Saint Exupéry 1946) could be seen as the specific quality of what really matters to people and thus the sign of great value for social change. If so, "accounting for the unaccountable" (Boiral 2016) should be considered an important research direction for developing a positive approach to accounting performativity. How, for example, to account for the value of silence (Bigo 2018)? Or the value of not-for-(immediate)-profit behaviors such as gifts (McKernan 2012) and help (Tang et al. 2008, 2015)? Can meditation, generosity, benevolence become manageable, accountable, and profitable acts of communication?

3 Conclusion

This chapter (1) presented work dealing with accounting as a form of management communication, (2) invited consideration of management communication as a form of accounting, and (3) discussed the practical implications of this theoretical argument for accounting and management communication. It notably emphasized the organizing role of the accounting triad (the accountor, the accountee, and the accountant) and showed how this triad could be adapted to a digital world (the likor, the likee, and the likant). These reflections not only pave the way for new research directions but could also be helpful in accounting education as well as management communication education. How to teach management communication without knowing how to calculate social scores? How to teach accounting without knowing how to calculate digital values? Figures 1 and 3 provide a common framework that could be used as a learning toolbox for this aim.

4 References

Aggeri, Franck & Morgane Le Breton. 2018. Counting before acting? The performativity of carbon accounting called into question – Calculation acts and dispositifs in a big French construction company. *M@n@gement* 21(2). 834–857.

Ahrens, Thomas. 1997. Talking accounting: An ethnography of management knowledge in British and German brewers. *Accounting, Organizations and Society* 22(7). 617–637.

Alvesson, Mats & Hugh Willmott. 2003. *Studying management critically*. Thousand Oaks, CA: Sage.

Ashcraft, Karen & Dennis K. Mumby. 2003. *Reworking gender: A feminist communicology of organization*. Thousand Oaks, CA: Sage.

Austin, John L. 1962. *How to do things with words*. Cambridge, MA: Harvard University Press.

Benoit-Barné, Chantal & François Cooren. 2009. The accomplishment of authority through presentification: How authority is distributed among and negotiated by organizational members. *Management Communication Quarterly* 23(1). 5–31.

Bigo, Vinca. 2018. On silence, creativity and ethics in organization studies. *Organization Studies* 39(1). 121–133.

Bloomfield, Robert J. 2008. Accounting as the language of business. *American Accounting Association* 2(24). 433–436.

Boiral, Olivier. 2016. Accounting for the unaccountable: Biodiversity reporting and impression management. *Journal of Business Ethics* 135(4). 751–768.

Boje, David. 2019. Water storytelling and dark side of sixth extinction denial. Paper presented at the 2nd International and Interdisciplinary Conference on Discourse and Communication in Professional Contexts, "The dark side of communication", Aalborg University, Denmark, 14–16 August.

Burchell, Stuart, Colin Clubb, Anthony Hopwood, John Hughes & Janine Nahapiet. 1980. The roles of accounting in organizations and society. *Accounting, Organizations and Society* 5(1). 5–27.

Catasús, Bino. 2008. In search of accounting absence. *Critical Perspectives on Accounting* 19(7). 1004–1019.

Chiapello, Ève. 2007. Accounting and the birth of the notion of capitalism. *Critical Perspectives on Accounting* 18(3). 263–296.

Cho, Charles H., Matias Laine, Robin W. Roberts, & Michelle Rodrigue. 2015. Organized hypocrisy, organizational façades, and sustainability reporting. *Accounting, Organizations and Society* 40(C). 78–94.

Cooren, François. 2016. Ethics for dummies: Ventriloquism and responsibility. *Atlantic Journal of Communication* 24(1). 17–30.

Deetz, Stanley. 1992. *Democracy in an age of corporate colonization: Developments in communication and the politics of everyday life*. Albany, NY: SUNY Press.

Espeland, Wendy Nelson & Mitchell L. Stevens. 1998. Commensuration as a social process. *Annual Review of Sociology* 24(1). 313–343.

Ezzamel, Mahmoud, Hugh Willmott & Franck Worthington. 2008. Manufacturing shareholder value: The role of accounting in organizational transformation. *Accounting, Organizations and Society* 33(2–3): 107–140.

Fauré, Bertrand, Boris H. J. M. Brummans, Hélène Giroux, & James Taylor. 2010. The calculation of business, or the business of calculation? Accounting as organizing through everyday communication. *Human Relations* 63(8). 1249–1273.

Fauré, Bertrand, Francois Cooren & Frédérik Matte. 2019. To speak or not to speak the language of numbers: Accounting as ventriloquism. *Accounting, Auditing and Accountability Journal* 32(1). 337–361.

Fauré, Bertrand & Linda Rouleau. 2011. The strategic competence of accountants and middle managers in budget making. *Accounting, Organizations & Society* 36(3). 167–182.
Gond, Jean-Pascal, Guido Palazzo & Kunal Basu. 2009. Reconsidering instrumental corporate social responsibility through the Mafia metaphor. *Business Ethics Quarterly* 19(1). 57–85.
Goody, Jack. 1996. *The East in the West*. Cambridge: Cambridge University Press.
Gray, Rob. 2002. The social accounting project: Privileging engagement, imaginings, new accountings and pragmatism over critique? *Accounting, Organizations and Society* 27(7). 687–708.
Harzing, Anne-Wil & Ron Van Der Wal. 2009. A Google Scholar h-index for journals: An alternative metric to measure journal impact in economics and business. *Journal of the Association for Information Science and Technology* 60(1). 41–46.
Hirsh, Jorge E. 2005. An index to quantify an individual's scientific research output. *PNAS* 102(46). 16569–16572.
Igalens, Jacques & Jean-Pascal Gond. 2005. Measuring corporate social performance in France: A critical and empirical analysis of ARESE data. *Journal of Business Ethics* 56(2). 131–148.
Ijiri, Yuji. 1975. *Theory of accounting measurement*. Sarasota, FL: American Accounting Association.
Macintosh, Norman B., Teri Shearer, Daniel B. Thornton & Michael Welker. 2000. Accounting as simulacrum and hyperreality: Perspectives on income and capital. *Accounting, Organizations and Society* 25(1). 13–50.
McKernan, John F. 2012. Accountability as aporia, testimony, and gift. *Critical Perspectives on Accounting* 23(3). 258–278.
Messner, Martin. 2009. The limits of accountability. *Accounting, Organizations and Society* 34(8). 918–938.
Miller, Peter. 2001. Governing by numbers: Why calculative practices matter. *Social Research* 68(2). 379–396.
Miller, Peter & Ted O'Leary. 1987. Accounting and the construction of the governable person. *Accounting, Organizations and Society* 12(3). 235–265.
Morgan, Gareth. 1988. Accounting as reality construction: Towards a new epistemology for accounting practice. *Accounting, Organizations and Society* 13(5). 477–485.
Mumby, Dennis K. 2019. (Re)branding the dark side: Communicative capitalism and neoliberalism. Paper presented at the 2nd International and Interdisciplinary Conference on Discourse and Communication in Professional Contexts, "The dark side of communication", Aalborg University, Denmark, 14–16 August.
Mumby, Dennis K. & Cynthia Stohl. 1996. Disciplining organizational communication studies. *Management Communication Quarterly* 10(1). 50–72.
Pfeffer, Jürgen, Thomas Zorbach & Kathleen M. Carley. 2014. Understanding online firestorms: Negative word-of-mouth dynamics in social media networks. *Journal of Marketing Communications* 20(1–2). 117–128.
Robichaud, Daniel, Hélène Giroux & James R. Taylor. 2004. The metaconversation: The recursive property of language as a key to organizing. *Academy of Management Review* 29(4). 617–634.
Robson, Keith. 1992. Accounting numbers as "inscription": Action at a distance and the development of accounting. *Accounting, Organizations and Society* 17(7). 685–708.
Saint Exupéry, Antoine de. 1946. *Le petit prince*. Paris: Gallimard.
Searle, John R. 1969. *Speech acts: An essay in the philosophy of language*. Cambridge: Cambridge University Press.
Shotter, John & Ann L. Cunliffe. 2002. Managers as practical authors: Everyday conversations for action. In David Holman & Richard Thorpe (eds.), *Management and language*, 15–37. London: Sage.

Simonsson, Charlotte. 2019. Managerialism – a threat to communication professionalism? Paper presented at the 2nd International and Interdisciplinary Conference on Discourse and Communication in Professional Contexts, "The dark side of communication", Aalborg University, Denmark, 14–16 August.

Sombart, Werner. 1930. Capitalism. In Edwin R. A. Seligman & Alvin Johnson (eds.), *Encyclopedia of Social Sciences*, vol. 3. New York: Macmillan.

Spicer, André, Mats Alvesson & Dan Kärreman. 2009. Critical performativity: The unfinished business of critical management studies. *Human Relations* 62(4). 537–560.

Sumner, Erin, Luisa Ruge-Jones & Davis Alcorn. 2018. A functional approach to the Facebook Like button: An exploration of meaning, interpersonal functionality, and potential alternative response buttons. *New Media & Society* 20(4). 1451–1469.

Tang, Thomas Li-Ping, Toto Sutarso, Mahfooz A. Ansari, Vivien K. G. Lim, Thompson S. H. Teo, Fernando Arias-Galicia, Ilya E. Garber, Randy Ki-Kwan Chiu, Brigitte Charles-Pauvers & Roberto Luna-Arocas. 2015. Monetary intelligence and behavioral economics: The Enron effect – Love of money, corporate ethical values, Corruption Perceptions Index (CPI), and dishonesty across 31 geopolitical entities. *Journal of Business Ethics* 148(4). 919–937.

Tang, Thomas Li-Ping, Toto Sutarso, Grace Mei-Tzu Wu Davis, Dariusz Dolinski, Abdul Hamid Safwat Ibrahim & Sharon Lynn Wagner. 2008. To help or not to help? The good samaritan effect and the love of money on helping behavior. *Journal of Business Ethics* 82(4). 865–887.

Taylor, James R. 1993. *Rethinking the theory of organizational communication: How to read an organization*. New York: Ablex Publishing.

Taylor, James R., François Cooren, Nicole Giroux & Daniel Robichaud. 1996. The communicational basis of organization: Between the conversation and the text. *Communication Theory* 6(1). 1–39.

Taylor, James R. & Elizabeth J. Van Every. 2000. *The emergent organization: Communication as its site and surface*. Mahwah, NJ: Lawrence Erlbaum.

Valéry, Paul. 1957. La crise de l'esprit. In *Variétés: Premier volume*. Paris: Éditions du Sagitaire.

Vollmer, Hendrik. 2007. How to do more with numbers: Elementary stakes, framing, keying, and the three-dimensional character of numerical signs. *Accounting, Organizations and Society* 32(6). 577–600.

Weber, Max. 1978. *Economy and society: An outline of interpretive sociology*. Berkeley, CA: University of California Press.

Wittgenstein, Ludwig. 1953. *Philosophical investigations*. Oxford: Blackwell.

Part III: **Contexts of management communication**

Susanne Tietze, Hilla Back, and Rebecca Piekkari

20 Managing communication in multilingual workplaces

Abstract: This chapter is concerned with the constitution of multilingual organizations through acts of agentic communication. Specifically, it focuses on the role of translation and non-verbal communication which are still mainly ignored in many streams of literature that focus on communication. Drawing on a layered iceberg model of communication, we propose that the use of multiple languages, translation, and non-verbal communication are fundamental to understanding the constitution of multilingual organization, yet they often remain hidden, silent, and unexplored. We argue that translation permeates all layers of communication and is a collective management practice. The chapter reviews selected examples from different streams of research to demonstrate how multilingual organizations are constituted. We advocate that future research should include phenomena and consequences of English, languages, translation, and non-verbal meanings as they unfold in multilingual workplaces and mingle with narratives, discourses, and authoring of organizations.

Keywords: multilingual organization; non-verbal communication; translation; English

This chapter is concerned with communication among diverse employees in multilingual workplaces. These employees belong to different cultural and language groups and collectively negotiate meaning and language use on a daily basis. They make decisions whether to use English as a bridge language, to engage in translation, or to rely on non-verbal communication. These acts of communication are expressive and constitutive of organizations as well as "processes of meaning production and negotiation" (Schoeneborn, Kuhn, and Kärreman 2019: 476). This chapter draws on the Communication Constitutes Organizations (CCO) tradition whose central tenet is that organizations come into being, persist, and are changed through communication practices (Cooren, Taylor, and Van Every 2006). According to this tradition, communication is not only about transmitting messages – it is also and especially about communication taking on a role of a performative, agentic force in organizations.

While the CCO tradition approaches communication as constitutive acts, this tradition is, in our view, monolingual in character. In other words, any considerations of organizations being constructed through translation or non-verbal communicative acts in "other languages" have been mainly ignored (Steyaert and Janssens 2013; Tietze 2018) with some exceptions within the CCO literature proving a case in point (e.g., Bencherki, Matte, and Pelletier 2016). Yet, many organizations such as multinational corporations (MNCs), non-governmental organizations (NGOs), or entrepreneurial organizations are *de facto* characterized by the existence of multiple languages, with English perhaps being the most dominant one.

Despite English's status as a global language (Crystal 2003) and the global lingua franca (ELF) (Rocci 2009), its use does not prevent miscommunication and misunderstanding. Instead, it has been argued that its use glosses over issues of inequality in terms of access, skewing group relations colored by historical-political processes. Indeed, some scholars have proposed re-labeling the *multinational* organization the *multilingual* organization (Luo and Shenkar 2006; Fredriksson, Barner-Rasmussen, and Piekkari 2006). Yet, to date organizational scholars have paid limited attention to how languages are an intrinsic part of meaning negotiations in multilingual workplaces.

In this chapter, we follow some of the tenets of the CCO approach with its emphasis on the constitutive, creative, and performative character of language but apply it to the multilingual workplace. We offer a perspective which includes other languages than English and which considers translation and non-verbal communication as constitutive of management. The communicative acts are part of the collective practice of authoring, networking, enacting, and managing organizations. In this setting, it is particularly interesting to explore whether it is possible to manage multilingual and intercultural communication in the first place, and if so, how this occurs.

According to the Oxford Dictionary, to *manage* is defined as to "[b]e in charge of (a business, organization, or undertaking); run". This definition assumes a top-down perspective; a notion of being in control of something. Our take on managing languages differs from this definition insofar as we understand language in multilingual organizations to be fluid and collectively negotiated. In this regard, a choice as to which language to speak, in which situation, when or whether to translate, or when to use English as the pre-given shared language constitutes an important part of management communications within multilingual organizations. We propose an iceberg model that displays the different layers of communication and shows which ones are relatively directly accessible and which ones are used in the more hidden arenas of organizational life. We propose that translation permeates all layers of communication and represents not only a concept of how to understand communicative practices between members of different and distinct cultural groups, but also a collective practice occurring among organizational members (Piller 2007, 2009).

The chapter is organized as follows: we first introduce the iceberg model which visualizes the different layers of communication in a multilingual workplace, including the role of translation as a collective management practice. Thereafter, we briefly and selectively review several streams of research that have made contributions to understanding multilingual and intercultural workplaces: language-sensitive international business literature; work on non-verbal aspects of intercultural communication, and translation studies of translatorial acts. The language-sensitive international business research has investigated the role of English and its relationship with other languages in multinational corporations central to its inquiry. Thereafter, we address non-verbal acts of communication in the process of negotiations and meaning making, intermingling them with spoken or written communications. Furthermore, we ask whether communication can be managed collectively through translation in multilingual workplaces. The concluding section brings the respective insights together, addresses the constitution of contemporary multilingual workplaces, and provides an agenda for future research.

1 Different layers of communication in multilingual workplaces

In order to understand how language use can be understood in multilingual workplaces, it is necessary to understand the different layers of communication: those visible and audible, negotiated and translucent, as well as the interpreted and inaudible. The audible common corporate language is often focused on and attempted to be managed. However, most language-related issues occur below the surface and are inaudible or translucent in character. This means they are difficult to be formally managed or even to be appropriated by senior management. They are often managed through collective negotiations, including translation. Figure 1 visualizes our iceberg model, showing the different layers of communication in a multilingual workplace.

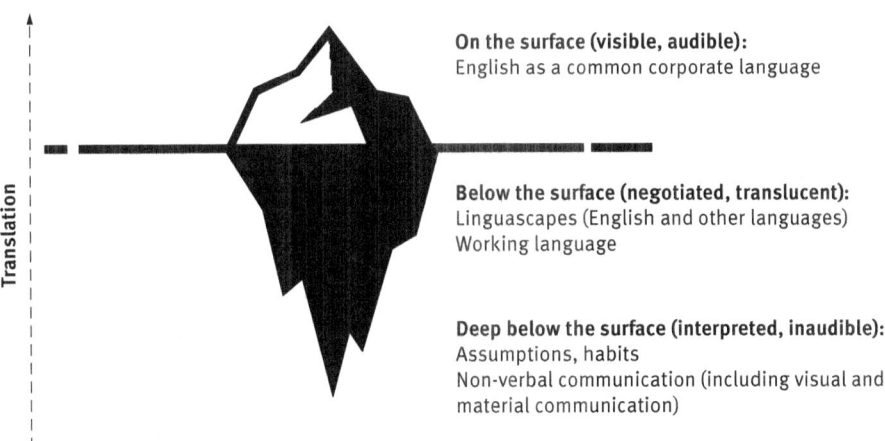

Figure 1: Layers of communication in a multilingual workplace

The purpose of this model is to visualize, i.e., to make explicit, the existence of different communicative areas. We have chosen this model to communicate to our readership that in multilingual organizations, these acts of constitutive communications exist and merit more attention. We acknowledge that these "layers" are interconnected with each other and in a mutually constitutive relationship – yet in this chapter we only outline some of these connections. We begin from the top of the iceberg and proceed down to the most inaudible facets of multilingual and intercultural communication. Throughout the review, we discuss the impact of these layers on the practices to influence, manipulate, shape, and sometimes control communication in multilingual workplaces.

1.1 On the surface: English as a mandated common corporate language

With scholarship focusing on the role of languages in international business and management research, it is by now an established field of inquiry (Karhunen et al. 2018; Tenzer, Terjesen, and Harzing 2017; Tietze and Piekkari 2020). This body of work can be divided into two broad areas: focus on a single language, typically English as a common corporate language and *lingua franca*; and focus on language diversity (Tietze and Piekkari 2020). In this chapter, we cover both areas.

As Figure 1 shows, we place the common corporate language in the visible section of the iceberg, because it represents a mandated language to be primarily used for internal inter-unit communications in the MNC. As Welch and Welch (2019: 624) explain, "[e]ssentially, a common corporate language is a form of language standardization introduced to reduce the potential for miscommunication arising from multilingualism". Through a unifying language, the top management seeks to gain benefits from facilitating information flow and knowledge transfer around the global entity, increasing efficiency (Luo and Shenkar 2006), creating a sense of belongingness within the MNC (Blazejewski 2006), as well as controlling and monitoring communications (San-Antonio 1987). A common corporate language can also be used for external purposes, for instance, to enhance employer branding (Kangasharju, Piekkari, and Säntti 2010) or facilitate communications with customers and suppliers (Neeley 2012b).

Figure 1 suggests that MNCs often (but not always) choose English as the common corporate language because it is assumed that everyone is able to draw on English to engage in communications. English enjoys the role and status of an established language in management knowledge and practice and is used as an international *lingua franca*, "an idiom that non-native speakers use with other non-native speakers" (Vandermeeren 1999: 276). The English language is also employed in exchanges between native speakers and non-native speakers (Tietze 2008). Thus, English is treated as the taken-for-granted language of international business (Nickerson 2005) and management (Tietze 2004).

We would argue, however, that the assumptions of everybody having equal access to English and of it being a universal language of knowledge are false. Critical investigations have shown that English alone is not able to capture all possible and existing knowledge in an unproblematic and objective way (e. g., Canagarajah [1999] for access to and teaching of English; Phillipson [1992] for its hegemonic influence; Steyaert and Janssens [2013]; Tietze [2018] for its influence on knowledge production). The literature we introduce next shows clearly that English as a common corporate language co-exists and blends with other languages. Its dominant and taken-for-granted status is perhaps *the status quo* for global corporate elites but not for others (Tietze 2004). The reality of multilingual workplaces features negotiations about which language to use with whom and why.

1.2 Below the surface: negotiated language use

In this section, we highlight collective negotiations of language use below the surface of the multilingual workplace and emphasize the contested position of English as a common corporate language. Indeed, any attempt to formally manage language diversity in a strict way is likely to fail or to be undermined. Steyaert, Ostendorp, and Gaibrois (2011) suggest that language use is always situated in contexts and driven by the language user. Instead of the concept of the common corporate language, they propose the term *linguascaping*. It captures the language decisions taken by language users *in situ* to manage and respond to language diversity as it prevails in their workplace.

While English plays an important and partly dominant role in local negotiations since other languages always exist in relation to English use, there are distinct discursive practices which shape the communicative encounter. These practices include, e. g., adaption to the language of the other, collective negotiations of a common language, and improvisation and changing of languages as used during encounters (Steyaert, Ostendorp, and Gaibrois 2011). They are constitutive of the relational, processual, and negotiated aspects of communications across language boundaries. As Figure 1 shows, the notion of linguascapes is useful to us because it highlights the various ways in which different languages are spoken alongside one another and how their space is negotiated in the multilingual workplace. This layer also represents communicative acts out of the reach of senior management's policy decisions about language use. Indeed, it can also be the place where such policies are deliberately flaunted.

Early studies in international business and management already questioned the intended integrating effect of a common corporate language (Piekkari et al. 2005; Vaara et al. 2005). Instead of promoting the integration between two previously separate organizations of a cross-border merger, the authors show how the choice and imposition of the common corporate language escalated disintegration and introduced language-based groupings alongside the traditional boundary of the acquired versus the acquiring organization. The new corporate language of the merged organization influenced staffing decisions and affected performance management of the

MNC. Language-based groupings were also found in another study, which looked at inter-unit communication in multinationals (Marschan-Piekkari, Welch, and Welch 1999).

These groupings formed a shadow structure which was hiding behind the formal organization chart, superimposing its own logic of interlinking foreign subsidiaries with each other. The above findings also point to a hierarchy of languages (involving English, Spanish, and Finnish as the main languages), which partly replaced a hierarchy of structure, and which exerted influence under the radar of corporate policy (Marschan-Piekkari, Welch, and Welch 1999). Taken together, while these studies do not explicitly articulate an interest in the constitutive use of language, they do so implicitly by focusing on agentic actions of employees who gain or lose power due to their language competence. In this sense, the early studies can serve as examples of how languages are part of negotiating the positioning of individuals and groups.

As mentioned above, in practice, it is highly unlikely that a common corporate language can be implemented from the top by senior management and that all employees (including knowledge workers) are in a similarly favorable position to use English in the pursuit of their work tasks. Instead, this management decision may be met with differing degrees of resistance and rejection (Lønsmann 2018; see also Kroon, Cornelissen, and Vaara 2015). Neeley's (2012a) empirical study set in a French MNC is a case in point as she investigated employees' responses to the introduction of English as the mandated language. Her findings attest to the emotive and partly dysfunctional consequences of such attempts to control language use. That said, English as the common corporate language of MNCs is not always introduced by the management fiat. Instead, language use may be driven by staffs' implicit assumptions that English is the default language, particularly in the absence of a formal language policy (e. g., Sanden and Kankaanranta 2018). Sanden (2018) proposes more local approaches to language management that are aligned with the specific language competences and communicative needs of each workplace.

To sum up, in all the above studies the language-based behavior is highly interactive and can be described as a collective (but still diverse) effort to work with languages constructively to establish relationships and to ensure that tasks are understood, executed, and targeted to meet shared objectives. These language phenomena are recurrent in multilingual workplaces and form an important part of the constitution of these organizations.

1.3 Deep below the surface: non-verbal communication

In this section we introduce the role of non-verbal communication – the interpreted and inaudible layers of communication, deep below the surface of the iceberg – in the multilingual workplace (see Figure 1). Non-verbal communication includes, e. g., body language, tone of voice, gestures, silences, as well as visual and material communication. In linguistically constrained environments, MNC employees often rely on gestures, symbols, and visual aids to ensure that the message gets across (Sunaoshi, Kotabe, and Murray 2005). We therefore consider non-verbal communication at least as important as verbal communication. While, on the one hand, difficulties in surface language communication are easily noticeable, on the other hand, tacit knowledge and assumptions underlying non-verbal communication are often bypassed as their meaning gets lost in intercultural communication; additionally, such loss of meaning is often not even noticed by the message producer.

In intercultural communication, "[m]ost miscommunication does not arise through mispronunciation or through poor uses of grammar [...] The major sources of miscommunication in intercultural contexts lie in differences in patterns of discourse" (Scollon, Scollon, and Jones 2011: xv). In other words, miscommunication primarily stems from different *ways* of communicating. This places demands on managing the multilingual workplace. Hall (1959) was one of the first researchers to shed light on the "silent language", asserting that it is not only the surface-level language that is used for communication. He discussed cultural differences in matters concerning the language of time, space, material possessions, friendship patterns, and agreements. For example, a delay in response in the United States implies a lack of interest, while in Ethiopia the time required to make a decision is directly proportional to its importance (Hall 1959).

Despite contemporary criticism of Hall's work – most of his work is relatively general and remains centered on differences in national culture as well as downplaying the significance of individual interpretations and agency – his insights into temporal and spatial dimension as constituting a silent language are still relevant for our purposes. Hall (1959) suggests that if one understands the basic cultural assumptions and non-verbal cues that accompany spoken communication, one is able to communicate effectively even without working knowledge of the local language. While we do not subscribe to this particular view, it is nevertheless important to understand how one's own and others' cultural assumptions are part of one's own and others' communicative actions.

One such cultural assumption was investigated in more detail by Henderson (2005) who found that members of a multilingual team continued to "hear" through their own respective cultural filters. Henderson (2005) defined language diversity to include not only a variety of mother tongues, but also a variety of ways of hearing and interpreting the tacit assumptions built into messages. According to Henderson (2005), individuals from different cultures also use differing interpretive mechanisms due to diverse backgrounds. This point is often overlooked as individuals assume they understand an issue in the same way, especially when using a common working language such as English. Henderson (2005) also described how members from different cultures have differing expectations when it comes to verbal exchanges that tend to be ritualized or predictable – greeting, thanking, taking leave, apologizing, distancing, or forms of address. If expectations are not met and there is a deviation from a predictable pattern, attitudes can be negatively affected. She explains how the potential negative consequence of language diversity is often attributed to the lack of language competence; yet, in intercultural communication it is the lack of communicative competence that is the culprit.

Non-verbal communication may sometimes be the only communicative resource available in intercultural exchanges. Sunaoshi, Kotabe, and Murray (2005) studied technology transfer on the factory floor in Japanese-owned automotive plants in the United States. Since the Japanese technical personnel and their American co-workers had extremely poor knowledge of each other's language and cultural background, a large part of teaching and learning the new technology took place by avoiding the use of English or Japanese altogether. Instead, the technical personnel relied on pictures, drawings, abbreviations, and numbers to convey meaning. They also demonstrated the new technology by showing, touching, and performing the tasks together using the actual tools and material. Yet, in such a linguistically constrained environment, some of the tacit knowledge was not conveyed at all (Sunaoshi, Kotabe, and Murray 2005).

In the above study, the Japanese and US technical personnel were physically co-located on the factory floor. However, when individuals representing different cultural groups do not share the same time or space, the risk of misinterpretation and other hurdles of communication increase even more. Many contemporary MNCs boast of their flexible work arrangements as an employment perk, competing for highly ranked positions on lists such as the annual Top 100 "FlexJobs". Interestingly, much, if not most, information exchange occurs through non-verbal communication via intonation, mimics, and gestures, much of which is lost if communication relies primarily on text or audio channels (DiStefano and Maznevski 2000; Maznevski and Chudoba 2000). Rich media, such as videoconferencing platforms, allow for transmitting non-verbal signs of support or disagreement but still cannot replace face-to-face contact (Andres 2002).

Although these studies are nearly two decades old, the same dilemmas prevail, especially during the current COVID-19 pandemic. More recent research findings show that global virtual communication can result in misinterpretations and difficulty in establishing relationships due to a loss of non-verbal communication (see, for example, Saarinen and Piekkari 2015). However, despite the increasing prevalence of dispersed global work and the dependence on virtual communication, understanding how the loss of non-verbal cues affects intercultural communication remains limited. Furthermore, questions related to how global virtual work ties in with the use of English versus other languages, efforts to translate and interpret, or with the use of visual materials call for additional research.

Another example of communication transcending time and space is the use of email. Louhiala-Salminen, Charles, and Kankaanranta (2005) offered concrete examples of how different discourse styles can induce negative emotions between members of cultural groups, especially when they occur outside face-to-face situations. In their study on language practices in two international companies established through a cross-border merger between a Finnish and a Swedish company, the authors found several discursive dissimilarities between Finnish and Swedish employees. While the Finns felt that their use of language was "efficient, straight to the point", the Swedes found it "blunt and direct" (Louhiala-Salminen, Charles, and Kankaanranta 2005: 411). Furthermore, the Finns felt that the Swedish way of communicating was "endless discussion, avoiding conflict", while, according to the Swedes, it was a "dialogue, consensus, everybody participates" (Louhiala-Salminen, Charles, and Kankaanranta 2005: 408). This difference was also apparent in email communication: the Finns tended to use direct requests (e. g., "please comment on this"), while the Swedes preferred indirect alternatives (e. g., "could you please comment on this"). Culture-bound discursive features seem to spill over to multilingual communication, particularly to email communication transcending time and space. This suggests that interpretations in line with particular cultural assumptions are more likely to arise when the counterparts are not face-to-face.

Emails and the use of virtual platforms are widely used forms of communication also in global virtual teams, where members communicate across language, cultural, temporal, and spatial boundaries. In terms of non-verbal communication, global virtual teams offer fruitful ground to explore how the electronic nature of communicating impacts expressions and interpretations across language boundaries. In their study, Saarinen and Piekkari (2015) explored the interactions of Finnish managers and Chinese team members in virtual teams. Communication occurred through email, videoconferencing, Lync, Skype, conference calls, as well as live meetings. They found that the lack of nuance, emotion, and tone of voice when communicating virtually induced confusion. In addition, due to the limited amount of time for communication, stories were often left untold and small-talk between team members was minimized. This resulted in Finnish team leaders coming across as hard managers instead of people-oriented leaders, with negative effects on relationship-building. The apparent efficiency of communicating virtually across borders may hide its negative consequences for leadership, management, and intercultural communication.

The study by Saarinen and Piekkari (2015) also showed that especially Chinese team members found it important to establish trust and face-to-face relationships, but in virtual communication, these aspects were lost. Consequently, one Finnish manager reverted to extensive travel to meet the Chinese employees face-to-face, to enable direct communication. Furthermore, using English in virtual contexts and adhering to culturally contingent interpretations may increase the potential for miscommunication and disengagement and decrease the value expected from these groups. Managers may have to consider more diverse ways of communication with their teams. This often means spending time developing effective communication strategies to overcome the shortcomings of virtual communication, as shown in this study. Thus, virtual communication transcending time and space may not only result in misinterpretations but also in the loss of non-verbal communication.

Non-verbal communication can also be expressive of differences and tensions between team members. Hinds, Neeley, and Cramton (2014) noted power struggles between the German and the US members of a software development team. The US-based team members felt that their position was less well established compared to their German counterparts and that the ownership of the project was predominantly German. This was largely due to the German team members setting the timeline of the project, which caused US members to work during their holidays. In addition, documentation was often in German only and the English translation took an unreasonably long time to actualize. Some team members also complained about others not using English – the formal corporate language – in email conversations but relying on German. Power can be displayed either unintentionally or intentionally through non-verbal communication such as giving precedence to the German calendar or the act of language choice (German or English). Such power struggles activate fault lines that define sub-groupings, resulting in an "us versus them" attitude amongst team members (Hinds, Neeley, and Cramton 2014). These examples demonstrate how non-verbal communication can have implications not only for the power dynamics of the group but also for transparent and effective communication.

While we have mainly discussed how non-verbal communication, or the lack of it, can result in misinterpretations or tensions, it can also have a unifying effect. Barmeyer, Mayrhofer, and Würfl (2019: 800) discussed how informal information flows in multilingual organizations on a *time-island*. In Italy, this time-island is the coffee break – a time and place where employees gather spontaneously and information is exchanged more informally. In the United States, the boundary objects are water coolers; in Sweden, 'kitchens or lounges' (*fika*). It appears that a transition from formal to informal discourse happens in a similar fashion across cultures, through a mutual understanding of what a coffee cup or a water cooler symbolizes: decelerated social time, or what the authors call a time-island. Although the type of beverage being consumed may differ, the non-verbal spatial cues conveyed by this type of social situation appear to converge across cultures.

Thus, the development of new technologies has a significant effect on mutual understanding and draws attention to the importance of multimodality, i.e., the use of non-verbal communicative resources alongside or instead of verbal languages in intercultural communication.

2 Translation as practice and change

So far, we have highlighted how the visible, common corporate language blends with other languages and communicative resources, forming the communicative landscape of the multilingual workplace. As the iceberg model suggests, what cannot be seen is indeed difficult to control, though it is possible to shape and influence by accessing the resources associated with each level (see Figure 1). In this regard, we would argue that managing communication below the surface of the iceberg is not an impossible task, albeit a difficult one, requiring continuous effort.

Employing translation is part of this effort as it can be seen as a common response to the simultaneous existence of several languages in the multilingual workplace. At the same time, it is a way for all members of the multilingual organization to participate in managing language by translating culturally bound communication. In doing so, they create a joint meaning for individuals from different cultures. In Figure 1, the idea of collective management is shown by having translation permeate all layers of communication in the multilingual workplace. It is a collective process where different individuals within groups of employees, team leaders, and managers engage in translating words, texts, and meanings. Translation is then seen as a practice (just like the use of English is a collective, sometimes policy-bound, practice), which is likely to be concurrent in most multilingual contexts. We offer, here, a more comprehensive understanding of translation.

In daily parlance, translation is often associated with the reverbalization of meaning in another language. We define translation more comprehensively and holistically to include transformation, change, and transference of human and material resources across languages, organizations, institutional fields, countries, and other borders (Piekkari, Tietze, and Koskinen 2020). Translation also means changing the original word or text to make it accessible to receiving audiences in local (i.e., other language) contexts (Westney and Piekkari 2020). In this regard, the concept of translation captures on-going change and transformation of products, services, strategies, management models, organizational practices, and knowledge when the global meets the local. Furthermore, translation highlights the importance of translators who make choices about what and how to translate. These include professional translators or interpreters, but also employees who perform the role of the local translator beyond their normal work responsibilities. Thus, our definition encompasses both the metaphorical and interlingual meaning of translation (Piekkari, Tietze, and Koskinen 2020).

We encourage CCO scholars to integrate translation as a key aspect of the communicative constitution of multilingual workplaces (Piekkari, Tietze, and Koskinen 2020). It can be applied to understand how meanings are constructed, negotiated, and resisted both when employed in multilingual contexts or when used to translate meanings as they derive from non-verbal communications. As an agentic force, translation has a strong performative function in these organizations through which decisions are either concluded or propelled into particular trajectories of action. Translation shapes emergent relationships and constellations between individuals, groups as well as organizational units. While the use of English or the employment of situated discursive practices enables communication across language boundaries, recent studies provide convincing evidence that *ad hoc*, localized translation work is widely spread and a common response to the existence of language diversity (Ciuk,

James, and Śliva 2019; Kettunen 2016; Logemann and Piekkari 2015; Piekkari et al. 2013; Tietze, Tansley, and Helienek 2017).

These studies share a common understanding that translation is much more than a mechanistic act of changing a text from language A to language B. Rather, translation activity is seen as a discursive practice through which the multilingual organization is performed, constituted, and negotiated. On-going individual acts (Logemann and Piekkari 2015) and collective acts (Ciuk, James, and Śliva 2019; Kettunen 2016) of translation are agentic in that they have the potential to transform meanings, practices, and relationships. Translation work is also deeply imbued in particular socio-political contexts (e. g., Tietze, Tansley, and Helienek 2017). Thus, this contemporary stream of research argues that multilingual workplaces are spaces of agentic translation where meaning is made, manipulated, and rejected through acts of translation.

3 Discussion and conclusion

In this chapter, we have applied the CCO approach to the multilingual workplace and argued for the inclusion of languages (in plural), translation, and non-verbal communication in the communicative constitution of contemporary organizations. We have highlighted how organizational scripts are negotiated across languages, how translators can be regarded as authors and multilingual workplaces as linguascapes. All of the investigations pertaining to these matters are, implicitly or explicitly, based on Deetz's position (2003: 425) that "language is not the mirror of nature" – this is also true for how the English language and translation are used. However, this insight is yet to be fully incorporated into studies of the communicative complex character of multilingual organizations. Using English or translation are practices in situated contexts and as such they are not universal, objective, or more valuable than other communicative practices. In multilingual workplaces, this means that communicative acts involving the use (or non-use) of English, other languages, translation, and non-verbal communication are agentic in nature. Our intent in this chapter was to show that the existence of several languages necessitates actions, responses, and decisions, which contribute to the constitution of multilingual workplaces.

In order to understand communicative behavior in these workplaces, we have departed from a review of a variety of mainly empirical studies, which concerned themselves with the phenomenon of language diversity. Our review has drawn attention to the challenges and opportunities of managing multilingual workplaces that are characterized by multilingual, intercultural, and multimodal forms of communication. Once management is defined more broadly to include both a historically situated occupational role (i. e., the formal role of managers) as well as a collective practice, it becomes possible to speak about the collective process of meaning. We have also emphasized that non-verbal communication concomitantly informs the way employees interpret and shape situations.

Many contemporary organizations, including those with a more domestic orientation, are situated in multilingual realities. They struggle to find and use a shared language (often English) with all the disagreements and opportunities that this language brings along. Likewise, the relationship between English and "other" languages will remain an important aspect of today's workplaces. We have shown how specific discursive acts and decisions align groups or keep them apart. These shadow structures enable the sharing of knowledge but can also hinder it or change the body of knowledge through translation. Thus, understanding the communicative behavior, including when and to what effect translation is drawn upon, is a key aspect of the functionality of the multilingual workplace.

Returning to Hall's (1959) notion that much communication is silent, we argue that English is indeed treated as silent in that it has not been investigated or problematized outside an established, but still small, community of scholars. Translation in all its manifold manifestations is treated similarly, remaining silent in terms of the scholarly interest it evokes. Non-verbal means of communication are silent, too, but have (ironically) been more visible and researched by communication scholars. We see the current *status quo* in terms of blindness toward the dominant role of the English language as a serious gap in organization and management studies. A thought-provoking parallel can be drawn with blindness about how whiteness as an ethnic privilege is inscribed in the production of management and organization studies (Al Ariss et al., 2014). Al Ariss et al. (2014) argued that although whiteness in research is being hidden and unacknowledged, it shapes the process and outcome of research in significant ways, reducing social justice.

Therefore, based on our discussion of the multilingual workplace, we advocate a more holistic and inclusive understanding of communications within the CCO tradition. For example, managers of multilingual teams may wish to discuss the use of English, translation, and local languages openly and directly and develop practices that support the understanding of language use beyond technical correctness and expertise.

There is a well-established body of work within language-sensitive international business studies to draw on with regard to the status of use of English as the global language of knowledge, business, and management and its relationship with other languages through which multilingual organizations are linguascaped. Language practices also need to include translation (and interpreting) as well as acknowledge the existence and effect of non-verbal meanings. Such an integrated approach poses huge challenges not least in terms of gaining access but also in terms of the researchers' own language competences (for a detailed discussion, see Piekkari and Tietze 2016; Tietze 2018; Piekkari, Tietze, and Koskinen 2020). We strongly advocate that scholarship interested in communication and its constitutive performance concerns itself also with the phenomena and consequences of English, languages, translation, and non-verbal meanings as they unfold in multilingual workplaces and mingle with narratives, discourses, and authoring of organizations.

Our message poses a critical challenge for scholarship and practice because even domestically oriented organizations are increasingly becoming multilingual as evidenced, for example, by patters of migration. The flow of people across the globe changes patterns in workforce composition so that even domestic settings have long ceased to be monolingual and become more complex. We believe that a more holistic understanding of communication that comprises different languages, non-verbal acts, and translation is a necessary next step for scholarship of management communication.

4 References

Al Ariss, Akram, Mustafa Özbilgin, Ahu Tatli & April Kurt. 2014. Tackling whiteness in organization and management. *Journal of Managerial Psychology* 29(4). 362–368.

Andres, Hayward. 2002. A comparison of face-to-face and virtual software development teams. *Team Performance Management: An International Journal* 8(1–2). 39–48.

Barmeyer, Christoph, Ulrike Mayrhofer & Konstantin Würfl. 2019. Informal information flows in organizations: The role of the Italian coffee break. *International Business Review* 28(4). 796–801.

Bencherki, Nicolas, Fredérik Matte & Émilie Pelletier. 2016. Rebuilding babel: A constitutive approach to tongues. *Journal of Communications* 66(5). 766–788.

Blazejewski, Susanne. 2006. Transferring value-infused organizational practices in multinational companies: A conflict perspective. In Mike Geppert & Michael Mayer (eds.), *Global, national and local practices in multinational companies*, 63–104. Houndmills, UK: Palgrave Macmillan.

Canagarajah, Suresh. 1999. *Resisting linguistic imperialism in English teaching*. Oxford: Oxford University Press.

Ciuk, Sylwia, Philip James & Martyna Śliva. 2019. Micropolitical dynamics of interlingual translation processes in an MNC subsidiary. *British Journal of Management* 30(4). 926–942.

Cooren, François, James Taylor & Elizabeth Van Every. 2006. *Communication as organizing: Empirical and theoretical explorations in the dynamic of text and conversation*. Mahwah, NJ: Lawrence Erlbaum Associates.

Crystal, David. 2003. *English as a global language*. Cambridge: Cambridge University Press.

Deetz, Stanely. 2003. Reclaiming the legacy of the linguistic turn. *Organization* 10(3). 421–429.

DiStefano, Joseph & Martha Maznevski. 2000. Creating value with diverse teams in global management. *Organizational Dynamics* 29(1). 45–63.

Frederiksson, Riika, Wilhelm Barner-Rasmussen & Rebecca Piekkari. 2006. The multinational corporation as a multilingual organization. *Corporate Communications: An International Journal* 11(4). 406–423.

Hall, Edward. 1959. *The silent language*. Garden City, NY: Anchor Books.

Henderson, Kassis Jane. 2005 Language diversity in international management teams. *International Studies of Management & Organization* 35(1). 66–82.

Hinds, Pamela, Tsedal Neeley & Catherine Cramton. 2014. Language as a lightning rod: Power, contests emotion regulation and subgroup dynamics in global teams. *Journal of International Business Studies* 45(5). 536–363.

Kangasharju, Helena, Rebecca Piekkari & Risto Säntti. 2010. Yritysten kielipolitiikka—missä se piilee? [The language policy in international firms: Where is it hiding?]. In Hanna Lappalainen, Marja-Leena Sorjonen & Maria Vilkuna (eds.), *Kielellä on merkitystä* [Language matters], 136–157. Helsinki: Suomalaisen Kirjallisuuden Seura.

Karhunen, Päivi, Anne Kankaanranta, Leena Louhiala-Salminen & Rebecca Piekkari. 2018. Let's talk about language: A review of language-sensitive research in international management. *Journal of Management Studies* 55(6). 980–1013.

Kettunen, Jaana. 2016. Interlingual translation of the international financial reporting standards as institutional work. *Accounting, Organizations and Society* 56(C). 38–54.

Kroon, David, Joep Cornelissen & Eero Vaara. 2015. Explaining employees' reactions towards a cross-border merger: The role of English language fluency. *Management International Review* 55(6). 775–800.

Logemann, Minna & Rebecca Piekkari. 2015. Localize or local lies? The power of language and translation in the multinational corporation. *Critical Perspectives on International Business* 11(1). 30–53.

Lønsmann, Dorte. 2018. Embrace it or resist it? Employees' reception of corporate language policies. *International Journal of Cross Cultural Management* 17(1). 101–124.

Louhiala-Salminen, Leena, Mirjaliisa Charles & Anne Kankaanranta. 2005. English as a lingua franca in Nordic corporate mergers: Two case companies. *English for Specific Purposes* 24(4). 401–421.

Luo, Yadong & Oded Shenkar. 2006. The multinational organization as a multilingual community: Language and organization in a global context. *Journal of International Business Studies* 37(3). 321–339.

Marschan-Piekkari, Rebecca, Denise Welch & Lawrence Welch. 1999. In the shadow: The impact of language on structure, power and communication in the multinational. *International Business Review* 8(4). 421–440.

Maznevski, Martha & Katherine Chudoba. 2000. Bridging space over time: Global virtual team dynamics and effectiveness. *Organization Science* 11(5). 473–492.

Neeley, Tsedal. 2012a. Language matters: Status loss and achieved status distinctions in global organizations. *Organization Science* 24(2). 319–644.

Neeley, Tsedal. 2012b. Global business speaks English: Why you need a language strategy now. *Harvard Business Review* May. 1–10. https://hbr.org/2012/05/global-business-speaks-english (accessed 14 November 2020).

Nickerson, Christine. 2005. English as lingua franca in international business contexts. *English for Specific Purposes* 24(4). 367–380.

Phillipson, Robert. 1992. *Linguistic imperialism*. Oxford: Oxford University Press.

Piekkari, Rebecca & Susanne Tietze. 2016. Doing research on power and politics in multinational corporations (MNCs): A methodological perspective. In Florian A. A. Becker-Rittersbach, Susanne Blazejewski, Christoph Dörenbächer & Mike Geppert (eds.), *Micropolitics in the multinational corporation: Foundations, applications and new directions*, 208–240. Cambridge: Cambridge University Press.

Piekkari, Rebecca, Susanne Tietze & Kaisa Koskinen. 2020. Metaphorical and interlingual translation in moving organizational practices across languages. *Organization Studies* 41(9). 1311–1332.

Piekkari, Rebecca, Eero Vaara, Janne Tienari & Risto Säntti. 2005. Integration or disintegration? Human resource implications of a common corporate language decision in a cross-border merger. *International Journal of Human Resource Management* 16(3). 333–347.

Piekkari, Rebecca, Denise Welch, Lawrence Welch, Jukka-Pekka Peltonen & Tiina Vesa. 2013. Translation behaviour: An explorative study within a service multinational. *International Business Review* 22(5). 771–783.

Piller, Ingrid. 2007. Linguistic and intercultural communication. *Language and Linguistic Compass* 1(3). 208–226.
Piller, Ingrid. 2009. Intercultural communication. In Francesca Bargiella-Chiappini (ed.), *The Handbook of Business Discourse*, 317–331. Edinburgh: Edinburgh University Press.
Rocci, Daniel. 2009. *Global linguistics: An introduction*. Berlin: Walter de Gruyter.
Saarinen, Johanna & Rebecca Piekkari. 2015. Management is back! Cross-cultural encounters in virtual team. In Nigel Holden, Snejina Michailova & Susanne Tietze (eds.), *Routledge companion to cross-cultural management*, 420–440. Abingdon, UK: Routledge.
SanAntonio, Patricia. 1987. Social mobility and language use in an American company in Japan. *Journal of Language and Social Psychology* 6(3–4). 191–200.
Sanden, Guro. 2018. Ten reasons why corporate language policies can create more problems than they solve. *Current Issues in Language Planning* 21(1). 22–44.
Sanden, Guro & Anne Kankaanranta. 2018. "English is an unwritten rule here": Non-formalised language policies in multinational corporations. *Corporate Communication: An International Journal* 23(4). 544–566.
Schoeneborn, Dennis, Timothy Kuhn & Dan Kärreman. 2019. The communicative constitution of organizations, organizing and organizationality. *Organization Studies* 40(4). 475–496.
Scollon, Ron, Susanne Scollon & Rodney Jones. 2011. *Intercultural communication: A discourse approach*. Chichester, UK: John Wiley & Sons.
Steyaert, Chris & Maddy Janssens. 2013. Multilingual scholarship and the paradox of translation and language in management and organization studies. *Organization* 20(1). 131–142.
Steyaert, Chris, Anja Ostendorp & Claudine Gaibrois. 2011. Multilingual organizations as 'linguascapes': Negotiating the position of English through discursive practices. *Journal of World Business* 46(3). 270–278.
Sunaoshi, Yukako, Masaaki Kotabe & Janet Murray. 2005. How technology transfer really occurs on the factory floor: A case of a major Japanese automotive die manufacturer in the United States. *Journal of World Business* 40(1). 57–70.
Tenzer, Helene, Siri Terjesen & Anne-Wil Harzing. 2017. Language in international business: A review and agenda for future research. *Management International Review* 57(6). 815–854.
Tietze, Susanne. 2004. Spreading the management gospel – in English. *Language and Intercultural Communication* 4(3). 175–189.
Tietze, Susanne. 2008. International *management and language*. Abingdon, UK: Routledge.
Tietze, Susanne. 2018. Multilingual research, monolingual publications: Management scholarship in English only? *European Journal of International Management* 12(1–2). 28–45.
Tietze, Susanne & Rebecca Piekkari. 2020. Languages and cross-cultural management. In Betina Szkudlarek, Lawrence Romani, Joyce Osland & Dan Caprar (eds.), *The Sage handbook of contemporary cross-cultural management*, 181–195. London: Sage.
Tietze, Susanne, Carole Tansley & Emile Helienek. 2017. The translator as agent in management knowledge transfer. *International Journal of Cross Cultural Management* 17(1). 151–169.
Vaara, Eeero, Janne Tienari, Rebecca Piekkari & Risto Säntti. 2005. Language and the circuits of power in a merging multinational corporation. *Journal of Management Studies* 42(3). 595–623.
Vandermeeren, Sonja. 1999. English as lingua franca in written corporate communication: Findings from a European survey. In Francesca Bargiela-Chiappini & Christine Nickerson (eds.), *Writing business: Genres, media and discourse*, 273–291. Abingdon, UK: Routledge.
Welch, Denise & Lawrence Welch. 2019. Coping with multilingualism: Internationalization and the evolution of language strategy. *Global Strategy Journal* 9(4). 619–639.
Westney, Eleanor & Rebecca Piekkari. 2020. Reversing the translation flow: Moving organizational practices from Japan to the US. *Journal of Management Studies* 57(1). 57–86.

Philipp Dreesen and Julia Krasselt

21 Exploring and analyzing linguistic environments

Abstract: This chapter introduces a discursive perspective on the communicative environment of organizations and demonstrates how applied discourse linguistics and management partners can jointly explore discourses in order to improve how stakeholders can be addressed. The approach is illustrated by a case study on the communication management of energy discourses in Switzerland. Even if there are only a few transdisciplinary approaches to discourse analysis, it is shown how applied linguistics could offer its data-driven perspective to change the digital practices of management communication. After presenting key theoretical assumptions, the first part of this chapter deals with the practitioners' tasks from a transdisciplinary perspective. As for the second part, it shows how to cope with them by using applied discourse linguistics, which is shown in the conclusion as a way to change the practice of management communication.

Keywords: discourse linguistics; corpus linguistics; transdisciplinarity; simulation; patterns of language use

The chapter begins with an introduction to environment, discourse, and organization (1) and points out potential misunderstandings in the cooperation between practice and science (2 and 3). Since such cooperation is difficult and is therefore often avoided, an excellent opportunity is presented to develop new perspectives and solutions for problems of actor positioning in discourses (4). The research method *Applied Linguistics Discourse Analysis* helps by providing exemplary evidence for an implementation of the four modules: modeling, measuring, interpretation, and simulation (5). The chapter ends by showing which changes in practices of management communication are required (6).

1 Environment as discursive construction

Organizations communicate with, for, in, and through the environment in which they operate. Perspectives focusing on "with", "for," and "in" have gained considerable attention in the last twenty years (McPhee and Zaug 2000). In particular, the communicative constitution of organizations (CCO) approach shows the importance of language in the constitution of organizations (for an overview see Brummans et al. 2014; Putnam and Nicotera 2009). As Schoeneborn et al. (2014: 286) pointed out, "the proponents of this theoretical perspective are unified by the idea that organizations are invoked and maintained in and through communicative practices" (see also Cooren et al. 2011). What all these different "schools" of CCO have in common is that they develop a constructivist idea of organizations and their environment (Cooren 2012; Craig 1999).

The discursive turn (for an overview, see Putnam and Fairhurst 2001; Cooren 2015) also enabled an inverted perspective on the relationship between organizations and discourse by showing that organizations also communicate "through" their environment. Organizations are not only positioned in discourses but discourses also create positions through public communication. These organizational positions in discourses can be identified by patterns of language use. Analogous to Taylor and Van Every (2011: 33–64) showing that organizations can increase their authority and authoring through their interaction with other actors, this phenomenon can also be identified by analyzing the specific positions that are ascribed to organizations by others in public discourse. Suppose that "*WWF criticizes …*" is a statistically significant pattern of language use found in mass media, conclusions can be drawn regarding the attributed position of this environmental protection organization in discourse (namely that of the critic of certain aspects of energy and environmental policy). This position and the image associated with it could not be created by WWF alone, but by many different voices in public discourse. Through recurring references to these meaningful positions, they appear to become more and more authorized and can thus unfold communicative effects. Organizational communication management is therefore to be understood as being shaped by these discursive conditions.

It can be assumed that organizations do not exist in isolation, but are in a reciprocal relationship with their environment (Luhmann and Baecker 2018). This is put into practice, for example, by the St. Gallen fourth generation Management Model (Rüegg-Stürm and Grand 2015): the mediation between the inside of the organization and the environment is considered as the central function of management. Value creation is directly dependent on successful communication between the inside and outside (Theis-Berglmair 2013: 34) and management can be seen as a bundle of communicative tasks. Value creation thus is directly dependent on successful communication between the inside and outside (Stücheli-Herlach et al. 2017). Management is therefore a communicative practice that is implemented in a specific way in relation to the environment, more precisely, the various spheres of environment (Rüegg-Stürm and Grand 2015).

The organizational as well as the scientific challenge is that the discursive environment is initially a black box, of which, however, fundamental modes of operation are known from practice and research. Usually, organizations do not consider discourses as public spheres, communication contexts, or stakeholder networks but as public debate, discussion, or dialogue. Discourses are to be understood as a complex bundle of actors (e. g., WWF), topics (e. g., solar power), media (e. g., official websites), arguments (e. g., X due to Y), and discursive events (e. g., the Fukushima Daiichi nuclear disaster). Topics and the relevance of discourse events are not determined autonomously by actors (as the term *agenda setting* connotes) but developed dynamically in discourses.

The constitution of a topic thus depends on common ground, which manifests itself in shared knowledge and recurring discourse patterns. Common ground can be understood as what is considered sayable (Foucault 1981) by an actor in a medium at a certain point. In discourses, concepts of actor roles (e. g., critic), knowledge (e. g., canonical knowledge) and relevance (e. g., nuclear phase-out after Fukushima) are ultimately conveyed through patterns of language use (Bubenhofer 2009). Such knowledge and language structures emerge as orders of speech and have to be reflected as power structures of public communication. For this reason, we understand the environment as a network of discourses that consists of patterns of language usage. Our approach to analyzing these patterns for communication management tasks is called Applied Linguistic Discourse Analysis (DIA) as described in Dreesen and Stücheli-Herlach (2019).[1]

2 Practitioners' needs, wants, and demands

It is essential to develop a basic understanding of the mutual expectations of practice and science. This is a matter of debate in B2B (business to business) marketing research, where the theory-practice gap and the effects of digital transformation are discussed as discrepancies "between what practitioners need and what academia is investigating" (Mora Cortez and Johnston 2017: 93). For applied sciences, an understanding of their own offerings, on the one hand, and the practice partner's needs, on the other hand, is essential. For this purpose, the differentiation into needs, wants, and demands originating in B2C (business to consumer) marketing is revealing (Kotler, Armstrong, and Harris 2019: 7).[2] From an economic and marketing perspective, the tension between demands and wants is crucial: "Demands are wants for specific products that are backed up by the ability and willingness to buy them" (Kotler 1994: 4). The situation is different with regard to aspects of applied linguistics for environmental analysis. However, the following can probably be observed in many cases: there is a tension between the needs, wants, and demands of actors' ability to manage complex communication problems.

It is up to applied sciences to identify these differences and, if necessary, solve the conflict. For organizations, environmental analysis and communication tasks are not

---

1 In German DIA = Diskurslinguistik in Anwendung.
2 The key idea is based on Maslow's (1971) hierarchy of needs and has been adapted for B2C and B2B sales. While "need" in B2C sales is oriented more towards the needs of products and services essential for survival, "need" in B2B is oriented more towards the growth and sustainability of the organization.

ends in themselves, even if (successful) communication is constitutive of their existence. In most cases, the organization's management is not interested in the analytical tool itself (the linguistic analysis of the environment), but in solving a real-world communicative problem (e. g., to attain an overview of a specific discourse to influence a group of stakeholders). However, environmental analysis is a required step in identifying topics and addressing stakeholders,

It is therefore crucial to understand the basic principles of discourse, e. g., the shaping of actions by discourse, which can often be linked to the agent's communication routines as shown by structuring theory: "What agents know about what they do, and why they do it – their knowledgeability as agents – is largely carried in practical consciousness" (Giddens 1984: xxiii). This means that "as social actors, all human beings are highly 'learned' in respect of knowledge which they possess, and apply, in the production and reproduction of day-to-day social encounters; the vast bulk of such knowledge is practical rather than theoretical in character" (Giddens 1984: 22). In contrast to practical consciousness and tacit knowledge even professional actors generally lack theoretically systematized and empirically based knowledge about the discursive conditions in which they evolve and thus about the relevant conditions for action and the possible consequences of their action. In particular, the discursive effect of using formulaic expressions like *Stromkonzern Axpo* ('electricity company Axpo') or *Stromriese Axpo* ('power giant Axpo') are usually not well-known to the actors. Therefore, the analysis of these imprints will not be recognized by actors as a want or demand.

What kind of environmental analysis is wanted depends on the perspective: organizations begin their environmental analyses primarily according to the criteria of their own organizational routine and the ideological perspective from which they perceive and evaluate their environment. Above all, this includes media monitoring, media clipping, and evaluation based on references to the organization and its stakeholders. This can be described as introspection. But knowledge resources *within* the organization are too limited for certain problems. This reflection on introspection is the initial step for a transformative effect of discourse linguistics (for the field of governance practices, see Stirling 2016): Applied Linguistic Discourse Analysis (DIA) counters introspection with the possibility of extrospection, firstly by focusing on other media contexts, actors, topics, and periods of time with the corpus of results leading to a broader understanding of the environment. And, secondly, by using complementary data-based and data-driven analysis methods in order not to be guided too much by (introspective) presuppositions. In this sense, DIA first explores the environment and then analyzes it. As a result, the initial need and thus the demand change.

On the one hand, it is an improvement that organizations often demand networks, frame and issue analysis based on big data sets that should be representative (Phillips-Wren et al. 2015). Introspection is, on the other hand, only compatible with a data-driven approach if this perspective is openly reflected upon and one's own knowledge and competence gaps are acknowledged. Therefore, organizations need assistance to find and demand suitable solutions for their environment analyses. This can be achieved by cooperation between discourse researchers and reflective management practitioners. Another solution could be that discourse research transforms practical knowledge, e. g., through consulting, executive education, etc. Due to the widely differing methodological steps (e. g., discourse modeling, digital data analysis, simulating, see Section 5 of this chapter) and to the goal that researchers should also learn from practice, in the following, we focus on transdisciplinary cooperation.

3 Organizational needs and tasks

One of the primary goals of an organization is value creation. Since organizations consist of communication, the success of communicative tasks is directly linked to value creation. In professional domains, writing, speaking, and other communicative practices create economic value (Jakobs and Spinuzzi 2014). The theoretical background for this assumption in regard to discourse analysis is as follows: every message generated by an organization can be located within a discourse that itself consists of a multitude of messages (Stücheli-Herlach 2018: 180–181; McPhee and Zaug 2000). Each message is sent by an emitter. A discursive environment can therefore be understood as a network with sending/receiving nodes (organizations) and links (messages). In contrast to many other communication models, the discourse-analytical conception of communication is not a sender-receiver model, since in a discourse each "speaking actor" (here, an organization) is shaped by the dynamics and patterns of the many received messages of its discourse environment (Foucault 1982; Spitzmüller and Warnke 2011).

Ultimately, every organization is dependent on what has already been said in the discourse insofar as it needs to relate to what has been said (Holtzhausen and Zerfass 2015). The notion of a fully autonomous actor and its relationship to the stakeholder is modified by the notion of a subject that is specifically made to speak through discourse conditions. Thus, what one needs to know is one's own position and the discourse position of those involved. The value of a message, e. g., a tweet promoting renewable energy by an official public relations account, depends on its position within the discourse: Who speaks about renewable energy in what way? What are the dominant terms, phrases, emblematic issues (Stirling 2016), discursive markers (Viehöver 2006) as patterns of interpretation, etc. (Stücheli-Herlach and Perrin 2013: 29)? This comes close to the structural perspective (Saussure 1959) that the value (*valeur*) of a meaning depends on its relation to other meanings. For this reason, the urgent organizational task is to find out what relevant words, topics, arguments, examples, etc. constitute the dominant patterns of the discourse and by which actors they are reproduced (Moffitt 1999).

By understanding the theoretical assumptions of discourse analysis, the organizational tasks change: value creation is dependent on successful stakeholder management (Post, Preston, and Sachs 2002) and communication with stakeholders is a means of organization leadership (Freeman et al. 2010). Stakeholders have different communicative practices and are connected in dynamic ways, which need to be identified first (Stücheli-Herlach et al. 2017), e. g., through discourse network analysis (see Section 5.3 "simulation" and Section 6 of this chapter). Stakeholder networks are the result of communication. Coalitions and controversies between stakeholders emerge through the use of language. Stakeholders (actors), however, can have several roles with sometimes conflicting interests (e. g., supervisory authority, creditors, regulators). This role- and position-oriented stakeholder management changes the communicative tasks of the organization: the aim of writing must be defined by determining the position of the future text in public discourse (Stücheli-Herlach and Perrin 2013: 23). The approach called "message design" (Moffitt 1999) describes the steps from a key message and the strategic planning of text production processes to the product of narrative and argumentative patterns.

4 Transdisciplinary approach to applied discourse analysis

Applied Linguistic Discourse Analysis (DIA) is a transdisciplinary approach, where transdisciplinary is characterized by the close cooperation of scientific disciplines with non-scientific actors in order to solve socially relevant problems (Mittelstraß 2003; Perrin and Kramsch 2018). This is also described as "research about, for and with" practitioners (Cameron et al. 1992: 14–22). From a practitioner's perspective, these problems are highly complex, such as "policy analysis", "agenda setting", "issue monitoring", or "stakeholder analysis" (see Stücheli-Herlach et al. 2015).

DIA focuses on actors involved in social and especially professional practice (on professionality see Mieg 2003), e. g., as represented by a larger organizational unit with professional management. These actors are neither a subject nor an object of discourse-linguistic research. Instead, the joint accomplishment of tasks by scientists and professional practitioners leads to an ephemeral (i. e., transient) community of practice (see Wenger 1998), in which decisions must be related to and coordinated with each other (Sarangi and Van Leeuwen 2003). As a consequence, considerably more time and effort must be invested in building a common knowledge base and work processes as compared to conventionally institutionalized research groups (Fleck 1979) or consulting (see above).

5 Applied Linguistic Discourse Analysis

The following sections give an overview of the research method in general and its individual modules (see Figure 1). The modules are exemplified by a case study on the communication management of energy discourses in Switzerland:[3] the public affairs management of an energy company wants to improve the position of its company in the context of energy and environmental discussions. As explained above, one of the first steps in transdisciplinary cooperation is to develop a common basic understanding of the wants, demands, and needs. The company wants to take a position in the public perception of energy transition in Switzerland that is compatible with the company's objectives. The company faces the task of positioning itself in public debates on important political and economic issues related to energy transition. Demand: the company is a client of a media monitoring company and uses media clippings to become informed about selected topics, the company's own presentation, and previously identified stakeholders in the German-speaking national and regional mass media in Switzerland. Need: it is jointly determined that, first, a discourse-analytical orientation on the current energy discourses in German-speaking Switzerland is needed. This includes actors and their roles, stakeholders and their networks as well as topics and their verbalizations within the energy discourses. These objects of study are operationalized as follows.

The DIA research process is structured by three main questions, leading from the modeling of a specific discourse via the analysis of this discourse up to the simulation of the discourse: (1) how must a discourse be modeled to answer research questions that are theoretically and practically applicable? (see Module 1); (2) under which conditions do actors manifest themselves in the discourse? (see Modules 2 and 3); and (3) what are the possibilities and limitations for actions that must be expected within the discursive structure? (see Module 4).

Discourse as the object of research can be conceived in a constructivist manner as a model of social sign processes (a simulacrum in Barthes's [1967: 215] sense; see also Foucault 1982), which can be simulated by means of a text corpus that allows for the recording, analysis, and evaluation of public language use. Since there is no objective way of determining the basic population of a specific discourse, quantitative and qualitative analysis always refers to the corpus and cannot be considered representative from a theoretical point of view (Biber 1993). This view of discourse as a model allows for different discourse perspectives to be taken into account and thus helps the decision-making in strategic communication management.

---

[3] The following empirical results are based on the research project "Energy Discourses in Switzerland. Prerequisites for Change" (2016–2019), financed by the Swiss Federal Office of Energy (Stücheli-Herlach, Ehrensberger Dow, and Dreesen 2018).

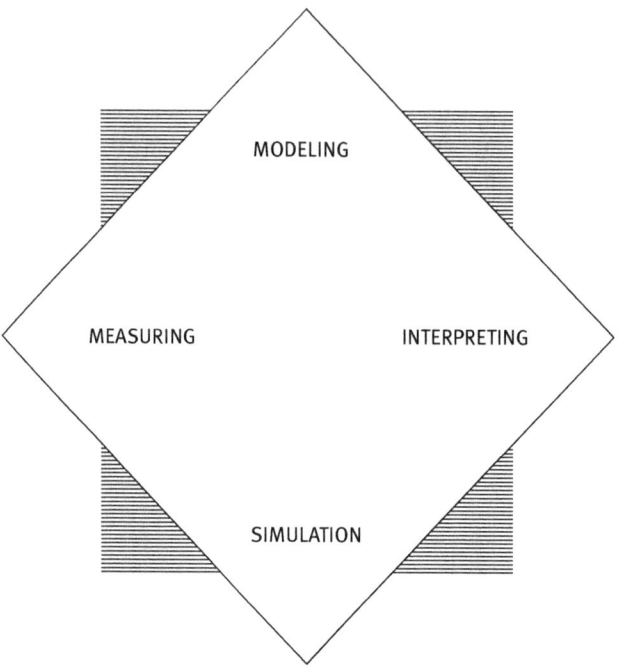

Figure 1: Modularized research method Applied Linguistic Discourse Analysis (DIA). The white diamond with the modules is incongruent with the hatched area, which symbolizes the transdisciplinary exchange between practice and research

5.1 Modeling (first module)

The first module serves to create a basis for the simulation of discursive formations and dynamics. It results in a corpus of texts of relevant discourse actors which will be used as a database for the identification of patterns of language use. Contrary to a decidedly self-referential perspective (e. g., manifested in typical media clipping tasks in which press articles mentioning the company are collected), an external perspective on the discourse under consideration is taken, which will be described in the following paragraphs.

Discourse modeling is more than a simple task of data collection. Firstly, it provides an initial orientation in an unmanageable number of utterances. Secondly, and even more importantly, modeling takes place in the collaboration of practitioners and research experts by defining parameters that determine the selection of relevant contributions to the discourse. The resulting corpus will form the basis for the solution of professional communicative problems. By making references to events and objects (such as political votes, law changes, environmental disasters, etc.), semantically relevant areas of discourse (i. e., words referring to important discourse concepts such as energy supply), relevant individual languages (Barthes 1967), and relevant discourse actors and their voices (Spitzmüller and Warnke 2011: 172–187) are identified. Media and text types that are situationally relevant to a specific discourse are considered (Clarke 2012). The aim is to create a snapshot of discourse processes on which the discourse actors' management decisions appropriate to the subject matter can be based (Rüegg-Stürm and Grand 2015: 46). Overall, the research module is carried out by reconstructing statements in contexts (Busse 2007) as a genesis of discourse.

Discourse modeling leads to an extensive list of relevant discourse actors which can be considered as the basic population for the planned discourse analysis. In order to allow for an abstraction above the level of individual actors, approaches such as traditional policy field analysis can be applied to achieve a manageable set of actor categories (Knoepfel et al. 2011). In the example of Swiss energy discourses, this results in the distinction between actors in policy formulation and implementation, actors as policy addressees and those affected by policy, actors in policy development and consultancy, and those involved in policy monitoring and mediation. The allocation of actors to categories enables not only the analysis of individual actors, but also of individual sub-areas of discourses.

Possible text sources include official websites, social media accounts, or official press releases that can be processed by using state-of-the-art data-crawling techniques or by using application programming interfaces that allow access to the relevant text data (Krasselt et al. 2020). Copyright and data protection issues as well as questions regarding the inclusion of paid or pay-walled content need to be considered. Annotating the texts that feed into the corpus with available metadata allows for downscaling this research module, e. g., by focusing on different time periods, topics, or categories of actors. In the example of Swiss energy discourse, 360 actors were sampled from the aforementioned policy fields. Their websites were taken as a textual database and were processed with a corpus linguist pipeline described in Krasselt et al. (2020).

Since actors in public communication take part in more than one discourse,[4] criteria need to be defined in order to include only those texts which are thematically connected to the discourse under consideration. Similar to media-clipping approaches, this can be achieved either by using a list of keywords that need to be present in a text or by applying machine learning algorithms such as topic modeling (Blei 2012) to a large discourse-unspecific corpus in order to find topics that point towards the discourse under consideration (see Table 1). Since texts referring to such topics do not necessarily need to contain typical keywords, they would have been missing in a traditional search-word-based approach to corpus compilation.

---

[4] This is, e. g., obviously the case with mass media actors who publish articles on a plethora of discourses.

Table 1: Selection of algorithmically determined topics containing words specific to energy discourses in Switzerland. Topics were calculated for a large, thematically unspecific corpus (Krasselt et al. 2020)

Topic No.	Words
topic 1	*Energie* ('energy'), *Schweiz* ('Switzerland'), *hoch* ('high'), *erneuerbar* ('renewable'), *verschieden* ('different'), *Entwicklung* ('development')
topic 2	*Energieforschung* ('energy research'), *Projekt* ('project'), *Gemeinde* (municipality'), *Energie* ('energy'), *CO2* ('CO2'), *hoch* ('high'), *Ziel* ('aim')
topic 3	*Abfall* ('waste'), *radioaktiv* ('radioactive'), *Schweiz* ('Switzerland'), *Nagra* ('Nagra'), *Risiko* ('risk'), *Schweizer* ('Swiss'), *Kanton* ('canton')
topic 4	*Wald* ('forest'), *Klimawandel* ('climate change'), *hoch* ('high'), *Land* ('country'), *Schweiz* ('Switzerland'), *Massnahme* ('measure'), *heute* ('today')

5.2 Measuring (second module) and Interpreting (third module)

In order to understand the linguistic and communicative conditions for actors' discourse contributions, the corpus is analyzed for patterns of language use. The carefully modeled corpus provides access to the textual surface of the discourse, which is characterized by exemplary language use that serves as a basis for understanding in public communication (Bubenhofer 2009). Patterns of language use become manifest as *re*curring words and phrases (e. g., the same word is frequently used by the majority of actors over a certain period of time) as well as frequently *co*occurring words and phrases, which refers to the frequent joint occurrence of two or more words in a text. They serve as syntagmatic manifestations of paradigmatic statements in a specific discourse (Bubenhofer 2009: 105–110). To a certain extent, such patterns of language use are already familiar to practitioners of management and are described by using notions like "buzzword" or "familiar expression". Such discourse characteristics that are already known can serve as a basis for formulating hypotheses about the discourse or for testing certain assumptions, e. g., regarding the prevalence of specific lexemes.

Measuring serves as an umbrella term for quantitative approaches, mainly elaborated in modern corpus linguistics but also in the field of natural language processing (Baker 2006; Bubenhofer 2009). Typical methods include the calculation of statistically significant keywords and collocations, the analysis of frequency and distribution of words and phrases, or the algorithmically driven calculation of topics. Depending on the way the corpus data is related to theories and categories existing prior to corpus analysis, those methods can be applied in either a corpus-driven or a corpus-based manner (McEnery and Hardie 2012; Tognini-Bonelli 2001). In a corpus-driven approach to discourse, the data forms the basic evidence for the inductive formation of hypotheses, generalizations, and theories. For instance, a list containing the frequency of *all* nouns in a corpus can point towards important concepts in the discourse. On the other hand, in a corpus-based approach, the data is used in a deductive manner to test hypotheses and to search for specific, pre-defined instances. A typical example would be the frequency analysis of pre-defined nouns denoting important concepts in a discourse. Following Bubenhofer (2009), Module 2 is conceptualized as a combination of both approaches, complemented by qualitative, non-standardized analytical methods.

In the example of Swiss energy discourses, the comparison of the vocabulary used by each actor category against a large, discourse-unspecific corpus (a so-called reference corpus) led to the identification of characteristic and actor-group-specific word usage, so-called keywords. A keyword in a corpus linguistic/data-driven understanding is conceptualized as a word that is "statistically more frequent in a particular corpus or text, when compared against another corpus" (Baker 2012: 255). Keywords can thus be utilized to measure a salient lexis characterizing the language use of discourse actors or groups of actors. Figure 2 shows the top fifty keywords for all four actors' categories in the corpus on energy discourses in Switzerland (A, B, C, D), as compared to a thematically unspecific Swiss reference corpus. Authorities and enforcement partners (B) show a rich departmental and institutional technical vocabulary reflecting the action being taken by and regulatory perspective of policy-related actors. Contrary, the keywords of business actors and interest groups (A) reveal evidence that addressees of energy policy and those affected by energy policy use their websites for self-representation by publishing business reports and success stories.

Interpreting: This third module provides a qualification of the functional meaning of these patterns within the discourse model. The module aims at understanding and explaining such patterns not only against the background of contexts and genealogy, but now also with regard to the formation in discourse, to the transformation in individual or several family-like discourse contributions, and to the composition in individual texts or sentences. The results are interpreted and weighed by relating them to situational discourse genealogy and individual findings. This results in a multilayered discursive network that explains and interprets interesting phenomena of language use in relation to other phenomena of language use (Dreesen et al. in press; Spitzmüller and Warnke 2011; Stücheli-Herlach et al. 2017). In addition, qualitative methods from interdisciplinary discourse studies are used (see Angermuller et al. 2014; Keller and Truschkat 2013). The use of patterns in single sources is interpreted as the discourse actors' role-specific, systemic-strategic action, which is why the methods deal extensively with questions related to the status of the actor in discourse (Dreesen et al. in press; Müller 2015; Roth 2014; Taylor and Cooren 1997).

By systematically capturing all words occurring within a certain distance to a specific actor's name (in the form of commonly used spellings and abbreviations – e.g., BFE and *Bundesamt für Energie* for the 'Swiss Federal Office of Energy'), patterns (so-called collocations) can be identified that reveal how actors are perceived by other discourse actors, which actions are attributed to them, and what meanings are

Figure 2: Top fifty keywords for all four actor categories in the corpus on energy discourses in Switzerland (A: economy, B: politics, C: journalistic media, D: science)

constructed around them. Table 2 shows the collocation profiles obtained for words denoting large Swiss energy suppliers. Firstly, the profiles contain typical economic action verbs such as *verkaufen* ('to sell'), *investieren* ('to invest'), and *übernehmen* ('to take over'). Secondly, the profiles share the same or similar descriptive terms, such as *Energiekonzern* ('energy company'), *Stromriese* ('power giant'), or *AKW-Betreiber* ('NPP operator'). Thirdly, a series of expressions relating to withdrawal from nuclear power are typical. The actor profiles obtained from the analysis are strongly economic in nature but are politicized with the associated emblem "nuclear power" (on this emblem concept in sociolinguistics, see Agha 2006: 235). The economic and political aspects are also reflected in the terms *Energiekonzern* ('energy company'), which bears a neutral connotation, and *Energieriese* ('electricity giant'), which bears an evaluative connotation.

Patterns of language use furthermore emerge from discourse actors' mutual references. Such mutual referencing in texts can be analyzed by means of social network analysis, a classic paradigm in social and political sciences, with a focus on the rela-

Table 2: Collocation profiles of words denoting large Swiss energy suppliers

Action verbs	Descriptive terms	Emblems
verkaufen 'to sell'	*Energiekonzern* 'energy company''	Beznau
beteiligen 'to participate'	*Betreiberin* 'operator'	Kaiseraugst
abkaufen 'to buy'	*Stromkonzern* 'electricity company'	Fessenheim
investieren 'to invest'	*Stromriese* 'power giant'	AKW
Entscheiden 'to decide'	*Energieriese* 'energy giant'	*Sicherheitsnachweis* 'safety certificate'
übernehmen 'to take over'	*AKW-Betreiber* 'NPP operator'	*Abschaltung* 'decommissioning'

tionships between actors, on patterns in these relationships, and on the theoretical modeling of these patterns (Carrington, Scott, and Wasserman 2005; Freeman 2004; Scott and Carrington 2011). In a discourse-linguistic understanding, such relationships can, for example, be operationalized in a network that is based on the mutual mentioning of actors. By applying network analytical measures, classical roles such as gatekeeper/broker, star, and coordinator (Friemel 2008: 185) can be quantitatively determined and interpreted in terms of discourse linguistics (Dreesen et al. in press).

Figure 3 shows a directed network in which nodes represent actors and arrows represent the reference of one actor by another actor (e.g., when the Swiss Federal Institute of Technology, ETHZ, is mentioned in a text from the BFE, then both nodes will be connected by an arrow pointing from BFE to ETHZ). The size of each node is a function of its centrality (so-called *eigenvektor* centrality, a typical network theoretical measure signaling the importance of nodes in networks, Bonacich and Lloyd 2001). Actors belonging to the category "policy addressees and those affected" (i.e., business and interest groups) stand out, especially energy service providers and manufacturers (Swissgrid, BKW, Axpo, Alpiq). In addition, a number of actors from "policy formulation and implementation" (authorities and enforcement partners in particular individual Swiss cantons (e.g., kanton_zh, kanton_ag).) stand out, in particular individual Swiss cantons. Centrality can therefore be used as a measure to identify stars in the energy discourse. These stars include the Swiss Federal Office of Energy (SFOE), which is remarkable from a Swiss perspective because energy policy is primarily implemented at a cantonal level (e.g., all cantons have their own energy laws and regulations).

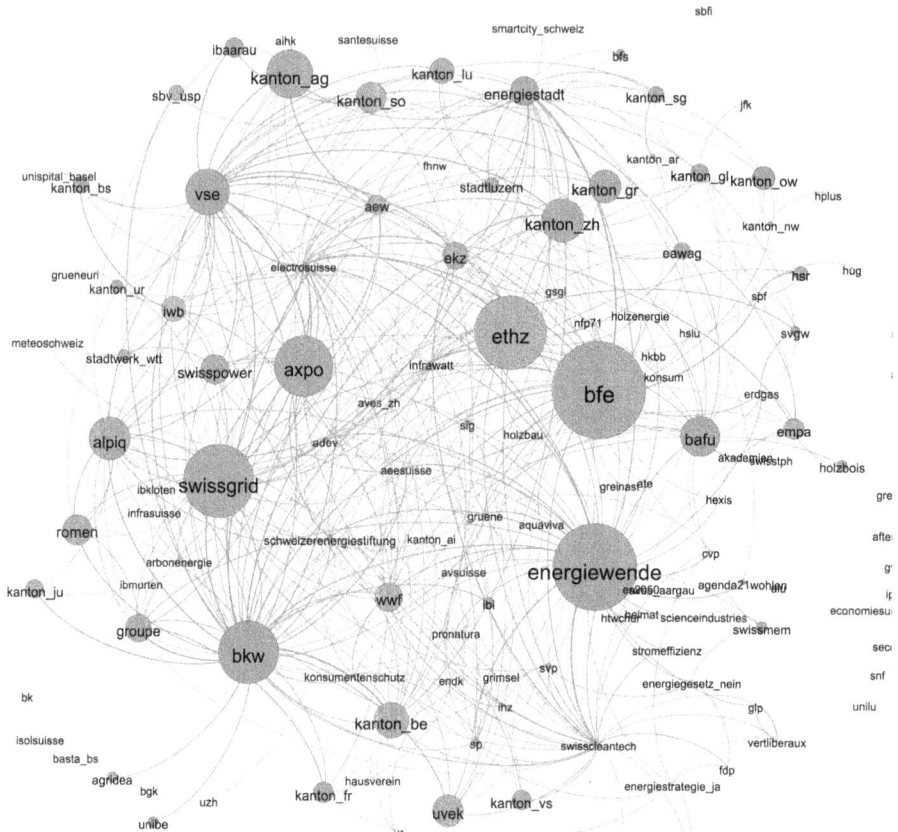

Figure 3: Directed network of mutual actor references. Nodes symbolize actors. The larger a node, the more often the corresponding actor is mentioned in the texts of other actors

5.3 Simulation (fourth module)

The last module aims to simulate discourses. This is the practical perspective on discourse outlined above as a model of social sign processes. The measurement and interpretation findings are triangulated (Denzin 2009; Flick 2011) by reflecting on the discourse against the background of scientific and practical perspectives (described in detail in Dreesen and Stücheli-Herlach 2019: 128, 137–139). We integrate the findings and challenge them with practical questions, e. g., how do we manage to communicate in a similar way as a successful organization? Which linguistic expressions are somewhat unsuitable because they are hardly ever used?

Simulation is achieved by means of "joint displays" (Kuckartz 2014: 136–148), i.e., condensed diagrammatic representations of results obtained in Modules 2 and 3. Such forms of presentation allow the visualization of *more than one* discourse characteristic (e.g., regarding keywords, collocations, and mutual references) and reveal the option of adopting different perspectives on the same question. The simulation takes place in presenting and explaining the theoretical assumptions and discussing the data collection, methods, and results with the practitioners. In the face of complex environmental and discourse-related decision-making situations, actors in practice have to simulate various possible solutions in order to compensate for the inevitable lack of knowledge about success factors. In this practical-theoretical context, simulation does not mean prediction (i.e., empirical forecasting), but rather experimental testing of both possible and desirable solution perspectives for a practical problem:

Case 1: an actor can reflect on similarities to other actors that arise due to the similar use of language patters (e.g., keywords, collocations) and can decide whether similar representations (e.g., between competitors) are wanted. Simulation then means taking up new perspectives by playing through several discourse positions.

Case 2: conversely, it is possible to simulate discourse positions on the basis of discourse networks, e.g., by finding out which discourse position is hardly represented at a certain national or federal level.

Regarding the question of communication strategies, a simulation of different procedures of "occupying terms" or of the competition of meanings with regard to important concepts such as *Ausstieg aus der Atomkraft* ('phasing out nuclear power') or *Förderung nachhaltiger Energie* ('promoting renewable energies') could be helpful (Klein 2014). To this end, the roles of the various actors could be determined on the basis of the actor network presented above and developed with regard to desired discourse coalitions with individual actors.

6 Current and future changes in practices of management communication

Applied Linguistic Discourse Analysis has two goals: (1) to understand the communicative conditions of a discursive environment and (2) to improve the communicative actions of practitioners by approaching relevant forms of professional communication in a transdisciplinary way. In order to achieve these goals, specific changes in tasks and practices of management communication are required that have an impact on wants, demands, and needs.

6.1 Extrospection

(1) The change from introspection to extrospection proceeds in the shift from data collection (media monitoring/media clipping) to the compilation and use of digital text corpora. Linguistically annotated corpora offer a wide range of analysis options that go far beyond data-based analysis. The continuous creation of digital text corpora is a central task for modern communication management.

(2) Nearly all search options (e. g., search engines, media archives, media clippings) for stakeholders, relevant topics, or mention of one's own organization in media are based on pre-defined search terms. Thus, a certain idea of what is relevant and possibly causal in the organizational environment is defined *a priori*. However, it is necessary to determine (e. g., by topic modeling) which objects, topics, and events shape the discursive conditions under which stakeholders express themselves.

6.2 Dynamics

(3) The continuous compilation of a digital text corpus prevents the organization from imagining its environment as static. While daily media monitoring can identify the current situation, the changeability and variability of discourses only become visible through larger data volumes over time.

(4) The stakeholder concept should be modified in such a way that actors from domains that seem irrelevant at first glance – e. g., in the case of energy discourses not only actors from economy and politics, but also civil society (NGOs) and science – should also be taken into account. The answer to the question of the relevance and role of actors and the status of stakeholders should come at the end, not at the beginning of an environment analysis.

Extrospection and dynamics are reflected in the discourse model, which can be used to locate organizations in a larger network. Simulations can be used to demonstrate how the use of language leads to positioning within the discourse.

7 References

Agha, Asif. 2006. *Language and social relations*. Cambridge: Cambridge University Press.
Angermuller, Johannes, Martin Nonhoff, Eva Herschinger, Felicitas Macgilchrist, Martin Reisigl, Juliette Wedl, Daniel Wrana & Alexander Ziem (eds.). 2014. *Diskursforschung: ein interdisziplinäres Handbuch* (DiskursNetz), vol. 2. Bielefeld: Transcript.
Baker, Paul. 2006. *Using corpora in discourse analysis*. London & New York: Continuum.
Baker, Paul. 2012. Acceptable bias? Using corpus linguistics methods with critical discourse analysis. *Critical Discourse Studies* 9(3). 247–256.
Barthes, Roland. 1967. The structuralist activity. In Roland Barthes, *Critical Essays*, 213–220. Evanston, IL: Northwestern University Press.

Biber, Douglas. 1993. Representativeness in corpus design. *Literary and Linguistic Computing* 8(4). 243–257.

Blei, David M. 2012. Probabilistic topic models. *Communications of the ACM* 55(4). 77.

Bonacich, Phillip & Paulette Lloyd. 2001. Eigenvector-like measures of centrality for asymmetric relations. *Social Networks* 23(3). 191–201. https://doi.org/10.1016/S0378-8733(01)00038-7.

Brummans, Boris H. J. M., François Cooren, Daniel Robichaud & James R. Taylor. 2014. Approaches to the communicative constitution of organizations. In Linda L. Putnam & Dennis K. Mumby (eds.), *The Sage handbook of organizational communication: Advances in theory*, 173–194. Thousand Oaks, CA: Sage.

Bubenhofer, Noah. 2009. *Sprachgebrauchsmuster. Korpuslinguistik als Methode der Diskurs- und Kulturanalyse* (Sprache Und Wissen 4). Berlin & New York: De Gruyter.

Busse, Dietrich. 2007. Diskurslinguistik als Kontextualisierung. Methodische Kriterien. Sprachwissenschaftliche Überlegungen zur Analyse gesellschaftlichen Wissens. In Ingo H. Warnke (ed.), *Diskurslinguistik nach Foucault. Theorie und Gegenstände*, 81–105. Berlin & New York: De Gruyter.

Cameron, Deborah, Elizabeth Frazer, Penelope Harvey, M. B. H Rampton & Kay Richardson. 1992. *Researching language: Issues of power and method*. London: Routledge.

Carrington, Peter J., John Scott & Stanley Wasserman (eds.). 2005. *Models and methods in social network analysis*. Cambridge: Cambridge University Press.

Clarke, Adele E. 2012. *Situationsanalyse: Grounded Theory nach dem Postmodern Turn*. Wiesbaden: Springer.

Cooren, François. 2012. Communication theory at the center: Ventriloquism and the communicative constitution of reality. *Journal of Communication* 62(1). 1–20.

Cooren, François. 2015. *Organizational discourse: Communication and constitution*. Cambridge: Polity Press.

Cooren, François, Timothy Kuhn, Joep P. Cornelissen & Timothy Clark. 2011. Introduction to the special issue: Communication, organizing and organization: An overview. *Organization Studies* 32(9). 1149–1170.

Craig, Robert T. 1999. Communication theory as a field. *Communication Theory* 9(2). 119–161.

Denzin, Norman K. 2009. *The research act: A theoretical introduction to sociological methods*. New Brunswick, NJ: AldineTransaction.

Dreesen, Philipp, Julia Krasselt, Maren Runte & Peter Stücheli-Herlach. In press. Operationalisierung der diskurslinguistischen Kategorie "Akteur". Triangulation und Reflexion eines drängenden Desiderats der angewandten Forschung. In Matthias Meiler & Martin Siefkes (eds.), *Linguistische Methodenreflexion im Aufbruch. Beiträge zu einer aktuellen Diskussion im Schnittpunkt von Ethnographie und Digital Humanities, Multimodalität und Mixed Methods* (Linguistik – Impulse & Tendenzen). Berlin & Boston, MA: De Gruyter.

Dreesen, Philipp & Peter Stücheli-Herlach. 2019. Diskurslinguistik in Anwendung. Ein transdisziplinäres Forschungsdesign für korpuszentrierte Analysen zu öffentlicher Kommunikation. *Zeitschrift für Diskursforschung* 7(2). 123–162.

Fleck, Ludwik. 1979. *Genesis and development of a scientific fact*. Chicago, IL: University of Chicago Press.

Flick, Uwe. 2011. *Triangulation: Eine Einführung* (Qualitative Sozialforschung 12). Wiesbaden: VS Verlag.

Foucault, Michel. 1981. The order of discourse. In Robert Young (ed.), *Untying the text: A post-structuralist reader*, 51–78. Boston, MA: Routledge & Kegan Paul.

Foucault, Michel. 1982. *The archaeology of knowledge*. New York: Pantheon Books.

Freeman, Linton. 2004. *The development of social network analysis: A study in the sociology of science*. Vancouver, BC: Empirical Press.

Freeman, R. Edward. 1984. *Strategic management: A stakeholder approach*. Boston, MA: Pitman.
Freeman, R. Edward, Jeffrey S. Harrison, Andrew C. Wicks, Bidhan L. Parmar & Simone de Colle. 2010. *Stakeholder theory: The state of the art*. Cambridge: Cambridge University Press.
Friemel, Thomas N. 2008. Netzwerkanalytische Methoden zur Identifizierung von Kommunikationsrollen. In Christian Stegbauer (ed.), *Netzwerkanalyse und Netzwerktheorie. Ein neues Paradigma in den Sozialwissenschaften*, 179–190. Wiesbaden: Springer.
Giddens, Anthony. 1984. *The constitution of society: Outline of the theory of structuration*.
Holtzhausen, Derina & Ansgar Zerfass. 2015. Strategic communication: Opportunities and challenges of the research area. In Derina Rhoda Holtzhausen & Ansgar Zerfass (eds.), *The Routledge handbook of strategic communication*, 3–17. New York: Routledge.
Jakobs, Eva-Maria & Clay Spinuzzi. 2014. 20 Professional domains: Writing as creation of economic value. In Eva-Maria Jakobs & Daniel Perrin (eds.), *Handbook of writing and text production*. Berlin & Boston, MA: De Gruyter.
Keller, Reiner & Inga Truschkat (eds.). 2013. *Methodologie und Praxis der Wissenssoziologischen Diskursanalyse. Band. 1: Interdisziplinäre Perspektiven* (Theorie und Praxis der Diskursforschung). Wiesbaden: Springer VS.
Klein, Josef (ed.). 2014. *Grundlagen der Politolinguistik. Ausgewählte Aufsätze* (Sprachwissenschaft). Berlin: Frank & Timme.
Knoepfel, Peter, Corinne Larrue, Frédéric Varone & Sylvia Veit. 2011. *Politikanalyse*. Opladen: Budrich.
Kotler, Philip. 1994. *Marketing management: Analysis, planning, implementation, and control*, 8th edn. Englewood Cliffs, NJ: Prentice Hall.
Kotler, Philip, Gary Armstrong & Lloyd C. Harris. 2019. *Principles of marketing*, 8th European edn. Hoboken, NJ: Pearson.
Krasselt, Julia, Philipp Dreesen, Matthias Fluor, Cerstin Mahlow, Klaus Rothenhäusler & Maren Runte. 2020. Swiss-AL: A multilingual Swiss web corpus for applied linguistics. In *Proceedings of the 12th Language Resources and Evaluation Conference*, 4138–4144. Marseille, France. https://www.aclweb.org/anthology/2020.lrec-1.510/ (accessed 29 November 2020).
Kuckartz, Udo. 2014. *Mixed Methods: Methodologie, Forschungsdesigns und Analyseverfahren*. Wiesbaden: Springer VS.
Luhmann, Niklas & Dirk Baecker (eds.). 2018. *Organization and decision*. Cambridge: Cambridge University Press.
Maslow, Abraham H. 1971. *The farther reaches of human nature*. New York: Viking Press.
McEnery, Tony & Andrew Hardie. 2012. *Corpus linguistics: Method, theory and practice* (Cambridge Textbooks in Linguistics). Cambridge & New York: Cambridge University Press.
McPhee, Robert D. & Pamela Zaug. 2000. The communicative constitution of organizations: A framework for explanation. *Electronic Journal of Communication* 20(1–2). http://www.cios.org/EJCPUBLIC/010/1/01017.html (accessed 5 December 2019).
Mieg, Harald A. 2003. Problematik und Probleme der Professionssoziologie. In Harald A. Mieg & Michaela Pfadenhauer (eds.), *Professionelle Leistung – professional performance: Positionen der Professionssoziologie* (Wissen und Studium Sozialwissenschaften), 11–46. Konstanz: UVK Verl.-Ges.
Mittelstraß, Jürgen. 2003. *Transdisziplinarität: Wissenschaftliche Zukunft und institutionelle Wirklichkeit* (Konstanzer Universitätsreden 214). Konstanz: UVK, Univ.-Verl.
Moffitt, Mary Anne. 1999. *Campaign strategies and message design*. Westport, CT: Praeger.
Mora Cortez, Roberto & Wesley J. Johnston. 2017. The future of B2B marketing theory: A historical and prospective analysis. *Industrial Marketing Management* 66. 90–102.
Müller, Marcus. 2015. *Sprachliches Rollenverhalten: Korpuspragmatische Studien zu divergenten Kontextualisierungen in Mündlichkeit und Schriftlichkeit* (Sprache Und Wissen 19). Berlin & Boston: De Gruyter.

Perrin, Daniel & Claire Kramsch. 2018. Introduction: Transdisciplinarity in applied linguistics. *AILA Review* 31. 1–13.
Phillips-Wren, Gloria, Lakshmi S. Iyer, Uday Kulkarni & Thilini Ariyachandra. 2015. Business analytics in the context of big data: A roadmap for research. *Communications of the Association for Information Systems* 37.
Post, James E., Lee E. Preston & Sybille Sachs. 2002. Managing the extended enterprise: The new stakeholder view. *California Management Review* 45(1). 6–28.
Putnam, Linda L. & Gail T. Fairhurst. 2001. Discourse analysis in organizations: Issues and concerns. In Fredric M. Jablin & Linda L. Putnam (eds.), *The new handbook of organizational communication: Advances in theory, research, and methods*, 78–136. Thousand Oaks, CA: Sage.
Putnam, Linda L. & Anne M. Nicotera. 2009. *Building theories of organization: The constitutive role of communication*. London: Routledge.
Roth, Kersten Sven. 2014. *Diskursrealisationen: Grundlegung und methodischer Umriss einer pragmatisch-interaktionalen Diskurssemantik*. Berlin: Erich Schmidt Verlag.
Rüegg-Stürm, Johannes & Simon Grand. 2015. *Das St. Galler Management-Modell. 4. Generation*, 2nd edn. Bern: Haupt.
Sarangi, Srikant & Theo Van Leeuwen. 2003. Applied linguistics and communities of practice: Gaining communality or losing disciplinary autonomy? In *Applied linguistics and communities of practice: Selected papers from the annual meeting of the British Association for Applied Linguistics, Cardiff University, September 2002*, 1–8. London & New York: British Association for Applied Linguistics, in association with Continuum.
Saussure, Ferdinand de. 1959. *Course in general linguistics*. New York: Philosophical Library.
Schoeneborn, Dennis, Steffen Blaschke, François Cooren, Robert D. McPhee, David Seidl & James R. Taylor. 2014. The three schools of CCO thinking: Interactive dialogue and systematic comparison. *Management Communication Quarterly* 28(2). 285–316.
Scott, John & Peter J. Carrington (eds.). 2011. *The Sage handbook of social network analysis*. Thousand Oaks, CA: Sage.
Spitzmüller, Jürgen & Ingo H. Warnke. 2011. *Diskurslinguistik. Eine Einführung in Theorien und Methoden der transtextuellen Sprachanalyse*. Berlin & Boston: De Gruyter.
Stirling, Andrew. 2016. Knowing doing governing: Realizing heterodyne democracies. In Jan-Peter Voss & Richard Freeman (eds.), *Knowing governance*, 259–289. London: Palgrave Macmillan.
Stücheli-Herlach, Peter. 2018. Message Design: Der Prozess zur wirkungsvollen Botschaft einer Organisation. In Annika Schach & Cathrin Christoph (eds.), *Handbuch Sprache in den Public Relations*, 171–190. Wiesbaden: Springer.
Stücheli-Herlach, Peter, Caroline Brüesch, Sandra Fuhrimann & Anna Schmitt. 2015. Stakeholder-Management im Netzwerk politischer Kommunikation. Forschung für ein integriertes Führungsmodell im öffentlichen Sektor. *Jahrbuch der Schweizerischen Verwaltungswissenschaften*. 77–101.
Stücheli-Herlach, Peter, Caroline Brüesch, Sandra Fuhrimann & Anna Schmitt. 2017. *Stakeholder-Management im Netzwerk politischer Kommunikation. Forschung für ein integriertes Führungsmodell im öffentlichen Sektor*. Winterthur: ZHAW Zürcher Hochschule für Angewandte Wissenschaften.
Stücheli-Herlach, Peter, Maureen Ehrensberger-Dow & Philipp Dreesen. 2018. *Energiediskurse in der Schweiz. Anwendungsorientierte Erforschung eines mehrsprachigen Kommunikationsfelds mittels digitaler Daten* (Working Papers in Applied Linguistics 16). Winterthur: ZHAW Zürcher Hochschule für Angewandte Wissenschaften.
Stücheli-Herlach, Peter & Daniel Perrin. 2013. Schreiben mit System. In Peter Stücheli-Herlach & Daniel Perrin (eds.), *Schreiben mit System*, 15–38. Wiesbaden: Springer Fachmedien Wiesbaden.

Taylor, James R. & François Cooren. 1997. What makes communication 'organizational'? How the many voices of a collectivity become the one voice of an organization. *Journal of Pragmatics* 27(4). 409–438.

Taylor, James R. & Elizabeth J. Van Every. 2011. *The situated organization: Case studies in the pragmatics of communication research*. New York: Routledge.

Theis-Berglmair, Anna Maria. 2013. Why "public relations", why not "organizational communication"? In Ansgar Zerfass, Lars Rademacher & Stefan Wehmeier (eds.), *Organisationskommunikation und Public Relations. Forschungsparadigmen und neue Perspektiven*, 27–42. Wiesbaden: Springer VS.

Tognini-Bonelli, Elena. 2001. *Corpus linguistics at work*. Amsterdam: John Benjamins. https://doi.org/10.1075/scl.6 (accessed 5 June 2020).

Viehöver, Willy. 2006. Diskurse als Narrationen. In Reiner Keller, Andreas Hirseland, Werner Schneider & Willy Viehöver (eds.), *Handbuch sozialwissenschaftliche Diskursanalyse*, vol. 1, 2nd edn., 179–208. Wiesbaden: VS Verlag.

Wenger, Etienne. 1998. *Communities of practice: Learning, meaning, and identity*. Cambridge: Cambridge University Press.

Jody L. S. Jahn
22 Managing high reliability organizations

Abstract: Theorizing on high reliability organizations (HRO) explains how members construct an interpretation system to notice emerging problems and take responsive actions to avoid failures. HRO theorizing tends to under-explain the role of structures (e.g., texts) and hierarchy in how HROs and members interpret and act on *weak signals* (i.e., easy-to-ignore errors or fragments of information). This chapter highlights the roles of materiality- and status-related communication barriers (e.g., texts, hierarchy) in high reliability processes. Specifically, the chapter considers how practical knowledge about weak signals is constituted in communication practice. The first half of the chapter reviews HRO literature explaining how members *interpret* and *voice* weak signals, and *structure* their actions around them. The chapter then applies an agential realism lens to theorize how organizational actors, objects (and other forms of materiality) combine their agencies to co-construct weak signals and what to do about them, through processes of *positioning*, *ventriloquization*, and *presentification*.

Keywords: high reliability organization (HRO); weak signal; communication constitutes organization (CCO); ventriloquization; presentification; positioning

The primary contribution of this chapter is that it addresses management communication regarding weak signals in the high reliability organization (HRO) context. The role of structures (e.g., texts) and hierarchy in how HRO/members interpret and act on *weak signals* – that is, small problems or operational developments that are easy to ignore – remains underexplored in HRO theorizing, which is largely formulated outside the communication field. This chapter brings materiality- and status-related communication barriers (e.g., texts, hierarchy) back into the picture to better consider how practical knowledge about weak signals is constituted in the communication practice. A view that considers that communication is constitutive of organizing processes (CCO) refines our theoretical explanations of management processes in HROs. In particular, an agential-realist lens draws attention to interaction dynamics that impact how HRO members co-construct weak signals and what to do about them, which can help managers gain self-reflexivity about how HRO communication is enabled or hindered.

This chapter proceeds as follows: the first section defines and introduces the importance of weak signals in HRO theorizing. The second section summarizes extant HRO theorizing explaining how members *interpret* and *voice* weak signals, as well as *structure* their actions to notice and address them. To contribute to the HRO work, I suggest viewing weak signals through an agential-realist CCO lens. Agential realism considers how organizational actors, objects (and other forms of materiality) combine their agencies to influence the direction of a conversation as they are made present in ongoing talk. The final section theorizes a relational view of communicating weak signals as members: (1) *position* the importance of weak signals, which sheds light on why it might be face threatening for organization members to communicate them, (2) *ventriloquize* structures (e. g., rules, roles) that assert jurisdiction over weak signals, which helps explain how members might negotiate authority over deciding what to do about them, and (3) *presentify* structures (e. g., rules, roles) to decide how to act on weak signals, which addresses how members situate the meaning of weak signals and how to manage them.

1 High reliability organizations

High reliability organizations (HROs) are characterized by their ability to avoid catastrophic failures in fluctuating, ambiguous conditions that make accidents and fatalities likely (Rochlin 1993; Weick and Sutcliffe 2015). High reliability organizations are unique because they must – and regularly do – operate without error amid varied, highly consequential hazards, and under time pressure (Rochlin 1993). Examples include aircraft carriers, nuclear power plants, and wildland firefighting (among others). Success for HROs is a "dynamic non-event" (Weick 1987: 119), meaning that when operations run smoothly, it is difficult to detect exactly which actions contributed to success; conversely, it is difficult to know how close members came to failures. Therefore, HROs manage a precarious tension between avoiding accidents but potentially not knowing why, and experiencing failure events that provide valuable lessons but might endanger lives. As such, one of the central safety challenges HROs face is making hazards, as well as mistakes and successful actions visible.

Value creation for HROs lies in how their operations *reliably* avoid catastrophes, particularly through members exercising their practical knowledge and drawing from organizational resources to catch and respond to *weak signals*. Weak signals refer to information that is easy to ignore due to its potential to blend in with other "noise", and can include minor mistakes or subtle operational developments (Brizon and Wybo 2009). For example, Weick and Sutcliffe (2007) described a case in which Davis-Besse nuclear power plant workers noticed "mysterious" rust particle build-up that required them to change their air and water filters every two days over the course of a few years. However, the workers did not know the filters were supposed to last two months; thus, they did not know that the amount of rust particle accumulation they were seeing was abnormally high. It turned out the rust particles came from corrosion from the metal lining of a storage area meant to house radioactive material. In effect, the rust build-up was a weak signal that the critical power plant infrastructure was breaking down.

As this example illustrates, weak signals are important because they could comprise a cascade of small errors or minor actions possibly leading to a catastrophic failure. Such signals are difficult to detect because they might not be salient to organization members who are not already attuned to look for them, making one's practical knowledge and experience essential for detecting them. Weak signals also are difficult to act on because they might be construed as unimportant, partial information, or as tentative conclusions during the time when it is most crucial to take action on them (Weick 1987). Both their lack of salience, and their potential failure to garner a threshold of interest from multiple organization members, makes weak signals one of the key safety and communication challenges in high reliability organizing.

Overall, extant theorizing on HROs seizes on communication and action that interpret circumstances (e. g., sensemaking, interpretation), voice the importance of weak signals (e. g., employee voice and silence), and structure action in anticipation of weak signals (e. g., incident command system, safety rules). The next section reviews this array of work and provides critiques. After that, I propose a view of management communication that considers that detecting and managing weak signals in HROs is a form of practical knowledge that members cultivate through particular discursive moves occurring at the intersections of interpreting, voicing, and structuring practices. Specifically, the chapter theorizes how members develop practical knowledge through: *positioning* (interpreting and voicing), *ventriloquizing* (structuring and voicing), and *presentifying* (interpreting and structuring) possible trajectories of events and actions.

1.1 Interpreting weak signals

One key practical challenge for HRO members is the need to maintain vigilant awareness of ongoing operations to make salient weak signals that might point to emerging problems. As such, prominent HRO theorizing is process oriented. In particular, Weick and Sutcliffe (2001, 2007, 2015) identified principles of *mindfulness* (also referred to as principles of HRO) by which individuals can remain vigilant in everyday action, thereby contributing to the mindfulness of the organizational system broadly. Specifically, (1) members manage hierarchical relationships in ways that empower the most knowledgeable members to make decisions about an issue or problem, regardless of rank (referred to as deference to expertise). (2) Members actively discover and discuss what they do not know, through looking for complexity in their surroundings (reluctance to simplify interpretations). (3) Members also are attentive to the big picture of what their organization aims to accomplish, and they make deliberate efforts to maintain awareness of ongoing activities and emerging problems (sensitivity to operations). Further, (4) members generate a collective understanding about previous actions and events to keep lessons relevant to the ongoing practice. In particular, members report mistakes and try to learn as much as possible from organizational catastrophes (preoccupation with failure). Finally, (5) they sharpen their ability to bounce back from mistakes, and deal with surprises as they happen (commitment to resilience). These five principles reflect HRO efforts to make successful and unsuccessful actions and hazards visible, and to remain open to changing course spontaneously as conditions unfold.

The mindfulness/HRO principles have their roots in Karl Weick's notions of *sensemaking* (Weick 1995) and *interpretation* (Weick 2001); both of these concepts address how members cultivate vigilance in observing unfolding circumstances, and in communicating their insights to others. Sensemaking involves the "ongoing, retrospective development of plausible images that rationalize what people are doing" (Weick, Sutcliffe, and Obstfeld 2005: 409). Sensemaking (Weick 1995; Weick, Sutcliffe, and Obstfeld 2005) involves, for individuals, taking action in their environment while scanning it for the most meaningful information among numerous cues. Members *notice* cues emerging from both their own actions and their surroundings and *bracket* them as potentially important. Members then *label* the cues according to what they might suggest and *presume* an explanation of the events. After that, they act on their presumption and then assess how well their presumptions and action aligned with the situation they faced. Retrospective reflections guide them to change future assessments and actions if initial responses disconfirmed what they thought (Weick 1995; Weick, Sutcliffe, and Obstfeld 2005).

Similar to sensemaking, Weick (2001) proposed that *interpretation* processes translate emerging events into a model for understanding. In Weick's (2001) view, *interpretation* is a system-level process accomplished through "scanning" by many members at all organization levels to detect weak signals – or emerging problems – that could be caught while they are still small. The "data" derived from scanning are then passed onto the few upper-level managers who interpret the observations and give the data meaning. Weick (2001) contended that organizations whose operations heavily rely on the external environment, or for which the environment is considered hostile, allocate the most resources to gathering intelligence or conducting "scanning". For example, large wildland fires often involve such an interpretation process because they are spread across a geographic landscape. Because no single person is able to monitor the entire fire, fire managers ask their field-level personnel to *scan* or observe their own surroundings and then pass along their *data* (e. g., observations about localized fire behavior or weather conditions) to them so they can begin to construct a big-picture understanding of what the fire is doing, and anticipate how it might progress (Jahn, Myers, and Putnam 2018).

HRO research that attends to vigilant awareness of weak signals tends to assume that noticing weak signals is the core activity facilitating reliability. However, this work often assumes that communicating weak signals to others would be relatively unproblematic – unconstrained by status or hierarchy barriers, and unfolding autonomously in relation to formal safety texts like rules or procedures (Jahn, Myers, and Putnam 2018). Research in related disciplines sheds light on such concerns.

1.2 Voicing weak signals

While research on sensemaking and interpretation helps explain how members look for and contextualize weak signals, research on employee voice can help explain why HRO members might notice weak signals but fail to communicate about them. Employee voice refers to typically pro-social behaviors by which members express constructive opinions and ideas meant to benefit the organization (Botero and Van Dyne 2009; Morrison 2011). This work has examined factors making an industry or organization a welcoming (or hostile) place for voice, including how leader behaviors encourage or silence voice (Detert and Burris 2007), and ways members react to working in a hierarchy (Morrison 2011). Employee voice research is particularly valuable for examining ways that participation in safety and other organizational processes is risky for members who suspect their supervisor might reject their recommendations or ignore their concerns (Barton and Sutcliffe 2009; Blatt et al. 2006).

Similarly, research on safety communication addresses the extent to which subordinates feel able to openly discuss safety issues with supervisors even when faced with production pressure, or management prioritizing output over safety (Hofmann and Stetzer 1998). Studies show that team supervisors set the tone for how the entire group interacts through ways they implement formal procedures, manage competing demands, and balance safety with productivity (Hofmann and Stetzer 1998; Jahn and Black 2017). Because production pressure often comes from worker expectations expressed and reinforced through organizational hierarchies, research on safety communication suggests that managers' level of openness to discussing members' safety concerns indicates how much managers value employee wellbeing and safe behavior over production output (Hofmann and Stetzer 1998).

Additional employee voice research contributes insights about how role-related identities provide a sensemaking frame influencing whether and how members choose to voice concerns. For instance, Blatt et al. (2006) studied medical residents' accounts of mishaps, probing whether residents voiced opinions at critical moments or remained silent. These authors found that medical residents often were inclined to remain quiet because their role identity was in flux (i. e., they were transitioning from medical student to physician). They noted residents remained quiet when they anticipated speaking up would anger their conversation partner, and when it might jeopardize efforts to enact their precarious physician identity. Similarly, Barton and Sutcliffe (2009) found that wildland firefighters tended to remain quiet about safety concerns when they questioned their own expertise. Referencing the research on employee voice, both of these studies (Barton and Sutcliffe 2009; Blatt et al. 2006) attend to ways that professional identities provide a sensemaking frame that guides whether and how individuals voice their concerns – even in professions in which safety and reliability depend on workers talking about weak signals.

Literature on employee voice complements the HRO research because it addresses how individuals might feel enabled or constrained to voice weak signals when faced with status or hierarchical differences relative to other members. Both HRO theorizing and the work on employee voice would benefit from considering how organizations structure activity to anticipate weak signals, and provide guidance in communicating about and managing them, namely through organizational structures and texts.

1.3 Structuring to anticipate and respond to weak signals

HRO theorizing is partly grounded in systems thinking, emphasizing how action emerges from coordination among interrelated subsystems, and ways activities of small units contribute to the larger units in which they are embedded (Grabowski and Roberts 1997). Early HRO research contends that the safest, most accident-avoidant HROs are those in which individual members can imagine the "big picture" of what their organization seeks to accomplish. Subsystems are *loosely coupled* allowing for varying degrees of decentralized decision making (Grabowski and Roberts 1997). In effect, HRO members gain schemas about the broader system and consider how their individual roles help script their contribution to it (Grabowski and Roberts 1997; Jahn, Myers, and Putnam 2018). The purpose and value of these schemas and scripts is that they decentralize authority and enable organization members at any level to adjust their actions to remain safe.

Continuing with systems thinking, Weick and Roberts (1993) discussed the ideas of collective mind and heedful interrelating on aircraft carrier flight decks. Collective mind refers to individuals acting as though they are a group. This concept pertains to the relationship between how individuals act and their understanding of the patterns of related activities comprising the collective goal. *Heedfulness* refers to the degree to which individuals act carefully and mindfully. Weick and Roberts (1993) viewed the heedful interrelating process as the mechanism by which members act out their collective understanding of the organizational system.

While systems thinking imposes a schema for an organizational structure onto high reliability operations, the notion of organizational structure is mostly treated in a figurative manner in foundational HRO theorizing. Only a few researchers have explored the actual organizational structure some HROs use. One example is Bigley and Roberts (2001), who studied how the incident command system (ICS) – a bureaucratic arrangement employed by emergency responders (US Federal Emergency Management Agency, wildland fire) – provides a scalable hierarchical structure allowing a flexible organizational response during emergencies. Their study found that the ICS platform enables an emergency response operation to configure a management structure tailored to the size and complexity of an incident's demands. ICS provides a scaffold of consistent designated roles, which enables responders to confidently switch among the roles as an incident's size, conditions, or operational configurations shift. However, improvisation within ICS is only possible insomuch as supervisors permit and direct authority to migrate (Bigley and Roberts 2001).

A crucial drawback of hierarchy-based structures in HROs is that stratified relationships can obstruct members' willingness to communicate weak signals. It can be difficult for subordinates to share partial information and tentative conclusions – the exact kind of information HROs depend on so members can catch and address emerging problems early (Weick 1987). With this concern in mind, Jahn and Black (2017) modeled how the wildland firefighting HRO, operating within the ICS framework, generates a respectful interactional culture that fosters the kind of free-flowing communication assumed in the HRO/mindfulness principles. The study found that organizational members might overcome common hierarchy-based constraints to HRO by considering how leaders throughout a chain of command communicate to cultivate the necessary cross-level awareness of an operation. The study also demonstrated ways in which supervisors, members, and groups might attend to removing communication barriers by carefully attending to their interactional climate.

Implicit in theorizing that attends to structuring HRO operations through systems or hierarchies is the notion that once members understand the structure and their roles in it, they will exchange information about weak signals with one another unproblematically. Thus, a critique of this theorizing is that knowledge and information are considered neutral without regard to the ways in which status differences and social pressures enable and constrain members' communication about weak signals (Jahn, Myers, and Putnam 2018).

In addition to organizational systems and hierarchies, high reliability organizing also is structured through organizational texts, such as safety rules. Because HROs must respond to changing circumstances, members constantly need to translate safety rules into action. A study by Zeigler (2007) showed how the meaning and uses of safety rules shifted throughout nearly 100 years of wildland firefighting practice. Zeigler (2007) noted that the purpose of the list of wildland firefighter safety rules has always been to guide how workers approach ambiguous fire conditions. However, her analysis illustrated how the meaning of the safety rules' guidance changed over time, signaling different meanings for generations of wildland firefighters. Zeigler (2007) used a Foucaultian genealogical method to track discourses shaping the list's symbolic meaning. She showed how the list initially served the symbolic purpose of praising *coolheaded* actions (rather than embracing risks). She then traced a shift in the list's meaning, showing an era in the 1990s to early 2000s when several major fatality cases resulted in the list being used as a checklist of operating procedures that carried punishment if workers deviated from them.

More recently, and also in the wildland firefighting context, Jahn (2019a) studied how a safety rule policy change altered expectations for how wildland firefighters should use safety rules in practice and to learn about hazards. The study mapped the cycle of technical documentation stemming from wildland firefighter Doctrine, a US Forest Service safety policy that allowed firefighters to bend and disregard safety rules according to their judgment. Jahn's (2019a) text analysis examined twelve years of organizational policy, safety, and training documents associated with Doctrine, tracking how language in the texts redefined how safety rules and other documents were to be used on scene and within accountability processes (i. e., fatality investigation procedures and report narratives attributing accident causality). In particular, safety rules have long been associated with a *rationalist* or compliance/violation logic, meaning that workers must *comply* with rules, and can expect disciplinary action if they *violate* them. However, Doctrine represents a new logic for using rules that fall into an *adaptation* safety paradigm, in which rules can be bent and broken, and in which rules enable flexible responses (rather than restrict action). The analysis illustrated how documents were linked with each other in the policy texts, training manuals, and accident investigation processes and reports comprising the organization's technical documentation cycle. It also directed management and scholarly attention toward developing better understandings about how rules are incorporated into "normal" safety practice, when rules enter and inform decision processes, and how organizations investigate accidents to determine cause and accountability.

Each of the HRO practices reviewed previously – interpreting, voicing, and structuring – sheds important light on how organizations remember and plan for weak signals, and how members interpret and communicate them. However, each area poses barriers to acting on weak signals that are not adequately resolved through the lines of theorizing from which they emerged. The central thesis of this chapter is that weak signals become evident and manageable through practical knowledge. Because practical knowledge is tacit and difficult to codify, we need to better capture the communication processes by which it is enacted and we need to consider how figures (objects, texts, organizational formal structures; defined in the next section) mediate the development and mobilization of practical knowledge regarding weak signals in HRO theorizing.

2 Reconceptualizing weak signals as practical knowledge

The central value creation for HROs is in noticing and managing weak signals in such a way that they contribute to *reliably* avoiding catastrophic failures. Much HRO research reviewed in the previous section explains ways members notice and communicate about weak signals, and it highlights particular objects that aid in these efforts, namely structures (e. g., ICS system) and texts (e. g., safety rules). However, by assuming that weak signals exist just "out there" – that is, external to HRO members – to be noticed and managed, extant HRO theorizing relies on explaining member vigilance in noticing them and communicating their observations in a transmission/information exchange manner. This type of explanation lends itself well to unpacking *reliable* avoidance of accidents as being a process of ongoing vigilance on the part of individual organizational members within a community. However, a key drawback of theorizing is the assumption that weak signals exist just "out there" in the first place as information or cues that *should* or even *could* be noticed.

An alternative way to think about weak signals is to reconceptualize the discovery of them not only as a process of noticing and communicating, but also as a constitutive process in which they are brought into being in the first place through communication. Under a constitutive view, then, *weak signals* would be defined as *practical knowledge about possible trajectories of events or actions that is talked into being through participation among various figures* (rather than just as cues or information that is noticed and passed along to others). Thus, weak signals are not only noticed, but also constructed. Further, constructing possible *trajectories* of events/actions (i. e., the content that weak signals suggest under extant HRO theorizing) occurs through mobilizing various *figures* while participating in intersecting organizational *practices*. Before defining and explaining the roles of figures, practices, and trajectories, I will first provide an overview of *agential realism*, the ontological orientation undergirding the subsequent ideas presented in this chapter.

2.1 Grounding weak signals in an agential-realist ontology

Agential realism holds that social and material aspects of organizational action are intertwined – a condition referred to as *hybrid* action (Latour 1994), among other labels. To view organizational action as fundamentally hybrid means that scholars consider that humans and objects co-act as a "third actor" able to accomplish something different than any of the comprising actors could accomplish alone (Robichaud 2006). Moreover, there is no "external" reality; rather, organizational actor's experiences consist of intertwined connections among other people, objects, spaces, ideas, and so on, in a given moment. That is, agential-realists are concerned with analyzing what occurs in the *flatland* of ongoing interactions (Latour 2005), which means that this approach is primarily interested in the various *figures* (objects, ideas, discourses, texts, symbols, etc.) made present during an episode of interaction (Cooren 2010).

Adopting an agential-realist ontology for explaining how possible trajectories of events or actions are constituted through communication involves decentering human agency such that we more thoroughly take into account the roles of materiality (e. g., objects, sites, bodies, media infrastructures, texts as artifacts) in social action. Analysts, then, examine *sociomaterial* organizational action. The term *sociomaterial* is unhyphenated to denote the inherent inseparability between social and material elements. To *see* sociomaterial phenomena, we have to look differently than we are perhaps used to at the ways objects, sites, bodies, and so on participate in action. In particular, Latour (2005: 5) explained that sociomaterial analyses involve "tracing associations between heterogeneous elements". It considers "social" action to be less about purely intentional human behaviors, and more about looking at the "connections between things that are not themselves social" (Latour 2005: 5). That is, analyzing social action is neither about considering ways humans *appropriate* objects or texts – that would be too human-centered an explanation nor is it about unpacking ways objects or sites *enable/constrain* human action – that would be too object-focused an analysis. Instead, the task of "tracing connections" between heterogeneous elements involves paying attention to *hybrid co-action*. Robichaud (2006: 106) described imagining hybrid co-action as a third actor:

> a third actor emerges out of the connection between the human [and the object] [...] the point is that the intention, the script, the path, the direction, and the program of action of the new "hybrid agent" called an actor-network is neither that of the essentially material [object] nor that of the essentially human citizen, but is channeled by a new goal path that redefines the interest, the will, the functions, the roles, and the identities of the two agents involved.

To reconceptualize weak signals as a form of practical knowledge means to consider how possible trajectories are constructed in communication practices involving various sociomaterial actors or *figures*. A figure is an idea or physical object pertaining to collective experiences or understandings that is invoked (implicitly or explicitly) in talk in such a way as to make a difference in a conversation's direction or the trajectory of further collective organizational efforts (Cooren et al. 2011). A figure can include objects, professional titles, and organizational positions (Bergeron and Cooren 2012). For example, workers might reference safety rules in their everyday communication with each other to make present the lessons that safety rules inscribe, or they might invoke the organizational authority of the rules to propose (or dissent against) a course of action. An organizational practice provides a site in which to track the co-participation of sociomaterial elements/actors (Nicolini 2011). Practices combine actor agencies in ways that develop new meanings, change meanings, and instantiate long-standing meanings of objects and sites. Thus, possible trajectories of events or action emerge through the ongoing communication comprising an organizational practice.

2.2 Constructing trajectories of events and actions through intersecting practices

Under an agential-realist view, practices are sites at which multiple sub-practices intersect through ongoing "flatland" interactions that mobilize various figures. To connect with and build from previous HRO theorizing, we might consider that interpreting, voicing, and structuring relative to weak signals (the first part of the chapter) are general practices associated with high reliability organizing. We might consider that there are key *figures* addressed in that literature as well, including ICS and generic forms of communication like safety rules and maps. We might also consider additional figures briefly referenced in that section, including occupational or organizational roles and identities, and organizational discourses.

The next sections explore how practices intersect to: (1) *position* weak signals, which sheds light on why it might be face threatening for organization members to co-construct an interpretation of them, (2) *ventriloquize* weak signals, which helps explain how members might negotiate jurisdiction over deciding what to do about them, and (3) *presentify* weak signals, which addresses how members situate the meaning of weak signals and how to manage them.

2.2.1 Positioning: interpretation and voice

An agential-realist approach helps us move away from individual observations and communication about weak signals. Instead, by decentering human agency and being inclusive of who or what might be acting in an interaction, we can explain why certain trajectories of action might emerge through communication. Positioning lies at the intersection of interpretation (e.g., sensemaking) and voicing practices. Positioning, then, involves being inclusive of how organizational roles script how members approach (i.e., interpret) their work depending on the responsibilities, preoccupations, and identities associated with their role (e.g., physicians versus medical students). Positioning also considers that complementary relationships (e.g., supervisor/subordinate) script interactions between organizational counterparts, which further shapes expectations for voicing in the context of a given relationship.

The concept of *positioning* (Davies and Harré 1990; Spitzmüller 2019) can shed light on the ways in which individuals view themselves relative to others and, importantly, how subject position is dynamic, making some discourses accessible when occupying some positions, and making the same discourses unavailable when occupying other positions. According to Davies and Harré (1990), organizational actors are constituted and reconstituted as they participate in various discursive practices. Thus, an individual does not hold a static position. Rather, individuals shift positions depending on who they interact with (and the positions made available through those interactions), and depending on the discursive practices by which people are able to make sense of their own and others' roles. The idea of discursive positioning constituting the subject positions of organizational roles, and providing role-related scripts, can help to explain why the medical residents (Blatt et al. 2006) and firefighters (Barton and Sutcliffe 2009) discussed previously avoided voicing concerns with their organizational counterparts.

Positioning can be further elaborated by considering Labov and Fanshel's (1977) idea that interactants are arranged into asymmetric *head-complement* relationships in which there is an implicit understanding, rooted in language, that defines the head's *responsibilities* and the complement's *rights*. For example, because we use language, we understand not only the meanings of the words *supervisor* (head) and *subordinate* (complement), we also understand that the two words have meaning only in relation to each other (e.g., there cannot be a supervisor without a subordinate and vice versa).

By extension, we know that these labels are associated with particular scripts for action such that communicative interactions between head and complement reflect negotiations around the head's responsibilities relative to the complement (e. g., the supervisor has the responsibility to make safe decisions) and the complement's rights relative to the head (e. g., the subordinate has the right to be protected).

Weak signals, then, are constructed at the site where complementary relationships and their associated organizational scripts (or expectations) intersect. That is, positioning involves both interpreting and voicing weak signals within the understood rights and responsibilities of the complementary relationship. If the higher-ranking member (i. e., the head) initiates the conversation about a weak signal, then the responsibilities and rights between the head and complement are preserved. However, the asymmetry of the head-complement relationship might impose an obstacle to member's efforts to co-construct the meaning of weak signals, namely by making communication between parties unequal, and possibly face threatening.

For example, weak signals might include information a novice observes (e. g., rust build-up in an air filter) but might not feel confident is important (e. g., nobody seems concerned that we change the filters every 48 hours). Raising the issue with a higher-ranking member could be face threatening for the novice because it might expose their own naïveté (e. g., if what they think is a problem really is not one), or it might expose a higher-ranking member's negligence (e. g., if he or she did not notice the weak signal first). In this case, the incomplete information and tentative observations that characterize weak signals collide with member's understandings of the rights and responsibilities associated with their complementary relationship. While the intersection of weak signals and complementary relationships can create face threats, Jahn (2019b) also found that lower-ranking members gained valuable, empowering experience – especially when engaging in face-threatening repartee with higher-ranking members regarding weak signals. These interactions helped lower-ranking members build self-reflexivity about both challenging communication situations and uncertainties they face on the job.

2.2.2 Ventriloquizing: structure and voice

The previous section explained why positioning weak signals might be face threatening (or empowering) for interacting organization members. The idea of *ventriloquization* can help us understand how organization members might sidestep face threatening exchanges by drawing from other organizational resources to situate the importance of weak signals or their own jurisdiction over the interpretation of the weak signal, by invoking organizational structures (e. g., rules, procedures, positions, professional identity). Ventriloquization lies at the intersection between structuring and voicing practices, such that members draw from structures (e. g., texts) to assist them in voicing a possible trajectory of events or actions and lending legitimacy to their concerns. *Ventriloquism* considers how various *figures* (e. g., safety rules) participate in organizing processes (Benoit-Barné and Cooren 2009; Cooren 2004, 2010).

For example, Benoit-Barné and Cooren (2009) found that members in a distributed organization acquired authority through ventriloquizing, or invoking, the central mission/goals of their organization to make a difference in how their interactions unfolded. Members might also gain authority in a situation through invoking the organizational authority of rules, thus changing the complementarity of a relationship (Benoit-Barné and Cooren 2009; Cooren 2004). While complementary relationships link organization members to one another through implicit and explicit mutual practices and obligations, authority is not given and must be communicatively negotiated (Benoit-Barné and Cooren 2009). Ventriloquizing a figure (e. g., document, policy, position) can challenge the complementarity of a relationship as members mobilize the figure's legitimacy to lend authority to what they say (Bergeron and Cooren 2012).

Ventriloquization contextualizes a weak signal in relation to an organizational structure that lends meaning about who or what has authority to decide the action trajectory. For example, Jahn (2016) compared how two wildland firefighting workgroups incorporate safety rules into communication practices, specifically, how they *ventriloquized* them, thus considering how safety rules *participated* in organizing. The study illustrated how firefighters navigated authority by citing particular rules to highlight the importance of weak signals and suggest what should be done about them. In particular, invoking rules to dissent from action based on weak signals firefighters observed enabled parties to diffuse face-threatening personal challenges, while wrestling authority over the situation from a co-worker.

For example, Jahn's (2016) study describes a situation in which a group of firefighters had to decide how to begin fighting a nighttime wildfire. Most members of the group felt the situation was unsafe and leaned toward waiting until daylight to begin. However, one "gung-ho" (i. e., overly motivated) member of the group passionately advocated to begin fighting fire immediately in the dark. To counter the gung-ho member, a firefighter invoked, or ventriloquized, the standard risk management checklist to highlight the risks of their situation and override the suggestion to fight the fire at night. Aligning with the safety checklist allowed firefighters to push a safer trajectory of action while avoiding a face-threatening confrontation.

2.2.3 Presentifying: interpretation and structure

Presentification lies at the intersection between interpretation and structuring practices. Presentification captures the idea that collectives (e. g., groups, organizations) exist through the various figures that represent it, thus speaking or acting on their behalf; such figures might include mission statements, safety procedures, or logos, among others (Cooren, Brummans, and Charrieras 2008). Presentification refers to "activities involved in making something or somebody present to something or somebody else" (Cooren, Brummans, and Charrieras 2008: 1343). When members pre-sentify various figures (e. g., knowledge, missions, procedures), they transport their organization across space and time.

For example, generic texts (e. g., rules, maps) are examples of objects that carry long-standing, but not deterministic, meanings about an organization's missions or goals. A map, for instance, might carry specific generic features (e. g., roads, property boundaries, scale, legend). Maps might also carry expectations for how to use it (Bhatia 2010). Both the generic features and the expectations for use are long-standing meanings that might get reproduced in hybrid co-action. How a text participates in practice might also include the sequencing or patterning of activity, which, in turn, might shape the temporal unfolding of the activity and ultimately what the trajectory produces (Geisler 2001). Because it is not given how a text might participate in co-action, it is possible that multiple trajectories of co-action are possible even if members hold relatively standardized notions of how to use a given text (or other generic object).

One example of bringing together interpretation and voice practices, to understand how HRO members construct practical knowledge about hazards and possible trajectories of action, was Jahn (2018), which examined how the textual agency of safety rules (i. e., co-participation of humans and documents) shifted when the US Forest Service introduced the Doctrine policy to re-imagine how safety rules should be used in practice, thus changing the safety rules genre. The study drew from rhetorical genre studies, proposing that generic texts like safety rules mediate social action, contributing to professional epistemologies for seeing and approaching work. When a genre changes, so does its professional epistemology or how workers prioritize aspects of their job. The study showed how the co-action between firefighters and safety rules before the genre change allowed members to learn passively about hazards and invoke rules to voice dissent. After the genre change, firefighters used safety rules flexibly to justify their actions, which altered the sequence in which rules participated in making firefighting decisions, and resulted in expanding the scope of the job and closing off opportunities to invoke rules to bolster dissent when they felt unsafe.

In summary, there are several benefits of taking an agential-realist view of constructing trajectories of events and actions (rather than focusing on noticing and communicating weak signals) in HRO theorizing. One benefit is that this theoretical shift moves us away from relying on explaining organizational action as being a consequence of individuals' discretionary decisions, and instead urges us to consider how organizational roles are scripted in terms of both their preoccupations and their reliance on complementary roles. Another benefit is that this approach adds nuance to explanations about how members negotiate authority between their organizational roles while drawing from various figures to gain the upper hand when needed.

3 Conclusion

This chapter redefines a central preoccupation with HRO theorizing: that members' vigilant efforts to interpret, voice, and structure actions around weak signals contributes to an organization's ability to *reliably* avoid catastrophic failures. This chapter proposes an alternative understanding of weak signals as possible trajectories of events or actions that become salient through intersecting practices involving various organizational figures (e. g., workers, structures, genres, occupational discourses). An agential-realist CCO perspective on management communication helps explain why weak signals might be face threatening as they intervene on a complementary relationship (positioning). The perspective also shows how members flip the complementarity of their relationship through situating a weak signal in relation to an organizational structure (e. g., procedure, role) to claim authority over it (ventriloquization). Additionally, it shows how members might deflect face threats associated with weak signals through contextualizing them in relation to a figure (presentification) that pushes the communicators toward a different course of action.

The value of taking an agential-realist approach to the study of management communication in HRO contexts is that it decenters human agency and brings into sharper focus how dealing with dangerous organizational complexity (e. g., nuclear power plants, aircraft carrier flight operations) or emerging problems (e. g., natural disasters) involves hybrid actions among organization members, texts, discourses, and so on. The highlighted studies demonstrate the value of this approach by illustrating various concerns that become salient when we decenter human agency and consider instead a *plenum of agencies* (Cooren 2006).

4 References

Barton, Michelle A. & Kathleen M. Sutcliffe. 2009. Overcoming dysfunctional momentum: Organizational safety as a social achievement. *Human Relations* 62(9). 1327–1356.

Benoit-Barné, Chantal & François Cooren. 2009. The accomplishment of authority through presentification: How authority is distributed among and negotiated by organizational members. *Management Communication Quarterly* 23(1). 5–31.

Bergeron, Caroline D. & François Cooren. 2012. The collective framing of crisis management: A ventriloqual analysis of emergency operations centres. *Journal of Contingencies and Crisis Management* 20(3). 120–137.

Bhatia, Vijay K. 2010. Interdiscursivity in professional communication. *Discourse and Communication* 4(1). 32–50.

Bigley, Gregory A. & Karlene H. Roberts. 2001. The incident command system: High-reliability organizing for complex and volatile task environments. *Academy of Management Journal* 44(6). 1281–1299.

Blatt, Ruth, Marlys K. Christianson, Kathleen M. Sutcliffe & Marilynn M. Rosenthal. 2006. A sensemaking lens on reliability. *Journal of Organizational Behavior* 27(9). 897–917.

Botero, Isabel C. & Linn Van Dyne. 2009. Employee voice behavior interactive effects of LMX and power distance in the United States and Colombia. *Management Communication Quarterly* 23(1). 84–104.

Brizon, Ambre & Jean-Luc Wybo. 2009. The life cycle of weak signals related to safety. *International Journal of Emergency Management* 6(2). 117–135.

Cooren, François. 2004. Textual agency: How texts do things in organizational settings. *Organization* 11(3). 373–393.

Cooren, François. 2006. The organizational world as a plenum of agencies. In James R. Taylor, François Cooren & Elizabeth J. Van Every (eds.), *Communication as organizing: Empirical and theoretical explorations in the dynamic of text and conversation*, 81–100. Mahwah, NJ: Lawrence Erlbaum.

Cooren, François. 2010. *Action and agency in dialogue: Passion, incarnation and ventriloquism* (Dialogue Studies 6). Philadelphia, PA: John Benjamins.

Cooren, François., Boris H. J. M. Brummans & Damien Charrieras. 2008. The coproduction of organizational presence: A study of Médecins Sans Frontières in action. *Human Relations* 61(10). 1339–1370.

Cooren, François, Timothy Kuhn, Joep P. Cornelissen & Timothy Clark. 2011. Communication, organizing and organization: An overview and introduction to the special issue. *Organization Studies* 32(9). 1149–1170.

Davies, Bronwyn & Rom Harré. 1990. Positioning: The discursive production of selves. *Journal for the Theory of Social Behaviour* 20(1). 43–63.

Detert, James R. & Ethan R. Burris. 2007. Leadership behavior and employee voice: Is the door really open? *Academy of Management Journal* 50(4). 869–884.

Geisler, Cheryl. 2001. Textual objects: Accounting for the role of texts in the everyday life of complex organizations. *Written Communication* 18(3). 296–325.

Grabowski, Martha & Karleen Roberts. 1997. Risk mitigation in large-scale systems: Lessons from high reliability organizations. *California Management Review* 39(4). 152–162.

Hofmann, David & Adam Stetzer. 1998. The role of safety climate and communication in accident interpretation: Implications for learning from negative events. *Academy of Management Journal* 41(6). 644–657.

Jahn, Jody L. S. 2016. Adapting safety rules in a high reliability context: How wildland firefighting workgroups ventriloquize safety rules to understand hazards. *Management Communication Quarterly* 30(3). 362–389.

Jahn, Jody L. S. 2018. Genre as textual agency: Using communicative relationality to theorize the agential-performative relationship between human and generic text. *Communication Monographs* 85(4). 515–538.

Jahn, Jody L. S. 2019a. Shifting the safety rules paradigm: Introducing Doctrine to US wildland firefighting operations. *Safety Science* 115. 237–246.

Jahn, Jody L. S. 2019b. Voice enactment: Linking voice with experience in high reliability organizing. *Journal of Applied Communication Research* 47(3). 283–302.

Jahn, Jody L. S. & Anne E. Black. 2017. A model of communicative and hierarchical foundations of high reliability organizing. *Management Communication Quarterly* 31(3). 356–379.

Jahn, Jody L. S., Karen K. Myers & Linda L. Putnam. 2018. Metaphors of communication in high reliability organizations. In Rangaraj Ramanujam & Karleen Roberts (eds.), *Organizing for reliability: A guide for research and* practice, 169–193. Palo Alto, CA: Stanford University Press.

Labov, William & David Fanshel. 1977. *Therapeutic discourse: Psychotherapy as conversation*. New York: Academic Press.

Latour, Bruno. 1994. On technical mediation. *Common Knowledge* 3(2). 29–64.

Latour, Bruno. 2005. *Reassembling the social: An introduction to actor-network-theory*. Oxford: Oxford University Press.

Morrison, Elizabeth W. 2011. Employee voice behavior: Integration and directions for future research. *The Academy of Management Annals* 5(1). 373–412.

Nicolini, Davide. 2011. Practice as the site of knowing: Insights from the field of telemedicine. *Organization Science* 22(3). 602–620.

Robichaud, Daniel. 2006. Steps toward a relational view of agency. In James R. Taylor, François Cooren & Elizabeth J. Van Every (eds.), *Communication as organizing: Empirical and theoretical explorations in the dynamic of text and conversation*, 101–114. Mahwah, NJ: Lawrence Erlbaum.

Rochlin, Gene I. 1993. Defining high reliability organizations in practice: A taxonomic prologue. In Karleen Roberts (ed.), *New challenges to organization research: High reliability organizations*, 11–32. New York: Macmillan.

Spitzmüller, Jürgen. 2019. 'Sprache' – 'Metasprache' – 'Metapragmatik': Sprache und sprachliches Handeln als Gegenstand sozialer Reflexion. In Herausgegeben von Gerd Antos, Thomas Niehr, & Jürgen Spitzmüller (eds.), *Handbuch Sprache im Urteil der Öffentlichkeit*, 11–30. Berlin: De Gruyter.

Weick, Karl E. 1987. Organizational culture as a source of high reliability. *California Management Review* 29(2). 112–127.

Weick, Karl E. 1995. *Sensemaking in organizations*. Thousand Oaks, CA: Sage.

Weick, Karl E. 2001. *Making sense of the organization*. Oxford: Blackwell.

Weick, Karl E. & Karleen H. Roberts. 1993. Collective mind in organizations: Heedful interrelating on flight decks. *Administrative Science Quarterly* 38(3). 357–381.

Weick, Karl E. & Kathleen M. Sutcliffe. 2001. *Managing the unexpected*. San Francisco, CA: Jossey-Bass.

Weick, Karl E. & Kathleen M. Sutcliffe. 2007. *Managing the unexpected: Resilient performance in an age of uncertainty*, 2nd edn. San Francisco, CA: Jossey-Bass.

Weick, Karl E. & Kathleen M. Sutcliffe. 2015. *Managing the unexpected: Sustained performance in a complex world*, 3rd edn. Hoboken, NJ: John Wiley and Sons.

Weick, Karl E., Kathleen M. Sutcliffe & David Obstfeld. 2005. Organizing and the process of sensemaking. *Organization Science* 16(4). 409–421.

Zeigler, Jennifer A. 2007. The story behind an organizational list: A genealogy of wildland firefighters' 10 Standard Fire Orders. *Communication Monographs* 74(4). 415–442.

Shiv Ganesh, Mohan Dutta, and Ngā Hau
23 Building communities

Abstract: Power relations are impossible to suspend in community building; consequently, such efforts are always dialectical, tension-laden and ongoing. In this chapter we outline a set of four communicative tensions that help animate and position community organizing as praxis, each of which implicates power relations differently. These are: local versus global domains, reformatory versus revolutionary change, persuasive versus coercive means, and immanent versus external loci of control. We expand on these tensions before turning our attention to community building as philosophy and praxis. Our effort here is to highlight the work of the culture-centered approach to change in yoking together theory, method and efforts at social change and community-building. We do so by highlighting two efforts at community building, each of which foregrounds the four tensions articulated earlier, in different ways. The first case describes anti-poverty organizing in Singapore, and the second illustrates indigenous resistance in Aotearoa New Zealand. In concluding we discuss the implications of community building as praxis.

Keywords: community building; culture-centered approach; power; praxis; resistance

Scholars of organizational and management communication have known for over fifty years just how devastating the impact of capitalism has been upon the ability of communities to assert themselves as thriving democratic spaces. Deetz's (1992) much-lauded work on the corporate colonization of the lifeworld for instance, established how communities had been reshaped by corporate logics and the acute communicative dependencies that ensued. As a starting point, then, the notion of community building needs to take into account the fact that communities *require* building (or rebuilding), assertion, and communicative labor in the first place. That this is a challenging task is particularly evident from the large literature on neoliberalization and individualization, which establishes that building community and group identities in the face of regimes that encourage atomization is especially fraught (Ganesh, Zoller, and Cheney 2005). Community building is also the fulcrum for decolonization efforts and attempts to procure social justice, and as such is a foundational aspect of collective resistance (Dutta 2012, 2015).

What, though, is community building? We understand communities to be everyday sites of communal articulation, constitution, negotiation, dialogue, and transformation. In turn, we theorize community building in culture-centered terms, defining it as a form of reflexive organizing that is deeply attentive to ongoing processes of marginalization as part of a project to create democratic communication spaces, infrastructures, and futures (Dutta 2004a, 2004b; Dutta et al. 2019). Of the various historical orientations to community organizing (Rothman 1970), community building makes most sense in a social action orientation, which frames community participation in terms of engagement, mobilization, justice, and advocacy (Ganesh and Stohl 2014). Thus, we position community building as a form of praxis: an integration of philosophy, method, and action.

We also position power relations and dynamics as an inevitable feature of community building. While, in some ways, theories of power preclude a theory of community inasmuch as the degree to which we can build any egalitarian community depends upon the degree to which we can suspend or erase power differences, in others, community building involves directly addressing and naming power relations. Our view tends towards this latter position: we hold that power relations themselves are constitutive of social formations and are thus impossible to suspend (Laclau and Mouffe 1985), and in this sense, communities have never been places of innocence. That is, there is always already injustice and hierarchy in communities by virtue of their being a social formation in the first place. Addressing this central contradiction is a critical aspect of community building: innocence, once lost, cannot be found, and yet, that is precisely what community-building efforts must set out to do. Consequently, such efforts are always dialectical, tension-laden, and ongoing.

So, in this chapter we turn our attention to four central dialectics and tensions that organizers continually attend to as they attempt to build community. Tensional approaches to organizing now have a rich history in organizational communication studies, particularly as regards democratic process (Stohl and Cheney 2001), but it is not our aim to address the entire breadth of this theoretically diverse literature. Our approach is much more closely aligned with a Marxist dialectic: that modes of economic and social production and reproduction generate their own internal contradictions, and resistance; in turn, those efforts, as they reify, diachronically generate their own contradictions (Marx 1967). This is not to say, of course, that power automatically produces resistance; instead, community-building efforts are always arduous and effortful attempts at praxis. Moreover, they are by definition precarious, never guaranteed to procure the survival of communities themselves.

Our aim is, therefore, to outline a set of communicative tensions that help animate and position community organizing as praxis, in line with the emphasis in this handbook upon communicative action, practice, and their forms. We proceed by outlining four tensions in community building that characterize most efforts. We then turn our attention to praxis itself, in the form of highlighting culture-centered efforts at community building that merge theory, research, methods, and action as they attempt to obtain transformative social goals. Here, we focus upon two cases; one based in Singapore, and the other based in Aotearoa New Zealand.[1]

---

[1] *Aotearoa New Zealand* signifies "the bicultural identity of this country". *Aotearoa* is one Māori name for 'the country', although there are several others.

1 Tensions in community building

> Life seems to lack rhyme or reason or even a shadow of order unless we approach it with the key of converses. Seeing everything in its duality, we begin to get some dim clues to direction and what it's all about. It is in these contradictions and their incessant interacting tensions that creativity begins. As we begin to accept the concept of contradictions we see every problem or issue in its whole, interrelated sense. We then recognize that for every positive there is a negative, and that there is nothing positive without its concomitant negative, nor any political paradise without its negative side. (Saul Alinsky, *Rules for Radicals*, 1989: 29)

Alinsky's (1989) *Rules for Radicals* continues to be a pivotal text for activists and community organizers. The lessons it teaches resonate for theory and research as well as praxis and help us come to grips with the broad swathe of problematics that community organizing, understood as democratic social practice, implicates. As his comment above suggests, the very recognition of contradictory processes of marginalization in global, regional, national, and local spaces inaugurates the creative and dialogic co-construction of identities and communicative infrastructures, and enables raising claims into local, regional, national, and global structures.

In communication studies, the culture-centered approach to community building (CCA) proposes a framework for organizing communities, constituted, as Alinsky's work implies, within and in solidarity with academic-activist relationships at the global margins (Dutta 2004a, 2004b, 2014, 2015). Such an approach centers the principle of communicative equality, implying the equitable distribution of communicative resources for community building. The CCA also emphasizes, as Alinsky suggests, that problems need to be seen in whole and interrelated senses: that communities at the margins are both constituted by inequalities in the distribution of communicative resources in mainstream society, as well as constitutive of embedded inequalities within the community itself.

Thus, communities inevitably reproduce the classed, raced, and gendered distributions of power, as both reflections and extensions of global capitalist formations. An attunement to the "margins of the margins" in community-building work can mitigate these exigencies. Such a sensibility enables the exposure of spaces and sites of violence and erasure within community infrastructures, hidden inequalities in the distribution of communicative resources, and the ongoing work of power in constituting the margins (Dutta 2014). The classed structures of exploitation at work for instance are reproduced in the classed organizing of communities, which are further exacerbated through the structures of gender, race, ethnicity, caste, religion, and citizenship (Dutta and Thaker 2019).

The broad scope of these problematics can be articulated in terms of four sets of tensions. In what follows, we describe, contextualize, and illuminate these tensions with studies from organizational communication and cognate fields. Our discussion is not meant as an exhaustive account or literature review; neither are we claiming that the four tensions discussed below represent a complete account of the communicative problems that inhere in community building. Instead, our aim in attending to these tensional features is to provide the reader with an applied sense of how communicative tensions might manifest themselves in practice. The four tensions we foreground are: local versus global, reformatory versus revolutionary, persuasive versus coercive, and immanent versus external.

1.1 Local versus global

In a sociological sense, *local* and *global* describe distinct but mutually constitutive domains. The local versus global tension is easily articulated in terms of the cliché that the global is manifested locally (Robertson 1997). In more complicated terms, research that implicates local and global tensions in community organizing has engaged with the issue in terms of scales of contention, locations of organizing, solidarity, and intersectionality. Tarrow's (2005) work on scales of contention in social movements, for instance, identifies six processes through which contentious claims are articulated locally and then made global: global framing of local issues, internalizing contention, diffusion and modularity, scale shifts, externalization, and transnational coalition formation. In the contemporary era, global issues are always and already intertwined with local ones, and as Tarrow says, most global movements are actually very local.

In Aotearoa New Zealand, the Save Happy Valley Campaign, a series of protests against open coal cast coal mining in the South Island, that took the form of an occupation, articulated their concerns not only in terms of local environmental issues and those of indigenous justice, but also in terms of global climate change. The implication of the local is always necessary in articulations of the global. Else, movement organizers will struggle to make globally framed issues immediate, accessible, and urgent enough to facilitate mobilizing and community building (Ganesh 2018b).

Tensions between local and global also throw into relief the question of the spaces *where* community building takes place, an issue that also involves the age-old debate about what counts as a community in the first place, its spatial articulation, and crucial questions of who is included and who is excluded by these definitional processes (Shepherd and Rothenbuler 2000). Community building is spatially complex, situated between the local and the global. It can involve neighborhood associations and localities mobilizing against global corporate malfeasance (Zoller and Tener 2010). On the other hand, it can also involve the building of connections across nations, as Dempsey, Parker, and Krone (2011) showed in their study of transnational feminist networks.

The question of location and inclusion and the extensive boundary work it suggests also surfaces the issue of solidarity and its central place in determining how community building and coalition work can take place. For instance, there has been considerable critical attention paid to the term *ally* and its limitations in attempts to build the kind of deep inter-community solidarity required to sustain anti-racist movements such as Black Lives Matter. Greenberg (2014: 14) for instance, argued that the term *allyship* paradoxically prevented people from bringing their "full self to the table in multiracial activism", thereby preserving a kind of elitism, which in turn makes it difficult to build deep solidarity around community causes.

Building effective solidarity ultimately involves recognizing the intersectionality (Crenshaw 1989) of oppressive experiences around and against which community organizing should occur, and the co-vulnerability of a range of marginalized groups in the face of oppression. Chávez (2013), for instance, argues that effective movement building necessarily invokes coalitional politics across communities and groups. She makes that case persuasively in her study of queer migration across national boundaries, which identifies "coalitional moments" in organizing that can both expand the scale of community organizing while keeping issues alive, specific, and actionable for vulnerable communities affected by them.

1.2 Reformation versus revolution

A second communicative tension in community building lies in the relationship between social change efforts geared towards revolutionary, structural, and radical change on the one hand, and those geared towards reformative and relatively contained change efforts, on the other. Aberle's (1966) now classic distinction between reformative and revolutionary change, based on his study of Peyote amongst Navajo communities, rested not on how many people the movement was attempting to change, but on the *extent* of the change involved. Equally classic is the critique of this formulation which recognizes that revolution and reformation are not separate social goals, but part of a duality.

Alinsky (1989: 32), for instance, argued that "the converse of revolution on one side is counterrevolution and on the other side, reformation, and so on, in an endless chain of connected converses". In strategic terms, Alinsky meant that organizers needed to accept that revolutionary and radical outcomes almost inevitably needed to be preceded by reformative or even redemptive moves; or that reformative goals could be revolutionary, and that revolutionary goals, even if they were not met, could be reformative. As the iron law of oligarchy (Michels 1962) suggests, and to paraphrase Eric Hoffer (1967), unless we work to prevent it, every noble cause will begin as a social movement, turn into an organization, and end as a racket.

The goals of community building, like any other organizing effort, are, of course, complex, and involve not only synchronic but also diachronic tensions between radical and institutional goals. Harter et al.'s (2004) study of Streetwise, a community organizing effort around homelessness, demonstrates vividly how survival goals exist in dialectical tension with a radical social change goal. The study found that for women and men without homes, the urgent need to survive, find income and support both preceded and stood in tension with the broader and more radical social goal of eliminating impoverishment.

It is also critical to recognize that the instrumental aspects of organizing can obfuscate affective and constitutive dimensions of community building, and that affect and constitution are critical dimensions of revolutionary and reformative tensions (Ganesh 2015, 2018a). The Occupy movement may not have achieved the revolutionary goals that it aspired to, but it had the nascent effect of building solidarity between portions of the left that had drifted into relatively autonomous spheres of action (Ganesh and Stohl 2013). Conversely, as studies grounded in the CCA have demonstrated time and again, even a small community-building act – such as asserting a community's right to water or sexual health – can have powerful and potentially revolutionary outcomes when it comes to developing collective identity, efficacy, and pride (Basu and Dutta 2009).

1.3 Persuasion versus coercion

The tension between persuasion and coercion and attendant specters of violence has been written about by a considerable number of communication scholars (e. g., Freeman, Littlejohn, and Pearce 1992). At the heart of the tension lies not only what counts as symbolic, but also the question of agency. In traditional formulations, persuasion and communication methods aimed at procuring change rely on voluntary action, whereas coercion is non-symbolic and implies force or its threat. Violence, thus, is traditionally understood as extra-communicative. Stretching across both these domains is the question of agency. Agency has been written about considerably in organizational studies in recent years (e. g., Brummans 2018), and such writing demonstrates that how agency is theoretically positioned affects how one might consider and constitute communication itself.

For example, direct action as an activist tactic has historically been considered non- communicative inasmuch as it involves organizers eschewing traditional communication activities such as lobbying and education, and encouraging communities to engage in action rather than words to achieve their goals (Ganesh and Wang 2015). If, however, communication itself is understood in radically relational terms that imply the relations constituted by people, events, objects, and places (Kuhn, Ashcraft, and Cooren 2017), then what counts as "direct action" is itself a communication method because it implies reterritorializing relations between communities, place, and resources. From this standpoint, according a natural entity legal agency is a powerful rhetorical move.

Feminist new materialism in organizational studies has considerable potential in demonstrating the utility of non-dualistic approaches to communication for community organizing. Lockwood Harris' (2019) work, for instance, advocates feminist dilemmatic theorizing, focusing attention upon both the performative and non-performative qualities of language. In doing so, it shows how a sophisticated material theory of communication makes a difference, forcing organizations and communities to come to a reckoning with embodied historical violence in their midst that discourse may have named and not named; or simultaneously enabled and disabled. Cruz's (2014) work on trauma, the memory of violence, and organizing, while not strictly speaking in this tradition, also demonstrates how violence and trauma are inextricably caught up with and inaugurate local and postcolonial forms of feminist organizing and praxis.

1.4 Immanent versus external

Immanent versus external tensions implicate the locus of control in community building. These tensions are most visibly articulated in two broad streams of research. One set of studies focuses on the dynamics of community empowerment and assertion where power, efficacy, and control stem from carefully and arduously cultivated community-building efforts, i.e., where the locus of control is immanent. Another set illustrates how loci of control in community building are inevitably external. Here, scholars argue that community-building efforts have to contend with the idea that every effort to create change is often constituted through externals, through capitalist and colonial dynamics and pressures.

This latter idea has two dimensions: constitution and erasure. Scholars who have emphasized the first approach are prone to discuss community identity itself as an assemblage or *agencement* (Kuhn, Ashcraft, and Cooren, 2017), where what appears to be an organically asserted community identity is actually constituted through externals. Ganesh and Barber's (2009) work on the *silent community*, for instance, shows how NGOs work to construct marketized, rationalized, and informatized representations of communities that may not even contain actual people.

Over the last thirty years, a considerable body of literature in organizational communication and organizational studies more broadly has also established multifarious ways that community autonomy has been eroded and erased. These include not only Deetz's (1992) comprehensive thesis regarding the corporate colonization of everyday communication praxis, but also many specific studies of community and cooperative building – perhaps the most well-known of these being Cheney's (1999) work on the Mondragon cooperatives. More broadly, postcolonial approaches to organizational communication (Broadfoot and Munshi 2013) bear considerable promise in investigating the dynamics whereby, in Castoriadis' (1987) terms, the ability of collectives of people to imagine autonomous futures, has been colonized and erased by colonial capital.

Juxtaposed against these studies, a considerable body of literature in organizational communication studies focuses on *immanent* dynamics involved in community empowerment, often through the lens of resistance, but also through collective assertion. Trethewey's (1997) study of clients at a human service organization, for example, identified multiple, albeit fragmented ways that women were able to resist and subvert the passive subject positions that they had been assigned. Research on the notion of empowerment is complex and is heavily inflected by the theoretical sensibility of the study.

For instance, poststructural work on empowerment (e. g., Ashcraft and Kedrowicz 2002) has shown that empowerment is a paradoxical process that can inaugurate its own sets of inequities. Research inspired by social exchange and collective theories also argues that the heart of community empowerment begins when people start organizing groups to obtain social change that they could not achieve as individuals (e. g., Rogers and Singhal 2016). Studies that are more explicitly grounded in a critical tradition and a discourse of suspicion, however, are prone to question the discursive function of empowerment itself, as well as terms related to it. Dempsey's (2010) critique of the notion of "community engagement", for instance, identifies how a term ostensibly designed to describe democratic participation devolved into a means to garner compliance.

2 Community building as philosophy, method, and praxis

In this section, we turn our attention to praxis, a term that brings together our concerns with theory, transformation, and practice. Once again, we draw from Marx (1963) in understanding praxis as the production and transformation of collective subjectivity that results from material action. For Marx (1963), philosophy itself is, after all, the abstraction of contradictions encountered in practice. Understood in those terms, praxis is close to synonymous with the term community building itself. Our effort here is to highlight the work of the culture-centered approach in yoking together theory, method, and efforts at social change and community building, and we do so by highlighting two efforts at community building that drew their theoretical and practical insight from the approach (Dutta, 2014). As we do so, we surface multiple tensions and contradictions, paying particular attention to processes of erasure, voice, and materiality.

2.1 Organizing the poor in Singapore

The "Singaporeans Left Behind" advocacy campaign was designed as a communicative infrastructure for challenging and dismantling the extreme neoliberal symbolic-material architecture constructed by the state (Dutta et al. 2019). Advisory groups of community members from low-income households co-created the campaign, seeking to build a communicative register for poverty in Singapore. The naming of poverty as the site and substance of the intervention reflected the desire of low-income households to build transformation around this register. The project came about through what is now a well-known and signature method of the CCA: to use the research process itself as a means of community building. This process involves an initial reflexive research engagement with marginalized voices and issues, through the use of a wide range of methods, including interviews, dialogues, focus groups, and even autoethnography. These methods become part of a facilitative process whereby community voices design campaigns for action through the creation of a community advisory group or board. The community advocacy campaigns as infrastructural arrangements are thus led, designed, implemented, and even evaluated by the community.

In the case of the Singaporeans Left Behind campaign, organized by the Center for Culture-Centered Approach to Research and Evaluation (CARE), a series of 180 interviews, participant observation, and food drives helped the community and the researchers identify key themes in impoverishment, including housing access and affordability, precarity regarding the provision of basic services, food insecurity, as well as alienation and stigma (Dutta, Tan, and Rathina-Pandi 2016). This became the basis of the advocacy campaign, which took largely digital forms, contained a widely shared Facebook and social media link, featured creative and innovative videos by both researchers and the community, and enabled online discussions by community members and Singaporeans about poverty and precarity, as well as critical assessments of official community organizations that functioned as state organs. Its effectiveness was evident not only in the conversations and discursive registers around poverty but also, critically, in the repressive response from the system, seeking to shut down or change/modify the intervention while orchestrating various forms of screening and audit targeting the center running the interventions, subjecting it to organized attack (Dutta et al. 2019).

Working at the margins of the margins and foregrounding systemic impoverishment tarnishes the Singaporean dream. More to the point, it challenges the very notion of a Singaporean community as a homogenous and apolitical resource, constructed through the externals of the hegemonic People's Action Party (PAP) (Dutta 2020; Dutta et al. 2019). Community participation in these hegemonic constructions is formulated as the state-directed community engagement, mediated through a wide array of state-sponsored and approved service organizations and civil society organizations. This actually works to deplete the democratic spaces for voices and ownership, and was in fact the impetus for culture-centered organizing in the first place, and the need to locate the intervention specifically outside the organizing logics of the state and civil society. Immanent power thus is rooted in community voices seeking to interrogate, resist, and transform the hegemonic organizing deployed by the neoliberal-authoritarian state. Co-creating narrative registers at the community margins for the articulations of everyday challenges with health and wellbeing in Singapore disrupts the total control in/over community life held by organizations such as the Community Centers (CCs) and Resident Centers (RCs) as extensions of the authoritarian state.

Moreover, the campaign dismantled the state-driven work of depoliticizing community by reducing it down to the recipient of services delivered by the neoliberal-authoritarian structure by foregrounding issues and identities around working-class struggles in Singapore. It did so by attending to the challenges with minimum wage, price rise, and high cost of living in Singapore (Dutta et al. 2019). Organizing, building, and supporting community identity was thus constituted around the question of social class, voicing working-class issues, and co-constructing class-based solutions. The potential of revolutionary structural transformation in community organizing is salient because of its capacity to disrupt the active work of depoliticizing the community which in turn is constructed in terms of Confucian harmony. This direct confrontation with the structure served as the axis for the negotiation of power.

Simultaneously, however, the campaign enabled the visibilizing of inequalities within Singaporean communities, and complexified the terrain of class politics with issues connected to gendered and raced marginalization in Singapore. For instance, discussions foregrounded racism within communities and in the organizing logics of the CC and RC structures. Malay articulations of raced marginalization in particular served as the basis for voicing and organizing around the disenfranchising practices of racial capitalism, attending to the ways in which the racist portrayal of the "lazy Malay" worked to keep the hegemonic colonial capitalist structure intact. Everyday struggles with livelihoods amidst multiple jobs performed by members of low-income households, constituted in relationship with the precarities of rental housing, food insecurity, and struggles to afford healthcare thus served as registers for constructing community identities in resistance to hegemonic state narratives of self-help and individualized responsibility.

2.2 Māori organizing at the margins

These raced, classed, and gendered inequalities were also evident in the context of Māori organizing in Aotearoa New Zealand. A culture-centered process of organizing assumes significance in the context of an indigenous land occupation project, developed through an ongoing ethnographic participatory partnership. At the heart of the culture-centered intervention depicted here is the Ōroua river, which is approximately 140 kilometers long and flows southwards from the headwaters out of the Ruahine ranges to the Feilding township and out to the Manawatū river, south of Palmerston North. *Whānau, hapū*, and *iwi*[2] consider both the Ōroua river and the Ruahine mountain ranges as significant landmarks in community life. The Feilding advisory group,

---

2 *Whānau, hapū*, and *iwi* are terms that denote social and kinship groupings in Māoridom, with *iwi* being the largest collective group, and *whānau* on the other hand, referring most often to family members.

comprising the "margins of the margins" of the Ngāti Kauwhata *iwi*, outlined their meanings of health and wellbeing as intertwined with the land, the river, and the environment, drawing on the longstanding relationship of Ngāti Kauwhata with the Ōroua river. The co-constructed research process began in June 2019, with in-depth interviews of thirty *whānau* participants that were guided by the advisory group. The findings were co-analyzed by the collective of advisory group members, community researchers, and academics, pointing to the key role of the river to the health and wellbeing of community members.

Just over six months into the ethnographic research guided by the advisory group, in early January 2020, Horizons Regional Council, the regional regulatory authority, invoked the 1941 Soil Conservation and Rivers Control Act to take possession of ancestral Māori land near the banks of the Ōroua river and construct a stopbank, or compacted earth dam, to prevent flooding. One of the ways that communication inequalities are expressed is through council consultation processes (Harmsworth 2005). While on the face of it, local government organizations appear to be keeping the community informed and garnering their opinions, it can also be used as a tool to prop up council agendas. We found that this was the case with the Ōroua stopbank construction, where potential dissent was suppressed. Not all *iwi* members were notified of the council's consultation process about the construction, and more importantly, not all *whānau* who were landowners were notified. Those that were notified and attended the council consultation *hui* ('meeting'), reported that their voices were not listened to. Particularly salient here was the erasure of the voices of the classed margins.

Against this backdrop, several Ngāti Kauwhata *whānau*, including members of the Feilding advisory group and the legal owners of the land, Te Ara o Rehua Ahu Whenua Trust, decided to occupy the land on the banks of the river at the construction site on 20 January 2020. The aim was to disrupt the communication erasure and to stop the illegal development. With little to no resources and no power, water, or shelter on the land, *whānau* collectivized their approach. *Kuia* (female elders) regularly sent baked food to the frontliners on the land. Workers stayed there at night and went to work during the day. Kauwhata *marae* (village courtyard and surrounding buildings) opened its bathroom facilities to the *whānau*, and other *whānau* supplied makeshift cooking facilities, shelters, and tents.

Horizons Regional Council then quickly agreed to meet with the *whānau*, in the hope that there was still a possibility that the stopbank construction would proceed. *Whānau* highlighted to the council that the written notice it had provided under the Soil Conservation and Rivers Control Act 1941 did not fully comply with section 137 of the act. The errors were pointed out to council and the *whānau* deemed the council's possession of their ancestral land to be unlawful. The council then delivered a verbal apology in the first face-to-face meeting held between the *whānau* and its representatives in January 2020 and acknowledged that they had not been fully consulted. Notwithstanding the apology, *whānau* members issued the council with a verbal and written trespass notice under the Trespass Act 1980, with a warning to stay off their ancestral land.

The culture-centered approach thus served as a basis for community building, bringing together members at the "margins of the margins" of the Māori *iwi* in Feilding, and articulating their voices in constructing the challenges to wellbeing and the solutions to these challenges (Dutta 2014, 2015; Dutta and Elers 2020). The advisory group of *iwi* members from the "margins of the margins" in Feilding noted the ongoing erasure of their voices and connected this erasure to their displacement from land. Their narratives articulated how their erasure from claims to land and the ecosystem was tied to the process of colonization, the attack on their dignity, and the ongoing erasure of their voices.

The principles of the CCA as the basis of organizing the collective turned to the concept of communicative equality, seeking to co-create infrastructures for voices. As the group started collaborating on identifying strategies for addressing this erasure, it came to learn about the illegal stopbank construction on the Ōroua river which, in the understanding of advisory group members, violated the sovereignty of the *whānau*, challenged the health and wellbeing of members, and erased them by eliminating them from the participatory process. Against this backdrop, the advisory group decided to engage in direct action and occupy the land on the banks of the river at the sites of the construction, to stop the illegal development and disrupt erasure. Through meetings held within the group, strategies were developed for the physical occupation of the land as a tactic to disrupt communicative erasure of *whānau* voices. The occupation illustrated how voices from the margins emerged into discursive spaces, disrupting the colonizing logics of occupation as development.

3 Conclusion: can innocence, once lost, be found?

Our aim in this chapter was to outline a set of communicative tensions to help position community building as a communicative praxis. The central metaphor we have worked with is that of innocence lost. In raising questions about whether communities can be seen (or ever were) sites innocent of inequality, injustice, and marginalization, we have implicitly questioned the ideal of communities as places of equity, camaraderie, as well as deep and extensive horizontal connections amongst equals. This insight is certainly not new. Network studies of community (Stohl 1995), for instance, have shown that community networks exhibit similar patterns of centralization, disconnectedness, bridging, and isolation as one might expect to find in corporations or public organizations. Rather, in outlining four dialectical tensions, we wished to illustrate how community building, as an attempt to recover an innocence that may never have existed, is a dilemmatic and, in many senses, impossible task.

The editors of this volume asked us to consider three pivotal questions about community organizing regarding its contextualization, functionality, and features, and it is helpful to address them explicitly. We understand contextualization to refer to the milieu in which ideas are realized and made material. Community organizing acquires meaningful context and significance by virtue of its implicit emphasis upon power relations and the constitutive and assertive role it plays in social formation. As a communicative activity, community building is both an activity designed to excavate immanent inequity, as well as one that is designed to challenge hegemonic interests. Functionality, for us, refers to the notion that ideas and concepts have unique generative and material force. Here, community building is significant because it is centered squarely around issues of justice, democracy, and the (impossible) restitution of equity. And finally, the structural features of community organizing are evident in the four tensions identified in this chapter.

The four dialectical tensions we have illustrated – local versus global, reformative versus revolutionary, persuasive versus coercive, and immanent versus external – draw together a considerable amount of work in organizational and management communication studies that represent a variety of theoretical traditions on the study of community and organizing. The notion of community building, however, brings an inevitably critical sensibility to our rendition of these four tensions. As we said at the outset of the chapter, the tensions we have highlighted here are not an exhaustive representation of the literature itself. Rather, they are designed to illustrate the insight we derived from Alinsky's (1989) work: that the potential for community building cannot be unlocked unless we "approach it with the key of converses".

The culture-centered approach is an ideal exemplar of community building because it features community building as a form of praxis: an integration of philosophy, method, and action. The two cases we featured here each illustrate various aspects of multiple contradictions in community building and bring a necessary anchor to what we believe would otherwise be a theoretically abstract and disengaged treatment of the term. Ultimately, we hope that the cases complicate the role of the academic in the ongoing negotiations between community advisory groups, community researchers, and activists (Dutta et al. 2019). The labor of generating theory should place the body of the academic on the line, work through the tensions we have identified to co-create spaces of solidarities with the margins, and build registers that transform the structures that perpetuate inequalities. In other words, if community building is truly to become praxis, it must involve placing the body of the academic in the negotiation of and resistance to power in order to co-create registers for structural transformation. It is in this sense that we see the work of community building as an overtly political labor. Even a cursory glance at the world around us today reminds us of how necessary that labor has become.

4 References

Aberle, David. 1966. *The Peyote religion among the Navajo*. Chicago: Aldine Publishers.
Alinsky, Saul D. 1989. *Rules for Radicals: A practical primer for realistic radicals*. New York: Random House.
Ashcraft, Karen Lee & April Kedrowicz. 2002. Self-direction or social support? Nonprofit empowerment and the tacit employment contract of Organizational Communication Studies. *Communication Monographs* 69(1). 88–111.
Basu, Ambar & Mohan Dutta. 2009. Sex workers and HIV/AIDS: Analyzing participatory culture-centered health communication strategies. *Human Communication Research* 35(1). 86–114.
Broadfoot, Kirsten & Debashish Munshi. 2014. Postcolonial approaches. In Linda Putnam & Dennis K. Mumby (eds.), *The Sage handbook of organizational communication: Advances in theory, research and methods*, 151–171, Newbury Park, CA: Sage.
Brummans, Boris H. J. M. (ed.). 2018. *The agency of organizing: Perspectives and case studies*. New York: Routledge.
Castoriadis, Cornelius. 1987. *The imaginary institution of society*. Cambridge: Polity Press.
Chávez, Karma R. 2013. *Queer migration politics: Activist rhetoric and coalitional possibilities*. Urbana, IL: University of Illinois Press.
Cheney, George. 1999. *Values at work: Employee participation meets market pressure at Mondragón*. New York: Cornell University Press.
Crenshaw, Kimberle. 1989. Demarginalizing the intersection of race and sex: A black feminist critique of antidiscrimination doctrine, feminist theory and antiracist politics. *University of Chicago Legal Forum* (1). 139–167.
Cruz, Joëlle. 2014. Memories of trauma and organizing: Market women's susu groups in postconflict Liberia. *Organization* 21(4). 447–462.
Deetz, Stanley. 1992. *Democracy in an age of corporate colonization: Developments in communication and the politics of everyday life*. Albany, NY: SUNY Press.
Dempsey, Sarah. 2010. Critiquing community engagement. *Management Communication Quarterly* 24(3). 359–390.
Dempsey, Sarah, Patricia Parker & Kathleen Krone. 2011. Navigating socio-spatial difference, constructing counter-space: Insights from transnational feminist praxis. *Journal of International and Intercultural Communication* 4(3). 201–220.
Dutta, Mohan. 2004a. Poverty, structural barriers and health: A Santali narrative of health communication. *Qualitative Health Research* 14(8). 1107–1122.
Dutta, Mohan. 2004b. The unheard voices of Santalis: Communicating about health from the margins of India. *Communication Theory* 14(3). 237–263.
Dutta, Mohan. 2012. *Voices of resistance: Communication and social change*. West Lafayette, IN: Purdue University Press.
Dutta, Mohan. 2014. A culture-centered approach to listening: Voices of social change. *International Journal of Listening* 28(2). 67–81.
Dutta, Mohan. 2015. Decolonizing communication for social change: A culture-centered approach. *Communication Theory* 25(2). 123–143.
Dutta, Mohan. 2020. COVID19, authoritarian neoliberalism, and precarious migrant work in Singapore: Structural violence and communicative inequality. *Frontiers in Communication* 5. https://www.frontiersin.org/articles/10.3389/fcomm.2020.00058/full (accessed 14 November 2020).
Dutta, Mohan & Steve Elers. 2020. Public relations, indigeneity and colonization: Indigenous resistance as dialogic anchor. *Public Relations Review* 46(1). 1–9.

Dutta, Mohan, Asha R. Pandi, Raksha Mahtani, Ashwini Falnikar, Jagadish Thaker, Dyah Pitaloka & Kang Sun. 2019. Critical health communication method as embodied practice of resistance: Culturally centering structural transformation through struggle for voice. *Frontiers in Communication* 4(67). https://doi.org/10.3389/fcomm.2019.00067 (accessed 14 November 2020).

Dutta, Mohan, Naomi Tan & Asha Rathina-Pandi. 2016. *Singaporeans Left Behind: A culture-centered study of the poverty experience in Singapore*. Care: White Paper Series 1. Singapore: CARE: Center for Culture Centered Approach to Research and Evaluation, National University of Singapore, 1–26.

Dutta, Mohan & Jagadish Thaker. 2019. 'Communication sovereignty' as resistance: Strategies adopted by women farmers amid the agrarian crisis in India. *Journal of Applied Communication Research* 47(1). 24–46.

Freeman, Sally A., Stephen W. Littlejohn & Barnett W. Pearce. 1992. Communication and moral conflict. *Western Journal of Communication* 56(4). 311–329.

Ganesh, Shiv. 2015. The capacity to act and the ability to move: Studying agency in social movement organizing. *Management Communication Quarterly* 29(3). 1–7.

Ganesh, Shiv. 2018a. Logics of mobility: Social movements and their networked others. *International Journal of Communication* 12. 3997–4010.

Ganesh, Shiv. 2018b. What's new about global social justice movements? In Jolanta A. Drzewiecka & Thomas K. Nakayama (eds.), *Global dialectics in intercultural communication*, 287–301. New York: Peter Lang.

Ganesh, Shiv & Kirsty F. Barber. 2009. The silent community: Organizing zones in the digital divide. *Human Relations* 62(6). 853–876.

Ganesh, Shiv & Cynthia Stohl. 2013. From Wall Street to Wellington: Protests in an era of digital ubiquity. *Communication Monographs* 80(4). 425–451.

Ganesh, Shiv & Cynthia Stohl. 2014. Collective action, community organizing and social movements. In Dennis K. Mumby & Linda L. Putnam (eds.), *Sage handbook of organizational communication*, 3rd edn, 743–765. Newbury Park, CA: Sage.

Ganesh, Shiv & Ying Wang. 2015. An eventful view of organizations. *Communication Research and Practice* 1(4). 375–387.

Ganesh, Shiv, Heather Zoller & George Cheney. 2005. Transforming resistance, broadening our boundaries: Critical organizational communication studies meets globalization from below. *Communication Monographs* 72(1). 169–191.

Greenberg, Julie. 2014. Beyond allyship: Multiracial work to end racism. *Tikkun* 29(1). 11–17.

Harmsworth, Garth R. 2005. Good practice guidelines for working with tangata whenua and Māori organisations: Consolidating our learning. *Landcareresearch*. https://www.landcareresearch.co.nz/publications/researchpubs/harmsworth_good_practice_tanagata_whenua.pdf (accessed 14 November 2020).

Harris, Kate Lockwood. 2019. *Beyond the rapist: Title IX and sexual violence on US campuses*. Oxford: Oxford University Press.

Harter, Lynne, Autumn Edwards, Andrea McClanahan, Mark C. Hopson & Evelyn Carson-Stern. 2004. Organizing for survival and social change: The case of Streetwise. *Communication Studies* 55(2). 407–424.

Hoffer, Eric. 1967. *The temper of our time*. New York: Harper & Row.

Kuhn, Timothy, Karen Lee Ashcraft & François Cooren. 2017. *The work of communication: Relational perspectives on working and organizing in contemporary capitalism*. New York: Routledge.

Laclau, Ernesto & Chantal Mouffe. 1985. *Hegemony and socialist strategy: Towards a radical democratic politics*. London: Verso.

Marx, Karl. 1963. *Economic and philosophical manuscripts*. London: C. A. Watts.

Marx, Karl. 1967. *Capital*. New York: International Publishers.
Michels, Robert. 1962. *Political parties: A sociological study of the oligarchical tendencies of modern democracy*. New York: The Free Press.
Robertson, Roland. 1997. Glocalization: Time-space and homogeneity-heterogeneity. In Mike Featherstone, Scott Lash & Roland Robertson (eds.), *Global modernities*, 25–44. Thousand Oaks, CA: Sage.
Rogers, Everett & Arvind Singhal. 2016. Empowerment and communication: Lessons learned from organizing for social change. *Annals of the International Communication Association* 27. 67–85.
Rothman, Jack. 1970. Three models of community organization practice. In Fred M. Cox, John L. Erlich & Jack Rothman (eds.), *Strategies of community intervention: A book of readings*, 20–36. Itasca, IL: Peacock.
Shepherd, Gregory & Eric W. Rothenbuhler. 2000. *Communication and community*. Oxford: Taylor & Francis.
Stohl, Cynthia. 1995. *Organizational communication: Connectedness in action*. Thousand Oaks, CA: Sage.
Stohl, Cynthia & George Cheney. 2001. Participatory processes/paradoxical practices: Communication and the dilemmas of organizational democracy. *Management Communication Quarterly* 14(3). 349–407.
Tarrow, Sidney. 2005. *The new transnational activism*. Cambridge: Cambridge University Press.
Trethewey, Angela. 1997. Resistance, identity, and empowerment: A postmodern feminist analysis of clients in a human service organization. *Communication Monographs* 64(4). 281–301.
Zoller, Heather & Meagan Tener. 2010. Corporate proactivity as a discursive fiction: Managing environmental health activism and regulation. *Management Communication Quarterly* 24(3). 391–418.

Dennis Schoeneborn and Verena Girschik
24 Managing CSR Communication

Abstract: In this chapter we elaborate on how corporate social responsibility (CSR) strategies and practices both produce and are produced by CSR communication. We outline three main characteristics of CSR communication as a particular form of management communication, that is, CSR communication's institutionalized, contested, and moralized character. From this basis, we derive key theoretical and practical implications for CSR-related management communication. We structure our considerations along three different orientations: (1) communication from the top-down (e.g., a firm's aspirational talk), (2) communication from the bottom-up (e.g., internal activism), and (3) communication around the organization (e.g., how to develop resonance capacities for the multiplicity of external/societal voices). The chapter closes with a brief conclusion and outlook in which we address the need for further research on the actionability, consequentiality, and bindingness of CSR communication.

Keywords: corporate social responsibility (CSR); CSR communication; management communication; communicative constitution of organization (CCO); institutional theory

More and more business firms are declaring commitments to fulfilling their responsibilities to society at large, promising to contribute in various ways to the alleviation of pressing societal issues such as ending human rights abuses and minimizing pollution (Matten and Moon 2020). Some firms take on these social responsibilities defensively: for instance, when they engage in corporate social responsibility (CSR) as a means of countering pressure and criticism from stakeholders or activists (den Hond and de Bakker 2007; McDonnell, King, and Soule 2015). In the face of such pressures, firms identify the need to account for their impacts on societies and to assume social and environmental responsibilities in order to maintain their legitimacy.

Other firms approach CSR proactively: for instance, when they calculate that CSR might pay off by contributing to their long-term competitive advantage. Indeed, many firms are seeking to develop new business models that aim at doing well by doing good, creating value for both business and society (Porter and Kramer 2011). Such proactive CSR strategies are considered useful by some firms as a means of differentiating their products as socially responsible and for building brand and reputation (Du, Bhattacharya, and Sen 2010). In developing countries and emerging markets, a further reason for proactively taking on CSR arises when firms confronted with governance gaps take on social responsibilities that address these gaps in order to enable or support their market strategies (Marquis and Raynard 2015).

The perception that many firms adopt CSR policies with the primary goal of fostering their own reputation and legitimacy (Du, Bhattacharya, and Sen 2010) has given rise to accusations that CSR is used primarily as a form of greenwashing or window-dressing. Importantly, the suspicion and very notion of greenwashing rests on a clear-cut distinction between CSR-related communication and CSR-related practices; or, to put it differently, CSR *talk* (in the form of CSR reports, brochures, and advertising campaigns, etc.) tends to be seen as decoupled – whether intentionally or carelessly – from CSR *walk* (i.e., the actual implementation of CSR in business practices and procedures).

This distinction has been problematized, however, in recent works from the field of organizational communication studies that adopt a less cynical viewpoint on CSR (e.g., Christensen, Morsing, and Thyssen 2013, 2019), emphasizing that decoupled forms of CSR talk could in fact become conducive to CSR walk, and thus should not be prematurely condemned as immoral or malevolent. According to Schoeneborn, Morsing, and Crane (2020), these different viewpoints are grounded in two distinct understandings of the talk-action relation. While suspicions of greenwashing imply that a firm's CSR communications are in an exclusively *representational* relation with CSR practices (typically, as reported retrospectively), other studies also emphasize the *constitutive and formative relation* between CSR talk in predating and lending meaning to CSR walk, in this sense "talking [CSR] into existence" (Haack, Schoeneborn, and Wickert 2012: 817).

Whichever viewpoint is adopted, both underscore the crucial role of organizational and managerial communication for CSR, showing that CSR communication can be used *both* as an effective smokescreen and means of manipulation to shield off illegitimacy concerns *and* as an important resource with the potential for actual organizational and social change. In this chapter we elaborate on how firms' CSR strategies and practices both produce and are produced by CSR communication. As a first step, we outline the characteristics of CSR communication as a particular form of management communication. On the basis of these considerations, we derive key theoretical and practical implications for CSR-related management communication. The chapter closes with a brief conclusion and outlook.

1 What characterizes CSR as a particular form of management communication?

Almost half a century ago, Mintzberg (1973) demonstrated that managers spent about 80 percent of their day-to-day activities on different forms of communication such as giving presentations, participating in meetings, and writing documents. This percentage can be presumed to be even higher today, facilitated by digital and mobile communication technologies. One of the main communicative activities of managers and leaders now pertains to CSR communication and other forms of interaction with relevant stakeholders (Voegtlin, Patzer, and Scherer 2012). Given that managers engage in a wide variety of genres of communication (on strategy, leadership, change, etc.), it is important to identify what characterizes CSR as a form and genre of management communication in particular, that is, in the sense of genre as a recurrent and typified mode of practicing communication in organizational settings (Bhatia 1993). Below we therefore elaborate briefly on the following three defining characteristics: (1) CSR as an inherently institutionalized form of communication; (2) CSR as a contested form of communication; and (3) CSR as a moralized form of communication.

1.1 CSR as an institutionalized form of communication

For many decades, the dominant perspective on companies' responsibilities maintained that firms first and foremost had a responsibility to generate *economic* value (Friedman 1970). This narrative held that companies contributed to social value creation by generating economic wealth, for example by producing employment and encouraging innovation. This prevailing narrative was challenged, however, with companies accused of abusing their economic power for accumulating and concentrating wealth in the hands of a tiny minority at the expense of society at large (Klein 2000). CSR is often considered a response to these accusations in that it holds out the promise of companies using their economic wealth and power to boost contributions to society and to solve pressing social problems (in line with the so-called "Spiderman" principle: with great power comes great responsibility). Indeed, most firms have now come to realize they need to engage in some form of CSR communication and stakeholder dialogs if they are to secure the societal license to operate (Scherer and Palazzo 2011), that is, to secure legitimacy in the eyes of crucial stakeholders, regulators, and society at large. CSR is thus driven by the institutionalized expectation that companies can no longer just mind their (own) business.

With the further institutionalization of CSR, the global CSR discourse has converged on one dominant narrative that positions firms as part of the solution to social problems rather than as the creators of these problems. However, a key challenge for firms working with CSR arises from the need to balance economic and social value creation. In the past, many firms engaged in CSR by using their profits to address social problems, for example through philanthropic initiatives, while leaving their core business unchanged (Matten and Moon 2020). More recently, by contrast, more and more firms espouse a commitment to integrating CSR in their core business practices, seeking to craft synergies that will enable the creation of value both for their business and for society (Porter and Kramer 2011).

Despite the inherent challenge involved in this endeavor, the promise is that such strategies and new business models may enable firms to attain direct and measurable benefits on the bottom line while securing legitimacy at the same time. As Feix and

Philippe (2020) have highlighted, however, the dominant institutionalized narrative of CSR incorporates a number of internal paradoxes and ambiguities in the concept. For example, firms portraying CSR as a synergistic solution to social problems that benefit businesses and society may aim in this way to pre-empt and buffer criticism from societal observers (for critical accounts, see Crane et al. 2014; Hoffmann 2018).

These considerations lead us to identify the first specific characteristic of CSR, that is, to be an *institutionalized* form of management communication. This means that managers who engage in CSR communication need to understand that they are operating within a highly institutionalized setup, as it has become a taken-for-granted expectation that firms will have some form of CSR department, will report on their CSR and sustainability practices (Etzion and Ferraro 2020), and engage in interactive conversations with their stakeholders (Palazzo and Scherer 2006). In this sense, firms experience isomorphic pressures to mimic what other firms do (Scherer, Palazzo, and Seidl 2013).

This institutionalization process is further fueled by an increasing focus on CSR and sustainability in the education of management students at universities and business schools (Høgdal et al. 2019) and the gradual entry of these students into the job market. This professionalization of CSR and its ever more highly institutionalized character have resulted in limited freedom as to what can be said or done in the now established genres of CSR and sustainability reporting, stakeholder dialogs, etc. We return to this point later in this chapter when we discuss the implications of CSR for management communication.

1.2 CSR as a contested form of communication

Despite its highly institutionalized character, CSR is also a highly contested concept. Indeed, Curbach (2009) argues that the domain of CSR is shaped by struggles over how to define the meaning of the concept, between what she calls the "corporate social responsibility movement" (i.e., business firms in alliance with moderate NGOs) and the "corporate social irresponsibility movement" (i.e., radical activists such as Greenpeace). The latter movement tends to criticize CSR for projecting an overly corporate-centric version of the scope of a firm's responsibility. Importantly, in this view it is the communicative struggle over meanings that in itself constitutes the existence of CSR as an institution.

Because the meaning of the concept is contested, CSR is sometimes accused of being an "empty signifier" (Zueva and Fairbrass 2019) that can mean everything and nothing because it does not clearly define the scope of corporate responsibilities. For instance, while CSR often involves environmental and human rights concerns, other issues such as corporate tax evasion have so far typically fallen outside the scope of CSR (see Dowling 2014). Furthermore, CSR is often used more or less interchangeably with the concept of corporate sustainability. While sustainability historically pertained primarily to environmental issues, the concept is now used to refer to the achievement of environmental, social, and economic objectives, as for example in the notion of the Triple Bottom Line (Bansal and Song 2017). On the one hand, the somewhat abstract and almost all-encompassing character of CSR makes it relatively easy for firms to generate CSR talk (e. g., to communicate versions of the institutionalized narrative in their CSR reports); on the other hand, the abstractness of the term may also render it devoid of meaning at the level of practice, especially when applied in different local contexts.

By virtue of the embeddedness of their market activities in local, social, and political contexts, business firms have typically been ascribed certain roles and responsibilities. The division of labor regarding the fulfillment of these social responsibilities between business and societal actors such as governments and NGOs differs across countries, with firms in some countries implicitly taking on social responsibilities by virtue of their embeddedness in the local institutional environment (Matten and Moon 2008). Companies in Scandinavia, for instance, are known to maintain strong relations with their stakeholders and have historically assumed a crucial role in co-creating not only economic but also social value (Strand, Freeman, and Hockerts 2015). While contextually bound and historically contingent, local divisions of labor are renegotiated and evolve as firms increasingly engage in CSR and take on new social roles and responsibilities (Matten and Moon 2020).

Moreover, because firms operate across national borders and their impacts extend to distant countries, their social responsibilities are also renegotiated in arenas of transnational governance. Grounded in the observation that firms often fill gaps in governance, for example, when they provide healthcare or education in developing countries, the CSR literature has long acknowledged that companies take on responsibilities traditionally undertaken by governments (Matten and Crane 2005). The literature on *Political CSR* in particular focuses on how the division of labor between business and governments is renegotiated (Scherer and Palazzo 2011; Scherer et al. 2016), finding that such re-negotiations most saliently take place transnationally through multi-stakeholder initiatives (de Bakker, Rasche, and Ponte 2019). As a form of transnational governance, these initiatives bring together a variety of stakeholders to discuss solutions to global issues such as human rights abuses and environmental degradation. In order to enable collective action and produce social value, however, such cross-sectoral initiatives face the challenge of moving beyond the contestation of corporate responsibilities and of developing a communicative co-orientation over time (Koschmann, Kuhn, and Pfarrer 2012).

1.3 CSR as a moralized form of communication

Because CSR pertains to business firms taking on responsibilities in the societal sphere, and because their actions have impacts on public goods, firms engaged in CSR are no longer evaluated solely according to norms that govern their market activities. In the societal sphere, legitimacy is ascribed on the basis of the extent to which corporate practices are "the right thing to do" (Palazzo and Scherer 2006). For this reason, corporate social responsibilities ought to be defined through deliberation and public will formation. The key evaluation criterion by which firms are evaluated in terms of CSR, therefore, is the moral value of their practices.

CSR as a "morally charged" practice (Caruana and Crane 2008: 1512) is special in that it tends to attract particular media attention (see also Schultz 2011). As Haack, Schoeneborn, and Wickert (2012) showed in their empirical study of the Equator Principles, a CSR standard in the international project finance industry, public communication about firms can lead to what the authors of the study term "moral entrapment". In other words, once a firm has publicly committed to adopting a certain CSR practice in substantive ways, such as by adopting a sustainability standard, it will be hard for the company to turn back from that established commitment and abandon the CSR practice at a later point. Haack, Martignoni, and Schoeneborn (2020) have further illustrated the notion of moral entrapment in the case of Apple, which in 2012 announced it would withdraw from the EPEAT program, a sustainability standard in the electronics industry, only to be compelled to re-adopt the standard soon after in the face of widespread criticism from activists and the media. The authors conclude from this case that it is the morally charged character that distinguishes CSR, at least in the eyes of public beholders, from other less sensitive organizational practices such as the adoption of technical standards.

Taken together, CSR communication can be seen as a particular genre of organizational and managerial communication (see Bhatia 1993; Orlikowski and Yates 1994), a genre shaped, as we have shown, by its institutionalized, contested, and moralized character. Given these three main features, CSR and sustainability communication imposes a particular burden on managers, requiring them to give serious consideration to stakeholder claims in their day-to-day decision-making (Voegtlin, Patzer, and Scherer 2012). Such consideration also entails developing sensitivities to the voices and viewpoints of societal observers (Trittin and Schoeneborn 2017) who are ultimately the ones who bestow legitimacy on an organization (Bitektine and Haack 2015; Suchman 1995).

2 What are the key theoretical and practical implications for CSR as a form of management communication?

On the basis of what we have identified as the specific characteristics of CSR as a form of management communication, in the following section, we derive the key implications for the theory and practice of CSR communication. We structure our considerations according to three different orientations: (1) communication from the top down, (2) communication from the bottom up, and (3) communication around the organization.

2.1 Top-down

Although societal expectations regarding the responsibilities of firms have become highly institutionalized over recent decades, these expectations may nonetheless directly contradict each other as the expectations of different groups of stakeholders can significantly diverge. Leaders and managers are thus recurrently forced to choose amongst a portfolio of three basic strategic options of legitimation, as Scherer, Palazzo, and Seidl (2013) highlight: (a) *strategic manipulation* (i.e., attempting to influence societal expectations in such a way that they conform with existing business practices); (b) *isomorphic adaptation* (i.e., altering existing business practices so that they conform with societal expectations); or (c) *moral reasoning* (i.e., engaging in deliberative dialog with stakeholders that will ideally generate mutual change and closer approximation of existing business practices with societal expectations). While moral reasoning is usually seen as the most advanced form of attaining legitimacy (see also Morsing and Schultz 2006), it also tends to involve considerable costs. For this reason, Scherer, Palazzo, and Seidl (2013) argue that firms may need to embrace a "paradox strategy" to cope in the face of complex and partly contradictory expectations, that is, by simultaneously combining the three legitimation strategies according to different audiences.

Many firms manage to escape immediate societal expectations and to buffer potential criticisms from external constituents by engaging in what has been termed "aspirational talk" (Christensen, Morsing, and Thyssen 2013). Such talk takes the form of communicative projections to accomplish an idealized state of alignment with societal expectations in the future (typically in the long-term future). Driven to a great extent by the Paris Climate Agreement of 2016 and the UN's Sustainable Development Goals set for 2030, more and more large firms have started to proclaim ambitious climate goals in recent years: for example, the Scandinavian Airline SAS aims to have its carbon emissions cut by half by 2050, while the German car manufacturer Volkswagen aims to become completely carbon-neutral by 2050. However, such bold claims have often been seen as a form of decoupling or greenwashing since these idealized, future goals are often rather distant from current business practices. Nevertheless, Christensen, Morsing, and Thyssen (2013, 2019) argue that, under certain conditions, such aspirational talk can serve as an important driver of organizational change toward sustainability by projecting a future for which the firm can subsequently be held accountable (for further empirical evidence of this claim, see studies in Haack, Schoeneborn, and Wickert 2012 as well as Penttilä 2020).

While aspirational talk is pursued as a tactic by one group of firms, another group of firms are heading in the opposite direction of "strategic silence" (Carlos and Lewis 2018). For example, in a study based on data on actual greenhouse gas emissions generated by US investor-owned electric utility companies, Kim and Lyon (2015) were able to show that some firms had underreported their achievements in reducing emissions. The authors interpreted this communicative strategy as a form of undue modesty in sustainability communication that they termed *brownwashing*, being, in some senses, the opposite of greenwashing. Similarly, Font, Elgammal, and Lamond (2017) provided evidence from an interview-based study of the hotel industry of what they termed *greenhushing*, which occurs when a firm deliberately withholds information about its CSR practices.

An important question arising from these observations is why some firms and managers opt for aspirational talk while others opt for greenhushing. One line of reasoning posits that some firms attempt to minimize public exposure on matters of CSR and sustainability in order to avoid too demanding public expectations and scrutiny (see also Eisenegger and Schranz 2011). Given the "morally charged" character of CSR business practices (Caruana and Crane 2008; Schultz 2011), public re-negotiations of responsibilities are often contentious and can pose a risk to companies' legitimacy and reputation (Reinecke and Ansari 2016). Firms may therefore opt to remain silent in order to shield themselves from contestation, especially when they deem their reputation to be at risk. Firms pursuing such tactics may still continue undertaking CSR practices in the meantime, further seeking to develop their presentation of such practices in ways they hope will withstand public scrutiny (Girschik 2020a).

A second line of reasoning proposes that the size of firms is the key explanatory variable for these two diametrically opposed orientations in CSR communication (Wickert, Scherer, and Spence 2016). This is because for large firms it is comparatively inexpensive (relative to their overall cost structure) to maintain a dedicated unit to take care of CSR communication, while it is comparably costly to implement CSR in their actual business practices and complex multi-layered value chains. On this basis, Wickert, Scherer, and Spence (2016) posited that large firms tend to feature what they term an "implementation gap" in the form of a discrepancy between CSR communication and actual implementation. For small and medium-sized firms (SMEs), by contrast, the relative costs of maintaining a dedicated unit for CSR communication are comparably high while the relative costs of implementing CSR in less complex business practices and value chains are comparably low. Accordingly, we can expect that smaller firms are more likely to suffer from a "communication gap", since, although such firms may perform well in terms of CSR implementation, they typically lack the resources to inform the world about these activities. Consequently, firms are more likely to engage in aspirational talk whereas small firms are more likely to engage in modes of greenhushing.

2.2 Bottom-up

With the aim of complementing existing explanations of firms' CSR strategies and activities, the CSR literature has recently turned attention to the micro-level, intra-organizational dynamics of CSR, focusing especially on the roles of individuals in these processes (for an overview, see Gond and Moser 2019). By zooming in on individuals, the micro-level literature has afforded a closer look at how CSR managers work with and juggle the competing demands of social value creation and economic value creation (and specifically the profit imperative). Such research has consistently shown that the institutionalized narrative of CSR as a synergistic solution is problematic at the level of implementation and that CSR managers struggle to navigate the tensions and paradoxes inherent in CSR (see also Hahn et al. 2014). In doing so, managers construct and negotiate the meaning of CSR for their respective firms (Mitra and Buzzanell 2017). Such micro-level bottom-up studies thus serve to highlight the formative potential of CSR communication (see Schoeneborn, Morsing, and Crane 2020).

In intra-organizational politics, CSR communication plays a crucial role in drawing attention to social issues and in pushing for action to address these issues. For example, CSR managers may "sell" social issues to management by engaging in "behaviors that are directed towards affecting others' attention to and understanding of issues" (Dutton and Ashford 1993: 398), ultimately aiming to gain management's attention and persuade them to commit resources to social issues (Alt and Craig 2016; Sonenshein 2016). In addition to mobilizing higher echelons, issue-selling may also be used to cultivate awareness and influence decision-making throughout an organization (Wickert and de Bakker 2018). In doing so, CSR managers may draw on a firm's CSR-related aspirations and commitments. Indeed, the efforts of CSR managers to push societal issues in their companies is likely to be one of the key mechanisms by which a company's CSR aspirations gain traction over time and begin to influence decision-making, ultimately driving substantive implementation.

While CSR is most prominently driven by CSR managers or other professionals who enjoy legitimacy in promoting social issues by virtue of their roles within companies, other employees may also engage in CSR-related communication. Recent contributions to the field have revived the idea of activism in organizations by drawing attention to social movements emerging in or extending into companies (Briscoe and Gupta 2016; Scully and Segal 2002). Many companies host "tempered radicals" (see also Skoglund and Böhm 2019), that is, employees who pursue their passion under the umbrella of management in order to use corporate channels and resources to drive their social goals. Such activist employees may be well-positioned to promote CSR understandings and activities that appeal to both external stakeholders and internal decision-makers (Girschik 2020b).

A key question around bottom-up processes pertains to the extent to which these processes challenge a company's dominant discourse and practices, especially since companies are often quick to manage dissent by firing or otherwise immobilizing employees who do not fit in. In a related context, Costas and Kärreman (2013) have shown that CSR can be used to construct an idealized image of a company's identity and activities, thereby making these companies attractive to employees who may identify with such idealized images and merely enact already laid-out paths. Such "decaf" enactment of CSR (Costas and Kärreman 2013: 410; see Contu 2008) is problematic, reducing the space for critical discourse and thus increasing the likelihood that social issues will simply be co-opted into the managements' strategic agenda. In this way, social issues may be turned into minor, innocuous concerns while the company continues business as usual (Wright and Nyberg 2017).

2.3 Around

While our discussion of the top-down and the bottom-up processes has so far presented organizations, managers, and employees as the primary originators of CSR-related communication, in this section we address how external voices around a firm can fundamentally shape its CSR communication, as well. In their reconceptualization of diversity management from a communication-centered perspective, Trittin and Schoeneborn (2017) have argued that firms need to become more responsive to the multiplicity of voices and societal concerns surrounding them (see also Cooren 2020). This view ascribes a new role to diversity managers and/or CSR managers, whose main task becomes that of funneling in and "ventriloquizing" (Cooren 2020) external voices *vis-à-vis* internal audiences.

The effectiveness of these managerial efforts in turn depends on the degree to which they are able to translate external voices and make them connective to other existing conversations that constitute an organization, for example, by translating CSR-related terminologies in ways that make them compatible with and comprehensible to core corporate functions such as finance, operations, and marketing (see Schoeneborn and Trittin 2013). While these considerations may seem abstract at first glance, their immediate practical relevance becomes clear when we consider that some CSR managers do succeed in mobilizing societal discourses (e.g., on climate change) to leverage their standing within organizations and thereby increase their chances of bringing about change (see van Aaken, Splitter, and Seidl 2013).

In focusing on external factors that shape CSR communication, it must be acknowledged that the clear-cut distinction between a firm's internal and external communication has become increasingly blurred in recent decades (Schoeneborn and Trittin 2013). For example, the sophisticated mimicry and persiflage now made possible by digital media (Etter, Ravasi, and Colleoni 2019) has made it more and more difficult to identify who is authorized to speak on behalf of an organization (see also Dobusch and Schoeneborn 2015). Such ambiguities are furthermore reflected in media reports around organizations, as illustrated in the case of a past controversy involving the Danish shipping giant Maersk and an infrastructure project for the Nicaragua Canal. This project had been proposed by Chinese investors and its implementation threatened to have significantly harmful social and environmental impacts. In an interview about the project, an engineer working for Maersk declared that the firm would be generally supportive of these "infrastructure improvements" as they would serve to foster global trade. This statement was swiftly picked up by both the media and critical NGOs that accused Maersk of not using their influence as a responsible corporate citizen to stop the realization of the Nicaragua Canal project before it got off the ground (The Guardian 2014). The controversy created a challenge for Maersk's sustainability managers to "come through" with their corporate voice, to publicly affirm they would not support the construction of the project and to distance themselves credibly from their own employee's statement for the sake of preserving stakeholder relations.

Such external challenges and pressures for CSR communication become even more pronounced when considering that the majority of firms studied by current research are multinational companies (MNCs). This is important because, while many studies of CSR and communication have focused on the activities of top management or CSR departments at corporate headquarters, the fact that MNCs operate across national borders means their subsidiaries are actually embedded in a wide variety of external environments (Kostova, Roth, and Dacin 2008). The cross-border aspect of MNCs is a major cause of intra-organizational complexity, as indicated by Kostova, Roth, and Dacin (2008: 997): "MNCs have complex internal environments, with spatial, cultural, and organizational distance; language barriers; inter-unit power struggles; and possible inconsistencies and conflict among the interests, values, practices, and routines used in the various parts of the organization". Recognizing the global and local dimensions of firms' activities and their interplay draws attention to intra-organizational dynamics that most recent research has only begun to explore.

On the one hand, this perspective highlights how CSR strategies and ideas are diffused globally and negotiated with local subsidiaries. As ideas diffuse across contexts, they need to be "translated" so as to appeal to, fit, and be useful in idiosyncratic local environments and their context-bound terminologies (Sahlin and Wedlin 2008). As a result, global CSR strategies are converted into hybrid ideas and practices as managers on the ground try to implement them locally (Acosta, Acquier, and Gond 2019; Gutierrez-Huerter et al. 2019). On the other hand, recent research has shown that local CSR practices may feed back into and shape global CSR strategies. Attempting to gain legitimacy in their local environments, subsidiaries may co-construct solutions to pressing social problems together with key stakeholders and thereby redefine their roles and responsibilities from the bottom up (Girschik 2020a). CSR communication may then play a crucial role in detecting local solutions and framing them in ways that enable them to travel and inspire new ways of thinking about and doing business throughout a firm (Girschik 2020b).

3 Concluding remarks

In this chapter we have argued that CSR represents a special genre of management communication that comes with peculiar challenges originating in the institutionalized, contested, and moralized character of CSR. Our discussion has elaborated on the multi-layered complexities (top-down, bottom-up, and around the organization) that managers need to consider when working with CSR communication. We have also highlighted how debates about CSR, both in academia and in practice debates, tend to revolve around a fundamental distinction between CSR walk and CSR talk. As Schoeneborn, Morsing, and Crane (2020) have recently proposed with their notion of "t(w)alking", however, it can make sense to shift the focus of attention from talk-walk relations to talk-talk relations, i.e., to ask how different forms of CSR communication can best create traction for follow-up communication, thereby adding to the actionability, consequentiality, and bindingness of such talk (see also Ford and Ford 1995; Christensen, Morsing, and Thyssen 2019; Winkler, Etter, and Castelló 2020). The pressing societal issues of our times, above all the global challenge of climate change, require that firms and managers not only deliver short-term actions but also effective communication that lends meaning to long-term change. This is all the more necessary given the power of anticipatory communication and narratives as major vectors of rapid organizational, economic, and societal dynamics (see also Shiller 2019).

4 References

Aaken, Dominik van, Violetta Splitter & David Seidl. 2013. Why do corporate actors engage in pro-social behaviour? A Bourdieusian perspective on corporate social responsibility. *Organization* 20(3). 349–371.

Acosta, Pilar, Aurélien Acquier & Jean-Pascal Gond. 2019. Revisiting politics in political CSR: How coercive and deliberative dynamics operate through institutional work in a Colombian company. *Organization Studies*. https://doi.org/10.1177%2F0170840619867725 (accessed 14 November 2020).

Alt, Elisa & Justin B. Craig. 2016. Selling issues with solutions: Igniting social intrapreneurship in for-profit organizations. *Journal of Management Studies* 53(5). 794–820.

Bakker, Frank G. A. de, Andreas Rasche & Stefano Ponte. 2019. Multi-stakeholder initiatives on sustainability: A cross-disciplinary review and research agenda for business ethics. *Business Ethics Quarterly* 29(3). 343–383.

Bansal, Pratima & Hee-Chan Song. 2017. Similar but not the same: Differentiating corporate sustainability from corporate responsibility. *Academy of Management Annals* 11(1). 105–149.

Bhatia, Vijay K. 1993. *Analysing genre: Language in use in professional settings*. London: Longman.

Bitektine, Alex & Patrick Haack. 2015. The "macro" and the "micro" of legitimacy: Toward a multilevel theory of the legitimacy process. *Academy of Management Review* 40(1). 49–75.

Briscoe, Forrest & Abhinav Gupta. 2016. Social activism in and around organizations. *Academy of Management Annals* 10(1). 671–727.

Carlos, W. Chad & Ben W. Lewis. 2018. Strategic silence: Withholding certification status as a hypocrisy avoidance tactic. *Administrative Science Quarterly* 63(1). 130–169.

Caruana, Robert & Andrew Crane. 2008. Constructing consumer responsibility: Exploring the role of corporate communications. *Organization Studies* 29(12). 1495–1519.

Christensen, Lars T., Mette Morsing & Ole Thyssen. 2013. CSR as aspirational talk. *Organization* 20(3). 372–393.

Christensen, Lars T., Mette Morsing & Ole Thyssen. 2019. Talk-action dynamics: Modalities of aspirational talk. *Organization Studies*. https://journals.sagepub.com/doi/full/10.1177/0170840619896267#articleCitationDownloadContainer (accessed 14 Novemver 2020).

Contu, Alessia. 2008. Decaf resistance: On misbehavior, cynicism, and desire in liberal workplaces. *Management Communication Quarterly* 21(3). 364–379.

Cooren, François. 2020. A communicative constitutive perspective on corporate social responsibility: Ventriloquism, undecidability, and surprisability. *Business & Society* 59(1). 175–197.

Costas, Jana & Dan Kärreman. 2013. Conscience as control: Managing employees through CSR. *Organization* 20(3). 394–415.

Crane, Andrew, Guido Palazzo, Laura J. Spence & Dirk Matten. 2014. Contesting the value of "Creating Shared Value". *California Management Review* 56(2). 130–154.

Curbach, Janina. 2009. *Die Corporate-Social-Responsibility-Bewegung*. Wiesbaden: VS Verlag.

Dobusch, Leonhard & Dennis Schoeneborn. 2015. Fluidity, identity, and organizationality: The communicative constitution of Anonymous. *Journal of Management Studies* 52(8). 1005–1035.

Dowling, Grahame R. 2014. The curious case of corporate tax avoidance: Is it socially irresponsible? *Journal of Business Ethics* 124(1). 173–184.

Du, Shuili, C. B. Bhattacharya & Sankar Sen. 2010. Maximizing business returns to corporate social responsibility (CSR): The role of CSR communication. *International Journal of Management Reviews* 12(1). 8–19.

Dutton, Jane E. & Susan J. Ashford. 1993. Selling issues to top management. *Academy of Management Review* 18(3). 397–428.

Eisenegger, Mark & Mario Schranz. 2011. Reputation management and corporate social responsibility. In Øyvind Ihlen, Jennifer Bartlett & Steeve May (eds.), *Handbook of communication and corporate social responsibility*, 128–146. Malden, MA: Wiley-Blackwell.

Etter, Michael, Davide Ravasi & Elanor Colleoni. 2019. Social media and the formation of organizational reputation. *Academy of Management Review* 44(1). 28–52.

Etzion, Dror & Fabrizio Ferraro. 2020. The role of analogy in the institutionalization of sustainability reporting. *Organization Science* 21(5). 1092–1107.

Feix, Aurélien & Déborah Philippe. 2020. Unpacking the narrative decontestation of CSR: Aspiration for change or defense of the status quo? *Business & Society* 59(1). 129–174.

Font, Xavier, Islam Elgammal & Ian Lamond. 2017. Greenhushing: The deliberate under communicating of sustainability practices by tourism businesses. *Journal of Sustainable Tourism* 25(7). 1007–1023.

Ford, Jeffrey D. & Laurie W. Ford. 1995. The role of conversations in producing intentional change in organizations. *Academy of Management Review* 20(3). 541–570.

Friedman, Milton. 1970. A Friedman doctrine: The social responsibility of business is to increase its profits. *The New York Times Magazine*, 13 September. 32–33.

Girschik, Verena. 2020a. Managing legitimacy in business-driven social change: The role of relational work. *Journal of Management Studies* 57(4). 775–804.

Girschik, Verena. 2020b. Shared responsibility for societal problems: The role of internal activists in reframing corporate responsibility. *Business & Society* 59(1). 34–66.

Gond, Jean-Pascal & Christine Moser. 2019. The reconciliation of fraternal twins: Integrating the psychological and sociological approaches to 'micro' corporate social responsibility. *Human Relations* 74(1). 5–40.

Gutierrez-Huerter O, Gabriela, Jeremy Moon, Stefan Gold & Wendy Chapple. 2019. Micro-processes of translation in the transfer of practices from MNE headquarters to foreign subsidiaries: The role of subsidiary translators. *Journal of International Business Studies* 51(3). 389–413.

Haack, Patrick, Dirk Martignoni & Dennis Schoeneborn. 2020. A bait-and-switch model of corporate social responsibility. *Academy of Management Review*, https://doi.org/10.5465/amr.2018.0139 (accessed 14 November 2020).

Haack, Patrick, Dennis Schoeneborn & Christopher Wickert. 2012. Talking the talk, moral entrapment, creeping commitment? Exploring narrative dynamics in corporate responsibility standardization. *Organization Studies* 33(5–6). 815–845.

Hahn, Tobias, Lutz Preuss, Jonatan Pinske & Frank Figge. 2014. Cognitive frames in corporate sustainability: Managerial sensemaking with paradoxical and business case frames. *Academy of Management Review* 39(4). 463–487.

Hoffmann, Jochen. 2018. Talking into (non)existence: Denying or constituting paradoxes of corporate social responsibility. *Human Relations* 71(5). 668–691.

Høgdal, Catharina, Andreas Rasche, Dennis Schoeneborn & Levinia Scotti. 2019. Exploring student perceptions of the hidden curriculum in responsible management education. *Journal of Business Ethics*, https://doi.org/10.1007/s10551-019-04221-9 (accessed 14 November 2020).

Hond, Frank den & Frank G. A. de Bakker. 2007. Motivated ideologically activism: Activist groups influence corporate social change activities. *Academy of Management Review* 32(3). 901–924.

Kim, Eun-Hee & Thomas P. Lyon. 2015. Greenwash vs. brownwash: Exaggeration and undue modesty in corporate sustainability disclosure. *Organization Science* 26(3). 705–723.

Klein, Naomi. 2000. *No logo: Taking aim at the brand bullies*. New York: Picador.

Koschmann, Matthew A., Timothy R. Kuhn & Michael D. Pfarrer. 2012. A communicative framework of value in cross-sector partnerships. *Academy of Management Review* 37(3). 332–354.

Kostova, Tatiana, Kendall Roth & M. Tina Dacin 2008. Institutional theory in the study of multinational corporations: A critique and new directions. *Academy of Management Review* 33(4). 994–1006.

Marquis, Christopher & Mia Raynard. 2015. Institutional strategies in emerging markets. *Academy of Management Annals* 9(1). 291–335.

Matten, Dirk & Andrew Crane. 2005. Corporate citizenship: Toward an extended theoretical conceptualization. *Academy of Management Review* 30(1). 166–179.

Matten, Dirk & Jeremy Moon. 2008. 'Implicit' and 'explicit' CSR: A conceptual framework for a comparative understanding of corporate social responsibility. *Academy of Management Review* 33(2). 404–424.

Matten, Dirk & Jeremy Moon. 2020. Reflections on the 2018 Decade Award: The meaning and dynamics of corporate social responsibility. *Academy of Management Review* 45(1). 7–28.

McDonnell, Mary-Hunter, Brayden King & Sarah Soule. 2015. A dynamic process model of contentious politics: Activist targeting and corporate receptivity to social challenges. *American Sociological Review* 80(3). 654–678.

Mintzberg, Henry. 1973. *The nature of managerial work*. New York: Harper & Row.

Mitra, Rahul & Patrice M. Buzzanell. 2017. Communicative tensions of meaningful work: The case of sustainability practitioners. *Human Relations* 70(5). 594–616.

Morsing, Mette & Majken Schultz. 2006. Corporate social responsibility communication: Stakeholder information, response and involvement strategies. *Business Ethics: A European Review* 15(4). 323–338.

Orlikowski, Wanda J. & JoAnne Yates. 1994. Genre repertoire: The structuring of communicative practices in organizations. *Administrative Science Quarterly* 39(4). 541–574.
Palazzo, Guido & Andreas G. Scherer. 2006. Corporate legitimacy as deliberation: A communicative framework. *Journal of Business Ethics* 66. 71–88.
Penttilä, Visa. 2020. Aspirational talk in strategy texts: A longitudinal case study of strategic episodes in corporate social responsibility communication. *Business & Society* 59(1). 67–97.
Porter, Michael & Mark Kramer. 2011. Creating shared value: How to reinvent capitalims and unleash a wave of innovation and growth. *Harvard Business Review* 89(1–2). 62–77.
Reinecke, Juliane & Shaz Ansari. 2016. Taming wicked problems: The role of framing in the construction of corporate social responsibility. *Journal of Management Studies* 53(3). 299–329.
Sahlin, Kerstin & Linda Wedlin. 2008. Circulating ideas: Imitation, translation and editing. In Royston Greenwood, Christine Oliver, Kerstin Sahlin & Roy Suddaby (eds.), *The Sage handbook of organizational institutionalism*, 218–242. London: Sage.
Scherer, Andreas G. & Guido Palazzo. 2011. The new political role of business in a globalized world: A review of a new perspective on CSR and its implications for the firm, governance, and democracy. *Journal of Management Studies* 48(2). 899–931.
Scherer, Andreas G., Guido Palazzo & David Seidl. 2013. Managing legitimacy in complex and heterogeneous environments: Sustainable development in a globalized world. *Journal of Management Studies* 50(2). 259–284.
Scherer, Andreas G., Andreas Rasche, Guido Palazzo & Andre Spicer. 2016. Managing for political corporate social responsibility: New challenges and directions for PCSR 2.0. *Journal of Management Studies* 53(3). 273–298.
Schoeneborn, Dennis, Mette Morsing & Andrew Crane. 2020. Formative perspectives on the relation between CSR communication and CSR practices: Pathways for walking, talking, and t(w)alking. *Business & Society* 59(1). 5–33.
Schoeneborn, Dennis & Hannah Trittin. 2013. Transcending transmission: Towards a constitutive perspective on CSR communication. *Corporate Communications: An International Journal* 18(2). 193–211.
Schultz, Friederike. 2011. *Moral–Kommunikation–Organisation: Funktionen und Implikationen normativer Konzepte und Theorien des 20. und 21. Jahrhunderts*. Wiesbaden: VS Verlag.
Scully, Maureen & Amy Segal. 2002. Passion with an umbrella: Grassroots activists in the workplace. *Research in the Sociology of Organization* 19. 125–168.
Shiller, Robert J. 2019. *Narrative economics: How stories go viral and drive major economic events*. Princeton, NJ: Princeton University Press.
Skoglund, Annika & Steffen Böhm. 2019. Prefigurative partaking: Employees' environmental activism in an energy utility. *Organization Studies* 41(9). 1257–1283.
Sonenshein, Scott. 2016. How corporations overcome issue illegitimacy and issue equivocality to address social welfare: The role of the social change agent. *Academy of Management Review* 41. 349–366.
Strand, Robert, R. Edward Freeman & Kai Hockerts. 2015. Corporate social responsibility and sustainability in Scandinavia: An overview. *Journal of Business Ethics* 127(1). 1–15.
Suchman, Mark. 1995. Managing legitimacy: Strategic and institutional approaches. *Academy of Management Review* 20(3). 571–610.
The Guardian. 2014. Nicaragua canal will wreak havoc on forests and displace people, NGO warns. *The Guardian*. https://www.theguardian.com/global-development/2014/sep/30/nicaragua-canal-forest-displace-people (accessed 14 November 2020).
Trittin, Hannah & Dennis Schoeneborn. 2017. Diversity as polyphony: Reconceptualizing diversity management from a communication-centered perspective. *Journal of Business Ethics* 144(2). 305–322.

Voegtlin, Christian, Moritz Patzer & Andreas G. Scherer. 2012. Responsible leadership in global business: A new approach to leadership and its multi-level outcomes. *Journal of Business Ethics* 105(1). 1–16.

Wickert, Christopher & Frank G. A. de Bakker. 2018. Pitching for social change: Towards a relational approach to selling and buying social issues. *Academy of Management Discoveries* 4(1). 50–73.

Wickert, Christopher, Andreas G. Scherer & Laura J. Spence. 2016. Walking and talking corporate social responsibility: Implications of firm size and operational cost. *Journal of Management Studies* 53(7). 1169–1196.

Winkler, Peter, Michael Etter & Itziar Castelló. 2020. Vicious and virtuous circles of aspirational talk: From self-persuasive to agonistic CSR rhetoric. *Business & Society* 59(1). 98–128.

Wright, Christopher & Daniel Nyberg. 2017. An inconvenient truth: How organizations translate climate change into business as usual. *Academy of Management Journal* 60(5). 1633–1661.

Zueva, Anne & Jenny Fairbrass. 2019. Politicising government engagement with corporate social responsibility: "CSR" as an empty signifier. *Journal of Business Ethics*. https://doi.org/10.1007/s10551-019-04330-5 (accessed 14 November 2020).

Brigitte Bernard-Rau

25 Rating social and environmental performances

Abstract: Social rating agencies (SRAs) use corporate social performance (CSP) metrics to evaluate the way business organizations deal with social and environmental issues. In producing their social ratings, SRAs can operate as 'economic actors' or 'social actors'. As very little is known on how they construct their metrics, this chapter lifts the veil on the rating practices of a well-established social rating agency (SRA), oekom research AG. Key aspects of this SRA's relationships and interactions with internal and external actors show how the construction process of social ratings becomes standardized, and how the communicative practices around the making of these ratings offer new insights into CSP scholarship, and into management and organization studies. The chapter comprises four sections: 1) an overview of the literature addressing SRAs, 2) the sociogenesis of oekom research AG (oekom), 3) an overview of oekom's rating practices, and 4) a discussion and conclusion.

Keywords: social rating agencies; social ratings; corporate social performance (CSP); internal and external stakeholders; relational and communicative dynamics

In the last two decades, the business world has been marred by financial scandals, corporate reputational crises, and business failures. Many investors believe that their investment decision-making process should therefore not only be guided by the financial success of a company but also by its social performance. To know which companies to invest in, investors rely on third-party assessment organizations to provide them with corporate social performance (CSP) tools such as in-depth research on non-financial aspects of a company as well as benchmark analyses, social ratings, rankings, and indices (Graves and Waddock 1994; Orlitzy, Schmidt, and Rynes 2003; Searcy and Elkhawas 2012; Waddock and Graves 1997). These third-party providers are referred to as social rating agencies (SRAs).

SRAs generate metrics, grades, rankings, and ratings based on non-financial information to evaluate companies' organizational structures, policies, and practices in relation to environmental, social, and governance (ESG) issues. SRAs feed investors' demand for non-financial information by offering ESG research, ESG analysis, and ESG evaluation under the form of social ratings. Through their analysis and assessment, they not only provide valuable ESG information to the investment market, they also incentivize rated firms to improve their corporate social behavior.

Many scholars rely on this ESG information to conduct their empirical studies, notably when trying to establish a link between corporate social performance and corporate financial performance (Margolis and Walsh 2003; Orlitzky, Schmidt, and Rynes 2003; Wang, Dou, and Jia 2016). These studies use a variety of performance metrics, indices such as the Dow Jones Sustainability Index and the FTSE4Good Index (FTSE), as well as rankings or ratings provided by SRAs such as ARESE, Asset4 (Bloomberg), Innovest, KLD Research and Analytics (MSCI ESG Ratings), oekom research (ISS-ESG), and Vigeo-Eiris (Moody's) (e. g., Alberola and Giamporcaro-Saunière 2006; Chatterji et al. 2016; Chatterji, Levine, and Toffel 2009; Delmas, Etzion, and Nairn-Birch 2013). However, little is known on how these corporate social performance metrics are constructed.

This chapter lifts the veil on the production of social ratings at one of these SRAs, namely oekom research AG, as a single case. It proposes insights on the way the agency understands what it means to be a responsible organization and how this understanding supports the construction, operationalization, and evaluation of ESG performance indicators. It also draws particular attention to how the agency communicates regarding ESG issues and how its rating practices actively shape relationships around societal issues.

The chapter comprises four sections. The first section offers an overview of the literature addressing SRAs, clarifying the different epistemological approaches. The second section focuses on the sociogenesis of oekom research AG and explains why this SRA is a specific case in the social rating industry. The third section lifts the veil on the rating practices, including the conceptualization and operationalization of ESG measurements at oekom research AG, and shows how this SRA engaged in constant critical dialogue, both internally and externally. Finally, the fourth section highlights the transformative role of SRAs in the relationships between society and business and discusses the dynamic account in which social ratings can serve as vehicles for action and change towards addressing societal concerns.

1 Assessing epistemological and ontological positions on SRAs

The terms *social rating agencies*, *sustainability rating agencies*, *CSR rating agencies*, or *ESG rating agencies* have been used interchangeably in the literature to designate rating organizations measuring CSP (Bessire and Onnée 2010; Graves and Waddock 1994; Igalens and Gond 2005; Mattingly and Berman 2006; Schaefer et al. 2006; Sharfman 1996). Their theoretical approaches are broadly encompassed under the umbrella of the corporate social responsibility (CSR) and corporate social performance (CSP) literature.

CSR and CSP scholars conceptualize CSP as the relationship between firms' economic and social objectives, firmly establishing an epistemological position as regards this relationship (Carroll 1979; Wartick and Cochran 1985; Wood 1991). More often than not, they adopt a positivist and functionalist approach to study the CSP-CFP link and consider non-financial metrics as "taken-for-granted" (Entine 2003; Igalens and Gond 2005). For them, an SRA can be defined as "any organization that rates or assesses corporations according to a standard of social and environmental performance that is at least in part based on non-financial data" (Scalet and Kelly 2010: 70).

Studies using a constructivist or a socio-constructivist approach are driven by a quest to describe and understand several phenomena around the nascent social rating industry. They explore, for instance, the conditions explaining the emergence of SRAs, their historical evolution, their growth strategies, and their legitimacy as a new profession (Alberola and Giamporcaro-Saunière 2006; Avetisyan and Ferrary 2013; Avetisyan and Hockerts 2017; Bessire and Onnée 2010; Déjean, Gond, and Leca 2004; Waddock 2008). This approach suggests that SRAs should be looked at not only as mere providers of "taken-for-granted measures of CSP" but also as entrepreneurial actors or institutional entrepreneurs.

For some scholars, SRAs form part of a social movement, the socially responsible investment movement, which is, therefore, socially constructed. Arjaliès' (2010) empirical study describes SRAs as "challengers" who, from within economic and financial institutions, employed a mainstreaming strategy to drive change towards a more ethical or sustainable approach. In that vein, what matters to an SRA is to exert pressure on firms to behave more responsibly towards society. SRAs are, then, "ideologically motivated", ready to "step forward to articulate societal preferences about the level and nature of corporate social change activities, and they challenge firms to comply with these preferences" (den Hond and de Bakker 2007: 917).

Furthering the theoretical and empirical debates around the nature of SRAs, Elbasha and Avetisyan (2018) draw on Strategy-as-Practice and Neo-Institutional Theory research to conceptualize SRAs not only as "economic actors" but also as "social actors". Their view on SRAs as socially constructed takes them a step further in their understanding of SRAs as "supra-individual actors". As a result of their constant interactions with powerful and legitimate actors in the CSR field (e. g., investors, companies, field experts, government, academia), SRAs have established themselves as "strategic actors" who "actively engage in defining and revisiting the structural parameters", by materializing, integrating, and reshaping social and environmental issues in their rating schemes (Elbasha and Avetisyan 2018: 44).

Comprehensive information on SRAs' actual rating schemes and structural parameters, and in particular the construction process behind the development of social rating practices, is, however, not widely spread. A general question is how do SRAs operate to provide the yardstick against which companies' CSP is measured? More precisely, how do SRAs integrate societal issues in their measurement frameworks, specifically how their non-financial performance metrics and their CSP measurement practices are determined, constructed, and developed to deliver CSP data. Yet, SRAs' approach to assessing social performance and to generate the metrics behind this performance is not always clear.

The scarcity of research describing what SRAs actually do and how they do it may be explained by the difficulty to access proprietary data on the methodologies covering their rating practices. To this end, the following section offers to open the "black box" of a well-established SRA by exploring the procedures surrounding the operationalization of ESG data into measures of CSP. Taking a socio-constructivist perspective, it thus acknowledges that SRAs are social actors and also actors for social change in the realm of society and business relationships.

2 oekom research AG: a specific case in the social rating industry[1]

2.1 oekom research AG: its sociogenesis

The two men behind oekom research AG are Jacob Radloff and Robert Hassler. Born in the 1960s not far from Lake Starnberg in Bavaria, Jacob Radloff was a free thinker already in his youth, distinguishing himself as an anti-nuclear activist and leading an Anti-Chemicals-Club at age 10, then as an environmental activist resisting the building of an expressway through the hills near his home at age 13. Radloff left school at the age of 17 and launched an ecologically minded magazine entitled *Politische Ökologie* ('Political Ecology') in 1987 when he was only 21. Two years later he started the 'oekom publishing house' (oekom Verlag), which still exists today.

In 1993, Radloff invited Robert Hassler, another young environmentally-minded enthusiast freshly graduated in Business Administration from Ludwig-Maximilians University in Munich (Germany) to launch oekom Gesellschaft für ökologische Kommunikation GmbH ('oekom – private limited liability company for ecological communication'), an independent information provider for ecology and sustainability, furnishing ecologically oriented publications and journals, and providing ratings of enterprises according to ecological criteria. Both activities continued under the same legal entity and many journals, including *Ökologisches Wirtschaften* ('Ecological Economy') since 1997, *GAIA* since 2001, as well as *Informationsdienst Der Umweltbeauftragte* ('Information Service – The Environmental Officer'), and *Ökologie & Landbau* (Ecology and Farming) since 2004, have sprung from this venture.

In 1999, the environmental rating activities were spun off from the publishing house and incorporated as a new legal entity, oekom research AG (oekom). At this date, oekom started to produce ratings for the investment community.

---

[1] Since March 2018, the social rating agency has been a subsidiary of Institutional Shareholder Services (ISS), operating under the brand ISS-oekom and ISS-ESG (oekom research 2018). The agency failed to stay true to the strong desire of its founders to remain financially independent and has been unable to resist the wave of mergers and acquisitions in the ESG rating industry (Avetisyan and Hockerts 2017).

2.2 A unique set of data

The case study benefited from access to unique data. For just over four years, I worked as an ESG analyst at oekom. During this total immersion, I actively participated in all the activities and projects of my research team, which included doing corporate ratings and country ratings, attending in-house trainings and analysts' meetings, and participating in working group discussions and annual workshops. This opportunity enabled me, as an "insider-researcher", not only to gain access to privileged documents but also to develop a detailed level of experience in the rating domain. I observed the agency's practices, experiencing the ESG rating processes from the elaboration of the rating methodology to the corporate social performance assessment, benefiting from a thorough knowledge of the work practices, methodology, schemes, and procedures surrounding the production of ESG ratings. From this privileged standpoint, and only after a cooling period of a little over eighteen months after I resigned from my position at oekom, I started this research as a scholar. I was then able to complement my quasi-ethnographic observations with interviews conducted with oekom employees and its management.

Finally, in order to put these data into context, I analysed important original texts and documents produced by oekom to better support its rating approach. Four foundational documents were considered: (1) the agency's mission statement, (2) its understanding of sustainability, (3) its principles of sustainability rating, and (4) the Ethical-Ecological Rating – The Frankfurt-Hohenheim Guidelines. These documents constituted the basis on which oekom was disseminating its vision, theorizing its purpose, and setting out the principles that were relevant to rate a company.

3 Lifting the veil on oekom's rating practices

To investigate oekom's rating practices, the study takes a closer look at how the process of constructing ESG metrics became standardized. This helps trace the practices of *becoming* an SRA, *being* an SRA, and *doing* SRA ratings (Anteby, Chan, and Dibenigno 2016).

3.1 Becoming an SRA: the accidental occurrence of a skilled profession

When oekom research AG was created in 1993, its founders, Jacob Radloff and Robert Hassler, had as their primary objective the motivation of companies to become more environmentally friendly. The idea of developing an environmental rating germinated when the German chemical and consumer goods company Henkel & Cie published its first environmental report in 1992, leaving oekom research's two ecologically oriented founders intrigued. They wanted to be able to determine whether what Henkel communicated on their environmental performance was truly the expression of a real responsibility and commitment to protect the natural environment or was just the result of a PR campaign. Shortly after they gained access to the report, they set out to explore the market of environmental ratings and conducted a basic desk research. They soon discovered that, in the UK and USA, some investors were buying ethical screenings in order to exclude sin stocks from their portfolio – e.g., no tobacco, no pornography – but that no similar research effort focused on environmental issues. oekom's first Environmental Rating was created.

The oekom founders' active personal involvement in the environment and climate issues was instrumental in the design and development of their rating activity. For them, assessing firms' level of environmental responsibility presented an opportunity to promote environmental performance from a management perspective and to stimulate competition between companies. However, the oekom founders ignored much of the investment field. They then had to face strong competition from asset managers and asset owners who were more familiar with the financial world.

The founders persevered and, with their distinct pioneering spirit in the field of environmental research and sustainability rating, participated in as well as won an international tender for a four-year rating project involving global financial players such as Bloomberg. As of 1995, various financial service providers started launching eco- and sustainability funds on the financial markets using oekom's environmental research. Given these developments in the field, the two *ecological advocates* turned *social entrepreneurs*.

Academic research led by social ethics professor Dr. Johannes Hoffman at Johann Wolfgang Goethe University in Frankfurt (Germany) and consumer affairs economist professor Dr. Gerhard Scherborn at the Hohenheim University in Stuttgart (Germany) represented a turning point in the process of oekom becoming an established social agency. In 1991, the two professors created a project group named *Ethical-Ecological Rating* (ECR), which aimed to develop a set of criteria to identify investments for ethically and ecologically motivated investors. For the elaboration of their criteria, the scholars adopted value-tree analysis (VTA) and identified three main dimensions as the basis of their ethical evaluation of companies: (1) 'cultural sustainability' (*Kulturverträglichkeit*), (2) 'social sustainability' (*Sozialverträglichkeit*), and (3) 'environmental sustainability' (*Naturverträglichkeit*). Their choice of theoretical foundation was determined by their willingness to "influence the movements of capital from a 'moral reasoning' and a 'normative moral understanding', such as that reflected in the ecological movement, and make it fruitful for the structuring of socio-economic life and for cultural development" (Balz et al. 2002: 18). In 1997, the ECR project group presented its theoretical set of criteria, the Frankfurt-Hohenheim Guidelines (FHG) (Balz et al. 2002).

In 1999, a contract between the ECR project group and oekom research AG was signed. oekom developed a new rating product for the investment community, the

Corporate Responsibility Rating (CRR), which, based on the FHG, added social and cultural dimensions to their already existing Environmental Rating. With the CRR, oekom emerged, therefore, as a skilled professional organization, turning its founders' commitment to the natural environment into social entrepreneurship and becoming a social rating agency almost by accident.

3.2 Being an SRA: setting sustainable development as a guiding principle

Within a mix of methodological, organizational, and communicational structures, oekom analysts had to operationalize oekom's rating schemes following methodologies and rating practices embedded in the concept of sustainable development as a normative construct. Based on their ecologically oriented agenda, oekom's founders, together with the ECR project group, developed a set of principles setting sustainable development as a guiding principle, at the heart of oekom's philosophy, when producing social ratings. Standing up for the natural environment, the agency adopted a position that defined the SRA's organizational core values and identity. oekom's motivation to pressure firms to be transparent about the societal outcomes and impacts of their business practices prompted the SRA to be transparent about its holistic approach.

In 2010, the agency formalized its approach in a document titled *oekom research's Understanding of Sustainability*, in which oekom detailed its intrinsic values and beliefs as regards the protection and development of human society as well as the conservation of the natural environment for which the key players in politics and civil society, the economy and financial markets bear joint responsibility. Following the concept of sustainable development as a guiding principle, the agency assessed and evaluated firms' policies, measures, and actions with an assumed normative perspective for sustainable development, which formed the basis for the SRA's internal critical dialogue. Every analyst was required to learn and master oekom's ecological approach as developed in these specific sustainable development principles in order to measure CSP accordingly. By being transparent about the set of principles upon which firms were being measured, the agency adopted the role of a values-based watchdog in the field with the same normative approach.

Viewing itself as a social actor with a clear socially and ecologically oriented perspective, oekom decided, based on its own values, beliefs, and principles, what is good CSP performance and what is bad CSP performance. In the words of oekom's founder and CEO, "[Investors] want us to enable them to invest according to THEIR values and not to OUR values … We [at oekom] have a holistic logic. We say: this is good or this is bad".

In another key oekom document *Principles of Sustainability Rating*, analysts were informed about their duties and responsibilities. In this document, oekom informed all interested parties, particularly the firms they were rating, the investors buying their ratings, and all employees, on the beliefs and values upon which their rating framework was operationalized. Three fundamental principles were highlighted: independence, completeness, and comparability. However, whether economically sustainable or not, the principle of independence was the foundation on which the quality of their ratings had to rely. For one of oekom's directors, only an *independent authority*, that is, financial independence, could guarantee independent ESG research. In fact, although the SRA originally had ecological and societal motives, it was a for-profit company that had to meet economic imperatives and participate in the economy with external actors. The agency acknowledged the traditional narratives of capitalism and a free market while, at the same time, making room for analysis based on principles of freedom, rights, and stakeholder responsibility.

3.3 Doing by communicating: the communicative constitution of the SRA

The rating process implied operationalizing a sustainability approach and applying ESG knowledge to the SRA's rating structure. This required setting up standardized structures and documented processes and dedicating organizational structures to discussing questions related to the rating methodology and the rating process. By fostering a culture of regular dialogue, the SRA was putting communication at the centre of its activities.

3.3.1 Standardized structures and documented processes

Standardized structures and documented processes ensured the quality of oekom's social ratings. Mandatory handbooks gave comprehensive directions on rating guidelines and processes, including the indicator assessment approach. Analysts had to strictly follow very clear instructions regarding the assessment and grading process as well as the evaluation standards outlined in this documentation. All members of the research team started at oekom as research assistants (the entry-level analyst position, also referred to as junior analysts) and were first enrolled in a six- to ten-month training period. During this time, they were tested on their ability to evaluate ESG topics and indicators in accordance with oekom's understanding of sustainability and oekom's rating rules and methodology. A pool of long-standing analysts familiar with both oekom's sustainability approach and the practice of rating facilitated the training. Steps in the rating process included: company profile updates, negative criteria, strengths and weaknesses, media screening, external research for interim reports, full update reports, or event-driven reports.

The main challenge for the analyst was to learn and to integrate oekom's position towards all ESG issues addressed in the rating framework and to implement the methodology as accurately as possible. With the guidance of several analysts, the new recruit did research on a broad spectrum of ESG issues such as industry-wide sustainability trends, always looking for information that might trigger changes in the rating framework. This research was later used to formulate oekom's position as regards key ESG issues and to inform all relevant parties. oekom position papers on subjects ranging from climate change to human rights were made publicly available in order to foster transparency in the rating evaluation standards (e. g., Carbon Capture and Storage, Nuclear Energy, Corporate Green Bonds, GMOs and Agro-Biotechnology, Working Conditions in the Supply-Chain).

The good execution and implementation of the instructions written in a set of key documents was of outmost importance to become an analyst. One such document was the *Top Research Rules*, which comprised oekom's rating methodology and played a central role throughout the rating process. During the training period, the research assistant was expected to have read the rating methodology *in extenso*, to have studied it with attention, and to show that she was able to implement it in all stages of the rating process.

The *Top Research Rules* detailed standard procedures about how to operationalize oekom's approach in the rating framework. They explained, for example, how and when to adapt standardized selection options, how to adapt the wording of the standardized content phrase, and how and when an analyst could downgrade or upgrade the assessment. They also instructed analysts regarding what source documents (company sources and external sources) to use for the evaluation/grading. All information that formed the basis for the score given to an indicator had to be very well documented in the "Source" field, including, for instance, stating the page number in long documents. While the documented instructions on the rating processes were exportable in an MS Word document, the evaluation/grading grid with the choices of standardized selection options was only available on a logbook database.

3.3.2 Operationalizing ESG data in the rating structure

A standardized rating structure framed the assessment of positive criteria as well as of controversies in all three ESG dimensions based on company and non-company information sources. The information sources subjected to the continuous screening process included industry- and country-specific sources focusing on alerts, newsletters, and reports from NGOs, press releases from governmental authorities, publications by experts or consumer organizations, and information from the media. The use of an internet search engine was instrumental to screening ESG information and was conducted by analysts using a list of pre-defined keywords for all relevant indicators. The identification of relevant ESG performance indicators within each industry was central to operationalizing a rating, and all information likely to impact a company's rating was included in the rating structure.

3.3.3 ESG dimensions and ESG performance indicators

The SRA's rating system was operationalized through two main pillars: (1) Society, which included the corporate governance dimension, and (2) Environment. The Society pillar focused on firms' actions regarding the protection and development of human society and the Environment pillar on the conservation of the natural environment.

From a pool of approximately 700 indicators, *general* and *industry-specific*, the agency developed a rating framework with two parts (environmental dimension (E); social and governance dimensions (S and G)), using an average of 100 criteria for each industry, to assess firms' societal behavior. Drawn from the Frankfurt-Hohenheim Guidelines (Balz et al. 2002), these criteria were sometimes very complex and difficult to assess on one's own. They covered a large number of societal issues, where facts and circumstances were researched, collected, and evaluated, strictly following the above-mentioned standardized structures and documented processes. Each category represented a societal issue and was divided into three sub-categories: topics, indicators, and assessment and evaluation criteria. Categories, topics, and indicators could in turn be sub-divided. In the assessment and evaluation criteria section, two elements were evaluated: content and coverage. An overview of this rating framework is presented in Table 1.

Table 1: ESG performance indicators commonly assessed at oekom research

E	for Environmental Performance Indicators	– ECO-EFFICIENCY • Energy use • GHG emissions • Total waste • Water use • Paper use
S	for Social Issues Performance Indicators	– STAKEHOLDER MANAGEMENT – **STAFF:** Freedom of association, Work-life balance, Job security, Health and safety, etc. – **SOCIETY:** Human rights, Community involvement, Influence on public policy, etc. – SUPPLIERS
G	for Corporate Governance Performance Indicators (including Business Ethics)	– CORPORATE GOVERNANCE: Compliance, Board independence, Executive compensation, etc. – BUSINESS ETHICS: Code of ethics, Codes of conduct, Compliance programmes

3.3.4 Rating processes relying on discussion processes

Before a decision on any aspect of the methodology and rating process was taken, numerous meetings between research team members were held. During periodical research meetings, methodological inputs and updates regarding what ESG information to collect, how to deal with the sources of information, how to write relevant content, or how to grade the assessment were discussed. By promoting a culture of knowledge and expertise transfer, the agency helped analysts not only to follow internal principles, guidelines, and procedures but also to define, redefine, and co-construct them in interaction. The goal of such organizational structures and communicative dynamics was to empower analysts in their capacity to deliver reliable ratings and sound corporate rating reports. Each analyst was, therefore, in a position to do, to communicate, and to co-construct in a joint common spirit. In order to allow analysts to co-construct the rating methodology and the rating processes, oekom created the conditions for such dialogues and discussions. These communication episodes were hence defining oekom.

3.4 Communicating and relating

3.4.1 Engaging in dialogue with firms and investors

Throughout its written and verbal communication, the SRA's leitmotiv was to "have an impact on society through the economy". Based on their motivation to act as social actors for a sustainable world, the SRA engaged regularly with two types of actors from the business world: investors (their clients) and investee companies (the rated companies). As reported, the agency was endowing its social ratings with a communicative agency: "In a direct way, we try to achieve that our clients get meaningful information. Indirectly, we also want to make the economy sustainable on the whole" (COO, former Head of Research). Thus, by interacting on two sides (clients/investors and rated companies), as an educator and as an expert interpreter of non-financial information, one of the agency's central roles was relational.

3.4.2 Relating with investors

Very early on, oekom's founders were prompted to believe they could succeed in their social and ecological goal by helping investors "understand what are the key issues for specific industries and therefore for specific companies" so that these investors could directly influence the companies trying to attract their investments. Therefore, oekom's analysts had to perform an educational and pedagogical role with the companies they were rating, not only with regard to ESG issues but also concerning the instrumental motives of actors in the investment field.

> We manage to make them see the positive impact of sustainability and to show that it has a positive impact on the economic performance of the company, [...] that sustainability is not only [...] a moral thing but has an important impact on the company [...] on share prices, on profit, and at the end, also on shareholders. (Senior Analyst)

Such information was often qualitative, therefore difficult to analyze and estimate objectively, and was sometimes written in technical language, often incomplete, concealed, or not easily accessible. This interpreter role was therefore essential for investors.

3.4.3 Relating to rated companies

From a social entrepreneur's perspective, oekom was acting as a social advocate, using its social ratings as effective communicative instruments to penalize or reward business practices. The SRA expected the firms it rated to become more socially and environmentally friendly through their evaluation of ESG performance indicators, but at the same time avoided affiliations or business agreements that could risk the validity, objectivity, and reliability of its assessments. Thus, to comply with one of the SRA's core principles, independence, oekom did not conduct consulting services to help companies improve their ratings. The SRA's core clients being the investors and not the firms, the SRA opted to deliver independent social performance analysis and social ratings.

However, firms could buy either standardized Corporate Rating Reports or an Industry Report, which contained comparative presentations and detailed analyses of companies as well as benchmark information (oekom research 2017). These were designed to encourage dialogue with rated companies on professional ratings and thereby to trigger social performance. As firms were able to compare their sustainability performance with their peers, and to better identify their strengths and weaknesses, the SRA was acting true to its original social objective of "transforming the economy".

The rating process proceeded through various steps (data collection, data analysis, assessment, and evaluation/grading) before a final CSP or ESG rating outcome was assigned. An essential part of the rating process, however, was the feedback process. During this feedback process, analysts engaged in a dialogue with the assessed companies about their social and environmental performance. Each analyst in charge of a company rating would use this opportunity to raise the awareness of their contact person regarding specific ESG issues. Analysts managed their relationship with this contact person by picking up on "objective" and "corporate" sensitivities. The agency thus acted as a *persuader* and a *disseminator*.

oekom management viewed this communicative dynamic as a key step in the rating process, and thus, each new member of the research team received, in the form of a flowchart, a detailed description of how to identify and verify who at a rated company would be the right contact. Once the first draft of the rating report was completed by the analyst, the rated firm received targeted information containing details of the qualitative and quantitative assessment (content and coverage) and the evaluation/grading (individual and aggregated grades), including their assessment weight in percentage points. This gave firms an opportunity to contact oekom, ask questions on the rating process or the rating methodology, contest the rating assessment, provide clarifications, and make corrections when necessary. At the end of the procedure, each rated firm received a complimentary full draft of their rating report. After the feedback process was concluded, and the final rating communicated to both oekom clients and the rated firms, the CSR or sustainability officer, who was the point of contact at the rated firm, had the opportunity to continue the dialogue with oekom via a questionnaire titled *Now it's your turn to rate us!*.

4 Discussion and conclusion

The specific case of the German SRA oekom sheds light on the social reality of its CSP measurement tools. oekom's foundational principles of sustainability lay behind the construction process of its ESG metrics and of its rating processes. The agency was involved in various dialogical exchanges, which influenced organizational outcomes both internally and externally. Central to the SRA's organization were the discussions held during regular meetings between analysts at all levels, and within their respective organizational structure, with the objective of educating investors and influencing firms' behavior. Together with the feedback process between analysts and CSR/sustainability managers, these discussions were part of the communicative dynamics underlying the SRA's activity.

An analysis of these communicative dynamics helps illuminate how debates about rating translations and interpretations are constitutive of organizational and social change. The practices initiated by oekom's founders and enacted by the members of its research team created lines of dialogue between firms and investors in order to advance sustainable development as a guiding principle towards "a more sustainable economy". With its culture of both internal and external discussion, the SRA adopted a "communicational perspective on ethics and corporate social responsibility" (Cooren 2018) and a "communicational way of approaching the world" (Cooren 2012).

In that sense, oekom's rating approach attempted to bridge the gap between society and business and to take a transformative role. Analysts used and interpreted information they considered relevant to measure ESG performance indicators thus emphasizing the interaction between financial and ethical or societal dimensions. The "becoming" of oekom as an SRA is a process by which its members socialize and develop thoughts and actions for social change (Anteby, Chan, and Dibenigno 2016).

SRAs should be seen not only as "economic actors", providing taken-for-granted social metrics, but also as "social actors", "advocates", or "activists" with a clear agenda for how the world should be (Arjaliès 2014; Déjean et al. 2013; Elbasha and Avetisyan 2018; Gond 2006; den Hond and de Bakker 2007).

The model presented in Figure 1 illustrates how oekom opened lines of dialogue between society at large on the one side, and firms and investors on the other, bridging the gap between society and business.

Figure 1: SRA practices as lines of dialogue between society and business

Through its rating practices, oekom brought societal concerns to the forefront of the discussion within firms and in the investment world, thus advocating according to society's expectations that the business world act responsibly. Four types of dialogues took place. First, the agency was in a direct dialogue with society on social concerns, selecting the relevant environmental, social, and governance (ESG) issues to include in its rating framework. Second, setting sustainable development as a guiding principle of responsibility, the agency fostered a culture of critical internal dialogue to continuously improve its rating practices. Third, the SRA analysts assessed, evaluated, and measured firms' CSP, and as such entered into dialogue through a feedback process with managers about their CSR practices. Finally, as investors were relying on the social ratings for their investment decisions, they needed to enter into a dialogue with the SRA concerning the non-financial information, its translation, and interpretation.

Through the communicative agency of its social ratings and the process of interaction, the SRA spoke with one voice, "ventriloquising", in Cooren's (2018, 2012) terms, society's needs and ESG challenges. Internal and external open dialogues were an integral part of the assessment and evaluation of firms' behavior. The SRA put communication about ESG issues at the center of its rating process, ready to be attacked and debated. What this SRA had ventriloquized from society as "matters of concern" were then translated into ratings to become "matters of authority" for business (Vásquez et al. 2018). Interested parties should acknowledge SRAs' transformative power and pressure for greater interaction in the fields of CSR and CSP. The internal and external lines of dialogue that the agency developed (training, meetings, discussions, feedback) can be seen as a transformative power in which the SRA becomes the advocate of society's interests.

Since the final and key step in this rating process for users of such measurement tools is the grading of ESG information, actors need to be aware of the fact that, paralleling traditional quantitative financial statements, the evaluation of non-financial measures can also be based on normative statements. It is, thus, the duty of SRAs to make a conscious effort to clarify their objective when evaluating firms' social performance and to require of its analysts a high level of qualification, expertise, and experience. In conclusion, this empirical study of oekom research AG and its rating practices further develops the debate around the nature of SRAs, and around SRAs' rating processes, methodologies, and measurement tools. It highlights the role of SRAs as translators and interpreters of societal issues, thus acknowledging their legitimacy and transformative power in the business-society relationship.

5 References

Alberola, Emilie & Stéphanie Giamporcaro-Saunière. 2006. Les agences d'analyse et de notation extra-financière: Quels services pour quels investisseurs? *Revue d'économie financière* 85. 171–189.

Anteby, Michel, Curtis K. Chan & Julia Dibenigno. 2016. Three lenses on occupations and professions in organizations: Becoming, doing, and relating. *Academy of Management Annals* 10(1). 1–62.

Arjaliès, Diane-Laure. 2010. A social movement perspective on finance. How socially responsible investment mattered. *Journal of Business Ethics* 92(1). 57–78.

Arjaliès, Diane-Laure. 2014. Challengers from within economic institutions: A second-class social movement? A response to Déjean, Giamporcaro, Gond, Leca and Penalva-Icher's comment on French SRI. *Journal of Business Ethics* 123(2). 257–262.

Avetisyan, Emma & Michel Ferrary. 2013. Dynamics of stakeholders' implications in the institutionalization of the CSR field in France and in the United States. *Journal of Business Ethics* 115(1). 115–133.

Avetisyan, Emma & Kai Hockerts. 2017. The consolidation of the ESG rating industry as an enactment of institutional retrogression. *Business Strategy and the Environment* 26(3). 316–330.

Balz, Bernd-Christian, Claudia Döpfner, Klaus Rainer Forthmann, Peter Grieble, Johannes Hoffmann, Claus F. Lücker, Konrad Ott, Lucia A. Reisch, Thomas Schardt, Gerhard Scherhorn & Hans-Albert Schneider. 2002. The Frankfurt-Hohenheim Guidelines. In Project Group Ethical-Ecological Rating & oekom research AG (eds.), *Ethical-ecological rating – The Frankfurt-Hohenheim Guidelines and their implementation via the Corporate Responsibility Rating*, 15–57. Schriftenreihe zur ökologischen Kommunikation, Bd. 8, 2nd extended version. Munich: ökom Verlag.

https://www.cric-online.org/images/individual_upload/div_infos/fh_guidelines_engl.pdf (accessed 2 October 2020).

Bessire, Dominique & Stéphane Onnée. 2010. Assessing corporate social performance: Strategies of legitimation and conflicting ideologies. *Critical Perspectives on Accounting* 21(6). 445–467.

Carroll, Archie B. 1979. A three-dimensional model of corporate social performance. *Academy of Management Review* 4(4). 497–505.

Chatterji, Aaron K., Rodolphe Durand, David I. Levine & Samuel Touboul. 2016. Do ratings of firms converge? Implications for managers, investors and strategy researchers. *Strategic Management Journal* 37(8). 1597–1614.

Chatterji, Aaron K., David I. Levine & Michael W. Toffel. 2009. How well do social ratings actually measure corporate social responsibility? *Journal of Economics and Management Strategy* 18(1). 125–169.

Cooren, François. 2012. Communication theory at the center: Ventriloquism and the communicative constitution of reality. *Journal of Communication* 62(1). 1–20.

Cooren, François. 2018. A communicative constitutive perspective on corporate social responsibility: Ventriloquism, undecidability, and surprisability. *Business & Society* 59(1). 75–197.

Déjean, Frédérique, Stéphanie Giamporcaro, Jean-Pascal Gond, Bernard Leca & Elise Penalva-Icher. 2013. Mistaking an emerging market for a social movement? A comment on Arjaliès' social-movement perspective on socially responsible investment in France. *Journal of Business Ethics* 112(2). 205–212.

Déjean, Frédérique, Jean-Pascal Gond & Bernard Leca. 2004. Measuring the unmeasured: An institutional entrepreneur strategy in an emergent industry. *Human Relations* 57(6). 740–765.

Delmas, Magali A., Dror Etzion & Nicholas Nairn-Birch. 2013. Triangulating environmental performance: What do corporate social responsibility ratings really capture? *The Academy of Management Perspectives* 27(3). 255–267.

Elbasha, Tamim & Emma Avetisyan. 2018. A framework to study strategizing activities at the field level: The example of CSR rating agencies. *European Management Journal* 36(1). 38–46.

Entine, Jon. 2003. The myth of social investing: A critique of its practice and consequences for corporate social performance research. *Organization and Environment* 16(3). 352–368.

Gond, Jean-Pascal. 2006. *Contribution à l'étude de la Performance Sociétale de l'Entreprise. Fondements théoriques, construction sociale, impact financier.* Toulouse: University Toulouse I.

Graves, Samuel B. & Sandra A. Waddock 1994. Institutional owners and corporate social performance. *Academy of Management Journal* 37(4). 1034–1046.

Hond, Frank den & Frank G. A. de Bakker. 2007. Ideologically motivated activism: How activist groups influence corporate social change activities. *Academy of Management Review* 32(3). 901–924.

Igalens, Jacques & Jean-Pascal Gond. 2005. Measuring corporate social performance in France: A critical and empirical analysis of ARESE data. *Journal of Business Ethics* 56(2). 131–148.

Margolis, Joshua D. & James P. Walsh. 2003. Misery loves companies: Rethinking social initiatives by business. *Administrative Science Quarterly* 48(2). 268–305.

Mattingly, James E. & Shawn L. Berman. 2006. Measurement of corporate social action: Discovering taxonomy in the Kinder Lydenburg Domini ratings data. *Business & Society* 45(1). 20–46.

oekom research. 2017. *oekom impact study 2017.*

oekom research. 2018. oekom research to Join Institutional Shareholder Services. http://oekom-research.com/index_en.php?content=Pressemitteilung-15-03-2018- (accessed 5 August 2018).

Orlitzky, Mark, Frank L. Schmidt & Sara L. Rynes. 2003. Corporate social and financial performance: A meta-analysis. *Organization Studies* 24(3). 403–441.

Scalet, Steven & Thomas F. Kelly. 2010. CSR rating agencies: What is their global impact? *Journal of Business Ethics* 94(1). 69–88.

Schaefer, Henry, Jana Beer, Jan Zenker & Pedro Fernandes. 2006. *Who is who in corporate social responsibility rating? A survey of internationally established rating systems that measure corporate responsibility.* Gütersloh & Stuttgart: Bertelsmann Foundation & University Stuttgart.

Searcy, Cory & Doaa Elkhawas. 2012. Corporate sustainability ratings: An investigation into how corporations use the Dow Jones Sustainability Index. *Journal of Cleaner Production* 35. 79–92.

Sharfman, Mark. 1996. The construct validity of the KLD social performance ratings data. *Journal of Business Ethics* 15. 287–296.

Vásquez, Consuelo, Nicolas Bencherki, François Cooren & Viviane Sergi. 2018. From 'matters of concern' to 'matters of authority': Studying the performativity of strategy from a communicative constitution of organization (CCO) approach. *Long Range Planning* 51. 417–435.

Waddock, Sandra A. & Samuel B. Graves. 1997. Quality of management and quality of stakeholder relations. *Business & Society* 36(3). 250–279.

Waddock, Sandra. 2008. Building a new institutional infrastructure for corporate responsibility. *Academy of Management Perspectives* 22. 87–108.

Wang, Qian, Dou Junsheng & Jia Shenghua. 2016. A meta-analytic review of corporate social responsibility and corporate financial performance: the moderating effect of contextual factors. *Business & Society* 55(8). 1083–1121.

Wartick, Steven L. & Philip L. Cochran. 1985. The evolution of the corporate social performance model. *Academy of Management Review* 10(4). 758–769.

Wood, Donna J. 1991. Corporate social performance revisited. *Academy of Management Review* 16(4). 691–718.

Anne M. Nicotera, Melinda Villagran, and Wonsun (Sunny) Kim

26 Managing in hospitals

Abstract: This chapter examines the hybridity of hospitals' organizational meaning structures and the resulting hybridity of hospital managers, who sit at the interplay between organization and communication. Hybrid practices polarize hospital managers between *clinical management* and *general management* priorities. This chapter focuses on management communication implications of hospitals' unique and enduring paradoxical characteristics: conflicting missions, interaction of multiple professions, multiple external stakeholders, and an ambiguous and complex external environment. These characteristics are illustrated with excerpts from hospital employee interviews and discussions. Hospitals' essential structure is based in communication in these domains. Illustrations reveal that the organizational uniqueness of hospitals lies in the communicational implications of their social structures. Finally, a conceptual framework for hospital management communication is offered that provides tools for examining paradox through hybridity to prevent impasse and provide agency, conceptualizing hospital-unique characteristics as intersecting communication paradox domains.

Keywords: paradox; hybridity; hospital management; structurational divergence; communicative constitution of organization

Hospitals and healthcare systems are rapidly becoming more complex and less linear. The international trend is toward *patient-centered*[1] designs, "with the aim of moving from functional towards process-oriented organizational forms, focusing on the process of care instead of on functional, self-referential departments within the hospital" (Fiorio, Gorli, and Verzillo 2018: 2; see also Gabutti, Mascia, and Cicchetti 2017). Hospitals are vertically integrating into healthcare networks, complex systems of care across the spectrum of inpatient and outpatient services (Ridgely et al. 2019; Giancotti, Guglielmo, and Mauro 2017; Lega and De Pietro 2005). In the United States, this may increase administrative overhead (Hoffer 2019).

---

[1] *Patient-centered* care organizes care delivery structures and procedures around the movement of the patient through the healthcare system. Patient-centered care privileges the values of the patient in making care decisions and it depends on a well-informed patient who is active in her own care. This should not be confused with *person-centered* or *person-directed* care. Person-centered care is a clinical model that considers all aspects of personhood in treatment (social, emotional, and spiritual in addition to biomedical concerns). Person-directed (sometimes called patient-directed) care gives the patient direct control over medical decisions. (See Lines, Lepore, and Wiener 2015; Kumar and Chattu 2018.)

Factors in the organizational environment drive changes, pressuring administrators to ensure ever-greater depths and varieties of progressively coordinated services with shrinking resources. Mounting complexity is also driven by medical/clinical advances, growing clinical specializations, and demands from increasingly educated patients. Change is constant, both in the environment and in the sophistication of organizational functions, and can create more problems than it solves (Ommaya et al. 2018; Overton 2020). Although organizational designs continually evolve, hospitals have distinctive, enduring characteristics. They are more complex, fast-paced, and exigent (Barret 2014) than other human service organizations (e. g., schools, social agencies). Intersecting categories of hospital types include public/private/community-based, for-profit/non-profit, teaching/non-teaching, urban/rural/regional, and administrative type (Bevan and Ruttan 1987; Newhouse 2007).

In addition to values-creation to address operational and financial needs, hospital managers also face clinical demands, creating complex tensions. Because of unique organizational features explicated below, hospitals are rife with incompatible meaning structures. Structurational divergence (SD) theory explicates communication challenges stemming from these conditions (Nicotera and Clinkscales 2010). The *SD-nexus* is an interpenetration of contradictory structures that simultaneously impose equally compelling oppositional action demands. SD-nexuses create recurrent conflict cycles that sap agency (the *SD-cycle*): unresolved conflict, immobilization, and development erosion, rendering the conflict intractable. Nicotera and Clinkscales (2010) describe communication problems encountered by a nurse-manager of a geriatric care unit (GC) embroiled in SD from interpenetration of a patient-centered care clinical model and an efficiency/documentation operational model. To streamline admissions, patients were transported from the emergency department (ED) to the GC to wait. They often became unstable, requiring immediate care by GC nurses. Yet, since there was no GC admission, records could not accurately document who provided care, complicating management review and negatively impacting GC nursing reviews. The documentation system could not account for actual events.

Hospitals are constructed from hybrid meaning structures, creating communication domains susceptible to impasse and relational damage. Hospital managers, especially middle managers, must therefore communicate with staff, peers, and upper management to prevent intractable problems created by intersecting contradictory meaning structures. They do so from within their own hybrid positioning. Such structuring drives communication, which, in turn, (re)produces the structuring. Hybrid middle managers are the fulcrum of interplay between organization and communication. *Hybrid management* is indeed the common practice whereby non-medical healthcare professionals engage in clinical and general/generic management (Savage and Scott 2004), typically clinicians who transition from clinical practice to management.

Hybrid management practices often polarize these managers between priorities: *clinical management* (focusing on workload and responsibilities of a profession directed by professional values) and *general management* (concentrating on operational and strategic issues that shape the organization and its functioning). Polarization generates friction because training/education in clinical and general management come with contradictory socializations. Different, often competing, objectives drive the two sets of imperatives (e. g., subjecting clinicians to corporate rather than professional agendas). Managerial hybridity necessitates identity negotiation and engenders identity politics (McGivern et al. 2015). Hybrid managers therefore work in SD-susceptible conditions.

Hybrid managers are knowledge brokers (Burgess and Currie 2013) and integrators (Chreim et al. 2013) of paradoxical missions (clinical versus operational) and values (public-service versus market-based). They span boundaries between executives and front-line staff and coordinate support across boundaries. As clinicians, they negotiate competing understandings of quality (Savage and Scott 2004). Practitioners prioritize one-to-one encounters with patients/clients; general managers look to equity, relevance to need, cost-efficiency, effectiveness, and consumer acceptability; and patients prioritize professional communication, cleanliness, food, and privacy. These hybrid professionals communicate across these discourses, integrating them into consistent messages while creating and maintaining systems for values-integration and goal accomplishment. The physician-manager or nurse-manager faces these challenges paradoxically positioned at intersections of at least three competing discourses (Iedema et al. 2004): clinical medicine/practice's profession-specific discourse, management's resource-efficiency and systematization discourse, and interpersonalizing discourse devoted to hedging/mitigating contradictions.

Despite its importance, there is no cohesive literature on hospital management communication. This chapter focuses on management communication implications of hospitals' enduring characteristics. First, we illustrate a widely cited model of those characteristics (Ramanujam and Rousseau 2006) from a *Journal of Organizational Behavior* special issue. Articles in the issue conclude that the direct application of organizational theory to hospitals is unwise (see also Mintzberg 1997 for a complexity model of hospital organizational issues). Second, we provide a conceptual framework for hospital management communication, combining Ramanujam and Rousseau's (2006) model, hybridity, and SD theory. This approach provides tools for examining paradox through hybridity to prevent SD and provide agency, conceptualizing hospital-unique characteristics as intersecting communication paradox domains.

1 Unique organizational features of hospitals

Ramanujam and Rousseau (2006) propose a hospital-specific organizational theory,[2] observing that hospitals fall short in applying state-of-the-art clinical and managerial practices. Their four unique organizational features highlight hospitals' fundamental pluralism: conflicting missions, interaction of multiple professions, multiple external stakeholders, and an ambiguous and complex external environment. These common features grounded in empirical research findings are broad, enduring, and still quite relevant.

First, hospitals have multiple *conflicting missions* (i.e., patient care, community service, medical education, health research, and, in some countries, profit and religious values), creating the need for a multi-dimensional assessment of the mission-achievement. Second, hospital workforces consist of multiple professions with a multitude of differing training and licensing requirements, salary structures, and power roles (Körner et al. 2015). These professionals are socialized pre-employment in other organizational systems, so hospital-based organizational socialization is often neglected. Third, hospitals face a complex external environment with multiple stakeholders (e.g., third-party payers, consumers, government, and professional associations). Finally, the hospital task environment is complex, ambiguous, dynamic, local, and subject to simultaneous standardization and flexibility demands (Maxwell et al. 2019).

To illustrate these four characteristics, we drew excerpts from existing transcripts of hospital employee interviews and discussions in a nurses' training course. The interviews gathered narratives illustrating communication processes from eighteen hospital employees (fourteen female; four male) at three southwestern US hospitals (a large urban teaching hospital, a smaller private hospital in the same city, and a suburban community hospital in a large for-profit chain). All had previous experience in other facilities. The interviews, conducted by the second author, explored experiences inside and outside hospitals to demonstrate commonality and uniqueness across healthcare settings. The discussion transcripts originated from a continuing education (CE) course on communication and conflict directed by the first author. They include conversations among thirty-six nurses (thirty-five female; one male) from various institutional settings, meeting in groups of six. All had hospital experience; twenty-three were currently hospital-employed.

As mentioned previously, the characteristics identified by Ramanujam and Rousseau (2006) distinguish hospitals from other organizations. They illustrate that hospitals have an essential structure *based in communication* in these four domains. Our

---

[2] They use the term *healthcare organization* synonymously with *hospital*, but subsequent changes in healthcare systems have made this equivalency inaccurate.

illustrations show that the organizational uniqueness of hospitals lies in the communicational implications of their social structures.

1.1 Conflicting missions

Mission statements reflect organizational culture, embodying beliefs about the organization. An interviewee explained,

> There's just something about working in a hospital that's different from any other setting in healthcare. We all handle paperwork, meetings, and budgets, but somehow being in a hospital brings the "why" home in a very direct way. The hospital setting brings us face to face with the human side of the equation, and helps keep us in touch with the importance of the work we do.

Hospitals' mission to treat acute biomedical issues is unique, even from other healthcare organizations (HCO). The underlying value of alleviating human suffering resonates for all members. This value can be integrated into communication with every organizational role. From neurosurgeons to custodians, everyone's work translates to patients' clinical outcomes.

Weaving this value into organizational discourse is a valuable management communication tool. Unity of purpose creates common ground that builds relationships among employees and with patients, allowing the hybrid manager to integrate meaning differences. This crucial component of SD prevention (Nicotera, Mahon, and Wright 2014) is compromised because ongoing patient relationship-building is irrelevant to acute biomedical treatment. The curative mission drives a patient-discharge goal without relationship-building incentive with few exceptions (e. g., obstetrics, whose patients return for subsequent deliveries). Contrary to developing a repeat-client base, employees are driven to achieve patients' successful exit without return in tension with ongoing patient relationship-building.

There are also tensioned patient definitions: medical-need and consumer-oriented. One CE course nurse commented on definitions held by management, nurses, and patients, illustrating tension between customer-service and medical-need demands:

> There is a patient and what their expectations of healthcare system are and consumerism then there is the management and the business model and then there is the staff nurse [...] [Patient] feedback is very important that they give at the end of their hospital stay that does a lot and that is a big part of you know, medicine.

Another CE participant addressed the patient-as-consumer model in labor and delivery, with its managerially imposed repeat-customer imperative:

> The patient should be treated as a consumer because patients are really our guests in a way [...] to please the patients because they are your guests. We will, the employees should act like cast members and they do their best or [...] so that the guests will come back [for their next baby].

The person-centered (not patient-directed) approach is a key tool to manage this tension. Perceptions of patient demands may be reframed as patients' emotional or cognitive need to feel in control, whole, and empowered – evoking compassion (Kumar and Chattu 2018). A person-centered approach thus frames patients as more than their biomedical problems. Interview narratives illustrate how competing missions must be coordinated with the patient-care mission. Understanding secondary missions depends on knowing the motivations driving them. An interviewee noted, "the altruistic ideal of medicine – do no harm – is certainly the prevailing advertised motivation, but the reality seems to be a mixture of capital-driven models of collaboration with altruistic motives of individual members".

Conflicting missions of hospitals are complicated by unique divisional and authority structures. Hospitals' bureaucracy and multiple missions require parallel hierarchies – in addition to already-nested operational, financial, and clinical hierarchies. These structures carry implicit communication rules. Interviewees agreed that while channels and forms of patient-care communication were highly regulated, other hospital missions were less discussed. One illustrates the hierarchically structured nature of communication:

> When you work in the medical profession: getting the correct orders from the physician, carrying out those orders, making sure that your team that you are working with is aware of what is going on with that patient, making sure that everyone is doing what they're supposed to be doing. We can't go off on our own and do our own thing.

Despite rules-orientation and patient-care mission, interviewees noted a lack of training on how to communicate to achieve that mission.

> There is not training on specific verbiage to use in patient care. Hospitals do expect staff to use a certain tone of voice with the patients and families. They should be upbeat and [...] avoid anything, topics or tones that might raise anxiety. There are also rules of communicating ethically, no gossiping, no pre-judgment.

Yet, the lack of specificity in these expectations creates an opportunity for contradictions to arise.

1.2 Multiple professions and socialization processes

Ramanujam and Rousseau (2006) discuss the socialization and interaction of multiple professions but not their distinctive hierarchies. In addition to a variety of diverse employees, hospital hierarchies also centrally include non-employees. In the US, physicians who are not hospital employees can be primary patient care decision-makers authorized to issue directives to hospital employees. Rarely in other settings would a non-employee fulfill such a central role. This authority status comes with interesting language; the formal agreement granting authority to practice at the hospital gives physicians *privileges*.

The rule structures guiding communication among stakeholders may be incompatible. Volunteers serve in roles essential for patient care (intake, patient mobility) but are not subject to the same rules governing the paid workforce or physicians with practice privileges. In teaching hospitals, patient care (primary mission) also functions as a professional socialization tutorial for medical residents (secondary mission). External stakeholders, such as accrediting agencies, dictate rules for medical education that may not coincide with patient care (Safarani et al. 2018), which means that hospital managers must communicate with multiple stakeholders. Managers who understand value systems and languages of diverse groups can thus communicate across meaning systems to unite them by articulating shared values. The ethic of care for ill and injured creates a common ground that can prevent or alleviate SD and its intractable tensions (Nicotera, Mahon, and Wright 2014).

Yet even this common ethic can be implicated in SD without attention to managerial hybridity. In our previous example, hybridity complicated the relationship between the two department managers. Although operational peers, the ED physician-manager held higher clinical status than the GC nurse-manager, complicating their relationship. Because their relative clinical statuses are clear, communication about this problem should have been rooted in clinical issues. Communication based on their shared clinical ethics could have resulted in an agreement to privilege clinical over operational goals. Focusing on unmet clinical needs of elderly patients (at higher destabilization risk than other populations), rather than GC's bureaucratic sanctions, offers better ground for collaboration to design operational practices that follow rather than direct clinical practices – keeping patients under direct observation of the documented department. Since the reverse (operational directing clinical) compromised patient care, it is easy to see how privileging the clinical structure eliminates the contradiction and fulfills their shared clinical ethics. Communication that explicitly identifies paradox and rests on common ground is a hospital management communication imperative.

1.3 Complex external stakeholders

External stakeholders play significant functional roles. Hospital policies are complex and mandated from multiple sources (e. g., government and accrediting agencies, professional associations, and corporations like insurance companies). Medical residents are deliberately temporary employees who serve patients, hospital administrators, and attending physicians directing their education while navigating a unique maze of rules and responsibilities that goes beyond socializations from multiple professions. Externally driven certifications provide another example. CE participants discussed imperatives to achieve Magnet status from the American Nurses Credentialing Center (ANCC) – the most prestigious distinction available for nursing excellence and high-quality patient care. Yet, one nurse observed how changes to satisfy these demands had no connection to patient care or the quality of current practices. "There is a lot of hoo-ha about we have to change this, we have to change that, and we are coming up with all these great names for things and stuff", but she saw little connection to patient-care improvement. She described changes in nursing assignments that met Magnet demands but did not work as well for patient care. External stakeholder certification requirements for high-quality care superseded local environmental requirements that would have actually provided high-quality care.

Magnet criteria are entirely operational/organizational rather than clinical: Transformational leadership; structural empowerment; exemplary professional practice; new knowledge, innovation, and improvement; and empirical outcomes. These are desirable but disconnected from idiosyncratic local environmental needs. Magnet status can create inadequate standardized responses to nonstandard demands. Magnet criteria are organizationally valid, so implementation without goal displacement presents a management dilemma. Management communication must mobilize shared values that connect daily practices to Magnet requirements. Some employees view certifications/accreditations as a necessary evil brought on by increasing hospital competition.

Whether competition is necessary is currently debated (Hoffer 2019). External stakeholders are concerned about skyrocketing costs – resulting in hospital reform in the US to increase profitability through competition. Depending on perspective, competition is either the spine or underbelly of hospital economics, as it creates excellence incentives that do not directly translate to better care. Excellence measures vary, are often subjective, and rarely consider employee needs or wellbeing. Competition can lead to duplication of care, driving up costs across the national system (Hoffer 2019). A medical educator interviewed addressed the tension between patient care and profits:

> The [medical] students with whom I interact have great values. They care deeply about patients and becoming great at their profession. They show professionalism. They worry about the structure of the healthcare system, but they love patient care. I often tell them that payment and bureaucracy may impact our income, but once you go into the room (either in the clinic or the hospital) it becomes you and the patient. You cannot explain the reward of caring for patients to those who have never done it. Our students understand that.

Family members and caregivers are key external stakeholders who must be included in communication. They control dialogue about patient progress with a tremendous stake in patient outcomes. With multiple care providers, inclusion of family members in communication creates unique requirements for hospital employees. An interviewee noted,

> On occasion a family might request to be informed about the patients' status by telephone or email when they do not live in the area. It's really important to have strong communication with them [the patient] and more so with the family. The caregivers that are taking care of that patient [...] we include all of that; not just normal hospital doctor to nurse type communication, but the family communication.

Rarely in another kind of organization would someone with such indirect ties have such a central role in organizational communication. To effectively include these stakeholders, managers must navigate intersecting and often contradictory clinical, operational, and legal structures.

1.4 Dynamic/ambiguous tasks

Although hospitals are divisional bureaucracies, cross-professional teams are common and divisions (e. g., radiology, anesthesia, dietary, PT) function across medical-surgical units (e. g., intensive care, pediatrics, geriatrics, maternity, orthopedic, etc.). Multiply-crossed divisions of labor muddle professional roles and can lead to SD due to differing patient-care perspectives. Role conflict is rampant. Even mundane tasks, like transferring patient care between units, are complicated by applying standard procedures to nonstandard tasks. Patients' unique combinations of clinical and non-clinical issues are relevant to care. Many employees resist the hierarchy casting physicians as superior – often enforced by physicians. In describing the shift allowing more nurses and physicians' assistants to provide primary patient care, one interviewee implicitly perpetuated this hierarchy, "The losers in this situation are not so much the doctors but the patients who would benefit from more skilled doctors".

Some CE discussions focused on unique demands of hospital work. Demand is round-the-clock ("we work weird hours, we work 7–7, we work 11–11, work 3–3, we work 7pm to 5am, we have all different shifts"), and can be overwhelming ("I can't even go to the bathroom"). Patient-care regulations/procedures are standard, but patients' needs are not; bureaucratic procedures often interfere with patient care.

> Now we need to fill out a daily schedule with our patient, find out what they like to eat and what time they want to rest and not be disturbed. Also a good idea, except for we are in acute care facility and I can't tell when the doctors are coming in and anyway it is a [...] and we are needing to round with the doctors now; which is also great, but my concern that I voiced is, "When are we going to do any nursing care? What happens to the patient when we are so busy filling out the forms?"

Here, the bureaucratic attempt to standardize the nonstandard is quite clear.

CE participants discussed standardized responses to nonstandard problems, such as processing admissions to inpatient units from the ED only during shift change for more efficient care transition. The following quotes illustrate this and similar experiences:

> At shift change we are pushing beds and then the ER is admitting onto our floor and there is this huge chaos on our floor at like 3 o'clock and you know, it really could be the chaos could be more orderly if you know, [the nurse-manager] could open up a few beds before 3 o'clock, and that is every day. We are just in a real chaos state all the way from three to seven because that is the busiest time, you know the ER, they've triaged their patients, they've treated them and they are ready to move them. Around 3 o'clock there is a lot of activity, so if we could get our patients moved to the medical unit earlier, it would just help our staff. There just wouldn't be this chaos of beds moving this way, beds moving that way and it is wild. It is a circus and our nurses really get frustrated, our charge nurses get frustrated.

> Many procedures are not done on Saturdays and Sundays, so patients are admitted on Friday, they are hanging out all weekend just to get a procedure done [...] there is a clear contradiction here between scheduling according to days of the week and when actual patient need happens.

> Lactation services are offered only during business hours, as if babies are never born at night or on weekends, as if babies only feed on a 9:00–5:00 schedule. These new moms need lactation support, so post-partum nurses end up giving a bottle or giving contradictory advice and literally undoing overnight what it took a lactation consultant all day to achieve with a mom and baby. So, I come back the next morning and I have to start all over or a baby born on Friday night is home before I even get to work and the mom may give up on breastfeeding because she did not have proper lactation support in hospital.

Inability to predict demand creates shortages. Several CE participants described sending nurses home in compliance with the required patient-census rubric (patient/nurse ratio), only to have new admissions elevate the patient census, resulting in a dangerously short shift.

An interviewee offered advice to nurses who find ambiguous role structures, hospital rules, and vertical structures "restrictive and counter-productive". "Don't give up on nursing! Just try to get a job outside of a hospital. I use the term 'outside the box' to say that nurses need to work outside of hospitals – hospitals are the box".

We would not counsel a manager to advise their own staff to seek employment elsewhere to relieve job-related frustrations. Rather, SD-mitigation strategies explicitly confront frustration and frame it as a challenge – a shared problem for joint problem-solving rather than an obstacle. Directly confronting an SD-impasse together, framing relationships as partnerships, is a crucial first step to transcending it. The manager should explicitly acknowledge challenges, create dialogues that find common ground, and empower others to discuss their meaning/values contradictions to find ways to prioritize actions. This restores agency to mitigate existing SD-cycles and prevent new ones (Nicotera, Mahon, and Wright 2014).

2 Recommendation: a conceptual framework for management communication

We now propose a framework combining managerial hybridity, SD theory, and hospital-distinct characteristics to provide grounding for hospital management communication scholarship and practice. The four organizational features are re-conceptualized as overlapping domains of paradox. Each holds multiple sets of meaning structures that interpenetrate to pose communication challenges with potential for SD-nexuses – simultaneous, oppositional, equally compelling action demands. Managerial hybridity frames identity and is a fulcrum that cultivates ability to discern contradictory meaning intersections. Rather than sacrificing agency to polarization, embracing hybridity as a set of reference frames provides insight on paradoxes and ways to navigate them. Hybridity imparts the ability to analyze communication challenges posed by contradictions in each of the domains, problem-solve, and construct action protocols. Through hybridity, managers can switch frames of reference to analyze a problem from multiple vantage points, find the common ground among them, and facilitate consensus that transcends the contradictions (see Figure 1).

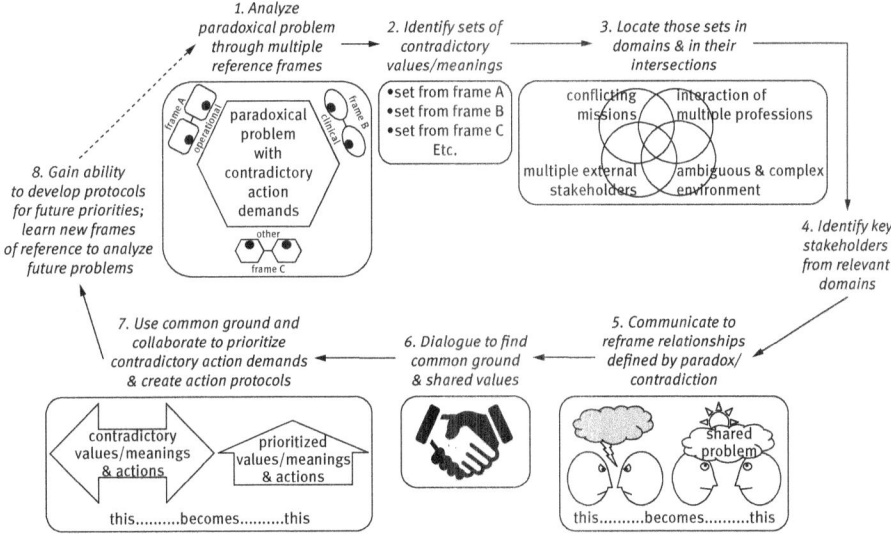

Figure 1: Framing paradox and contradictory action demands through hybridity

We first examine the contradiction/paradox through multiple reference frames (i.e., clinical, operational, and other) to identify meaning/value contradictions, then identify the domains those contradictions inhabit. Taking each relevant domain in turn, we identify the relevant stakeholders on whom contradictory demands are imposed and (to the extent possible) identify the underlying meaning structures (legal, operational, clinical, etc.). The challenge is then to communicate in dialogical ways to identify potential SD-nexuses, help others understand the contradictions, re-frame those contradictions as shared problems, and find common ground (Nicotera, Mahon, and Wright 2014).

From that common ground, managers can collaborate with stakeholders to prioritize action demands and create action protocols, restoring agency. Here, management communication functions to facilitate mutual translations of structure and action to navigate and transcend paradox. Each iteration of this cycle provides new reference frames to analyze future paradoxes and builds managerial ability to develop protocols for future priorities/actions. This conceptual combination of hybridity, SD theory, and hospital-distinct organizational characteristics offers a framework for hospital/healthcare management communication theory, research, and practice.

2.1 Implications for management communication theory and research

This framework provides a structure for analyzing day-to-day administrative complexity. It categorizes hospitals as unique organizations phenomenologically inseparable from the social processes that constitute them, centering the role of management communication in creating values that advance organizational success through mutual translations between structures and actions. The framework can specify hospitals' necessary tensions, as it clarifies and problematizes their paradoxically multiple (often nested) hierarchies. Hospitals' inherent tensions carry particular communicative challenges, as we have shown (e. g., balancing financial/operational and clinical goals; standardizing the nonstandard; navigating multiple nested hierarchies; and negotiating the complexity of hospital subtypes).

This framework provides a mechanism to identify paradoxical processes for analysis. It highlights managerial identity negotiation. Tensioned identity is the primary force driving managerial communication. This framework can provide important theoretical linkages to major theoretic traditions in organizational studies that can help apply them to hospital management communication (e. g., critical management theory, communicative constitution of organization, paradox theory, structuration, and institutional theory).

2.2 Implications for management communication practice

Management communication must create and sustain values that share common ground, are commensurate across missions, resonate with internal and external stakeholders' myriad values, and promote flexibility to meet the demands of a dynamic environment. Hospital outcomes are generally measured by patient satisfaction and patient experience,[3] clinical outcomes, cost controls, and staff turnover. While managers are responsible for facilitating these, none are under their direct control. Often, they are not even under their indirect control. Management communication must create and sustain structures of responsibility and accountability. This includes the creation and maintenance of quality-monitoring systems and environmental scanning systems (for such things as regulation changes, patient-demand trends, insurance caps, pharmaceutical pricing developments, and emerging community health needs). Finally, hospital managers must be mindful of their own discursive hybridity. Hybrid identity and management communication must be mutually supportive. This framework provides a set of analysis, communication, and planning tools for continuous learning and improvement.

3 Conclusions

Along with hybridity, the organizational features illustrated herein impede hospitals' ability to overcome difficulties in learning. Ramanujam and Rousseau (2006: 818) cited hospitals' "limited track record in adopting and sustaining organizational improvements and innovations"; slowness in both translating research into clinical practice and adopting effective organizational practices from other industries (or even from unit-to-unit in the same institution); and organizational disorder. Yet, these things are beginning to change as hospital organizational designs shift to more care-centered models (Fiorio, Gorli, and Verzillo 2018).

Hospital managers have traditionally failed to implement contemporary organizational practices such as team structures, deeper and expanded competencies, explicit goal setting, dedicated structures for patient safety, feedback and redesign, "thinking organizationally" across professions, and shifting to high-involvement practices (Ramanujam and Rousseau 2006: 822). These dynamics are changing as organizational designs evolve (e.g., see Smith et al. 2018). Hospitals' unique struc-

---

3 *Patient satisfaction* depends on whether the patient's expectations have been met. This is problematic when expectations are unrealistic, uninformed, or based on outdated clinical practices. Hence, *patient experience* is becoming an additional standard for measuring quality of health care encounters. Unlike patient satisfaction, which measures how happy a patient is with her care, patient experience measurements use more directed questions that gain a patient's perspective on the extent to which the provider has met pre-determined aspects of quality care. For example, rather than asking how satisfied a patient was with a care provider's explanation of treatment, a patient experience item would ask questions that target specific clinical standards known to improve clinical outcomes, such as "Did the doctor provide clear discharge instructions?" Both patient satisfaction and patient experience are important outcome measures. Hospital management needs to know both how happy people are with their care and how well standard procedures are being followed in the patients' experience.

tures are constituted through communication. Such things as complex roles and task structures, distinctive external stakeholders, and competing missions are embedded in structures. Hospital managers need strategies based on an understanding of how these features interact with organizational functions to (re)produce enduring structures. They must mindfully manage their own hybrid identities, so their communication transcends rather than (re)produces paradoxical structures that lead to organizational impasse (Nicotera, Mahon, and Wright 2014). Our framework provides a set of tools.

Organizational scholars must expand their thinking. First, general organizational scholarship should not be applied to hospitals, and hospital-based research should not be generalized beyond hospitals. Both are currently common practice in the organizational studies literature. Second, we need hospital-focused organizational theory, management communication theory, and organizational communication theory to better integrate the healthcare and organizational literatures. Third, the challenges of hospitals are centered in a unique interplay between communication and structure. Finally, hospital management communication, and the ways it can address these problems, must be conceptualized from a theoretical structure grounded in structurational intersections, identity and discursive hybridities, and paradox.

4 References

Barrett, Ashley K. 2014. Breaking boundaries: Temporality and work-life practices in hospital organizations. *Western Journal of Communication* 78(4). 441–461.

Bevan, Gwyn & Frans Ruttan. 1987. The organisation and functions at university hospitals in different countries. *Financial Accountability & Management* 3(2). 77–115.

Burgess, Nicola & Graem Currie. 2013. The knowledge brokering role of the hybrid middle level manager: The case of healthcare. *The British Journal of Management* 24(1). 132–142.

Chreim, Samia, Ann Langley, Mariline Comeau-Vallée, Jo-Louise Huq & Trish Reay. 2013. Leadership as boundary work in healthcare teams. *Leadership* 9(2). 201–228.

Fiorio, Carlo V., Mara Gorli & Stefano Verzillo. 2018. Evaluating organizational change in health care: The patient-centered hospital model. *BMC Health Services Research* 18(1). 95.

Gabutti, Irene, Daniele Mascia & Americo Cicchetti. 2017. Exploring "patient-centered" hospitals: A systematic review to understand change. *BMC Health Services Research* 17(1). 364.

Giancotti, Monica, Annamaria Guglielmo & Marianna Mauro. 2017. Efficiency and optimal size of hospitals: Results of a systematic search. *PLoS ONE* 12(3). e0174533. https://doi.org/10.1371/journal.pone.0174533 (accessed 14 November 2020).

Hoffer, Edward. 2019. America's health care system is broken: What went wrong and how we can fix it. Part 3: Hospitals and doctors. *The American Journal of Medicine* 132(8). 907–911.

Iedema, Rick, Pieter Degeling, Jeffrey Braithwaite & Les White. 2004. 'It's an interesting conversation I'm hearing': The doctor as manager. *Organization Studies* 25(1). 15–33.

Körner, Mirjam, Marcus A. Wirtz, Jürgen Bengel & Anja S. Göritz. 2015. Relationship of organizational culture, teamwork and job satisfaction in interprofessional teams. *BMC Health Services Research* 15. 243. https://doi.org/10.1186/s12913-015-0888-y (accessed 14 November 2020).

Kumar, Raman & Vijay Kumar Chattu. 2018. What is in the name? Understanding terminologies of patient-centered, person-centered, and person-directed care! *Journal of Family Medicine and Primary Care* 7(3). 487–488.

Lega, Federico & Carlo De Pietro. 2005. Converging patterns in hospital organization: Beyond the professional bureaucracy. *Health Policy* 74(3). 261–281.

Lines, Lisa M., Michael Lepore, Joshua M. Wiener. 2015. Patient-centered, person-centered, and person-directed care: They are not the same. *Medical Care* 53(7). 561–563.

Maxwell, Jim, Angel Bourgoin, Michelle Savuto, Joanne Crandall, Zoe Lindenfeld & Rachel Tobey. 2019. *Health center coalition: The federally qualified health center urban health network*. The Delta Center for a Thriving Safety Net. JSI Research & Training Institute.

McGivern, Gerry, Graem Currie, Ewan Ferlie, Louise Fitzgerald & Justin Waring. 2015. Hybrid manager-professionals' identity work: The maintenance and hybridization of medical professionalism in managerial contexts. *Public Administration* 93(2). 412–432.

Mintzberg, Henry. 1997. Toward healthier hospitals. *Health Care Management Review* 22(4). 9–18.

Newhouse, J. J. 2007. Hospital strategic planning for diversity integration based on organizational type and CEO tenure. *Hospital Topics: Research and Perspectives on Health Care* 85(1). 11–16.

Nicotera, Anne M. & Marcia J. Clinkscales. 2010. Nurses at the nexus: A case study in structurational divergence. *Health Communication* 25(1). 32–49.

Nicotera, Anne M., Margaret M. Mahon & Kevin B. Wright. 2014. Communication that builds teams: Assessing a nursing conflict intervention. *Nursing Administration Quarterly* 38(3). 248–260.

Ommaya, Alexander K., Pamela F. Cipriano, David B. Hoyt, Keith A. Horvath, Paul Tang, Harold L. Pa, Mark S. DeFrancesco, Susan T. Hingle, Sam Butler & Christine A. Sinsky. 2018. Care-centered clinical documentation in the digital environment: Solutions to alleviate burnout. *NAM Perspectives*. Discussion Paper. National Academy of Medicine, Washington, DC. https://nam.edu/care-centered-clinical-documentation-digital-environment-solutions-alleviate-burnout/ (accessed 14 November 2020).

Overton, Barbara Cook. 2020. *Unintended consequences of electronic medical records: An emergency room ethnography*. Lanham, MD: Lexington Books.

Ramanujam, Ranga & Denise M. Rousseau. 2006. The challenges are organizational not just clinical. *Journal of Organizational Behavior* 27(7). 811–827.

Ridgely, M. Susan, Erin Duffy, Laura Wolf, Maria Vaiana, Dennis Scanlon, Christine Buttorff, Brigitt Leitzell, Sangeeta Ahluwalia, Lara Hilton, Denis Angiel, Amelia Haviland & Cheryl Damberg. 2019. Understanding U.S. health systems: Using mixed methods to unpack organizational complexity. *eGEMS (Generating Evidence & Methods to Improve Patient Outcomes)* 7(1). 39.

Safarani, Samaneh, Pouran Raessi, Hamid Ravaghi & Mohammadreza Malecki. 2018. Managerial challenges of teaching hospital, a review of the existing literature. *Journal of Evolution of Medical and Dental Sciences* 7(43). 4686–4692.

Savage, Jan & Cherill Scott. 2004. The modern matron: A hybrid management role with implications for continuous quality improvement. *Journal of Nursing Management* 12(6). 419–426.

Smith, Cynthia D., Celynne Balatbat, Susan Corbridge, Anna Legreid Dopp, Jessica Fried, Ron Harter, Seth Landefeld, Christina Y. Martin, Frank Opelka, Lew Sandy, Luke Sato & Christine Sinsky. 2018. Implementing optimal team-based care to reduce clinician burnout. *NAM Perspectives*. Discussion Paper. National Academy of Medicine, Washington, DC. https://nam.edu/implementing-optimal-team-based-care-to-reduce-clinician-burnout/ (accessed 14 November 2020).

Amanda J. Porter, Damla Diriker, and Ilse Hellemans
27 Crowdsourcing

Abstract: In this chapter, we argue that crowdsourcing can be a promising tool for addressing societal challenges by harnessing the knowledge and creativity of the crowds. Comparing the design elements and communication assumptions of crowdsourcing for well-structured organizational problems with that of ill-structured societal challenges, we analyse how crowdsourcing can be adapted to enable the integration of diverse knowledge. We offer an illustration of diverse knowledge integration in collaborative crowdsourcing used to co-create solutions to the problem of food waste. Future research directions include the role of problem framing and participatory architectures to harness crowdsourcing for greater societal impact. This chapter begins with a review of the existing crowdsourcing literature, followed by our analysis and illustration, and concludes with a discussion of future research directions.

Keywords: collaborative crowdsourcing; knowledge integration; societal problems; grand challenges

Contrary to the belief that crowdsourcing is a phenomenon of only the last decade, seeking solutions to seemingly intractable problems from a large group of individuals is nothing new. One of the early successful cases of crowdsourcing dates back to the eighteenth century when several sea-captains and merchants petitioned the British Parliament to find a solution to a deadly problem for sailors: a "Longitude Prize" of £20,000 was offered to anyone who could find a way to determine the longitude at sea (Johnson 1989). Many assumed that the solution would be the work of scientists, but a self-educated carpenter and clockmaker, named John Harrison, won the prize by developing a new marine watch that made it possible to locate ships at sea.

Today, our ability to communicate with many minds for generating novel ideas is much easier with digital technologies. This has spawned a growth in the use of crowdsourcing as a tool for tackling a wide range of problems, ranging from outsourcing repetitive tasks to a large number of individuals (e.g., Amazon Mechanical Turk), to generating innovative ideas with the help of the crowd (e.g., Fiat designed Fiat Mio based on the ideas collected from the crowd). A recent but more rare application of crowdsourcing entails tackling large societal problems, like poverty and climate change, through collaborative crowdsourcing platforms (e.g., OpenIDEO).

This chapter aims to show how crowdsourcing can be designed and adapted by organizations as a tool for addressing societal challenges, which are increasingly relevant for the processes of value creation promoted by organizations. We then compare the design elements and communication assumptions underpinning two applications of crowdsourcing: one aimed to solve well-structured, organizational problems, and another aimed at tackling ill-structured, societal problems. Our comparison shows how extant crowdsourcing literature on solving well-structured problems assumes a rather linear information-processing view of management communication (Putnam, Phillips, and Chapman 1996), while the growing literature on crowdsourcing as a tool for tackling societal challenges and organizational value co-creation necessitates a much richer view of communication, one that can foster multivocal coordination and problem-solving (Furnari 2014). We do not aim for an exhaustive review of the predominant crowdsourcing literature on product innovation but rather seek to elucidate how the basic elements of crowdsourcing design can be adapted to suit the complex, multi-stakeholder settings that comprise societal challenges.

The chapter is structured as follows: first, we review the existing literature on crowdsourcing, highlighting key design elements in the setting of well-structured problems. Second, we examine the emerging subfield on crowdsourcing as a tool for tackling ill-structured societal challenges, comparing the key design elements in this domain. We then offer an illustration of multivocal communication dynamics that underpin collaborative crowdsourcing for tackling societal problems. Finally, we conclude with directions for future management communication research on crowdsourcing in the domain of societal problem-solving.

1 The benefits of solver diversity for generating novel ideas

The term crowdsourcing was first coined by Howe (2006), who defined it as the act of outsourcing a task traditionally performed by a specific actor (i. e., employee or group of experts) to an undefined group of individuals (i. e., the crowd). Over the years, we have seen many different applications of the concept, resulting in a rather heterogeneous literature. Reviewing the existing definitions in the literature, Estellés-Arolas and González-Ladrón-de-Guevara (2012) came up with the following unifying definition: "a type of participative online activity in which an individual, an institution, a non-profit organization, or company proposes to a group of individuals of varying knowledge, heterogeneity, and number, via a flexible open call [i. e., announcement], the voluntary undertaking of a task" (Estellés-Arolas and González-Ladrón-de-Guevara 2012: 197). This definition moves beyond Howe's (2006) original conceptualization of crowdsourcing as simply outsourcing tasks to a broader audience, merely for financial returns, to facilitating problem-solving and value co-creation for scientific and creative breakthroughs (Brabham 2017).

At the core of crowdsourcing as a method for problem-solving is a strong belief that the "wisdom of crowds" can provide solutions to problems that may outperform that of individuals or groups of experts (Surowiecki 2004). Crowdsourcing enables the widespread involvement of actors from different disciplines, fostering the diversity of problem-solvers (Malhotra and Majchrzak 2014). When the crowd is composed of diverse individuals with different perspectives, they may provide the building blocks for generating more innovative solutions (Boudreau and Lakhani 2013).

While the process by which diverse stakeholders engage in problem-solving is of clear importance to management communication scholarship (Koschmann 2016; Kuhn 2008), the majority of crowdsourcing research has not adopted an explicit management communication perspective. The predominant approaches in the literature assume a rather linear information transmission-based view of the crowdsourcing process (for an exception see Brabham 2008). In the next sections, we review this literature to elucidate the design elements that constitute the crowdsourcing process to provide the baseline from which we introduce approaches that focus more centrally on the importance of communication in the domain of crowdsourcing for tackling societal challenges.

2 Engineering crowdsourcing to solve well-structured organizational problems

In this section, we present the main design elements that appear to be the common denominators for crowdsourcing scholars. This list of design elements is not exhaustive, but rather selected for enabling later comparison between this form of crowdsourcing and the more recent, yet less studied, applications of crowdsourcing for societal challenges.

2.1 The problem: what is the nature of the challenge?

A key element that defines the crowdsourcing process is the nature of the problem that a host organization sets out to solve. Current research has typically focused on two main types of problems: (1) micro-tasks, that are routinized and repetitive (e.g., Amazon Mechanical Turk asking the crowd to read a restaurant review and answering a survey about it) and (2) innovation-type problems and creative tasks (e.g., LEGO asking the crowd to submit their product ideas, for the winning ideas to be produced by the company later on) (Estellés-Arolas and González-Ladrón-de-Guevara 2012; Boudreau and Lakhani 2013).

In both cases, the problem is well-structured, meaning that it is divisible into smaller tasks that can be performed by individual crowd members (Estellés-Arolas and González-Ladrón-de-Guevara 2012; Ghezzi et al. 2018). Accordingly, most crowdsourcing research emphasizes that the problem should be easy to delineate and transmit to the crowd, and have clear objectives for solutions (Afuah and Tucci 2012; Barbier et al. 2012). This allows the host organization to control the process and stimulate the desired type of solutions.

2.2 The solution: what knowledge is required?

Depending on the type of problem, the knowledge required from the crowd will vary (Ghezzi et al. 2018). While well-structured innovation-type problems require solvers with specific skills, micro-tasks do not require particular skills or expertise (Kittur 2010). For instance, in a recent task in Amazon Mechanical Turk, participants were asked to identify the object in an image, which does not require high cognitive effort (Estellés-Arolas and González-Ladrón-de-Guevara 2012).

Another related decision is whether to broadcast the task to a large or a small-sized crowd. While attracting a larger crowd may increase the chance of finding breakthrough ideas, it may also cause each participant to exert less effort (Boudreau, Lacetera, and Lakhani 2011). Typically, the optimum size of the crowd depends on the crowdsourcing initiative, given that input provided by the crowd will subsequently need to be consolidated and evaluated. Broadcasting the tasks to a larger or smaller crowd may also influence the decision to issue a private call to invite an exclusive and defined group of individuals, or to have an external call open to anyone.

2.3 Incentives: how to attract the crowd?

Given that participants spend time and effort voluntarily to accomplish a task, it is generally agreed that their investments need to be compensated (Dahlander, Jeppesen, and Piezunka 2019). Although monetary incentives are often the norm, studies show that such incentives are not the only way to attract participants. Financial incentives can even have an adverse effect for individuals with an intrinsic motivation to participate (Huang, Singh, and Mukhopadhyay 2012), such as deriving personal enjoyment from participation (Frey, Lüthje, and Haag 2011) or showing off their skills and building reputation (Dahlander, Jeppesen, and Piezunka 2019). In such cases, non-monetary incentives, for instance, providing more interesting tasks or promoting learning (Kaikati and Kaikati 2013), can incentivize participants more effectively. Thus, a dual incentive structure may be useful, with both a fixed-price award linked to the outcome and a performance-contingent award, such as recognition of those participants who make the highest number of contributions (Terwiesch and Xu 2008).

2.4 Rules: how to induce contributions from the crowd?

The crowd members' willingness to participate not only depends on the incentive scheme, but also on the underlying social principles and rules on the platform (Ghezzi et al. 2018). For instance, in crowdsourcing for innovation-type problems, participants are often clearly instructed to post an idea, and occasionally, to provide communicative feedback on others' ideas through their comments, or to evaluate ideas by providing upvotes or downvotes on the platform (Malhotra and Majchrzak 2014).

A key decision is to choose between a collaborative crowdsourcing platform, where the crowd works together to achieve an outcome and a crowdsourcing contest, where the crowd competes to provide the winning solution (Boudreau and Lakhani 2013). Encouraging both cooperation and competition between the crowd participants increases the chances that the crowd will provide higher-quality inputs (Hutter et al. 2011). While most crowdsourcing relies on technical features of the platform to enable this interaction, a platform *moderator* may also be useful for stimulating interactions among the crowd participants and improving the content quality (Wise, Hamman, and Thorson 2006). Moderators monitor the interactions to reinforce the rules or to encourage participants to share their knowledge. Regardless of what method is used, most crowdsourcing research agrees that the guidelines for contributing ideas or solutions must be clear for all participants (Ghezzi et al. 2018).

2.5 Phases: how to structure the process?

Although the crowdsourcing process may take different forms based on the type of problem and the skills required from the crowd, from executing simple tasks (e. g., Amazon Mechanical Turk[1]) to sourcing new product design ideas (e. g., Starbucks' "My Starbucks Idea" Campaign[2]), most of them tend to follow a similar pattern. Typically, the process starts with the host organization defining the task and the knowledge required, which is then communicated to a group of individuals, either through an open or targeted call. Next, during the *idea generation* phase, the crowd accomplishes the task or provides solutions to the problem through an online platform. The ideas, or solutions, are then evaluated during the *idea evaluation/selection* phase based on the evaluation approach defined by the host organization. Finally, the *implementation phase* includes the diffusion of ideas (Rossen and Lok 2012) or the consolidation of ideas into a product or service (Brabham et al. 2014).

Crowdsourcing research on well-structured problems has depicted this as a highly structured, sequential, linear process where the host organization harnesses

---

[1] https://www.mturk.com/.
[2] https://ideas.starbucks.com/.

the intelligence of the crowd in an open yet controlled manner (Brabham et al. 2014). Schematically, this process is similar to the classic *input-process-output* (IPO) model in the communication literature (Pavitt 1999), where the clearly defined problem is the input, the idea generation and evaluation is the process, and the "best" idea is the output. Such an IPO model has even been used as a preferred structure for organizing the body of crowdsourcing research (for example, see Ghezzi et al. 2018).

2.6 Selection: how to choose the best ideas?

There are two main approaches identified in the literature for the evaluation and selection of ideas in crowdsourcing: structured and unstructured. In the structured approach, evaluation metrics are defined *ex-ante*; when they are defined precisely and communicated clearly, these metrics are seen to usefully limit the problem-solution space and prevent ambiguity (Sieg, Wallin, and von Krogh 2010). When it is difficult to define metrics *ex-ante*, due to either the characteristics of the task or difficulty in identifying the desired features of the solutions, organizations may choose to make judgment calls, allowing them a greater flexibility to select unconventional solutions (Dahlander, Jeppesen, and Piezunka 2019).

Evaluations can be performed by selected experts or the crowd itself, for instance, by allowing the crowd to vote for their favorite idea (Ghezzi et al. 2018). Moreover, it can follow a one-off or sequential model (Dahlander, Jeppesen, and Piezunka 2019). In the one-off model, the selection is made drawing on the evaluation input of the crowd or selected experts, while in the sequential model, a first selection is made based on the evaluation input, then the crowd is asked to provide a new set of inputs, which are evaluated once more (Levinthal and Posen 2007).

However, it is common that the final selection of ideas is performed internally by experts within the host organization. A key consideration for the host organization in choosing the evaluation and selection method is how to avoid information overload, which is a common pitfall that can lead organizations to inadvertently choose more familiar ideas over more distant yet novel ones.

2.7 Implementation: realizing crowdsourced solutions?

The implementation of solutions to well-structured problems is where the inputs from the crowd are disseminated, finalized, and transformed into actual products or services (Cui, Wu, and Tong 2018). Typically, the implementation is handled internally within the host organization without the involvement of the crowd (Poetz and Schreier 2012). In most cases, the details about the implementation are not even shared with the crowd, which has led some to argue critically that crowdsourcing is merely an idea generation tool, falling short of producing ideas that are realized in practice (Bloodgood 2013).

From a communication perspective, it could be argued that crowdsourcing without implementation merely gives participants the illusion of making contributions, amounting to little more than "crowdwashing" (Cherry 2018). This concern, among others alluded to above, provides the impetus for an emerging stream of crowdsourcing research that critically examines how it may be adapted to tackle ill-structured problems of societal relevance. In the remainder of the chapter, we review the empirical research in this domain to examine how we may enrich and extend crowdsourcing to go beyond the linear communication model that dominates the existing literature described above.

3 Orchestrating crowdsourcing to tackle ill-structured societal challenges

Many of today's pressing societal challenges are too complex to be solved by a single individual (Ferraro, Etzion, and Gehman 2015). As society is being faced with challenges that resist easy fixes, such as environmental crises or poverty, organizations have found them at the center of the discussion: not only are they involved as they contribute to many of these challenges, but they are also taking an increasingly active role in solving them (George et al. 2016). As crowdsourcing allows an approach to harness diverse individuals' knowledge, it is not surprising to see many organizations experimenting with it to address societal challenges, such as public health (Brabham et al. 2014), civic problems (Brunswicker, Bilgram, and Fueller 2017), and ocean sustainability (Porter, Tuertscher, and Huysman 2020). The aim of such initiatives is not only economic value creation for the host organization but the broader aim of creating value for society as well (Porter and Kramer 2011).

Existing studies in this domain have shown that complex societal problems can be tackled by individuals with complementary knowledge when they are allowed to understand the problem collaboratively and to brainstorm on its different aspects for co-creating multiple solutions (Malhotra and Majchrzak 2014; Porter, Tuertscher, and Huysman 2020). However, while crowdsourcing may be a suitable approach for tackling societal problems by connecting diverse actors from multiple knowledge domains to engage in joint problem-solving, the literature suggests that crowdsourcing elements may require significant re-orientations to tackle these problems successfully (Brabham 2017; Majchrzak and Malhotra 2019).

In the remainder of this section, we provide an overview of the extant literature on crowdsourcing to tackle societal challenges to facilitate a useful comparison with crowdsourcing for solving well-structured problems. For an overview of this comparison, see Table 1.

Table 1: Comparison of crowdsourcing design by nature of the problem

	Well-structured organizational problems	Ill-structured societal problems
The problem: *What is the nature of the challenge?*	– Well-defined, well-structured, with clear objectives – Defined by the host organization – Modularizable – Can be performed by individual crowd members independently	– Ill-defined, ill-structured – Defined with the (sub) crowd-stakeholders – Not divisible into smaller, simpler tasks – Cannot be understood and solved by a single individual
The solution: *What knowledge is required?*	– Specific skills/expertise may be required for innovation-type problems, and not for micro-tasks – Codified and explicit knowledge required – Larger crowd increases access to breakthrough ideas dispersed among independent individuals – Pool of participants can be defined based on the desired outcome	– Knowledge required cannot be defined *ex-ante* – Collaborative integration of knowledge and collaborative idea generation – Diverse group of crowd participants
Incentives: *How to attract the crowd?*	– Mainly monetary, outcome-based incentives – Secondary non-monetary, performance-related incentives, like social recognition for the highest number of contributions, but these are not required to be present	– Both outcome-based and performance-based incentives are needed to promote knowledge integration – Both monetary incentives and non-monetary incentives are important to promote different participant roles for effective knowledge integration
Rules: *How to induce contributions from the crowd?*	– Clear guidelines and instructions were given to the crowd to post their ideas, typically without interacting with each other – Technical features of the platform influence the interactions among crowd members, while moderation is not always necessary	– Clear guidelines and instructions to promote a transparent, multivocal dialogue, as well as effective knowledge integration – Active management by moderators to enable deeper communicative interactions
Phases: *How to structure the process?*	– Structured approach following the linear process of problem definition, idea generation, evaluation, and implementation	– Dynamic process where problem definition, idea generation, and evaluation co-evolve simultaneously
Selection: *How to choose the best ideas?*	– Possible to define an evaluation criteria *ex-ante* – Typically performed by host organization without the involvement of the crowd – A "best" or "winning" idea	– Difficult to define criteria *ex-ante* – Integrate crowd knowledge into evaluation – Select multiple solutions to develop
Implementation: *Realizing crowdsourced solutions?*	– Ideas integrated and implemented by host organization without crowd involvement	– Need to involve selected idea holders in development

3.1 The problem: what is the nature of the challenge?

Understanding the nature of societal challenges is key for utilizing crowdsourcing in tackling them. Unlike simple or well-structured problems, complex societal problems cannot be easily defined. They transcend boundaries, influence many stakeholders from different disciplines, and are characterized by many interactions and trade-offs (Ferraro, Etzion, and Gehman 2015). Moreover, as the future manifestations of the problem and its consequences are uncertain, it is difficult for actors to forecast their evolution (Ferraro, Etzion, and Gehman 2015). Take, for example, the problem of food waste. This involves a complex network of different players – seed producers, farmers, traders, retailers, and consumers – that all operate on a global scale and are heavily reliant on each other. The communication and information supplies between a consumer and a farmer will be inadequate to navigate through their varying evaluations on how to tackle food waste. This results in a highly uncertain situation for all stakeholders involved, even though collaborative actions are required to move forward (George et al. 2016).

Given their ill-structured nature, it is near impossible to divide these problems into simpler and well-structured sub-problems (Majchrzak and Malhotra 2019). Further, it is not possible for an individual or a small group of experts inside an organization to understand the complexities associated with the wicked problems. By openly inviting key stakeholders to define the problem, a host organization utilizes crowdsourcing for a critical function: defining the problem itself (Majchrzak and Malhotra 2019). By *not* providing the crowd with a structured problem definition, the crowdsourcing architecture may allow them to hold multiple interpretations of the problem simultaneously and foster critical thinking towards more innovative solutions (Majchrzak and Malhotra 2019). Therefore, unlike well-structured problems, the aim here is to involve the crowd as a "partner" in constructing the meaning of the problem itself (Porter, Tuertscher, and Huysman 2020).

3.2 Solutions: what knowledge is required?

Unlike simple tasks or well-structured problems, it is difficult to identify the exact knowledge required for tackling complex societal problems, as there may be a myriad of trade-offs and interdependencies that could unfold as the problem is being tackled (Majchrzak and Malhotra 2019). Further, while a host organization with a simple or well-structured problem often has clear desired outcomes, ill-structured societal challenges will likely have multiple and possibly conflicting solution paths (Majchrzak and Malhotra 2019). Thus, rather than targeting solvers with specific skills, it is important to build a truly diverse crowd of requisite variety (Weick 1979) that mirrors the nature of such problems, as diverse knowledge, perspectives, and expertise are needed to understand their complexities, and consider innovative solutions. Based on their observations of different social media sites, Brunswicker, Bilgram, and Fueller (2017) proposed a mixed recruitment strategy that combines targeted recruiting with word of mouth. By generating excitement around the societal problem, participants should feel like it is a "rare event bringing together the best knowledge available" (Majchrzak and Malhotra 2019: 274).

3.3 Incentives: how to attract the crowd?

Previous studies have shown that whether the crowd members have intrinsic or extrinsic motivations may have different effects on the quality of the submitted solutions (Boudreau, Lacetera, and Lakhani 2011; Frey, Lüthje, and Haag 2011), and thus, the incentive mechanisms must be designed accordingly. Given the problem complexity and potential intangibility of desired outcomes (Battistella and Nonino 2012), intrinsic incentives may be more powerful in motivating the crowd to participate in tackling societal challenges and engage in value co-creation with host organizations.

Further, the host organization should aim to promote collaborations among crowd participants, which can be stimulated by offering dual incentives, with small monetary awards as well as recognition awards (Malhotra and Majchrzak 2014). Studies on crowdsourcing for tackling wicked problems have found that when only "best" solutions are rewarded, the crowd may be less inclined to collaborate (Malhotra and Majchrzak 2014). Thus, a range of crowd members' performances, such as the quality of their comments or the persistence of their efforts to integrate knowledge exchanged by the other participants, should be recognized when designing the incentive structure for the process.

3.4 Rules: how to induce crowd contributions?

The emerging research on crowdsourcing for ill-structured problems shows that when the crowd is simply asked to provide their ideas, they may fail to offer novel, feasible, or well-thought-out solutions (Malhotra and Majchrzak 2014). Instead, a crowdsourcing process should be adopted, where communication and knowledge integration among the crowd members is promoted (Maholtra and Majchrzak 2014). Here, we contend that multivocal coordination is critical, and by this, we mean any "discursive and material activity that sustains different interpretations among various audiences with different evaluative criteria, in a manner that promotes coordination without requiring explicit consensus" (Ferraro, Etzion, and Gehman 2015: 373; Furnari 2014). For instance, by formulating the problem statements broadly, crowdsourcing platforms may allow the crowd members to preserve their own interpretations and apply their unique perspectives when proposing innovative ideas or solutions to the wicked problem (Porter, Tuertscher, and Huysman 2020).

However, communicating openly and sharing such a variety of knowledge may be considered as unnatural by the participants (Davenport and Prusak 1998), either because they cannot envision their "piece" in the overall puzzle or because they find dialogue difficult to spark on their own. As a result, transparent, multivocal dialogue among the crowd members needs to be promoted through instructions and design features to encourage them to share their perspectives about the problem and solution (Brunswicker, Bilgram, and Fueller 2017), even if they are contradictory. When participants are given specific instructions, for instance, to post not only well-developed solutions but any kind of knowledge they may possess or to vote on comments not based on their "liking" but based on how useful they are for finding a solution to the wicked problem, they may generate more innovative solutions compared to challenges with conventional instructions (Malhotra and Majchrzak 2014). Consequently, the role of platform moderators, those that facilitate the crowdsourcing process, becomes an important element to promote the necessary "deeper" communicative interactions on the platform.

3.5 Phases: how to structure the process?

The traditional linear approach to the crowdsourcing process (i.e., the definition of the problem, generation of ideas, evaluation of ideas, and implementation of a solution) does not seem to be entirely effective when tackling societal challenges (Porter, Tuertscher, and Huysman 2020). This approach has many disadvantages, such as leading to fixation with one facet of the problem or one specific solution (Jansson and Smith 1991). Further, when their involvement is limited to the idea generation phase, the crowd members may not be able to suggest what aspects of the problem need to be solved or give important local knowledge for the implementation of solutions (Majchrzak and Malhotra 2019).

A host organization needs to experiment with the design of the process itself (Porter, Tuertscher, and Huysman 2020) to move away from the predominant sequential phases towards a process that upholds the importance of interpretive flexibility (Bijker 1987) needed for addressing such problems. Studies have suggested several adaptations to the crowdsourcing process, for instance, designing a process that allows for solving and defining the problem to occur simultaneously as two intertwined sub-processes (Majchrzak and Malhotra 2019). Rather than taking a sequential approach, it may also be necessary to return to phases once they have already passed. For instance, knowledge generated during ideation may be helpful in the later evaluation of solutions, as participants contributing to ideation may be in a better position to evaluate the ideas as they would be exposed to the diverse issues and perspectives surfaced by the crowd (Porter, Tuertscher, and Huysman 2020).

3.6 Selection: how to choose the best ideas?

While crowdsourcing for well-structured problems often sees selection as an internal process performed by the host organization, as diverse individuals may hold different values and interpret the problems differently, reaching a consensus on what is the best solution for a societal challenge is near impossible (Ferraro, Etzion, and Gehman 2015). It is, therefore, unlikely that the desired solution can be known in advance, making the definition of evaluation criteria *ex-ante* difficult. Porter, Tuertscher, and Huysman (2020) found that host organizations can benefit from reviewing ideas on the platform to learn about the preferences of the diverse participants, suggesting that evaluation criteria may be developed *after* the idea generation so that diverse perspectives can be included in the evaluative judgments of ideas.

When involving the crowd in evaluation, all ideas and dialogues on the platform must be transparent for the crowd participants to compare the knowledge shared, as well as evaluate and re-evaluate the proposed solutions (Baralou and Tsoukas 2015). Finally, rather than selecting a single "winner", the host organization may benefit from selecting multiple solutions to foster "distributed experimentation", or the development of multiple ideas simultaneously, which is found to be important in the context of societal challenges where the likelihood of failure, when relying on one type of solution, is high (Ferraro, Etzion, and Gehman 2015).

3.7 Implementation: realizing crowdsourced solutions?

While crowdsourcing for well-structured problems often assumes that the host organization develops the "winning" solution internally, without the involvement of the crowd, engaging the crowd in the implementation phase has several advantages. Crowd members often possess the local knowledge that is critical for the successful implementation of solutions and may be able to further develop the solutions using their diverse perspectives, backgrounds, and expertise. For instance, in the crowdsourcing initiative to tackle ocean sustainability, Porter, Tuertscher, and Huysman (2020) found that the host organizations involved diverse actors in the development of the ideas, including their employees and the idea holders themselves. As a result, some solutions became more robust, while others were discovered to be less feasible to realize in practice. Given that one single "best" solution to a societal problem does not exist (Ferraro, Etzion, and Gehman 2015), the involvement of key stakeholders in the implementation process may be critical for distilling the actual value of solutions, while also generating a widespread commitment to the solution (Gray and Stites 2013).

4 An illustration of crowdsourcing for societal problems: the Food Waste Challenge

In this section, we zoom in on the communicative interactions within a crowdsourcing platform designed to tackle societal challenges, OpenIDEO, to illustrate *how* solutions are generated through sharing and integrating multivocal knowledge. OpenIDEO addresses social issues with the involvement of participants from around the world. Specifically, we focus on the challenge of food waste, which posed the following question to the crowd: "How can we dramatically reduce food waste by transforming our relationship with food?" (OpenIDEO). During three-months, more than 20,000 people contributed over 726 ideas and 4,500 comments to this challenge. Next, we illustrate multivocal coordination in a sample of comments derived from the Food Waste Challenge.

4.1 Multivocal knowledge sharing

In the Food Waste Challenge, multivocal knowledge sharing was focused on exposing multiple facets of the problem, even if these did not directly pertain to the suggested idea/solution itself. For instance, participants often shared their varying perspectives on the root causes of the problem, illustrated by comments such as the following: "People do not educate themselves on food waste in a way they should" or "Involving the youth in the problem is key in transforming our relationship with food!" Such comments provided a space for exploring and constituting a multivocal understanding of the different aspects of the problem itself.

Second, through multivocal knowledge sharing, participants were not only able to share the elements of the ideas they liked, but also to raise concerns. For instance, one idea submitted to the challenge was about developing a box with a "first-in-first-out" system for household refrigerators to better identify foods close to expiring. While participants from family households liked the large-size of the box with multiple compartments, others commented that it was precisely the large-size that precluded the box from working for their single-person or shared refrigerator households. As a result, multivocal knowledge sharing helped to reveal opposing perspectives when considering different solutions to the problem.

Finally, collaborative platforms can support multivocal knowledge sharing through different forms of communication. For instance, participants often encouraged contributions by showing gratitude or commenting on their usefulness: "This is pure genius! Just thinking of the possibilities or the impact this could have on world hunger is very exciting!" Moreover, they often asked clarification questions to guide their contributions. In some cases, the participants also included their specific expertise in their comments: "Great idea! I am in the bay area, and I can help with app wireframes, user flows, prototyping …". Overall, multivocal coordination within the platform encouraged participants to further build collaborations.

4.2 From sharing to integrating multivocal knowledge

While multivocal knowledge sharing offers a useful starting point, this knowledge also needs to be integrated to generate innovative solutions to societal challenges (Malhotra and Majchrzak 2014). In the Food Waste Challenge, participants often *highlighted* which knowledge was most relevant through their comments: "Some people here have already mentioned that it would be hard for people to remember what produce needs to be stored, where and how in the market". Furthermore, some participants *combined* the varying perspectives exchanged. For instance, recall how some participants preferred a smaller box for their individual living situations, whereas family households preferred a larger one. Further down in this discussion thread, a third participant who read these concerns suggested designing multiple sizes of the box to accommodate these varying needs.

In rare cases, idea holders proposed to combine their original ideas into one larger solution, as they realized that similar ideas would merge into a more complete solution, or could benefit from collaborations among different idea holders. However, it is important to consider that this "higher-level" form of combining two or more ideas was observed much less frequently than the integration of knowledge within the comments for a single idea. This can be identified as a key development point, as this integration of top-level ideas could help to create more robust, impactful solutions.

5 Conclusion and directions for future research

The aim of this chapter was to show how crowdsourcing can be extended for problem-solving in the domain of societal challenges. A focal attribute of crowdsourcing is its ability to harness and leverage a diversity of knowledge and perspectives. However, this promise may go unrealized if changes to the communication assumptions underlying the predominant approaches to crowdsourcing design are not made. Specifically, we contend that crowdsourcing to solve well-structured organizational problems often assumes an information-transfer model of communication, one in which the host organization "controls" a linear process engineered towards the desired outcome (Pederson et al. 2013). In this case, management communication is dominated by concerns such as clarity regarding the problem formulation, gathering the right information from the crowd, and extraction of the "best" solution for internal organizational usage.

In contrast, crowdsourcing to tackle ill-structured societal challenges necessitates a multivocal management communication approach. Specifically, the design of crowdsourcing for multivocal coordination is less about engineering the process to capture the desired solution and more about orchestrating its various elements to involve diverse stakeholders. In this case, management communication is concerned with gaining a plurality of perspectives on the problem, facilitating collaborative ideation with crowd-stakeholders, and jointly integrating diverse knowledge to develop ideas towards the implementation in a local context.

Crowdsourcing in the domain of societal problems presents several unique challenges for future management communication research. Specifically, we focus on three areas: (1) problem framing, (2) inclusive, participatory architectures, and (3) organization of the process.

First, an important direction for future communication research is the investigation of how to approach the problem. This debate extends across the crowdsourcing literature as the framing of the problem is particularly salient in the setting of societal challenges. While previous research indicates that a modular approach may exclude important perspectives on the problem, future research is needed to understand all variations of problem framing that are possible and their relationship with the societal value creation for societal challenges.

Second, research is needed to shed light on what constitutes an inclusive, multivocal participatory crowdsourcing architecture. More specifically, future studies can investigate which technical features stimulate multivocal knowledge integration, not only for a single idea but also for integrating multiple ideas across an entire challenge into higher-level solutions. For example, how can we design a platform so that highlighting and combining is facilitated, for instance, by leveraging technologies such as categorization algorithms to assign labels and make suggestions? In addition to technical features, future research is also needed on how to bolster the skills and capabilities of the various participants to engage in multivocal knowledge sharing and integration. What are the specific management communication skills needed for moderators to generate the multivocal engagement of diverse stakeholders in this setting? How do particular sequences of communicative interactions foster enhanced multivocality?

Finally, more research is needed on the crowdsourcing process itself and how it is organized in practice. Given that societal challenges often lack clear solutions, crowdsourcing for societal challenges should not focus on generating a single solution but rather on ensuring the prolonged engagement of stakeholders (Ferraro, Etzion, and Gehman 2015), such that solutions can be continuously (re)generated over time. Given that many crowdsourcing challenges use a limited timeframe to induce "urgency" and generate momentum, future research should explore the appropriate design for a crowdsourcing process that serves both short-term and long-term time horizons. Should management rethink "winners" and "losers", and, if so, how can the process be designed to realize more cycles of multivocality and progression of impact? By posing questions such as these, we aim to encourage management communication research with impact (Keyton et al. 2010) that plays an integral role in understanding and solving some of our world's most pressing societal challenges.

6 References

Afuah, Allan & Christopher L. Tucci. 2012. Crowdsourcing as a solution to distant search. *Academy of Management Review* 37(3). 355–375.
Baralou, Evangelia & Haridimos Tsoukas. 2015. How is new organizational knowledge created in a virtual context? An ethnographic study. *Organization Studies* 36(5). 593–620. https://doi.org/10.1177/0170840614556918 (accessed 28 February 2020).
Barbier, Geoffrey, Reza Zafarani, Huiji Gao, Gabriel Fung & Huan Liu. 2012. Maximizing benefits from crowdsourced data. *Computational and Mathematical Organization Theory* 18(3). 257–279.
Battistella, Cinzia & Fabio Nonino. 2012. What drives collective innovation? Exploring the system of drivers for motivations in open innovation, web-based platforms. *Information Research* 17(1). http://www.informationr.net/ir/17-1/paper513.html (accessed 28 February 2020).
Bijker, Wiebe E. 1987. The social construction of Bakelite: Toward a theory of invention. In Wiebe E. Bijker, Thomas P. Hughes & Trevor J. Pinch (eds.), *The social construction of technological systems*, 159–187. Cambridge, MA: MIT Press.
Bloodgood, James. 2013. Crowdsourcing: Useful for problem solving, but what about value capture? *Academy of Management Review* 38(3). 455–457.
Boudreau, Kevin J., Nicola Lacetera & Karim R. Lakhani. 2011. Incentives and problem uncertainty in innovation contests: An empirical analysis. *Management Science* 57(5). 843–863.
Boudreau, Kevin J. & Karim R. Lakhani. 2013. Using the crowd as an innovation partner. *Harvard Business Review* 91(4). 60–99.
Brabham, Daren C. 2008. Crowdsourcing as a model for problem solving: An introduction and cases. *Convergence* 14(1). 75–90.
Brabham, Daren C. 2017. How crowdfunding discourse threatens public arts. *New Media and Society* 19(7). 983–999.
Brabham, Daren C., Kurt M. Ribisl, Thomas R. Kirchner & Jay M. Bernhardt. 2014. Crowdsourcing applications for public health. *American Journal of Preventive Medicine* 46(2). 179–187.
Brunswicker, Sabine, Volker Bilgram & Johann Fueller. 2017. Taming wicked civic challenges with an innovative crowd. *Business Horizons* 60(2). 167–177.
Cherry, Miriam A. 2018. Corporate social responsibility and crowdwashing in the gig economy. *Saint Louis University Law Journal* 63(1). https://scholarship.law.slu.edu/lj/vol63/iss1/3 (accessed 3 July 2020).
Cui, Tingru, Yi Wu & Yu Tong. 2018. Exploring ideation and implementation openness in open innovation projects: IT-enabled absorptive capacity perspective. *Information and Management* 55(5). 576–587.
Dahlander, Linus, Lars Bo Jeppesen & Henning Piezunka. 2019. How organizations manage crowds: Define, broadcast, attract, and select. In Jörg Sydow & Hans Berends (eds.), *Managing inter-organizational collaborations: Process views* (Research in the Sociology of Organizations 64), 239–270. Bingley, UK: Emerald.
Davenport, Thomas & Laurence Prusak. 1998. *Working knowledge: How organizations manage what they know*. Cambridge, MA: Harvard Business School Press. https://doi.org/10.5860/choice.35-5167 (accessed 28 February 2020).

Estellés-Arolas, Enrique & Fernando González-Ladrón-de-Guevara. 2012. Towards an integrated crowdsourcing definition. *Journal of Information Science* 38(2). 189–200.
Ferraro, Fabrizio, Dror Etzion & Joel Gehman. 2015. Tackling grand challenges pragmatically: Robust action revisited. *Organization Studies* 36(3). 363–390.
Frey, Karsten, Christian Lüthje & Simon Haag. 2011. Whom should firms attract to open innovation platforms? The role of knowledge diversity and motivation. *Long Range Planning* 44(5–6). 397–420.
Furnari, Santi. 2014. Interstitial spaces: Micro-interaction settings and the genesis of new practices between institutional fields. *Academy of Management Review* 39(4). 439–462.
George, Gerard, Jennifer Howard-Grenville, Aparna Joshi & Laszlo Tihanyi. 2016. Understanding and tackling societal grand challenges through management research. *Academy of Management Journal* 59(6). 1880–1895.
Ghezzi, Antonio, Donata Gabelloni, Antonella Martini & Angelo Natalicchio. 2018. Crowdsourcing: A review and suggestions for future research. *International Journal of Management Reviews* 20(2). 343–363.
Gray, Barbara & Jenna P. Stites. 2013. Sustainability through partnerships: Capitalizing on collaboration. *Network for Business Sustainability*. December 2. https://www.nbs.net/articles/sustainability-through-partnerships-a-systematic-review.
Howe, Jeff. 2006. The rise of crowdsourcing. *Wired Magazine*, 1 June.
Huang, Yan, Param Vir Singh & Tridas Mukhopadhyay. 2012. Crowdsourcing contests: A dynamic structural model of the impact of incentive structure on solution quality. *International Conference on Information Systems* [ICIS], vol. 3. 2505–2521. https://aisel.aisnet.org/icis2012/proceedings/EconomicsValue/6 (accessed 28 February 2020).
Hutter, Katja, Julia Hautz, Johann Füller, Julia Mueller & Kurt Matzler. 2011. Communitition: The tension between competition and collaboration in community-based design contests. *Creativity and Innovation Management* 20(1). 3–21.
Jansson, David G. & Steven M. Smith. 1991. Design fixation. *Design Studies* 12(1). 3–11.
Johnson, Peter. 1989. The Board of Longitude 1714–1828. *Journal of the British Astronomical Association* 99(2). 63–69.
Kaikati, Andrew M. & Jack G. Kaikati. 2013. Doing business without exchanging money: The scale and creativity of modern barter. *California Management Review* 55(2). 46–71.
Keyton, Joann, Stephenson J. Beck, Amber S. Messersmith & Ryan S. Bisel. 2010. Ensuring communication research makes a difference. *Journal of Applied Communication Research* 38(3). 306–309.
Kittur, Aniket. 2010. Crowdsourcing, collaboration and creativity. *XRDS: Crossroads, The ACM Magazine for Students* 17(2). 22–26.
Koschmann, Matthew. A. 2016. A communication perspective on organisational stakeholder relationships: Discursivity, relationality, and materiality. *Communication Research and Practice* 2(3). 407–431.
Kuhn, Timothy. 2008. A communicative theory of the firm: Developing an alternative perspective on intra-organizational power and stakeholder relationships. *Organization Studies* 29(8–9). 1227–1254.
Levinthal, Daniel & Hart E. Posen. 2007. Myopia of selection: Does organizational adaptation limit the efficacy of population selection? *Administrative Science Quarterly* 52(4). 586–620.
Majchrzak, Ann & Arvind Malhotra. 2019. *Unleashing the crowd: Overcoming the managerial challenges*. Cham: Springer.
Malhotra, Arvind & Ann Majchrzak. 2014. Managing crowds in innovation challenges. *California Management Review* 56(4). 103–123.
OpenIDEO. https://www.openideo.com/ (accessed 27 February 2020).

Pavitt, Charles. 1999. Theorizing about the group communication-leadership relationship. In Lawrence R. Frey, Dennis Gouran & Marshall Scott Poole (eds.), *The handbook of group communication theory and research*, 313–334. Thousand Oaks, CA: Sage.

Pedersen, Jay, David Kocsis, Abhishek Tripathi, Alvin Tarrell, Aruna Weerakoon, Nargess Tahmasbi, Jie Xiong, Wei Deng, Onook Oh, Gert Jan De Vreede 2013. Conceptual foundations of crowdsourcing: A review of IS research. *Proceedings of the 46th Annual Hawaii International Conference on System Sciences, HICSS 2013*. 579–588.

Poetz, Marion K. & Martin Schreier. 2012. The value of crowdsourcing: Can users really compete with professionals in generating new product ideas? *Journal of Product Innovation Management* 29(2). 245–256.

Porter, Amanda J., Philipp Tuertscher & Marleen Huysman. 2020. Saving our oceans: Scaling the impact of robust action through crowdsourcing. *Journal of Management Studies* 57(2). 246–286.

Porter, Michael E. & Mark R. Kramer. 2011. Creating shared value. *Harvard Business Review* 89(1–2). 62–77.

Putnam, Linda L., Nelson Phillips & Pamela Chapman. 1996. Metaphors of communication and organization. In Stewart R. Clegg, Cynthia Hardy & Tom Lawrence (eds.), *Handbook of organization studies*, 375–408. Thousand Oaks, CA: Sage.

Rossen, Brent & Benjamin Lok. 2012. A crowdsourcing method to develop virtual human conversational agents. *International Journal of Human Computer Studies* 70(4). 301–319.

Sieg, Jan Henrik, Martin W. Wallin & Georg von Krogh. 2010. Managerial challenges in open innovation: A study of innovation intermediation in the chemical industry. *R&D Management* 40(3). 281–291.

Surowiecki, James. 2004. *The wisdom of crowds*. New York: Anchor.

Terwiesch, Christian & Yi Xu. 2008. Innovation contests, open innovation, and multiagent problem solving. *Management Science* 54(9). 1529–1543.

Weick, Karl E. 1979. *The social psychology of organizing*. Reading, MA: Addison-Wesley.

Wise, Kevin, Brian Hamman & Kjerstin Thorson. 2006. Moderation, response rate, and message interactivity: Features of online communities and their effects on intent to participate. *Journal of Computer-Mediated Communication* 12(1). 24–41.

Sarah E. Riforgiate and Samentha Sepúlveda

28 Managing and being managed by emotions

Abstract: Simultaneously, communication is used to manage emotions and emotions manage interactions in organizations. This chapter explores emotional management from culture, organizational, and interpersonal perspectives. Specifically, the chapter discusses concerns and benefits to managing emotions, as well as the relationship between verbal/nonverbal communication and emotional management. Later sections delve into how communication and emotional management intersect with myriad organizational processes including organizational socialization, emotional labor, emotional intelligence, emotional contagion, technology use, and destructive emotional management. Throughout each section, the chapter emphasizes areas that warrant further exploration to extend understanding of emotions and management.

Keywords: emotion regulation/management; emotion communication; emotion theories; emotions in organizations; organizational communication

Communication of and about emotions has far reaching implications for organizations and their members. This chapter synthesizes research across management, communication, business, linguistics, psychology, and related disciplines to explain how emotion is managed by and manages communication. The chapter begins by explaining what emotions are and the mutual influence language and emotion have in shaping organizational understandings and practices. It then explores emotional management from cultural, organizational, and interpersonal perspectives.

1 Importance of emotions and management

Emotions are woven tightly into the fabric of organizational life and have gained increased scholarly attention over the last thirty years (Ashkanasy and Dorris 2017). From Hochschild's (1983) introduction of emotional labor in her seminal book *The Managed Heart*, to the popularization of emotional intelligence (Goleman 2006), the management of emotional displays and communication of emotion has been explored from a variety of organizational, leadership, and employee perspectives. Importantly, while emotions are felt internally, they are communicatively interpreted, shared, and managed (Riforgiate and Komarova 2017). Individuals express, suppress, modify, exchange, and spread emotions through verbal and nonverbal communication processes (Waldron 2012). The language individuals use and nonverbal communication expressions matter. Further, the management of emotional expressions has noteworthy implications, making this a significant topic to explore.

1.1 Negative implication of emotion management

The very idea of managing emotions and emotional expressions for work, as well as the deep and automatic feelings within individuals, can be somewhat concerning. After all, emotional reactions to frightening situations such as fight, flight, or freeze act as a protection mechanism (Floyd and Afifi 2011). Work requiring individuals to suppress specific emotions to appear brave or stoic can contribute to dangerous work conditions and practices. For example, Scott and Myers (2005) detailed how rookie firefighters were trained in boot camp to minimize feelings and expressions of fear when entering burning structures. Rivera and Tracy (2014) described how border patrol agents suppressed feelings of sadness to appear stoic, even when they felt deeply for undocumented immigrants who were dehydrated, injured, raped by bandits, or lost children during dangerous crossings. While bravery and stoic strength may be necessary for this work, suppressing these emotional displays can toughen emotions (Rivera and Tracy 2014) and remove important warning cues for safely approaching this work (Scott and Myers 2005).

Emotional management concerns also occur for client-facing employees. Employees directed to communicate positively with clients may enhance company profits at personal costs. Hochschild (1983) illustrated how female flight attendants were instructed to tolerate inappropriate advances made by male customers and show compassion by reframing the situation to think of customers as frightened children. Attendants engaged in emotional labor to tactfully navigate sexual harassment behaviors without organizational support. Similarly, Hall (1993) noted the dangers waitresses faced when managing their own and others' emotions. Waitresses were indeed expected to smile and be congenial despite male customers' suggestions that these servers were dessert or a piece of meat to consume as part of the dining experience.

Further, employees who adjust authentic emotions (*real* self) to enact organizational expectations (*fake* self) can alter their self-identity, making it difficult to know what emotions and identity characteristics are genuine (Tracy and Trethewey 2005). When individuals espouse fabricated emotions, they can lose a sense of naturally felt emotions that are important for decision making. Fully suppressing emotions can reduce individuals' ability to make decisions at all. Without emotions people are unable to make choices and instead become trapped in an endless process of creating alternatives and weighing options (George 2000).

Constantly self-monitoring one's own emotions and adjusting communication to manage others' emotions requires effort, can be exhausting (Chu, Baker, and Murrmann 2012), and leads to burnout (Tracy 2017). Ethically, managing emotions is problematic when management is manipulative (Dougherty and Krone 2002). Supervisors with high emotional intelligence, a strong ability to detect and manage their own and others' emotions, may manipulate emotions for personal gain, disregarding the organization's and employees' best interests (Fineman 2000). Even darker, workplace bullying occurs when an organizational member subjects an employee to long-term systematic abuse inducing ongoing negative emotions that ripple beyond the targeted worker to co-workers, family, and friends (Lutgen-Sandvik 2018).

1.2 Positive implications of emotional management

There are also positive implications of adjusting one's emotional expressions. Communicating positive emotions verbally and nonverbally (e. g., smiling, upbeat language), even when individuals do not initially feel positive, often enhances their own happiness and wellbeing (Grandey 2000). Employees can "catch" positive emotions from others, making the workplace more pleasant and enhancing employee creativity (Fredrickson and Branigan 2005). Additionally, faking positive emotions to overcome challenging situations can increase feelings of pride and job security (Brotheridge and Grandey 2002). Positive emotions are related to increased job satisfaction and motivation (Fineman 1996), and workers can spread positive emotions to others through emotional cues (Ashkanasy and Daus 2002).

Emotional management can also be taught and lead to positive outcomes. Lewis, Neville, and Ashkanasy (2017: 38) reported that developing emotional intelligence skills in nursing students enhanced their ability "to understand and manage anger, frustration, and anxiety during interactions with patients". Similarly, by paying attention to communication patterns, hospice workers can enact strategies to relate compassionately with patients in sustainable ways, benefiting workers and patients alike (Way and Tracy 2012). While organizations profit from employees' emotional displays, individual employees can also increase their income. Salespeople who communicate positivity enhance client interactions to increase sales commissions (Cialdini 2009). Similarly, waitresses who smile genuinely can increase their tip income (Bujisic et al. 2014).

Leaders can also positively manage followers' emotions. Little, Gooty, and Williams (2016: 93) found that leaders who effectively regulate followers' emotions to "alleviate and minimize goal-obstructive work events" help followers navigate work challenges, develop stronger leader-member relationships, and increase job satisfaction. Additionally, leaders who generate positive emotions enhance work enjoyment, foster loyalty, and increase leader-follower trust (Lutgen-Sandvik, Riforgiate, and Westerman 2015). Considering the myriad implications of managing emotions, it is necessary to consider how communication and emotions intersect. The next section defines emotions and explicates how emotions and language shape each other.

2 Conceptualizing emotions

Emotions are a short-term response to a stimulus; individuals respond to an event – we are excited *about*, angered *by*, or frustrated *with* an occurrence (Hodder 2016). Emotions are different from moods in that emotions are a short-term response to a stimulus, whereas moods are less intense and shift over time (Barsade 2002). Emotions involve a physiological arousal quickly followed by an assessment. When an event occurs, the amygdala, or feeling center of the brain, activates and receives information slightly before the frontal cortex, which manages executive functioning (Swidler 1986). Recognizing the stimulus, individuals quickly assess the valence (positive or negative) and intensity (amount of arousal) of the emotion (Waldron 2012). Heelas (1996: 172) explains that once the emotion is felt, "biologically generated elements have to be 'enriched' by meanings [...] before becoming emotional experiences". After the initial event and appraisal, individuals consider relevant factors in interpreting the emotion, such as the event cause, threat level, and ability to handle the situation (Fisher 2019).

For example, when an individual experiences the emotion of fear, her pupils dilate, her pulse rate increases, and her body prepares for flight, fight, or freeze responses (Floyd and Afifi 2011). Flight (leaving the context) is marked by communication avoidance; freeze responses are marked by silence and inaction; and fight responses generate defensive communication (e. g., harsh words, increased speaking volume/rate). When the individual interprets the emotion and behaviors, the experience may be categorized in a variety of ways, such as terrifying if danger existed or funny if the response was an overreaction with no danger present.

2.1 Nonverbal communication of emotion

The most recognized emotions include "enjoyment, anger, disgust, fear, surprise, and sadness" and are shared through nonverbal and verbal communication (Hodder 2016: 426). While there are many nonverbal communication cues for emotions, facial expressions are studied the most and are considered a pan-cultural phenomenon (Ekman and Friesen 2003). Research using facial recognition software to measure valence, arousal (intensity), and dominance (amount of control) across sixty nonverbal facial expressions of English and Chinese individuals narrowed the six most recognized expressions to four emotions: "happy, sad, surprise/fear, and disgust" (Jack et al. 2016: 725). Specifically, communicating happiness (e. g., "joy" or "pleasant surprise") is associated with lip corners pulled and cheeks raised; sadness (e. g., "shame" or "anguish") is associated with closed eyes, stretched lips, and lowered brows; surprise/fear (e. g., "amazed" or "ecstatic") is associated with the upper lip raised and the jaw dropped; and disgust (e. g., "rage" or "furious") is associated with wrinkling of the nose and raising of the upper lip (Jack et al. 2016: 725).

Emotions are also relayed through other nonverbal communication cues (Planalp 1998). Vocal cues convey emotions through variations in vocal pitch, volume, guttural tone, and speech rate. Posture, gestures, and other body language provide additional emotional information. Some nonverbal cues are difficult or impossible to control, such as pupil dilation, sweating, and blushing. Research often considers nonverbal communication cues independently, but the cues work together simultaneously to convey emotions (Planalp 1998).

2.2 Verbal communication of emotions

While nonverbal cues are important, they do not always provide enough information for an interpretation of emotions. Individuals rely on words to act "like conceptual glue" to categorize emotions (Barrett, Lindquist, and Gendron 2007: 328). When individuals are provided with emotional words, the words change the way the facial expressions are perceived, making some emotions, such as anger, seem even more intense (Barrett, Lundquist, and Gendron 2007). Additionally, Herbert et al. (2018: 2) report that emotional words "increase neural activity in the ventral visual processing stream (involved in object recognition) [...] which may also lead to changes in approach and avoidance behavior" responses. In addition to enhancing meanings and activating physiological responses, emotional words are a symbol that captures a complex set of feelings (Schnall 2005).

Words and the way words are used to describe emotions are also important to consider. In studies of word origins, "anger" and "guilt" have been identified as the first emotion words created across languages and may have been developed to enforce rules of social conduct (Schnall 2005). There are more negative emotion words compared to positive emotion words in the English language (Fisher 2019). Language availability calls attention to the salience of negative emotions reflected by and as a reflection of language. Further, when measuring emotional intensity, Argaman (2010) found that Hebrew speaking individuals used a similar number of lexical modalities (e. g., verbal reducers, intensifiers, emotional words, etc.) when describing low and high intensity negative events. However, fewer lexical modalities were used to describe low intensity positive events compared to high intensity positive events. Accordingly, negative events trigger more emotional language use regardless of intensity while low intensity positive events are less marked by emotional language. As Argaman (2010: 98) explained, "words are always the mediators between real emotion and the perception of the emotion".

2.3 Emotional patterns managing communication

Language manages emotions as individuals use words to interpret experiences in specific contexts and cultures (Heelas 1996). Weick's (1988: 307) question, "How can I know what I think until I see what I say?" captures how communication is central to sensemaking and allows individuals to organize meaning to understand emotions in context. Communication is an action; "what I say" signifies *enactment* where individuals use language to bracket the event as noteworthy based on previous assumptions and experiences (Weick 1988). What is said then prompts *selection* through "see[ing]" and *retention* occurs when "I know what I think" as individuals store information for future events and interpretations (Hall 2011). The sensemaking experience is a "social interactional process in which participants jointly construct meaning" and "language is a resource for negotiating meaning" (Darics and Clifton 2018: 918). Individuals recognize, interpret, and manage emotions throughout interactions with others.

Emotions are not isolated as they prompt responses which manage ongoing patterns of behavior across people. When individuals experience positive emotions, they are more cooperative and creative (Lutgen-Sandvik, Riforgiate, and Fletcher 2011) and these emotions can spread to others (Ashforth and Humphrey 1995). Complementary communication patterns occur when individuals interact and mirror each other's nonverbal communication (Canary and Lakey 2013). Communication patterns can unfold in ways that build positive emotions and compassion (Huffman 2017) or they can be destructive (Andersson and Pearson 1999). For example, if one person is angry, verbal patterns (such as accusations and excuses) along with nonverbal cues (such as interrupting and increased volume) are often reciprocated by the individual's conversation partner in a pattern that can escalate the emotions in the exchange (Canary and Lakey 2013). When negative emotions are engaged in a turn-taking pattern, communication triggers hormonal flooding, which can exacerbate the situation (Penberthy et al. 2018). Rumination occurs when individuals dwell on problems or concerns, creating a spiral of increasingly negative emotions (Boren 2014). However, communication can de-escalate negative emotions if one party is able to engage the other party calmly and effectively through listening and communicating empathy (Fisher and Ury 1991).

On a broader scale, emotions are socially reinforced and managed in organizations through interactions and observed feeling rules (Paul and Riforgiate 2015). Miller, Considine, and Garner (2007: 231) identified five ways emotions are experienced in regard to work, explaining that (1) inauthentic emotions are fabricated as "emotional labor" to engage in customer/client interactions; (2) "emotional work" involves genuine emotions in working with customers/clients; (3) "emotions with work" occur through co-worker interactions; (4) emotions outside of work that flow into the workplace constitute "emotions at work"; and (5) "emotion toward work" occurs when the work causes emotions. In each instance, emotions are evaluated and managed in relation to the organizational context and culture. The remainder of this chapter considers the ways emotions are managed through communication broadly at a societal level, as well as through organizational and interpersonal practices.

3 Societal level emotional management

Communication is "a symbolic process of creating and sharing meaning" with words representing objects and ideas (Nicotera 2020: 4). Single words can stand for complex feelings. For example, Schnall (2005: 29) explained that "envy" describes the complexity of the experience of "a person's desire to achieve a particular outcome, that person's inability to achieve that outcome, while witnessing another person's success at achieving that very outcome". While individuals can experience envy in nuanced ways, there is general agreement of the meaning of the word envy and the associated emotion. Words also stand in for societal level expectations that fundamentally shape how emotions are enacted in organizations. Emotional heuristics are enacted at a subconscious level to manage behavior. Below, we describe two words that shape assumptions and discourses to manage and reinforce emotions in terms of work: professionalism and care-work.

3.1 Professionalism

The word professionalism is attached to understandings of what it means to behave like an ideal or preferred worker and doing work that is valued (Cheney and Ashcraft 2007; Drago 2007). While nuances of professionalism vary across cultures and organizations, professionalism is associated with efficiency, rationality, and the absence of emotions. Mumby and Putnam (1992: 469) explain that rationality involves "intentional, reasoned, and goal-directed behavior". Fineman (2000: 10) further describes assumptions that employees should "think and act rationally to maximize their gains" and "efficiently and economically produce goods and services". Ultimately, emotions are perceived as problematic and disruptive of rational, measured decision making (Dougherty and Drumheller 2006).

While professionalism is associated with Western discourses (Tracy and Malvini Redden 2020), emotion management also occurs in Eastern cultures. For example, Krone and Morgan (2000: 96) studied Chinese executive and deputy executive directors of state-owned enterprises and concluded that "their discourse about emotion suggest[s] that emotional control is an ongoing process of adaptation and learning" where managers talked about de-intensifying feelings (pleasant and unpleasant) to calm down, gain self-control and learn from the experience.

Professionalism encourages employees to downplay or suppress emotional expressions. "Good organizations are places where feelings are managed, designed out, or removed" privileging "behavior control and cognitive processes" (Fineman 1996: 545). However, organizations are not completely devoid of emotions or even neutral. While "expressions of negative emotions, such as fear, anxiety and anger tend to be unacceptable except under fairly circumscribed conditions", other emotions are more acceptable (Ashforth and Humphrey 1995: 104). Professionalism includes neutral and moderately positive emotions but discourages negative and extreme emotional displays (Riforgiate and Tracy 2021).

Several challenges occur with connections between professionalism, rationality, and emotions. First, emotions can "*serve* rationality" by allowing individuals to weigh the importance of ideas in making decisions (Fineman 2000: 10). Emotions are also important for identifying issues and solving problems (Garner and Poole 2009). Garner and Poole's (2009) study of problematic group members illustrated how leaders who acknowledged emotions and confronted problematic members moved their group to progress. Further, decision making while in a slightly negative mood is associated with less susceptibility to persuasion (Ashkanasy and Dorris 2017). Therefore, emotion can be beneficial to organizations and members.

Second, professionalism places additional emotional constraints on minority group members. Wingfield (2010: 257) explained that, like their white co-workers, "black professionals understand that the feeling rules of their jobs mandate displays of congeniality and likability" but "this feeling rule is difficult to sustain given the racism they encounter in their work environments". Further, white professionals' expressions of anger or frustration are generally interpreted as passion for work, whereas black professionals' similar emotional expressions are perceived as dangerous, making it hard for black professionals to communicate commitment to work (Rao and Neely 2019).

Race, sex, and class intersect in terms of emotion work and minority members often feel they must carefully monitor their emotions to change social perceptions of minority groups (Mirchandani 2003). Additionally, Gist-Mackey's (2018) research demonstrated how working-class job search training programs promoted communication and emotion management behaviors to teach marginalized individuals (race and class) to assimilate to mainstream professional expectations, even when the work they sought did not fit a professional workplace and involved physical labor. Taken as a whole, these findings underscore how powerful societal expectations are in managing emotional display rules and enactment, even when the rules disadvantage groups and are not appropriate for the type of work.

Finally, linking professionalism and rationality manages emotions by accentuating masculine values and ideologies (Mumby and Putnam 1992). Women are stereotyped and often perceived as emotional, "weak, irrational, and dangerous" (Lutz 1996: 154). These assumptions manage emotions, particularly for women who face a greater stigma for expressing emotions in "professional" spaces. Lively's (2000) research on paralegals in a privately owned law firm pointed out how women experienced a "crying taboo" because those who cried were deemed weak. Further, Lutz's (1996) interviews over four time-points found that women discussed the need to control emotions twice as often as men. Another disadvantage of the rational/emotional split is that emotion-related work, particularly care-work, is not recognized or rewarded in the same ways as professional work (England and Folbre 1999).

3.2 Care-work

While professionalism discourages emotions, societal level expectations connect emotion-related work to women (Kirby et al. 2016). Women occupy the majority of care-work positions that attend to the wellbeing of others (England and Folbre 1999). Care-work occupations include childcare, teaching, nursing, and customer care, among others. *Care* implies that workers will feel emotional connections to others and communicate genuine concern. Nurses trained to understand their own and other's emotions were able to "manage anger, frustration and anxiety during interactions with patients", which improved patient care (Lewis, Neville, and Ashkanasy 2017: 38). Non-profit workers who communicated compassion through immediacy behaviors provided better support for homeless young adults (Huffman 2017). Hospice workers who recognized emotions, related, and (re)acted were more resilient, enhancing patient care (Way and Tracy 2012).

Despite the importance of and need for care-work involving emotions, contrasting professionalism/rationalism and care-work/emotion creates concerning societal level differentiations. First, care-work is not financially compensated as well as work in male dominated fields (England and Folbre 1999). England and Folbre (1999) explained that this financial discrepancy occurs because emotional work is seen as (1) natural rather than skilled work, (2) offering intrinsic rewards as part of the compensation, (3) part of one's civic service rather than employment, (4) serving those who are unable to pay (e. g., children, elderly, poor, etc.), and (5) impossible to put a price value on because care-work is a function of love.

Second, despite resistance to compensating care-work, organizations have commodified care-work to increase revenue, particularly in the service industry. Hotel frontline employees are expected to "portray friendly emotions" (Shapoval 2019: 78), airline attendants are expected to be welcoming (Hochschild 1983), and cruise ship employees are told to "turn [their] smile on" (Tracy 2000: 91). The combination of lower compensation while simultaneously profiting from employee emotion illustrates the complex ways emotions are managed and potentially exploited.

4 Organizational and interpersonal emotion management

Societal level discourses broadly shape emotional expectations that are reinforced at the organizational level through interpersonal interactions. This section discusses how emotions are managed and spread in organizations through socializing members, emotional labor, emotional intelligence, emotional contagion, and organizational processes and structure. We also discuss destructive emotion management patterns.

4.1 Organizational socialization and emotions

Individuals learn expectations for organizational members through multiple stages of organizational socialization (Jablin 2001). Before individuals join an organization, they develop expectations about work and how that work should make them feel through the *anticipatory socialization stage.* Ruder and Riforgiate (2019: 38) found that young adults learned in college classes that non-profit work should be "personally meaningful work" that "gets you out of bed in the morning". The expectation that work should generate positive emotions, passion, and a sense of purpose helped some students find fulfilling jobs but created frustration and disappointment when students' expectations were unmet (Ruder and Riforgiate 2019). Employers can screen for emotional fit during the interview process, but screening is complicated when employers and job candidates accentuate positive impressions during interviews (Huffcutt, Culbertson, and Riforgiate 2015). Internships are another way to assess skills and emotional fit and are most effective when employers and interns work together to manage emotional tensions resulting from the learning experience (Woo, Putnam, and Riforgiate 2017).

The *encounter stage* occurs when individuals join the organization and learn about the work, culture, and emotional rules through orientation, training, and daily interactions (Kramer 2010). Anderson (2018: 80) described her orientation experience at a for-profit homebuilder that emphasized feeling rules connected to religiosity, including a folder labeled "honor God in all we do" and a laminated wallet-sized values card. Scott and Myers (2005) detailed how new recruits at a municipal fire department were trained to compartmentalize and emotionally detach through repeated exposure to emotional events, formal training emphasizing professionalism, and hazing to test recruits' trustworthiness. Smith and Kleinman (1989) explained how medical students were socialized to display neutral emotions to communicate power and discourage patients from challenging them. Each organization and industry has specific emotional expectations that employees must learn and either embrace or change as they become full organizational members (*metamorphosis stage*).

4.2 Emotional labor

In many industries, employees are trained and expected to perform emotional labor, which involves "the management of feeling to create a publicly observable facial and bodily display" for the benefit of the organization (Hochschild 1983: 7). Emotional labor occurs through surface acting (faking emotions to align with sanctioned emotions) or deep acting (changing felt emotions to match expected emotions) (Grandey 2003). Surface acting involves communication that fabricates, suppresses, amplifies, downplays, or masks (substituting one emotion for another) emotions (Malvini Redden 2013). Communicating emotions that employees disagree with can threaten employees' preferred identity and trigger emotional dissonance. Tracy (2004) explained how correctional officers experienced emotional dissonance when they were expected to be strong to enforce authority while simultaneously serving inmates (e. g., bringing meals, cleaning up), which increased employee experiences of burnout (Tracy 2004). However, social support can reduce emotional dissonance and enhance job satisfaction, offering a potential avenue to address dissonance (Abraham 1999).

Managing emotions through emotional labor can also be beneficial. Conrad and Witte (1994: 420) noted that "the mere act of saying positive things or acting cheerful even if one does not feel cheerful leads to healthier individuals". Further, Scarduzio and Malvini Redden (2015) reported that negative emotions can allow employees to distance themselves from clients, feel a sense of camaraderie with co-workers, and enhance teamwork. Taken as a whole, emotional labor research has expanded from customer service to other work sectors and continues to tease out the nuances of how the emotional performance is managed and manages the emotions of workers and clients.

4.3 Emotional intelligence

Emotional intelligence (EI) is another concept related to emotion management. Mayer, Caruso, and Salovey (2016: 2) explained that "emotionally intelligent people (a) perceive emotions accurately, (b) use emotions to accurately facilitate thought, (c) understand emotions and emotional meanings and (d) manage emotions in themselves and others". EI is associated with positive outcomes. For example, project managers with high EI are better able to manage relationship, task, and process conflict, which enhances project performance (Khosravi, Rezvani, and Ashkanasy 2020). Further, EI is associated with higher project manager job satisfaction and trust in others, contributing to project success (Rezvani et al. 2016).

In addition to EI, social intelligence and personal intelligence involve managing emotions. Social intelligence is the ability to "understand social rules, customs, and expectations, social situations and the social environment, and to recognize the exercise of influence and power in social hierarchies. It also includes an understanding of intra- and inter-group relations" (Mayer, Caruso, and Salovey 2016: 10). However, social intelligence is highly correlated with general intelligence, creating difficulty in separating the two concepts. Personal intelligence involves maintaining self-control and being able to identify and manage "motives and emotions, thoughts and knowledge, plans and styles of action" (Mayer, Caruso, and Salovey 2016: 10). While EI involves recognizing another's emotion (e. g., happy, sad, frustrated), personal intelligence involves the ability to predict motives and behavioral patterns (e. g., identifying an employee's frustration will result in a co-worker confrontation). Each of these intelligences contribute to emotional management.

4.4 Emotional contagion

Because emotions are social and communicative, emotions spread across workplace interactions through emotional contagion (Banerjee and Srivasta 2019). Emotional contagion can be intentionally managed. Employees may be directed to be welcoming and to spread positive emotions to encourage a pleasant hotel stay (Shapoval 2019) or be trained to be gruff and directive to evoke passenger anxiety when moving through airport security (Malvini Redden 2013). Emotional contagion can also occur unintentionally and spread spontaneously. Employees spread positive emotions when they experience happiness working with co-workers (Lutgen-Sandvik, Riforgiate, and Fletcher 2011) and can spread negative emotions when venting (Paul and Riforgiate 2015) or ruminating on negative events (Boren 2014).

4.5 Organizational process and structures

Organizational processes and structures manage how emotions are experienced and spread. For example, Wang et al. (2020) studied a global organization that standardized language use across international sites to coordinate workflow and collaboration. This structural decision evoked emotions of frustration with language barriers, embarrassment from not being able to communicate and perform quickly in a non-native language, and confusion from misunderstanding communication (Wang et al. 2020).

Technology structures designed to manage client and co-worker interactions also influence emotions. Ishii and Markman (2016) studied customer service employees who used phone, email, and chat technology to address client concerns. Employees felt the highest emotional presence and engaged in less surface acting when interacting via phone, which positively predicted job satisfaction (Ishii and Markman 2016). Additionally, technology may limit nonverbal cues, but still promote emotional contagion (Cheshin, Rafaeli, and Bos 2011). Cheshin, Rafaeli, and Bos (2011) found that remote workers associated text-based word combinations that sounded resolute with the emotion of anger, while word combinations indicating flexibility were associated with happiness. Organizational processes and structures deserve attention because of the ways they manage members' emotional experiences.

4.6 Destructive emotion management

Finally, it is important to acknowledge destructive communication practices that manage emotions. Frost (2004: 11) explained that workplace toxicity occurs when organizational members "feel stripped of their confidence, hope or self-esteem through the harshness or disrespect in the message they get from others" (Frost 2004: 11). Daily interactions contribute to larger problematic patterns. For example, Paul and Riforgiate (2015) illustrated how traditional justice (authoritarian and rules-based) leadership fostered destructive communication practices such as employees "stuffing" negative emotions and "venting" outside of work, resulting in lower employee satisfaction, higher turnover, and contentious workplace conflicts. Employees also contribute to negative emotions. Mancl and Pennington (2011: 8) detailed interviews with women who explained their experiences of "poppy clipping" designed to "cut [high achieving women] down to size" through passive-aggressive nonverbal and verbal exchanges.

Even more concerning, harassment, and bullying occur as perpetrators systematically provoke targets who experience increasingly negative emotions sustained over long periods (Lutgen-Sandvik 2003). Tracy, Lutgen-Sandvik, and Alberts' (2006: 159) metaphor analysis detailed how bullying targets felt like a "prisoner" and "slave" as they described their bullies as "narcissistic dictators", "demons", and "evil". While perpetrators are responsible for direct acts of bullying, organizations also contribute by enabling cycles of bullying to occur through grievance processes that silence targets, dismiss concerns, and justify abuse (Lutgen-Sandvik 2003). When targets seek advice to overcome bullying, recommendations place the burden of change on individual agency and rational (professional) solutions that ignore the erratic nature of bullying behaviors (Tye-Williams and Krone 2017). Understanding the management of destructive emotional processes is necessary to facilitate change.

5 Conclusion

As illustrated in this chapter, societal, organizational, and individual emotions manage and are managed through communication in complex and nuanced ways. Language shapes emotional expression and simultaneously influences how emotions are communicated, perceived, and interpreted. Considering the positive and negative implications related to emotion management and the myriad ways emotions manage and are managed, researchers and practitioners will continue to benefit from understanding and exploring this important topic.

6 References

Abraham, Rebecca. 1999. The impact of emotional dissonance on organizational commitment and intention to turnover. *The Journal of Psychology* 133(4). 441–455.

Anderson, Lindsey B. 2018. When the Lord builds the house: An autoethnographic account of working in an evangelical for-profit organizational culture. *Culture and Organization* 24(1). 74–93.

Andersson, Lynne M. & Christine M. Pearson. 1999. Tit for tat? The spiraling effect of incivility in the workplace. *Academy of Management Review* 24(3). 452–471.

Argaman, Osnat. 2010. Linguistic markers and emotional intensity. *Journal of Psycholinguist Research*. 39(2). 89–99.

Ashforth, Blake E. & Ronald H. Humphrey. 1995. Emotion in the workplace: A reappraisal. *Human Relations* 48(2). 97–125.

Ashkanasy, Neal & Catherine S. Daus. 2002. Emotions in the workplace: The new challenge for managers. *The Academy of Management Executive* 16(1). 76–86.

Ashkanasy, Neil M. & Alana D. Dorris. 2017. Emotions in the workplace. *Annual Review Organizational Psychology and Organizational Behavior* 4(1). 67–90.

Banerjee, Poulami & Manjari Srivastava. 2019. A review of emotional contagion: Research propositions. *Journal of Management Research* 19(4). 250–266.

Barrett, Lisa F., Kristen A. Lindquist & Maria Gendron. 2007. Language as context for the perception of emotion. *Trends in Cognitive Sciences* 11(8). 327–332.

Barsade, Sigal G. 2002. The ripple effect: Emotional contagion and its influence on group behavior. *Administrative Science Quarterly* 47(4). 644–675.

Boren, Justin P. 2014. The relationships between co-rumination, social support, stress, and burnout among working adults. *Management Communication Quarterly* 28(1). 3–25.

Brotheridge, Céleste M. & Alicia A. Grandey. 2002. Emotional labor and burnout: Comparing two perspectives of "people work". *Journal of Vocational Behavior* 60(1). 17–39.

Bujisic, Milos, Luorong L. Wu, Anna Mattila & Anil Bilgihan. 2014. Not all smiles are created equal: Investigating the effects of display authenticity and service relationship on customer tipping behavior. *International Journal of Contemporary Hospitality Management* 26(2). 293–306.

Canary, Daniel J. & Sandra Lakey. 2013. *Strategic conflict*. New York: Routledge.

Cheney, George & Karen L. Ashcraft. 2007. Considering "the professional" in communication studies: Implications for theory and research within and beyond the boundaries of organizational communication. *Communication Theory* 17(2). 146–175.

Cheshin, Arik, Anat Rafaeli & Nathan Bos. 2011. Anger and happiness in virtual teams: Emotional influences of text and behavior on others' affect in the absence of non-verbal cues. *Organizational Behavior and Human Decision Processes* 116(1). 2–16.

Chu, Kay H., Melissa A. Baker & Suzanne K. Murrmann. 2012. When we are onstage, we smile: The effects of emotional labor on employee work outcomes. *International Journal of Hospitality Management* 31(3). 906–915.

Cialdini, Robert B. 2009. *Influence: Science and practice*, 5th edn. Boston, MA: Pearson.

Conrad, Charles & Kim Witte. 1994. Is emotional expression repression oppression? Myths of organizational affective regulation. *Annals of the International Communication Association* 17(1). 417–428.

Darics, Erika & Jonathan Clifton. 2018. Making applied linguistics applicable to business practice: Discourse analysis as a management tool. *Applied Linguistics* 40(6). 917–936.

Dougherty, Debbie S. & Kristina Drumheller. 2006. Sensemaking and emotions in organizations: Accounting for emotions in a rational(ized) context. *Communication Studies* 57(2). 215–238.

Dougherty, Debbie S. & Kathleen J. Krone. 2002. Emotional intelligence as organizational communication: An examination of the construct. *Annals of the International Communication Association* 26(1). 202–229.

Drago, Robert W. 2007. *Striking a balance: Work, family and life*. Boston, MA: Dollars & Sense.

Ekman, Paul & Wallace V. Friesen. 2003. *Unmasking the face: A guide to recognizing emotions from facial clues*. Los Altos, CA: Melor Books.

England, Paula & Nancy Folbre. 1999. The cost of caring. *Annals of the American Academy of Political & Social Science* 561(1). 39–51.

Fineman, Stephen. 1996. Emotion and organizing. In Stewart R. Clegg, Cynthia Hardy & Walter R. Nord (eds.), *Handbook of organizational studies*, 543–564. London: Sage.

Fineman, Stephen. 2000. Emotional arenas revisited. In Stephen Fineman (ed.), *Emotion in organizations*, 2nd edn., 1–24. London: Sage.

Fisher, Cynthia. 2019. Emotions in organizations. *Oxford research encyclopedia of business and management*. 1–41. https://oxfordre.com/business/view/10.1093/acrefore/9780190224851.001.0001/acrefore-9780190224851-e-160?rskey=TzRvm7&result=1 (accessed 14 November 2020).

Fisher, Roger & William Ury. 1991. *Getting to yes: Negotiating agreement without giving in*, 2nd edn. New York: Penguin Books.

Floyd, Kory & Tamara D. Afifi. 2011. Biological and physiological perspectives on interpersonal communication. In Mark Knapp & John Daly (eds.), *Handbook of interpersonal communication*, 4th edn. 87–130. Thousand Oaks, CA: Sage.

Fredrickson, Barbara L. & Christine Branigan. 2005. Positive emotions broaden the scope of attention and thought-action repertoires. *Cognition and Emotion* 19(3). 313–332.

Frost, Peter J. 2004. Handling toxic emotions: New challenges for leaders and their organization. *Organizational Dynamics* 33(2). 111–127.

Garner, Johny T. & Marshall Scott Poole. 2009. Opposites attract: Leadership endorsement as a function of interaction between a leader and a foil. *Western Journal of Communication* 73(3). 227–247.

George, Jennifer M. 2000. Emotions and leadership: The role of emotional intelligence. *Human Relations* 53(8). 1027–1055.

Gist-Mackey, Angela N. 2018. (Dis)embodied job search communication training: Comparative critical ethnographic analysis of materiality and discourse during the unequal search for work. *Organization Studies* 39(9). 1251–1275.

Goleman, Daniel. 2006. *Emotional intelligence*. New York: Bantam.

Grandey, Alicia A. 2000. Emotion regulation in the workplace: A new way to conceptualize emotional labor. *Journal of Occupational Health Psychology* 5(1). 95–110.

Grandey, Alicia A. 2003. When "the show must go on": Surface acting and deep acting as determinants of emotional exhaustion and peer-rated service delivery. *Academy of Management Journal* 46(1). 86–96.

Hall, Elaine J. 1993. Smiling, deferring, and flirting: Doing gender by giving "good service". *Work and Occupations* 20(4). 452–471.

Hall, Maurice L. 2011. Sensing the vision: Sense making and the social construction of leadership in the branch office of an insurance company. *Atlantic Journal of Communication* 19(2). 65–78.

Heelas, Paul. 1996. Emotion talk across cultures. In Rom Harré & Gerrod Parrott (eds.), *The emotions: Social, cultural and biological dimensions*, 171–199. Thousand Oaks, CA: Sage.

Herbert, Cornelia, Thomas Ethofer, Andreas Fallgatter, Peter Walla & Geog Northoff. 2018. The Janus face of language: Where are the emotions in words and where are the words in emotions? *Frontiers in Psychology* 9. 1–5.

Hochschild, Arlie R. 1983. *The managed heart: Commercialization of human feeling.* Berkeley, CA: University of California Press.

Hodder, Ruppert. 2016. Emotion, organization and society. *Culture and Society* 53(4). 425–434.

Huffcutt, Allen I., Satoris S. Culbertson & Sarah E. Riforgiate. 2015. Functional forms of competence: Interviewing. In Annegret F. Hannawa & Brian H. Spitzberg (eds.), *Communication competence* (Handbooks of communication science 22), 431–448. Boston, MA: De Gruyter Mouton.

Huffman, Timothy P. 2017. Compassionate communication, embodied aboutness, and homeless young adults. *Western Journal of Communication* 82(2). 149–167.

Ishii, Kumi & Kris M. Markman. 2016. Online customer service and emotional labor: An exploratory study. *Computers in Human Behavior* 62. 658–665.

Jablin, Fredrick M. 2001. Organizational entry, assimilation, and exit. In Fredrick M. Jablin & Linda L. Putnam (eds.), *The new handbook of organizational communication*, 732–818. Thousand Oaks, CA: Sage.

Jack, Rachael E., Wei Sun, Ioannis Delis, Oliver G. B. Garrod & Philippe G. Schyns. 2016. Four not six: Revealing culturally common facial expressions of emotion. *Journal of Experimental Psychology* 145(6). 708–730.

Khosravi, Pouria, Azadeh Rezvani & Neil M. Ashkanasy. 2020. Emotional intelligence: A preventative strategy to manage destructive influence of conflict in large scale projects. *International Journal of Project Management* 38(1). 36–46.

Kirby, Erika L., Sarah E. Riforgiate, Isolde K. Anderson, Mary P. Lahman & Alison M. Lietzenmayer. 2016. Working mothers as "jugglers": A critical look at popular work-family balance films. *Journal of Family Communication* 16(1). 76–93.

Kramer, Michael W. 2010. *Organizational socialization: Joining and leaving organizations.* Malden, MA: Polity.

Krone, Kathleen J. & Jayne M. Morgan. 2000. Emotion metaphors in management: The Chinese experience. In Stephen Fineman (ed.), *Emotion in organizations*, 2nd edn., 83–100. London: Sage.

Lewis, Gillian M., Christine Neville & Neal M. Ashkanasy. 2017. Emotional intelligence and affective events in nurse education: A narrative review. *Nurse Education Today* 53. 34–40.

Little, Laura M., Janaki Gooty & Michelle Williams. 2016. The role of leader emotion management in leader-member exchange and follower outcomes. *The Leadership Quarterly* 27(1). 85–97.

Lively, Kathryn J. 2000. Reciprocal emotion management: Working together to maintain stratification in private law firms. *Work and Occupations* 27(1). 32–63.

Lutgen-Sandvik, Pamela. 2003. The communicative cycle of employee emotional abuse: Generation and regeneration of workplace mistreatment. *Management Communication Quarterly* 16(4). 471–501.

Lutgen-Sandvik, Pamela. 2018. Vicarious and secondary victimization in adult bullying and mobbing: Coworkers, target-partners, children, and friends. In Maureen K. Duffy & David Yamada (eds.), *Workplace bullying and mobbing in the United States*, 171–200. Santa Barbara, CA: ABC–CLIO.

Lutgen-Sandvik, Pamela, Sarah Riforgiate & Courtney Fletcher. 2011. Work as a source of positive emotional experiences and the discourses informing positive assessment. *Western Journal of Communication* 75(1). 2–27.

Lutgen-Sandvik, Pamela., Sarah E. Riforgiate & Catherine Westerman. 2015. "My boss is wonderful, and I'll do anything for him!": Positive managerial communication and employee emotion-action tendencies. Paper presented at the Central States Communication Association Conference, Madison, WI, 15–19 April.

Lutz, Catherine A. 1996. Engendered emotion: Gender, power, and the rhetoric of emotional control. In Rom Harré & W. Gerrod Parrott (eds.), *The emotions: Social, cultural and biological dimensions*, 151–170. Thousand Oaks, CA: Sage.

Malvini Redden, Shawna. 2013. How lines organize compulsory interaction, emotion management, and "emotional taxes": The implications of passenger emotion and expression in airport security lines. *Management Communication Quarterly* 27(1). 121–149.

Mancl, Anne C. & Barbara Penington. 2011. Tall poppies in the workplace: Communication strategies used by envious others in response to successful women. *Qualitative Research Reports in Communication* 12(1). 79–86.

Mayer, John D., David R. Caruso & Peter Salovey. 2016. The ability model of emotional intelligence: Principles and updates. *Emotion Review* 8(4). 1–11.

Miller, Katherine I., Jennifer Considine & Johny Garner. 2007. "Let me tell you about my job": Exploring the terrain of emotion in the workplace. *Management Communication Quarterly* 20(3). 231–260.

Mirchandani, Kiran. 2003. Challenging racial silences in studies of emotion work: Contributions from anti-racist feminist theory. *Organization Studies* 24(5). 721–742.

Mumby, Dennis K. & Linda L. Putnam. 1992. The politics of emotion: A feminist reading of bounded rationality. *Academy of Management Review* 17(3). 465–486.

Nicotera, Anne M. 2020. Study of organizational communication. In Anne M. Nicotera (ed.), *Origins and traditions in organizational communication: A comprehensive introduction to the field*, 1–21. New York: Routledge.

Paul, Gregory D. & Sarah E. Riforgiate. 2015. "Putting on a happy face," "getting back to work," and "letting it go": Traditional and restorative justice understandings of and emotions at work. *Electronic Journal of Communication* 25(3–4). http://www.cios.org/ejcpublic/025/3/025303.html (accessed 19 January 2021).

Penberthy, Jennifer K., Dinesh Chhabra, Dallas M. Ducar, Nina Avitabile, Morgan Lynch, Surbhi Khann, Yiqin Xu, Nassima Ait-Daoud & John Schorling. 2018. Impact of coping and communication skills program on physician burnout, quality of life, and emotional flooding. *Safety and Heath at Work* 9(4). 381–387.

Planalp, Sally. 1998. Current issues arising at the confluence of communication and emotion. *Australian Journal of Communication* 25(3). 65–80.

Rao, Aliya Hamid & Megan Tobias Neely. 2019. What's love got to do with it? Passion and inequality in white-collar work. *Sociology Compass* 13(12). 1–14.

Rezvani, Azadeh, Artemis Chang, Anna Wiewiora, Neal M. Ashkanasy, Peter J. Jordan & Roxane Zolin. 2016. Manager emotional intelligence and project success: The mediating role of job satisfaction and trust. *International Journal of Project Management* 34(7). 1112–1122.

Riforgiate, Sarah E. & Maria Komarova. 2017. Emotion at work. In Craig R. Scott & Lori K. Lewis (eds.), *International encyclopedia of organizational communication*. Chichester, UK: Wiley-Blackwell.

Riforgiate, Sarah E. & Sarah J. Tracy. 2021. Management, organizational communication and emotion. In Gesine L. Schiewer, Jeanette Altarriba & Ng Bee Chin (eds.), *Handbook on language and emotion*. Boston, MA: De Gruyer Mouton.

Rivera, Kendra D. & Sarah J. Tracy. 2014. Embodying emotional dirty work: A messy text of patrolling the border. *Qualitative Research in Organizations and Management: An International Journal* 9(3). 201–222.

Ruder, Emily M. & Sarah E. Riforgiate. 2019. Organizational socialization of millennial nonprofit workers. In Mary Z. Ashlock & Ahmet Atay (eds.), *Examining millennials reshaping organizational cultures*, 33–50. New York: Lexington.

Scarduzio, Jennifer A. & Shawna Malvini Redden. 2015. The positive outcomes of negative emotional displays: A multi-level analysis of emotion in bureaucratic work. *Electronic Journal of Communication* 25(3–4). http://www.cios.org/ejcpublic/025/3/025305.html (accessed 19 January 2021).

Schnall, Simon. 2005. The pragmatic of emotion language. *Psychological Inquiry* 16(1). 28–31.

Scott, Clifton & Karen Kroman Myers. 2005. The socialization of emotion: Learning emotion management at the fire station. *Journal of Applied Communication Research* 33(1). 67–92.

Shapoval, Valeriya. 2019. Organizational injustice and emotional labor of hotel front-line employees. *International Journal of Hospitality Management* 78. 112–121.

Smith, Allen C. III & Sherryl Kleinman. 1989. Managing emotions in medical school: Students' contacts with the living and the dead. *Social Psychology Quarterly* 52(1). 56–69.

Swidler, Ann. 1986. Culture in action: Symbols and strategies. *American Sociological Review* 51(2). 273–286.

Tracy, Sarah J. 2000. Becoming a character for commerce: Emotion labor, self-subordination, and discursive construction of identity in a total institution. *Management Communication Quarterly* 14(1). 90–128.

Tracy, Sarah J. 2004. The construction of correctional officers: Layers of emotionality behind bars. *Qualitative Inquiry* 10(4). 509–533.

Tracy, Sarah J. 2017. Burnout in organizational communication. In Craig Scott & Lori Lewis (eds.) *International encyclopedia of organizational communication*. Chichester, UK: Wiley-Blackwell.

Tracy, Sarah J., Pamela Lutgen-Sandvik & Jess K. Alberts. 2006. Nightmares, demons, and slaves: Exploring the painful metaphors of workplace bullying. *Management Communication Quarterly* 20(2). 148–185.

Tracy, Sarah J. & Shawna Malvini Redden. 2020. The structuration of emotion and organizational communication. In Anne M. Nicotera (ed.), *Origins and traditions in organizational communication: A comprehensive introduction to the field*, 348–369. New York: Routledge.

Tracy, Sarah J. & Angela Trethewey. 2005. Fracturing the real-self/fake-self dichotomy: Moving towards crystallized organizational identities. *Communication Theory* 15(2). 168–195.

Tye-Williams, Stacy & Kathleen J. Krone. 2017. Identifying and reimagining the paradox of workplace bullying advice. *Journal of Applied Communication Research* 45(3). 218–235.

Waldron, Vincent R. 2012. *Communicating emotion at work*. Malden, MA: Polity Press.

Wang, Qui, Jeremy Clegg, Hanna Gajewska-DeMattos & Peter Buckley. 2020. The role of emotions in intercultural business communication: Language standardization in the context of international knowledge transfer. *Journal of World Business* 55(6). 1–21.

Way, Deborah & Sarah J. Tracy. 2012. Conceptualizing compassion as recognizing, relating and (re) acting: An ethnographic study of compassionate communication at hospice. *Communication Monographs* 79(3). 292–315.

Weick, Karl E. 1988. Enacted sensemaking in crisis situations. *Journal of Management Studies* 25(4). 305–317.

Wingfield, Adia H. 2010. Are some emotions marked 'whites only'? Racialized feeling rules in professional workplaces. *Social Problems* 57(2). 251–268.

Woo, DaJung, Linda L. Putnam & Sarah E. Riforgiate. 2017. Identity work and tensions in organizational internships: A comparative analysis. *Western Journal of Communication* 81(5). 560–581.

Samir L. Vaz, Eduardo A. Figueiredo, and Gabriela X. Maia

29 Changing through communication

Abstract: This chapter explores the role of communication for managing organizational change. We illustrate how the CEO statements, concepts, terms and expressions relate to the way middle managers make sense of a change management program that took place at the Brazilian subsidiary of a large Multinational Company. Our theoretical background consequently assumes that sensemaking is a discursive process situated in interactions, conversations, and actions between organization members, representing specific ways of speaking and constructing social reality. Based on the extant knowledge, we believe such interplay between discourses and sensemaking can shed further light on a complex reality that both top managers and middle managers must deal within the course of organizational change.

Keywords: organizational change; communication; discourse; sensemaking; middle managers

There is a growing scholarly interest in exploring the role of discourses for managing organizational change (Akarsu, Gencer, and Yıldırım 2018; Ernst and Jensen Schleiter 2019; Näsänen 2017). Discourse is a "connected set of statements, concepts, terms and expressions which constitutes a way of talking or writing about a particular issue, thus framing the way people understand and act with respect to that issue" (Watson 1994: 113). It thus represents one of the main social practices that drives organizational change, due to its capacity to shape actors' attention, define roles, agency, and consequently act as a mechanism of power and control (Laine and Vaara 2007).

Sensemaking also represents a social practice with significant importance for organizational change (Lüscher and Lewis 2008; Lockett et al. 2014; Balogun and Johnson 2004). When confronted with uncertainty or ambiguity, over time, organizational actors engage in sensemaking to understand novel, unexpected, or confusing situations, clarifying what is going on by extracting and interpreting cues from their work environment (Maitlis and Christianson 2014; Dougherty and Drumheller 2006). They do this through a collective process of thinking and talking about organizational issues that creates a shared meaning regarding questions like "what is happening?", "what does this mean?", and "what do we do now?". Therefore, sensemaking allows groups of individuals to accept and understand change (Maitlis, Vogus, and Lawrence 2013).

Sensemaking is not only an individual and cognitive process but a communication practice based on interactions between organizational actors (Allard-Poesi 2005). It involves peoples' interpretation of cues linked with their past frames of references and experiences to create a shared sense of meaning (Weick 1995). Communication is central for sensemaking because people interpret change through their everyday experiences, that is, through conversations, discussions, stories, jokes, rumors, gossip, and even non-verbal signs (Balogun and Rouleau 2017).

Top and middle managers are two of the most important groups of actors who influence organizational change by means of their discursive and sensemaking practices. Top managers are those members from the upper echelons that are usually responsible for making strategic decisions (Amason 1996) while middle managers distinguish themselves by having both access to top managers and knowledge of operations (Wooldridge, Schmid, and Floyd 2008). These different groups of actors can therefore engage in a dispute for identity and control during organizational change: top managers, by mobilizing discourses to reproduce their hegemony and middle managers, by displaying resistance through discourses meant to create more room for maneuver (Laine and Vaara 2007). Likewise, discourses represent a practice used by top managers to frame middle managers' accounts of responsibility (Sillince and Mueller 2007) and to foster middle managers' commitment by means of contradictory objectives related to organizational change (Jarzabkowski and Sillince 2007). Thereby, top managers tend to employ discourses to influence the way middle managers make sense of organizational change by legitimating (Erkama and Vaara 2010) their acceptance of a changing context (Sillince and Brown 2009).

Managing organizational change therefore depends, we contend, on a mutual and interconnected relationship between top managers' discourses and middle managers' sensemaking. Using change narratives and rhetorical strategies, top managers resonate with middle managers as sensemakers, creating "plausible" meanings that legitimate organizational change programs (Thurlow and Mills 2015). Thus, middle managers' sensemaking is situated in a political context, demarked by top managers' legitimizing discourses about dominant ideologies or decision-making assumptions (Geppert 2003). Based on the extant knowledge, we believe such interplay between discourses and sensemaking can shed light on a complex reality that both top managers and middle managers must deal within the course of organizational change. Communication emerges then as a significant aspect affecting change, which can foster or inhibit the transformation of any organization.

In what follows, we clarify the conceptual perspectives around discourses and sensemaking, by presenting our theoretical background. Our focus here is on change management rather than organizational development, since the first includes a wide range of intervention strategies that directly or indirectly contribute to a larger organizational change effort (Worren, Ruddle, and Moore 1999). Thus, we provide additional evidence of this phenomenon by presenting a case study about a change management program that was strongly influenced by top managers' discourses and middle managers' sensemaking.

1 Theoretical background

Among the different perspectives developed by multiple scholars on sensemaking, we choose to investigate this phenomenon as a discursive process (Gephart 1993). From this perspective, sensemaking is created through interactions, conversations, and actions between organization members (e. g., Weick, Sutcliffe, and Obstfeld 2005; Allard-Poesi 2005; Balogun et al. 2014). Sensemaking thus reveals itself through words in written or spoken texts, which materialize socially constructed meanings (Weick, Sutcliffe, and Obstfeld 2005) or even "descriptions of the world" (Brown 2000: 46). For instance, Balogun and Johnson (2004: 524) define sensemaking as a "conversational and narrative process" and give examples of a variety of communication genres through which sensemaking could occur, like gossip, conversations, stories, and rumors. Thus, this discursive view promotes a "socio-constructionist turn" on sensemaking research by focusing on "detailed, situated and concrete practices and interactions" (Allard-Poesi 2005: 170).

Discourses are key aspects related to sensemaking processes in organizations. To illustrate this, Maitlis and Lawrence (2003) explored the role played by discourses in the social construction of an artistic strategy in a symphony orchestra. Their results reveal that organizational sensemaking derives from an interplay of how people talk and write about strategy, which provides a basis for strategic actions. Several other scholars also associate sensemaking with the production of discourses (e. g., Vaara, Kleymann, and Seristö 2004). They usually understand that the constitution of an environment is enacted through conversation and interactions, which generates an agreed-upon "text-world" that enables consistent and collective action for organizational members.

Discourses here act as a guide for the way people make sense of social reality, transforming it from a subjective perspective into their very own tangible reality (Nicholson and Anderson 2005). Accordingly, language helps to "construct organizational reality through texts that are produced, consumed and disseminated by individuals" (Sonenshein 2006: 1159–1160). As pointed out by Weick, Sutcliffe, and Obstfeld (2005: 409), "sensemaking is, importantly, an issue of language, talk, and communication. Situations, organizations, and environments are talked into existence". Hence, organizational actors mobilize discourses as a resource to construct intersubjective meanings in organizations (Maitlis and Christianson 2014), which means that their "performative power is central to sensemaking" (Balogun and Rouleau 2017: 113).

From a communicational perspective, this means that discourses represent "specific ways of speaking and constructing social reality" (Vaara, Kleymann, and Seristö 2004: 4). Organizational actors henceforth demonstrate a discursive ability when they are able to construct and engage in convincing accounts of their world (Maitlis and Lawrence 2007). Consequently, we choose to study discourses because of their relevance as triggers and correlates for sensemaking, particularly when managing organizational change. Next, we give more details on our case study, which explores the context of a change management program where top managers' discourses and middle managers' sensemaking played a significant role.

2 Case study: managing change at ICARUS

Our case study involves a change management program that took place at ICARUS, a fictitious name we use here to protect the identity of the company (e. g., Küpers, Mantere, and Statler 2013). ICARUS is a subsidiary operating in Brazil and is part of a global multinational, whose headquarters are located in Europe. We began our data collection in 2019. At that time, ICARUS almost had six thousand direct employees and eleven business units, distributed in different regions of Brazil. Despite its history of leadership and competitiveness in the Brazilian industry of fast-moving consumer goods, the company had started to face losses in market shares and profits since 2014. Significant changes also started to challenge the industry attractiveness due to the entrance of new players and the rise of substitute products. Political and economic uncertainties in Brazil were affecting the life of low-income people and thus orienting customers to choose products with lower prices.

A huge change management program emerged then as a reaction to this uncertain environment and poor company performance, with two main objectives: first, to better adapt the company by redesigning its organizational structure, reducing costs, modifying the approach for sales, and revising all distribution channels; second, to develop new competences and fostering new values to shape the organizational culture and consequently improve the company's performance. The CEO (chief executive officer) was the main sponsor of this change management movement. In 2017, he launched a formal change management program under the name *Action*, which was expected to last until 2022. Using an extensive and active communication strategy, he started to encourage all employees to commit to change, by means of face-to-face meetings, online broadcasts, videos, presentations, and other communication channels. The Action program achieved somewhat positive results after two years of implementation. However, a global and unexpected restructuring abruptly interrupted the program, which was specific to the Brazilian subsidiary. This period represented a hiatus in the change management, particularly after an executive succession removed the previous CEO from his position. Thus, employees had to deal with a transitioning phase, without all the guidance he provided.

We had privileged access to primary data because one of us was working for ICARUS during the change management process. Our data consisted of fifteen hours of videos comprising the CEO's speeches and presentations, in addition to more than fifty corporate communications through email, social media, and meeting minutes. We also compiled notes from participative observation on multiple occasions, such as meetings and informal conversations with middle managers as well as senior members of the C-Suite (e. g., chief financial officer – CFO, chief operating officer – COO, and chief information officer – CIO). Finally, we conducted fifteen semi-structured interviews with middle managers to better explore their understandings of the change management program as well as the CEO's discourses. These interviews, which were recorded, lasted an average of fifty minutes and were later transcribed for analysis. We provide a synthesis of our data in Tables 1 and 2.

Table 1: Sources and descriptions for collected data

Sources	Description	Dates
Video recordings	Launching of the Action program: presentation made by the CEO about the business context, reinforcing its importance to overcome corporate challenges	Sep/2017
	Follow-up meeting about the results of the Action program	Aug/2018
	Meeting to present the results for the first year of the Action program	Dec/2018
	CEO presentations with updates and changes in the Action program	May/2019
		July/2019
Corporate communication channels	A total number of fifty-four formal communications made by the CEO using formal channels like email, social media, and minutes of meetings	Jan/2018 to Oct/2019
Fieldnotes from participative observation	Notes created from participative observations on multiple occasions, like formal meetings, working groups, and informal conversations with middle managers and top managers	May/2019 to Dec/2019

Table 2: Interviews with top and middle managers

	Interviews	Dates
1	Portfolio Manager A	Oct/2019
2	Manager for National Merchandising	Oct/2019
3	Portfolio Manager B	Oct/2019
4	Portfolio Manager C	Nov/2019
5	Communication Manager A	Dec/2019
6	Manager for Logistics and National Distribution	Jan/2020
7	National Manager for Business to Consumer (B2C)	Jan/2020
8	National Sales Manager	Jan/2020
9	Communication Manager B	Mar/2020
10	Communication Manager C	Mar/2020
11	Head of Innovation	Mar/2020
12	National Sales Manager	Mar/2020
13	Manager for Industrial Quality	Mar/2020
14	Manager for National Information Technology	Mar/2020
15	Head of Human Resources	Mar/2020

We analyzed these data using open coding to explore multiple concepts as well as their properties (Strauss and Corbin 1998). Next, we grouped these first-order concepts into broader second-order categories and, later, in more abstract as well as comprehensive dimensions of analysis. We describe in more detail the case story and our analysis in the following section.

3 Managing change through the CEO discourses

We begin our analysis by presenting the CEO's discourses that emerged as recurrent practices he mobilized for managing the organizational change program. The CEO launched the Action program in his first ninety days in the position. He personally announced the change initiative by broadcasting a video simultaneously for all the company's business units, using different communication channels. In this video, the CEO spoke about the current challenges faced by ICARUS and the importance of starting a transformation for the future sustainability of the businesses. In the subsequent months, the CEO himself led face-to-face meetings with teams from all units, sharing more details about his plan with employees. Speeches, presentations, emails, social media, and meeting minutes elaborated and presented by the CEO were almost a "mantra" for managing the organizational change program. He enacted his role of the main sponsor and often spoke personally with middle managers. Our analysis revealed six main categories of discourses produced by the CEO to manage his planned organizational change. As we will show, these six categories were then grouped into two broader dimensions of analysis.

Our first emerging category relates to the dissemination and promotion of the organizational change for middle managers, which we classified as *Presenting the Plan*. By presenting the plan, the CEO signaled that ICARUS needed to change in order to recover performance and grow again. At the same time, this kind of discourse reinforced the need for a cultural transformation that could support this recovery. While trying to generate greater engagement and identification on the part of middle managers, the CEO made it clear that the company's employees had to share many of his perceptions.

> We live in a constantly changing market and we know that the coming years will be challenging. We have seen years of decline in performance and we need to make ICARUS grow again. [...] Moreover, we hear a lot that ICARUS is slow, bureaucratic and hierarchical. We agree and want to change, and we have to change together, but it cannot be done by decree, but rather by changing the company's culture. To overcome these challenges and deliver on our goals, we are launching the Action program (CEO's speech given in September 2017, as part of the Action program launch video)

The CEO subsequently used this challenging context of an uncertain environment and poor company performance to promote and detail his plan for the entire organization. His discourse delimited different stages of the plan and what would be the main courses of action for achieving results. Among other aspects, some of the main concerns of his discourses were sharing with employees more information about the change management initiative as well as detailing aspects like scope, length, and deadlines to assess the initial results. Such alignment was an important attempt to shape the shared sense people were starting to make and thus reduce possible frustrations due to false expectations.

> Our plan will last four years. It is clear that the first year will be focused on investments, allocating resources to sustain results. In the following year, we hope these investments will start to pay off, and from the third year onwards, the country and ICARUS will start to grow, the economy should improve and we will benefit from it, growing our business again. (CEO's speech given in September 2017, as part of the Action program launch video)

Beyond the presentation of the plan, we identified other emerging categories associated with the CEO's discourses, particularly after the change program completed its first two years. The first is called *Justifying Results*, a type of discourse that was commonly used by the CEO to share with employees negative results that were below expectations. Most of the time, discourses that were meant to justify results consisted of attributing unexpected performance to external factors, which were presented as uncontrollable and unpredictable.

> The world outside was much more difficult than we expected. We expected a drop in the level of unemployment, GDP growth and a clearer political situation, but none of this happened. The political situation was very confused, at the same time economic growth was below expectations and unemployment did not fall. This directly affected the consumer's pocket, making a difference when choosing products in our category. It was absolutely because the economy did not behave as we expected, and it was not just because of ICARUS, the market as a whole failed. Everyone is suffering because this was not a problem for the consumer in our category, but for the Brazilians as a whole, which affected all categories. (CEO's speech given in November 2018, during a meeting with middle managers)

To balance these negative results attributed to external aspects, the CEO also produced discourses with a more positive approach, which we named *Valuing Achievements*. These discourses usually consisted of presenting qualitative and more subjective factors that were supposed to shed light on somewhat positive results. Conversely, the CEO mainly attributed these positive results to the organization by presenting these achievements as resulting from the employees' efforts and commitment:

> We are on the right way! We have a lot to celebrate! Everything we said we were going to do, we did! ICARUS has a clear plan, we worked very hard to deliver the plan and we succeeded. (CEO's speech given at a celebration for the completion of the Action program's second year)

Presenting the plan, justifying results, and valuing achievements are discourses that represent attempts made by the CEO to move his change management forward, via constant follow-up providing somewhat satisfactory reasons why certain things happened and others did not, together with (non) responsibilities for it. We therefore grouped these discourses in a broader analytical category called *Discourses for Accountability*. These emerging categories and aggregate dimensions of analysis are illustrated in Figure 1.

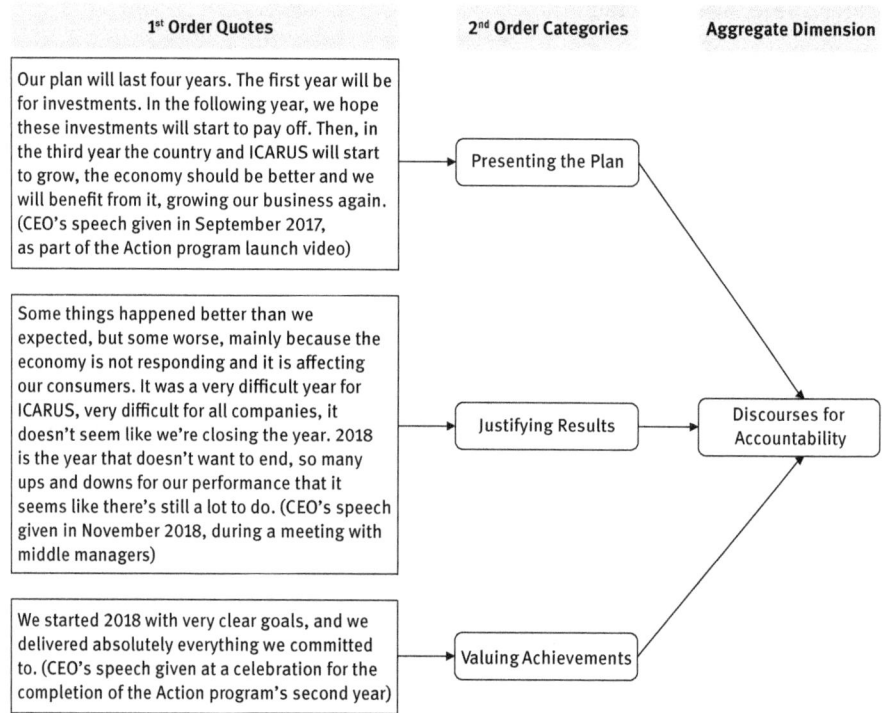

Figure 1: Illustrative quotes and emerging categories of analysis associated with *Discourses for Accountability*

Despite the possible influence accountability discourses could exert on middle managers' sensemaking, we also observed different discourses employed by the CEO for managing change through communication. These discourses were meant to instigate in each employee a desire for change and so promote their personal engagement. Hence, discourses like these were mostly oriented to behavioral attributes.

For instance, the CEO constantly produced discourses associated with inspiring individual values and behaviors, aimed at reinforcing cultural aspects that started to be praised in the context of his change management. The CEO consequently mentioned middle managers as role models for people at other hierarchical levels, by presenting them as central agents for driving the expected cultural transformation.

> There is a fundamental component to our success: our winning culture, our leadership, the ability to reinvent ourselves and act in a responsible manner. Excellence is what guides us; we need people with courage, who question the status quo. (CEO's speech given at a celebration for the completion of the Action program's second year)

We also found another type of discourse, which we labeled *Encouraging Employee's Participation*. This type of discourse especially targeted middle managers by making them feel responsible for achieving the expected organizational change.

> Be sure that we are all committed to making the Action program happen. However, this will only be possible if we count on the attitude and participation of each one of us. So, let's go together! (CEO's speech given in May 2019, during a presentation for sales managers)

Inspiring individual values and behaviors and encouraging participation represent discourses intended to motivate each individual personally in a process of particular devotion towards the organizational change. Therefore, we grouped these analytical categories in a broader dimension named *Discourses for Engagement*. Engagement here is about passion and commitment, regarding managers' willingness to invest discretionary effort to help the change management succeed. Figure 2 consequently illustrates our main emerging categories of analysis.

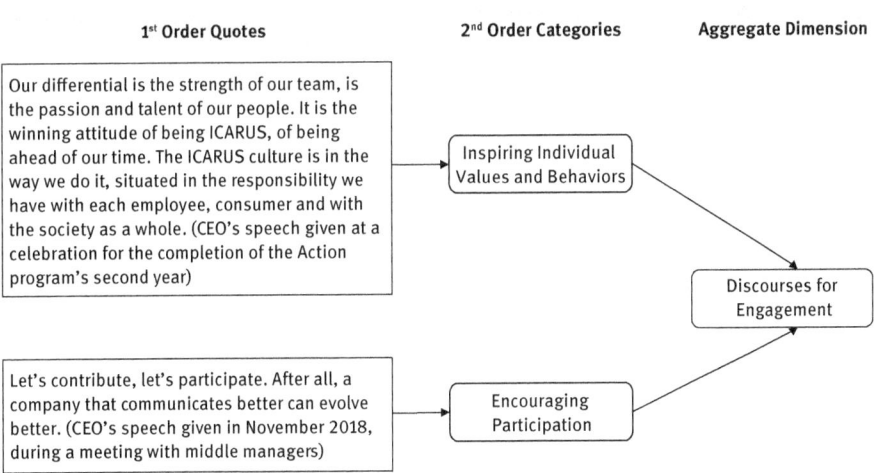

Figure 2: Illustrative quotes and emerging categories of analysis associated with *Discourses for Engagement*

After more than two years of managing the organizational change program, the European headquarters of ICARUS announced a global restructuring that would merge offices of several countries into regional units, subsequently reducing costs and the number of employees. In this context, the headquarters abruptly interrupted the Action program, while ICARUS faced the forced executive succession of its CEO, the main champion of the change management initiative. We were actively collecting data through participative observation when this happened. We noticed an informal closure of the plan while a new group of board members took control of the company. At that moment, after a leadership hiatus, the recently appointed CEO thanked all employees for the time they had dedicated to the program, saying that it had so far generated important results for the businesses, but informing that this initiative was no longer a priority in the face of the new reality that the company had to deal with. In the following, we present our analysis of how the middle management made sense of this whole change management process.

4 Managing change through middle management sensemaking

Middle managers from ICARUS initially demonstrated a certain confidence regarding the change management program proposed by the (former) CEO. Among this group of individuals, there was a consensus that ICARUS needed to undergo a transformation due to bad performances the company has been facing in recent years.

> The company's context before the change management program made us feel that our leadership was weakening, without expectations about a promising future [...]. Our feeling was that we were sailing by following the wind, without a clear direction [...]. The CEO then addressed a common anxiety among us, everyone knew that we needed to change, but nobody knew how to do that, so he was able to give us a direction. (Middle manager interview, October 2019)

This initial alignment around the proposed organizational change reveals a shared meaning among middle managers regarding what they called a "relevant plan". At that time, middle managers recognized the importance and ambition of the CEO's intention, identifying it as an opportunity for ICARUS as well as for themselves.

> I had never seen what ICARUS managed to do, opening its doors to the new. The company had enough maturity to say that a renewal was mandatory; otherwise, we would be screwed in a few years. Yes ... I never saw a multinational get this done. (Middle manager interview, October 2019)

Middle managers also shared a common interpretation that change management at ICARUS was happening with some transparency in communication. Data from interviews and notes suggested that middle managers perceived a complementarity between the CEO discourses and aspects that employees could observe during their daily routines, so this leveraged a sense of transparency.

> He always had a very transparent communication with the team. Communication was periodic, we actually had a lot of information about the program, very transparent. This means that our CEO was always saying what was working, what the challenges were ahead, what was going wrong, where he had to improve [...]. Therefore, I really think there was a great transparency in communication, and this motivated me. (Middle manager interview, March 2020)

Curiously, middle managers commonly mentioned that the CEO was a *charismatic leader*. This could also explain why the change program found fertile terrain for initial acceptance on their part. The CEO himself was the main sponsor of the Action program from its launch and consequently was at the forefront of most presentations and communications. He had a long history of working at ICARUS, as he had started his career at the operational levels until reaching the highest executive position in the country business unit. This apparently afforded him credibility among employees and the ability to talk easily about various organizational issues. Altogether, the CEO usually demonstrated his interest and concern for the company's operation, for instance, by participating in meetings with employees that were not from the managerial ranks.

> There is nothing to discuss about how much his presence was necessary. Moreover, he came from below, [...] this gives a feeling that this is possible for everyone. If the president arrived there, starting as an office boy, I also have a chance. (Middle manager interview, October 2019)

We also noticed some middle managers' predisposition to believe and listen to the CEO, something that was not commonly observed in previous change management programs implemented by other leaders in the company. The CEO leveraged this predisposition by displaying empathy, trying to put himself in the middle managers' place, interpreting their feelings and concerns.

> What was cool is that there was a charismatic factor in the CEO. He was the face of this program. There were times we noticed a greater engagement because of that. Therefore, I think he had a fundamental role in our accepting the plan. (Middle manager interview, December 2019)

Throughout the change management process, we also observed that middle managers sometimes developed a *feeling of accomplishment* associated with the change management initiative. Such feeling relied on interpretations of positive results connected to some expected milestones that were in the CEO's original plan. However, going beyond these objective measures or goals, the CEO usually promoted moments of celebration, sharing a positive image about what was going on in the organization.

We therefore identified four main expressions that appeared to summarize the way middle managers initially made sense of the organizational change they were experiencing: relevant plan, transparency in communication, charismatic leadership, and feeling of accomplishment. Middle managers engaged in conversations, rumors, gossip, discussions, and even jokes that revealed their confidence towards how the CEO was managing the organizational change. Curiously, our observations and interviews suggested that this confidence was more based on the CEO as a symbol and inspiring individual rather than on concrete evidence related to achieving goals or driving performance. Thus, we grouped these emerging categories in a broader dimension of analysis, named *Subjective Confidence*, as illustrated in Figure 3.

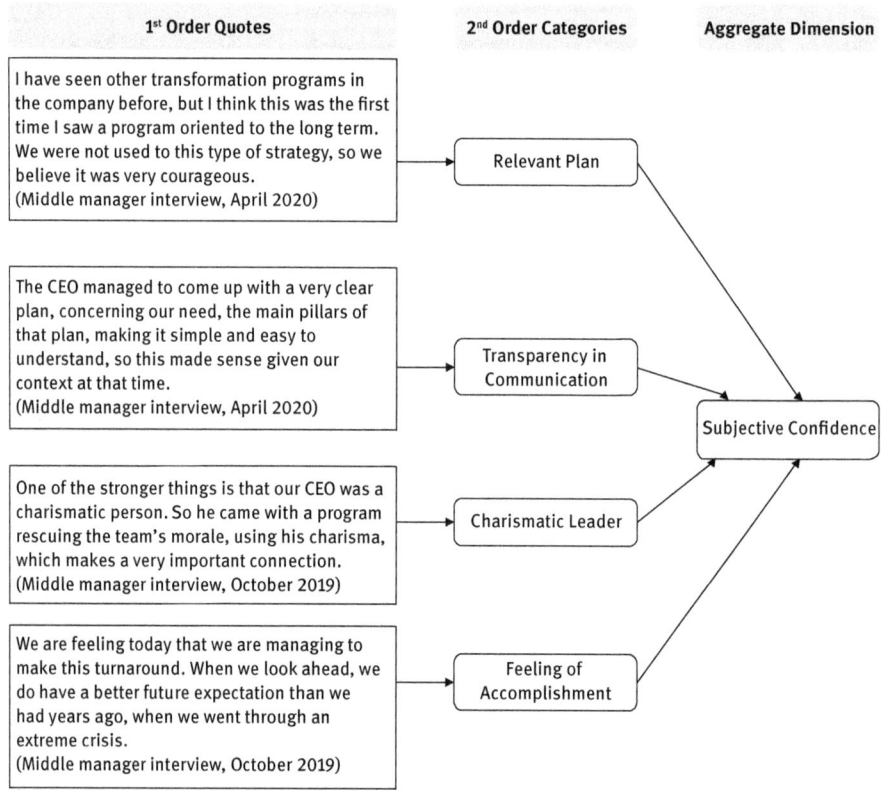

Figure 3: Emerging categories of analysis about middle managers' sensemaking around subjective confidence

However, particularly when the change management initiative was completing its first two years, middle managers developed a collective understanding with negative views regarding the Action program. In some situations, middle managers talked about and elaborated on more objective and concrete aspects of the change management. For instance, sometimes we observed a shared sense of meaning regarding what middle managers perceived as a *program failure*. Despite all the discursive efforts made by the CEO to attribute challenges and difficulties to external and unmanageable issues, middle managers sometimes doubted what he was saying and if he was clearly focusing on objective analysis of the key performance indicators.

> The program does not deliver the ambition and results that were expected [...] I do not think the program has started to generate discredit, but in the third year it no longer had the impact it had before. (Middle manager interview, April 2020)

Middle managers sometimes associated this shared sense of program failure with a collective understanding that the CEO was demonstrating an incoherence between discourse and practice. Apparently, middle managers perceived that the CEO's discourses were vague and did not correspond with their daily routines. They then started to challenge the credibility of his change management, arguing that his discourse was contradictory.

> People tend to question discourses when they do not see 100 percent engagement. I'll give you an example that relates with our culture. The discourse was "we won't work until late anymore", but everyone keeps sending emails later. The narrative is "we won't work after hours", but everything comes back. Therefore, here comes a discourse that says, "we will have a better life quality", "we will work less". However, after a while, these things end up not being credible anymore, because the message is not consistent with the action. (Middle manager interview, October 2019)

Middle managers additionally developed a shared sense that there was a *lack of clarity* regarding the change management approach promoted by the CEO. This lack of clarity was actually related to the decision-making assumptions that were at the origin of the organizational change initiative, going further than what was happening during its implementation. Middle managers sometimes criticized the organizational change, arguing that it was more a maneuver for the CEO to manage impressions than a real driver of company performance.

> Our start of the program was in fact quite "top-down", because not everyone was involved in building the plan. In the beginning, the CEO came down presenting all the departmentalized initiatives; you received these initiatives a lot like a cascade-down, without contributing at that moment. (Middle manager interview, October 2019)

This collective sense of a *lack of clarity* grew over the years since modifications to the program were perceived as not being properly communicated to all the teams, generating doubts and uncertainty, and reducing credibility. From our participative observation and informal conversations with middle managers we noticed that they lacked an understanding of the reasons why things were being altered. They wondered if these could represent top management's attempt to hide problems, for example, or even whether top managers did not properly recognize middle managers as important "change agents". "I think the main issues were about some initiatives that happened, for example, due to cuts in investments. This generally weakened our feeling of confidence in the change plan" (Middle manager interview, October 2019). We consequently identified three different emerging categories to outline how middle managers collectively developed a shared sense of meaning around the change management initiative: program failure, incoherence between discourse and practice, and lack of clarity. Here, we have meanings mostly derived from middle managers' skepticism towards the change management, which were based more on objective and concrete aspects of the organizational results. This allowed us to group these analytical categories into a broader dimension, concerning middle managers' *objective skepticism* about the change management, as illustrated in Figure 4.

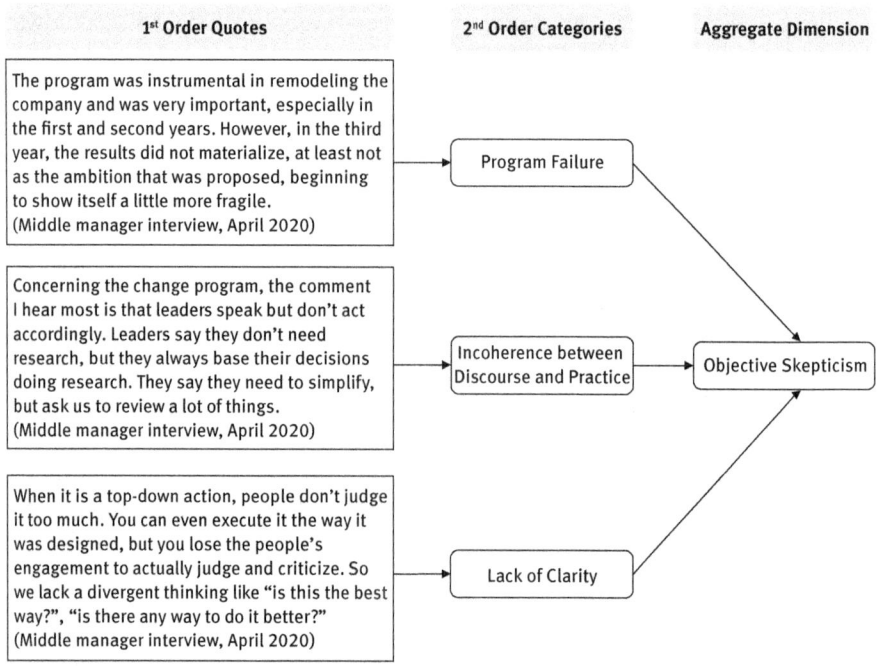

Figure 4: Emerging categories of analysis about middle managers' objective skepticism

5 Discussion and conclusions

What can we infer from this case study of change management? To begin with, the CEO's discourses on *accountability* and *engagement* appeared to have in common two primary and opposite ways of communicating during the course of his change management program. One type of communication usually consisted of attributing results considered negative or below expectations to factors that were external to the organization. The CEO argued that these factors – such as the economic crisis, political instability, and market consumption – were "unpredictable" and "uncontrollable". In contrast, at other times, the CEO attributed positive results to factors that were internal to the organization, such as members' work, effort, or even the quality of his plan.

Attribution is a mechanism by which people explain their own behaviors, third-party actions, and events. Through attributions, it is possible to establish a cause-and-effect relationship for a given situation, transforming an ambiguous event into a more plausible or clear context, which helps people understand what they are observing. Chaudhry, Wayne, and Schalk (2009) suggest that attributions have two purposes: first, to make the environment more predictable and controlled; second, to define the most appropriate actions in response to a given event. Attribution is consequently closely related to sensemaking, as it consists of creating meaning for a context marked by ambiguous interpretation (Cardon, Stevens, and Potter 2011; Parker, Arthur, and Inkson 2004).

According to Heider (1958), attribution involves people's judgment about the level of responsibility that something or someone has regarding observed results. This premise implies that responsibility is associated with internal or external attributions. Internal attribution means that the organization or an individual directly caused what happened, while external attribution associates what happened with occurrences that are external to the actor or the organization. These forms of attribution generate different perspectives regarding responsibility, including *intentionality* and *justification*. On the one hand, intentionality is at stake when actions performed by the organization or by people are supposed to explain results. On the other hand, justification means that some actors do not take complete responsibility, which makes the observed results appear reasonable. Thus, the attribution of an event to external or internal factors will possibly influence the attitudes, motivations, and cognition of all people involved (Eberly et al. 2011).

Our findings corroborate previous research by suggesting that the attribution of successes or failures does not occur neutrally and impartially. On the contrary, attribution appears to be a convenient discursive practice displayed by some actors, particularly in the context of managing organizational change (Vaara 2002). Based on attribution theory, it thus appears possible to infer that the CEO's discourses at ICARUS were meant to frame results of the Action program in order to protect and preserve his original plan, foster the employees' commitment, spread a sense of security, and justify bad performance. These practices partially allowed the CEO to exempt himself from responsibility for not achieving the expected results of his change management initiative.

We also identified that middle managers' sensemaking about organizational change reflected both what we called first a *subjective confidence* and then an *objective skepticism*. According to Cramer, Van Der Heidjen, and Jonker (2006), the objective aspect of sensemaking focuses on translating meaning into clear and tangible intentions, and thus defining limits for individual actions. In contrast, the subjective aspect of sensemaking is oriented towards values and beliefs, connecting more with the organization's ethical and moral principles (Cramer, Van Der Heidjen, and Jonker 2006). In our study, this objective component of middle managers' sensemaking involved aspects related to the concreteness of the organizational change, such as goals, quantitative metrics, and procedures. The subjective component in our study conversely relates with values such as courage, ambition, sense of accomplishment, in addition to the importance of the CEO as a representative symbol of the change plan.

Our results allow us to explore the interplay between subjectivity and objectivity as inherent aspects of sensemaking, with a relevant impact on change management efforts. Objectivity is understood here as a managerial mechanism enacted to maintain impartiality in decision making, under the belief that the achievement of organizational goals relies on a rational approach (Hurst 1997). By subjectivity, we refer to actors' interpretations of their values and behaviors as meaningful for themselves or others (Hurst 1997). The change management at ICARUS demonstrates the importance of middle managers balancing the possible tensions and contradictions stemming from this interplay between objective and subjective aspects of sensemaking. Regarding the subjective aspect, change management generates a sense of identity and new frames of reference for behaviors and attitudes, which were particularly represented by the charismatic figure of the CEO. Regarding the objective aspect, we observed a shared meaning created by middle managers around the importance of evidence-based results, with the focus on achieving impartial and reliable facts that the change management would in due course be working and generating good performance.

The ICARUS case study also has implications for the practice of corporations and managers. An initial insight is the importance of involving middle managers in change management programs. Our analysis indeed reveals that the middle managers were translating the CEO's discourses while dealing with emerging conflicts and contradictions over the organizational change. Top managers then need to promote a transparent and continuous dialogue with middle managers, even in the absence of expected and tangible results. Our study also contributes to promoting discourses as a strategic practice that must receive special attention on the part of executives who need to conduct change management initiatives. Discourses should be planned by managers, who must be concerned with how the sequential order of facts will be presented as well as with avoiding contradictions that significantly affect the way the audience will make sense of change events. Ensuring consistency between discourse and practice is accordingly essential.

Therefore, while leaders are often told to "walk the talk", the existence of multiple realities of organizational life will possibly make their subordinates link that walking with a different set of words, and thus cause them to perceive leaders' talk as insincere. As stated by Weick (1995: 182–183): "those best able to walk the talk are the ones who actually talk the walking they find themselves doing most often, with most intensity, and with most satisfaction".

6 References

Akarsu, Ozgur, Mehmet Gencer & Savaş Yıldırım. 2018. Listening to the organization: Change evaluation with discourse analysis. *Journal of Organizational Change Management* 31(5). 1040–1053

Allard-Poesi, Florence. 2005. The paradox of sensemaking in organizational analysis. *Organization* 12(2). 169–196.

Amason, Allen C. 1996. Distinguishing the effects of functional and dysfunctional conflict on strategic decision making: Resolving a paradox for top management teams. *Academy of Management Journal* 39(1). 123–148.

Balogun, Julia, Claus Jacobs, Paula Jarzabkowski, Saku Mantere & Eero Vaara. 2014. Placing strategy discourse in context: Sociomateriality, sensemaking, and power. *Journal of Management Studies* 51(2). 175–201.

Balogun, Julia & Gerry Johnson. 2004. Organizational restructuring and middle manager sensemaking. *Academy of Management Journal* 47(4). 523–549.

Balogun, Julia & Linda Rouleau. 2017. Strategy-as-practice research on middle managers and sensemaking. In Steven W. Floyd & Bill Wooldridge (eds.), *Handbook of middle management strategy process research*, 109–132. Northampton, UK: Edward Elgar.

Brown, Andrew D. 2000. Making sense of inquiry sensemaking. *Journal of Management Studies* 37(1). 45–75.

Cardon, Melissa S., Christopher E. Stevens & D. Ryland Potter. 2011. Misfortunes or mistakes? Cultural sensemaking of entrepreneurial failure. *Journal of Business Venturing* 26(1). 79–92.

Chaudhry, Anjali, Sandy J. Wayne & René Schalk. 2009. A sensemaking model of employee evaluation of psychological contract fulfillment: When and how do employees respond to change. *The Journal Applied Behavioral Science* 45(4). 498–520.

Cramer, Jacqueline, Angela Van Der Heijden & Jan Jonker. 2006. Corporate social responsibility: Making sense through thinking and acting. *Business Ethics: A European Review* 15(4). 380–389.

Dougherty, Debbie S. & Kristina Drumheller. 2006. Sensemaking and emotions in organizations: Accounting for emotions in a rational(ized) context. *Communication Studies* 57(2). 215–238.

Eberly, Marion B., Erica C. Holley, Michael D. Johnson & Terence R. Mitchell. 2011. Beyond internal and external: A dyadic theory of relational attributions. *Academy of Management Review* 36(4). 731–753.

Erkama, Niina & Eero Vaara. 2010. Struggles over legitimacy in global organizational restructuring: A rhetorical perspective on legitimation strategies and dynamics in a shutdown case. *Organization Studies* 31(7). 813–839.

Ernst, Jette & Astrid Jensen Schleiter. 2019. Organizational identity struggles and reconstruction during organizational change: Narratives as symbolic, emotional and practical glue. *Organization Studies* June. 1–20.

Gephart, Robert Jr. 1993. The textual approach: Risk and blame in disaster sensemaking. *Academy of Management Journal* 36(6). 1465–1514.

Geppert, Mike. 2003. Sensemaking and politics in MNCs: A comparative analysis of vocabularies within the global manufacturing discourse in one industrial sector. *Journal of Management Inquiry* 12(4). 312–329.

Heider, Fritz. 1958. *The psychology of interpersonal relations*. New York: Wiley.
Hurst, David K. 1997. When it comes to real change, too much objectivity may be fatal to the process. *Strategy and Leadership* 25(2). 6–12.
Jarzabkowski, Paula & John Sillince. 2007. A rhetoric-in-context approach to building commitment to multiple strategic goals. *Organization Studies* 28(11). 1639–1665.
Küpers, Wendelin, Saku Mantere & Matt Statler. 2013. Strategy as storytelling: A phenomenological collaboration. *Journal of Management Inquiry* 22(1). 83–100.
Laine, Pikka-Maaria & Eero Vaara. 2007. Struggling over subjectivity: A discursive analysis of strategic development in an engineering group. *Human Relations* 60(1). 29–58.
Lockett, Andy, Grame Currie, Rachael Finn, Grahan Martin & Justine Waring. 2014. The influence of social position on sensemaking about organizational change. *Academy of Management Journal* 57(4). 1102–1129.
Lüscher, Lotte S. & Marianne W. Lewis. 2008. Organizational change and managerial sensemaking: Working through paradox. *Academy of Management Journal* 51(2). 221–240.
Maitlis, Sally & Marlys Christianson. 2014. Sensemaking in organizations: Taking stock and moving forward. *Academy of Management Annals* 8(1). 57–125.
Maitlis, Sally & Thomas B. Lawrence. 2003. Orchestral manoeuvres in the dark: Understanding failure in organizational strategizing. *Journal of Management Studies* 40(1). 109–139.
Maitlis, Sally & Thomas B. Lawrence. 2007. Triggers and enablers of sensegiving in organizations. *Academy of Management Journal* 50(1). 57–84.
Maitlis, Sally, Timothy J. Vogus & Thomas B. Lawrence. 2013. Sensemaking and emotion in organizations. *Organizational Psychology Review* 3(3). 222–247.
Näsänen, Jaana. 2017. Two versions of nomadic employees: Opposing ways to employ the same discourse in talking about change. *Discourse and Communication* 11(3). 259–275.
Nicholson, Louise & Alistair Anderson. 2005. News and nuances of the entrepreneurial myth and metaphor: Linguistic games in entrepreneurial sense-making and sense-giving. *Entrepreneurship Theory and Practice* 29(2). 153–172.
Parker, Polly, Michael B. Arthur & Kerr Inkson. 2004. Career communities: A preliminary exploration of member-defined career support structures. *Journal of Organizational Behavior* 25(4). 489–514.
Sillince, John A. A. & Andrew D. Brown. 2009. Multiple organizational identities and legitimacy: The rhetoric of police websites. *Human Relations* 62(12). 1829–1856.
Sillince, John & Frank Mueller. 2007. Switching strategic perspective: The reframing of accounts of responsibility. *Organization Studies* 28(2). 155–176.
Sonenshein, Scott. 2006. Crafting social issues at work. *Academy of Management Journal* 49(6). 1158–1172.
Strauss, Anselm & Juliet Corbin. 1998. *Basics of qualitative research techniques*. Thousand Oaks, CA: Sage.
Thurlow, Amy & Jean Helms Mills. 2015. Telling tales out of school: Sensemaking and narratives of legitimacy in an organizational change process. *Scandinavian Journal of Management* 31(2). 246–254.
Vaara, Eero. 2002. On the discursive construction of success/failure in narratives of post-merger integration. *Organization Studies* 23(2). 211–248.
Vaara, Eero, Birgit Kleymann & Hannu Seristö. 2004. Strategies as discursive constructions: The case of airline alliances. *Journal of Management Studies* 41(1). 1–35.
Watson, Tony J. 1994. *In search of management: Culture, chaos and control in managerial work*. London: Routledge.
Weick, Karl E. 1995. *Sensemaking in organizations*. Thousand Oaks, CA: Sage.
Weick, Karl E., Kathleen M. Sutcliffe & David E. Obstfeld. 2005. Organizing and the process of sensemaking. *Organization Science* 16(4). 409–421.

Wooldridge, Bill, Torsten Schmid & Steven W. Floyd. 2008. The middle management perspective on strategy process: Contributions, synthesis, and future research. *Journal of Management* 34(6). 1190–1221.

Worren, Nicolay A. M., Keith Ruddle & Karl Moore. 1999. From organizational development to change management: The emergence of a new profession. *The Journal of Applied Behavioral Science* 35(3). 273–286.

About the contributors

Florence Allard-Poesi is Professor of Management and member of the Institute de Recherche en Gestion (I. R. G) at the Université Paris-Est Créteil Val-de-Marne. Her research focuses on sensemaking and the role that discursive practices play in these processes. Her area of expertise also includes the performativity of discourses and scientific methods, in particular those that aim to measure work stress and suffering or well-being. Her work has been published in *Human Relations*, *Organization*, *M@n@gement*, *Méthodes de Recherche en Management* (R. A. Thiétart ed.), and *The Social Construction of Stress* (M. Lauriol, Ed.).

Rickard Andersson (PhD, Lund University, 2020) is an Assistant Professor in the Department of Strategic Communication at Lund University, Sweden. His research interests include strategic communication, organizational communication, and organizing.

Hilla Back is a Doctoral Candidate in International Business at the Department of Management Studies at Aalto University School of Business. Her doctoral thesis concerns the link between language diversity and social inclusion from the perspective of migrants. Particularly, she is interested in the experiences of individuals who do not understand the majority language of the workplace or university. She has an avid research interest in language, social psychology, and diversity and inclusion issues. Hilla has recently been awarded a competitive two-year Young Researcher Grant by the Emil Aaltonen Foundation to encourage her research.

Zhuo Ban is an Associate Professor in the Department of Communication at University of Cincinnati. Her research takes a global, critical perspective to contemporary issues in organizational communication and public relations. Her work has been published in international peer-reviewed journals including *Organization*, *Management Communication Quarterly*, *Journal of Applied Communication Research*, *Public Relations Inquiry*, and *Journal of International and Intercultural Communication*.

J. Kevin Barge (Ph.D., University of Kansas) is Professor of Communication at Texas A & M University and an Associate with the Taos Institute. He is also a member of the planning team for the Aspen Conference, a community of engaged organizational communication scholars focused on developing practical theory and collaborative research that bridge academic-practitioner interests. Kevin's major research interests center on developing a social constructionist approach to leadership, articulating the connections between appreciative practice and organizational change, as well as exploring the relationship between discourse and public deliberation, specifically practices that facilitate communities working through polarized and polarizing issues.

Mariaelena Bartesaghi is Associate Professor of Communication at the University of South Florida. Her work as a discourse analyst examines accountability and authority in institutional settings and, most recently, in dynamics of crisis.

Nicolas Bencherki is an Associate Professor of Organizational Communication at Université TÉLUQ, Montréal, Canada, and an Affiliate Professor at Université du Québec à Montréal. He studies the role of communication and materiality in constituting organizational reality, thus revisiting classic notions of management such as strategy, membership and authority, as well as property. Empirically, his work mostly focuses on non-profit organizations and inter-organizational collaboration. He has published in outlets such as *Academy of Management Journal*, *Organization Studies*, *Human Relations*, *Journal of Communication*, and *Communication Theory*. He co-edited *Authority and Power in Social Interaction: Methods and Analysis*, published in 2019 by Routledge.

Brigitte Bernard-Rau is an Affiliated Researcher at the Institute for Management Research, Radboud University, Nijmegen/The Netherlands, from where she earned her PhD in Management Sciences. Brigitte's research draws on insights from organization theory and economic sociology to explore the field of Corporate Social Responsibility (CSR). She investigates how social rating agencies engage in relationships with internal and external actors, and use social ratings to bring about change in organizations.

Patrice M. Buzzanell is Professor and Chair of the Department of Communication at the University of South Florida and Endowed Visiting Professor at Shanghai Jiaotong University. She served as President of the International Communication Association (ICA), Council of Communication Associations, and Organization for the Study of Communication, Language and Gender. She is an ICA Fellow and National Communication Association Distinguished Scholar. Her research focuses on career, resilience, gender, and engineering design. She received ICA's Mentorship Award and the Provost Outstanding Mentor Award at Purdue, where she was University Distinguished Professor and Endowed Chair/Director of the Butler Center for Leadership Excellence.

Laure Cabantous is Professor of Strategy and Organization at the Business School (formerly Cass), City, University of London. Her areas of expertise include performativity, Actor-Network Theory, embodied cognition, decision making and strategy-as-practice. She is a former Editor in Chief of M@n@gement. Her work has been published in such journals as the *Academy of Management Review*, *Human Relations*, *Journal of Management*, *Journal of Management Studies*, *Organization Science*, *Organization Studies*, *Organization*, *Strategic Organization*.

Theresa Castor (Ph.D., University of Washington) is a Professor of Communication at the University of Wisconsin-Parkside (USA). She researches organizational decision-making and crisis through a discourse analytic lens, examining the interplay of language, interaction, and materiality in constituting crises. She serves on the board of the International Association for Dialogue Analysis, is the author of *Climate Risks as Organizational Problems*, co-edited *Water, Rhetoric, and Social Justice: A Critical Confluence*, and is a National Society for Experiential Education Fellow.

François Cooren, PhD (Université de Montréal, 1996), is a professor at the Université de Montréal, Canada, where he is chair of the Department of Communication. His research focuses on organizational communication, language and social interaction, and communication theory. He is past president of the International Communication Association (ICA, 2010–2011), president of the International Association for Dialogue Analysis (IADA, 2012–2021) and former editor-in-chief of *Communication Theory* (2005–2008).

Damla Diriker is a PhD Candidate at the KIN Center for Digital Innovation, School of Business and Economics, Vrije Universiteit Amsterdam. She has been a researcher at KIN Center since 2018. She holds a Research Master degree in Business in Society from the University of Amsterdam and the Vrije Universiteit Amsterdam. She is interested in studying how digital technologies and collaborative approaches can allow diverse actors to address grand societal challenges. For her PhD research, she explores the use and organization of open innovation for tackling grand challenges.

Christine Domke is Professor of Social Communication at Fulda University of Applied Sciences, Germany, at the department of Social and Cultural Studies. She holds a PhD in linguistics from the University of Bielefeld and got her habilitation (postdoctoral degree) with a study on in public communication in cities, railway stations and airports. Her research interests include organizational communication, pragmatics, media linguistics and semiotic landscapes. Current research projects investigate cultural changes due to the covid pandemic based on digital crowd research (together with Matthias Klemm) and new digital forms of communication in organizations such as multimodal storytelling.

Philipp Dreesen is Professor of Digital Linguistics and Discourse Analysis at the School of Applied Linguistics at Zurich University of Applied Sciences, Switzerland. His research interests include discourse linguistics, corpus linguistics, digital transformation, language criticism, and connections between language, politics, and law. He has published widely in the field of sociolinguistics. He developed methodologies for the new field of comparative discourse linguistics. Currently he co-leads a research project on COVID-19 discourses in Switzerland, funded by the Swiss National Science Foundation.

Mohan J. Dutta is Dean's Chair Professor of Communication. He is the Director of the Center for Culture-Centered Approach to Research and Evaluation (CARE), developing culturally-centered, community-based projects of social change, advocacy, and activism that articulate health as a human right. Mohan Dutta's research examines the role of advocacy and activism in challenging marginalizing structures, the tropes of whiteness that perpetuate violence, the relationship between poverty and health, political economy of global health policies, the mobilization of cultural tropes for the justification of neo-colonial health development projects, and the ways in which participatory culture-centered processes and strategies of radical democracy serve as axes of global social change.

Bertrand Fauré is an Associate Professor in Information and Communication Sciences at the University Toulouse 3, Paul Sabatier (Technological Institute of Tarbes). He is the author of the book *La communication des organisations* published in 2014 with Nicolas Arnaud. His research, which is about the performativity of the language of numbers in organizations, has been published in international peer-reviewed journals such as *Human Relations*, *Accounting Organizations and Society*, and *Management Communication Quarterly*. His current research deals with the performativity of social media metrics and how to use the performativity of numbers for social change

Eduardo A. Figueiredo has a Master in Business Administration at Fundação Dom Cabral, Brazil. His research interests are strategy-as-practice, sensemaking and middle management, particularly in contexts of organizational change. Since 2004, he has been working for British American Tobacco with marketing management, as well as with leadership development.

Alicia Fjällhed is a PhD student at the Department of Strategic Communication, Lund University. Her research interests include strategic communication, public communication ethics, and philosophy of communication.

Shiv Ganesh (PhD, Purdue University) is Professor in the Department of Communication Studies in the Moody College of Communication, at the University of Texas at Austin. He studies and writes about issues of collective action and social justice organizing in the context of global and technological processes. His writing engages with these issues in a range of locations, including India, Aotearoa New Zealand, Sweden and the United States, all of which are places he has lived and worked.

Ursina Ghilardi is a Research Associate in the Research Group "Organizational Communication and Public Sphere" at Zurich University of Applied Sciences. She also teaches at the Institute for Applied Media Sciences. Formerly she worked as a consultant for digital public relations (with management functions). Her areas of research include management and counselling communication, corporate newsrooms and social media.

Verena Girschik is Assistant Professor of CSR, Communication and Organization at Copenhagen Business School (Denmark). She adopts a communicative institutionalist perspective to understand how companies negotiate their roles and responsibilities, how they perform them, and with what consequences. Empirically, she is interested in activism in and around multinational companies and in business-humanitarian collaboration. Her research has been published in the *Journal of Management Studies*, *Human Relations*, *Business & Society*, and *Critical Perspectives on International Business*.

Ngā Hau (LLM with distinction, Waikato University) belongs to Ngāti Kauwhata in the Manawatū, where she was born and has lived most of her life. She is a Junior Research Officer at CARE, the Center for Culture-Centered Approach to Research and Evaluation in the School of Communication, Journalism and Marketing, Massey University, Palmerston North. She is also a PhD student utilising the Culture-Centered Approach to build infrastructures for voice amongst Māori with lived realities of multiple socioeconomic and communicative disparities.

Ilse Hellemans is passionate about bringing research and practice together. She was engaged in a position as Junior Researcher at the KIN Center for Digital Innovation, School of Business and Economics, Vrije Universiteit Amsterdam. For this position, she studied how large crowds share their diverse knowledge and perspectives on crowdsourcing challenges, in order to solve societal challenges such as food waste. She divides her time between research and consulting and aims to facilitate knowledge exchanges wherever possible.

David Hollis is Senior Lecturer within the Human Resource Management Department at Nottingham Business School, Nottingham Trent University. His research focuses on the communicative constitution of organization, performativity, power, authority, and aesthetics.

Geert Jacobs is a Professor at the Department of Linguistics at Ghent University, where he teaches Business and Professional Discourse and directs the Master programme in Multilingual Business Communication. He is President of the Association for Business Communication (ABC). He has researched widely in the fields of media linguistics, news production and institutional discourse.

Jody L. S. Jahn (PhD, University of California, Santa Barbara) is an Associate Professor in the Department of Communication at University of Colorado at Boulder. She uses mixed methods to examine how members of hazardous organizations communicate to negotiate action, and how members interface with organizational safety policies and documents. Recent research examines wildland firefighting workgroups.

Dr. **Wonsun (Sunny) Kim** is a health communication/health services scholar by degree, with extraordinary training in health communication, behavioral medicine and psychosocial oncology, and intervention research with strong quantitative and qualitative methods design and analysis skills. She is an Associate Professor in the Edson College of Nursing and Health Innovation at Arizona State University, and a Research Affiliate and Associate at the Mayo Clinic. Her scholarship has focused primarily on understanding mechanisms to promote better psychosocial health and quality of life for cancer patients and family caregivers, including those who are members of underserved and vulnerable populations.

Matthias Klemm is Professor of Sociology of Work, Organization and Intercultural Relations at the Department of Social and Cultural Studies, University of Applied Sciences, Fulda, Germany. He studied Sociology, Political Science and Psychology at the Friedrich-Alexander-University of Erlangen-Nürnberg and holds a PhD and a habilitation in Sociology. He is head of the centre of Intercultural and European studies (Cinteus) at the Fulda University. Current fields of scientific investigation are the integration of migrant workers in the German health care sector and the establishment of digital "crowd research" regarding cultural change in the course of the covid pandemic (together with Christine Domke).

Susanne Knorre is an independent management consultant and part-time Professor at the Institute of Communication Management at Osnabrück University of Applied Sciences, Germany. She specializes in strategic communication in the context of business management and leadership. Susanne has longstanding management and leadership experience both in business and politics and is a member of the supervisory boards of renowned German companies. From 2000 to 2003 she was Minister of Economics in Lower Saxony.

Julia Krasselt, PhD, is a Research Associate at the School of Applied Linguistics at Zurich University of Applied Sciences, Switzerland. Her research interests include corpus linguistics, discourse linguistics and computational linguistics. Her research focusses on the application of quantitative/data driven methods for the identification of patterns of language use.

Salla-Maaria Laaksonen (D.Soc.Sc.) is a researcher in the Centre for Consumer Society Research, University of Helsinki. Her research focuses on technology, organizations, and new media, including social evaluation of organizations in the hybrid media system, the organization of online social movements, and the use of data and algorithms in organizations. She is an also expert in digital and computational research methods.

Philippe Lorino is Emeritus Distinguished Professor at ESSEC Business School. He advises the French Nuclear Safety Authority about organizational factors of risk. He served as a senior civil servant in the French Government and as a director in the finance department of an international manufacturing company. He draws from pragmatist philosophy (Peirce, Dewey, Mead) and dialogism theory (Bakhtin) to study organizations as organizing processes rather than organizational structures, "inquiries" in the pragmatist sense, i.e., actors' ongoing dialogical exploration and experimentation of the possible futures of their own cooperative activity. He has published articles in top-ranking journals and the book *Pragmatism and Organization Studies* (Oxford University Press, 2019 EGOS Book Award).

Gabriela X. Maia has a Master in Business Administration at Fundação Dom Cabral, Brazil. Her research interests are strategy-as-practice and sensemaking, particularly in high reliability organizations that operate under extreme contexts. Since 2006, she has been working for Petrobras with oil platform operations and maintenance, as well as with leadership development.

Dr. **Anne M. Nicotera** is a Professor and the Chair of the Department of Communication at George Mason University. Her research is grounded in a constitutive perspective and focuses on management/leadership communication, recurrent/cyclic conflict, diversity, race and gender, and aggressive communication, with a particular interest in healthcare organizations. She has published her research in numerous national journals. She has also published five books and several scholarly chapters. She is also an active organizational consultant, designing and delivering organizational communication based management and leadership training, with a special interest in serving health professionals in the developing world.

Howard Nothhaft (PhD, University of Leipzig, 2010) is Associate Professor in the Department of Strategic Communication at Lund University, Sweden. His research interests include strategic communication and strategy theory, theory of science, cognitive science and personality psychology, disinformation and counter-disinformation.

Daniel Perrin is Professor of Applied Linguistics, Vice President at Zurich University of Applied Sciences, President of the International Association of Applied Linguistics AILA, as well as Editor of the *International Journal of Applied Linguistics* and the De Gruyter *Handbook of Applied Linguistics* series. His areas of research include media linguistics, methodology of applied linguistics, text production research, and analysis of language use in professional communication. www.danielperrin.net

Rebecca Piekkari is Marcus Wallenberg Professor of International Business at the Aalto University, School of Business in Finland. She has a long-standing interest in language diversity both as a management challenge for multinational corporations and contemporary universities as well as a methodological challenge for researchers doing fieldwork. Her current work focuses on the practices of linguistic inclusion and exclusion; the shifting meaning of location for management activities; the use of translation approach in international business; cross-language research and the future of qualitative research methodologies. She is Fellow of the Academy of International Business and the European International Business Academy.

Amanda J. Porter is Associate Professor at the KIN Center for Digital Innovation, School of Business and Economics, Vrije Universiteit Amsterdam. Her research examines how digital technologies can support open, multi-stakeholder, problem-centered forms of organizing. Her current project examines how organizations employ crowdsourcing to tackle grand societal challenges. She has published research in the *Journal of Management Studies*, *Organization Studies*, the *Journal of Computer Mediated Communication*, and *Management Communication Quarterly*, among others.

Lars Rademacher (MA, PhD) is a Professor of Public Relations at Darmstadt University of Applied Sciences, Germany, and Adjunct Lecturer & Researcher at Munster Technological University, Ireland. His research interests cover public legitimacy, PR ethics, digital leadership, CSR and compliance communication.

Sarah E. Riforgiate (PhD, 2011, Arizona State University) is an Associate Professor in the Department of Communication at University of Wisconsin-Milwaukee. Her research and teaching concentrate on the intersections of organizational and interpersonal communication, particularly regarding public paid work and private life, to increase understanding and develop practical solutions to improve interactions. Dr. Riforgiate's research projects include work-life concerns, emotions in organizations, conflict, leadership, and policy communication. Her work has been published in *Communication Monographs*, *Journal of Family Communication*, *Management and Communication Quarterly*, *Western Journal of Communication*, and the *Electronic Journal of Communication*, among other journals

Dennis Schoeneborn is a Professor of Organization, Communication and CSR at Copenhagen Business School (Denmark) and a Visiting Professor of Organization Studies at Leuphana University of Lüneburg (Germany). His research is focused on exploring the constitutive and formative role of communication for phenomena of organization, organizing, and organizationality. Dennis served as head coordinator of the Standing Working Group "Organization as Communication" at the European Group of Organizational Studies (EGOS) from 2015–2020. His work has been published in the *Academy of Management Review*, *Business & Society*, *Human Relations*, *Journal of Management Studies*, *Management Communication Quarterly*, and *Organization Studies*, amongst other outlets.

Christian Schwägerl is a Professor of Communication Management at the Institute of Communication Management at Osnabrück University of Applied Sciences, Germany. He specializes in strategic communication, internal communication as an organizational function, management communication, and organizational change. His main research interests are in exploring direct and mediated interpersonal communication in organizations and language in strategic processes.

Samentha Sepúlveda (MA, 2017, Northeastern Illinois University) is a Doctoral Candidate in the Department of Communication at University of Wisconsin-Milwaukee. She is a critical qualitative scholar who focuses on interspecies communication. Her research examines communication with, for and about animals to discover how these discourses are used to validate the exploitation of animals and disempowered humans. Exposing these issues aids efforts to dismantle exploitative and oppressive practices related to gender, race, class, and species. Her work has been published in *Women & Language* and appears in edited books.

Viviane Sergi is Associate Professor in Management in the Department of Management at ESG UQAM in Montréal, Canada. Her research interests include process thinking, performativity, the transformation of work, leadership, and materiality. Her recent studies have explored how communication is, in various settings, constitutive of organizational phenomena, such as new work practices, strategy and leadership. She also has a keen interest in methodological issues related to qualitative research. Her work has been published in journals such as *Academy of Management Annals*, *Human Relations*, *Scandinavian Journal of Management*, *Long Range Planning*, *M@n@gement* and in *Qualitative Research in Organizations and Management*.

Peter Stücheli-Herlach is Professor of Organizational Communication, Head of the Research Group "Organizational Communication and Public Sphere" and actual President of the University Conference at Zurich University of Applied Sciences (Switzerland). He headed and co-directed projects of applied research and scientific counseling at the Institute of Applied Media Studies for more than 15 years. Formerly he worked as a newspaper editor and public relations consultant. His areas of research include discourse analysis, process analysis of management communication and design analysis of public storytelling practices.

Susanne Tietze, PhD, is Professor of Multilingual Management at Sheffield Hallam University, UK. She has a long-standing interest in language, discourse and meaning, including the exploration of hegemonic practices enacted through language. She is researching the role of English, language diversity and translation in the production of management knowledge. Her latest book, *Management Research: A Language and Translation Perspective on Knowledge Production*, is an innovative, language-and translation-sensitive take on research philosophies, research methods and the epistemology of writing in English. She has recently led a funded research project about the agency of translators within multilingual business communities.

Consuelo Vásquez (Ph. D., Université de Montréal) is an Associate Professor in the Département de Communication Sociale et Publique at the Université du Québec à Montréal in Canada. Her research interests include ethnography, project organizing, volunteering and the communicative constitution of organizations. Her work appears in such venues as *Communication Theory*, *Human Relations* and *Qualitative Research in Organizations and Management*. She is the co-founder of the Research Group Organizing and Communication (ReCOr) and the Latin-American Network of Organizational Communication Scholars (RedLAco). She is head researcher of "Volunteering on the move," a research program funded by the Social Sciences and Humanities Research Council of Canada.

Samir L. Vaz is Associate Dean for Master Degree Programs as well as Professor of Strategic Management and Organizations in Fundação Dom Cabral, Brazil. His research examines the various ways in which collective interpretations, activities and communication allow individuals to enact the organizational reality that is associated with strategy implementation, organizational change and extreme contexts.

Dr. **Melinda Villagran** is the Director of Texas State University's Translational Health Research Initiative, a Professor in the Department of Communication Studies, and Principal Investigator of Networx, an mHealth program for women. Her research and teaching seek to improve health outcomes and quality of life for at-risk populations through more effective health communication. She is the author of two books and over 65 peer-reviewed publications. She has served as a guest editor for national and international journals, won several top paper awards, and has served as a scientific grant reviewer and editorial board member for regional, national, and international journals.

Peter Winkler is a Full Professor of Organizational Communication at the University of Salzburg, Austria. His research focuses on the societal conditions and consequences of organizational communication. His articles have appeared in such journals as *Business & Society*, *International Journal of Strategic Communication*, *Management Communication Quarterly*, *Science, Technology, & Human Values*, and *Social Studies of Science*.

Alex Wright is Senior Lecturer in Strategy and Organization at Sheffield University's Management School. His research interests center on communication, routines, performativity, qualitative approaches, and critical literature reviews. He has published in *Organization*, *Journal of Management Inquiry*, *Long Range Planning*, and *M@n@gement*.

Heather M. Zoller is a Professor at the University of Cincinnati. Her research addresses organizing and the politics of public health and appears in journals such as *Communication Monographs, Journal of Applied Communication Research, and Communication Theory*. She is a former Associate Editor at *Human Relations* and *Management Communication Quarterly*.

Index

accountability 69, 70, 75, 82
accounting 14–15
- accountability 354, 355
- performativity 347, 357, 358
- triad 349, 350, 351, 358
- (un)accountable 357, 358
- zero carbon 357
action 69, 70, 75, 82
- see also self-action
actors 461, 473
- economic 459, 471, 472
- entrepreneurial 461
- social 462, 471, 472
- supra-individual 461
actor network theory 218–219, 224
affordance, see technological affordance
agency 69, 70, 75, 82, 232–235, 239–242, 263, 264, 273, 274, 418, 422, 423, 478, 479, 486, 487–488
- agents 240–241
- ecological 102
- hybrid co-action (or agency) 418
- plenum of agencies 423
- textual 422
- see also reflexive agency
agential realism 417
agility 339–340
algorithms 102–103, 173
alignment 285
Alinsky, Saul 429, 431
Allen, Branda 130
Alvesson, Mats and Karreman, Dan 195–196, 207
ambiguity (of strategy discourse) 198, 200–201, 208
analysis
- see also keyword analysis
- practices of 319
applied linguistics 3–5
artificial intelligence in mentoring 305–306
Ashcraft, Karen 128, 129, 133
aspirational talk 443, 449–450
attribution 543
- intentionality and justification 543
- internal and external 543
- purpose 543
- and sensemaking 543

Austin, John L. 4, 28, 34–35, 195–196, 199–200, 252–254, 347, 351, 354–355
authority 482, 483
automation 181–182
autonomy 91

Bakhtin, Mikhail 343
Barnard, Chester 70–71
Barthes, Roland 395–396
Baxter, Leslie 74
belief 90–92, 98
Boden, Deirdre 31, 32, 39, 72
boundaries 101–102
boundary spanning 479
Bourdieu, Pierre 2, 146
brand/branded/branding 12, 263–264, 270, 271, 285–289
- corporate branding 263–265
- ethical 274–275
- communities 267, 268
- corporate 265
- dialectic of 268, 274
- higher education, university 270–272
- managers and management 263
- organizing properties of 266–267
- value 263, 268
- web model 269
brownwashing 450
bureaucracy 125, 482, 483, 484, 485, 486
Butler, Judith 34–35, 254–255, 260

Callon, Michel 196, 202
Catholic Church 235–236
- Catholicism 235–236
change management 341–343
- change communication 19–20, 341–343
- emergent change 337, 340
- leadership in, see leadership 339
- learning organization and change 337–338
- see also management
- see also organization development
- planned change 337, 340–342
chatbot mentoring 306
Cheney, George 427–428, 433
Christensen, Lars T. 264, 276, 282, 289–290, 444, 449, 454
citationality 254–255, 260

citation index 354
client systems 314
Clifton, Jonathan 215, 217, 220
co-creation 484, 489, 492
collaboration 178–180, 186, 482, 483,
    487–488
– collaborative crowdsourcing 483, 484, 487,
    489
collective responsibility 279, 287–288
collocation
– analysis 399–400
– profile 401
commissive 234
committing 47, 49, 56, 62, 63
commonality 95
common ground 391, 481, 483, 486, 487–488
communication 93, 101, 483, 484, 485,
    487–488, 493, 495–498
– see also change communication
– see also computer-mediated communication
– see also creating by communicating
– course 47, 51, 56, 58, 59
– linear model 263, 264–265
– conversation, conversational 267, 268, 272,
    273
– communicative capitalism 268, 269, 276
– interpreted and inaudible 378
– negotiated and translucent 375
– see also non-verbal communication
– open communication 341, 348
– virtual 380, 381
– visible and audible 375
– see also visual communication
– see also team communication
communication management 279, 280–290
– communication managers 279, 281, 283,
    286–289
– corporate communication 281–282
– public relations 281
– strategic communication 282
communication responsibility 286–288
communicative constitution of organi-
    zations 161, 167, 169, 171, 173, 185–186,
    232, 237–241, 243, 250–251, 263, 264,
    265, 266, 285–289, 290, 409, 418, 423,
    488
– author 286
– authoritative texts 280, 286
– authorize 286

– central tenet 373–374, 385
– in multilingual workplaces 373
– consubstantialization 240
– as conversation and text 247, 249–255, 257,
    259
– figures, reconfigurations 271
– language and communication as
    constitutive 368–369
– matters of authority 239, 285, 287–288
– matters of concern 237, 239, 285, 287–288
– presentify 286
– representation practices 270
– smoke and crystal 241
communicative dynamics 469, 471
community 16–17
– immanent vs external 433–444
– local vs global 430–431
– persuasion vs. coercion 432–433
– reformation vs. revolution 431–432
– tensions in 430–431
– community manager 356
– community of inquiry, see inquiry 92, 95, 102
competition 114, 115, 117–118
computer-mediated communication, see
    communication 182–183
conflict (interpersonal) 478
consulting 314
– systems 314
contradiction 478–479, 482, 483, 485, 486,
    487–488
control 90–91, 94
controlling 8
conversation 343, 344–345
– analysis 30–32, 37, 321, 345–346, 347
– conversational lamination 32, 39, 40
convincing 47, 49, 56, 62, 63
Cornelissen, Joep 264, 265, 272, 273, 276, 282,
    289–290
corporate rating reports 469, 470
corporate social performance (CSP) 465,
    470–473
– CSP-CFP link 461
– literature 460–462
– metrics 459–461, 463, 471, 472
corporate social responsibility (CSR)
– communication 17
– communicational perspective on ethics 471
corpus 395, 396–397
cosmetics 255–256

cost 479, 484, 489
counseling 13–14, 313–334
– communication 314–317
– communication, practices of 318
– research 321–322, 330–331
– schemes, interactive 321
– system 317
COVID-19 70, 76, 80–82
creating by communicating, *see*
    communication 7
creativity 91, 93, 97, 98, 101
crowdsourcing 18–19
– for ill-structured problems 489, 491–495
– *see also* incentive schemes in crowd-
    sourcing
– for well-structured problems 485–489
culture management 126–127

Dahl, Robert 127
data-based 398–399
data-driven 398
datafication 183, 187–188
deciding 6–7, 47, 49, 55, 59, 62, 63, 69–70,
    71, 74
– in crisis settings 76
– vs. decision-making 70–71, 74
– discursive 72–74
– framework 70, 75
– metaconversations in 70, 75
– metapragmatics of 70, 75
– overlapping contexts of 70
– rational metamodel 69–70
decision-making 143–145, 147, 157
– contingency 339–340, 348
– emergence 339–340
decisions 147, 153, 155–157
decoupling/decoupled 444, 449
deliberation, practices of 317
demand 391–392, 395, 403
Derrida, Jacques 27, 29, 34
design 232–242
– designing 11, 48, 49, 59, 63, 232–242
– *see also* patient-centered hospital design
– practices of 319
developing organizations 14
Dewey, John 90–91, 92–93, 100
Dewey, John and Bentley, Alfred F. 93–95, 96,
    101–102
diagrammatic representation 403

dialogue 94, 95, 98, 465, 466, 469–473, 484,
    486, 487–488
– critical 460, 465
– dialogical space 274
digital
– communication 143, 156–157
– discourse 182–183
digitalization 173
directive 234
disciplinary power, *see* power 128–129
discourse 389–404, 479, 481, 529, 531
– applied linguistic discourse analysis
    (DIA) 391, 395–403
– critical discourse analysis 272
– analysis 168
– interpretation 398
– measuring 398
– modeling 396–398
– discursive agency 4
– discursive environment 393
– discursive practice 263, 264, 268, 269, 271
– *see also* leadership
disorder 133
disruption 96, 97
documentary reconstruction 321–322
documenting 9
– accumulative effect of 172–173
– as performative 165, 172
– practice of 164, 318
documents
– as actors 169
– etymology 163
– fixity of 166
– mundane nature 165, 172
– objectifying capacity 169
– ordering effect 167
– organizing effects 166–167
– as products 168
– as sites 168
– value of 170–171
doubt 90–92
Drucker, Peter 48
Dunbar, Robin 236

education 47, 59
Edwards, Richard 127
emergence 93–94, 97, 101
emotions 19
endurance 171

English
- bridge language 373
- common corporate language 377–379
- dominant role 374
- lingua franca 374, 376
- mandated corporate language 376–377
- shared language 385
enterprise social media, enterprise social network, enterprise social platform 177–180
- *see also* social media
- *see also* social network
environment 478, 480, 484, 489
- environmental performances 17
- environmental, social, and governance (ESG) 459–463, 466–473
- dimensions 467–468
- performance indicators 460, 467–468, 470–471
- research 459, 466
ESG, *see* environmental, social, and governance
ethic of care 483
ethnomethodology 30–32, 37
European Communication Monitor 284
executive management, *see* management 314
extrospection 392, 404

Fairhurst, Gail T. 214, 215, 216, 218, 219, 220, 221
Feldman, Martha 248–249, 252, 254
feminist management research, *see* management 129–130
Ferraro, Fabrizio, Etzion, Dror, and Gehman, Joel 489, 491– 494, 497
figures 418–419
Fleck, Ludwig 394
Follett, Mary P. 101, 102
Foucault, Michel 128–129, 197, 202, 391, 393, 395
framing 216, 217
Furnari, Santi 484, 492,
future 231–232, 243–244

Garfinkel, Harold 31, 72, 250, 259, 317
genre 445–446, 448, 454
Giddens, Anthony 128, 249, 392
global South 130
goals 483, 488
governance 102

Gramsci, Antonio 128
Greimas, Algirdas Gremian 219
greenhushing 450
greenwashing 444, 449–450
Grunig, James, and Hunt, Todd 281

habit 92, 96, 97, 98–99, 101
Hall, Edward 379, 385
hashtag 148–149, 152–153, 155
hegemony 128
heteronomy 90–91
heteronormativity 129
hierarchies 184, 186, 482–483, 485, 488
high-reliability organizations 16, 410–411, 414
Hobbes, Thomas 231–232, 243
Hoffer, Edward 477, 484
hospitals' enduring characteristics 480–486
human relations school of management 124
Hurricane Katrina 70, 76–80
Hybridity/hybridization 222 478–479, 487
Hymes, Dell 73–74
- SPEAKING mnemonic 73–75

iceberg model
- overview 373–374
- layer of communication practices 374, 375–376
- interconnected of layers 376
idea
- generation 487, 488, 490, 493, 494
- evaluation/selection 487, 488, 490, 494
- implementation 488, 490, 494
identity 479, 487, 488–489
- organizational members' identities 196, 201
- strategist's identity 203–204
ideology 128
imagination 101
immutable mobiles 166
incident command system 414
incentive schemes in crowdsourcing, *see* crowdsourcing 486, 487, 490, 492
informing 47, 49, 52, 62, 63
inquiry 91, 92–93
- *see also* community of inquiry
- trans-actional 93–95, 97, 102
inscriptions 166
institutionalization/institutionalized 445–446
integrating 47, 49, 63
inter-action 93–94

internal activism/activists 451
intersectionality 130
introspection 392, 404

Jaki, Stanley L. 235–236
Joas, Hans 2, 5
joint display 403

keyword analysis, *see* analysis 399
Knights, David and Morgan, Garet 195, 197
knowledge 479, 484
– diversity 489, 491, 493, 494, 496, 497
– integrating 496, 489, 490, 492, 497
– sharing 178, 180, 184, 486, 487, 489, 490, 491, 494–497
– transformation 47
Krippendorff, Klaus 319
Kuhn, Timothy 38, 280, 283, 286, 288, 373

language 253
– games 314
Latour, Bruno 38, 165–166, 218, 248, 417
leadership 314
– communication 184, 186
– discursive 214, 215, 217
– *see also* discursive environment
– discursive leadership and research methods 220–222, 225
– *see also* discursive practice
– hierarchical and shared 219
– training programs 223, 225
– presence 218, 222, 218
– reflexive agency, *see* agency 215
– systemic constructionist leadership 223
leading 10–11, 313–314
legitimacy 443–445, 448–451, 454
Leonardi, Paul 177, 180–181
Lewin, Kurt 337
liking 356
linguascape
– explanation 377
– negotiated language use 377
linguistic environments 15–16
linguistic turn 126
Luckmann, Thomas 4
Luhmann, Niklas 69, 108, 143–144, 145–146, 314

Macnamara, Jim 284
macroacting 218
management 143–144, 145–149, 279
– *see also* change management
– definition of 2
– emotions 19
– etymology of 1
– *see also* executive management
– *see also* feminist management research
– high-reliability organizations 16
– in hospitals 18
– *see also* managerial best practices
– managerial role set 143, 149–150, 156
– rehabilitation of 2
management communication 1–2, 12–13, 15, 232, 241–242, 279, 336, 341, 348–349
– contexts of 15–20
– definition of 1–2
– forms of 10–15
– linguistic perspective on 2–3
– poststructuralist 125–126
– practice perspective on 2–3
– practices of 6–10
– structuralist 124
March, James G., and Simon, Herbert A. 143
Marx, Karl 125, 428, 434
materialization 170–172
Mayo, Elton 124
McLeod, John 314–315
McPhee, Robert, and Zaug, Pamela 145, 389
meaning 478
– production of 47, 57, 62
means-ends dichotomy 90–91
measurement 187–188
mentoring 13, 296–302
– complexities 304–307
– cultural differences 306–307
– managerial best practices, *see* management 307–308
– prototypical 296–297, 301
– formal 295, 297–299, 302, 303, 305, 306
– informal 295, 299–300, 303, 305
– episodic 295, 300–301, 303, 305, 306
– blended 301–302
– network (also distributed) 305
– language
  – advice-giving 303
  – directives and requests 303–304
meso level 148–150, 153

metaconversation 339, 348
metrics 459, 460, 461, 463, 471, 472
microblogging 143, 147, 150–151, 156–157
middle manager 530
mindfulness 411
Mintzberg, Henry 1, 3, 4, 22, 28, 48, 70, 146, 251, 444–445
mission(s) 480–482
modeling 389–393, 395–397, 401, 404
moderators 487, 490, 493, 497
Montreal School, see communicative constitution of organizations 218–219
motivating 47, 49, 57, 58
multivocality 484, 490, 492–497
Mumby, Dennis 72, 128, 263, 268, 269, 271, 273, 275, 277, 352, 354, 357
mundane 248

need 391–395, 403
network
– analysis 400–402
– centrality 401
– disciplines 113–115
– initiation 109–113
– maintenance 113–119
– see also social networks
networking 7–8, 178
non-verbal communication 373, 378, 379, 382
– see also communication
– explanation 378–382
– use of email 380
– silent language 378, 385
– virtual groups 381, 382
non-verbal cues 182–183

observation 102
oekom research AG 459–473
– being 463, 465–466
– communicating 469
– communicative constitution 466–469
– rating practices 463–472
– sociogenesis 462
– relating 469–471
Ong, Walter J. 28–30
online collaboration software, see enterprise social media
OpenIDEO 483, 495
orality 29–30

organization 389–394, 404
– ambidexterity 338–339
– heterarchy 338
– hierarchy 338, 347
– learning organization 337–338
– organization development 336–341
– organization development practices research 348
– see also partial organization
organizational change
– interplay between discourses and sensemaking 530
organizational culture 184–186, 188
organizational discourses 315
organizational tensions, contradictions, and paradoxes 131

paradox 479, 483, 487–488
Paret, Peter 237–239
partial organization, see organization 108–109
participatory formats 116–118
patient-centered hospital design, see design 477, 478
patterns of language use 317, 321–330, 390–391, 398–402
Peirce, Charles S. 91–92, 93, 96
Pentland, Brian 248–249, 252, 254
performance 351, 354, 356
– see also rating social and environmental performances
performative
– effects 258
  – illocutionary 200–203
  – perlocutionary 203–206
– and ostensive 248, 249
– and performance 248–249, 254
– power 253
performativity 34, 39, 195–196, 253–255, 260
person-centered care 477, 482
photographs 257–258
planning 11, 232–235, 237, 239–244
– plan 232–235, 237, 239–243
platform 177–179, 181–182, 188
Plato 28
pluralism 94, 95, 97
pluralist model of power 127
polarization 479, 487
polyphony 289–290
– (of voices) 443, 452

Porter, Michael E. 285
positioning 419
"positive" management research 133–134
postcolonial theories 130
posting 9
power 179, 186–187
– critical/interpretive approach to 124–125
– see also disciplinary power
– practice and 51, 59, 64, 428, 434
– tensions in 429–434.
– good/best practice 58, 65
– practices 417–419
– professional practice 47, 50, 62
– see also scientific approach to power
– turn 317
– writing practice 62, 65
practitioner 47
pragmatism 91, 93, 96
precarity 133
– resistance to 133
presentification 421–422
problem-solving 484, 485, 489, 496
progression analysis 64
project map 329
Prussian army 237–239
purpose 234–235, 243–244
Putnam, Linda 125, 126, 131, 132

quality 479, 484, 489

racial privilege 130
Ramanujam, Ranga, and Rousseau, Denise 479, 480, 482,489
rating social and environmental performances, see performance 17
relationality 251–253, 259
resistance 8, 131
– everyday forms of 131
   – hidden forms of 132
   – collective forms of 133
rhetorical features 169
role conflict 485
routines/routinizing 11, 247–262
– see also culture management
– as communicative constitutions 255
– management 255
– organizational 249, 253
– routinization 250–251
rules 482, 483, 484, 486

Sacks, Harvey 28
Schatzki, Théodore 2, 3, 314, 336
Schumpeter, Joseph 146
scientific approach to power, see power 124
Searle, John 4, 34, 234, 344, 355
self-action, see action 93
self-presentation 143–144, 151, 153, 156–157
semiotic mediation 95–96
sensemaking 217, 529, 531
– communication practice 529
– language 531
– objectivity and subjectivity 543–544
sexuality, construction of 129–130
shared values 483, 484, 487
Simon, Herbert A. 71–72, 319
simulation 402–403
situation 91, 92, 100
Smith, Dorothy E. 162, 165, 169, 172
social capital 106, 109–110, 114
socialization 479, 480, 482–483
social media, see twitter 173, 182–183, 187, 257–258
social networks, see networks 355
social power 127
social ratings 459, 460, 465,
– communicative agency 472
– construction process 459, 461, 471
– methodology 463, 466–467, 469, 471
– rating structure 466, 467
– practices 459–472
social rating agencies 459–460
– definitions 460, 461
– epistemological approaches 460–462
societal problems 483–485, 489, 491–498
sociomateriality 417–418
speaking 6
– speech 27–40
– speech acts 336, 344
stakeholder 389, 391–395, 404, 480, 483–485, 490, 487–488
– stakeholder theory 102
standardization 480, 484, 185, 486, 488
St. Gallen Management Model 390
strategic ambiguity 111–113
strategies of control 127–128
– simple 127
– technical 127
– bureaucratic 127–128
– concertive 128

strategizing 10
strategy 234–235
– deliberate approach 282
– strategic approach 281
– strategy formulation 281
– strategy implementation 281
– strategic plan 234
strategy discourse 195–196
– as body of knowledge 197–198
– as conversations 198–199, 204–205
– as narratives 198
structurational divergence (sd) 478–479, 481, 483, 485–488
structure 478, 480–481, 482, 483, 485, 486, 488–490
surveillance 129, 187–188
Sutcliffe, Kathleen 410–411, 413, 419
systemic approach 314

talk 232, 239
Taylorism 90, 91
Taylor, Frederick 71
Taylor, James R. 30, 33, 39–40
Taylor, James R. and Van Every, Elizabeth. J. 4, 167, 172, 390
team communication, see communication 177, 181
technological affordances 179–181, 184–185, 187–188
technological interface 179, 183
technology-mediated 177, 179, 182, 184
temporality 171–172
tensions in hospital management 481–484
text, see textual 32–33, 252, 255–260
text-conversation dynamic 167
textual
– agency 167
– nature of organizations 162, 169, 172
– reality 167
– see also text
thinking 47, 49, 50, 52, 62
time and temporality 182
tool 47, 59, 62, 64, 65
topic modeling 397

top manager 143, 154, 530
traces 163–164, 167
– value of 170–171
trans-action 93–96, 100–102
transdisciplinary 394
translation
– definition 383
– agentic force 384
– meaning making, see meaning 384
– translation as collective management 375
t(w)alking 454
tweeting 8–9, 147–152
twitter, see social media 143, 147–149

uncertainty 107
unity of purpose 481

Vaara, Eero 196–198, 201, 205, 207
value 248, 250, 252, 256
– creation and valuation 109–110, 115, 264, 266, 267, 272, 284–285
ventriloquism 38, 218, 420–421, 452, 472–473
visual communication, see communication 183
voicing 178, 184–185, 188

want 391–392, 395, 403
WAYS 58–62, 64
weak signals 409–410, 417, 420
Weber, Max 125, 235
Weick, Karl 3, 4, 24, 143–144, 239–240, 242–243, 410–411, 414, 516, 529
White, Harrison C. 106–115
white paper 52–55
Wittgenstein, Ludwig 34, 126, 314, 347, 352, 353, 360–361
worker-owned cooperatives 134
writing 6, 29–30, 33, 38–40, 47, 49, 57
– collaborative 47, 52
– competence 47
– domain-specific 47, 50, 52, 55, 59, 64, 65
– multilingual 47, 52
– process 47, 50, 51, 65
– technique 47, 58, 59, 62
– tool 47, 52, 59, 62, 64, 65

www.ingramcontent.com/pod-product-compliance
Lightning Source LLC
Chambersburg PA
CBHW060256240426

43661CB00060B/2808